LANGUAGE AND THE STATE
THE LAW AND POLITICS OF IDENTITY

LANGUE ET ÉTAT
DROIT, POLITIQUE ET IDENTITÉ

CENTRE FOR CONSTITUTIONAL STUDIES

Proceedings of the Second National Conference
on Constitutional Affairs

CENTRE D'ÉTUDES CONSTITUTIONNELLES

Actes de la deuxième conférence
sur les affaires constitutionnelles

LANGUAGE AND THE STATE
THE LAW AND POLITICS OF IDENTITY

LANGUE ET ÉTAT
DROIT, POLITIQUE ET IDENTITÉ

Edited by / Sous la direction de
David Schneiderman

LES ÉDITIONS
YVON BLAIS INC.

C.P. 180 Cowansville (Québec) Canada J2K 3H6
Tél.: (514) 263-1086   Fax: (514) 263-9256

Données de catalogage avant publication (Canada)

Conférence sur les affaires constitutionnelles (2ᵉ : 1989 : Edmonton, Alb.)

Language and the state: the law and politics of identity: proceedings of the second National Conference on Constitutional Affairs = Langue et État: droit, politique et identité : actes de la deuxième conférence sur les affaires constitutionnelles

Tenue du 27 au 29 avr. 1989 à Edmonton, Alb.
Texte en anglais et en français
Comprend des références bibliographiques : p.

ISBN : 2-89073-756-X

1. Politique linguistique — Canada — Congrès. 2. Droits linguistiques — Canada — Congrès. 3. Langage et culture — Canada — Congrès. 4. Minorités linguistiques — Canada — Congrès. I. Schneiderman, David. II. University of Alberta. Centre d'études constitutionnelles. III. Titre. IV. Titre : Langue et État.

KE4413.N37   1991   344.71'09   C91-096383-5F

Canadian Cataloguing in Publication Data

National Conference on Constitutional Affairs (2nd : 1989 : Edmonton, Alta.)

Language and the state: the law and politics of identity: proceedings of the second National Conference on Constitutional Affairs = Langue et État: droit, politique et identité : actes de la deuxième conférence sur les affaires constitutionnelles

Held Apr. 27-29, 1989 in Edmonton, Alta.
Text in English and French
Includes bibliographical references : p.

ISBN : 2-89073-756-X

1. Language policy — Canada — Congresses. 2. Linguistic minorities — Legal status, laws, etc. — Canada — Congresses. 3. Language and culture — Canada — Congresses. 4. Linguistic minorities — Canada — Congresses. I. Schneiderman, David. II. University of Alberta. Centre for Constitutional Studies. III. Title. IV. Title : Langue et État.

KE4413.N37   1991   344.71'09   C91-096383-5E

Dépôt légal : 2ᵉ trimestre 1991
Bibliothèque nationale du Québec
Bibliothèque nationale du Canada

ISBN : 2-89073-756-X

PREFACE

Canada has a lengthy record of experimenting with the constitutional recognition of collective rights. Constitutional guarantees for the continued provision of denominational education, for example, were entrenched to safeguard the continued existence of certain religious communities. With the passage of the *Charter of Rights and Freedoms* in 1982, the focus of constitutional concern shifted predominantly to the relationship between the individual and the state, creating concern for Québecers who feared that individual rights would override Québec's collective concerns regarding language. Even those Charter rights which arguably may be characterized as collective rights, such as rights to English and French language education, are viewed by some as threatening to the interests of the Francophone collectivity in Québec. The shift also occurred as much contemporary constitutional theory attempted to reconcile collective interests with the traditional liberal political order, with its emphasis on the individual.

In view of these events, and the recurring linguistic tensions which predominate the Canadian constitutional scene, the Centre for Constitutional Studies decided to devote its second national conference on the constitution to the issue of language and the state. Twenty-five years after the Report of the Royal Commission on Bilingualism and Biculturalism, in the midst of the debate over Meech Lake, and the emerging language claims from "unofficial" language groups, it was considered timely to examine how Canada and other countries have tried to accommodate the linguistic tensions they each face.

The Centre for Constitutional Studies was founded in 1987 as a result of the collaborative efforts of the Faculty of Law and Departments of History and Political Science at the University of Alberta, and the financial support of the Alberta Law Foundation. The Centre was designed to facilitate and pursue the interdisciplinary study of constitutional matters on a national and bilingual basis. For this, the Centre's second, conference over thirty scholars from a wide variety of disciplines gathered together, along with some one hundred and fifty registrants, in Edmonton on April 27-29, 1989.

The conference structure, which parallels that of the book, was very much a collective effort. The organizing committee was led by A. Anne McLellan, Chair of the Centre for Constitutional Studies Management Board, and was composed of Edmund Aunger, David Bai, Todd Ducharme, Mary Moreau, Alain Noel, and June Ross. They deserve much of the credit for the high quality and thoughtful scope of the conference. Todd Ducharme, former Executive Director of the Centre for Constitutional Studies, ably took on much of the conference organization. He was assisted by Christine Urquhart, also of the Centre. The conference was given generous financial support by the Alberta Law Foundation and the Secretary of State for Canada.

The publication of this monograph, which incorporates virtually all of the presentations, could not have been undertaken without more collective effort. Most notably, Christine Urquhart transcribed, amended, and transformed much of the text into its present form. The editors of the Alberta Law Review 1990-91 aided by checking citations. While most citations are uniform with Canadian legal style, others have been left consistent with the author's own discipline. The Alberta Law Foundation contributed generously towards the cost of this publication and their continuing support of Centre activities is gratefully acknowledged.

Each of the contributors, with an abundance of cooperation and goodwill, withstood my editorial badgering. Thanks are due as well to François Chevrette, Yvon Fontaine, and Deni Lorieu who participated at the conference. I am extremely grateful to the Management Board of the Centre for Constitutional Studies, with whom it has always been a pleasure working, and who kindly entrusted to me the task of editing this volume.

David Schneiderman

PRÉFACE

Depuis longtemps déjà, le Canada travaille à la reconnaissance constitutionnelle des droits collectifs. Les garanties constitutionnelles protégeant l'éducation dispensée par les écoles confessionnelles, par exemple, ont été enchâssées pour assurer la survie de certaines collectivités religieuses. Avec l'adoption de la *Charte des droits et libertés* en 1982, les préoccupations constitutionnelles se sont déplacées pour porter sur la relation entre l'individu et l'État. Les Québécois ont alors craint que les droits individuels surpassent les préoccupations linguistiques de la majorité. Même les droits de la *Charte* que l'on peut à juste titre caractériser de collectifs, tels que les droits à l'éducation dans la langue de la minorité anglaise et française, sont perçus par certains comme constituant une menace envers les intérêts de la collectivité francophone au Québec. Ce changement de direction résulte également de la démarche actuelle des juristes de droit constitutionnel, qui tentent de concilier les intérêts collectifs et l'ordre politique libéral traditionnel, ce dernier accordant une importance prédominante à l'individu.

À la lumière de ces événements et des tensions linguistiques renouvelées qui dominent la scène constitutionnelle canadienne, le Centre d'études constitutionnelles a décidé de consacrer sa deuxième conférence nationale à la question de l'État et de la langue. Vingt-cinq ans après la publication du Rapport de la Commission royale sur le bilinguisme et le biculturalisme, au milieu des débats du lac Meech, et des revendications linguistiques qui émanent des groupes linguistiques « non officiels », on a estimé qu'il était opportun d'étudier comment le Canada et les autres pays se sont efforcés de régler leurs tensions linguistiques respectives.

Le Centre d'études constitutionnelles a été fondé en 1987, grâce aux efforts conjugués de la faculté de droit, des départements d'Histoire et de Sciences politiques de l'Université de l'Alberta, et avec le soutien financier de l'Alberta Law Foundation. Le Centre a été institué afin de promouvoir l'étude interdisciplinaire des questions constitutionnelles à l'échelle nationale et dans une perspective bilingue. Ainsi, du 27 au 29 avril 1989, la seconde conférence du Centre a rassemblé plus de trente spécialistes représentant une grande variété de disciplines, ainsi que quelque cent cinquante congressistes.

La structure de cet événement, parallèle à celle du livre qui en est issu, est une oeuvre collective. Le comité organisateur a oeuvré sous la direction d'Anne McLellan, présidente du Conseil d'administration du Centre d'études constitutionnelles, auquel siègent Edmund Aunger, David Bai, Todd Ducharme, Mary Moreau, Alain Noel et June Ross. Tous doivent être félicités de la qualité et de l'envergure de la conférence. Avec l'assistance de Christine Urquhart, Todd Ducharme, ancien Directeur administratif du Centre d'études constitutionnelles, a assumé en grande partie l'organisation de la Conférence. L'Alberta Law Foundation et le Secrétariat d'État du Canada ont apporté leur généreux soutien financier.

La publication de cette monographie, qui comprend la presque totalité des communications, n'aurait pu être entreprise sans une mesure supplémentaire de collaboration collective. Mentionnons notamment la participation de Christine Urquhart, qui a transcrit et révisé les textes pour donner au présent ouvrage sa forme définitive ; le comité de rédaction de l'Alberta Law Review 1990-91 a assumé la vérification des citations. Si la plupart d'entre elles sont conformes au style juridique canadien, d'autres reflètent davantage le domaine de leur auteur. L'Alberta Law Foundation a généreusement contribué à défrayer les coûts de publication et nous la remercions du soutien fidèle qu'elle apporte aux activités du Centre.

C'est avec infiniment de générosité et de bonne volonté que chacun des contributeurs a subi mes incessantes « suppliques » éditoriales. Je voudrais encore exprimer ma gratitude à François Chevrette, à Yvon Fontaine et à Deni Lorieu, qui ont participé au congrès. Je suis extrêmement reconnaissant aux membres du Conseil administratif du Centre d'études constitutionnelles, avec qui il est toujours agréable de travailler et qui m'ont confié la tâche de préparer ce volume.

David Schneiderman

TABLE OF CONTENTS / TABLE DES MATIÈRES

Comments
Comments

Partie I / Part I

Une communauté peut-elle avoir des droits?

La façon dont nous résolvons la tension existant entre les droits individuels et les droits collectifs est déterminée en grande partie par notre caractérisation de leurs fondements philosophiques respectifs. Les intérêts collectifs peuvent l'emporter sur les préoccupations individuelles à condition que les collectivités puissent se prévaloir de droits au même titre que les individus. Il est donc nécessaire de déterminer si les communautés détiennent bien des droits.

Michael McDonald propose une série de questions et de réflexions sur le sujet. Il suggère une théorie des droits qui s'efforce d'être juste et raisonnable, non seulement pour l'ordre social établi mais aussi pour le groupe minoritaire et la façon dont il perçoit ses droits. Il oppose les droits collectifs définis en tant qu'ensemble de *choix* protégés, pour lesquels la communauté agit à titre d'agent de choix, aux droits perçus comme une série d'avantages protégés, où la collectivité devient le bénéficiaire passif de certains avantages. Dans un exposé incisif traitant des droits individuels et collectifs, l'auteur examine les deux aspects de la question.

Bien que les diverses versions du libéralisme aient refusé de reconnaître la notion de droits collectifs, McDonald suggère qu'il est souvent possible de concilier individualisme libéral et collectivisme. Dans les cas de conflits insolubles, il existe parfois des motifs de résolution en faveur de la collectivité. McDonald reconnaît que le seul fait d'établir ainsi la distinction entre les deux notions constitue une simplification exagérée, la reconnaissance des droits collectifs équivalant souvent à la valorisation des droits des membres individuels de la collectivité.

Bryan Schwartz refuse d'analyser les réalités morales en termes collectifs. Pour lui, les communautés ne sont que des collectivités composées d'individus. Il refuse également la caractérisation que McDonald applique au libéralisme. Si le libéralisme traditionnel a toujours eu une vision limitée des droits collectifs, il a cependant fait une place importante aux droits des groupes dans les documents tels que la Constitution canadienne. Schwartz adopte une vue pragmatique

1

et tente de résoudre le conflit existant entre l'individu et la collectivité mais il se déclare en faveur de l'individu dans les cas de conflits insolubles.

Les deux auteurs explorent donc la notion libérale traditionnelle de droits collectifs et répondent par l'affirmative à la question posée.

Can a Community Have Rights?

The ways in which we resolve the tension between individual and collective rights are determined, to a large extent, by the way in which we characterize the philosophical foundations for each of them. Collective interests may be able to prevail over individual concerns if communities can claim rights as do individuals. It is necessary, therefore, to address the question of whether communities can have rights.

Michael McDonald offers a series of questions and reflections on community rights. He suggests an outline for a theory of rights that seeks to be fair and reasonable, not only to the dominant social order, but to the minority group's understanding of their own rights. He contrasts the conception of collective rights as a series of protected *choices*, where the community acts as an agent of choice, with the conception of rights as a series of protected *benefits*, where the community is a passive recipient of benefits. An insightful account of individual and collective rights will involve an examination along both lines.

Even though versions of liberalism have resisted recognition of a notion of collective rights, McDonald suggests that liberal individualism and collectivism are often reconcilable. And, in the case of intractable conflict, there are grounds in some instances for resolving the dispute in favour of the collectivity. McDonald recognizes that even characterizing the dispute in this way is an oversimplification, for the recognition of collective rights can often enhance the rights of the individual members of that collectivity.

Bryan Schwartz resists analyzing moral realities in collective terms. For him, communities are no more than collectivities of individuals. He also resists McDonald's characterization of liberalism. While liberalism traditionally has had a limited vision of collective rights, it has accommodated important group rights in such documents as the Canadian constitution. Schwartz takes a pragmatic view that seeks to reconcile conflict between the individual and collectivity but his fall-back position, in the case of irreconcilable conflict, is in favour of the individual.

The two authors, therefore, expand on the traditional liberal notion of collective rights so as to answer the question posed in the affirmative.

QUESTIONS ABOUT COLLECTIVE RIGHTS[1]

Michael McDonald

I used to have a sign on my office door that said: "I have all the correct answers if only you ask the right questions." My intention in this paper is to raise at least some of the right questions. I leave to my learned friends in law and the social sciences the challenge of providing the right answers.

I begin with two crucial questions: first a "can" question, *can* communities have rights; and second a "should" or "ought" question, *should* communities have rights?

Figure 1

CAN A COMMUNITY HAVE RIGHTS?

Analytical Issues:

[a] Rights questions: What are rights? What is it to have a right? What is the point of rights?

[b] Communities questions: What are communities? How can we differentiate communities from mere collections of unrelated individuals? What is the relation between communities and their members?

1. This paper is part of a larger project on collective rights that has been undertaken over the past several years. Some of that work has been supported by grants from the Social Science and Humanities Research Council. I have also received encouragement and assistance from colleagues in both philosophy and law, including particularly Pierre Carignan, Ernie Weinrib, Denise Réaume, Wil Kymlicka, Robert Ware and members of the Canadian Section of the International Association for Philosophy of Law and Social Philosophy. For this paper, I am grateful for the remarks of my two commentators: Professor Bryan Schwartz (University of Manitoba) and Professor François Chevrette (Université de Montréal). Dr. Joseph Pestieau of Cégep de Saint-Laurent has also sent me a number of valuable comments.

[c] Metaphysical issues: what are the existence conditions for being a rights-holder? What sorts of communities, if any, can satisfy these conditions?

SHOULD A COMMUNITY HAVE RIGHTS?

Normative Issues:

[a] Conventional Context: How do collective rights fit into various legal and social contexts? In particular, how do collective and individual rights interface in liberal democratic theory?

[b] Critical Context: If communities have rights, what happens to the rights of others: be they members of that community, members of other communities, or other communities in their own right? What is the value of collective rights: instrumental or intrinsic?

The "can" question raises conceptual questions concerning the natures of rights and communities, as well as metaphysical questions about the existence conditions for both rights and communities. Assuming that it is plausible to say that at least some sorts of communities can have collective rights, then the "should" question can be entertained. This, I take it, is a question about justification in a normative context: be it the conventional context of legal rules and social mores or the critical context of moral and political argument.

To pose analytical questions about rights, let us begin on familiar ground with the sort of material about rights that we provide students in their first classes in jurisprudence and philosophy of law. First in the broad sense of the term, 'rights' are relational in that they are correlated with duties. Each right implies the existence of a duty on the part of an obligant. Or to put this another way, the possession of a right confers "a normative advantage" on its possessor and "a normative disadvantage on the obligant".[2] Thus, in our subsequent discussion of rights, we must deal with relationships. We must not forget that the attribution of a right to one party involves the imposition of a duty or duties on at least one other party.[3]

Second, again in the broad sense of the term, 'rights' are usefully divided into Hohfeldian types: liberties, powers, immunities, and rights in the narrow sense of claim-rights. Each Hohfeldian-type is correlated

---

2. W. Sumner, *The Moral Foundation of Right* (Oxford: Clarendon Press, 1987) at 32.
3. So the multiplication of *Charter* rights carries a price in the correlative multiplication of *Charter* duties upon governments.

with duty-types: no-rights, liabilities, and disabilities and 'duties' in the narrow sense. The resultant rights-duties pairs can be further divided into two sets. The first set contains primary normative relations which can be understood in terms of the deontic modalities of the permitted and non-permitted.[4] This yields the familiar square:

Figure 2A

Right ----------------Liberty

Duty ----------------No Right

The remaining set contains secondary normative relations. In effect, it allows its possessors ways of establishing, extinguishing, or blocking primary relations. This makes a static normative order into a dynamic one. It is constructed from alethic modalities which tell us what it is possible, impossible or necessary for agents to do.[5] Hence, the second familiar square:

Figure 2B

Power -------------- Immunity

Liability ------------ Disability

I am now in a position to introduce what I take to be a very useful recent advance in the analysis of rights, which has been presented in two recent and important books on right by the American philosopher Carl Wellman and the Canadian philosopher Wayne Sumner.[6] This is the idea that legal, conventional, and moral rights, like those found in the *Charter*, are best understood as complexes of Hohfeldian elements designed to protect some core Hohfeldian element.[7]

---

4. This can be expressed in terms of either the forbidden and not-forbidden or the required and not-required.
5. Sumner, *supra*, note 2 at 23 and 28. See H.L.A. Hart, *The Concept of Law* (Oxford: Oxford University Press, 1961).
6. Carl Wellman, *A Theory of Rights: Persons Under Laws, Institutions, and Morals* (Totowa, N.J.: Rowman & Allenheld, 1985). Sumner, *supra*, note 2.
7. See Wellman, *supra*, note 6 at 81 ff and Sumner, *supra*, note 2 at 45ff. In Carl Wellman's terms, rights establish a domain in which the possessor of a right has dominion over others in virtue of the various Hohfeldian elements she has in her possession: "The

According to this view, the right of a minority language store-owner to post signs in her own language has at its core the liberty of posting a sign in whatever language she chooses. This core is protected by powers, including that of being able to bring suit against the government; immunities against various legal actions by government and private individuals including, in the case of a constitutional right, an immunity from government's extinction of the core liberty; and claim-rights, say, to police protection against the linguistic majority.

By contrast, the core of the collective right to French signs only in public places in Québec is a power over those who place signs in languages other than French, who thus labour under the correlative disability. This power is exercised through the Office of the French Language (Office de la langue française and Commission de la surveillance de la langue française); it may compel observance through generating specific claim-rights against those who post such signs. The exercise of the power by the Bureau is surrounded by associated Hohfeldian elements including immunities (against minority interference), claim-rights (to the removal of signs), and liberties.

Taking seriously this conception of legal and moral rights as consisting of clusters of Hohfeldian elements arranged around a core Hohfeldian element allows us to raise some important questions about the point or purpose of particular rights and rights as a general class. For particular rights, pointing to the core element provides an informative answer about the function of that right, for example, that the point of section 23 Charter rights is to be found in core element of a claim of linguistic communities against governments to minority language education. The apparatus of control over school boards and the like is designed to protect that core claim.[8]

By asking about the function of rights in general we enter the current philosophical debate about whether rights are best understood as

---

dominion conferred upon a right-holder by a respected legal right is essentially similar [to the Roman *dominus* and the feudal lord]. It is a two-sided freedom-control concerning a limited domain defined by the core of the right and in face of the second party or parties to the right. To the extent that it is realized, this dominion enables the will of the right-holder to prevail over the will or wills of the second parties in any confrontation to which the right is relevant." (96)

8. There are a series of Canadian cases illustrating this point. See, for example, *Reference re Education Act of Ontario* (1984), 47 O.R. (2d) 1 and *Commission des Écoles Fransaskoises Inc. et al.* v. *Government of Saskatchewan* (1988), 48 D.L.R. (4th) 315. Also see my paper "Respect for Individuals Versus Respect for Groups: Public Aid for Confessional Schools in the United States and Canada" in Diana Meyers and Kenneth Kipnis, eds, *Philosophical Dimensions of the Constitution* (Boulder, Co.: Westview Press, 1988) at 180-195.

protected choices (Wayne Sumner, Carl Wellman, and Joel Feinberg) or as *protected benefits* (Joseph Raz, Neil MacCormack and David Lyons).[9] Let me use an analogy I have employed elsewhere in talking about collective rights to illustrate the debate.[10] I have suggested that we might think of rights as involving, at a minimum, relationships among three parties: the rights-holder, an obligant, and a beneficiary.[11] An illuminating analogue to this is a delivery system like a post office or courier company, in which there are also three essential parties: the sender, the deliverer, and the recipient.[12]

Figure 3

Rights-Holder [RH] ---------- Sender [S]

Obligant [O] ----------------- Deliverer [D]

Beneficiary [B] ---------------- Recipient [R]

Protected Choice Aims at *Control*:

RH's control over O
S's control over D

Protected Benefit Aims at *Securing Interests*

B's interest in the benefit in question
R's interest in receiving the package

Are we to describe delivery systems as essentially choice or benefit oriented? Is the aim to give the sender control over the deliverer, or

---

9. Sumner, *supra*, note 2 at 32-53; Wellman, *supra*, note 6 at 185-220; Neil MacCormick, "Children's Rights: A Test-Case for Theories of Right" in *Legal Right and Social Democracy: Essays in Legal and Political Philosophy* (Oxford: Oxford U.P., 1982) at 154-166; Joel Feinberg, "The Nature and Value of Rights" in *Rights, Justice and the Bounds of Liberty* (Princeton: 1980) at 143-158; Joseph Raz, "On the Nature of Rights" (1984) 93 *Mind* 370; Joseph Raz, "Legal Rights" (1984) 4 *Oxford Journal of Legal Studies* 1; David Lyons, "Rights, Claimants and Beneficiaries" (1969) 6 *American Philosophical Quarterly* 2.

10. Michael McDonald, "Collective Rights and Tyranny" (April and June 1986) 56 *University of Ottawa Quarterly* 2 and published simultaneously in Guy Lafrance, ed., *Pouvoir et Tyrannie*, (Ottawa: University of Ottawa, 1986) 118-119.

11. The same person may be both a rights-holder and a beneficiary.

12. As before, the first and third parties may be the same person since one can send packages to oneself. There may be more than three parties in either a rights system or delivery system, including those like judges or supervisors who are to rectify misfirings of either system.

is it to put the package in the hands of the recipient? On the first conception, the choice of the sender is emphasized; while on the second, it is the benefit to the recipient. Since our main concern is with the charter of collective rights and their possessors, we are asking if the appropriate model to use for collective rights should be one based on choice or benefit; are we to think of the possessors of collective rights as primarily either agent-choosers or recipient-beneficiaries?

Debate between adherents of the protected choice and protected benefits analyses of rights has centred on cases in which rights seem to do one task to the exclusion of the other. Thus, the core of a child's right to a compulsory education is its provision of a benefit but not a choice. For this reason, the advocate of a protected choice analysis will treat such rights as peripheral or deviant cases of rights.[13] Whereas, the advocate of a protected benefit analysis will regard such rights as paradigmatic. Sumner notes that the analytic commitment to either a protected choice or benefit [=interest] analysis has important normative implications:

> The interest conception treats rights as devices for promoting individual welfare. Thus the dominating image here is of the right-holder as the passive beneficiary of a network of protective and supportive duties shared by others, from which it follows that a being can be a right-holder only if it possesses interests. On the other hand, the choice conception treats rights as devices for promoting freedom or autonomy. Thus the dominating image here is of the right-holder as the active manager of a network of normative relations connecting her to others, from which it follows that a being can be a right-holder only if it possesses these managerial abilities.[14]

Sumner goes on to point out that the protected choice theory of rights is likely to be more restrictive in granting rights since it requires the possessors of rights to be autonomous beings; whereas, the protected benefit theory can grant rights to all those who stand to benefit from their possession, which includes non-autonomous as well as autonomous beings. Thus, one might well prefer presenting and defending animal rights in terms of a protected benefit analysis rather than a protected choice analysis; for on the former, rights as protected benefits can be directly possessed by animals; while on the latter, animals could only have rights derivatively as protected by the choices of autonomous agents, for example, as their pets or livestock.

We might be initially inclined to think that the choice of a protected choice or a protected benefit conception of rights is dictated by the

---

13. Feinberg, *supra*, note 9 at 157-8 says such rights contain half-liberties rather than the full-liberties associated with normal rights.
14. Sumner, *supra*, note 2 at 47.

choice of basic normative positions. Thus, we might naturally assume that defenders or rights-centred conceptions of morality (advocates of deontic theories) would adopt the protected choice conception of rights, while advocates of goal-centred notions of morality (consequentialists) would choose the protected benefits conception of rights. So Rawls, who believes that the right brackets or limits the good, would take the view that rights protect choices, while his utilitarian adversaries would adopt a protected benefits view of rights. While this is by no means atypical, it is not the case that there is such a tight fit between one's analysis of rights and one's basic normative position. Thus, in *The Moral Foundation of Rights*, Wayne Sumner advances a consequentialist case for rights as protected choices. That is, Sumner holds that the best analysis of rights, both conventional and moral, is in terms of protected choices. But the best justification of rights available is consequentialist. On the other hand, Neil MacCormack advances a protected-benefit analysis of rights, while adopting at various times a deontic and specifically Kantian justification for rights.[15] Both Sumner and MacCormack would, I think, defend this mix-and-match strategy in terms of demonstrating the explanatory and justificatory *reach* of their basic theories.

In weighing the protected choice and protected benefits accounts of rights, we must understand the often intimate connections between having a choice and being in a position to benefit. Often having a choice available to an individual or a group provides a benefit to the possessor. Thus, the right to vote or hold office protects or provides its possessors the benefit of participation in public life. In this case, the benefit is active and not passive. Having a protected choice can also bring about the enjoyment of certain benefits. Thus, linguistic educational rights can be sought because such rights open up a variety of social and economic opportunities. Similarly, the exercise of choices guaranteed by rights can be primarily intended to bring about the enjoyment of certain benefits, as when one exercises a stock option to secure profits or minimize losses. There are then important intentional and causal relations between choices and benefits.

Furthermore, both choice and benefit theories have important commonalities. Both present rights as *distributive* and *not aggregative*. The immediate aim of a right is the distribution of something, whether conceived as choices or benefits, rather than the maximization of either choices or benefits indiscriminately. Both also assume a *confrontational*

---

15. See Neil MacCormick, *Legal Right and Social Democracy: Essays in Legal and Political Philosophy*, (Oxford: Oxford University Press, 1982) especially "Children's Rights: a Test-Case for Theories of Rights" at 154-166 and "Nation and Nationalism" at 247-265.

context or background in which the valued commodity is in short supply. Both these features are essential to any adequate analysis of rights. Rights function like a delivery system and not a lottery or slot machine with random payoffs. The context of rights is one in which the focus is on winners and losers — a zero sum game as it were!

This confrontational context helps us understand why majority rights should not be described as collective rights, while minority rights can be so described. Thus, we would be reluctant to describe the linguistic rights of the Francophone majority in Québec as collective rights except in the context of a larger collectivity, Canada, in which that Francophone majority is a minority. It becomes less odd, I think, to talk about the collective rights of the majority insofar as the dominant normative order limits the rights of the majority to get its way.[16] This can come about because, as in the case of Québec, the majority in one jurisdiction is a minority in a more inclusive jurisdiction. But it also can come about when there are entrenched limits on majority rule embodied in a constitution, which is also the situation that Québec finds itself in today.

My own sense of the dispute about the analysis of rights as protected choices or as protected benefits is that protected choice theorists currently have the lead due to the recent publications of Wellman and Sumner. In terms of analyzing legal rights, I believe the protected choice theory is simply more convincing. While for some purposes it is useful to think of legal rights as distributing and protecting benefits, most often the bottom-line concern is with control or choice. Indeed, the movement in political philosophy from utility-centred justifications to those based on rights has been a move away from a political and legal conception of humans as welfare-consumers (*homo patiens*) to one of humans as autonomous agents (*homo agens*).[17]

Nonetheless, while we usually focus on the right-holder's choice, there are situations in which we are concerned with the recipient's benefits. It would then be cumbersome and unprofitable to insist that we grant a monopoly to one of these theories. Hence, I would suggest that an insightful account of individual and collective rights will involve an examination of rights along both the choice and the benefit dimensions. Moreover, collective rights in their strongest form would include both choices and benefits for the groups in question.

We can now get some insight into our initial question "Can a community have rights?" by asking two key sub-questions.

---

16. See below on the notion of a double understanding. Pestieau has reminded me that these contextual limits on collective rights are not just legal but also ideological.

17. See H.L.A. Hart, "Between Utility and Rights" in Alan Ryan, ed., *The Idea of Freedom* (Oxford: Oxford U.P., 1979) at 77-98.

Figure 4

[1] Can communities exercise rights?

    a. Model = Protected Choice
    b. Capacity = Cognitive and Practical Capacities for exercising rights.

[2] Can communities be the beneficiaries of rights?

    a. Model = Protected Benefit
    b. Capacity = Having interests

The first [1] points us in the direction of the protected choice conception of rights; the second [2] fits within the protected benefit conception of rights. Both questions lead to an enquiry into the nature of communities, in particular whether communities exercise and benefit from rights in the same ways as individuals do? Responding to this question requires, in turn, an enquiry into the conceptual relationships between individuals and their communities.[18] It raises, in particular, the question of whether the collective exercise of, or collective benefit from, rights can be reduced to the individual exercise of, and benefit from rights by members of the group in question. At least some of these questions concern legal existence and were much debated in English, American, and Continental jurisprudence around the turn of the century.[19] This debate has been revived in recent years by Peter French's philosophical analysis of corporations and in jurisprudential work by Meir Dan-Cohen's work on the legal theory of complex organizations.[20]

---

18. Such an enquiry would address a number of questions. One question is whether our models of choice and benefit are individual or collective. That is, do we model collective choice and benefit on individual choice and benefit or the reverse? A second question concerns the logical relationships of collective and individual rights. A third concerns the fit between such rights, in particular the way in which a core element in one kind of right can be protected by peripheral elements from another.

19. Here, see Frederick Hallis, *Corporate Responsibility: A Study in Jurisprudence* (London: Oxford University Press, 1930) [Reprinted 1978 by Verlag] for a comprehensive survey and especially the debate on the case of *Free Church of Scotland* v. *Lord Overton*, [1904] A.C. 515; also see Meir Dan-Cohen, *Rights, Persons, and Organizations: A Legal Theory for Bureaucratic Society* (Berkeley: University of California Press, 1986) and my review-article "The Personless Paradigm" (1987) 37 *U.T.L.J.* 212-226. My own position is like that of the legal realists who opposed treating collectivities as merely legal fictions.

20. See Peter French, *Collective and Corporate Responsibility* (New York: Columbia University Press, 1984) and M. Dan-Cohen, *ibid.* For criticisms of this position see, for example, Michael Keeley, "Organizations as Non-Persons" (1981) 15 *Journal of Value Inquiry*, also in D. Poff and W. Waluchow, *Business Ethics in Canada* (Scarborough: Prentice-Hall Canada, 1987) at 45-49, and Patricia Werhane, "Formal Organizations, Economic Freedom, and Moral Agency" in D. Poff and W. Waluchow, *id.* at 39-44.

I will try to disentangle some of the leading questions with a series
of short reflections on the relationship between communities and their
members centring on the relationship between the community's exercising
and enjoying rights and the members of that community exercising and
enjoying rights.

Reflection #1. While there can be groupings of social groups, it
must be the case that, in the last analysis, groups are composed of
individual members and not the reverse. A pride of lions is made up
of individual lions, a flight of birds of individual birds, and a nation
of its citizens.

Reflection #2. Yet this does not mean that what we predicate of
groups can necessarily be predicated of the group's members. Because
a nation can declare war or a pride of lions survive a hundred years
does not mean that each individual citizen can individually or severally
declare war or that lions normally live to be a hundred. Similarly, we
may meaningfully attribute characteristics to members of a group that
cannot be attributed to the group itself. Thus, while all the members
of a German friendship society in Kitchener-Waterloo may be blond,
over six feet tall, and drive Mercedes, it is not the case that the society
has these characteristics. Similarly, to say that group A has the right
X is not to say that each member of A has the right to X. Thus, to
say that a jury can find the accused guilty as charged is not to say
that each member of the jury has this power. Or to say that each member
of the jury has a right to vote on the guilt or innocence of the accused
is not to say that the jury somehow has such a right as a group.

Reflection #3. Exercising or benefiting from a right Q is a matter
of making or having something happen under conventional, legal, or
moral rules.[21] So I exercise my right to vote by marking an X on a
ballot or I benefit from an inheritance by receiving my designated portion
of the estate. What counts as exercising or benefiting from the right
is rule-determined.[22] There is no difference here between collective and

---

21. I am following Feinberg here. As Kurt Baier made clear in his now classic *The Moral
    Point of View* (Ithaca N.Y.: Cornell U.P., 1958) at 178-180 that while both the law
    and morality consist of rules, only law has an authoritative source of such rules.
22. In his "Notes for Comments" on this paper, Professor Schwartz says, "As a matter
    of law, we can assign rights to just about anyone or anything." He then goes on
    to claim that shows the "limited prospects" of the sort of conceptual analysis of rights
    provided in this paper. However, if one takes seriously the idea that rights involve
    exercising or benefitting under a rule, it is plain that there are reasonably clear limits
    to the plausible attribution of rights. If, for example, the law says that cats have
    the right to vote, there must be some aspect of feline behaviour which is conventionally
    taken to be casting a ballot. The law in effect must attribute to cats those cognitive
    and practical capacities that it will count as voting. Now either it is the case that
    legal officials believe that cats have this capacity or not. If they have the belief, then
    it is plausible to give cats the right to vote; if they do not have the belief, then it

individual rights. It is not the case that collective rights are rule-bound, while individual rights are not. All rights are rule-bound.

Reflection #4. Yet group rights typically require individual members to act on behalf of or represent the group. Thus, a corporation acquires or disposes of assets through the actions of its President and Board of Directors; they represent the corporation, which is to say that their individual actions count under the rules of corporate law as the actions of the collective.[23] This seems to push us toward reducing the whole to its parts.

Reflection #5. Yet as we have seen (in #3), rights are a matter of making something happen under rules. Rules are a social phenomenon. Only in a derivative way, do we talk about rules in isolation from a social context, as Kant does when he talks about "self-imposed maxims". Even Kant's notion of autonomy was appropriated from the context of collective self-rule. We move back in our reflections from parts to the whole. With minority rights, a minority is recognized as a rights-holder or beneficiary under some conventional, legal, or moral set of rules. In a constitutionally unlimited democracy, the majority determines which minorities are recognized and how they are recognized.[24]

Reflection #6. But it may be said that anything is possible under rules. Can the rule-maker arbitrarily designate any random collection of individual persons as a collectivity and attribute to them either collective rights or duties? Thus, Japanese Canadians at the beginning of World War II had their property seized and were removed to concentration camps because they were regarded as a part of a treasonous group — a fifth column. In response, one can note that there have been legal systems in which vases, cats, and, much more cruelly, the wholly or partially incompetent have been found guilty of capital offenses. From this point of view, groups are no more or no less arbitrarily rule-designated than are individuals. This provides a partial antidote to one kind of scepticism about collective rights, namely, the view that collectives and their rights are nothing but legal (or conventional) fictions.[25]

is implausible to make the attribution. Of course, it is possible that in the latter case, the assignment of the right to vote to cats could be a cheat designed to secure additional rights, say, to the owners of cats. In my view then, the end-result is that a conceptual analysis of rights nicely displays our shared cognitive commitments in the assignment of rights. Thus, we can focus on the key question of whether groups can be so organized that they can as a group either exercise or enjoy rights.

23. The difference between a person representing a group and a person being a representative or a typical member of a group is useful for understanding the notion of self-collection discussed shortly.

24. Pestieau has reminded me that often non-democratic imperial powers have been better at recognising rights of peoples than have liberal democracies. Thus, for example, there were extensive collective rights regimes in the Ottoman and Austro-Hungarian Empires as well as in Imperial Russia and China.

25. See Hallis, *supra*, note 19.

Reflection # 7. The two key questions are : which rules are *reasonable* and *fair* in their attributions of rights and responsibilities to groups and individuals ? In our prevailing liberal ideology the reasonable and fair attribution of rights and responsibilities to individuals is well worked out. For those of us who want to explore and defend collective rights the intellectual challenge is to work out criteria for the reasonable and fair attribution of rights and responsibilities to communities. Whether or not this sends us beyond the liberal paradigm remains to be seen.

In the remainder of this paper, I would like to offer some suggestions about how we might address both these problems. I will highlight the key issues.

Reasonableness. Consider again the attribution of collective responsibility for treasonous activities to Japanese Canadians. What would have made such an assertion a reasonable one, whether or not it was fair ? Surely there would have to be some evidence of conspiratorial activities. That is, there would have to have been both shared goals and coordinated activities. It would not be enough then to show that several Japanese Canadians independently of each other wanted Japan to win the war and tried to secure that end. Neither is it sufficient to have shared goals without coordinated activities. Nor can there be the meaningful attribution of coordinated activities without shared goals. For there to have been a conspiracy there must have been a *shared understanding* in the sense of shared goals and coordinated activities.[26] Acting on a shared understanding requires an explicit or implicit collective decision procedure. So in the case of the conspiracy, there must be some conventional way in decisions are reached. Perhaps, the conspirators let Person A decide or take a vote.

Since the term "understanding" can be used to designate an agreement ("coming to an understanding") as well as a cognitive state ("understanding that" something is the case), talking about "a shared understanding" may tempt us to think of it arising from a kind of explicit or implicit compact or contract between individuals. This might be reinforced by a commitment to methodological individualism, which would require the reconstruction of a shared understanding from goals and aspirations of the members of the group in question but not the reverse. Perhaps, the conspiracy arises because person A wants to get revenge for the racist behaviour of his neighbours ; person B because she wishes to do what the Emperor commands ; person C because he

---

26. See A.M. Honoré, "Groups, Laws, and Obedience" in A.W.B. Simpson, ed., *Oxford Essays in Jurisprudence* (Oxford : Clarendon Press, 1973) at 1-21 ; *id.*, "What Is A Group ?", (1975) 61 *Archiv fur Rechts-und Sozialphilosophie* 161-179.

is young and restless, and so on. Now none of this is in itself implausible (though of course it was quite palpably false in the actual case). The danger lies in thinking that the reconstruction of individual behaviour in terms of group intentions is unilluminating and eliminable. It would be a mistake then to forego the possibility of explaining actions of individual conspirators (spying, sabotaging, and the like) in terms of the joint enterprise, namely that each was doing her part in the conspiracy. If we then ask, "Which is first, the individual or the group?", we raise a proverbial chickens-or-eggs question. Of course, understanding eggs helps us to understand chickens; nonetheless, we may also learn a great deal about eggs from looking at chickens.

I have already illustrated the danger of overlooking the eggs with the case of Japanese Canadians. Let me point out the danger of ignoring the chickens with our record of handling native rights. Again, my concern is not with the unfairness of this treatment, but with its unreasonableness in terms of a persistent tendency to dismiss or misconstrue native peoples' community-constituting understandings. Now the problems here go well beyond the failure to attribute rights and responsibilities to native communities. Thus, it is not enough to say that the provincial or federal governments will respect a given band's title to land in the same way that it respects any corporations's title to property. If aboriginal title is reduced to a fungible, alienable resource, then a main aspect of aboriginal rights vanishes. Moreover, if the mode of claiming aboriginal title is in deep conflict with native modes of dispute settlement, then the collective act of asserting such title may well undermine the community that it is meant to protect.[27] This raises an important set of questions about the articulation and recognition of shared understandings in law and, especially in our constitutional context, the role that collective rights play in not only respecting but also at the same time reshaping the community in question.[28] The difficult task is to find ways of attributing such rights while respecting the underlying social realities.

A more general point is appropriate here. With minority rights, the picture is of minority groups that exercise and benefit from rights in a given society's legal system.[29] As a claimant or beneficiary, the

---

27. See Linda Medcalf, *Law and Identity: Lawyers, Native Americans, and Legal Practice.* (Beverly Hills, Calif.: Sage Publications, 1978).

28. See Robert Cover, "Nomos and Narrative" (1983-4) 97 *Harvard Law Review* 4.

29. Analogous remarks can be made about the recognition of collective rights in international law. For a discussion of this topic, see my paper "Collective Rights in International Relations" in Wesley Cragg, Laurent Larouche, and Gertrud Lewis, eds., *Challenging the Conventional: Essays in Honour of Ed Newberg* (Burlington, Ont.: Trinity Press, 1989) at 115-127.

minority group has standing in a more encompassing normative order — "the social order". However, a space or gap is left or created in society's shared understanding for the minority to occupy. In that shared social understanding, the group is represented as having such characteristics of a community-constituting understanding as are necessary to the exercise or enjoyment of the right in question. But the group with its shared understanding also presents a normative order or set of rules concerning its own and its members activities. So, with minority rights, there is the minority group's understanding of itself and society's recognition of the minority as a rights-holder and beneficiary. There is then, with minority rights, a *double understanding*; two normative orders are involved.

Figure 5

DOUBLE UNDERSTANDING

Social Understanding [U_s]: Putatively shared by all Members of Society S including S's constitutional order, which contains a gap or space for the minority's understanding to operate. S attributes to M the capacities necessary for the exercise and enjoyment of various collective rights.

Minority Understanding [U_m]: Putatively shared by all members of the Minority M, including an acceptance of the constitutional order of S at least to the extent of being able to exercise and enjoyment the collective rights permitted in U_s.

Key Issue: The fit between U_s and U_m:

— Are they congruent conceptually and morally?

— Their acceptability to both S and M.

— Does U_s distort U_m? Does U_m distort U_s?

There may well be conceptual or practical conflicts between the two. Society's norms may be inconsistent with the minority's shared understanding. Perhaps the recognition of minority rights will in this case initiate a process that leads to the dissolution of that society. Or the minority may well see that it will destroy itself if it tries to exercise the collective rights afforded in that social order.[30] So, from the central

---

30. The perception of serious inconsistencies on the part of either society or the minority can well initiate a destructive process.

law-giver's perspective, the question is whether and in what ways to recognize a minority consistent with the encompassing shared understanding; while from the minority perspective, it is whether and in what ways to seek recognition from the central legal order consistent with the minority's understanding of itself.[31] For the former, we would do well to think of the arguments advanced by those who wanted New Brunswick, Manitoba, and Newfoundland to withhold or withdraw assent of the Meech Lake Accord. For the latter, we might reflect on the strongly negative reaction in Québec to the decisions in *Brown's Shoes* and *Allan Singer, Ltd.*[32]

There is a further complication that must be introduced. Thus far, I have talked about groups as if they all could be identified in terms of their purposes. However, the most important candidates for collective rights, families, minority groups, nations and the like, could well be described as *purposeless*.[33] Their goals are extremely broad; their shared understandings encompass ways of life and a set of social meanings for their members. That is, shared understandings in this case provide a context for shared purposes. They are purposeless too in the sense that they standardly have goals which do not refer to ulterior purposes; a primary goal is simply being together. Think of friendships and the like in this connection. In brief, there is an important subcategory of groups that it is harder to describe or define in terms of ulterior purposes. I will describe these as communities, in contrast with other groups that can largely be defined in terms of their purposes, such as corporations, labour unions, and sports associations.

Communities present, what I would call, *formation questions*. These are questions about the interaction of individual and group identities: how individuals form and are formed by their communities. On social contract models of justice, formation is standardly pictured[34] as a one-way process in which asocial individuals have only instrumental interests in establishing a common normative order.[35] Without denying the interest and ingenuity of contractarian theories presented by philosophers like

---

31. It should be noted that some groups like corporations exist solely in order to get recognition and rights within the encompassing normative order; others, which can be plausibly labelled "communities" have reasons for their existence independently of such recognition. This latter category is not a simple one; it consists of a continuum or spectrum of groups.

32. [1988] 2 S.C.R. 711; [1988] 2 S.C.R. 790.

33. See Roger Scruton, *The Meaning of Conservatism* (Harmondsworth: Pelican Books, 1980) at 141-160 on "the autonomous institution".

34. I use this term because I am concerned here with the social contract as a metaphor.

35. Michael McDonald, "Ideology and Morality in Hard Times" in W. Cragg, ed., *Contemporary Moral Issues* (Toronto: McGraw Hill-Ryerson, 1983) at 598-610.

John Rawls and David Gauthier, I believe that we should be sceptical about using the state of nature as a universal departure point or *point d'appui* for addressing formation questions.[36] Contractarianism deforms formation questions in two ways. The first is by locating the 'real self' outside a social context. This is a point that a number of philosophers, including notably Michael Sandel and Bernard Williams, have raised concerning the conceivability of state of nature or original position arguments as ways of assessing our fundamental normative position.[37] The second is a rather less metaphysical and more political concern about the sort of individual and social alienation such a perspective promotes. It is not accidental that libertarianism, which is one of the least sympathetic positions to collective rights, has received its best defence from such hard-line contractarians as David Gauthier and, most recently, my colleague Jan Narveson.[38]

In any case, my purpose is to raise questions rather than load the agenda by presupposing certain answers. Let me then ask the assistance of social scientists and legal scholars in addressing the issues that arise out of this double understanding conception of collective rights. First, from social scientists, I would ask for help in modelling what I assume to be a continuum from purposeful associations to identifying communities. I would then ask for help in understanding communities from within, from the minority community's perspectives, and from without, from the larger community's perspective. Understanding another community from within raises acute problems in the translatability of perspectives — in particular in the philosophy of the social sciences.[39] But perhaps social scientists can provide at least approximate notions of how the potential subjects of collective rights — "communities" or "peoples" — see themselves. They can also help by providing ways of conceptualizing and imaginatively reconstructing differences in a minority's understanding of itself and the majority's understanding of the minority.[40]

---

36. John Rawls, *A Theory of Justice* (Cambridge: Harvard University Press, 1971).
37. Michael Sandel, *Liberalism and the Limits of Justice* (Cambridge: Cambridge University Press, 1983). Bernard Williams, "Persons, Character and Morality" in A.O. Rorty, ed., *The Identities of Persons* (Berkeley: University of California Press, 1976).
38. I do not think that libertarians are the only or even the worst ideological opponents of collective rights. Fascism with its forced identification of the people or nation with the state are even worse theoretical (and far worse political) opponents of collective rights for minorities. See Jan Narveson, *The Libertarian Idea* (Philadelphia: Temple University Press, 1989).
39. See Peter Winch, *The Idea of a Social Science and Its Relation to Philosophy* (London: Routledge and Kegan Paul, 1966).
40. Though even this formulation understates the complexity of the challenge. In functioning minority rights regime, the minority's self-conception is not insulated from its participation in the larger normative order: in itself it is a community; in relation to, say, the law, it is a right-holder or beneficiary.

From legal scholars, I would ask for help in thinking through the notions of legal agency and patiency (my term for the capacity for being a patient or object of others' actions) to see how well they can apply to diverse kinds of groups. I have tried to do this in terms of the notion of self-collection based on a shared understanding. But I must confess that notion has its origins in two, perhaps culturally bound, sources: one is the notion of legal personhood found in the law of associations and corporations and the other is what might be described as a philosophical reconstruction of a proto-legal community along Hartian lines.[41] The first has the advantage of linking the notion of communities to familiar classes of rights-bearers; the second has the advantage of tying it to a paradigmatic notion of a rule-creator. My worry with both approaches is that they may result in trying to force a variety of different shaped pegs into two extremely narrow holes: that of the legal person as the bearer of legal rights and the self-governing community as the source of law.[42]

Fairness. I now want to move from questions which arise from trying to find ways of treating communities reasonably to those which arise from trying to treat communities fairly or justly. Let me do this by discussing what I see as liberalism's strong *prima facie* presumption against collective rights. Standardly, this presumption arises as a corollary of arguments which purport to establish the moral priority of individual rights. These arguments have been expressed in two philosophically different forms; these are the foundational analogues of the protected choice and protected benefit analyses of rights discussed earlier.[43] The first seeks to ground liberal institutions and practices in the actual or, more standardly, hypothetical informed and voluntary choices of citizens.[44] The second is a benefit-centred conception, which tests conventional rules in terms of payoffs to those under the rules.[45] The

---

41. H.L.A. Hart and especially A.M. Honoré's 1975 paper, "What Is a Group?", *supra*, note 26. See Hallis and Dan-Cohen on the legal nature of corporations, *supra*, note 19. Another useful source here is Samuel Stoljar, *Groups and Entities: An Enquiry Into Corporate Theory* (Canberra: Australian National University, 1973).
42. The result may be unfortunate in both theoretical and practical terms. In terms of theory, the use of an all purpose metaphor like that of the legal person may lead us into misdescribing important legal issues (vide Dan-Cohen). As already noted, in terms of practice, the manner and mode in which we recognize communities as bearers (or deny that they can be bearers) of collective rights may distort those communities and deny them the autonomy they need to survive and flourish.
43. Recall though my earlier warning that a "mix and match" strategy is possible and even desirable.
44. Locke, Hobbes, and Rawls are leading examples of this way of grounding individual rights. I should note that for the sake of simplicity I am ignoring attempts to defend individual rights as natural rights. For a philosophically acute account of the problems with natural rights theories see Sumner, *supra*, note 2, c. 4.
45. I would include classical and contemporary utilitarian attempts to ground individual rights, such as, Bentham, Mill, Sidgwick, Brandt, and Parfit. Professor Brian Schwartz

choice and benefit rationales have been combined in various ways, such
as through the assumption that the conditions of social interaction are
essentially those of classical economics, such as Sidgwick's *Principles
of Political Economics*, or that self-centred maximizers would do best
by becoming constrained maximizers, as in Gauthier's *Morality and
Advantage*.[46]

With regard to collective rights, this presumption in favour of
individual rights commits the liberal to a kind of normative reductionism.
The only collective rights that can pass the test are those that derived
from the exercise or enjoyment of individual rights. This generates what
I would describe as a class-action model of collective rights. One authority
defines a class or representative action as:

> A lawsuit brought by representative member[s] of a large group of persons
> on behalf of all members of the group. The number of the persons
> represented must be so numerous that it is not practicable to join them
> as plaintiffs. The class must be ascertainable, the members must share
> a common interest in the issues of law and the action must satisfy a number
> of special requirements before the trial court will certify the action to
> be one maintainable as a class action.[47]

Notice that class actions involve *non-voluntary* groups. Thus for
the liberal, the key moral questions raised by class actions concern (a)
*the need for proceeding without the express consent of all members
of the group*, and then (b) *the extent to which those in the group genuinely
share "a common interest in the issues of law"*.[48] The model of the group
provided by the class action is "thin" in that the answer to question
(a) is usually that while it is impractical to actually secure each and
every individual's consent, there is every indication that it would be

---

also seems to fall into this camp as well when he says, "The only thing of ultimate
moral importance is subjective experience — what living beings think, feel, sense."
I would invite him to engage in a quasi-Humean introspective test by looking into
his own subjective experiences to see whether he finds there some pure, essential
individuality or whether what he labels as individual is deeply socially rooted. Even
to use a language to describe one's subjective experiences is to engage in a fundamentally
social activity. Even to say that "I am more than the sum of my social roles" is to
locate oneself within a social context.

46. Sidgwick, *Principles of Political Economics*, 3rd ed. (London: Macmillan, 1901);
Gauthier, *Morality and Advantage* (Oxford: Oxford University Press, 1986).

47. John C. Yogis, *Canadian Law Dictionary* (Toronto: Barron's Educational Services,
1983), at 39. Also see *Black's Law Dictionary*, Abridged Fifth Edition, (St. Paul,
Minn.: West Publishing Co., 1983), at 129, which defines a class action as "provid[ing]
a means by which, a large group of persons are interested in a matter, one or more
may sue or be sued as representatives of the class without needing to join every member
of the class".

48. See, for example, David M. Beatty, *Putting the Charter to Work: Designing a
Constitutional Labour Code* (Kingston: McGill-Queens University Press, 1987).

forthcoming; the answer to question (b) is that whatever their other differences, the parties have on the issues in question a sufficient convergence of interests so that a class action would not significantly disadvantage particular members of the group. Hence, the class action provides a realistic model of the group as a convenient device for advancing the parallel wills and interests of its members. Crucially, both the exercise and interest dimensions of self-collection are absent from the class action concept. A class action is called for because the individuals in questions are *not* united in such a way as to be able to otherwise exercise the right. They lack a shared understanding and a collective decision-procedure. Thus, the individuals represented in the class action cannot advance their interests in the way that they could have provided they had been members of a corporation, union, or association in pursuit of common interests. The interests of those in a class action are severable or disjoint in that an obligant could satisfy the interests of some beneficiaries without satisfying the interests of all. The members of the class in question are neither taken to have interlocking interests in each others' interests, nor to have some literally or metaphorically common interest, like a common fund or assets.[49]

This thin, class-action sense of collective rights provides a foil against which can be constructed thicker notions of collective rights. In this area, Denise Réaume has done a brilliant job of providing a richer conception of shared goods in the area of linguistic rights.[50] The thin concept also provides a useful yardstick of how seriously we as Canadians take collective or community rights. My quite unsystematic sampling of students and popular literature in English Canada is that while there is considerable sympathy for the individual rights of minority members, there is precious little sympathy for their collective rights. What most English Canadians want then is "a level playing field" on which only one kind of game can be played — the rough and tumble game of individual rights.

Now if you hadn't already noticed, let me state my conviction that we miss a great deal by retaining this thin class-action notion of collective rights. In terms of collective agency, there is the loss of what Benjamin Constant labelled "the liberty of the ancients" — the positive liberty of participation in collective self-rule or "autonomy" in its original sense.[51]

49. See Stoljar, *supra*, note 41.
50. Denise Réaume, "Individuals Groups and Rights to Public Goods" (1988) 38 *U.T.L.J.* 1.
51. I owe this valuable insight to Joseph Pestieau's recent paper, "Droits des personnes, des peuples, et des minorités", which I have commented on at the annual meetings of the Canadian Philosophical Association during the Learned Societies in May 1989.

Moreover, there is a failure to recognize the non-voluntary, identifying community as a morally significant decision-maker and right-holder. In terms of a loss of benefits, *the cost of liberal individualism is deracination.* We see this in an extreme form for native people on the skid rows of Winnipeg, Edmonton, and Saskatoon. Of the need for roots in a purposeless identifying community, the French philosopher Simone Weil wrote:

> To be rooted is perhaps the most important and least recognized need of the human soul. It is one of the hardest to define. A human being has roots by virtue of his real, active and natural participation in the life of a community which preserves in living shape certain particular treasures of the past and certain particular expectations for the future. This participation is a natural one, in the sense that it is automatically brought about by place, conditions of birth, profession and social surroundings. Every human being needs to have multiple roots. It is necessary for him to draw wellnigh the whole of his moral, intellectual and spiritual life by way to the environment of which he forms a natural part.[52]

This raises a crucial question: can we in Canada rise to the challenge of respecting community as well as individual rights? Let me close by listing what I take to be some of the primary intellectual challenges this question poses. I leave to others the task of posing more concrete practical challenges.

1. Minority collective rights require a double understanding — a minority's shared understanding within a more encompassing understanding shared by majority and minority communities. There is always then a question of balance: preserving the whole without destroying the parts. But neither the whole nor the parts remain static. Even in constitutional matters there is no eternally right balance to be struck once and for all time.

---

52. Simone Weil, *The Need for Roots: Prelude to a Declaration of Duties Towards Mankind* (London: Ark, 1987) at 41 [1952 translation of L'enracinement 1949]. On pp. 7-8, Weil says: "The degree of respect owing to human collectivities is a very high one, for several reasons. To start with, each is unique, and if destroyed, cannot be replaced. One sack of corn can always be substituted for another sack of corn. The food which a collectivity supplied for the souls of those who form part of it has no equivalent in the entire universe. Secondly, because of its continuity, a collectivity is already moving forward into the future. It contains food, not only for the souls of the living, but also for the souls of beings yet unborn which are to come into the world during the immediately succeeding centuries. Lastly, due to this same continuity, a collectivity has its roots in the past. It constitutes the sole agency for preserving the spiritual treasures accumulated by the dead, the sole transmitting agency by means of which the dead can speak to the living." This emphasis on the place of the individual in an identifying community is also present in Neil MacCormick's "Nation and Nationalism", *supra*, note 15 at 247-264 in which he explores the concept of nationalism and defends Scottish nationalism.

2. This can be reinforced by reminding ourselves that communities differ in their needs and wants. While the overall objective of having identifying communities flourish is a worthy one, the conditions for the flourishing of a small Francophone community in Manitoba are not the same as for the Anglophone minority in Montréal. These in turn are quite different than the elements essential to the well-being of Micmacs in Nova Scotia. The communities in question need different clusters of rights to protect different domains. Moreover, as communities, they need to be recognized in different ways. At the level of a theory of collective rights, it is essential to have an array of alternative models of communities as agents and beneficiaries so that the law's understanding of divergent communities does not amount to a substantial misunderstanding.

3. One characteristically liberal worry is whether affirming the collective rights of a group vitiates the individual rights of its members. Can we work out with the communities in question a shared understanding of such vital matters as exit-rights and entrance-rights?[53] Obviously, in some cases, compromise is impossible for us: we would not grant to fanatical defenders of patriarchy the Roman right of the *paterfamilias* over the welfare and even the lives of family members. In other cases, compromise is impossible for minority communities: old order Mennonites will not send their older children to modern secondary schools or to serve in our defence forces. But I would urge us not to conceive every attempt to reach an accommodation as a zero-sum game. Without denying that individual members have sometimes to be protected from their communities, most of us would hold dear conceptions of individual well-being, which place a high premium on integration into communities in which our individual lives have their significance and savour. Thus,

---

53. An important part of the thin model of collective rights is that dissociation is seen as a crucial right. The liberal concedes that in not all cases is it practicable or just to let individuals completely dissociate themselves from groups. Sometimes there are free-rider problems which necessitate the use of devices like the Rand Formula in regard to membership in labour unions. In other cases, liberals are willing to allow opt-out, as opposed to opt-in, formulas for determining group membership. The presumption though is against such devices: individuals must be free to leave as well as to join groups. Now I do not want to deny that the right to dissociate is an important individual right, but I would suggest that insistence on this right has kept us from taking seriously minority collective rights. For one thing, it exacerbates conflicts with more traditional cultures if we emphasize the exit-rights of their members, particularly their youth. (See *Yoder* v. *Wisconsin* (1972) 406 U.S. 205 in this connection). Second, it makes it too easy to destabilize emerging groups in which the sense of solidarity is just beginning to form. Third, emphasizing exit-rights leads us to a test for the legitimacy of groups which is alternatively too broad or too narrow. Some voluntary groups are obnoxious, but members stick with them for want of better alternatives. More importantly, we overlook the needs that self-collection serves, particularly the collective or shared aspirations of a people.

while in some cases either society's [U_S] or the minority's [M_S] shared understanding makes agreement on this issue impossible, it is often the case that collective minority rights enhance the individual rights of members through providing a strong identifying community.

4. A second characteristically liberal worry has to do with how a minority community will treat its own minorities. Hence, it might be argued that there is a moral presumption in favour of a minority extending to parallel minorities within it the same rights which the minority thinks have been justly accorded to it. That is, the principle says that as the minority [M_a] is to society as a whole [S] so is a sub-minority [M_k] to the minority [M_a]. It is important to stress that this principle only applies directly to what can be labelled parallel *(sub)minority*; this is a (sub)minority [M_k] which is in the same position vis-à-vis the minority [M_a] as that minority stands to the whole of society. Thus, it would be incongruous for the union of Canadian Automobile Workers (CAW) to try to organize office workers at automobile parts manufacturing companies into a union, while refusing the right of its own office workers to organize a union at the CAW head office. Nonetheless, this would not thereby commit the CAW to recognizing a union of its top management personnel. It is also important to notice that there can be reasons, especially historical reasons, for treating minority A more favourably than an apparently parallel (sub)minority B. A may be owed compensation for past collective injustices that B has not experienced.

Moreover, we cannot in all fairness expect minorities to commit suicide.[54] It is essential for a community to maintain a critical mass sufficient to have the rights vital to their continuity.[55] Since I am not a demographer, I cannot speak with any authority on the often expressed concerns in Québec about the gradual erosion of the fully functioning Francophone community. I would only say that these worries strike me as far more plausible than the claims one hears from English-rights activists in Ontario and Alberta. Similarly, I believe that there are few valid points of comparison between the situation of Anglophone minority community in Québec and Francophone minorities elsewhere in Canada. There are perhaps then more reasons for allowing significant asymmetries in regard to collective rights than there is in the case of individual rights.[56]

---

54. It is important to stress that the principle stated in the antecedent applies to parallel minorities, i.e., minorities who are in the same position vis-à-vis the minority as the minority stands to the majority. It is also important to notice that there can be historical reasons for treating minority A more favourably than a parallel minority B. As already mentioned, A may be owed compensation for past collective injustices that B has not experienced.
55. McDonald, *supra*, note 10 at 121.
56. These asymmetries arise from the pronounced differences in the size, structure, and type of various collective right-holders.

5. Both these liberal worries, (3) and (4), point to basic tensions between individualists, who advocate collective rights only to advance individual rights, and collectivists, who ground the case for collective rights on a thicker notion of the community.[57] These tensions manifest themselves at two key stress points: (a) in the idea of the state and (b) in the idea of the citizen. For the individualist, the state is fundamentally a collective means to individual ends; citizenship is not an end in itself. For the collectivist, the notions of state and citizenship are richer in their intertwining of individual and social well-being; there is not the gulf that the individualist assumes to exist between the public and the private.[58]

6. Hence, there are two different defences of collective and, particularly, minority rights in both domestic and international law.[59] On the individualist view, collective rights, like individual rights, protect essentially private areas of concern in which individual members of minority groups may find shelter.[60] On the collectivist view, collective rights are essential to public life and to individual self-identification; they provide the vital means whereby we express our true natures as members of identifying communities. To put the issue starkly, the individualist is with regard to public life a monotheist: there shall be "no strange gods" in public — only individual rights and/or interests. The collectivist is a polytheist in politics — welcoming into her pantheon almost every community's household gods.

I would leave you then with a final question: can the individualist and collectivist ideals be reconciled intellectually and practically? This is key to our future as a country. I have however no answer to it. But then I didn't promise answers; as a philosopher, I only offer questions.

---

57. I have chosen the terms "individualists" and "collectivists" in preference to that of "liberals" and "communitarians" for two reasons. First, a case can be made out that some liberals, like Mill and Hobhouse, have recognized the importance of identifying communities; see William Kymlicka's, *Liberalism, Community, and Culture* (Oxford: Oxford University Press, 1989). Second, communitarians have not, as far as I know, said much about collective rights. So while they share with, what I have labelled, "collectivists" a certain view of politics, they are not committed to the same strong defence of minorities.

58. Pestieau sees the individualist notion as having its roots in protestantism; whereas, collectivism has an ancestry which is more in the Russian Orthodox and, to a lesser extent, the Catholic tradition.

59. For international law, see my paper "Collective Rights in International Relations" in Cragg, Larouche, and Lewis, eds., *supra*, note 29 at 115-127.

60. See Jan Narveson, "Have We a Right to Non-Discrimination" in D. Poff and W. Waluchow, eds., *Business Ethics in Canada* (Scarborough: Prentice-Hall Canada, 1987) at 183-198.

COMMENTS

Bryan Schwartz

Can communities have rights? If you ask me as a lawyer, I will give you a very simple answer: yes. Of course communities can have rights: sticks can have rights, birds can have rights, the devil can have rights, God can have rights, anyone or anything can have rights. In theory and practice, it can be done. But the assignment of rights depends partly on considerations of convenience and practicality, sometimes on considerations of political compromise, and I hope, to some extent, on the basis of underlying moral vision. That is how one has to start — with underlying moral vision, not with the structural analysis of rights.

Rights are not a primary philosophical, or political, concept. The way you assign rights depends on what your underlying moral vision is. In fact, I do not think that there is such a thing as a fixed concept of rights that has a particular meaning. It is not only that we have varying conceptions of what rights are, but that we have divergent understandings of what the concept of right is to begin with. In different systems of philosophy or politics, rights serve much different roles and mean much different things. Engaging in exercises about analyzing and parsing the structural and formal characteristics of rights is, therefore, a philosophical enterprise of some value but with definitely limited prospects. As a matter of fact, some moral visions are not based on rights at all. It is somewhat ironic that, as much as the collectivist literature calls us to surmount our ethnocentricism, it does not recognize that a lot of social and political cultures are not based on rights. I happen to be inculcated in a religious and moral system that is based almost entirely on obligations.

So the question I want to start with is what is our underlying moral vision? What sort of good and just society are we working towards? Based on our answer, we can decide how we want to assign rights on the basis of principle or practicality.

To answer questions about moral vision, one also has to ask what philosophers call 'ontological questions', questions about what it means to be. Probably the leading article on "groupism" in law is by Professor Ronald Garet of the University of Southern California, who purports to tell us that groups are just as intrinsically important as individuals on the basis of what he purports to be an existential analysis. Existential analysis is a right place to start, but I think Garret has obscured anything interesting about existence in a welter of jargon.[1]

The starting point for me is simply this: absolutely nothing counts, absolutely nothing is of moral significance, except what living beings experience. Absolutely nothing else. What living beings think, feel, and what they care about — that is what counts. Nothing else, *intrinsically*. I do not think that the environment has any intrinsic rights. A mountain may have value, but that value is entirely derivative of the fact that maybe birds live on it, or people appreciate it, or climb on it, or whatever. I cannot imagine anything that is dead to itself having intrinsic moral significance. What counts are things that are alive to themselves.

The location of existence as far as I can see, is in individuals. A married couple may consist of two individuals, it may behave in certain ways that you can describe collectively, but ultimately it consists of two individual consciousnesses travelling through time. In fact the point about travelling through time is one of the great mysteries of metaphysics, but it's something you all believe, even if you never thought about it. You not only exist in your own unique world of consciousness at any moment in time, you also exist in it through time. The child you were at six and the adult you will be when you are sixty have something in common with who you are now. That is different from all the other realms of experience that ever have been or ever will be.

So I am an individualist first and foremost because I believe that the nature of the universe is individualistic, and that any attempt to analyse moral realities primarily in terms of collective realities is inevitably crude and will not do justice to the underlying individual realities. I am not only an individualist, but also liberal. I believe that every individual should have the right to define herself or himself to the maximum extent possible, with freedom and dignity. Even if that sometimes means damage being done to the members of other groups who would prefer to maintain themselves in a more closely defined structure. There is a very unfair rap that is laid against us liberal individualists, which is, that we favour

---

1. Garet, Communality and Existence: The Rights of Groups, (1983) 56 S. *Cal. L. Rev.* 1001. A more extended critique is contained in my article, "Individual and Community", forthcoming in *Journal of Law and Religion*.

the atomistic lifestyle, the lifestyle of the individual. As a liberal, I no more prefer the lifestyle of a hermit to the lifestyles of people who live in communes. Those are the choice of individuals. If individuals want to get together and live in the neo-colony or form the muni-colony, that is just as much to be respected as people who want to go off and watch the stars from an isolated observatory. Individualists who say the primary unit of moral account is the individual, surely do not deny that individuals may want to seek self-realization by forming all sorts of organizations, from a family to a cultural organization, to a religion, to a country, or not collectively at all.

As a matter of fact, I think that liberal individualism has tremendous resources to carry out the process of reconciliation that Professor McDonald calls for. That was the burden of my book *First Principles, Second Thoughts*[2]: to try to show that one can, consistently with the liberal individualist framework, accommodate a great many, indeed most, of the demands that groups make upon society, for example, those that aboriginal people have made in the constitutional process. *First Principles, Second Thoughts* is not only a philosophical study; it attempts as well to be a study in constitutional pragmatics. It is not my view that the aim of constitution building is to make one moral vision prevail over another. We should avoid unnecessary battles over ultimate symbolism. On the contrary, the aim is to try in a principled way to build a just society which, to the maximum extent possible, does not require people to abandon their ultimate philosophical beliefs. I would like to see the problem of aboriginal peoples resolved in a way which does not require anyone to abandon their particular underlying moral philosophy. Rather we should seek common ground: practical solutions which are acceptable from both the liberal individualist standpoint and to those who understand the world in collectivistic or groupist terms.[3]

Part of my philosophical writing has been an attempt to expand the resources available to the liberal individualist vision of the world in accommodating group claims. Historically, one can almost view the development of mainstream liberalism in a number of steps. First of all, there is negative liberty: nobody can stop me from sleeping under the bridge, and nobody can stop me from going to Paris, but of course that does not mean I have the money or the opportunity to do either. Today, mainstream liberalism is social-welfare liberalism, which

---

2. *First Principles, Second Thoughts: Aboriginal Peoples, Constitutional Reform and Canadian Statecraft* (Montreal: The Institute for Research on Public Policy, 1986).
3. Even with imaginative efforts to create common ground, however, some cases of irreconcilable conflict may remain. In these cases, I believe that the principles of liberal individualism should prevail.

recognizes that it is just not enough to have freedom and individual self-determination, or negative liberty. I think a social-welfare liberal should also recognize that part of social welfare, for those who choose it, is to have supportive human relationships. An example I like to give is the work of United States Senator Daniel Patrick Moynihan who has written that the leading cause of inner-city poverty in the United States is the breakup of families in the inner-city. I believe that we should regard that as another form of poverty: the poverty of human deprivation. We should recognize that there is a denial of social justice when people grow up without fathers, just as there is a denial of social justice when people grow up without money.[4]

Looking at a community as ultimately consisting of individuals, each with his or her own special characteristics, is a way of humanizing collectivities which is likely to conduce to their being respected. One of the aims of a tolerant society is to get people to see each other not just as one more example of the "Slurbians" or the "Yungolians", but as individuals who have something very special and unique to offer, not only in the context of the group affiliation but in addition to the group affiliation. It is also to see each other as ones who can choose ultimately to redefine the group affiliation.

Contrary to Professor McDonald's view, I do not regard groupism or collectivism as going against the mainstream of Canadian constitutional thought or practice. On the contrary, some critics of Canadian political life have characterized us as a neo-feudal society. Gerald Vano in *Neo-feudalism: The Canadian Dilemma*,[5] argues that Canada has historically understood itself primarily as an agglomeration of groups and not as individuals, and, he argues that is precisely what is wrong with this country. As a matter of constitutional law, if you read the *Constitution Act, 1867*[6] you will find a lot of group rights. You will find the establishment of state religion for a few privileged churches, but you will not find much in the way of individual rights. If you look at the *Constitution Act, 1982*[7] you will find a raft of concessions to group rights, s. 15(2) (affirmative action programs), s. 27 (multicultural heritage), s. 23 (minority language education), and s. 25 (the shielding of aboriginal rights). So the collectivist stream is not only realized in Canadian social practice through time, it is also a very important element of social practice and belief that has crystallized in our fundamental constitutional document.

---

4. This idea is developed further in "Individual and Community", *supra*, note 1.
5. (Toronto: Anansi, 1981).
6. (U.K.) 30 & 31 Vict., c. 3.
7. Being Schedule B of the *Canada Act, 1982* (U.K.), 1982, c. 11.

Contrary to what some of the collectivists may tell you, it is often untrue that these minority groups are the poor waifs of politics, unable to defend themselves — it depends on the group. Some groups have enormous political advantages over other groups or unorganized individuals. This is a point that is made very strongly and effectively in an article by Professor Bruce Ackerman.[8] If you are standing for the principle that every individual should be treated equally and you do not belong, for that purpose, to an organizational structure, it is not easy to mobilize others to your cause. Everybody else who believes in it has a lot of other concerns or they do not identify themselves primarily as dedicated to the cause of individual equality. Whereas if you belong to a particular ethnic or religious group, you are likely to have an in-built organization that will very effectively help you to mobilize and lobby. And calling that minority group a special interest may cause you to look a little bit more deeply into exactly how Canadian politics are played out.

I have called the Canadian branch of collectivism "history-based groupism". This collectivism raises another question which Professor McDonald might add to his list. Should we have a collectivist attitude which assigns different rights to different groups on the basis of their different histories? French Canadians in Québec claim certain right because they were sort of here first. Aboriginal people claim certain rights because many of them actually were here first, although not all of them. Groups claim rights to a certain share of representation in society because the group was oppressed in the past, regardless of the circumstances of particular individuals. I have strong objections to trying to accommodate group claims in a way that gives special privileges to different groups on the basis of their different histories. On the contrary, what we should be trying to do is finding ways to accommodate group-oriented aspirations while assuring equal dignity and equal respect for the members of all groups. For example, the multicultural language program in the public schools in my own province of Manitoba gives every group, whether they are Ukrainians or Jews or whatever, the opportunity to have their children spend half the school day being educated in their heritage language. I find that a much more attractive model, one which gives people the opportunity to choose to maintain their cultures and contribute to the richness of human experience without signalling out certain groups for special privilege. The former approach is not fair nor is it politically an attractive way to go. It provokes enormous resentment from those of us who were not on the earlier airplane.

---

8. "Beyond Carolene Products" (1985), 98 *Harv. L. Rev.* 713.

I now want to discuss a very hard question, since I do not want to pretend that there is always going to be the possibility of reconciliation and accommodation between my vision and the groupist vision. My work does adopt the perspective that there is tremendous scope for accommodation: that these are not sharply contrasting visions in which no congruence is possible. In practice, there are large areas of common ground. Practical solutions can be found that are consistent with the symbolic and philosophical aspirations of both sides. But sometimes there are going to be hard cases and in those hard cases I would have a different hard answer than would Professor McDonald. If you would ask me, should a group be able to maintain its viability, its population bases, by limiting the educational opportunity of its own children, I would say no. The resources a group has in maintaining the group identity of its children should be commensurate with the moral vision that the group offers its children. A group does not have the right, and the individuals within that group do not have the right, to maintain their particular lifestyle by suppressing the opportunity for their children to define themselves in the way they see fit.

One should also ask some hard questions about language policy towards a linguistic majority. Usually we think in terms of protecting minority language rights. For example, in the Québec situation we are concerned with the limitation of English-speaking minority rights. But there is another very pressing question, which is how the Québec majority treats the other members of the Québec majority. Is it right and proper to deny local school boards the opportunity to expose Francophone children to English as a second language? Is it right for us to have a society that says to working class people, whose children go to public schools, "we're going to fight assimilation by making sure that your kids do not acquire a fluent knowledge of the other official languages"? I think it is a very important question and I hope that we can confront it.

What does the future hold for us? Well I do not have the sense that my side is winning big. On the contrary, I am very worried about a society that is increasingly balkanized on the basis of rigid ethnic lines and increasingly intolerant towards minorities and towards individual members of those minorities. The liberal vision is far from being the predominant one. Even though it is the one most likely to succeed, it is endangered and has to be fought for. It is very much worth fighting for.

Partie II / Part II

Vers une théorie des droits linguistiques

Les théories des droits linguistiques sont traditionnellement fondées sur les relations de pouvoir *de facto*. Les droits linguistiques ne sont souvent reconnus que lorsque sont présentes à la fois une assise territoriale importante, une longue histoire et une influence politique. Voilà qui offre un terrain peu propice à la résolution des querelles linguistiques.

Denise Réaume élabore une fondation théorique mieux motivée. Elle rejette la justification traditionnelle issue d'un modèle de «survie» selon lequel on peut invoquer, en faveur du droit à l'existence d'une langue, des droits moraux qui existent indépendamment du sujet qui la parle et qui autorisent à une certaine coercition. Elle lui préfère la notion de «sécurité linguistique», qui vise à créer un environnement juste pour les personnes qui pratiquent la langue, sans déformer les pratiques linguistiques de qui que ce soit.

Réaume poursuit ses propos en établissant des distinctions entre les deux régimes qui favorisent la sécurité linguistique au Canada; chacun d'eux comporte ses avantages individuels et collectifs. Sous le régime de la «tolérance linguistique», cette sécurité est favorisée par les garanties constitutionnelles qui assurent la liberté d'expression, la liberté d'association et les droits à l'égalité. Sous le régime des «langues officielles», les gouvernements offrent services et éducation dans la langue officielle de la minorité, favorisant ainsi à la fois le développement individuel et la sécurité collective. Reconnaissant que le régime des langues officielles ne protège que quelques communautés minoritaires, Réaume définit des critères permettant de déterminer quelles seront les collectivités susceptibles d'en bénéficier.

Michael MacMillan propose deux directions de base à une théorie des droits linguistiques. L'une, semblable à celle de Réaume, passe de la théorie à la pratique et classe les droits linguistiques parmi les droits de la personne. MacMillan distingue trois catégories de revendications de droits : les droits à la tolérance (qui correspondent plus ou moins au régime des langues officielles proposé par Réaume), et les droits de promotion active (qui incluent le régime des langues officielles et plus encore; par exemple la *Charte de la langue française* du Québec). MacMillan affirme que la théorie de Réaume bascule vers les droits de promotion active et qu'elle autorise de ce fait des mesures qui outrepassent les motifs de sécurité linguistique. C'est dans cette dernière catégorie que l'on se trouve parfois en conflit fondamental avec les revendications des autres groupes linguistiques.

La direction opposée, qui va de la pratique à la théorie, exige que l'on rassemble et que l'on définisse un consensus sur la façon dont les droits sont perçus. Dès lors, la théorie des droits linguistiques reflète les réalités fondamentales sous-jacentes partagées de tous — le *statu quo*, essentiellement. En s'appuyant sur une série de sondages publics, MacMillan démontre comment, à cause de l'appui limité accordé aux droits linguistiques des minorités, la théorie résultante serait de portée beaucoup plus restrictive que la théorie évoluant dans le sens opposé.

Towards a Theory of Language Rights

The foundations for theories of language rights have traditionally been grounded in *de facto* power relationships. Often, language rights have been recognized only when the circumstances of a significant territorial base, a lengthy history, and political influence, converge. This provides a weak foundation from which to reconcile language disputes.

Denise Réaume constructs a more principled theoretical grounding for language rights. She rejects the traditional theoretical justification, based on a 'survival' model. That model assumes there are moral claims to the existence of a language irrespective of who speaks it, at times requiring the coercion of others to speak the language. Rather, she advances the notion of "linguistic security" which aims to create a fair environment for present language speakers and does not distort the linguistic practices of anyone.

Réaume expands on the theory by distinguishing between the two regimes which foster linguistic security in Canada, each of which provide both individual and collective benefits. In the regime of "linguistic tolerance", security is enhanced through the constitutional protections of freedom of expression, freedom of association and equality rights. In an "official languages" regime, government provides services and education in the minority official language, enhancing both individual development and collective security. Recognizing that an official languages regime protects only a few minority communities, Réaume develops criteria for determining which communities may be given the benefit of inclusion in that regime.

Michael MacMillan suggests two basic directions for a theory of language rights. One, such as Réaume's, moves from theory to practice, taking the view of language rights as a human right. MacMillan specifies three categories of rights claims: toleration rights (roughly equating Réaume's regime of linguistic tolerance), promotion-oriented rights (roughly equating Réaume's official language regime), and strong promotion rights (which includes the official languages regime and more: for example, Québec's *Charter of the French Language*). MacMillan argues that Réaume's theory spills over into strong promotion rights and is, therefore, permissive of measures beyond those enhancing linguistic security. It is in this latter category that one occasionally finds fundamental conflict with the claims of other linguistic groups.

The opposing direction, moving from practice to theory, calls for the collection and identification of the shared understandings of rights. The resulting theory of language rights reflects these basic underlying shared realities — essentially a reflection of the *status quo*. Drawing upon a series of Canadian public opinion polls, MacMillan shows how, due to limited support for minority language rights, the resulting theory would be far more restrictive in focus than would be a theory moving in the opposite direction.

THE CONSTITUTIONAL PROTECTION OF LANGUAGE: SURVIVAL OR SECURITY?*

Denise G. Réaume

As central as the question of language is to Canadian political history, we are still lacking a comprehensive theory of language rights. Under what circumstances and to what extent should the use of particular languages be legally protected? My objective in this paper is to outline the main pillars of such a theory through four stages. First, I will discuss the nature of the interest that is capable of grounding rights to use a particular language; second, I will consider what might be called the social dimension of language rights, i.e. the importance of the fact that language use is a collective practice; third, I will examine the main language rights recognized in Canada in light of the first two points; and finally, I will touch on the issue of which linguistic communities should receive special protections and consider the moral implications of the possible under-inclusiveness of the present regime.

1. THE NATURE OF THE INTEREST IN LANGUAGE

I begin by adopting an account of rights which makes human interests central. Following Joseph Raz, I will say that a right to X exists if and only if some person's interest is sufficient reason for holding others to be under a duty to provide or secure X.[1] From this perspective any

* This paper presents, in abbreviated form, some ideas being developed in a larger project of which Dr. Les Green, of the Department of Philosophy and Osgoode Hall Law School, York University, is co-author. I am grateful to him for permission to use some of our joint research here. We are both indebted to the Connaught Programme on Legal Theory and Public Policy, University of Toronto, and the Human Rights Fund of the Department of Justice for financial support. The opinions expressed here are solely those of the author. I am also grateful to the Editor of the *McGill Law Journal* for permission to use some material which was first published in (1989) 34 *McGill L.J.*

1. J. Raz, "On the Nature of Rights", *Mind* 93 (1984) 194-214. See also, Raz, *The Morality of Freedom* (Oxford: Clarendon Press, 1986) c. 7, and Raz, "Right-based Moralities", in Waldron, ed., *Theories of Rights* (Oxford: Oxford University Press, 1984).

theoretical account of language rights must begin by attempting to identify an interest in language that could plausibly be thought sufficiently urgent to warrant holding others to be duty-bound. Now, there is a sense in which our interest in language is one of the most important we possess.[2] Without language, without a sophisticated means of communication, we would scarcely be human; we would certainly be unable to formulate the terms of our life together. But this tells us little about the nature of our interest in speaking some particular language. It merely shows that it would be wrong to deprive a human being of language altogether; wrong, for example, to raise a child in isolation from human speech. Since we know that human infants have the capacity to learn any of the world's languages, denial of the opportunity to speak a particular one is not an infringement of the basic right to be treated like a human being. In the sense in which I shall use it, a theory of language rights is not about this foundational interest in language. Rather, in the most general terms, it is about the interest in using a particular language, namely, one's mother tongue. Thus, we start after the foundational right has already been secured; after people have already acquired a language in the normal way. Our concern, then, is the extent to which their ability to use this language should be further protected.

I shall distinguish between two overlapping, but nonetheless quite different, interests in using one's mother tongue. Employing a distinction identified by Leslie Green[3] and elaborated in a joint paper,[4] I shall say that the interest in language may be understood as either linguistic survival or linguistic security. The first focusses on the importance of the survival of one's language group over time. Much of what has been written on language rights in Canada implicitly or explicitly accepts this view.[5] Nevertheless, I shall argue against it, and suggest that language rights are better grounded in the value of linguistic security.

a) Survival

To understand the survival model it may help to recall something of the intellectual history of language policy in Canada. The dominant conception of the interest in language in Canadian literature on language

---

2. L. Green, "Are Language Rights Fundamental?" (1987) 25 *Osgoode Hall L.J.* 639 at 651.
3. *Ibid.*
4. L. Green and D. Réaume, "Education and Linguistic Security in the Charter" (1989) 34 *McGill L.J.* 777.
5. See for example, J.E. Magnet, "Collective Rights, Cultural Autonomy and the Canadian State" (1986) 32 *McGill L.J.* 170 at 184; André Braën, "Language Rights" at 21, Pierre Foucher, "Language Rights and Education" at 257, and Emmanuel Didier, "The Private Law of Language" at 327, all in Michel Bastarache, ed., *Language Rights in Canada* (Montreal: Les Éditions Yvon Blais, 1987).

policy comes from demographers and the political scientists who have been influenced by them. Demographers are professionally interested in long-term trends and in language communities considered as a whole. Their predictions and prescriptions make sense only in this context. For some time the demographic data has indicated a decline in the number of francophones in Canada, both in English speaking Canada and in Québec. (The most immediate causes of this trend are the extraordinarily low birth rate amongst francophones and assimilation to English.) This has led to predictions that before very long there will be no francophones left on this continent. The prescriptive response has been a variety of recommendations designed at least to halt this trend.

Politically speaking, the most influential recommendation has been that regional majorities, or more exactly, provincial majorities, should be given wide powers to determine language policy within their boundaries. (The most extreme variant of this argument has been that Québec should secede from Canada and, as a sovereign country, have unlimited power over its own language policy.) In this way, vulnerable language groups will have the power to protect their language. This is immediately recognizable as the territorial approach to language policy.[6] It rests on the view that a language must have a territorial base and political sovereignty within that territory in order to survive.

The question these writers have failed explicitly to address is this : what is so valuable about the survival of languages that warrants imposing duties on possibly unwilling citizens to preserve or promote them? One possible answer is that languages should be enabled to survive for their own sakes. Thus, one frequently hears from demographers and Québec politicians that the objective of language policy is the preservation of the French language in North America. Yet this seems problematic as a normative basis for language rights. Any theory of rights based on human interests must focus on the speakers of a language rather than on the language itself. A claim put on behalf of a language as such tends either to be ultimately aesthetic in nature or to anthropomorphize language.[7] It is not languages that have rights, but people.[8] Furthermore, there is a crucial equivocation in this approach about the correct object

---

6. Cf. J.A. Laponce, *Langue et territoires*, Québec : les Presses de l'Université Laval, 1984 [travaux du centre international de recherche sur le bilinguisme : A-19].

7. Green, *supra*, note 2 at 656.

8. This is an argument about the justification of rights, not their wording in legal documents. For example, s. 133 of the Constitution Act, 1867 simply says that the French and English languages may be used in some contexts and must be used in others. Despite the fact that the languages themselves are referred to, I shall argue that these provisions must be understood from the point of view of the benefit or capacity they confer on speakers of those languages.

of protection. As I said, the objective is frequently said to be the preservation of French in North America. But if the focus were really on the language itself, it would be difficult to understand why it is so important that it survive in a certain geographical area. If we were merely concerned that French survive, that there continue to be people who speak that language, there would be little call for any special protections that might be counted as language rights. The French language, as such, is in little danger of dying out. Throughout the world there are millions of speakers and most are not under any pressure to abandon their mother tongue. The call for special protections for French only makes sense if we assume that French must survive in North America. But surely languages are quite indifferent as to where they are spoken. It is hard to imagine that its preservation here is of importance to the language itself.

What this suggests is that it is implausible to think that we should protect language use for the sake of the language itself. The politicians and demographers are not concerned about French, but about its speakers who are located on the North American continent. It can only be for their sake that French should be enabled to survive here. But this brings to the surface a moral problem concealed by the equivocation between a language and its speakers. If it is the speakers of a language who have a right that it survive, there is no justification for protecting speakers of one language in preference to those of another where their interests conflict. For example, unlimited provincial jurisdiction over language policy obviously carries a potential threat to the survival of the anglophone community within Québec. (We have already seen other provinces with more power over language than Québec currently has use it to weaken their francophone communities.) One cannot appeal to the fact that the English language as such is not endangered as an excuse for sacrificing its speakers in Québec without illegitimately shifting back to the language itself as the focus of protection.[9] As long as our moral concern is with the speakers of languages the claims of minority groups within provinces cannot be brushed aside. The interest of English speakers in speaking English is no less real, or urgent, than the interest of French speakers in speaking French.

Recently, advocates for Québec anglophone groups and francophone groups within the predominantly English provinces have adopted the demographers' survival language, but, in recognition of the equivocation in the territorialist position, have maintained a focus on the speakers

---

9. This does not preclude, of course, policies which simply take account of the fact that the anglophone community in Québec can draw on the existence of anglophones elsewhere in Canada to sustain itself.

of the language themselves, and insisted that these speakers have the right that their language survive. This position is at least coherent, but incurs certain other problems. Firstly, on a rhetorical level it is not clear that it will be possible to pry the survival ideal away from the territorialist approach which has monopolized it for the better part of thirty years, and it is clear that the territorialist approach is antithetical to the programme of the minority language groups of either language. Secondly, this approach again brings to the surface important ambiguities in the objective of survival. We must first clarify how good a prognosis for survival a language group need have in order to claim the right to survive. We must also investigate the importance of the identity of the speakers of the protected language to the survival objective. Exploring this latter question in particular will in turn require us to flesh out the interest in survival that is alleged to be in issue, and this will raise further moral concerns about adopting this model as a normative basis for an account of language rights.

But first we may eliminate one possible sort of interest one might be thought to have in the survival of a language. One might want a language to survive out of concern for preserving the rich texture of human society by protecting a variety of different ways of life. This is certainly an understandable human interest, but is too general to ground rights to use one's mother tongue. There is no reason I cannot be just as concerned with the contribution to the texture of Canadian society of Cree in Saskatchewan or Gaelic in Nova Scotia as with that of my own language group.[10] We must therefore look for an interest in continuity which is more closely tied to one's own language. Before probing this further, we should be more precise about the goal of survival in this context. The argument that provincial control over language is the best way to ensure the survival of French in North America frequently carries with it an attitude of resignation about the fate of francophones outside of Québec.[11] Their provincial governments might be generous enough to permit their language communities to continue, but they have no right to such support. This abandonment of these communities is often justified by the claim that there is no possibility that the language can survive there, so there is no point in protection, but there is a chance in Québec provided that the provincial government can control language policy. It would seem that if minority groups are going to adopt this

10. The same is true of the 'ecological' argument for the protection of language made by David Marshall and Roseann Gonzalez, "Why We Should Be Concerned About Language Rights: Language Rights from an Ecological Perspective" in this volume.
11. This is frequently accompanied by inflated optimism about the ability of the anglophone community in Québec to survive even in the face of provincial governmental hostility.

model, this argument must be addressed. How long must the life-expectancy of a language group be before it acquires a right to survive? If we choose a sufficiently short life-span, many minority groups will qualify, but the rhetorical force of calling our aim group 'survival' quickly evaporates.

At the other extreme, if one takes a sufficiently long term as one's reference point, it is unclear that even Québec francophones would qualify, even with a plenitude of legislative powers to protect language. It is sobering to recall that Lord Durham justified his proposed policy of assimilation in part by his conviction that there was no hope that the French 'race' could survive in North America.[12] Was Lord Durham clearly wrong, since the French culture continues to thrive? Or is the jury of history still out? If in another two hundred years French has all but disappeared on this continent, should we say that Durham was right all along and therefore judge Canadian language policy to have been a tragic mistake, merely painfully prolonging the inevitable? Or is survival for three hundred years sufficient to have justified protection over that period? The length of time during which a language community can continue and the likelihood of such continuation are issues that must be more carefully addressed by survivalists to make the model not only plausible, but intelligible.

Furthermore, the practical and political difficulties of a model grounded in predictions about the future should not be underestimated. It is obvious to us now that Durham's prediction was self-serving and likely based in no small part on wishful thinking. No doubt, however, some policy makers of the time thought it was an objective assessment of the situation. Present predictions are based on more data, but it can hardly be hoped that they are entirely uninfluenced by some political agenda. The line between objective prediction and self-fulfilling prophecy is likely to be very fine here. Yet the survival model makes language policy and rights entirely vulnerable to such predictions.

Other aspects of survival as an objective also need to be clarified. It might be construed as the desire that our children and grandchildren continue to identify with our practices, our way of life. Most generally this is a desire for cultural continuity, but frequently language is an important aspect of a broader cultural identity.[13] However, it must involve, at least derivatively, an interest in others in addition to one's own descendants because a language cannot survive unless more than

---

12. Gerald M. Craig, ed., *Lord Durham's Report* (Toronto: McClelland and Stewart Ltd., 1963) at 146-152.
13. Green, *supra*, note 2 at 656-7.

one family continues to speak it. But what is the precise nature of this desire for continuity? Its most notable, and I think most problematic, feature is its future orientation. It means that it is vital to the well-being of existing people that they be assured that future persons continue their language. But languages change over time. If we understand the interest in survival to require that future generations continue to speak the language as we do, as an aspect of preserving our culture, this would freeze an essentially fluid practice. I think this is impossible as well as undesirable. But as a language changes it becomes something that earlier generations could have identified with less and less. It is hard to see how the Romans could have had an interest in the existence, today, of the distant relative that modern Italian is. No doubt a Roman would find it easier to identify with modern Italian than with modern Chinese, but then so would a modern French, Spanish, or even English speaker. And this is even more true of the cultures of which language is a bearer. The interest in survival thus diminishes as the distance between present and future users of the language increases. So, the interest in survival must allow for the normal changes that take place in the development of a language, and extends only a limited distance into the future.

Secondly, the ethnic composition of language communities normally changes over time. Some new members join and some old ones leave. This fact requires us to clarify whether the alleged interest is in one's own descendants continuing to speak one's language, or in the continued existence of a language group of which one's descendants may or may not be members. I suspect that most people who are tempted by the survival model would not think that the right to survival of the existing community of speakers would be adequately protected by gradually relocating descendants of the existing members into other language communities and replacing them with new speakers assimilated from other language groups. Certainly, this would not appeal to those Québec nationalists who feel it important to distinguish between assimilated allophones and *Québécois de vieille souche*. Rather, people are attached to the idea that their own descendants should carry on their practices, including language. Is this best expressed by claiming a right to the survival of the language group?

We may be willing to concede that this desire for continuity is an important human interest, but I doubt that a right to survival can be derived from it. To begin with, the last point shows that the objective must be described in a more personal way than that with which we started out. It is not just the continued existence of a group of people speaking a certain language that people are interested in; it is linguistic continuity through time with a particular group of people with whom one already feels a certain affinity. More importantly, there are serious moral concerns with treating this interest as a right. The interest in linguistic continuity would undoubtedly be sufficient to motivate people to teach their children their language and participate in cultural events which help improve the chances that the language will survive. But I am doubtful that it is sufficiently strong to justify imposing duties on others who may have different and competing cultural ambitions to secure this outcome.

To pursue this problem, let us return to the challenge posed by the demographers. Strictly speaking, it is probably not true that survival is impossible for minority language communities. A great variety of measures could be taken to ensure their continuation. Laws could be passed requiring all existing speakers to pass their language on to their children. Existing speakers could be required to have more children in order to increase the number of speakers. If this still was not enough, measures could be taken to force some outsiders to become members of the community and further bolster its numbers. Perhaps these kinds of measures are not essential to the survival of minority communities. Nevertheless, the claim that the members of such communities have a right that their language survive would seem to imply that such measures have at least a prima facie justification. This seems to me implausible. People are certainly entitled to raise their children so as to maximize their chances of continuing the community's traditions, but they do not have a right, not even one that is defeated by a competing right, to force their own children to do so, much less to coerce non-members of the group into participation. This problem arises because the claim to a right to survival is a claim to a certain future state of affairs which necessarily requires the participation of other people who may or may not want to participate. Once we reject the idea that language rights have to do with protecting languages themselves, we cannot ignore the potential for conflicting interests amongst the speakers of a particular language. If language rights protect speakers and not languages, all speakers and all languages are entitled to equal protection.[14]

I do not think that the objectives of those who use the rhetoric of survival are quite as bold as wanting such firm control over the fate of future generations. Let me now contrast the survival model with the interest in security. This will allow me to show that the security conception provides a more plausible account of the interest in language, one which also captures the kernel of sense in the survival theme. Those claims justifiably made in the name of survival can in fact be accounted for

---

14. This does not mean that identical measures are appropriate in every community irrespective of social circumstance, but it does at least mean that no group of speakers can be wholly ignored.

under the rubric of security, without appeal to the morally repugnant and conceptually confused ideal of group survival.

b) Security

The future-oriented focus of the survival model overlooks two much more immediate, and, I think, more central, interests in the use of one's mother tongue. Here, I adopt Green's distinction between the instrumental interest in communication and the expressive interest in language as a marker of cultural identity.[15] Since it is difficult to learn a second language, and even those who succeed are rarely as comfortable in it as in their mother tongue, there is a powerful interest in being able to communicate with others in one's own language. This is especially so if the context makes being properly understood important. Secondly, and perhaps more importantly, most people regard their language as a marker of identity, a cultural inheritance which they value. Even if they can speak another language, they prize the community in which they have been raised and aculturated and regard the use of their language as an important sign of this affiliation.

Here, then, are two present-oriented interests which persons have in the use of their mother tongue which are prior to and much weightier than any interest in the future success of one's language. In fact, survival might be understood as a projection of the expressive interest into the future. One's pride in one's community is extended to a pride in its future existence. But surely it is more important that living individuals be able to so express their identity as members of a language community than that they be confident that future generations will be able to do so. Furthermore, the latter is parasitic upon the former, since unless people now can use the language it is unlikely to survive into the future.

If one's right to identify with one's linguistic tradition is to be secured, one must not face a constant barrage of pressures to abandon one's community for another. Language use has a valuable expressive dimension only if rooted in a free and fair context. Those who are forced to use a particular language cannot be thought thereby to express their identity. While future generations may come to identify with a new language, this cannot justify any initial coercion required to bring about the change. The most brutal forms of coercion involve prohibitions on the use of a language and prescriptions to use another, such as occurred in Ontario's schools in the wake of Regulation 17.[16] But these are not

---

15. Green, *supra*, note 2 at 658-659.
16. This was issued as part of a Circular of Instructions by the Department of Education on 17 August 1913. The circular is reproduced in the trial judgment of Lennox J. in *Mackell* v. *Ottawa Separate School Trustees* (1914), 32 *Ont. L.R.* 245, at 252-54.

the only unfair tools influencing language use. Creating disincentives by making important opportunities unavailable to speakers of a particular language can be just as unfair as more directly coercive measures. This focus on unjust pressures on language choice does not mean that language must be consciously chosen, or that it is valuable only when chosen. Language is only partially a realm of free choice. Children have a mother tongue long before they develop the capacity for reflective and informed choice about ethnic identification, and parents typically transmit their mother tongues as a matter of course. But these normal processes of social development contribute value to their outcomes only in circumstances which are fair and unbiased. The point of language rights is to give speakers a secure environment in which to make choices about language use, and in which normal social processes of language transmission between generations can take place in a way that confers positive value on the resulting ethnic and cultural identification.

At the same time, language can become a matter for conscious choice. It is possible (though not probable under normal circumstances) that even in a completely secure environment, some members of minority language groups would still make free and informed decisions to integrate with a majority community. The need to identify with a community may be deeply rooted in human nature, but we know that there is nonetheless much flexibility regarding the community with which one identifies. To coerce someone to remain in a language community is no better than coercing one to leave. In both cases his interest in expressing affiliation with a language group is violated. Conscious choice, is thus only one way, and an unusual one, through which identification is exercised. While it deserves respect, it is no more valuable than the normal processes of socialization through which one becomes a part of a particular community.

In a flourishing language community, speakers normally have the opportunity, without serious impediments, to live a full life in a community of people who share their language. This is taken for granted by those in linguistically homogeneous societies and those who speak the majority language in pluralistic societies. Through sheer numbers they enjoy *de facto* linguistic security without need for special legal protections. No doors are closed, and no aspects of human fulfillment are unavailable on account of language. Abandoning one's mother tongue (oneself or on behalf of one's children) is, of course, a conceivable option for them, but not one to which they are driven by force of social circumstance and not one which will ever be considered in the normal course of life. It is otherwise for members of linguistic minorities. Without special protections, minority language speakers are inevitably placed under strong pressures to abandon their mother tongue. The more restricted the opportunities available in one's own language the more rational it becomes to take up the language that offers greater ones. This does not mean that minority language speakers do not value their language or communities, but simply that there are some burdens which outweigh the benefits of cultural identification. The important point is that there are some costs that it is unjust to expect linguistic minorities to bear for the sake of maintaining their community and linguistic security requires that they not be imposed.

Part of the environment which ensures linguistic security must be provided by the members of a particular language community themselves. Activities which require the participation of many people depend upon their choices converging. To the extent that linguistic security requires a social environment that includes such activities, the community is dependent upon its own efforts. The larger the community, the greater the range of options its members will have, simply because it is more likely that there will be sufficient numbers interested in a wide range of things. If a community is too small, much of this will not be feasible. But the right to linguistic security protects only against unfair or coercive pressures to abandon one's language. The voluntary choices of others not to participate may affect one's ability to continue one's own participation, but this is not coercive or unfair. If I want to play field hockey, but no one else does, I am not the victim of coercion.

The value of linguistic security is more attractive than is survival as the ground of language rights. It appeals to a more tangible and immediate interest which has more weight than our interest in what happens in the future. Further, one might think that the appeal of the survival model itself relies on something like the expressive interest in language — our desire to identify with a continuing language community. Yet, the focus on survival requires that a certain state of affairs exist, that a certain language continue to be spoken, which provides a reason for various intrusive policies to achieve that state of affairs. Some of these measures would clearly threaten other important values. Perhaps more importantly, some, by coercing affiliation, would be inconsistent with the very idea that identification with one's own language group is a good, an idea to which the survival model also wants to appeal. By contrast, the linguistic security model strives to ensure a different state of affairs. It holds that the ultimate fate of a language community is up to its members, but they should be protected from unfair or coercive pressures distorting normal practices of language use and transmission. While this may mandate government support for minority communities, it cannot justify intrusive measures to sustain a language community. The desired state of affairs described by the linguistic security model internally recognizes the equal standing of all languages and their speakers. This means that the exclusion of coercive measures are built into the value to be protected and do not rest on independent justifications.

The confusion of survival and security is easily made, for the conditions threatening security also make survival less likely. Evidence of assimilation and decline among the francophone minorities has made it clear[17] that the lack of adequate linguistic guarantees in the 1867 Constitution had exacerbated their demographic fragility.[18] Nonetheless, the decline of the minorities is a symptom and not itself a disease. It is presumptive evidence that there is strong and potentially unfair social pressure to abandon their language. Fostering linguistic security requires eliminating the unfair pressures and thus enables people to carry on with the normal social processes which usually result in the continued health of a language community. But by-product should not be confused with purpose. This puts survival in its proper perspective, as subordinate to more substantial and immediate concerns to provide a fair environment for present speakers of the language.

2. THE SOCIAL DIMENSION OF LANGUAGE RIGHTS

Linguistic security supports one's ability to live one's life in a particular linguistic milieu, within a language community. This underlying good is what I have called elsewhere a participatory good. Its production and, more importantly, its enjoyment require the existence of a social group.[19] Participation with others in the complex set of practices which comprise a language community gives its existence value. The point of the freedom to use one's mother tongue lies in sharing it and the culture it embodies with others. This interest cannot be satisfied for an individual in isolation from other speakers; it can be enjoyed only through participation with others. Different participatory goods require different levels of participation to give them value. The complexity of a flourishing language community means that extensive numbers are required to create the kind of good which has value. Linguistic demographers have long

---

17. This was first recognized by the francophone communities themselves when various provincial governments revoked the *de facto* freedom that denominational schools had previously had to use French as the language of instruction. See Pierre Foucher, *Constitutional Language Rights of Official Language Minorities in Canada* (Ottawa: Ministry of Supply and Services, 1985) for a survey of the history. See *The Heirs of Lord Durham* (Ottawa: Burns and MacEachern Ltd., 1978) for the views of *La Fédération des Francophones hors Québec*. See the *Royal Commission Report on Bilingualism and Biculturalism* (Ottawa: Queen's Printer, 1968) especially Book 2, for the beginning of serious efforts at constitutional reform in this regard.
18. The desire to remedy this was a driving force, not only of the language rights provisions, but of the Charter as a whole.
19. D. Réaume, "Individuals, Groups, and Rights to Public Goods" (1988) 38 *U. of T.L.J.* 1.

realized that the health of a language requires a critical mass of speakers. This participatory element justifies distinguishing this kind of right from those protecting individuals as such. To mark the distinction, I call them 'group rights'. By contrast, individual rights are often thought to be valuable precisely because the number of those who share one's interest is irrelevant to whether it ought to be protected.

This does not mean that whole communities are the only possible claimants of language rights. Given that language communities lack clearly identifiable representative bodies, enforcement of rights would be impossible if only group claims were allowed. The participatory nature of a language community has more to do with establishing preconditions of the existence of the right, and, as I will argue below, with the substance of those protections, than with the question of who has standing to put such claims. Whatever other language communities might be able to make similar claims (I shall return to this question in a moment), it is clear that, considered nationally, the English and French language communities are sufficiently robust and capable of providing a reasonably full range of experience for their members that we can be confident that these groups meet the threshold conditions. Thus there is a principled reason why these two communities ought explicitly to be mentioned as deserving of protection.

With respect to some language rights, no further conditions are necessary, and any individual can claim their benefits. These are services which, if provided at all, can readily be made available to each member of the community. For this reason, each individual has the right to use French or English in certain courts and legislatures. To accommodate the minority at all requires the courts to put in place mechanisms which, once operative, can serve each member of that community. Similarly with Parliament and the services provided by central federal government and New Brunswick government offices. With respect to the right to education and local government services, French and English are explicitly mentioned again because there are significant pockets in all parts of the country. However, the local nature of the service makes them conditional upon the local existence of a community large enough to warrant them. Once this is established, there is no reason why an individual member of this community may not enforce the right. (I leave aside the question of who should bear the onus of establishing the existence of such a community.) Thus, the good protected by these rights requires a community, yet it is possible, for enforcement purposes, legally to define the right-holder in individualistic terms.

Nor should this social dimension be mistaken for another sort of argument sometimes made in respect of group rights. Such claims are sometimes made on behalf of a society as a whole. But this usually either mistakes a collection of individual interests for a collective interest, or falsely assumes that one particular group right or interest automatically prevails over any other right or interest with which it competes. It is very rare that a society is wholly united in any particular interest. Thus talk of 'society's rights' is usually an obfuscatory way of disguising the fact that some members interests are being preferred to those of others. This seems to me to describe the suggestion in the preamble of the *Charter of the French Language* that the Québec people has articulated its identity through the French language.[20] This is a blatant attempt to conceal the linguistic division within the Québec people. This right of society is in fact only the right of the majority. But to accord rights to the majority, *qua* majority, makes nonsense of the whole notion of rights. Rights are needed to protect against the majority. Francophone Québécois can claim the right, as members of a linguistic community, to linguistic security, a group right in the sense here defended. But this claim is on the same footing as the right of the English minority, which is also a group right. The mere claim that one group has a right tells us nothing about the weight of this claim against that of a conflicting right of another group. We need not here explore how such competing claims should be evaluated; it is sufficient to guard against an abuse to which the notion of group rights is liable.

3. THE REGIME OF LINGUISTIC TOLERANCE AND THE REGIME OF OFFICIAL LANGUAGES

In considering the main provisions of the linguistic regime in Canada, one must distinguish between those provisions which fall within the regime of linguistic tolerance, and those falling within the regime of official languages. Both kinds can be demonstrated to foster linguistic security in different ways.

a) Tolerance

Linguistic security argues for supporting minority language groups in order to eliminate unfair pressures to conform to majority language practices. This support takes two forms. First, a secure environment is partly established by those general rights which establish what I shall call a regime of linguistic tolerance. This encompasses the usual rights of freedom of expression, association, non-discrimination, and natural justice, as applied to language use. These ensure that one's language is not made a ground of liability. They protect one's ability to use one's

---

20. R.S.Q. 1977, c. C-11.

language of choice in private life, to publish newspapers, to organize services etc. in one's own language. There are two important features to note about these tolerance rights. Firstly, they are completely universal: the speakers of any language can claim them. There is no more justification for prohibiting Chinese or Hindi in public places than for prohibiting French or English. Secondly, although there is a social dimension to some of these rights (such as freedom of association), the group threshold for their enjoyment is very small: two people are often enough. We may thus treat them effectively as protecting individuals in the use of their languages.[21] No community of any appreciable size is a necessary condition of this protection. It should be obvious how the regime of tolerance contributes to linguistic security. Some of the most coercive measures against the use of a particular language are exactly those that would be prohibited by these rights.

b) Official Languages

In the case of very small linguistic communities, there may be little more that can be done to support them. But when groups have the standing and vitality of the French and English communities in Canada, governments have the capacity and duty to do more. They may provide for services, counteract unfair bias, and generally facilitate their activities in ways that will have tangible and beneficial consequences. These facilitative actions may intervene quite vigorously in the customary linguistic order, without threatening security in the way the compulsory measures discussed above would. This creates what I shall call an official languages regime. In Canada, the features of this regime are familiar. Both French and English can be used before certain legislatures and courts. Federal government and New Brunswick government services must be provided in both official languages. And the minority in each province have a right that their children be educated in their language. This is by no means the only form an official language regime can take. Linguistic security can be fostered in many positive ways. These are simply the ones which seemed appropriate to the framers of the 1867 and 1982 Constitutions. Someone might argue that these choices were limited or mistaken in some way. My only objective here is to argue that they can and should be seen to promote linguistic security, understood as the protection of the participatory good of a flourishing language community.

---

21. Although the participatory nature of these rights may well have implications for their interpretation in certain contexts which would require them to be distinguished from strictly individual rights, for present purposes they are more like those individual rights than they are like the more complex participatory rights needed to positively protect linguistic security which will be examined in the next section.

Into this framework we may set each of the three main families of constitutional rights described above: the right to services, to participation in government, and to educational facilities. The contribution of each toward linguistic security in both the public and the private realm should be clear. The flourishing of a minority linguistic group requires that it be able to participate in public life in its language and that it have at its disposal the basic means of cultural reproduction. These resources are needed to enable the community freely to define itself as a collectivity and fairly to participate in Canadian society.

Let us first consider the contribution of a minority education system to linguistic security.[22] Provision for minority language education is a complex good with many different facets. For convenience, I distinguish two main aspects.

There are powerful *individual benefits* of children being able to learn in their mother tongue: it is easier to master other subjects when one knows the language and feels socially at ease in the classroom. It also opens doors to participation in one's community and fosters a positive attitude towards it. The absence of minority language education is quite obviously a powerful assimilationist force. Children grow up with a grasp of their mother tongue which is inadequate for the kind of adult pursuits which require strong communication skills. In such circumstances it is hardly surprising that people abandon their first language and do not teach it to their children. Before long, such a community ceases to be viable and its language, if it persists at all, has merely folkloric status.

Education cannot, however, be fully understood as an individual good.[23] Minority language instruction benefits the linguistic group as well. It has *collective benefits* which flow from the language being a vehicle of instruction. For example, it provides and renews cultural capital. This is true at the level of both 'high' and 'popular' culture: the productive and appreciative capacities must be nurtured and trained through a comprehensive education. Musicians, writers, artists obviously depend on and draw on common cultural capital in representing and contesting the life of the community. But even folk and oral tradition, sporting culture, etc. all draw on a stock of common forms and images. In modern societies, this capital is largely controlled by the educational

---

22. These points are developed more fully in L. Green and D. Réaume, *supra*, note 4.
23. Pierre Foucher, "Language Rights and Education", in M. Bastarache, ed., *supra*, note 5, emphasizes the individual benefits to highlight the individual's standing to enforce the right. However, as I have argued above, there is no good reason to tie the nature of a right to the issue of who may sue for its protection. The primary beneficiaries of minority language education rights are children, but control over the right is normally exercised by their parents.

system. Other direct collective benefits are more instrumental : it provides jobs for members of the minority community. Still others are by-products of the existence and administration of minority language instruction.[24] For one thing, a community with public institutions will have greater visibility and status. More importantly, an educational facility such as a neighbourhood school is an important focus of social and cultural activities for the community, especially in smaller towns. And managing a school system by electing trustees, hiring teachers, setting policy, etc. are all important parts of the political life of such communities and contribute to their richness and vitality. This analysis of the range of contribution to linguistic security made by education argues for the establishment of minority language educational systems comprehensive enough to provide all these benefits.

Next, consider language protection in the public sphere. What is the point of this kind of protection? Taken by themselves, it may seem unlikely that these provisions can be of much help in fostering linguistic security. Most people very rarely find themselves dealing with a court or the legislature. And although one's contact with various government offices may be more frequent, it would be hard to argue that the inability to buy stamps in one's own language is a major threat to linguistic security. But there is another dimension to these seemingly trivial activities which ties them more centrally to the flourishing of a language community. Linguistic security requires that the members of a community be able to live as fully as possible in their own language. Ideally, it should be possible to work, worship, and relax in one's own language. An important part of this picture is the language of the public life of one's society. It is probably beyond government's capacity to guarantee the right to use a particular language in all contexts, and in many its help is not needed and perhaps not even wanted. However, one area which is firmly within its control is the language of public life.

It is therefore appropriate that the *Constitution* seek to make the most important aspects of the country's political institutions bilingual and in doing so make these institutions part of the life of both official linguistic communities. The scope of life which can be conducted in one's own language is thereby importantly expanded to include

---

24. *Cf. Rapport de la commission ministérielle sur l'éducation secondaire en langue française / Report of the Ministerial Commission on French Language Secondary Education* (The Symons Report) (Toronto : Queen's Printer, 1972) "The school occupies a central role in the cultural life of the community... The French language schools must truly be community schools and easily accessible to the general population of the linguistic group they exist to serve...." (at 13).

participation in political institutions. This is important to linguistic security because no community is complete without political institutions. Bilingualism attempts to make important governmental bodies seem less like alien forces which control the minority without being accessible to them.[25] This means that the government must meet the specific responsibilities imposed upon it in a spirit of becoming a full participant in the linguistic life of both official language communities. It is not enough to refrain from interfering with the language use of the minority. The flourishing of a language community means that there must be full communication in that language within the community. If government is to be a part of this community, it must be prepared to communicate with its members in their own language. The more fully this is realized — the more the minority can feel comfortable with these institutions as representative of their linguistic community — the more they can feel that politics is fully open to them as a pursuit. If the government's participation is too grudging or artificial this will cut off from the minority a crucial aspect of social life. Linguistic security, therefore, requires that government services, including judicial services, be organized within minority language communities so that they are provided largely by members of that community.

4. WHICH COMMUNITIES SHOULD BE PROTECTED?

I have said that the regime of tolerance protects speakers of any language, without regard to the size of their community. In Canada, the official language regime is, however, limited to the protection of the French and English communities. Much of what I have already said will serve to justify the inclusion of at least these two groups. In Canada as a whole, they are the two largest and most dynamic language communities. Admittedly, some others have significant regional concentrations, but none on a national scale. The significance of size thus lies in the simple fact that the French and English constitute currently viable language communities, each able to sustain for its members a reasonably full cultural life. Since Confederation, this has always been so, and explains why the framers of the 1867 Constitution should have included language protections for both groups. Each group legitimately and reasonably expected that it would continue to flourish as a distinct

---

25. Raymond Breton, "Multiculturalism and Canadian Nation-Building", in Alan Cairns and Cynthia Williams, eds, *The Politics of Gender, Ethnicity and Language in Canada* (Toronto: University of Toronto Press, 1986) Vol. 2 of the Collected Research Studies of the Royal Commission on the Economic Union and Development Prospects for Canada.

linguistic community.[26] The 1867 Constitution included the supports for such flourishing as seemed most important and feasible at the time. In 1982, in light of the increased importance of education and governmental services to citizens, these supports were extended. But such support is meaningful only if there already exists a basically viable community.

The creation of a regime of official languages does in a sense mark those languages as special. Is this unfair to other language groups? Sometimes the exclusion of other groups is raised to suggest that it makes no sense to have an official language regime at all. It is clear, however, that abolishing it would not benefit any minority language group. Even without the regime of official languages, the French and English would still exercise massive *de facto* dominance in Canada. The elimination of that regime would only attack the linguistic security of French and English minority communities by putting their fate into the hands of regional majorities. It would do nothing to improve the position of other language groups. A more interesting argument is one which contends that other groups deserve to be added to the club of those enjoying official language protections. I have said nothing to tell against a sound claim being made on behalf of such groups. It is, however, a fact that the constitution refers exclusively to two groups. It could, instead, have included general criteria for recognition as an official language group. Assuming that there are other groups who have been wrongly excluded, what difference should this make to our moral support for the existing regime?

I believe that it should make none. Even if other groups deserve similar treatment, this cannot detract from the justice of according that treatment to the English and French. That others should be admitted to the club is no reason for revoking the membership of those already in, or in any way limiting the protections to which they are otherwise entitled. The moral entitlements of others provide only an argument for constitutional amendment to recognize their claims. We ought to distinguish between two kinds of political or moral arguments. The first is essentially comparative, so that the very fact that one individual or group has received a benefit is reason to confer it on others and therefore grounds a complaint by anyone who has not been favoured. The second

---

26. This provides an interpretation of the sense in which language rights are compromise rights: they are special rights created as a result of a constitutional bargain over interests which the parties rightly regard as legitimate. But that does not, of course, do anything to diminish their importance. For a fuller exposition of this argument see L. Green and D. Réaume, "Second Class Rights?: Principle and Compromise in the Charter", forthcoming, *Dalhousie Law Journal*.

kind of argument does not rely on such comparisons. It ties entitlement to attributes of the individual or group so that these attributes are grounds for receiving the benefit, irrespective of how others are treated. Each entity enjoying the appropriate attributes can therefore make a claim on its own behalf. Full justice is achieved by ensuring that all qualified entities receive the benefit in question, but each claim can be adjudged independently of all the others.

Language rights, as moral and political claims, fall into the non-comparative category. The argument that a language group deserves special protection is not based on the fact that other groups have it, but that this group needs it and can make use of it. The wrong, if any, which the existing regime of language rights does to speakers of non-official languages cannot be made good by restricting the rights of official language minorities, any more than the wrong done to women in being denied the vote could have been redressed by limiting the voting rights of (some group of) men. The same argument applies to the claims made by official minority groups in different provinces. There is an unfortunate tendency for governments to treat the claims of minorities as dependent upon the treatment accorded groups in other provinces. For example, the Québec government is fond of reminding the rest of the country that its minority is treated better than that in any other province. When used to deflect a valid claim that the rights of anglophones have been infringed, this amounts to a crude example of the *tu quoque* fallacy.[27] Minority groups should not be treated as hostages held by competing sides in a conflict, such that one side need refrain from cutting off its hostage's finger only if the other side's hostage remains unharmed. The claims of each group, whether an official group within a particular province or an unofficial group, can and must be considered on their own merits. In providing an account of the point and characteristics of a regime of official languages, my approach thus aspires to full generality, and applies to any other minority group whose language satisfies the appropriate threshold conditions for a group right. The regime of official languages is thus not a barrier to, but a model for, future change.

---

27. To be even-handed, Manitoba Premier, Gary Filmon's, response to the introduction of Bill 178 in the National Assembly of Québec could be interpreted as committing the same fallacy if one thought that the distinct society clause of the Meech Lake Accord was an appropriate recognition of the language rights of francophone Québécois. That one group has not been treated appropriately cannot justify withholding protection of the legitimate claims of another. Although such tactics are a common political bargaining tactic, no one should mistake them for sound public policy.

CONCLUSION

Language policy making has for too long been conducted solely as an aspect of power politics. The result has been a singular inattention to the development of a principled theoretical grounding as an important aspect of human rights. I have argued that much of the implicit grounding of the arguments for various policies that have held rhetorical sway in Canadian society is unsatisfactory, both conceptually and morally. We should abandon the survival model and instead think of language rights as the attempt to establish linguistic security for vulnerable communities.

LINKING THEORY TO PRACTICE: COMMENTS ON "THE CONSTITUTIONAL PROTECTION OF LANGUAGE"

C. Michael MacMillan

The concept of language rights, in some form or other, is a firmly established component of the Canadian political tradition. With the passage of the *British North America Act*, 1867,[1] language rights achieved a minimal expression in section 133. The content of language rights has evolved over the years, culminating in the significant expansion of language rights embodied in the *Canadian Charter of Rights and Freedoms* of 1982[2] and the passage of Bill C-72.[3] Despite its one hundred and twenty year history, we still know remarkably little about our notion of language rights beyond its expression in these documents and their judicial interpretation. Two different governmental inquiries have stated that language rights are "basic rights", without either making the case for such a significant claim, or fully exploring its implications.[4] At the same time, one recent study opined that the logic of language rights has not been developed, especially in relation to the attendant rights and duties associated with the concept of official bilingualism.[5] More recently, the Commissioner of Official Languages has remarked on the pressing need "... to clarify and structure the ongoing debate on Canadian bilingualism".[6]

---

1. Now *Constitution Act, 1867* (U.K.), 30 & 31 Vict., c. 3.
2. Part 1 of the *Constitution Act, 1982*, being Schedule B of the Canada Act, 1982 (U.K.), 1982, c. 11.
3. *The Official Languages Act*, S.C. 1988, c. 38.
4. Task Force on National Unity, *A Future Together: Observations and Recommendations* (Hull: Supply and Services, 1979) at 53; Royal Commission on Bilingualism and Biculturalism, *Report: The Cultural Contribution of the Other Ethnic Groups, Vol. 4*, (Ottawa: Queen's Printer, 1969) at 14.
5. Task Force on Official Languages, *Towards Equality of the Official Languages in New Brunswick* (Fredericton: Government of New Brunswick, 1982) at 117.
6. D'Iberville Fortier, "Bilingualism and Canadian Values" (Notes for the Falconbridge Lecture, 26 Nov. 1985) (Ottawa: Office of the Commissioner of Official Languages, 1985) at 12.

The same problem emerges when we move from the Canadian to the international stage. Language rights, or their effective equivalents by other names, have been recognized from the United States to Malaysia.[7] Yet, the growth in the practice of language rights has far outstripped the development of the theory. There is an increasingly apparent need to achieve some conceptual clarity about this intensely controversial concept. One important question then, is to identify the means by which a theory of language rights is to be linked to its burgeoning practice. Such a theory, it should be noted, is primarily normative, rather than empirical: it is intended to develop an argument for the recognition of language rights rather than to explain the existing variations in language rights.[8] In this commentary, I shall outline two basic directions for such an inquiry and suggest some issues which must be addressed stemming from their respective applications.

One approach is rationalistic and deductive. It involves an attempt to justify a set of language rights as belonging to the recognized set of human rights. This involves the identification of the essential features of a human right and the development of an argument to the effect that language rights meet those recognized criteria. This is, of course, the tactic pursued by Professor Réaume. The other is empirical and inductive. It attempts to construct a rationale and content for language rights from public attitudes and social practices. Thus, the former moves from theory to practice; the latter from practice to theory. Each approach suggests broadly similar conclusions, to wit, that language rights are unlike conventional human rights in certain key respects, and that any justification of language rights must recognize certain important restrictions on their assertion.

From Theory to Practice

There are a series of difficulties in the attempt to link the notion of language rights to the conventional literature on human rights. Initially, it is necessary to emphasize that there is no prevailing justificatory theory of human rights, but rather a series of individual arguments for the recognition of particular entities as human rights. One can speak, with some qualifications, of a set of core features of human rights which language rights must meet. One such set is that outlined by Maurice Cranston as practicability, paramount importance, and universality.[9] An

---

7. For a presentation of language policy in a variety of countries, see William R. Beer and James E. Jacob, *Language Policy and National Unity* (Totowa, N.J.: Rowman & Allanheld, 1985).

8. The latter task is pursued in J.A. Laponce, *Languages and Their Territories* (Toronto: University of Toronto Press, 1987), c. 3 and 4 especially.

9. I discuss these criteria and their application to language rights more fully in my "Language Rights, Human Rights and Bill 101" 90 *Queen's Quarterly* (Summer 1983) 344 at 351.

application of these criteria clarifies the manner in which language rights only partially meet some of these criteria. However, in terms of a broad justificatory argument, the case must be made for language rights individually.

Such an endeavour requires a prior definition of the meaning of language rights. As Professor Réaume has clearly indicated, a language right refers to a right to one's mother tongue or native language. It is not simply a right to speak a language *per se*, but rather the language of one's heritage. In fact, the term is more appropriately used in the plural rather than in the singular form, since the specification of such rights necessarily involves enumeration of occasions where one is entitled to use one's mother tongue. This specification may usefully be divided into three categories of linguistic rights claims. I would suggest a variation of the categories applied by Professor Réaume. The first category is constituted by what are often referred to as toleration rights, synonymous with liberty rights, meaning the right to be left alone. It is characterized by the absence of prohibitive legislation, and/or legislation specifying that such languages are permissible in the private realms (at home, in social clubs). The second category consists of a group of promotion-oriented rights, aimed at sustaining a particular language. This would include the right to an education, and to receive government services in the language. The final category is constituted by rights to a strong promotion of a language, best exemplified by the provisions of Québec's Bill 101,[10] which tend toward ensuring that individuals can live their lives in their own language. The right to work in one's own language is one such example.

These three categories are noteworthy in that they each require rather different rationales for recognition of the language rights claims, and they differ in their compatibility with the essential features of human rights. There is a rather ironical twist to the rationales and the justification for the various categories of rights. The less demanding the substantive claims for language rights, the less compelling the argument for them will be. However, the more demanding they are, the less they are able to meet some of the essential conditions of a human right. A particular case in point concerns the correlativity of rights and duties, which will be discussed below.

Beyond identifying the content of language rights, there is the important issue, alluded to by Professor Réaume and others, of identifying the bearer of such rights. Who is entitled to claim language rights? Is

---

10. Charter of the French Language, R.S.Q. 1977, c. C-11.

it all the individuals or all the citizens of a particular country, or only the native-born ones? Does it cover all the languages spoken in a country or only the historically established, dominant one(s)? Language rights admit of situations where they do not hold for all individuals. Tourists and immigrants are two obvious instances of categories excluded from the array of language rights claims identified above.[11] These examples suggest one of the distinctive features of language rights — that they are situationally grounded. The claim of linguistic minorities to language rights also illustrates the point further, in that the density of cultural and communal life attached to the particular language is relevant to the legitimacy of the claim as well. Consequently, one must conclude that language rights deviate from established human rights in the important respect that they are not universal. Only individuals in particular social contexts can claim them.

Professor Réaume quite properly emphasizes that people, rather than languages are the bearer of rights, and that the justification of language rights must be based upon the identification of an important individual interest in them. The former point has come to be expressed in Canadian federal legislation only recently, with the important consequence that individuals are in a position to claim services from government as a right. The latter point is also to be framed as Professor Réaume clearly perceives, in terms of the "flourishing" of individual and group identify insofar as it is based on language. This in turn raises an important question which is not developed in Professor Réaume's discussion — which groups may claim language rights? Professor Réaume has contented herself with presenting a rebuttal to the view that, if German or Ukrainian minorities don't have recognized language rights, then why should English and French minorities have them? Given recent developments in the province of Alberta, the presentation of such a rebuttal is entirely timely. However, one issue that increasingly deserves consideration is the extent to which other linguistic minorities may lay claim to language rights. This whole issue has been too long neglected. The pragmatic basis upon which language rights have been justified to date in Canada becomes rather unsteady, however, when one considers extending such rights to other groups, or, more immediately, when one proposes expanding the scope of existing language rights for the two official language groups. Moreover, the extension of language rights to other groups raises the issue of what the common content of recognized

---

11. At least one language right would be extended to these categories: the right to an interpreter in a court and other adjudicative proceedings. Such a right is recognized in the *Canadian Charter of Rights and Freedoms*, section 14.

language rights ought to be. If anything, it encourages a more restrictive specification of language rights. The point is well illustrated in the delineation of rights and duties attendant to language rights.

A compelling issue regarding language rights concerns the correlativity of rights and duties. It is generally accepted that rights involve the assignment of corresponding duties upon others to respect those rights. Conventionally, these "others" are understood to be every other individual, but it often includes such collective entities as governments. What kinds of duties are entailed upon others through a recognition of language rights? The first two categories are relatively unproblematic in that the toleration rights simply require non-interference, while the second category, involving education and government services, impose duties directly upon governments and only indirectly upon individuals.

The third category, which recognizes a right to live one's life in a particular language, encounters a fundamental conflict of rights and duties. If individual A has a right to live his life in his own language, then other individuals who do not share that language have a duty to communicate with him in that language. If individual B has a similar right to a different language, then they are inescapably confronted with a fundamental and irreconcilable conflict of rights and duties. For this reason, there cannot be a universal right to language in this third sense. It can only approximate the conditions of a human right in the first and second senses. To put it somewhat differently, there are important discontinuities in the apparent continuum of language rights claims, which suggest limits to the extent of such claims. In this regard, I was intrigued by Professor Réaume's claim that linguistic security requires government services by member's of one's own linguistic group.[12] This content of a language right appears to fall into category three of those I've just outlined, and I suspect that the rationale for it is rather different from the "linguistic security" basis that she has used to provide the general argument for a regime of language rights.

These considerations underscore the complexity of language rights as a form of human right. Nonetheless, these considerations must be addressed if a satisfactory justification of language rights is to be achieved via this route.

---

12. Denise Réaume asserts that "Linguistic security, therefore, requires that government services, including judicial services, be organized within minority language communities so that they are provided largely by members of that community" in "The Constitutional Protection of Language: Survival or Security", at 56 in this volume.

From Practice to Theory

An alternative approach to the justification of language rights is to identify and analyze their occurrence in the customs and practices of Canadian society. As used by Flathman, the concept of a practice refers to "...clusters, nodes, or foci of meaningful activity that form more or less distinct aspects of the life of a society or subsocietal social group".[13] In particular it is "...the acceptance, by participants in the practice, of rules according to which it is right, obligatory, proper, prudent, or simply expected that they act in certain ways and refrain from certain other actions."[14] Rules, in Flathman's perspective, are[15]

> " ... conduct-gilding [sic] devices (1) that presuppose forms of action susceptible of choice and guidance; (2) that are thought to be important; (3) about which criteria of right and wrong, good and bad, wise or unwise have developed and been widely accepted. (4) These criteria have been accepted for reasons that can be stated and that can and do serve as guides to the interpretation and application of the rules to particular cases."

Such rules are not captured for the most part in legal text. They consist of the working understandings of the participants, their rationales and behaviours in responding to particular claims and the kinds of criticisms they make of various justifications for various rights. The emphasis then is on the shared understandings of the participants.

Thus, there is a practice of rights in Western liberal democracies the content of which can be expressed in these rules. For example, in order to claim a right to strike and picket, the claimant, A, must understand and invoke a series of rules: 1) the general rule regarding rights in the society, 2) the specific rule regarding the particular claimed right, and 3) the rule regarding the application of the general and specific rights to the particular situation in which they are being claimed. As well, A advances in the process the argument that there is such a right as the one claimed (to strike and to picket), and that A's interests or objectives will be served by its recognition. These invocations and arguments are subject to dispute by others, and will often be disputed. These disputes in turn serve to clarify the rules to the participants in the practice as well as to observers.[16]

In this approach, the analyst attempts to elucidate the conventions and unwritten rules that govern communication and action within a

---

13. Richard Flathman, *The Practice of Rights* (London: Cambridge University Press, 1976) at 17.
14. *Id.* at 14.
15. *Id.* at 107.
16. *Id.* at 24-25.

particular domain. The task, as understood by Flathman, is "... to identify and give a systematic account and assessment of the assumptions, beliefs, ideas, values, expectations, and modes of action that are prominent in the practice as its participants understand it and engage in it".[17] The enterprise is more a process of clarification of that which is already known, or believed, than one of creation or discovery.

At the outset, it should be emphasized that this application of Flathman's approach is definitely of the "garden variety" sort. It eschews, for the most part, the language-games focus which is the basis of its inspiration (deriving from Wittgenstein), emphasizing instead the elucidation of the values, beliefs and understandings of the participants in the practice of language rights. The choice of topic in turn necessitates the fact that this analysis must be preliminary and exploratory, in no small measure because the associated practices are themselves relatively undeveloped and only now in the process of rule formation. Moreover, the same might be said of the general rules regarding rights in Canadian society, which have become a focus of attention only in the past two decades. This is to some extent advantageous, in that the practice is itself the object of substantial dispute, and therefore offers quite explicitly the values and beliefs which are the focus of contention.

In what follows, I shall draw upon public opinion polls, both national and regional, to determine regularities and conflicts in understandings of those issues. This discussion, it should be noted, will focus primarily upon debates outside the Québec context, partly for reasons of space, and partly because the Québec debates have followed rather distinctive lines regarding the practice of rights.[18]

Interest in public attitudes regarding language rights in Canada first emerged with the investigations of the Royal Commission on Bilingualism and Biculturalism in the 1960's (hereafter referred to as the B&B Commission). Since then, attention to public opinion has waxed and waned in conjunction with the outbreak of linguistic controversies at the federal or provincial levels. For the most part, the patterns of opinion are sufficiently consistent to suggest the existence of a continuing practice, or perhaps practices, of language rights in Canada.[19]

---

17. *Id.* at 17.
18. I have analyzed the Québec language rights debate from a rather different approach in my "Language Rights, Human Rights, and Bill 101", *supra*, note 9, 343-361.
19. The ensuing discussion draws upon several surveys of public opinion on language rights in Canada, notably, Jonathan Pool, "Mass Opinion on Language Policy: The Case of Canada" in Joshua A. Fishman, ed., *Advances in Language Planning* (The Hague: Mouton, 1974) 481-492; Goldfarb Consultants Ltd., *The Searching Nation* (Toronto: Southam Press, 1977); Stacy Churchill and Anthony H. Smith, "The Time Has Come" (1987) 19 *Language and Society* 4.

In exploring the extent of shared understandings through survey data, the question immediately arises as to what level of uniformity constitutes substantial agreement. Obviously, anything less than unanimity involves a certain measure of arbitrariness. However, in an area which is highly controversial, such as rights in general much less language rights, extremely high levels of agreement are virtually impossible. Recognizing this, I choose to accept a working figure of 66%, as the indicator of substantial agreement. My rationale is simply that a figure which is accepted as decisive for such important decisions as some constitutional revisions, fits nicely with established political practice.

If this working definition is accepted, the result is a fairly consistent, limited understanding of the practice of language rights. Taking the country as a whole, it would appear that there is a shared understanding regarding three particular areas of language rights: 1) access to federal government services in both official languages, 2) entitlement to minority language education for the residents of a province, and 3) entitlement to hospital services in the minority language for residents of a province.[20] If we wish to elicit underlying principles in these examples, we find only that they relate to governments rather than individuals or organizations. Secondly, they concern areas of vital interest to the individual. We might say that, where the vital interests of the individual are involved, the public recognizes the propriety of those interests being served in a manner which permits the individual to judge the extent of protection to those interests. This does not translate into a general obligation on all governments to respond to individuals in their own language, as the responses regarding provincial government services attests (57% support). This is somewhat surprising, since it is generally conceded that the provincial governments have greater visibility and importance in the daily lives of people.

The answer to this puzzle is partly to be found in another noticeable feature of these findings and that is the strong regional variation in the extent of agreement to those propositions. The Canadian Facts survey reported its results in relation to five regions of Canada as well — Québec, Atlantic, Ontario, Prairies, and British Columbia. In relation to the aforementioned agreement regarding language rights, none receive the

---

20. Churchill and Smith, *id.*, Tables 2 & 3. The support levels are, respectively, 74%, 74%, 71%. It should be noted that one other item nearly meets the criterion. 63% of Canadians believe that minority language residents of a province should be entitled to postal services in their own language. The 1965 study analyzed by Pool is broadly comparable only on the first item, regarding federal government services. In that instance, support was consistently over 80% in all groups. See Pool, *id.*, at 489.

required level of support in all regions. All three are substantially accepted in Québec, Ontario, and the Atlantic region. While a majority accept each of the three in British Columbia, none receive the required two-thirds level of support. In the Prairie region, there is substantial agreement only in regard to minority language schools. Only Québec and Atlantic Canada indicate substantial agreement with the propositions that similar entitlement should extend to provincial government services and to services from business.[21]

These results indicate that there are several practices of rights in Canada, corresponding to the different regions. It is virtually nonexistent in British Columbia, and quite extensive in Québec and, to a lesser extent, Atlantic Canada. It obtains its broadest sweep in Central and Atlantic Canada. This helps explain the apparent discrepancy in responses for federal and provincial government language services. In fact, only three regions of the country accept the notion of federal bilingualism, and while they also support provincial services, it is to a lesser degree and therefore insufficient to create a substantial majority. Not surprisingly, it is the regions of the country with substantial numbers and/or percentages of their populations as members of an official language minority which support these language claims. It is in these areas that minority languages form part of the everyday life of the immediately relevant political communities.

In summarizing the results of these findings, what stands out is the existing tensions between a general acceptance of these principles associated with language rights combined with a rejection of the principal means of implementation. It is hard to envisage how governments can meet an obligation to provide minority language services without hiring bilingual personnel or unilingual individuals from both language groups. Yet strong reservations were expressed on both options. Beyond that, it would appear that language rights attach to the individual primarily in the role of citizen-consumer of government services, and not as worker, or neighbour. These limitations strongly suggest sharply limited parameters to the prevailing notions of language rights.

In light of this evidence, I would again return to Professor Réaume's suggestion that linguistic security requires that groups be served by

---

21. Churchill and Smith, *id.* Unfortunately, these results cannot readily be compared with the Pool study, *supra*, note 19, which examined its findings in terms of the composition of individual electoral districts. In terms of regions, however, it did compare Québec results with the rest of Canada collectively, and observed the same pattern as well. Initially striking here is the fact that the highest levels of acceptance for language entitlements is almost invariably from Québec. This is in sharp contrast to the image generated by all the publicity surrounding Bill 101.

members of their own linguistic group. Applying the "practice" model of rights, this proposal would be sharply rejected as the basis for a regime of language rights.

Conclusion

More generally, it is apparent that these two basic approaches to developing a theory of language rights have very different inherent tendencies. The move from theory to practice is inherently expansive in that, given its emphasis on protecting an interest in linguistic security, it invariably inclines to the proposition that "more is better". But language rights taken to their logical conclusion encounter certain fundamental conflicts with the prevailing conditions of a human right. The move from practice to theory, on the other hand, is quite restrictive, in that there is general agreement on a limited set of rights. In particular, there is a striking gap between public opinion about language rights and the content of government legislation. Accordingly, the choice of approach to a theory of language rights has significant consequences for the content of language rights that will be ultimately recognized.

Développement historique d'une politique linguistique au Canada

La politique linguistique canadienne est issue de toute une série de vues mouvantes et conflictuelles sur la nature de l'expérience canadienne. L'une d'elles voit en la Confédération le sommet de la conquête de l'Amérique du Nord par les Anglais : préconisée par Lord Durham en 1839, l'assimilation des communautés de langue française était le but ultime de la politique britannique en Amérique du Nord. Il existe d'autre part une vue compacte de la Confédération, qui perçoit la Confédération comme un traité entre deux nations «fondatrices» et qui constitutionnalise les institutions religieuses et éducationnelles au Québec. Elle permettrait l'épanouissement du Québec de langue française dans un cadre fédéral.

Selon Ramsay Cook, la vision de Lord Durham continue à dominer l'évolution historique de la politique linguistique. Durham estimait que l'homogénéité linguistique était la condition préalable indispensable à toute nation-État aspirant à participer pleinement à l'économie de l'Empire britannique. Avec une bonne volonté toute paternelle, il exigeait donc l'assimilation des Canadiens français. L'homogénéité linguistique fut généralement réalisée au Canada et au Québec, mais pas dans la même langue. Grâce aux garanties constitutionnelles protégeant l'éducation catholique romaine, le Québec parvint à résister au courant de l'assimilation. Tout comme le rôle de l'État, les garanties linguistiques étendirent leur portée — des services publics au secteur privé.

Avec la force grandissante du gouvernement québécois, les points de vue divergents s'affirmèrent. Selon Louis Balthazar, on ne parvint plus à communiquer dans les débats qui suivirent, véritables dialogues de sourds. Tandis que le Québec s'efforçait d'accroître ses pouvoirs pour assurer sa sécurité linguistique, les politiques fédérales évoluèrent dans une autre direction, en renforçant les institutions bilingues et en instaurant un régime d'égalité linguistique entre le français et l'anglais. Il y a conflit entre l'objectif fédéral qui tient à ce que les Québécois se sentent chez eux dans le reste du Canada, et la quête du gouvernement du Québec qui aspire tout simplement à être « maître chez nous ».

Balthazar oppose les deux visions. Une politique d'assymétrie ou d'égalité formelle conduira inévitablement à l'assimilation. Une politique de concentration, par contre, renforcera l'assise territoriale du français au Québec, tout en résistant aux tendances centralistes de l'État fédéral. Selon Ramsay Cook, l'ironie est qu'il ne nous reste plus que la vision de Lord Durham, celle de deux nations-États linguistiquement homogènes : l'une francophone au Québec, l'autre anglophone dans le reste du Canada.

Historical Development of Language Policy in Canada

Canadian language policy has developed out of a series of shifting and conflicting views about the nature of the Canadian experiment. There is the view that confederation was the culmination of the English conquest of British North America. As Lord Durham recommended in 1839, the ultimate aim of British policy in North America was to assimilate the French-speaking communities. Alternatively, there is the compact view of Confederation which saw Confederation as a treaty between the two "founding" nations, constitutionalizing existing religious and educational institutions in Québec. This would enable a French-speaking Québec to thrive under a federal framework.

According to Ramsay Cook, Lord Durham's vision has continued to dominate the historical development of language policy. Durham saw linguistic homogeneity as a prerequisite for any nation-state to compete fully in the economy of the British Empire. With paternal goodwill, he called for the assimilation of French-speaking communities. Linguistic homogeneity was generally achieved in Canada and in Québec, but not in the same language. With constitutional guarantees for Roman Catholic education, Québec successfully resisted assimilationist tendencies. As the role of the state expanded, so too did linguistic guarantees, from government services to the private sector.

As the role of the Québec government strengthened, the divergent views began to be further entrenched. The resulting dialogue, according to Louis Balthazar, was one of miscommunication: a dialogue of the deaf. While Québec has sought greater powers to ensure linguistic security, the federal government's policy evolved in another direction, by strengthening bilingual institutions and creating a regime of linguistic equality between the two languages. A conflict exists between the federal goal of making Québecers feel at home in the rest of Canada and the Québec government's goal of simply being *maître chez nous*.

Balthazar contrasts these two visions. A policy of assymetry, or formal equality, will lead inevitably to assimilation. A policy of concentration, on the other hand, strengthens the territorial base for the French language in Québec, while resisting the centralist tendencies of the federal state. The irony, as Ramsay Cook suggests, is that we are left with Lord Durham's vision, one of linguistic homogeneous nation states, albeit a Francophone one in Québec and an Anglophone one in the rest of Canada.

LANGUAGE POLICY AND THE GLOSSOPHAGIC STATE
'Scappa, che arriva la patria'*

Ramsay Cook

The Supreme Court of Canada, in the *Reference re Manitoba Language Rights* stated that "the importance of language rights is grounded in the essential role that language plays in human existence, development and dignity. It is through language that we are able to form concepts; to structure and order the world around us. Language bridges the gap between isolation and community, allowing humans to delineate the rights and duties they hold in respect of one another, and thus to live in society."[1]

If one were to apply that principle as a measuring stick against which to test the historical development of language policy in Canada the shortfall would be more than a little embarrassing. Yet to measure the past by that principle would be an unhistorical exercise, for it represents a philosophy of language and language policy that is the product of the very evolution that is the focus of this discussion. Indeed, what I want to suggest in my survey of this broad subject is that insofar as there has been anything systematic enough in the language to be worthy of the label "policy" it has, until recently, been founded on a rather different understanding of the role of language in society. Even today, I will conclude, the implications of this new philosophy have barely been considered.

Language policy in Canada has been an attempt to answer the question: who has the right to use what language, when, and where? That question has been posed, and reposed, because Canada has never

---

* E.J. Hobsbawn, *The Age of Empire* (London: Weidenfeld and Nicolson, 1987), cited at 142. The source is "An Italian peasant woman to her son" and it is translated, "Run away, the fatherland is coming."
1. [1985] 1 S.C.R. 721 at 744.

73

been a linguistically uniform community. Language policy, then, has had as its goal the definition of relations between language groups or, to put that another way, to define group rights. Consequently, the need to define a language policy was first faced when New France was ceded to Great Britain in 1763. Prior to that date no policy was needed: the state spoke French, the Church used Latin and French, the world of work and play was French, and there was no decided policy about the linguistic basis for relations with the native peoples — though it is striking that many missionaries and traders acquired some command of one of the local languages. Having conquered New France the British first assumed that assimilation would naturally follow. But as every schoolgirl knows, that policy had to be abandoned when English-speaking settlement failed to materialize. In 1774 Québec was accepted as a "distinct colony" within an English-speaking Empire, one where the religion and legal system, though not the language, of the majority were given legal recognition. When that "catastrophe shocking to think of" — the American revolution — erupted, a new constitution became necessary due to the sudden arrival of large numbers of English-speaking settlers. The 1791 constitution, establishing Lower and Upper Canada, represented a return to the policy of 1763: Canada was to be an English-speaking colony in which French Canadians were to be gradually, and voluntarily, assimilated. English was established as the language of public affairs and an attempt was made to establish it as the language of education. The policy failed. From the outset Francophone members of the Legislative Assembly spoke in their own language and made it evident that they would use these new institutions to defend their culture. The Royal Institution of Education found no favour with Francophones, who preferred to leave education with their French-speaking Church. Numbers, in Lower Canada, proved more effective than policy.

That situation obtained for fifty years until, in the wake of the failed Rebellions of 1837-38, Lord Durham's famous *Report* vigorously reasserted the policy of assimilation in order to establish peace between the "two nations warring in the bosom of a single state." Durham's *Report* might well be called the first systematic statement of language policy in Canada, one which had no legitimate successor until the 1960s and 1970s produced the *Report of the Royal Commission on Bilingualism and Biculturalism* (1965-71), the *rapport de la Commission d'enquête sur la situation de la langue française et sur les droits linguistiques au Québec* (1972) (the Gendron Commission), the Québec White paper on language[2] and its federal counterpart, *Towards a National Understanding* (1977).

---

2. Camille Laurin, Minister of State for Cultural Development, *Québec's Policy on the French Language* (March 1977).

On language, as on all other matters, Durham's *Report* is a very impressive, carefully conceived document, a point recently re-affirmed by Janet Ajzenstat in *The Political Thought of Lord Durham*.[3] Durham's assumptions about language policy remained at the heart of most subsequent language debate in Canada. The first of those assumptions was that language policy was fundamental to nation-building. Durham subscribed to the nineteenth-century liberal view — one shared by John Stuart Mill, for example, but rejected by Lord Acton — that linguistic homogeneity was a requirement of the nation-state, even the colonial nation-state. The conclusion he drew about British North America, as everyone knows, was that if it was to remain British its inhabitants would have to speak English. Francophones would have to accept assimilation. The claim that linguistic and cultural homogeneity is a requirement of nationhood is one which resurfaced repeatedly in both English and French Canada during the language controversies of the century following Durham's mission.

Less commonly heard, at least until the 1960s, but no less important, was Durham's contention that language policy and social policy are intimately connected. It was Durham's view that social mobility in an English-dominated North American economic system depended on a thorough knowledge of English. If French Canadians were to avoid the status of a permanent underclass, they would have to acquire the language of the economy. "I desire to give the Canadians our English character," he wrote, "for the sake of the educated classes, whom the distinction of language and manners keeps apart from the great Empire to which they belong." And he continued that he was even more anxious that the "humbler classes" be "amalgamated" because "their present state of rude and equal plenty is fast deteriorating."[4] The great liberal principle of equality of opportunity, whether in Imperial politics or in the work place, demanded the removal of those linguistic distinctions which, in Durham's view, placed French Canadians in an unequal starting position.

It was not until the 1960s and 1970s that the important issue of the language of work returned to the centre of the stage in the language debate in Canada. First came the Bilingualism and Biculturalism studies demonstrating that French Canadians occupied a shockingly low position on the economic ladder, especially in Québec.[5] These were followed by

---

3. (Kingston, Ontario: McGill-Queen's University Press, 1988).
4. Sir C.P. Lucas, ed., *Lord Durham's Report on the Affairs of British North America* (Oxford: Clarendon Press, 1912) II, 292.
5. See, for example, A. Raynauld, G. Marion et R. Béland, "La Répartition des Revenus Selon Les Groupes Ethniques Au Canada", an unpublished Research Report prepared for the B & B Commission, reviewed in Kenneth McRoberts, *Quebec: Social Change and Political Crisis*, 3rd ed. (Toronto: McClelland and Stewart, 1988) at 176-77.

debate and studies in Québec which both confirmed the earlier conclusions and proposed responses.[6] All of these later studies confirmed Durham's prognosis, but most of them also turned him on his head. Where Durham had recommended that French Canadians be anglicized to fit the economy, later studies made the more sensible and humane suggestion that the world of work be francicized to fit Francophones. Durham would have understood the argument, though he would surely have rejected the goal, presented by the Québec *White Paper on Language* this way:

> The Québec we wish to build will be essentially French. The fact that the majority of its population is French will be clearly visible — at work, in communications, and in the countryside. It will also be a country where the traditional division of powers, *especially in matters concerning the economy*, will be modified (italics added).[7]

For Dr. Camille Laurin, as for Lord Durham, language was much more about power than about poetry. Each believed in what Jean Laponce in *Languages and their Territories* has called, in neither of our official languages, "a glossophagic state."[8]

The Union of 1841, though not the federal union Durham had recommended, had assimilation — glossophagia — as one of its goals, for English alone was recognized as an official language. But political reality — French power — defeated ideology and in 1849 Lord Elgin dramatized that reality by reading the speech from the throne in both French and English. That pragmatic acceptance was translated into the *British North America Act* of 1867 which, for the first time since the conquest, gave constitutional recognition to French as one of the two official languages of "the new nationality." Bilingualism was accepted in the federal parliament and its courts and in the government of the newly created province of Québec. Moreover, the *BNA Act* made provision for a denominational school system in Québec which, in practise, gave institutional support to lingualistic duality. Roughly similar arrangements were made in Manitoba in 1870 and in the Northwest Territories in 1874, though these became victims to the cultural wars of the 1890s.

The debates about language policy in the century following Confederation centred to a large extent on the issue of minority educational rights outside of Québec. The abolition of French as an

---

6. See Serge Carlos, *L'utilisation du français dans le monde du Travail du Québec* (Québec: Éditeur Officiel, 1973) and the discussion in McRoberts, *id.*, at 177-80.

7. *Supra*, note 2 at 52.

8. 2nd ed. (Toronto: University of Toronto Press, 1987) at 1.

official language in Manitoba, for example, attracted far less controversy and litigation than the abolition of state support for denomination schools, schools which were Catholic and, in many instances, Francophone. The argument about separate schools was both religious and linguistic and, although the two issues cannot really be divided, I will do so for purposes of my analysis of language policy. Four particular concerns dominated this debate.

First, there was the contention that if Canada was to become a "nation", then cultural and linguistic homogeneity was necessary at least outside of Québec. That was D'Alton McCarthy's contention in the 1890s in his campaign in Manitoba and the Northwest, and it would resurface in the debate over the 1905 Autonomy Bills establishing Alberta and Saskatchewan, and in the school controversies in Ontario, Manitoba, and Saskatchewan between 1912 and 1919. On the whole that argument carried the day. In defending French language and Roman Catholic rights, most nationalists made exactly the same equation between language and culture or "race", and added religion. Henri Bourassa's famous speech at the 1910 Eucharistic Congress entitled *Religion, Langue, Nationalité*[9] is only one of a multiplicity of possible examples.

Second, there was the contention and counter-contention about the nature of the Confederation settlement of 1867 which is summed up in the old query: act or compact? Those, chiefly English Canadians, who insisted on the "act" thesis contended that the *BNA Act*, insofar as language was concerned, meant exactly what it said: English was the language of Canada outside of Québec with limited recognition for French in federal institutions and a fuller bilingualism in Québec. That was what Henri Bourassa called the "reservation" theory of Confederation: French Canadians, *comme les sauvages*, could only exercise their rights when they remained on the Québec reservation. To that theory he opposed the idea of a "compact" or *entente* between cultures which implied equality of French and English Canadians from coast to coast, equality of communities. Until the 1960s Bourassa's theory remained exactly that — a theory supported by a large number of French Canadians and rejected by most English Canadians.

Third, the language debate was complicated by immigration which brought, particularly to the Canadian west, a number of additional languages sometimes spoken by people more numerous than those who spoke French. What claims could these groups make, on grounds of right or practicality, that their languages should be recognized at least

---

9. (Montreal: Imprimerie du "Devoir", 1910).

as languages of education? The Manitoba answer in the so-called Laurier-Greenway settlement of 1897 was that those languages had as much right to recognition as French — restricted but significant use as a language of instruction. By 1916 the Manitoba government decided — and the other prairie provinces followed suit — that a mistake had been made. Educational reforms in the prairie provinces placed all non-English languages on an equal footing: they were prohibited as languages of education, though they could be taught as subjects. (In rural areas, where non-English groups were concentrated, these requirements were often ignored except when the provincial inspector paid his visits!)[10]

The fourth issue, one which I will merely mention, was cost. How much could developing provinces, or even a developing country, afford to spend supporting education in languages other than English? The answer was almost always, not much. Québec, of course, was an exception because there the minority language was English supported by constitutionally-guaranteed Protestant schools and the financial resources of an economically powerful community.

Lord Durham's argument about cultural uniformity and nation-building was not the only one at work in this debate. It would be quite inaccurate to leave the impression that the insistence that English be accepted as the only official language of education outside of Québec was simply a matter of Anglo-Saxon prejudice or racism — though there was enough, more than enough, of that. Durham's second argument also was a factor. Men such as J.S. Woodsworth and J.W. Dafoe, for example, believed that getting ahead in an English-speaking country and continent required a knowledge of the dominant language and an immersion in the dominant culture. Non-English speakers were open to exploitation both economically and politically because they were not integrated into the system, and integration required, as the first necessity, a command of English. Those progressive educational reforms which resulted almost invariably in the reduction, even erasure, of minority language rights, were based not so much on bigotry as on paternalism: the conviction that the reformers knew what was best for the objects of reform, namely, the "foreigners", a term that could include French Canadians. The well-known argument presented in John Porter's *The Vertical Mosaic*,[11] that the price of the cultural mosaic is a class system in which the English, and to a lesser degree the French, are dominant would have won approval from early twentieth-century educational reformers. It was also Durham's concern.

---

10. Robert Craig Brown and Ramsay Cook, *Canada 1896-1921: A Nation Transformed* (Toronto: McClelland and Stewart, 1974) at 252-62.
11. (Toronto & Buffalo: University of Toronto Press, 1965).

Without simplifying the record too drastically, then, it can be said that prior to 1960 disputes about language and language policy focussed largely on educational rights, to a lesser extent on the language of government, and almost not at all on the language of the private sector, except in the sense that education was designed to prepare students for work in the private sector where English predominated at all but the unskilled level. There were minor exceptions such as the campaign by *La Ligue des Droits français*, supported by *Le Devoir*, to force Eaton's to issue its catalogue in French. If we believe Roch Carrier's wonderful story "The Hockey Sweater," we must conclude that the campaign failed !

What eventually changed the emphasis of this debate, bringing the language of work to the forefront, was the growth of the welfare state, at all levels of government. And that was accompanied by the gradual but insistent blurring of the line that once, at least theoretically, divided the private from the public sector whether in economics, social security, health care, or that vague area called "culture." The growth of government and government services meant that employment opportunities in the public sector multiplied rapidly. Consequently the language of work became an important criterion for employment, and one subject to political pressure. Though Francophones had long been dissatisfied with their under-representation, especially at the upper levels, in the federal public service, it was no accident that that discontent became more pronounced with the rise of the welfare bureaucracy. Nor was it an accident that once the Québec state, after 1960, moved to improve and expand its public service, the federal government had to pay more attention to the demands of its Francophone employees. Otherwise they could and often did seek careers in Québec. The second consequence of increased government activity was, of course, a rising demand from those to be served in their own language. The Royal Commission on Bilingualism and Biculturalism and the *Official Languages Act*[12] were responses to these concerns, among others.

In Québec the issue soon moved beyond public sector concerns. By 1960 it had become widely recognized that the state must play a role in preserving and promoting the French language in an urban-industrial society. The stages leading from the Lesage government's tentative efforts in the language promotion area through the controversies of the Bertrand and first Bourassa administrations to the enactment of Bill 101 in 1977 cannot be discussed in detail. But the point of all of the recent language legislation in Québec has been to ensure that Francophone Québecers will be able to live their lives, at work as well as at home, in French. It has also been designed to ensure that new

---

12. R.S.C. 1985, c. 0-3, repealed and replaced by S.C. 1988, c. 38.

immigrants will be assimilated into the French rather than the English stream in Québec, a goal whose urgency is increased with every drop in the Francophone birth rate. These concerns form the essence of the Report of the Gendron Commission.

Increasing state intervention in language matters has raised in a dramatic fashion the old question of the relation of language and culture. Are they distinct or inseparable entities? Part of the problem is that the definition of "culture" is almost infinitely expandable — at last count there were about 300 different definitions of the word. Successive attempts by both government and intellectuals in Québec to give the term acceptable content have been less than convincing. (A point made both by Jean Larose in his *la Petite Noirceur*[13] and in *Nationalism and the Politics of Culture in Québec* by Richard Handler.[14]) But differing theories of the relation of language to culture have underpinned contemporary language policies. In a bilingual state it is logical to designate language as a simple means of communication. That is the assumption of the *Official Languages Act*.[15] By contrast, the authors of Québec language policy have argued that language, culture, and identity are inseparable, and that is stated in the preamble to the *Charter of the French Language*.[16]

If those contrasting views of language policy seem straightforward, then a look at the arguments in the recent Supreme Court case over the language of signs in Québec — the *Brown Shoes*[17] case — suggests that the ground is slipperier than first appearances might suggest. In that case the Québec government lawyers, in defending the prohibition of English signs, argued that there was no connection between language and culture despite Bill 101's assertion to the contrary. In their decision, the Supreme Court Justices reaffirmed their opinion in the *Reference re Manitoba Language Rights*[18] and stated:

> Language is so intimately related to the form and content of expression that there cannot be true freedom of expression by means of language if one is prohibited from using the language of one's choice. Language is not merely a means or medium of expression; it colours the content and meaning of expression. It is, as the preamble of the *Charter of the French Language* indicates, a means by which a people may express its cultural identity. It is also the means by which the individual expresses his or her personal identity and sense of individuality.[19]

---

13. Jean Larose, *La Petite Noirceur* (Montréal: Boréal, 1987) at 65-71.
14. (Madison, Wisc.: University of Wisconsin Press, 1988).
15. *Supra*, note 12.
16. R.S.Q. 1977, c. C-11.
17. *Attorney General of Québec* v. *La Chaussure Brown's Inc. et al.* (1988), 54 D.L.R. (4th) 577.
18. *Supra*, note 1.
19. *Supra*, note 17 at 604.

Thus Joshua Fishman's *Sociology of Language*[20], controversial though it may be among language theorists, has become a central principle of Canadian jurisprudence on language policy. And, it should be noted in passing, language is made the key to both collective and individual identity as if neither claim were open to controversy. What would James Joyce or Joseph Conrad have thought?

Though the defenders of Bill 101's regulations respecting commercial signage were thus hoisted on their own petard, the full implications of enshrining the Fishman doctrine in our jurisprudence are far from having been explored. How, for example, does it apply to French language minorities in Alberta? Or for that matter to those whose maternal tongue is neither French nor English? Could the doctrine be used to justify the claim of Canada's native peoples to official recognition of some or all of their numerous languages? These, and other questions, remain for the future.

Let me conclude this rapid, and sometimes simplified, survey by noting, first, that language policy has moved from being a relatively minor item on the public agenda in the years prior to 1960 — relatively minor, but always volatile — to one of central importance. Secondly, as it has evolved, policies based on two distinct philosophies and designed to achieve different goals have been implemented. There is a federal policy of official bilingualism formulated in the *Official Languages Act*[21] and enshrined in the *Charter of Rights*.[22] It has been adopted by New Brunswick and to a lesser extent Ontario and Manitoba. Then there is the Québec policy of modified unilingualism followed, or more accurately preceded by, the other six provinces. To that mix is added a commitment, stated in both the *Charter of Rights* and the *Charter of the French Language*,[23] to multiculturalism, a commitment which has a whole range of largely unexamined implications for language policy, especially in education. How compatible these philosophies, goals and commitments are, no one would dare predict.

That said, the issues involved in language policy — those of nation-building, of cultural pluralism or uniformity, of economic opportunity and social harmony — are no different than they were when Durham laid them out in 1840. What we should have learned from Durham, I would argue, is that an impressive analysis does not automatically lead to a just, or even a workable, solution.

---

20. (Rowley, Mass.: Newbury House Publishers, 1972).
21. *Supra*, note 12.
22. *Canadian Charter of Rights and Freedoms*, s. 27, being Schedule B of the *Canada Act 1982* (U.K.) 1982, c.11.
23. R.S.Q. 1977, c. C-11, s. 11.

HISTORY AND LANGUAGE POLICY

Louis Balthazar

Jean de Lafontaine écrivait, il y a trois cents ans :

Selon que vous serez puissants ou misérables,

Les jugements de cour vous rendront blancs ou noirs.

Cette citation ne s'applique pas tout à fait à la situation canadienne. Fort heureusement, il est souvent arrivé que des groupes faibles ou misérables aient été blanchis par une cour canadienne, surtout récemment. Ce qui peut-être se produit moins souvent, c'est que l'on rende justice à des faibles qui veulent cesser d'être faibles.

Historical Landmarks

I was planning to go through the historical situation of language policy in Canada in the first part of my exposé but Ramsey Cook has done it so well[1] and I disagree so little with his account (although I may not agree with his interpretation) that I do not deem it necessary to come back to it except for a few points. Ramsey referred to the *Québec Act*[2] not mentioning anything about language and that is true. But the *Québec Act* provided for the old French laws to be enforced in civil matters and, if my recollection is correct, those laws were written in French and not translated. If the link is made between culture and language, the fact that the old French laws were preserved and the fact that the Catholic religion was recognized, allowed the French language to be used a lot in Québec after 1774 and even after the *Constitutional Act, 1791*.[3] Another point I want to make is about the *B.N.A. Act*.[4] Section 193 says that English and French may be used in Parliament and in the legislature of Québec, and also in the Courts. Well, the exact

---

1. Ramsay Cook, "Language Policy and the Glossophagic State" in this volume.
2. 14 Geo. III, c. 83.
3. 31 Geo. III, c. 31.
4. Now the *Constitution Act*, 1867 (U.K.), 30 & 31 Vict., c. 3.

result of that provision is that Québec became bilingual and Ottawa remained almost unilingual until recently. And, of course, as Ramsey Cook has documented, the status of the French language has experienced complete devastation in the rest of the country until the 1960's. This illustrates what I am going to say later: the fact that if you treat English and French on the same level officially, the result is very imbalanced as it was, indeed, following the *B.N.A. Act.*

Let me turn now to the 1960s when, due in great part to the quiet revolution, the Royal Commission on Bilingualism and Biculturalism (the B & B Commission) was set up. The historical statement of Jean Lesage in 1964 is to me very important: "Québec has become the political expression of French Canada and for all practical purposes the homeland of all those who speak our language in the country." That meant a sort of identification between Québec and the French language; it meant also that the development of the French language, in the eyes of Jean Lesage and most Québecers then and now, is very much tied to Québec and to a strong Québec. Thus, the Government of Québec has called endlessly for more power and more responsibility over the development of the French language and Francophone culture. The response to the B & B Commission started a sort of dialogue of the deaf. Whereas Québecers wanted to reinforce the status of the French language in Québec and build the network of communications and institutions that are necessary for a language and a culture to develop, the anglo-Canadian response was by and large: "What can we do to make the French-speaking people comfortable throughout the country?" Québecers, on the one hand, wanted a strong Québec. But the reply was always: "We're going to build a bilingual Canada". There was no reply to the idea of a strong Québec. Except that the B & B Commission, in spite of its composition which reflected very much the population of Canada and the mood of Canada, came up with conclusions that were not exactly sheer bilingualism throughout Canada. The two majorities concept, especially, was elaborated by André Laurendeau and formulated in the B & B Report. The idea that there had to be a particular weight for the French language in the province of Québec, the linkage of language with culture, all of that went in a different direction from the prevailing mood and, not surprisingly, these concepts were not applied in the *Official Languages Act*[5] which addressed only the issue of two languages but not of biculturalism and certainly not the concept of the two majorities. That simplification also prevailed in the *Constitution Act, 1982*[6], the *Canadian Charter of Rights and Freedoms*[7] and recently, Bill C-72.[8]

5. R.S.C. 1985, c. O-3.
6. Being Schedule B of the *Canada Act, 1982* (U.K.), 1982, c. 11.
7. Part 1 of the *Constitution Act, 1982, id.*
8. *The Official Languages Act*, S.C. 1988, c. 38, as rep. R.S.C. 1985, c. O-3.

On the other hand, in Québec the trend was always in the opposite direction: to build a stronger Québec, to build a French Québec, and we had Bill 22[9] and Bill 101,[10] which can be considered as the moral equivalent of independence. The latter was thus certainly more than a linguistic bill, and it is still seen today as something very symbolic of the French identity. Hence the concern of the Québec population with the slow erosion of Bill 101 year after year, so that it could become eventually completely insignificant. To balance the Charter which is seen as an instrument of centralization and a grasp of the federal power over linguistic issues, there is the notwithstanding clause, also considered in Québec as having a very symbolic importance (as it does, I imagine, in the western provinces who demanded it in return for their acceptance of the Trudeau constitutional deal).

First Lesson: Asymmetry

I draw two main lessons from the history of language rights in Canada, two main propositions. The first is that asymmetry is the main feature of the language rights problem in Canada, and it cannot be bypassed without completely falsifying the issue. My second proposition or lesson to be drawn from recent history is that a certain demographic concentration is the main way for a language to be preserved and promoted.

Let us first look at asymmetry. Considering French and English in strict terms of equality leads to very unequal treatment in practice as shown by the application of s. 133 of the *B.N.A. Act*. It's a little bit like entering a limp person and a normal person together as equals in a running competition. The truth and the reality is that the French language is threatened everywhere in North America and is even threatened in Québec. The English language is not threatened even in Québec. Let me quote Jacques Henripin, an excellent demographer, in the Fall 1988 issue of *Language and Society*, The Review of the Commissioner of Official Languages. "In truth", concludes Henripin from his reading of the 1986 census, "only English is really vigorous everywhere in Canada. In fact, it is making relatively significant gains in every province and in the course of time persons who have another mother tongue adopt English at home and this language of adoption becomes the mother tongue of their children. French just manages to hold its ground and only in Québec where its losses to English are almost exactly compensated for by the gains it makes at the expense of third languages."

---

9. *Official Language Act*, S.Q.1974, c. 6.
10. *Charter of the French Language*, R.S.Q. 1977, c. C-11.

In Québec, nonetheless, Anglophones say that they are threatened by Bill 101 and Bill 178.[11] But to this day linguistic transfers in Québec, as shown by the last 1986 census, are still in favour of the English language. In 1986, 10.4 percent of the Québec population reported being of English mother tongue but 12.3 percent reported using English as the home language.[12] So, if the proportion of Anglophones in Québec goes down, it is entirely due to the out-migration of that population. Bilingual signs are forbidden by the law in Québec but it must be pointed out that they actually proliferate in practice and in reality. Just walk along St. Lawrence Boulevard and you will see a lot of English and you will even see occasionally some unilingual English signs.

A whole school network exists for Anglophones. Bill 101 restrictions apply to elementary and secondary schools, but, at the higher level, Anglophone colleges and universities get more than 30 percent of the Québec students for a population of 12 percent Anglophones. We are confronted also with the consequences of the anachronistic provision of our Constitution which guarantees denominational rights as opposed to linguistic rights. Because of the division of the school system between Catholics and Protestants, the Protestant School Board of Greater Montréal includes a growing number of French Schools, due to the fact that a lot of immigrants don't want to go to the Catholic school system; and those French schools are run by a Board which is, for the time being, to my knowledge, composed entirely of Anglophones. So, in the province of Québec you have a good number of French schools controlled by the Anglophone board. Is it the same for the Catholic system? Not really, because for a long time the Catholic School Commission of Montréal has included an Anglophone section and there have always been Anglophones sitting on the Catholic School Board. This denominational division exists in great part because of the stubbornness of some Catholic conservatives and "intégristes" around the Bishop of Montréal, who still control the Catholic School Board of Montréal but oddly enough it is due also to the Protestant School Board people, who are also fighting for the religious status quo.

In the province of Québec 60 percent of the Anglophones are now bilingual. That represents an impressive progress. But that means also there are one-third of the Anglophone population of Québec who are still unilingual. It is amazing that after all the events of the last years that, according to the 1986 census, one third of the Anglophone population of Québec still does not want or does not speak French.

---

11. An Act to Amend the *Charter of the French Language*, S.Q. 1988, c. 54.
12. See Statistics Canada, *Language Retention and Transfer* (Ottawa: Supply and Services, 1989) at 1-23.

On the other hand, 80 percent of the Francophones outside Québec are bilingual whereas only 9 percent of the Anglophone population outside Québec is bilingual (as opposed to 30 percent of the Québec Francophones). Francophones outside of Québec would gladly exchange their rights to some signs in French for McGill University, Concordia University, the Protestant School Board of Greater Montréal, the Montréal Gazette, radio and television stations, the present status of the English language in downtown Montréal, etc.

Sometimes French-speaking Québecers are accused of wanting to have their cake and eat it too: to call for a unilingual Québec and a bilingual Canada. That makes us feel guilty and we may feel at times we have to choose between strengthening the French fact in Québec and helping the minorities outside Québec. If we choose the former we may sound very selfish indeed since the minorities are in such a bad situation. But I think that is a false dilemma. In fact, what you find in Canada, and you will find it for a very long time whatever happens and whatever the laws are, is bilingualism in Québec and unilingualism in the rest of Canada. In practice, I could testify that Québec has never been as bilingual as it is since 1977. Now the majority of Anglophones can speak French as well as English. The figures above (60 percent Anglophones being bilingual, 30 percent for the Francophones) are normal, given the French majority. What I experienced as a young person, when I went to school in downtown Montréal between 1942 and 1950, was a completely unilingual west-end Montréal. At the time official bilingualism would prevail, and that helps to understand how French-speaking people in Québec can get terribly sensitive when they hear that Québec ought to be officially bilingual. We all remember what official bilingualism meant for Québec. I'm ready to argue again that, right now, even under the empire of such a stringent law as Bill 101, for all practical purposes, Montréal is a bilingual city.

Second Lesson: Concentration

My second point is very important too. Language is essentially a social phenomenon. For a language to be protected, to make it possible to enjoy linguistic rights, there has to be a good number of persons speaking that language. There is no way for me to look at language rights outside a collective situation. In the past, French Canadians have survived due to the fact that they formed ghettos outside Québec, small pockets here and there in Canada and also because, as Ramsay Cook has pointed out, Québec constituted more or less a sort of reservation. This is no longer possible and this is no longer something to be wished for either. Integration is very strong. Québec is now a wide open society so that you cannot look at the linguistic situation of minorities or at the Québec situation as you did in the past when we were living in a closed society. Hence the aspiration of Québec to create a French network of communication and to control it. Hence the insistence on the majority status of the French language, the insistence on distinguishing between the Québec linguistic problem and the linguistic problem elsewhere in Canada. In Québec, Francophones want to build a whole full-fledged society; in the rest of Canada you may build little societies, little concentrations, but I don't think it is possible, even in New Brunswick, to create a global society as in Québec. Consequently the iron law of survival for the French language in Canada is the following: the closer you are to Québec, the more you are likely to survive. The more minorities can be somewhat connected to a Québec network of communication, or extend that network to Ontario and New Brunswick to some extent, the more the French language is likely to be alive in Canada. It is no coincidence that Paul Desmarais and Antonine Maillet live in Montréal. Paul Desmarais is certainly not ashamed of his Franco-Ontarian origin and Antonine Maillet is still proudly an Acadian, not a Québécoise, but, for all sorts of practical reasons, because the metropolis of the Francophone culture in North America is in Montréal, they have to live there.

A strong Québec cannot be harmful to minorities. On the contrary, minorities in Canada have been reinforced, reinvigorated due to the Québec contagion and also indirectly because of reactions to the Québec phenomenon which made the rest of Canada discover only in the last twenty years the fate of the minorities.

Hence the necessity of decentralization in Canada, the necessity of a recognition of Québec's special identity and the danger, in my opinion, of building a Canadian nation-state which would eventually level off linguistic and cultural differences in the name of national standards, equality for all, under a charter of human rights, with a concept of indivisible sovereignty. I will be happy to live in a Canada which would not be a nation-state and which would not go along with the tradition of the modern centralized state. But if one day I have to opt between a Canadian nation-state and a Québec nation-state, I am afraid I would choose the latter.

Partie IV / Part IV

Droits linguistiques : récents développements constitutionnels

Selon Pierre Foucher, c'est à l'absence de droits linguistiques exprès dans la *Loi constitutionnelle de 1867* qu'il faut attribuer le sort des communautés francophones hors Québec. Depuis lors, et surtout au cours des vingt dernières années, les Franco-Canadiens ont réalisé de modestes gains, attribuables à un civisme judiciaire accru et à l'enchâssement des droits linguistiques dans la *Charte canadienne des droits et libertés*. Au bout du compte, cependant, les minorités linguistiques sont tout autant menacées aujourd'hui que jadis. Essentiellement, elles restent à la merci des gouvernements provinciaux. S'il estime toujours nécessaire de chercher des solutions politiques à ces problèmes, Foucher appuie le rôle que la Constitution pourrait jouer pour faire progresser les droits linguistiques.

Wayne MacKay illustre de façon saisissante comment certains fonctionnaires élus localement agissent envers les revendications linguistiques portant sur les droits garantis par la Charte. Il évoque le procès intenté par un groupe de parents acadiens en vue d'obtenir que leurs enfants soient instruits en français au Cap-Breton. MacKay décrit les tactiques obstructionnistes du conseil scolaire et le manque de probité du ministère de l'Éducation provincial, lesquels ont donné lieu à une série d'audiences et ont conduit les parents jusque devant la Cour d'appel de la Nouvelle-Écosse. L'histoire souligne la précarité des litiges relevant de la Charte et l'attitude de certains gouvernements envers une réclamation légitime présentée en vertu des droits linguistiques constitutionnels.

Timothy Christian relate un autre cas troublant : le débat animé auquel a donné lieu, en 1987, l'usage du français à la législature de l'Alberta. Léo Piquette, député francophone, avait alors tenté d'établir le statut constitutionnel du français en posant une question en français au ministre de l'Éducation. Cette initiative peu appréciée devait conduire à l'adoption de résolutions limitant sévèrement l'usage du français à l'Assemblée législative albertaine.

Suite à certaines initiatives législatives fédérales et à l'adoption de la Charte, la Cour suprême du Canada fut disposée à affirmer les droits linguistiques des minorités. Selon Joseph Magnet, en déclarant l'invalidité de l'*Official Language Act de 1890* du Manitoba (1985), elle atteignit un des points culminants de son activisme. La décision de la cour devait être appliquée peu après. À cause de l'isolement du Québec et de son opposition à la Constitution de 1982, du soutien inconsistant du gouvernement fédéral envers les minorités linguistiques et de la signature de l'Accord du lac Meech, la cour préféra ensuite généralement que les litiges d'ordre linguistique restent du domaine des provinces. Comme le souligne Magnet, les provinces n'ont pas d'antécédents très encourageants à cet égard. L'une après l'autre, la Saskatchewan et l'Alberta abolirent l'usage officiel du français.

Malgré l'existence d'un régime de langues officielles officiellement enchâssé dans la constitution, les conflits linguistiques se multiplient et s'intensifient. Magnet conclut que le « Canada est en train de s'ouvrir à la couture ».

Language Rights : Recent Constitutional Developments

It was the absence of express language rights in the *Constitution Act, 1867* which, according to Pierre Foucher, led to the demise of Francophone communities outside of Québec. Since then, and particularly in the last twenty years, Franco-Canadians have seen modest gains as a result of increasing judicial activism and the entrenchment of language rights in the *Canadian Charter of Rights and Freedoms*. In the end, though, linguistic minorities face the same kinds of threats today as they did in earlier times. Essentially they are left vulnerable to the devices of provincial governments. While political solutions to these problems must continue to be sought, Foucher supports the role that the constitution may play in further advancing language rights.

Wayne MacKay provides a startling example of how some locally elected officials are reacting towards language claims under the Charter. He traces litigation begun by a group of Acadian parents to secure French-language instruction in Cape Breton. MacKay recounts the obstructionist tactics employed by the school board and the untrustworthiness of the provincial department of education, necessitating a series of judicial hearings and, ultimately, vindication for the parents before the Nova Scotia Court of Appeal. It is a cautionary tale about the precariousness of Charter litigation and the attitude of some governments to a legitimate claim of Charter language rights.

Timothy Christian writes about another unsettling claim; the heated debate in 1987 over the use of the French language in the Alberta legislature. Leo Piquette, a member of the Assembly, sought to test the constitutional status of the French language by addressing a question to the Minister of Education in French. The gesture was not warmly received, leading ultimately to the adoption of resolutions severely restricting the use of the French language in Alberta's Legislative Assembly.

As a result of federal legislative initiatives and enactment of the Charter, the Supreme Court of Canada was open to the idea of breathing life into minority language rights. According to Joseph Magnet, the highwater mark in the Court's activism was the striking down in 1985 of Manitoba's 1890 *Official Languages Act*. The Court's retrenchment began shortly thereafter. As a result of Québec's isolation and opposition to the 1982 *Constitution*, the federal government's inconsistent support for linguistic minorities, together with the signing of the Meech Lake Accord, the Court preferred generally that language claims remain the domain of the provinces. As Magnet argues, the provinces do not have an encouraging record in this regard. In quick succession, the provinces of Saskatchewan and Alberta abolished the official use of the French language.

In spite of the constitutional entrenchment of an official languages regime, linguistic conflict has ensued at even heightened levels. In view of all of the events described in this part, as Magnet writes, "Canada's seam is opening".

DROITS LINGUISTIQUES AU CANADA : RÉCENTS DÉVELOPPEMENTS CONSTITUTIONNELS

Pierre Foucher

La tâche de faire le bilan des récents développements constitutionnels dans le domaine linguistique est passablement difficile. Elle est difficile pour plusieurs raisons : d'abord parce que c'est récent, donc il nous manque le recul nécessaire à une évaluation calme de la situation ; ensuite parce que chacun connaît sans doute déjà la plupart de ces événements, lesquels seront par ailleurs abondamment discutés dans d'autres ateliers ; enfin parce qu'au-delà de la simple description, il faut bien dégager de tout cela un sens juridique et social cohérent, ce qui conduit à des interprétations. Or en ces domaines, les interprétations sont hasardeuses et forcément subjectives. C'est donc avec l'oeil d'un francophone de l'extérieur du Québec, observateur attentif et parfois participant indirect, que j'aborderai la dernière décennie constitutionnelle si féconde en débats linguistiques.

Si on commence à dénombrer les arrêts importants depuis 1975, et même en écartant ceux qui portaient sur des textes de loi par opposition à des dispositions constitutionnelles, on dénombre quand même plus de 50 jugements importants en dix ans, une moyenne de cinq par année. De ce nombre, la moitié provient du Québec et autant de l'extérieur du Québec. On peut prévoir encore sept ou huit jugements cette année et autant l'année prochaine avec les procès en cours un peu partout au pays.

On plaide donc beaucoup au Canada en droits linguistiques. Je n'ai pas l'intention de vous faire un résumé de tous ces jugements ; il me suffit d'évoquer les noms de *Jones, Blaikie, Quebec Association, Société des Acadiens, Mercure ou Renvoi manitobain* pour évoquer chez vous les principes importants dégagés par la Cour suprême. J'aimerais plutôt vous inviter à réfléchir sur ce que représentent pour l'intégrité de la Constitution canadienne ces multiples procès. Après avoir défini généralement ce que devrait faire une Constitution, nous passerons en revue les principaux éléments qui se dégagent des textes constitutionnels et de la jurisprudence, pour en troisième lieu relier ces deux parties entre elles et voir si la Constitution canadienne est un instrument qui remplit la mission que doit remplir une bonne constitution.

I- À QUOI SERT UNE CONSTITUTION ?

Voilà bien une question qui mériterait à elle seule des heures de discussions. Contentons-nous donc de rester sur un terrain assez sûr sans entrer dans des considérations purement philosophiques sur la nature et le rôle de l'État.

Une Constitution, c'est deux choses. C'est d'abord, au sens formel, un ensemble de règles qui sont au-dessus de toutes les autres, c'est la norme de base, celle qui légitime le pouvoir des institutions. On retrouve des exemples récents de cette fonction de la Constitution dans le renvoi manitobain[1], alors que la primauté de la norme constitutionnelle et de principes supérieurs a conduit la Cour suprême du Canada à invalider les lois adoptées en violation des exigences constitutionnelles, en maintenant toutefois leur efficacité pour éviter le vide juridique auquel conduisait la nullité pure et simple.

Mais une Constitution, c'est aussi, dans son sens matériel, l'ensemble des règles écrites et non écrites (qu'on pense aux conventions de la constitution) qui régissent les rapports des organes de l'État entre eux et avec les citoyens. Dans ce sens, on devrait retrouver dans une constitution complète trois types de règles : des règles qui créent des institutions ; des règles qui définissent les principaux pouvoirs de ces institutions ; et des règles qui contrôlent l'abus de ces pouvoirs en conférant, au bénéfice des citoyens, une gamme de droits fondamentaux. Cette dernière fonction de la Constitution n'est d'ailleurs pas universellement admise : plusieurs pays de tradition anglo-saxonne croient encore qu'une Charte constitutionnelle des droits est inutile, parce que les règles démocratiques suffisent à assurer le respect des droits de tous (c'est la vision de Dicey) et qu'une Charte constitutionnelle crée un gouvernement de juges, politise la fonction judiciaire et déresponsabilise les gouvernants. D'autres estiment qu'il est essentiel de définir les valeurs fondamentales et les droits inhérents à toute personne afin de préserver les libertés et la démocratie elle-même.

Si on revient un instant à la Constitution de 1867, on s'aperçoit que des droits linguistiques il n'y en a presque pas, pas plus d'ailleurs qu'il n'y a de droits fondamentaux. L'absence de droits fondamentaux

---

1. *Renvoi : droits linguistiques au Manitoba*, [1985] 1 R.C.S. 721.

s'explique facilement : il n'était pas de mise dans les colonies britanniques, à cette époque-là, de conférer des droits au moyen de chartes constitutionnelles. L'absence de droits linguistiques est plus curieuse : les dispositions constitutionnelles en matière de langue ne visent au fond que le Québec et le Parlement fédéral ; on les a étendus ensuite au Manitoba dans un souci de préserver les droits des Franco-Manitobains. Il faut comprendre qu'à cette époque personne n'a pris la défense de leurs intérêts, ni au sein de leur communauté privée de moyens et de représentants, ni au sein des délégations officielles de leurs provinces.

L'absence de droits linguistiques en 1867 est à la source de la perte par les minorités francophones du contrôle de leurs écoles, ce qui allait s'avérer si désastreux à long terme pour la survie de ces communautés. Les législateurs sont intervenus (dans la décennie 1870 en Atlantique, dans la décennie 1890 dans l'Ouest, dans la décennie 1910 en Ontario) pour retirer aux francophones le droit d'utiliser leur langue dans l'enseignement et le droit de gérer leurs établissements d'enseignement. On a bien tenté d'invoquer la protection des droits des minorités religieuses[2] pour stopper ce geste, mais en vain : le Conseil Privé statua que ces droits visaient les aspects religieux et non linguistiques[3]. On dut se résigner à un constat d'échec de la Constitution pour assurer les droits des minorités francophones ; cela marqua le début de l'assimilation de ces communautés. On croyait peut-être, à l'époque, à la protection du pouvoir de choisir localement la langue de l'instruction. À tort ou à raison, les tribunaux en jugèrent autrement, de sorte que la survie de la langue française à l'école se fit en dépit de la Constitution plutôt que grâce à elle[4].

Les droits linguistiques constitutionnels dont nous nous préoccupons aujourd'hui sont donc, pour une grande part, une réponse moderne à un problème ancien. Cependant, la façon dont on a procédé pour les accorder fut malhabile. On a réagi à des pressions politiques conjoncturelles, sans s'interroger minutieusement sur ce qu'il convenait de faire. Certes, les propositions et les idées n'ont pas manqué durant la décennie pré-rapatriement ; mais les constituants ont peut-être trop axé leur action sur la pression politique du moment et pas assez sur une réflexion profonde quant à la fonction de droits constitutionnels en matière linguistique, quant aux besoins des communautés minoritaires, quant au genre de garanties qu'on devrait rechercher.

---

2. La *Loi constitutionnelle de 1867* (R.-U.), 30 & 31 Vict., c. 3, art. 93.
3. *Ottawa Roman Separate School Trustees* c. *Mackell*, [1917] A.C. 63.
4. Pour un historique complet du dossier scolaire au Canada, voir P. FOUCHER, *Évolution des systèmes scolaires francophones hors du Québec*, conférence prononcée à l'Université Laval, Québec 5 octobre 1989 ; à paraître dans les actes de la conférence, publiés par le L.A.B.R.A.P.S. de la Faculté d'éducation de l'Université Laval.

La dualité linguistique fait partie du Canada depuis sa fondation. Les crises scolaires du dernier siècle en Ontario, au Manitoba, les crises linguistiques récentes en Saskatchewan et en Alberta, les problèmes linguistiques du Québec ont toujours ébranlé les fondements du pays. Il est donc juste de reconnaître que cette question fait partie intime de la «grundnorm» canadienne. Mais voilà: si la dualité a toujours ponctué notre histoire, le développement des droits linguistiques constitutionnels est récent. Et le problème vient du fait qu'on a, pour des raisons de conjoncture politique, adopté des solutions constitutionnelles inadaptées aux problèmes. On a défini des droits sans référence aux fondements (autres que politiques) de ces droits, sans non plus prévoir une extension de la dualité hors de la sphère des droits vers l'exercice des compétences et ultimement la structure des institutions centrales et locales.

Donc, une Constitution devrait créer des institutions, définir des pouvoirs et accorder des droits. Ce faisant, elle devrait refléter les valeurs essentielles du pays.

En matière linguistique, la Constitution canadienne remplit deux de ces trois rôles. Elle a commencé par accorder des droits, fort limités au demeurant[5]; elle devrait bientôt orienter l'exercice des compétences dans le sens indiqué par l'Accord du lac Meech; elle devra dans une troisième étape s'occuper de transcrire les principes dualistes dans les institutions.

Nous allons maintenant démontrer cette évolution en trois temps à la lumière des événements de la dernière décennie.

II- LES DROITS LINGUISTIQUES CONSTITUTIONNELS DURANT LA DERNIÈRE DÉCENNIE

a) Les institutions

L'analyse n'est pas bien longue ici: il n'y a aucune institution vraiment dualiste au Canada. Quant aux institutions propres des minorités linguistiques, elles sont créées par l'entremise de certains droits et non directement par un acte constitutionnel. Il y avait bien au début, des motions que le Sénat devrait assurer la représentation des droits des minorités linguistiques; mais le Sénat n'a pas rempli ce rôle, pas plus d'ailleurs que les autres rôles qu'on avait voulu lui donner.

---

5. La *Loi constitutionnelle de 1867 (R.-U.)*, 30 & 31 Vict., c. 3, art. 133; la *Loi sur le Manitoba de 1870*, art. 23; la *Charte canadienne des droits et libertés*, Partie I de la *Loi constitutionelle de 1982*, constituant l'annexe B de la *Loi de 1982 sur le Canada (R.-U.)*, 1982, c. 11, art. 16 à 20.

Si la dualité linguistique du pays est une valeur fondamentale, elle ne transparaît pas dans le tissu des institutions nationales. Les minorités contrôlent certaines institutions par le biais de politiques fédérales ou provinciales, par leur propre volonté d'organisation et par la conjoncture démographique qui parfois les avantage.

b) Pouvoirs

La Constitution n'attribue aux institutions du pays des pouvoirs linguistiques explicites que depuis 1982.

Puisque le partage des compétences ne fait pas mention de la langue comme telle, on a jugé que la compétence en matière linguistique est divisée entre le Parlement et chaque province, comme un accessoire aux compétences formelles[6]. La langue, le droit linguistique, ne semblent donc pas devoir être un objet législatif fédéral ou provincial en soi; ce sont les aspects linguistiques des compétences détenues par le Parlement et les législations, selon le cas. Ce partage des compétences satisfait sans doute les législateurs provinciaux mais il est la source d'une certaine confusion au sein de la population et des communautés minoritaires elles-mêmes. Comment expliquer à un simple citoyen, une simple citoyenne, que le Canada est un pays où il y a deux langues officielles[7], mais que le Québec est officiellement francophone[8] et l'Alberta officiellement anglophone[9], tandis que dans le Nouveau-Brunswick officiellement bilingue[10] les Acadiens se plaignent du manque de services[11] et qu'en Ontario, on fait des progrès importants en l'absence de toute garantie constitutionnelle[12]? Quelle image de la Constitution offre une telle situation? Voilà à mon avis une des conséquences néfastes de l'arrêt *Jones*, quoiqu'à d'autres égards il ait pu avantager le Québec.

L'arrêt *Jones* a donc établi dès 1975 qu'au-delà du minimum garanti par la Constitution, chaque pouvoir législatif était libre d'intervenir pour ajouter des droits et couvrir des secteurs non prévus par la Constitution. Cette position a été réaffirmée en 1986 dans l'arrêt *Société des Acadiens*[13], où on ajouta que depuis 1982, le mandat de faire progresser les langues officielles vers l'égalité de statut, de droits et de privilèges revenait aux

---

6. *Jones* c. *P.G. Nouveau-Brunswick*, [1975] 2 R.C.S. 182.
7. La *Charte*, art. 16(1).
8. La *Charte de la langue française du Québec*, L.R.Q. 1977, c. C-11, art. 2.
9. *Loi linguistique*, S.A. 1988, c. L-7.5.
10. *Loi sur les langues officielles du Nouveau-Brunswick*, L.R.N.B. 1973, c. 0-1, art. 2; la *Charte*, art. 16(2).
11. Poirier et Bastarache, *Rapport sur les langues officielles au N.B.*, Fredericton, Imprimeur de la Reine, 1983.
12. *Loi de 1986 sur les services en français*, S.O. 1986, c. 45.
13. *Société des Acadiens du Nouveau-Brunswick* c. *Association of Parents for Fairness in Education*, [1986] 1 R.C.S. 549.

pouvoirs législatifs et non au pouvoir judiciaire par l'inclusion à la Constitution du paragraphe 16(3). Si le paragraphe 16(3) est limité aux droits linguistiques proprement dits, l'Accord du lac Meech vient confirmer et élargir ce principe en statuant que le Parlement et les législatures ont le rôle de protéger la dualité canadienne[14]. Enfin, l'arrêt récent *Singer*[15] confirme directement la compétence provinciale sur la langue dans les domaines qui sont déjà de sa juridiction, sous réserve du respect des libertés fondamentales qui ont semble-t-il, une portée en matière linguistique. De plus, l'arrêt *Valérie Ford*[16] confirme que l'article premier de la Charte autorise un législateur à exiger l'emploi prédominant de la langue française et que c'est un objectif légitime de l'État qui est suffisant pour justifier une restriction aux droits et libertés classiques.

Il y avait donc des compétences constitutionnelles implicites; il y a depuis 1982 un mandat législatif de faire progresser les droits linguistiques vers l'égalité de statut et d'usage des deux langues officielles; et il y aura peut-être, après l'entente du lac Meech, un engagement de protéger la caractéristique fondamentale du Canada dans tout exercice d'un pouvoir constitutionnel. La compétence des législateurs demeure intacte, tant de par la Charte que de par l'Accord du lac Meech; cependant, son exercice est désormais orienté vers l'atteinte de certains objectifs, si telle est cependant la volonté des législateurs. Car ces mesures, pour en terminer avec elles, ne sont pas coercitives; elles indiquent la direction à prendre mais ne forcent pas les législateurs à s'y engager ni ne les condamnent s'ils s'en tiennent au minimum constitutionnel[17].

c) Les droits linguistiques

On distinguera ici trois types de droits: ceux de 1867; ceux de 1982; et les droits scolaires.

i) Les droits en 1867

On a mentionné que ces droits étaient réduits à leur plus simple expression: en fait, on disposait à l'époque du seul article 133 de la *Loi constitutionnelle*. L'objet de l'article 133 était, semble-t-il, de garantir un statu quo et maintenir l'équilibre fédéral/Québec. La Cour suprême a statué en 1975 dans l'affaire *Jones* que le Parlement pouvait rajouter à cette disposition. Elle a par ailleurs reconnu dans *Blaikie*[18] que l'article

---

14. Résolution de modification constitutionnelle de 1987, art. 2.
15. *Singer, Devine* c. *P.G. Québec*, [1988] 2 R.C.S. 790.
16. *Valerie Ford* c. *P.G. Québec*, [1988] 2 R.C.S. 712.
17. Pour une évaluation de l'Accord du lac Meech sur les minorités linguistiques, voir P. Foucher, *L'Accord du Lac meech et les francophones hors-Québec*, (1988) A.C.P.D. 1.
18. *Blaikie* c. *P.G. Québec*, [1979] 1 R.C.S. 1011.

133 faisait partie du compromis fédéral initial, de sorte qu'on ne pouvait pas le modifier unilatéralement. Remarquons encore que cette intervention judiciaire suivait, comme en 1975, une intervention législative et avait pour but de restreindre l'action d'un législateur au nom d'une norme constitutionnelle. L'affaire *MacDonald*[19] a précisé en 1986 que ces droits étaient de nature linguistique et non fondamentale au sens des droits classiques; il revenait donc aux locuteurs de les exercer. L'affaire du *Renvoi manitobain* a toutefois reconnu l'importance de ces droits comme on l'a mentionné.

ii) Les articles 16 à 20 de la Charte canadienne des droits et libertés

En 1982, on a inscrit dans la Charte les articles 16 à 20 et l'article 23. Nous traiterons ce dernier séparément, mais regardons l'objet des articles 16 à 20. Cet objet, nous a dit la Cour suprême dans *Société des Acadiens*, s'inspire directement de celui de 1867 : il s'agit de préciser, d'augmenter et d'étendre les droits et obligations initiales du compromis de 1867. Ce sont donc des compromis politiques qu'on doit interpréter restrictivement.

Ces compromis sont cependant suffisamment importants pour que la Cour se soit autorisée, un an plus tôt, à invalider 90 ans d'activité législative inconstitutionnelle par la province du Manitoba, dans une décision historique et novatrice. Pas plus qu'on ne peut modifier unilatéralement ce compromis, on ne peut le violer sans s'exposer à des sanctions.

Enfin, ce sont des compromis qui portent sur des droits fondamentaux, car la Cour a admis dans *Mercure*[20] que les droits linguistiques sont des droits fondamentaux de la personne au même titre que les autres droits classiques.

Il faut noter qu'aucune décision n'a vraiment interprété directement l'article 20 de la Charte, celui qui porte sur les services. Dans l'affaire *Gautreau*[21], les procureurs ont invoqué l'article 20 pour forcer un policier à émettre une contravention dans la langue de la personne arrêtée, mais la Cour a préféré considérer la sommation comme un acte qui émane de la Cour, donc assujetti plutôt à l'article 19.

iii) L'article 23 de la Charte

L'article 23 est celui qui a engendré le plus de jurisprudence, et la plus intéressante. La portée de ce droit varie selon la nature de l'analyste.

---

19. *MacDonald* c. *Montréal (Ville de)*, [1986] 1 R.C.S. 460.
20. *Mercure* c. *Saskatchewan*, [1988] 1 R.C.S. 234.
21. *La Reine* c. *Ricky Gautreau*, (29 janvier 1989) (C.p.).

Pour le gouvernement fédéral, c'est un article réparateur qui vient corriger le silence de 1867 sur la question, une conclusion d'ailleurs entérinée par la Cour suprême dans *Quebec Association*[22]. Pour les législateurs provinciaux, les commissions scolaires locales et les ministères de l'éducation, c'est un droit reconnu à des groupes minoritaires mais dans la mesure de ce qu'il est raisonnablement possible de faire, sous réserve des coûts, de la logistique des transports et des problèmes administratifs ; surtout, c'est un droit que les provinces doivent elles-mêmes mettre en oeuvre dans l'exercice de leurs pleines compétences constitutionnelles sous l'article 93. Pour les minorités enfin, c'est la planche de salut, le dernier espoir dans certaines régions, la garantie de quelque chose de simple et qui pourrait se réaliser simplement, sans trop de complications bureaucratiques et logistiques : des classes et des écoles françaises pour elles-mêmes, et qu'elles peuvent contrôler.

À date, la plupart des jugements des cours d'appel au pays ont reconnu le bien-fondé de la position des minorités[23]. On a statué que l'article 23 garantit aux minorités le droit à une instruction signifiante et de qualité dans leur langue, dans des écoles homogènes quand c'est possible, et avec un droit de regard sur la gestion de cette instruction. Mais on a accepté aussi que le rôle moteur de la mise en oeuvre de ces droits reste dévolu au législateur et au gouvernement provincial.

L'article 23 commence à produire des résultats. On assiste à l'ouverture de classes, à la construction de centres scolaires communautaires à l'aide d'ententes fédérales-provinciales-communautaires, à des jugements qui dépassent les déclarations de principe. Mais on est encore loin d'une mise en oeuvre complète et satisfaisante de l'ensemble de ces droits.

iv) Les droits fondamentaux classiques

Deux tendances jurisprudentielles ont appliqué les droits fondamentaux classiques en matière de langue : il s'agit des arrêts sur la liberté d'expression et sur les droits à l'égalité.

La liberté d'expression comprend le choix de la langue de l'expression. Cette liberté s'exerce dans les sphères privées, on ne pourrait pas vraiment l'invoquer en Cour (liberté d'expression des avocats) ou

---

22. *Quebec Association of Protestant School Boards* c. *P.G. Québec*, [1984] 2 R.C.S. 66.

23. Ce sont : *Re Education Act (Ontario) and Minority Language Education Rights*, (1984) 10 D.L.R. (4th) 461 (le « renvoi ontarien ») ; *Mahé* c. *Alberta*, (1987) 42 D.L.R. (4th) 514 ; *Re : Reference Respecting the Education Act P.-E.-I.*, and *Minority Language Educational Rights*, (1988) 69 N. & P.-E.-I.R. 236 ; *Lavoie* c. *Nova Scotia*, (1989) 91 N.S.R. (2d) 184.

au Parlement (liberté d'expression des députés). Elle a été invoquée par les Anglo-québécois plutôt que par les francophones hors-Québec pour une raison bien simple : il n'y a pas beaucoup de lois qui interdisent l'emploi de la langue française dans les activités privées. Pourtant, on ne voit pas plus de français sur les affiches commerciales... C'est la pression sociale qui rend cette liberté linguistique bien abstraite pour les minorités francophones.

Les droits à l'égalité n'ont pas encore été invoqués devant les tribunaux (sauf en matière scolaire, sans succès), pour fonder des plaintes de discrimination basée sur la langue. Toutefois, un débat a divisé les cours d'appel au pays sur le fait que le droit d'un accusé d'avoir son procès dans la langue de son choix n'était pas en vigueur dans toutes les provinces[24]. Ce débat est devenu académique depuis l'adoption de la nouvelle loi fédérale sur les langues officielles[25].

Encore une fois, ces droits classiques sont de peu d'utilité pour les minorités francophones dont les besoins sont bien différents.

Évaluons maintenant ce que ces divers textes et les jugements qui les ont analysés nous apprennent sur la Constitution canadienne.

III- IMPACT DE CES MESURES SUR LA CONSTITUTION CANADIENNE

Si on fait le bilan de cette décennie, on arrive à un constat évident : les Anglo-québécois ont réussi à faire tomber ce qu'ils estimaient être les principaux « irritants » de la *Loi 101* tandis que les francophones hors-Québec ont fait des gains modestes (Manitoba, Mercure, dossier scolaire) mais qui n'ont pas suffi à enrayer l'assimilation.

La politique canadienne en matière linguistique est personnaliste, ce que je ne considère pas mauvais du tout compte tenu de la réalité démographique et historique du pays ; la politique québécoise est plus territoriale. Or les Anglo-québécois, en raison de leur histoire, de leur position dans l'ensemble nord-américain, et de la composition même de leur communauté, revendiquent plutôt des droits individuels et adoptent une démarche *en réaction contre* des lois qu'ils estiment brimantes pour leurs droits fondamentaux classiques ou leurs droits

---

24. En faveur de reconnaître que cette mise en oeuvre différenciée viole l'article 15 de la *Charte : Reference re French Language Rights of an Accused Person in Saskatchewan Criminal Proceedings*, [1987] 5 W.W.R. 577 ; contre cette conclusion : *R.* c. *Paquette (no 2)*, (1987) 38 C.C.C. (3d) 353, *Ringuette* c. *Canada & Newfoundland*, (1987) 63 N. & P.-E.-I.R. 126, et indirectement *McDonnell* c. *Fédération des Franco-Colombiens*, (1986) 6 B.C.L.R. (2d) 390.
25. *Loi sur les langues officielles du Canada*, S.C. 1985, c. 38.

linguistiques spéciaux. Les minorités francophones ne disposent pas du même poids politique ni de la même histoire; leur communauté est différente et leurs objectifs très éloignés de ceux des Anglo-québecois. Ce qu'ils ont à combattre, c'est la pression de leur milieu et les vexations systémiques dont ils font les frais malgré leurs droits constitutionnels. Il leur faut non seulement des *freins* aux actions abusives des législateurs, mais surtout des *leviers* qui vont forcer ceux-ci à agir. Voilà ce que ne reconnaît pas encore la Constitution canadienne, sauf en matière scolaire.

Cette situation vient du fait qu'à la fondation du pays, les protections constitutionnelles se sont avérées beaucoup trop limitées et partielles. L'oubli des droits scolaires, répétons-le, s'avéra fatal. Le fédéralisme lui-même eut un effet négatif: il avantagea le Québec mais diminua le rôle constitutionnel du Parlement et du gouvernement du Canada[26] (qui se servit malgré tout des pouvoirs à sa disposition, depuis 1968 surtout, pour maintenir la dualité linguistique) et renvoya les minorités linguistiques devant leur gouvernement provincial. Ces derniers ne s'empressèrent pas d'agir pour corriger une situation difficile et prétendent aujourd'hui qu'il est trop tard, que les nombres sont insuffisants et que les fondements constitutionnels du Canada ont changé. Le fédéralisme a donc rendu difficile un consensus national sur la question linguistique, qui aurait permis d'inclure à la Constitution des garanties plus adéquates.

Ainsi, le silence constitutionnel relatif de 1867 est en grande partie la cause des problèmes actuels. On ne peut pas réécrire l'histoire, mais on peut préparer des réponses modernes à des problèmes présents... Or qu'a-t-on fait en 1982, en enchâssant les articles 16 à 20? On a repris le dispositif de 1867 dans les articles 17 à 19 — et nous venons d'expliquer pourquoi cela nous apparaît insuffisant maintenant; on a ajouté la déclaration des langues officielles — mais les tribunaux nous ont appris que la progression vers l'égalité linguistique appartenait au législateur et que telle était l'intention des Constituants de 1982; on a ajouté un droit aux services publics mais en truffant ce droit de multiples conditions. La mise en oeuvre de ce droit s'avère aussi difficile. On est donc en présence de droits parfois inadaptés, parfois inefficaces. Je soumets que c'est une situation néfaste pour le constitutionnalisme canadien. La valeur normative de la Constitution s'en trouve dépréciée; quant à sa valeur symbolique, elle perd beaucoup de crédibilité.

---

26. Cela fut particulièrement évident et pénible lors de la crise scolaire au Manitoba en 1895, alors que les Québécois portèrent Laurier au pouvoir parce que celui-ci s'opposait à l'intervention législative fédérale dans le domaine scolaire; ou en 1988 quand le Premier Ministre du Québec refusa de condamner ses homologues de Saskatchewan et d'Alberta lorsque ceux-ci abrogèrent les droits historiques de leur minorité francophone. Ottawa protesta et se mit en devoir de compenser cette perte par des ententes; succès en Saskatchewan mais échec et refus global en Alberta.

Le dossier scolaire est révélateur à cet effet. Si on progresse bien dans certaines provinces, surtout en Atlantique, dans les provinces de l'Ouest l'avance est beaucoup plus lente. Or l'article 23 est censé offrir un remède national à des problèmes qui se posent à l'échelle du pays, mais qui relèvent des provinces. Le fédéralisme joue donc encore au détriment des minorités les plus démunies provincialement. Or qu'arrivera-t-il si, dans quelques années, les droits de l'article 23 ne sont pas pleinement mis en oeuvre? Les minorités se souviendront des promesses que recelait l'article 23, promesses non tenues. Cette fois, il ne s'agira pas de promesses politiques comme à la fin du siècle dernier: il s'agira de promesses *constitutionnelles*. Je pense qu'on ne rend pas service à la Constitution en traitant à la légère des droits pourtant clairs dans leur texte et en cherchant à les restreindre par tous les moyens disponibles. Le Canada entier aura sous les yeux un texte constitutionnel qui n'aura pas rempli son rôle premier de réparation. On peut prévoir que le cynisme et l'irrespect remplaceront la fierté et la force morale que doit avoir un texte constitutionnel.

Est-ce à dire que les droits constitutionnels que nous avons maintenant ne sont pas appuyés par la majorité de la population, dont la sagesse populaire s'exprime par la voix des représentants politiques? Est-ce à dire que nous devrions chercher des solutions en dehors du cadre constitutionnel, comme nous le faisons depuis plus de cent ans?

Ce n'est pas mon avis. Je pense que la Constitution a un rôle utile à jouer parce qu'elle est plus qu'une norme comme les autres: elle est l'expression du contrat social du Canada. À entendre tous nos politiciens récemment, la dualité canadienne est une richesse qu'il convient de préserver. La Constitution devrait donc être le réceptacle naturel de cette valeur, à la condition de procéder correctement et de respecter le rôle propre d'un tel outil.

L'Accord du lac Meech est une première tentative en ce sens. Il tente de réconcilier la dualité linguistique (personnaliste, individuelle (article 2(1)a)), fédéraliste (article 2(2)) et le caractère distinct du Québec. Il tente aussi de déborder le cadre strict des droits linguistiques pour imprégner l'exercice des compétences (2(3)). C'est une première tentative qui maintient le cap suivi jusqu'ici et qui risque fort de ne pas produire les résultats escomptés si elle n'est pas suivie de mesures précises et concrètes.

Quel devrait donc être l'agenda de la prochaine décennie? À mon avis, on devrait se pencher sur quelques grands thèmes.

D'abord, il faut absolument chercher à réconcilier les intérêts constitutionnels du Québec et des francophones hors-Québec. C'est réalisable. Les Québécois ont besoin de pouvoirs spéciaux : l'Accord tente d'y remédier. Les minorités ont besoin non seulement de droits, mais aussi qu'on tienne compte de leurs besoins dans l'élaboration de tout programme et de toute politique quelle qu'elle soit.

En deuxième lieu, il faut travailler à améliorer les droits linguistiques précis et à mieux encadrer le rôle des tribunaux. Cela se fera par une réflexion sur les articles 16 à 20 et une meilleure reformulation. Il ne faut pas confondre droits linguistiques et dualité linguistique, quant aux droits fondamentaux, de nature collective même si l'application en est individuelle, et créer des recours efficaces pour les citoyens.

En troisième lieu, les principes constitutionnels doivent se transcrire par des lois. C'est le principe de la pyramide : au sommet se trouve la Constitution, mais elle est précisée et appliquée au moyen de lois et de mécanismes administratifs efficaces (un tribunal administratif pourrait remplir une fonction utile).

Quatrièmement, on devra en toute priorité donner une impulsion au dossier scolaire. L'échec de la mise en oeuvre de l'article 23 serait grave non seulement pour les minorités, mais aussi pour le constitutionnalisme canadien. Après huit ans d'opération, on en connaît bien le contenu et les principes ; il reste à créer les mécanismes d'application.

Enfin, je pense qu'on devra de plus en plus appliquer la dualité linguistique à tous les programmes et toutes les activités.

Les droits constitutionnels actuels sont un minimum inadapté aux besoins. Ils auront quand même servi à susciter les discussions les plus vives et les plus dignes sur l'avenir même du pays (pensons à toutes les suggestions faites depuis 1968 dans le domaine ; chacune de ces suggestions est le fruit de multiples discussions au cours desquelles émerge chez les personnes qui les expriment la conscience de la valeur de la dualité canadienne). Sans l'article 16 de la Charte (quelle que soit son utilité judiciaire) on n'aurait pas pu lire un paragraphe comme l'alinéa 2(1)(a) de l'Accord du lac Meech. La dualité canadienne n'est pas qu'une affaire entre le Québec et le reste du Canada, contrairement à ce que la Constitution de 1867 aurait pu laisser croire ; elle a toujours été et demeure une affaire qui intéresse le pays en entier. Le débat engendré par les incidents au Québec et dans les deux provinces des Prairies a ramené un problème que l'Accord du lac Meech cherchait à provincialiser à ses dimensions nationales. En ce sens, au-delà de l'efficacité judiciaire de la Constitution, son efficacité symbolique et philosophique est en voie d'être atteinte. J'espère avoir pu exprimer des pistes de réflexion qui permettront au Canada de sortir de la pente glissante de la dévaluation des droits constitutionnels fondamentaux au nom d'intérêts politiques à court terme. Si on continue encore pendant une décennie à faire croire aux minorités linguistiques et à tout le Canada que l'on a des droits linguistiques constitutionnels quand on s'aperçoit qu'ils sont inapplicables, on rendra un bien mauvais service à la Constitution canadienne. Mais si on adopte une politique constitutionnelle adaptée et multiple, dans laquelle la dualité imprégnera les institutions, les compétences et les droits spéciaux, de concert avec les autres valeurs fondamentales qui forment la société canadienne d'aujourd'hui, alors la Constitution sera un document vivant et réel, d'une valeur inestimable pour la nation.

L'AFFAIRE PIQUETTE

Timothy J. Christian

MR. PIQUETTE: Thank you, Mr. Speaker. To the Minister of Education, le ministre de l'Éducation. Mr. Speaker, these questions are pertaining to section 23 of the Constitution Act signed by this province on April 19, 1982. Les Franco-Albertains attendent impatiemment depuis 1982.

MR. SPEAKER: Order please, hon. member. The Chair rises with great hesitation, but the hon. member and the Chair had a discussion last June with respect to the use of the French language in the Assembly. Permission was indeed granted for that to take place within debates, but at that time there was mutual consent that would not occur during question period. En anglais, s'il vous plaît.

MR. PIQUETTE: Mr. Speaker, when I rose in the House last year, I claimed the right to be able to speak in French in this House, and I don't think that right has been abolished by your statement. Les Franco-Albertains attendent impatiemment depuis...

MR. SPEAKER: Order please, hon. member. The Chair directs that the questions will be in English or the member will forfeit the position. Order please.

MR. PIQUETTE: Okay, if you do wish the translation. But I want to rise on a point of order relating to this, because I think my rights are not being abided by, by this Legislature. To the Minister of Education: Francophone Albertans have been waiting since 1982,....[1]

This brief exchange on the floor of the Alberta Legislature touched off a heated debate in the context of the ongoing dispute over the status of the French language in Alberta. A few minutes later Mr. Piquette rose on a question of privilege and challenged the ruling of the Speaker. He argued that by ordering him to put his question in English the Speaker had breached the privilege of all members of the Assembly and had exceeded his authority. Mr. Piquette submitted that the

> basic right of all Albertans to conduct their business through and with the provincial government in either of Canada's two official languages

---

1. *Alberta Hansard* (7 April 1987) 631.

predates the constitutional statutes which created Alberta and was never
effectively extinguished by those statutes.[2]

The Speaker ordered that he be provided with written elaboration
of the challenge and Mr. Piquette set out his concerns in a letter to
the Speaker the next day. This letter was accidently[3] released to the
press, an action which the Speaker later characterized as a breach of
the privileges of all members of the Assembly.[4]

Reaction to the Speaker's refusal to permit Mr. Piquette to ask
his question in French was swift and negative, both locally and nationally.[5]

Local Reaction

A columnist wrote in the *Edmonton Sun* that:

To many people from outside this province, "Redneck Alberta" is still
considered to be an accurate descriptive term. And David Carter, the
Speaker of the Alberta Legislature yesterday ensured that description will
take longer to go out of vogue.[6]

The *Edmonton Journal* took an even stronger line, responding with
an editorial later alleged by the Speaker to be a breach of privilege.
The editorial board was critical of the Speaker's "...terrible error in
judgement...

Carter's knee-jerk, red-necked reaction to Piquette's reasonable request
has drawn national attention.

His decision embarrasses Alberta on the eve of a first minister's conference
aimed at bringing Québec into the Constitution. It lays bare Alberta's
flagrant disregard and lack of respect for language rights that are enshrined
in the Charter".[7]

National Reaction

In its concurring editorial a few days later, the *Globe and Mail*
concluded that the Speaker had "...acted unreasonably in cutting short
Mr. Piquette's question."[8]

Premier Bourassa observed that it was "ironic" that Premier Getty
wanted to deny Québec special constitutional status while his Speaker

2. *Alberta Hansard* (7 April 1987) 636-637.
3. *Alberta Hansard* (15 April 1987) 818. Mr. Piquette claimed that he had already apologized
   in private to the Speaker for the fact that the letter had been accidentally released.
4. The Speaker ruled that Mr. Piquette had published a document of the Assembly without
   first obtaining the permission of the Speaker. This was compounded by the fact that
   the letter, in raising objections to the Speaker's ruling, contained unfavourable reflections
   upon the Speaker. The assertion that the Chair was in error was said to walk "a perilous
   path of being in contempt of the House." *Alberta Hansard* (9 April 1987) 698.
5. The proceedings were witnessed by Ontario's Premier David Peterson who was present
   in the visitor's gallery. On account of his presence a larger than normal contingent
   from the national press was in attendance and this may in part explain the attention
   which Mr. Piquette received.
6. Don Wanagas, *Edmonton Sun* (8 April 1987).
7. *Edmonton Journal* (9 April 1987).
8. *Globe and Mail* (15 April 1987).

denied French-Canadians the right to speak in French.[9] An editorial in *Le Soleil* commented that the Piquette incident had given "...a weapon to supporters of Québec independence."[10] Québec Communications Minister Richard French contended:

> As an anglophone, it seems inconceivable that a duly elected member of an assembly doesn't have the right to use his own language. It goes against everything this country is supposed to be about.[11]

Even the Prime Minister responded and was reported to have "voiced dismay to national caucus" over the Speaker's ruling. He was quoted by a member of caucus as having said:

> Can you imagine how a unilingual French-Canadian from a small town in Québec must feel watching on French TV the denial of the right to speak French in the Alberta Legislative Assembly.[12]

Meanwhile, two events in Edmonton symbolized the depth of feeling aroused by Mr. Piquette's action. On the one hand, a sign urging Piquette to "move to Québec" if he wanted to speak French was hung on his Legislature office door. On the other hand, a hundred French-speaking school children and community leaders gave Mr. Piquette a "wildly enthusiastic welcome" following the Speaker's ruling.[13]

The Speaker Rules on Piquette's Challenge

On April 9th, the Speaker ruled on the questions of privilege. He began by suggesting that Mr. Piquette and the caucus of the New Democratic Party were walking "a perilous path of being in contempt of the House" for having released to the press the letter to the Speaker which raised the question of privilege and suggested the Speaker was in error.[14] The Speaker also observed that the *Edmonton Journal* "has come dangerously close if not exceeding the privileges of this Assembly by publishing a personal attack on the Speaker" in the editorial quoted from above.[15] He said he would refer both matters back to the House for its further consideration.[16]

The Speaker then went on to deliver a lengthy ruling on the question of the privilege to speak French in the Assembly. He summarized his judgement as follows:

---

9. *Canadian Press* (19 April 1987).
10. *Le Soleil* (19 April 1987).
11. *Montreal Gazette* (20 April 1987) A-4.
12. *Edmonton Journal* (11 April 1987).
13. *Globe and Mail* (10 April 1987).
14. *Alberta Hansard* (9 April 1987) 698.
15. *Alberta Hansard* (9 April 1987) 698.
16. Not surprisingly, the editor of the *Edmonton Journal* responded to the Speaker's remarks in strong terms, asserting that "if this is an attempt to muzzle us we will fight it with every means at our disposal." *Edmonton Journal* (10 April 1987).

1. the matter of the usage of the French language in the House is not a matter of law but one of privilege to be dealt with by the House itself,

2. even if it were a matter of law, the Chair is bound to believe that the use of French would not be an obligation of the House anyway,

3. that as a point of order, the Office of Speaker obliges the Chair to rule the use of the French language in the Chamber as out of order, based on the rules and practices which bind the Chair from making any decision to the contrary until such time as the House gives authority to the Chair to permit the use of French in the Chamber.[17]

Finally, the Speaker referred back to the House the question of whether Mr. Piquette's privileges had been abrogated. The Premier advised that the Assembly would await an apology from Mr. Piquette.

The next day, April 10, 1987, Mr. Piquette obtained the unanimous consent of the House to deliver a brief statement. He rose and attempted to read a prepared account essentially restating his position and apologizing for any misunderstanding. He was interrupted by the Speaker who warned that he was in danger of committing a further breach of privilege. The Premier, rising on a point of order, commented that Mr. Piquette had not been apologizing but "weaseling around."[18] This suggestion raised the temperature of the debate and led to further headlines.

The Issues Are Referred to the Standing Committee on Elections and Privileges

Five days later, on April 15, 1987, the Government introduced a motion referring the whole matter to the Standing Committee on Privileges and Elections, Standing Orders and Printing. The Committee's terms of reference as set out and passed in the Motion of the Assembly, over Opposition objections, were as follows:

(1) whether or not a question of privilege arises when the proceedings of the Assembly are conducted solely in English;

(2) whether or not the hon. Member for Athabasca-Lac La Biche has breached the privileges of the Assembly in remarks while speaking to the question of privilege at pages 636 and 637 in *Alberta Hansard* on April 7, 1987, or in remarks in the Assembly on April 10, 1987, or in respect of any other matter in connection therewith;

(3) should a breach of privilege be determined by the Committee to have occurred, to make such recommendations to the Assembly as necessary to provide for reparation or to supply a remedy; and

(4) any other question that the Committee deems is related to the matters of privilege arising under Question 1 and 2 of this motion and the

17. *Supra*, note 14.
18. *Alberta Hansard* (10 April 1987) 720.

Speaker's statement to the House as contained in pages 697-701 of
Alberta Hansard on April 9, 1987.[19]

The Committee, composed of fourteen government and six
opposition members, began considering the issues referred to it on May
6, 1987. The Committee decided to call a series of expert witnesses.
A brief summary of the evidence presented will place in context the
constitutional aspects of "L'affaire Piquette" as the incident came to
be described.

The main issue was whether the right to speak French in the legislative
assembly, as guaranteed by s. 110 of the *Northwest Territories Act*, had
been effectively repealed by a motion passed in the Territorial Assembly
on January 19, 1892 or whether it had been carried forward by sections
14 or 16 of the *Alberta Act*.

Section 110[20] contained the following components. First, English
or French could be used (i.e. "may") in the debates of the Legislative
Assembly, and in proceedings before the courts. Second, both languages
were required to be used (i.e. "shall") in the records and journals of
the Legislative Assembly, and in all ordinances.

These requirements could be altered or removed after the next general
election of the Assembly by ordinance or otherwise, provided that the
regulations were embodied in a proclamation and published by the
Lieutenant Governor in accordance with the law.

On January 19, 1892 the Assembly of the Territories limited the
use of French by passing what has become known as the Haultain motion
which provided :

> That it is desirable that the proceedings of the Legislative Assembly shall
> be recorded and published hereafter in the English language only.

In his ruling of April 9, 1987 the Speaker of the Alberta Legislative
Assembly determined that by this motion the Assembly of the Northwest
Territories had, "in accordance with its own mandate ..., changed the

---

19. *Alberta Hansard* (15 April 1987) 807.
20. Section 110 of the *North-West Territories Act*, as amended in 1891 (*An Act to Amend
   the Acts Respecting the North-West Territories*, 54-55 Victoria, c. 22, s. 18) provided
   as follows :
   "110. Either the English or the French language may be used by any person in the
   debates of the Legislative Assembly of the Territories and in the proceedings before
   the courts; and both these languages shall be used in the records and journals of
   such Assembly; and all ordinances made under this Act shall be printed in both those
   languages: Provided, however that after the next general election of the Legislative
   Assembly, such Assembly may, by ordinance or otherwise, regulate its proceedings,
   and the manner of recording and publishing the same; and the regulations so made
   shall be embodied in a proclamation which shall be forthwith made and published
   by the Lieutenant Governor in conformity with the law and thereafter shall have full
   force and effect."

effect and application of s. 110 in clear, unequivocal terms"[21] and had repealed the right to speak French in the Assembly. This conclusion was contested before the Committee on Privileges and Elections. It was argued that the Haultain motion could not have extinguished the right to speak French in the Assembly for two reasons. First, it did not purport to regulate the language of debate, but only the language of recording and publishing proceedings. Therefore, even if the Haultain motion were effective to limit the application of s. 110 to the records and journals of the Assembly, it would not affect the right to use the French language in debates in the Assembly. To extinguish the right to speak French in the Assembly, clear words would have to be used.

Second, it was contended that the Haultain motion had never been proclaimed as expressly required by s. 110. Therefore, it was argued that the language guarantees in s. 110 had been carried forward by the *Alberta Act*.[22] Section 16 of that Act was designed to continue in force those laws which were in force in the Northwest Territories immediately before the creation of Alberta. While the Legislative Assembly of the new province had full authority to repeal any such laws, until this was done, they continued with full vigour.[23]

Witnesses Before the Committee

A Canadian historian, Dr. Kenneth Munro, reviewed the evidence upon which he based his conclusion that the Haultain motion had never been proclaimed. In essence, he testified that, despite extensive archival research, no proclamation of the Haultain motion signed by the Lieutenant Governor had ever been found.[24]

This conclusion led to an inquiry into the formal requirements for proclamation. Dr. L.C. Green expressed the view that there were no formal criteria and that the requirement for proclamation had been met by merely making the motion publicly known. Alternatively, he claimed that the Speaker's Petition at the beginning of a session of the Assembly, by which the Speaker claimed the traditional privileges of the Assembly, had been effective to carry forward the Assembly's rules as to the language

21. *Alberta Hansard* (9 April 1987) 100.
22. S.C. 1905, c. 3
23. Section 16 of the *Alberta Act* provides: All laws... existing immediately before the coming into force of this Act in the territory hereby established as the Province of Alberta, shall continue... as if... the *Alberta Act* had not been passed;... subject... to be[ing] repealed, abolished or altered... by the Legislature of the said [Alberta] Legislature...
24. Dr. Munro quoted from his article, "Official Bilingualism in Alberta", (1987) 12 *Prairie Forum* 37 at 42 in which he traced the history of the Haultain motion relying upon the study by Claude-Armand Sheppard, in *The Law of Languages in Canada* (Ottawa: Information Canada, 1971) at 85, *Les héritiers de Lord Durham*, vol. 1 (Ottawa: Fédération des francophones hors Québec, 1977) at 53 and *Report of the Royal Commission on Bilingualism and Biculturalism*, Book I (Ottawa: Queen's Printer, 1967) at 51 and 52.

of debate as set out in the Haultain motion.[25] This argument proceeded on the assumption that the language of debate in the Assembly was a matter of privilege rather than law. However, Dr. Green went so far as to state that even if the statutory right to speak French had not been expressly repealed it had fallen into disuse, or had been effectively changed by contrary practice.[26] Dr. Eugene Forsey took strong exception to this last point, arguing that a statutory right could not lapse "even by centuries of long disuse".[27] He argued that, assuming a statutory right existed, it could only be taken away by statute and could not be repealed by a mere standing order of a Legislature or a ruling by the Speaker. In his view the *Northwest Territories Act* specifically required proclamation and could not be satisfied by a Speaker's Petition — a mere statement of the Lieutenant Governor acceding to the Speaker's claim for the privileges of the Assembly. Accordingly, Dr. Forsey was of the view that:

> ...Mr. Piquette had the statutory right to put his question in French and... when the Speaker prevented him from doing so, there was a breach of Mr. Piquette's privilege.[28]

Dr. W.F. Dawson, the editor of *Beauchesne's Rules and Forms of the House of Commons of Canada*,[29] was called and expressed the opinion that Mr. Piquette had breached no privilege when he attempted to speak French in the Assembly.[30] Further, he expressed the view that the release of Mr. Piquette's letter to the press could not be considered a breach of privilege — it might be rude, but if fell short of breach of privilege.[31]

The Committee's Recommendations

After hearing many hours of evidence and lengthy and interesting debate, the Committee framed its findings as motions to be brought

---

25. *Alberta Hansard* (25 May 1987) 49.
26. *Alberta Hansard* (10 June 1987) 94-96.
27. *Alberta Hansard* (10 June 1987) 97. Dr. Forsey's view was preferred by the Supreme Court of Canada in its subsequent decision in *R. v. Mercure*, [1988] 2 W.W.R. 577 where La Forest J., writing for the majority, said at page 624: "It is true, as the respondent maintained, that French in fact ceased to be used in the debates, statutes and proceedings in the courts in 1892 (see Sheppard, p. 83), some years before the establishment of the province [Saskatchewan], but statutes do not, of course, cease to be law from mere disuse. As Driedger puts it, "A statute is not effaced by lapse of time, even if it is obsolete or has ceased to have practical application": see E.A. Driedger, *The Composition of Legislation*, 2nd ed. rev. (1976), at p. 110. At any event it does not strike me as a particularly attractive argument to put before a court of justice that a majority can destroy the rights of a minority by simply acting in violation of those rights."
28. *Alberta Hansard* (10 June 1987) 98.
29. (Toronto: Carswell, 1989).
30. *Alberta Hansard* (3 June 1987) 79.
31. *Alberta Hansard* (3 June 1987) 79.

back before the Assembly.[32] The Committee essentially side-stepped the question of whether there was a legal or constitutional right to speak French in the Assembly, holding that such a decision could not be "determined by the Committee exclusively." In speaking in support of his motion the Attorney General argued before the Committee that it was in no position to resolve the conflicting evidence it had heard about the legal status of French in the Assembly.[33] The New Democrat justice critic, Mr. Gordon Wright, agreed with the Attorney General and suggested that the Lieutenant Governor in Council ought to send the question to the courts by way of a Reference.

This suggestion was not acted upon.

The Attorney General also moved that there had been no breach of Mr. Piquette's privileges because the proceedings of the Assembly were conducted solely in English. He argued that a breach of privilege arose when a Member was unable to carry out his duties and that since Mr. Piquette was fluently bilingual and could have carried out his duties in English his privileges had not been breached.[34] This motion, of course, begged the question of what would have happened had Mr. Piquette been unilingual.

The Committee then moved on to deal with the future use of French in the Assembly.[35] The motion put French on the same plane as any

---

32. Alberta, Legislative Assembly, Standing Committee on Privileges and Elections, Standing Orders and Printing, "Report in Response to Government Motion No. 9 in Relation to Matters Dealing with Order and Privileges of the Assembly" No. 343/87 in *Sessional Papers* (25 November 1987) at 5:
   1. BE IT RESOLVED THAT BECAUSE:
   (a) the constitutional rights of members to speak French in the Assembly cannot be determined by the Committee conclusively; and
   (b) the essence of the privilege is whether or not a Member has been deprived of any right, without which he is unable to carry out his functions as a Member;
   the Committee finds no breach of privilege arising by virtue of the proceedings of the Assembly being conducted solely in English.
33. It was pointed out that some of the issues were currently before the Supreme Court of Canada in the appeal taken from the Saskatchewan Court of Appeal in *R.* v. *Mercure* which is discussed at greater length below. *Alberta Hansard* (25 June 1987) 213.
34. *Alberta Hansard* (23 June 1987) 187.
35. *Supra*, note 32:
   2. BE IT RESOLVED that the Committee recommend to the Assembly that the Standing Orders of the Assembly be amended to provide that, while the working language of the Assembly and its publications remain English, languages other than English may be used on the following basis:
   (a) subject to the approval of the Speaker, languages other than English may be used in the Assembly and its Committees at any time other than proceedings where an immediate response is expected or requested from another Member; provided written advance notice of two hours together with an English translation is delivered to Mr. Speaker, the Clerk and to any other Member as the Speaker may direct;
   (b) Subject to the approval of the Speaker, languages other than English may be used in Question Period to ask a main question provided written advance notice of two hours together with the English translation is delivered to Mr. Speaker, the

language other than English and required that, before French could be spoken in the Assembly, a translation into English and written advance notice of two hours be given to the Speaker. During Question Period any supplementary questions were to be asked in English. While the Opposition members expressed reluctance to support this motion, it was ultimately passed with their approval. The sentiments of Opposition members were stated best by the New Democrat justice critic, Gordon Wright, who said:

> ...I will be voting in favour of this...resolution because it is a marked advance over what we have at present, which is nothing. Yet I will be doing so with a degree of sadness, because we have missed an opportunity of being progressive and fair and in line with the rest of Canada and also to strike some blow at those who have it that we have an extraordinary number of rednecks in the province of Alberta. We've missed that opportunity, and so I will vote in favour of this resolution with a fair amount of tristesse,...[36]

The debate in Committee was a good deal more heated concerning the next part of the motion which proposed that Mr. Piquette be found to have breached the privileges of all members and be required to apologize for having failed to accept the ruling of the Speaker.[37] Opposition members strongly opposed this motion to no avail as it was passed by the majority. Once again the Prime Minister intervened, stating:

> It is unacceptable that any Canadian anywhere, including in the Alberta Legislature, should be forced to apologize for speaking English or French.[38]

The *Globe and Mail* also weighed in, comparing the noble concepts in the Meech Lake Accord with the requirement that Mr. Piquette apologize for speaking in his native tongue. An editorial asked rhetorically:

> And was it not quite absurd that the Committee should, in its collective wisdom, conclude that [Mr. Piquette] owed the Speaker an apology?[39]

Finally, late on the afternoon of June 25, 1987, the Government brought forward its last motion before the committee, this, to admonish

---

Clerk and to any other Member as the Speaker may direct. Supplementary questions must be asked in the English language.

36. *Alberta Hansard* (24 June 1987) 205.
37. *Supra*, note 32:
    3. BE IT RESOLVED that because the Honourable Member for Athabasca-Lac La Biche has breached the privileges of all Members of the Assembly:
    (a) By his failure to uphold the absolute authority of the Speaker to rule on points of Order and to accept such rulings without debate or appeal;
    (b) By casting certain reflections upon the Speaker and his actions, and thereby attempting to undermine the position of Mr. Speaker;
    the Committee recommends that the Honourable Member unconditionally apologize to the Assembly in respect of such breaches of privilege at the first reasonable opportunity.
38. *Globe and Mail* (1 July 1987).
39. *Globe and Mail* (3 July 1987).

the *Edmonton Journal* for its editorial of April 9th.[40] This motion, which was distributed just before being read, took Opposition members of the Committee by surprise. It was passed by the majority despite the strong protests of the Opposition members that it was unfair to condemn the *Edmonton Journal* without notice and without first giving the paper an opportunity to appear before the Committee.[41] The feelings of Opposition members were forcefully expressed by the Liberal member, Betty Hewes, who said:

> Well, I think this whole thing is patently unfair. It's unfair to the Journal....
> It's unfair to members of this Committee the way it has been dropped
> on our heads, and frankly I want no part of it whatsoever. It is to me
> just so much muscle-flexing nonsense..., and I think the Committee should
> not be guilty of that.[42]

She went on to point out that it was difficult to single out the *Edmonton Journal* when there had been so much strong editorial reaction to the Speaker's ruling across the country.[43] Despite these and other strong submissions, the majority passed the motion.

The Committee's Recommendations Before the Assembly

Five months later, on November 27, 1987, the Government House Leader moved a motion incorporating the main recommendations of the Committee before the Assembly. Significantly, the recommendation to "admonish" the *Edmonton Journal* was not presented and, indeed, has never been seen since. Neither did the motion mention the requirement that Mr. Piquette apologize. In his remarks that day, Mr. Piquette stated his position as follows:

> Mr. Speaker, I want to emphasize that it was never my intention on April
> 7 to challenge your authority to make judgement on the proceedings therein.
> My concern was to clearly establish my constitutional right to speak in
> either official language in this Assembly.[44]

In later press reports Mr. Piquette said that this comment was as far as he would go in making an apology to the Speaker.[45] To the relief

---

40. *Supra*, note 32:
    4. BE IT RESOLVED that the editorial in the Edmonton Journal of April 9, 1987 entitled "Bilingual Rights" contains reflections upon the Speaker, and hence upon the Assembly, which constitutes a gross breach of the privileges of the Assembly and the Committee recommends that the Assembly admonish the *Edmonton Journal* in respect to same.
41. *Alberta Hansard* (25 June 1987) 224.
42. *Alberta Hansard* (25 June 1987) 226.
43. An example of a more direct attack on the Speaker was printed in a scathing article in the *Globe and Mail* on 22 June 1987 where, among other things, it was said:
    Telling people what to do and looking important have been the hallmarks of his year-long tenure as Speaker.
44. *Alberta Hansard* (27 November 1987) 2095.
45. "What you saw today — this is all you are going to get," Mr. Piquette told reporters. *Edmonton Journal* (28 November 1987) A5.

of many, this statement, though not materially different from that which he immediately attempted to make on April 10, 1987, was accepted by the Government as an adequate apology.[46]

The Opposition attack on the motion focused on the requirement that a member obtain the approval of the Speaker before using French. It was argued that notification rather than approval would be adequate to deal with concerns about translation and that the proposed procedure made the use of French a privilege rather than a right. One member commented that it was ironic that such a procedure should appear on the same order paper as the Meech Lake Accord, which recognized that "French-speaking Canadians... concentrated outside Québec,... constitute a fundamental characteristic of Canada." Indeed, *Hansard* in both the day before and the day after the debate on the Piquette matter contains the text of the Meech Lake Accord in both English and French.

Finally, the Government motion was put and carried over the objections of a united and unanimous opposition. Once again concern was expressed in the press. The director-general of Association Canadienne-Française de l'Alberta, said the new rules were "totally unacceptable" and that:

> We must insist on French being recognized as a language in the Legislature, first and foremost. What the Legislature decides on other languages is something else.[47]

Postscript

A continuing consideration in the proceedings of the Committee and before the Assembly was the fact that the decision of the Saskatchewan Court of Appeal in *Mercure* v. *A.G. Saskatchewan* was under reserve by the Supreme Court of Canada.[48] Indeed, one of the arguments supporting the decision that the Committee lacked competence to deal with the legal status of French in the Assembly was that related issues were before the Supreme Court.[49] That decision was delivered on February 25, 1988, three months after the Alberta Legislative Assembly changed its procedure governing the use of French. It is useful to review that judgement and consider its impact on l'affaire Piquette.

Father Mercure was charged with speeding contrary to the *Saskatchewan Vehicles Act*[50] and was issued a summons. When he

---

46. In a story in the *Globe and Mail* on 5 December 1987, Government House Leader, Les Young, was quoted as saying that the government was treating Mr. Piquette's explanation as an apology.

47. *Globe and Mail* (28 November 1987).

48. [1988] 2 W.W.R. 577.

49. In speaking to the motion before the Assembly, the Government House leader also mentioned the case. *Alberta Hansard* (27 November 1987) 2094.

50. R.S.S. 1978, c. V-3.

appeared in Provincial Court, his counsel sought leave to do three things: to plead to the charge in French; to have a trial in French; and to delay the trial until the clerk of the Legislative Assembly of Saskatchewan produced French translations of the relevant statutes. He based his claim on an argument similar to that raised by Mr. Piquette: that s. 110 of the *Northwest Territories Act* which provided that either French or English could be used in proceedings before the Courts, had been continued in full force and effect by ss. 16 and 14 of the *Saskatchewan Act* (S.C. 1905, c. 42), (the provisions of the *Alberta Act*, S.C. 1905, c. 3, are identical). Section 16 of the *Saskatchewan Act* provides that:

> All laws...existing immediately before the coming into force of this Act in the territory hereby established as the Province of Saskatchewan, shall continue...as if...the Saskatchewan Act had not been passed;...subject...to be[ing] repealed, abolished or altered...by the Legislature of the said [Saskatchewan] Legislature...

In a lengthy judgement, and after reviewing the history of the creation of Saskatchewan, LaForest J. concluded that s. 110 did in fact apply to the modern courts of Saskatchewan as the Legislature of that province had not passed any statute purporting to remove the right to use French in proceedings before the courts. In coming to this conclusion he placed the function of s. 110 on a high plane.

> I should observe here that, while s. 110 governs procedural matters, it does not serve merely procedural ends. It embodies procedural rules that give rights to individuals and, in fact, those rules are to some extent framed in terms of rights. "Either the English or French language", s. 110 reads, "*may be used by any person* in the debates of the Legislative Assembly of the Territories and in the proceedings before the courts"(emphasis added). As well, the printing of the records and the enactment, printing and publishing of the statutes in both languages are not merely mechanical rules of procedure but are obviously intended for the benefit of the individuals who use those languages....They are language rights or language guarantees....[51]

While this judgement deals with the rights to be accorded the French language in court proceedings, it passes over some of the same ground that would have to be covered if the question had concerned the right to speak French in the Legislative Assembly of Alberta. The finding that s. 110 continued in full force and effect would be critical in the "Piquette" context. While LaForest J. did not have to consider the effect of the Haultain motion he did note that "there is doubt whether that resolution was valid because the proper procedural steps were not followed."[52] He also said some important things about the status of the

---

51. *R.* v. *Mercure*, [1988] 2 W.W.R. 577 at 632.
52. *Id.* at 623. The Haultain motion was irrelevant because it dealt with the language in which the proceedings of the Assembly of the Northwest Territories were to be

rights contained in s. 110 and the requirements of any instrument that purported to extinguish them. After equating language laws with human rights laws, he commented as follows:

> The remarks I have referred to in the *Spooner* case, *supra* respecting vested rights had reference to mere property and financial concerns. The courts, and particularly this court, have expressed themselves in even stronger terms in the area of law giving expression to human rights which it has treated as being of an almost constitutional nature. Repeal of such laws requires "clear legislative pronouncement," to use McIntyre J.'s words in *Winnipeg Sch. Div. No. 1 v. Craton*, [1985] 2 S.C.R. 150 at 156.[53]

He went on to hold that provisions such as s. 110 could not be impliedly repealed but would require express words. All of these points lead one to conclude, if it had been argued, that it would have been highly unlikely the Court would have declared that the Haultain motion repealed the language rights contained in s. 110. Certainly the argument that repeal could have occurred by disuse or by something less than formal proclamation would not have received a warm reception.

In his speech to the Assembly on the day the new rules were adopted in Alberta, Mr. Piquette suggested that he might have a constitutional right to speak French in the Assembly that would survive passage of the motion. That possibility may be assessed in light of the *Mercure* decision. LaForest J. noted the significant difference between an entrenched provision and one like s. 110. He held that the Legislature "...has the power to amend its constitution by an ordinary statute" though that ordinary statute had to be in both French and English.[54]

It might be argued that the motion which was passed by the Alberta Legislative Assembly on November 27, 1987 and which regulates the use of the French language cannot satisfy the requirements of s. 110 because it was not simultaneously passed in the French Language. However, on July 6, 1988 the *Alberta Languages Act*[55] came into force. By s. 7 of that Act, which was a response to the decision of the Supreme Court in *Mercure*, the Alberta Legislature, in both English and French, declared that:

---

recorded and published, not the language of statutes or proceedings in the courts. In coming to the conclusion that the proper procedural steps were not followed, LaForest J. relied upon the same study by Claude Armand Sheppard, *The Law of Languages in Canada* (Ottawa: Information Canada 1971), on which expert witnesses appearing before the Committee on Elections and Privileges based their evidence.

53. *Id.* at 633.

54. LaForest J. at *id.* 642 observed:

Accordingly, the legislature may resort to the obvious, if ironic, expedient of enacting a bilingual statute removing the restrictions imposed on it by s. 110 and then declaring all existing provincial statutes valid notwithstanding that they were enacted, printed and published in English only.

55. S.A. 1988, c. L-7.5.

Section 110 of the North-West Territories Act, chapter 50 of the Revised Statutes of Canada, 1886, as it existed on September 1, 1905, does not apply to Alberta with respect to matters within the legislative authority of Alberta.

Following passage of this statute there would not appear to be any ground upon which to argue that there is a subsisting right to speak French in the Legislative Assembly of Alberta.

One further postscript may be of interest. In the general election of March 21, 1989 Mr. Piquette lost his seat. The man who had become a national hero for French-Canadians[56] was, perhaps in part because of the notoriety he gained on this issue, decisively defeated by a Progressive Conservative candidate.[57]

Conclusion

One of the themes evident in l'affaire Piquette was the tension between the inherently contradictory goals of bilingualism and multiculturalism. Official bilingualism emphasizes the importance of French and English at the expense of other languages. However, this is contradicted by the fact that Canada is supposed to be a cultural mosaic rather than a melting pot. The reality is that official bilingualism creates two, rather than one, melting pots. The cauldron of the English or French majority, depending on where one resides in Canada, melts away the cultural and linguistic distinctiveness of minority members. Despite the avowed commitment to multiculturalism the dominant fact is French or English cultural and linguistic hegemony.

In Alberta the composition of the population is such that persons whose mother tongue is French are in a tiny minority. Indeed, the evidence in the *Mahé*[58] case suggests that there are as many Albertans whose first tongue is Chinese as French. This may help to explain why the debates over Mr. Piquette's rights proceeded on two distinct levels. On one level, there was the question of the legal or constitutional status of French compared with English. On the other, there was a question of the moral entitlement of a member of a tiny minority to speak a language in the debates of the Legislative Assembly which the vast

---

56. A sampling of newspaper headlines supports this point:
     "Language stand wins hero status", *Winnipeg Free Press* (6 December 1987); "Albertan becomes francophone hero among Quebecers", *Toronto Star* (29 April 1987); "Quebec legislature throws support behind Piquette", *The Chronicle Herald* (29 April 1987); "Alberta French fight wins MLA friends", *Winnipeg Free Press* (20 April 1987).
57. The riding was won by a well known Metis leader, Michael Cardinal. It may have been significant that there had been a federal by-election the week before the provincial election in the riding of Beaver River which included Mr. Piquette's riding. A Reform candidate, Deborah Gray, was returned to Parliament. Her platform included restricting the use of French outside Quebec. *Globe and Mail* (22 March 1989).
58. *Mahé* v. *Alberta*, [1987] 6 W.W.R. 31 (Alta. C.A.); rev'd (1990), 68 D.L.R. (4th) 69 (S.C.C.).

majority of members could not understand. Based on a review of the debates and press reaction it is clear that, while there was support for the legal or constitutional argument, there was little for the straight moral claim.

The simple fact is that Mr. Piquette's fight was bad politics in Alberta. Throughout the affair, the New Democrats were concerned about the potential backlash from overly vigorous support of Mr. Piquette's cause. It was fine to explore the constitutional and legal context, particularly if mileage could be made from alleging that the government had failed in its constitutional obligations. However, it is significant that none of the opposition parties pressed the moral merits of Mr. Piquette's claim. At most, members observed that it was "ironic" that the right to speak French in the Assembly was being restricted at the very time the resolution approving the Meech Lake Accord was before the House. The fact is, that by deciding to place the French language on a level with all other non-English languages, the Alberta Legislature chose to adhere to the multicultural rather than bilingual model of Canada.

From a purely demographic perspective, given the numbers of Albertans whose mother tongues are something other than French or English, and given that the vast majority of Albertans communicate in English rather than French, it must be asked whether the bilingual model makes more sense than the multicultural one in modern Alberta. When s. 110 was originally passed there were large numbers of French-speaking persons in the Northwest Territories. That is why the French language was afforded special protection.

The demographic reality was recognized by Premier Bourassa in his comments concerning the statute adopted by the Saskatchewan Government to comply with the ruling of the Supreme Court in *Mercure* — a statute which effectively repealed the bilingualism requirements of s. 110 of the *Northwest Territories Act*.[59] On a visit to Saskatchewan shortly after the new statute was passed, Premier Bourassa generally endorsed the approach of the Saskatchewan government, saying that "a responsible attitude" had been taken to the problem.[60] For taking this position, the Québec Premier was branded a "traitor" by the president of the Association Canadienne-Française d'Alberta, and "one of the bitterest adversaries of francophone rights outside Québec" by the Parti Québécois whip, Jacques Brassard.[61] However, one regards the statements of the Québec Premier, it is clear that they provided at least some justification for the later claim by Premier Getty that the *Alberta Languages Act* was an attempt to recognize Alberta's "distinct society."[62]

59. See *supra*, note 21.
60. *Globe and Mail* (13 April 1988).
61. *Globe and Mail* (13 April 1988).
62. *Alberta Hansard* (23 June 1988) 1964.

Courtesy of *The Chronicle-Herald* and *The Mail-Star*.

MINORITY LANGUAGE EDUCATIONAL RIGHTS VINDICATED

Lavoie et al. v. Attorney General of Nova Scotia

A. Wayne MacKay*

I. INTRODUCTION

The vindication of constitutional rights through the courts is an arduous, lengthy, and expensive task. Courts are notoriously slow, procedural demands are high, and lawyers are expensive. Given the inherent limitations of the court process as a vehicle of societal change, it is generally preferable to pursue solutions outside of the judicial forum, through administrative and political avenues. However, should lobbying efforts fail to provide a solution, recourse to the courts may be necessary as a last resort to prod reluctant administrators or politicians.

The pursuit of minority language educational rights in particular presents difficult challenges for both litigants and their counsel. At the heart of the controversies surrounding minority language education is the historic tension between Francophones and Anglophones in Canada, which in its worst forms is manifested as outright bigotry. Second, the constitutionalized national standards of minority language education produce a potential clash with the constitutional authority of the provinces to legislate on education matters pursuant to Section 93 of the *Constitution Act, 1867*,[1] and the tradition of local control exercised by school boards and education authorities. Third, litigants must persuade judges to overcome their traditional deference to the decisions made by educational administrators in their own bailiwick.

An example of the inherent tensions and practical difficulties implicit in constitutional litigation generally and minority language educational

* Professor MacKay of Dalhousie Law School in Halifax made the original presentation of this paper at the conference, but he gratefully acknowledges that this version of the final text was prepared by him in conjunction with Paul Morrison, a 1990 graduate of Dalhousie Law School.
1. (U.K.), 30 & 31 Vict., c. 3.

rights in particular, is found in the case of *Lavoie et al.* v. *Attorney General of Nova Scotia*.[2] I participated in this case as co-counsel, along with Ray Riddell of the Halifax firm of Cooper & McDonald, to a group of parents who wish to provide education in French for their children in fulfilment of their constitutional rights under section 23 of the *Charter*.[3] The history of the *Lavoie* case provides an illuminating case study of the problems lawyers and litigants face in actually trying to implement constitutional language rights in Canada.

II. FACTUAL BACKGROUND

The genesis of the *Lavoie* decision was the formation of a Francophone parents group in 1983, the Committee for French Education. The goal of the Committee was the securing of French language education for their children.[4] The Committee, which comprised representatives of the Acadian community and other Francophone groups resident in Cape Breton, had become concerned about the increased assimilation of the Francophone minority in Cape Breton. The parents were convinced that the continued survival of the Francophone presence in Cape Breton could only be ensured by the provision of primary and secondary school instruction in French. However, at the time that the Committee was struck, the availability of instruction in French in the Cape Breton School District was quite limited, comprising only core French or instruction in the French language and grammar for Anglophones. Even French immersion classes, which are no substitute for true minority language education, was only available beginning in Grade 7, by which time Francophone children would have become largely assimilated.

In the early 1980s, the parents were provided with hope in the form of two legislative initiatives in the field of minority language education. One was in the form of an amendment to the *Nova Scotia Education Act*.[5] The other, of course, was the entrenchment of minority language educational rights in section 23 of the *Charter*.

In June of 1981, the *Education Act* was amended pursuant to the *Acadian Schools Amendment*[6] to provide for French language instruction through the implementation of Acadian schools. The amended Act reads as follows:

2. (1989), 58 D.L.R. (4th) 293; 91 N.S.R. (2d) 184 (N.S.S.C. — App. Div.).
3. *Canadian Charter of Rights and Freedoms*, Part 1 of the *Constitution Act, 1982*, being Schedule B of the *Canada Act, 1982* (U.K.), 1982, c. 11 (hereinafter *Charter*).
4. At various points in the negotiation and litigation process, it appeared to the lawyers that the Council on Social Development, which funded the endeavour, was more concerned about a legal precedent than in having children receive minority language education at the earliest possible time.
5. R.S.N.S. 1967, c. 81.
6. S.N.S. 1981, c. 20.

3. The Governor in Council has the general supervision of public schools and education in the province and, without restricting the generality of the foregoing, may; ...

(aa) upon the request of a school board, or the joint request of two or more school boards, and upon the recommendation of the Minister, designate

(i) As an Acadian school, a school that is within the jurisdiction of the board or one of the boards, and

(ii) As the area which is to be served by the Acadian school, an area in which there is a sufficient number of children, whose first language learned and still understood is French, to warrant provision of public funds for instruction to be carried out in the French language

and, where the request is from two or more boards, determine the responsibilities of each board in relation to the school;

(aaa) upon the recommendation of the Minister, designate an Acadian district and make determinations respecting the operation of and support for an Acadian district;...

4. The Minister may...

(kb) determine the ratio of instruction in French to instruction in English in Acadian schools, prescribe courses of study in French and authorize French language textbooks and related materials for use in Acadian schools;

....

5A. The principal language of administration of an Acadian school and communication of an Acadian school with the community it serves shall be French.

Thus, under the scheme set up under the *Education Act*, before the Cabinet can exercise its discretion, the relevant school board must first make a request for designation as an Acadian school. Second, the Minister must make a positive recommendation. Finally both the school board and the Minister must deem there to be sufficient numbers of children whose language first learned and still understood is French. Despite many requests from the Committee for French Education, the Cape Breton District School Board refused to make the initial request to provincial Cabinet for an Acadian school that would have set the process in motion.

In 1982, the *Charter* became law, and in section 23 thereof provided guarantees for minority language education. Section 23 guarantees to qualifying parents the right to have their children receive primary and secondary school instruction in French, and the right to have them receive that instruction in French language educational facilities provided out of public funds, where numbers warrant. The guarantees of minority language education in the *Charter* are far wider in scope than the provisions contained within the *Education Act*. First, whereas the *Education Act* requires a request from a local school board and ministerial approval as a prerequisite to any exercise of Cabinet discretion, the *Charter* guarantees the right to instruction "where numbers warrant". Second, the *Education Act* grants discretion to the Minister to determine the ratio of instruction in French to that in English, while the *Charter* guarantees instruction in the minority language. Third, the *Education Act* requires that children in Acadian schools be competent in French, while the *Charter* determines eligibility for minority language instruction by reference to the linguistic and educational background of the parents. The third distinction is especially vital, because the effect of the provisions in the *Education Act* is to deny access to minority language instruction to those children who have lost ability in the minority language through assimilation. These crucial differences between the *Charter* and the *Act* formed the basis of an ultimately unsuccessful challenge to the provincial legislation in the *Lavoie* case.[7]

The parents therefore requested that the Cape Breton District School Board provide their children with primary and secondary instruction in French in a facility administered in the French language, pursuant to section 23. In addition, the parents also repeated earlier requests under the *Education Act* for the establishment of an Acadian school under the different and more restrictive statutory formula. The Board, however, proved no more accommodating to this request from the parents for their constitutional rights than they had under the provincial statute. The reason given for this refusal was that the number of children of qualifying parents was insufficient to warrant instruction.

In response to the Board's position, the parents commissioned a survey of the area within the jurisdiction of the Cape Breton District School Board, and with funding from the Secretary of State, distributed questionnaires in the spring of 1984 to over 11,000 elementary school children and 1,200 pre-schoolers within the district. Impressive results were obtained. Under the criteria outlined in both section 23 of the *Charter* and the *Education Act*, more than 660 students were identified as having a constitutional claim to education in French. The results were presented to the Board in October 1984. A copy of this survey

---

7. This is one aspect of the Nova Scotia Appeal Court decision that we would like to have appealed to the Supreme Court of Canada but we felt that the speedy provision of instruction to the qualifying Cape Breton children was the more important matter.

was also sent to the provincial Department of Education, which later claimed to have no knowledge of it. The Board met in April 1985 and denied the request for an Acadian school. The Board professed skepticism as to the results of the parents' survey, and then embarked on a survey of its own to determine the number of children of qualifying parents in the area. The School Board survey indicated that only 97 children were eligible to attend an Acadian school. The Board stated that because of the ages of the children, there would be insufficient numbers to start up a school, nor would there be sufficient numbers to sustain a program in later years. The Board thus refused to request an Acadian school. The Board's decision rested on the results of its own survey, despite the fact that the number of responses obtained for their survey was far smaller than the number obtained for the parents' survey.[8]

Concerned parents continued to persist in their demands for recognition of their rights under the *Charter*, and were skeptical of the results of the Board survey. After more lengthy legal negotiations between lawyers for the parents and the School Board, another survey was commissioned by the Minister of Education. Dr. Brian Joseph was hired to survey the district for another determination of the number of qualifying students. The survey identified 245 families as being entitled under section 23 of the *Charter* to have their children receive primary and secondary instruction in French. These 245 families represented a total of 429 children. The survey indicated that this number was an absolute minimum and that further children of qualifying parents may exist in the district who had not been identified by the survey. As a result of the Joseph survey, the parents continued to press for French language instruction, but no steps were taken by the Board. The parents finally instructed their recently retained legal counsel, Wayne MacKay and Ray Riddell, to be prepared to pursue court action as a last resort. In 1986, the decision was made to file an action in the Supreme Court of Nova Scotia against the School Board and the Attorney General of Nova Scotia.[9]

Even after the action had been commenced, my co-counsel and I attempted to negotiate a settlement which would put a school or classes in place as soon as possible. A conscious decision was made to pursue both political and judicial avenues in the interests of forestalling further assimilation of the Francophone children in the district. Another factor

---

8. The School Board received and analyzed only 54 questionnaires, whereas over 7,151 surveys were returned for the parents' survey. In addition, notice of the School Board survey to the public consisted of a single newspaper ad. The survey appeared to be designed to elicit as few responses as possible.

9. S.H. No. 59252 (Nova Scotia Prothonotary's Office).

in this decision was our recognition of the reluctance of the Nova Scotia courts to provide a remedy if the traditional administrative and bureaucratic channels had not been exhausted. Months of negotiations with the Department of Education and the Board followed, but our efforts proved fruitless. During these negotiations we became aware that bad faith and obstructionism seemed to be motivating the Board. We were also acutely aware that every delay contributed to the further assimilation of Francophone children in the district. Therefore, in July of 1987 we filed an application in the Nova Scotia Supreme Court for an interim injunction to put temporary classrooms in place for grades primary to six, until the Province and the Board could make arrangements for a school.

III. THE INTERIM INJUNCTION — JULY 1987

We were aware that a court would be reluctant to provide any relief before the merits of the case were fully considered. However, we felt that further delay only played into the hands of the Board. The essence of our argument for the grant of the interim injunction, based on the decision of the Supreme Court of Canada in *A.G. Manitoba* v. *Metropolitan Stores*,[10] was that the vindication of constitutional rights represented a serious issue to be tried, and that the continual danger of assimilation represented a severe, intangible loss that could not be compensated with monetary damages. Justice Robert Macdonald summarily dismissed the application. His Lordship's remarks were indicative of the uphill task faced by the litigants in this case. His Lordship was not only reluctant to provide instruction before a trial on the merits, for fear of presenting the trial judge with a *fait accompli*, he also stated that instruction of Francophone children in an Anglophone school did not promote assimilation. This statement is difficult to support sociologically, and also is at odds with decisions of other courts which have recognized the pressures on Francophones to assimilate in anglophone schools. As Richard C.J. stated in *Société des Acadiens du Nouveau Brunswick Inc.* v. *Minority Language School Board No. 50*:

> From the evidence presented at trial, as well as from the whole of the expert testimony it appears...that the grouping of Francophone and Anglophone pupils under the same roof and in the same system, leads to linguistic interference, to the weakening of the first and second languages and, consequently, to assimilation.[11]

---

10. [1987] 3 W.W.R. 1, (S.C.C.). Beetz J., indicates that, for an interim injunction in a constitutional setting, the applicant must demonstrate: 1) a serious issue to be tried. 2) likelihood of irreparable harm that is not susceptible to compensation in money damages. 3) the balance of convenience to the parties.

11. (1983), 48 N.B.R. (2d) 361 at 390-391 (Q.B.).

After the denial of the injunction, we continued to negotiate in the months before the trial scheduled for January 1988, although clearly from a weaker bargaining position than before, as the commencement of another school year had passed.

Negotiations continued into December 1987. Following the denial of the interlocutory injunction, the Board and the Attorney General indicated a willingness to provide a school, but that the funding arrangements would continue to be a matter for negotiation. Negotiations continued upon the many complicated aspects of implementing a minority language program. During the discussions it became clear that the key issue would be the location of the proposed school. It appeared that there were at least two available places in the Sydney area in which a school could be established. However, the Board refused to provide these spaces, claiming that these locations had been earmarked for other uses such as storage and office space. This refusal was another indication of the low priority that the Board attached to minority language educational rights.

In the first two weeks of December it appeared that negotiations were at a standstill as the Board refused to budge from its position that no space was available in the Sydney area. It was at this point that the Department of Education was looking into the possibility of providing a facility through one of its own buildings in Sydney, and there was the glimmer of a hope of settlement. As we continued preparation for the trial in January, we awaited word from the Minister of Education. Finally, at the end of December, we received word from the Attorney General that the Minister was willing to renovate a wing of the Adult Vocational Training Centre in Sydney and offer it as a location, on the condition that the Board would administer this facility. The location was central enough to be suitable to the parents, and since the solicitor for the School Board had indicated to us in writing that his client would administer the school if the Province provided the necessary funding, we felt that an agreement was at hand.

Our hopes for settlement were dashed when we received word from the Board that it would not agree to any settlement, and that any settlement that their solicitor had purportedly made was made without authority. This information was provided to us within days of the commencement of the trial. The position of the Board was a remarkable development, given that the Board's solicitor had recommended accepting the proposed new facility. The incident provided confirmation of the bad faith of several members of the Board that we had long suspected to exist.

IV. THE TRIAL — JANUARY 1988

With the Board's refusal to settle, the trial on the merits began before Justice J. Doane Hallett on January 4, 1988. The trial had been scheduled for four court days, but the actual proceeding stretched into ten days in January, and two more days in August. The main reason for the length of the trial was that the School Board, and to some extent the Attorney General, fought every issue tooth and nail, refusing to concede even the most inconsequential points. As one example of the obstructionist tactics employed, on the first day of the trial we attempted to introduce the Joseph survey as evidence of the numbers of eligible parents and children in Cape Breton. However, the Attorney General and the School Board objected on the grounds that we had not provided them with 30 days notice of our intention to introduce expert evidence, as required by the Civil Procedure Rules,[12] and that they had not had an opportunity to discover Dr. Joseph. This was a surprising position, given that the Province itself had hired Dr. Joseph to research the numbers of eligible parents and children. Yet at trial the parties claimed no prior notice of this evidence, and even challenged the qualifications and abilities of their own expert. Mr. Justice Hallett decided to allow the report into evidence, but only if Dr. Joseph were brought to court to be available for cross-examination upon his report. We were forced to find Dr. Joseph, who was at that time living in Ottawa, and fly him in for the trial at the expense of the parents.

The Joseph incident was a good example of the approach taken by the defendants in challenging facts and procedures in the hope of defeating the parents' claims. We were put to strict proof of every issue, and the Board and the Attorney General endlessly cross-examined every witness and exploited every Civil Procedure Rule to impede our efforts and avoid a simple determination on the merits. One of the more extreme examples of this was the suggestion by the Board that the citizenship of the claiming parents should have been proven by documentation in court. Justice Hallett was willing to accept the sworn statement of our clients. The tactics of the Board and the Attorney General were clearly to stall long enough to require the trial to be adjourned and carried over to the next available court date. Any later date could have resulted in a decision being rendered too late to implement any instruction before the beginning of the school year in September, 1988, and thus resulting in another lost year for the parents and children. Fortunately, the next case Justice Hallett was scheduled to hear after the *Lavoie* case was settled at the last minute, and enough court time opened for our case to be presented.

---

12. Nova Scotia Civil Procedure Rule 31.08.

At the end of the January trial, Justice Hallett was satisfied on the evidence that there were three to four hundred potential students in the district. However, his Lordship was uncertain whether the eligible parents identified by the Joseph survey would actually enrol their children in a facility for French language instruction if one were to be provided. His Lordship was reluctant to order the provision of instruction by the Board without clear evidence of demand. The approach of Hallett J. on this point raises the important issue of whether actual, demonstrated demand is necessary before minority language education is provided. Professor Magnet believes that the existence of actual demand should not be a prerequisite to the establishment of minority language education.[13] On the other hand, the Prince Edward Island Court of Appeal in *Reference Re School Act of P.E.I.*[14] was clear in stating that there must be a demonstrated demand before minority language education will be provided. Justice Hallett was of the view that demonstrated demand was necessary. He ordered that a registration be held at a "suitable and reasonably accessible facility" before he would determine whether there were sufficient numbers to warrant establishment of a minority language educational facility. He also stopped short of ordering minority language educational instruction at this point in deference to the traditional discretion of legislators and administrators in this area.

V. THE LOCATION APPLICATION — FEBRUARY 29, 1988

Throughout the trial, the Board had suggested that the Breton Education Centre in New Waterford would be a suitable location for a minority language educational facility. This is a relatively new and under-utilized facility which the Board was eager to put to greater use. We had vigorously objected to this site, as it is approximately 40 kilometers from Sydney, where the majority of eligible children were located, and thus would involve a bus ride of close to an hour for most of the children. Location of the facility is a crucial question in section 23 cases. As Cape Breton has a relatively dispersed population, it was essential that any school be located at a reasonably central location where parents would be likely to send their children. Justice Hallett had strongly hinted during the trial that he did not consider the Breton Education Centre to be a suitable location. However, he did not rule it out expressly in his January registration order. His Lordship had also indicated that he considered the site proposed by the Province at the Adult Vocational Training Centre in Sydney to be suitable. The Board

13. J.E. Magnet, "Minority Language Educational rights" (1982) 4 *Sup.Ct.L.Rev.* 195 at 206.
14. (1988), 49 D.L.R. (4th) 499 (P.E.I.S.C. *In Banco*).

realized, however, that if a registration were held which designated the Breton Education Centre as the proposed location, few if any parents would register their children, and the judge would consequently not order the establishment of a school. The Board thus proposed that the Breton Education Centre was the most suitable location to carry out the registration.

The Board's proposal forced a further appearance in court at the end of February in order to challenge the location chosen by the Board and stop the registration from proceeding. In the course of this hearing, the Attorney General not only supported the Board's proposed location, but went further by bringing in a transportation expert to substantiate and rationalize the lengthy bus ride to the Breton Education Centre. In unorthodox fashion, the lawyer for the Board even suggested that he had always enjoyed the bus ride to school as a positive aspect of the educational process. The Province also withdrew its offer of the Adult Vocational Training Centre as an alternative school site. It became increasingly clear that the Attorney General was no friend to the parents in their dispute with the Cape Breton School Board.[15]

Justice Hallett accepted our reasoning with respect to the issue of location, and issued a declaration that the location proposed was not reasonably accessible within the meaning of the January 1988 order. In his decision of March 11, 1988, his Lordship stated :

> It is implicit in the section 23 *Charter* right that a facility for a minority language education be reasonably accessible. Where classroom facilities, albeit not the most perfect, are available, they should be utilized. I agree with the arguments advanced by plaintiffs' counsel that the Board...had its priorities out of order. Virtually everything is given priority over accommodating the right of the minority francophone parents to have their children educated in French if the numbers warrant...It is as if the Board were not conscious that the *Charter of Rights* has been passed and is the law of Canada.[16]

This is the first judicial pronouncement that section 23 contemplates a school that is reasonably accessible to the qualified parents. Justice Hallett chided the Board for its conduct throughout the case, and went so far as to "suggest" that a facility located on the Mira Road in Sydney would be an attractive option. His Lordship went on to state that in assessing what might constitute a reasonably accessible site, the members of the Board might want to imagine themselves living in Québec City and wishing to have their other young children educated in English.

---

15. (1988), 84 N.S.R. (2d) 387 (N.S.S.C. T.D.).
16. *Id.* at 400.

Would they want their five to eleven year olds bused in the range of twenty kilometers to another community when classroom space is available in the city?[17]

The forceful statement of Justice Hallett in his March decision gave the parents hope that they would finally see some positive action on the part of the Board towards putting a programme of instruction in place. However, the Board and the Attorney General refused to comply with the court-ordered registration by refusing to select an alternate site for the proposed registration. The Board changed solicitors and announced their intention to commence an appeal of all the decisions made to date. The parents and their lawyers were forced back into court again.

VI. THE COURT OF APPEAL — APRIL 1988

The Board applied to the Court of Appeal to seek leave to appeal both the January trial decision and the March decision on location. The Appeal Court would not grant leave to appeal the January ruling, as the Board had allowed the thirty day appeal period to expire. However, the Board was permitted to appeal the March decision regarding the location of the proposed school. The earliest date on which an appeal could be heard was in September 1988. The obvious implication of the September appeal dates would be that the Board would have been successful in thwarting the implementation of a programme for another school year. However, in what might be regarded as a strategic error on its part, the Board had failed to seek a stay of proceedings with respect to the January order, and thus were arguably vulnerable to contempt proceedings which could be instituted to force them to conduct a registration during the appeal period.

Leave to apply for a contempt order was obtained and a date for the contempt hearing was set for May 31, 1988. Faced with the prospect of fines or other possible penalties from the contempt proceeding, the Board's solicitor offered to discontinue the appeal and hold the registration in compliance with the January and March orders, if we would agree to drop the Board as a defendant in the action and pursue our claim only against the Attorney General. In addition, we were to discontinue the contempt proceedings. The decision of the Board to carry out the registration was made much easier as a result of the terms of a secret deal that the Board had struck with the Province. If the Board agreed to carry out the registration, the Province would cover all the

---

17. *Id.* at 404.

costs of implementing the school, including providing a new maintenance building, and provide extra funding to compensate for the children lost to the English system, if the French school were to be ordered as a result of the registration. In light of these assurances, the Board agreed to hold a registration for the facility at Mira Road and to drop the appeal proceedings. Considering our need to have the registration conducted as soon as possible, and given the fact that we would still be able to pursue the remedies we might need through the action against the Attorney General as a sole defendant, we agreed to the Board's terms, discontinued the contempt proceedings, and dropped them as a party to the litigation on appeal.

VII. THE REGISTRATION — JUNE 1988

The registration was carried out by the Board during June 1988. Disappointingly, only 50 of the more that 400 students identified in the Joseph survey registered, spread over nine grades.[18] However, these diminished numbers were understandable in many respect. First, the numbers indicate the difficulty in maintaining the commitment of a diverse group of plaintiffs over a five year period, a fact that undoubtedly played a large role in the strategy of delay and attrition adopted by a Board and the Province. The parents who had originally fought for and pioneered the cause of a French school when their children were in grade primary or pre-schoolers now had children in grades 4 and 5 who could speak no or very little French.

Other parents may have been reluctant to place their children in a minority language programme when their children were only a year or two away from eligibility for the Board's late immersion programme. Secondly, the political climate and obvious antagonism expressed by the Board did not inspire confidence that the proposed school would have a quality program. Third, the parents had been saturated with surveys and phone calls and promises for a school for the past four

---

18. The results of the survey were as follows:

Grade	No.
P	5
1	13
2	6
3	8
4	4
5	6
6	4
7	2
8	2

years, without anything having been achieved. The parents may have thought that the registration was just another inconvenience that would again provide no concrete results. Finally, the parents were required to attend an interview in which the Board would determine whether French was the first language learned and still understood by the parents. This type of testing is not common in other provinces and intimidated many parents who might have been willing to have their children registered. Dr. Brian Joseph is doing a study of the factors that produced the low enrolment for the school. Given all the negative factors, it is certainly understandable that so many of the parents adopted a 'wait and see' attitude towards the proposed school.

The results of the registration were submitted to the Minister of Education for a determination of the services they were prepared to provide, given that level of enrolment. The Minister, Ronald Giffin, offered nothing, stating that there were not enough children registered to maintain a quality program. This statement was made despite the fact that there were several schools in the Cape Breton School District that operated with fewer than fifty students. Provided with these numbers, we returned to the Nova Scotia Supreme Court before Justice Hallett on August 8 and 10, 1988, for a determination on the merits of the section 23 case.

VIII. THE TRIAL DECISION — AUGUST 1988

We returned to court to present the results of the registration to Justice Hallett, and to request that a school be put into place. Our argument for a school was based in part on the guarantee of equality contained within section 15 of the *Charter*. It was argued on behalf of the parents that if there were English schools functioning in Cape Breton with fewer than 50 students, then based on even the most formal view of the equality guarantee the Francophone minority was entitled to their own school.[19] In the alternative, it was argued that there were at least enough children registered to warrant classrooms for instruction, if not a free standing facility of their own.

In his final decision,[20] Justice Hallett reviewed the Minister's decision not to provide a school, and applied a very restrictive standard to judicial involvement in section 23 cases. His Lordship stated:[21]

> It can be inferred that the Legislature, by not enacting a "numbers" formula, has determined that the Minister of Education should exercise the

---

19. For an analysis of the distinction between "formal equality" and "substantive equality", see A. Wayne MacKay, "The Equality Provision of the Charter and Education: A Structural Analysis" (1986) 11 *Can. Journal of Education (No. 3)* 293.
20. (1988), 90 N.S.R. (2d) 16 (N.S.S.C. T.D.)
21. *Id.* at 24-25.

responsibility of making the determination under s. 23(3) of the *Charter*. The Minister has made a determination on this issue after being apprised of the registration results; that determination was made in the exercise of the powers conferred on him by the Legislature pursuant to the Education Act of this Province. Unless the Minister has acted with bias, bad faith, unfairness or unreasonably, the court should not intervene. The evidence does not warrant the intervention of the court.

The approach adopted by Justice Hallett ignores the recognition by other courts of the remedial nature of section 23,[22] and further ignores the recognized approach of purposive interpretation of the *Charter* in general.[23] His Lordship's approach to the interpretation of section 23 was reminiscent of the old administrative law approach of judicial deference to parliamentary and administrative authority. The restrictive approach proposed by Justice Hallett was also disappointing, considering the somewhat activist approach to the *Charter* found in his earlier decisions in the case. The restrictive reasoning of his Lordship on this point would form the substance of our subsequent appeal of his decision.

In his supplementary reasons concerning the *Acadian Schools Amendment*,[24] released subsequently, Hallett J. held that the legislation was not unconstitutional, despite its differences with section 23 which were outlined earlier in this paper. His Lordship held that the legislation was "complementary" rather than inconsistent with the rights guaranteed by section 23. We argued that as the amendment defines eligibility in terms of the linguistic competence of the child, and not the parents, the effect of the *Acadian schools amendment* was to provide for areas in which Francophones were in the majority locally, and did not recognize the situation of the minority as a whole within the province as required by section 23. Schools established under the amendment provisions would in effect siphon off children from any potential section 23 program. Children, who through no fault of their own had become assimilated, would be adversely affected by any schools set up under the amendment as they would not qualify under the statutory requirement of fluency in French. Furthermore, the numbers necessary to establish a section 23 programme would be diminished. Despite our arguments on this point, the judge stated that in reality the *Acadian Schools Amendment* provided the Francophone minority in Nova Scotia with an additional protection. The constitutionality of the provision was a further issue in our subsequent appeal.

---

22. See for example *A.G. Québec* v. *Quebec Association of Protestant School Board*, [1984] 2 S.C.R. 66 at 79; *Reference Re School of P.E.I.* (1988), 49 D.L.R. (4th) 499 (P.E.I.S.C.) *In Banco*.

23. *R.* v. *Big M Drug Mart* (1985), 18 D.L.R. (4th) 321 at 359. (S.C.C.).

24. (1988), 90 N.S.R. (2d) 26 (N.S.S.C. T.D.).

IX. DECISION OF THE COURT OF APPEAL — MARCH 1989

We filed an application to appeal the decision of Hallett J. in the Appeals Division of the Nova Scotia Supreme Court. In its decision,[25] the Court allowed the appeal in part, holding that there were sufficient numbers of students to warrant French language instruction, but not a separate facility. The Appeal Court made some important statements about section 23 in general which I would like to examine in some detail. Chief Justice Clarke made strong statements about the approach to be employed in the interpretation of section 23. His Lordship accepted that section 23 is a remedial provision aimed at correcting perceived defects in the educational systems of the provinces as they affect Anglophone and Francophone minorities. The Chief Justice accepted that following the decision of the Supreme Court of Canada in *R.* v. *Big M Drug Mart Ltd.*,[26] *Charter* analysis requires a purposive approach, and a generous rather than a legalistic interpretation of its guarantees. His Lordship stated:

> I agree with the submission of the appellants that s. 23 of the *Charter* was intended as a remedial provision and, in order to be effective as a remedy for past defects, it must be given a large and liberal interpretation. With the advent of s. 23, linguistic minorities have been granted a constitutionally guaranteed right and this right must not be restricted by a confined approach to its interpretation.[27]

His Lordship also stated that the decision of *Société des Acadiens du Nouveau-Brunswick et al.* v. *Minority Language School Board No. 50*[28] which states that the language rights contained within sections 16 to 23 of the *Charter* arose from a political compromise and thus should be interpreted with more restraint than other *Charter* rights, did not apply to the interpretation of section 23. He asserted that section 23 is a unique and new remedial provision of the *Charter*.

The decision of the Court also accepts the role that associated sections of the *Charter* such as the equality guarantee in section 15 and the acknowledgement of the multicultural nature of Canada in section 27 could play in the purposive interpretation of section 23. Given the vigorous approach to section 23 interpretation adopted by Clarke C.J.N.S., it is not surprising that the Court overruled the decision of Hallett J. that the Court should be deferential to decisions made by the Minister of Education. His Lordship stated:

---

25. (1989), 91 N.S.R. (2d) 184 (N.S.S.C. App. Div.).
26. (1985), 18 D.L.R. (4th) 321 at 359 (S.C.C.).
27. *Supra*, note 11.
28. [1986] 1 S.C.R. 549 at 578. In *Mahé et al.* v. *Alberta*, [1987] 6 W.W.R. 331, (Alta. C.A.), at 350 Kerans J.A. concluded that the comments of Beetz J. regarding ss. 16-22 were equally applicable to s. 23.

While it is appropriate to consider the opinion of the Minister of Education as part of the evidence adduced at trial, it is, with respect, inappropriate to rest the result primarily upon his determination. To do so is to deny the role of the courts in protecting linguistic minorities and fails to recognize the more generous interpretive approach that must be given to section 23 of the *Charter*. The test under section 23 is not the reasonableness of the Minister's decision, as would be considered in an administrative law setting, but rather whether there has been a violation of the rights of the appellants as citizens of Canada. Section 23(3) is designed to correct injustices that exist in the educational system, not to maintain the status quo. The rights of the linguistic minority population of Nova Scotia under s. 23(3) are not within the exclusive domain of the school board or the Minister even though the decision of each may be made in good conscience. It was, with respect, an error to conclude that the court should not intervene once the Minister made his decision even though on its face the decision appeared reasonable.[29]

With respect to the issue of numbers, the Court declined to set a number as to how many children would be necessary to satisfy the "numbers warrant" requirement in a particular situation. The Court recognized the "two-tier" nature of the numbers requirement in section 23, stating that while there were not enough students to justify a separate Francophone facility, there were enough students to warrant the provision of instruction.[30] With regard to the implementation of this instruction, Clarke C.J.N.S. adopted the reasoning in the *Ontario Reference*[31] that the instruction had to be provided in a way that would not promote assimilation:

> It follows that the province must provide suitable accommodation for the minority language instruction these children are entitled to receive. It must be made available in a surrounding that is "consistent with the preservation and enhancement" of the French culture. It cannot be designed in a way that permits assimilation or smacks of immersion. The instruction must be provided in a suitably structured environment. I agree with the view expressed by the court in *Reference Re Education Act of Ontario*, at p. 527:
>> ...para. (3)(a) of s. 23 provides the right to "minority language instruction" which must include, apart from the requisite teachers and teaching materials, either classrooms or other physical facilities, like television, for such instruction.[32]

---

29. *Supra*, note 25 at 195.
30. This sliding scale approach to the numbers warrant test was ultimately affirmed by the ruling in *Mahé* v. *A.G. Alta.* (1990), 68 D.L.R. (4th) 69 (S.C.C.). This decision also affirms an expansive role for the courts in s. 23 cases.
31. *Reference Re Education Act of Ontario* (1989), 47 O.R. (2d) 1; 10 D.L.R. (4th) 491 (Ont. C.A.).
32. *Supra*, note 25 at 197.

This approach raises interesting questions of implementation. The approach adopted by Clarke C.J.N.S. could mean that the Francophone students would have to have a separate facility, because much of our argument was that if you do not provide instruction in a separate facility, then you do not really provide the necessary Francophone ambience to forestall assimilation. At a minimum, the approach could require a separate wing in an existing facility in which the minority students would not be overpowered by the Anglophone student population. This is in fact what was implemented for the 1989-90 academic year in the Cape Breton district as a result of this decision. Early reports indicate that the experience was a positive one for the students concerned.

With respect to the *Acadian Schools Amendment*, the Court of Appeal upheld the decision of Hallett J. as to its constitutionality, agreeing with the trial judge that it is complementary to existing *Charter* guarantees.

Finally, it is extremely important to note that the decision of the Appeal Court did not close the subject of a facility completely. The Court stressed that its determination as to the numbers warranting instruction was made on existing facts and numbers. The decision made it clear that the relevant educational authorities should reassess the number of students on a regular basis and particularly when the annual registration takes place, to see if a separate facility is warranted. The court stated :

> If the province fails to act or acts in a manner which appears inadequate, the appellants may return to the court to determine the adequacy of the action taken by the province in complying with the declaration that should be issued.[33]

CONCLUSION

In sum, the decision of the Appeal Court was an encouraging statement of the judicial approach to minority language educational rights. While the decision could likely have been successfully appealed to the Supreme Court of Canada, particularly on the issues of the *Acadian Schools Amendment* and the refusal of the court to provide a school, we were not inclined to return to court. While the establishment of a useful precedent may be important, the bottom line for us as lawyers was ensuring that at the end of the day the children of our clients were being educated in the minority language. An appeal would very likely have delayed the implementation of any instruction. The cost of pursuing

---

33. *Ibid.*

an appeal also would have been prohibitive. Despite the fact that a large part of the costs of this case were provided by the Court Challenges Program of the Canadian Council on Social Development, the funding is not complete and is difficult to secure. Given the costs and delays involved in pursuing legal action, I would stress the need to proceed along bureaucratic and political channels concurrent with any court action, in order to get a program in place as quickly as possible. The lesson of the experience in the *Lavoie* case, however, has been that the spur of legal action is often necessary to prod the government into recognizing and acting upon its constitutional obligations. For parents facing the kind of barriers encountered by the Francophone parents in Cape Breton, courts may be not only the last resort but, also, the only resort for instigating governmental action.

COMMENTS

Joseph Magnet

I

During the Trudeau years, independence for Québec became a substantial and intimidating possibility. Language politics were supercharged with a significance. Each language conflict reminded everyone that the language pot could boil over unpredictably, incinerating all hopes for the grand Canadian experiment. The 1969 *Official Languages Act*[1] sought to make the Federal government open and accessible to Québecers by instituting a comprehensive program of language equality. At the same time, Ottawa provided new support for official language minorities in the provinces. The purpose of Ottawa's effort was to resist the blandishment of a Canada split along linguistic lines, to construct a society in which English and French minorities could conduct much of their lives in their own language.

The 1969 policy is complicated by the fact that it served two policy goals which are partially irreconcilable and two client groups that have conflicting objectives. The principal client group was Québécois. The goal was to remedy the virtual exclusion of French from the federal public service. By language of work and equitable participation goals the 1969 policy sought to appease long standing grievances of Québécois, attract their loyalties to the federal state, and co-opt them away from nationalism by giving them an important stake in the federal government machinery. The second client group of the 1969 policy was the official language minorities in the provinces. The goal was to maintain, and in some cases, to resuscitate them. This was meant to have symbolic value in Québec because it drew a portrait where Québécois could inhabit communities in Canada beyond Québec without feeling culturally and linguistically foreign. This portrait of Canada offered Francophones something tangible, just as Québec offered Anglophones the possibility of moving there and living and working in English.

---

1. R.S.C. 1985, c. 0-3, repealed S.C. 1988, c. 38, s. 110.

These two policy goals came into conflict. Support for official language minorities meant support for the Anglo-Québec community, since the 1969 policy meant equivalence between all official language minorities. This brought Ottawa into direct conflict with Québec. It was the goal of language planners in Québec to build the French fact in Québec and, consequently, to restrict the use of the English language in that province. In short, enhancing minority rights did not impress and, to a certain extent, offended Québec. Ignoring Francophone minorities, especially during overheated periods, added rhetorical fuel to the nationalists' fire.

Ottawa made tangible, substantial progress in appeasing Québecers by its plans to reform the linguistic complexion of the federal public service. By 1983 the Commissioner of Official Language could observe with justification that the linguistic face of the federal administration had been transformed. Ottawa's support for provincial language minorities, however, was somewhat symbolic. Ottawa's efforts never slowed demolition of Canada's linguistic minorities by the inexorable march of assimilation which eclipsed language minorities by as much as 88 percent in some provinces. Nevertheless, Ottawa did do something in 1969, and the symbolic import of its actions coupled with real changes in the federal public administration was considerable. The result was a profound transformation of attitudes, an increasing open-mindedness.

All of this activity, symbolic and real, made it seem as if Canada's habit of neglecting official language minorities was coming to an end. By 1983, even the Official Languages Commissioner, an official paid to complain about Canada's linguistic woes, could report, uncharacteristically, that "there is reason for Canadians to share a certain pride about how far we have come, that there is no turning back", and could point to "a brighter linguistic future there for the taking". Even if this was the bitter-sweet valedictory speech of a retiring official, still, the remarks did indicate just how profoundly optimistic many Canadians had become about relations between the two language communities.

II

Ottawa's actions, and the resulting change in public attitudes, impressed the Supreme Court of Canada. In *Jones* v. *Attorney General of New Brunswick*,[2] Chief Justice Laskin used emphatic language, describing language rights as providing "special protection" for language minorities. When in 1979 the Anglophone minority of Québec[3] and the

---

2. [1975] 2 S.C.R. 182.
3. *A.G. Québec* v. *Blaikie*; *A.G. Québec* v. *Laurier*, [1979] 2 S.C.R. 1016.

Francophone minority of Manitoba[4] appealed to the Supreme Court of Canada for special protection against hostile provincial governments, the Supreme Court reacted firmly, with tough remedial protection and tough talk to both provinces. Building on the special protection language of *Jones*, the Court expanded official bilingualism beyond the expressed language of s. 133. Section 133, said the Court, "ought to be considered broadly", it should not be read "overly technical". Section 133 contained a principle "of growth" and on that principle the Court augmented s. 133 beyond its expressed terms to subject a wide spectrum of institutions and statutory materials to the discipline of official bilingualism. As a final slap at Québec, the Court noted that Québec itself had taken an "enlarged appreciation" of the meaning of courts of Québec by stipulating for unilingualism therein. The Court rubbed Québec's nose in this, holding that the bilingualism rule of s. 133 would fasten throughout the range of institutions captured by Québec's "enlarged appreciation".[5]

With respect to Manitoba, the Court was icy-cold. Manitoba's 1890 *Official Language Act* was invalid, period! The Court said not a word regarding the consequences. This left the impression that all Manitoba statutes since 1890 were void, as in flagrant contradiction with constitutional requirements. The Court's studied silence brooded ominously in the Manitoba constitutional landscape, dominating Manitoba politics for the next five years and setting the Manitoba legislature on a collision course with constitutional requirements.

That the Supreme Court of Canada was set on breathing life into official bilingualism through a robust, expanding, purposeful interpretation of constitutional guarantees was made crystal clear in the *Manitoba Language Reference*.[6] The Court used impressive rhetoric. The purpose of constitutional guarantees for official bilingualism, the Court stated, was to ensure "full and equal access to the legislatures, the laws, and the courts for Francophones and Anglophones alike". The Court explained its previous ruling in *Blaikie* from the perspective of full and equal access for the minority. According to the Court, *Blaikie* required equal authority and status for English and French because "nothing less would adequately ensure that the law was equally accessible to Francophones and Anglophones alike". And, most interesting, was the development of the Court's "special protection" doctrine, first instituted in *Jones*. The Court went beyond special protection to read constitutional guarantees for official bilingualism purposively, finding in them "a specific

---

4. *A.G. Manitoba* v. *Forest*, [1979] 2 S.C.R. 1032.
5. *Supra*, note 3 at 1028.
6. *Reference re Manitoba Language Rights*, [1985] 1 S.C.R. 721.

manifestation of the general right of Franco-Manitobans to use their own language" and imposing upon the judiciary the responsibility of protecting the correlative language rights of the Franco-Manitoban minority. In short, the Court had found in the terse phrasing of ancient constitutional texts a system of minority protection, and through a purposive and dynamic interpretation, the Court set out to reconstruct these special protections so as to ensure that the minority enjoyed full and equal access to the machinery of government in a meaningful way.

Had Ottawa acted consistently and persevered, the new openness and the new Court protection probably could have translated into institutional reality for language minorities. Dramatic development of minority languages has occurred in other countries; probably it could have happened here. However, Ottawa did not act consistently. Ottawa was often incomprehensible, contradictory, fickle, even, too often, an aggressive advocate *against* linguistic minorities. There are many examples of cracked federal behaviour detailed in the reports of the Official Language Commissioner. It will suffice to mention here Ottawa's behaviour in court. Ottawa repeatedly intervened in the language litigation of this decade against the language minorities. Ottawa gave the minorities funds to take their grievances to court, and then sent in federal lawyers to knock the minorities down. In the *MacDonald* case,[7] Ottawa submitted, in the words of the federal factum, that "[a] broad and generous interpretation of language rights cannot be used." In that case Ottawa got everything it asked for, including the narrow, stingy interpretation of language rights. This brought language rights expansion to an end in the Supreme Court.

III

Members of the Supreme Court of Canada must have found Canadian constitutional processes deeply anxiety-provoking following Québec's constitutional defeat in 1982. Québec refused to participate in Canada's constitutional processes, boycotting First Ministers' meetings, and opting-out, to the extent possible, of the *Charter of Rights*. Québec's isolation was not attributable alone to the Parti Québécois. The Québec Liberals, in opposition, voted with the Parti Québécois to condemn the patriation reforms. In Government, the Québec liberals thundered in their own way. "No Québec Government", Québec's Minister of Intergovernmental Affairs, Mr. Remillard, stated, "regardless of its political tendencies could sign the *Constitution Act of 1982* in its present form".[8] Mr. Remillard warned that Québec's isolation cannot continue

---

7. *MacDonald* v. *City of Montreal*, [1986] 1 S.C.R. 460.
8. See Remillard, "Rebuilding the Relationship: Québec and Its Confederation Partners", May 9, 1986 in Anne F. Bayefsky, ed., *Canada's Constitution Act 1982 and Amendments* (Toronto and Montreal: McGraw-Hill Ryerson Limited, 1989), Vol. II at 945.

much longer without jeopardizing the very foundation of true federalism. Language rights were an important constitutional axis around which Québec's grievances orbited. In these circumstances, it is entirely understandable the Supreme Court might be rethinking its aggressive imposition of a language rights system on the provinces. The Meech Lake Accord sent the Court an additional signal because the Accord diminishes the fragile status of Francophones outside of Québec. Let us consider just how Meech Lake works against language minorities.

An important implication of the "distinct society" clause is that the rest of Canada is also a distinct society.[9] Alberta Premier Don Getty invoked Meech Lake in this sense to justify abolishing the French language in Alberta.[10] The duality clauses of Meech Lake describe Québec as "a society". By contrast, Francophones outside of Québec are described as a population that is also present elsewhere in Canada. The legal sources of the word "society" suggest an institutional structure through which a community is organized and can act.[11] The legal sources of a population refer to an aggregate of people without such an institutional structure.[12] Meech Lake, in other words, conceives of Francophones outside of Québec as existing without an institutional base. When Meech Lake talks about provinces preserving Francophones outside of Québec, it uses the language of preserving the population, that is French-speaking Canadians without any institutional structure. It does not talk about preserving a society as it does in the case of Québec.[13] It is possible to read the duality clauses as creating an obligation to preserve minority language populations, and populations only. Meech Lake can plausibly mean that Francophones outside of Québec should never become societies; they should be preserved as populations, scattered aggregates of persons without organized institutions. That is the way that Premiers have already read it and used it.

The duality clauses of Meech Lake contain a contrast between the word "preserve" and the words "preserve and promote". Québec has a role to "preserve and promote" its distinct identity; other provinces have a role to "preserve" the presence of the French speakers. The contrast between "preserve and promote" encourages the perception that Québec is the real homeland of Francophones. Those outside of Québec are of secondary significance. This suggests an unflattering constitutional

---

9. Swinton and Rogerson, eds., *Competing Constitutional Visions* (Toronto: Carswell, 1988) at 5.
10. Alberta, *Hansard* (23 June 1988) 1964.
11. *A Preliminary Report of the Royal Commission on Bilingualism and Biculturalism* (Ottawa: Queen's Printer, 1965) at 103.
12. *Ibid.*
13. *Supra*, fn. 9, s. 2.(2)(3).

portrait of Francophones outside of Québec, an unattractive picture which could infect the interpretation of the few constitutional guarantees that Francophone minorities already enjoy.

Meech Lake provides for annual First Ministers' conferences on the constitution. Francophones outside of Québec are not included as an item on the agenda. They can only get on to the agenda by unanimous agreement of the federal government and all provinces. Any premier can veto their inclusion on the constitutional agenda. This is a net loss for Francophone minorities because unanimity has not been necessary to put them on the agenda previously. Senate reform is on the agenda for forthcoming constitutional conferences as proposed under Meech Lake. Francophones outside of Québec should be protected by a requirement that any proposed bill with linguistic implication should require approval by a double majority of the Senate, i.e. approval of a majority of all senators and of a majority of Francophone senators.[14] Francophone minorities are not required to be invited to the constitutional table to discuss Senate reform and they have no obvious proxy around the table to advance their views. So, an issue central to their constitutional development may be decided in their absence, or they may be ignored completely. In sum, Meech Lake concocts an unattractive portrait of linguistic minorities, a further bizarre illustration of the contracting constitutional significance of the language minorities in the constitutional landscape.

IV

Canadian constitutional processes after 1982, as I said, obviously impressed the Supreme Court of Canada. The *Manitoba Language Reference* case[15] was the high-water mark of language rights development, and it really was not all that high. After 1985 the Court did an abrupt about face. Unwilling any longer to challenge Québec, the expanding and dynamic reading of constitutional language rights came to a curt halt. The Court withdrew from serious constitutional review of language controversies. This happened unequivocally in the *MacDonald*[16] and *Société des Acadiens*[17] cases, where the Court agreed with the Government of Canada's submission that a broad and generous interpretation of language rights cannot be sustained. Language rights were portrayed

---

14. See Canada, *Report of Royal Commission on the Economic Union and Development Prospects for Canada, Vol. 3* (Ottawa :Supply and Services Canada, 1985) 91.
15. *Supra*, fn. 6.
16. *Supra*, fn. 7.
17. *Société des Acadiens du Nouveau Brunswick* v. *Association of Parents for Fairness in Education*, [1986] 1 S.C.R. 549.

as a "constitutional minimum". The Court set out on a new path by reasoning in the *Société des Acadiens* case that developments in the area of language rights were to be left to the provinces. If the Court imposed constitutional norms, provinces could not be persuaded to opt into official bilingualism.

If this is the real reason for the Court's aforementioned reading of language rights, the Court seems to have travelled to the other side of the reality principle. The provinces are not in the mood, and never have been in the mood in Canadian history, to advance language rights. Canadian history is a history of bitter, dangerous conflict over language rights as a result of a stingy, vindictive spirit by provincial majorities. It is a dangerous history. Canada's political system cannot control the pathological crises which break out from time to time. Each new language conflict threatens the security of this country. That is why jurisdiction in language conflicts is given to the courts for constitutional review. The conflict is channelled into legal procedure; the courts are directed to enforce a strict, consistent line.

Just how misguided was the Supreme Court's new approach, to leave language controversies as much as possible to provincial politics, became apparent almost immediately in Father André Mercure's case.[18] The Court ruled that French survives in Saskatchewan but without constitutional protection, presumably under the Court's newly discovered principle that provincial politics should advance language rights. This ruling invited the Saskatchewan Legislature to advance language rights by making an appropriate deal with the Fransaskois. That was thoughtful. The Court should have realized that its ruling also invited the Saskatchewan Legislature to abolish French.

The Court's judgment set Canada off on another serious round of language pathology. Predictably, Saskatchewan abolished French,[19] although it sugar-coated its actions with vague promises to implement some French rights in the future. "The Fransaskois were lucky", said Premier Grant Devine.[20] Mr. Mulroney blamed Mr. Trudeau for the plight of the Fransaskois,[21] a remark that only provoked laughter from the President of the Fransaskois, Mr. Baudais. Québecers stood by impotently, watching while their tiny Fransaskois cousins were mauled in the grizzly Saskatchewan political machine.

---

18. *R.* v. *Mercure*, [1988] 1 S.C.R. 243.
19. *The Language Act*, S.S. 1988, c. L-6.1
20. *Globe and Mail* (20 April 1988) A-1.
21. *Ibid.*

The journalists predictably poured fuel on the flames by asking whether Québec would punish its Anglophone minority in retaliation. Two wrongs of course do not make a right, but the journalists rightly sensed a deep sense of frustration and anger gnawing away in Québec. To make matters worse, Québecers watched on television, while their Premier, Mr. Bourassa, sat with Saskatchewan's Premier Devine, praising Devine's stinginess to the Fransaskois as "prudent" and "responsible", and flattered Mr. Divine by calling him one of the most dynamic leaders in the country.[22] This prompted the president of the Association Canadienne Française de l'Alberta, Mr. Ares, to cancel a planned meeting with Mr. Bourassa, calling Mr. Bourassa a "traitor".[23] Mr. Bourassa was unfazed. He advised Alberta Francophones to trust their Premier, Mr. Getty. His words were: "Mr. Getty was one of the strongest supporters of Québec in reaching an agreement on the Meech Lake Accord. Why will you not trust him?"[24] Mr. Getty told Mr. Bourassa to mind his own business.[25] Then Mr. Getty abolished the French language in Alberta.[26] While western language problems raged out of control, Québecers felt not only wronged, they felt humiliated.

The language issue caused problems with acceptance of the Meech Lake Accord. As Canadians turned away from the Meech Lake Accord in increasing numbers, Québecers felt increasingly rejected, and powerless. Even Québec's minimal five conditions accommodated in Meech Lake appeared unobtainable. The climate of opinion in Québec turned nasty.

At this point, the Supreme Court of Canada stumbled again into the picture. The Court was asked to invalidate the French-only requirements in Bill 101 and to annul Québec's wholesale opting out of the *Charter of Rights*.[27] In keeping with its new approach, the Court returned the issue to provincial politics by rejecting federalist arguments invalidating Bill 101 under the *Charter* while inviting and legitimating use of the nonobstant clause. This opened the door immediately to an acrimonious debate within and without Québec, a further exercise in language pathology which still continues. Québec's Anglophone minority is now insecure, fearfully experiencing the shell-shocked dread upsetting Francophone minorities in other provinces.[28] The only comic relief in the entire picture has been provided by Prime Minister Mulroney. He

---

22. *Globe and Mail* (14 April 1988).
23. *The Citizen (Ottawa)* (14 April 1988).
24. *Ibid.*
25. *Globe and Mail* (11 April 1988) A3.
26. *Languages Act*, S.A. 1988, c. L-7.5.
27. *Ford* v. *Attorney General of Québec* (1988), 54 D.L.R. (4th) 577.
28. *The Citizen (Ottawa)*, December 19, 1988, p. A-3.

conjured up Mr. Trudeau again to blame him for the problems. Nevertheless the situation is unhealthy. Canada's seam is opening. Premier McKenna of New Brunswick summed up the situation. "Canadians", he said, "are adopting an attitude of to hell" with minorities that threatens to divide the nation and pit Anglophones against Francophones. Parliament, the legislatures, and the courts, have no serious policy to counteract assimilation.

V

In the absence of a determined linguistic policy to alter demographic forces, the numbers tell everything. The numbers are clear in Canada. They have been clear for a long time. They are consistent. The trends are unmistakable. They tell us where we are going. We are most of the way there already. Whether measured by maternal language or home language, Francophones outside of Québec are declining in real numbers and as a percentage of total provincial populations. Whether measured by maternal language, or home language, Anglophones in Québec are declining in real numbers and as a percentage of the total provincial population. The decline is rapid, steep, and alarming. The assimilation rates are extraordinary. Some examples might help to illustrate what is happening and what has happened.[29] In Manitoba, 40,000 people used French in the home in 1971. In 1981 that number dropped to 29,000; in 1986 to 23,000. In Saskatchewan, 16,000 people used French as the home language in 1971. In 1981 that number dropped to 9,000; in 1986 to 6,000. In the fifteen years between 1971 and 1986, as measured by language used in the home, Anglophones in Québec declined from 888,000 to 676,000 people, a 24 percent drop in the Anglophone population.

This is were we are going. A split Canada: French, Québec, English outside Québec. We are most of the way there already. Now is the time for a thorough re-evaluation of official languages policy. The revised Federal Act[30] is nothing more than the 1969 policy a little enlarged. The Meech Lake Accord contributes nothing to this problem, and probably exacerbates it by contracting linguistic minorities. These policy responses are inappropriate to our new realities. These are hard truths, but they are truths. Our new situation requires us to reinvent our linguistic future and to imagine ourselves through new perspectives, which reality requires and makes possible.

---

29. The numbers here reflect a summary prepared by the Federation des Francophones Hors Québec. See also Statistics Canada, 1971 *Census* (Ottawa: Supply and Services, (1974) (92-766) Table 27, and Statistics Canada, *Language Retention and Transfer* (Ottawa: Supply and Services, 1989) Table 1.
30. *Official Languages Act*, S.C. 1988, c. 38.

Partie V / Part V

Sociétés multilingues : structures et stratégies

Il existe divers modèles démocratiques réconciliant les sociétés linguistiquement fragmentées. Le modèle de « consociation » explique comment certains pays ont maintenu leur stabilité politique malgré les divisions et fragmentations de ce type. Selon Arend Lijphart, le modèle en question peut assumer deux formes politiques : celle d'une grande coalition parmi les groupes ou celle d'une autonomie segmentée, comme dans un État fédéral par exemple. Lijphart propose un système de représentation proportionnelle où les groupes définissent eux-mêmes leur propre circonscription. Il recommande plus particulièrement ce modèle pour l'Afrique du Sud, pays profondément divisé.

La Suisse constitue l'archétype de la démocratie de consociation. Selon Kenneth McRae, c'est une des démocraties les mieux gouvernées du monde. McRae examine les caractéristiques qui expliquent son succès durable malgré la multiplicité des groupes linguistiques qui la composent : égalité des langues et distribution du pouvoir politique parmi les régions linguistiques.

Le cas de la Suisse suggère que les groupes linguistiques peuvent prospérer à condition d'avoir une assise territoriale significative. Jean Laponce décrit comment, dans certains pays, les groupes linguistiques vivent des conflits constants, au rythme de leur ascendance et de leur déclin. Pour résister à l'assimilation, les groupes linguistiques minoritaires suisses ont été portés à se concentrer géographiquement afin de contrôler l'usage de la langue sur leur propre territoire. Le Canada, quant à lui, a choisi plus récemment de promouvoir les droits linguistiques rattachés à la personne plutôt qu'à une région donnée, et cela à la largeur du pays. Cette situation tend à augmenter les conflits linguistiques alors qu'une solution territoriale aurait été plus harmonieuse.

Gurston Dacks démontre en quoi le modèle de consociation ou d'association [partnership] peut tenir compte des pouvoirs politiques qui émergent dans le nord du Canada. Les immenses distances géographiques qui séparent les divers groupes linguistiques, chacun d'eux contrôlant sa propre base territoriale et tous entrecroisant des liens économiques, offrent une structure sociale favorable au modèle d'association. Tout comme les chefs autochtones qui aspirent à retrouver leur souveraineté, les élites non autochtones réaliseront peut-être que l'unité dans l'association est une solution appropriée, préférable à la division.

Multilingual Societies : Structures and Strategies

There exists a variety of democratic models for uniting societies fragmented along linguistic lines. The «consociational» model helps to explain how certain countries have maintained political stability amidst such division and fragmentation. According to Arend Lijphardt, the model can take two political forms : one of a grand coalition amongst groups or one of segmented autonomy, such as in a federal state. Lijphardt proposes a system of proportional representation where groups define for themselves their own constituency. More particularly, he proposes this model for the deeply divided country of South Africa.

Switzerland is considered an archetype of consociational democracy. According to Kenneth McRae, it is one of the best governed democracies in the world. McRae discusses the features which have led to its continued success notwithstanding the multiplicity of its language groups. They include the equality of languages and the distribution of political power amongst linguistic regions.

As the Swiss case suggests, language groups can thrive as long as there exists some meaningful territorial base. Jean Laponce discusses how language groups in certain countries are locked in conflicts resulting in their ascendancy or decline. In order to fend off assimilation, minority language groups, such as in Switzerland, will tend to concentrate geographically in order to control language use in their own territory. Canada, on the other hand, has chosen more recently to advance language rights which are vested in the person rather than in a region, providing for language rights nation-wide. This tends to increase conflict between the languages in dispute and may have been at the expense of the more peaceful territorial solution.

Gurston Dacks shows how the consociational, or partnership, model may be appropriate to accommodate the emerging political powers in Canada's north. The large geographic distances between language speakers, each controlling their own territorial base, and cross-cutting economic ties, provide a social structure conducive to the partnership model. The non-aboriginal elites, together with native leadership seeking to regain aboriginal sovereignty, may find that unity in partnership is an appropriate alternative to division amongst themselves.

SELF-DETERMINATION VERSUS PRE-DETERMINATION OF ETHNIC MINORITIES IN POWER-SHARING SYSTEMS

Arend Lijphart

INTRODUCTION

In this paper, I want to make three main points. The first of these is that the basic principles of consociational democracy — or power-sharing democracy — are so obviously the appropriate answer to the problems of deeply divided (plural) societies that both politicians and social scientists have repeatedly and independently re-invented and re-discovered them. Secondly, these principles must be thought of as broad guidelines that can be implemented in a variety of ways — not all of the which, however, are of equal merit and can be equally recommended to divided societies. My third and most important point will be that an especially important set of alternatives in applying the consociational principles is the choice between self-determination and pre-determination of the constituent groups in the power-sharing system, that is, the groups that will be the collective actors among whom power will be shared.

To give a brief preview of the last proposition, the terms "self-determination" and "pre-determination" describe the alternatives very well and in an almost self-explanatory way, but my use of the former differs from the most common usage. Self-determination deviates from the most common usage. Self-determination deviates from the concept of *"national* self-determination" — the idea that nations should have the right to form separate sovereign states — in two fundamental respects. It refers to a method or process that gives various rights to groups *within* the existing state — for instance, autonomy rather than sovereignty — and it allows these groups to manifest themselves instead of deciding in advance on the identity of the groups. Needless to say, my concept of pre-determination is completely unrelated to the superficially similar theological concept of predestination. Like self-determination, it refers to an internal process, but in contrast with self-determination, it means

153

that the groups that are to share power are identified in advance. Both in contemporary and historical cases of consociationalism, pre-determination is more common, but I shall argue that self-determination has a number of great advantages and ought to be given much more attention by constitutional engineers who are trying to devise solutions for divided societies.

As a final introductory remark, let me define a few other basic concepts. I shall use the terms *deeply divided society* and *plural society* as synonyms. A plural society is a society that is sharply divided along religious, ideological, linguistic, cultural, ethnic, or racial lines into virtually separate subsocieties with their own political parties, interest groups, and media of communication. These subsocieties will be referred to as *segments*. As the definition of plural society indicates, the segments can differ from each other in several ways : in terms of religion, language, ethnicity, race, and so on. The most common of these is *ethnicity*, but the different categories overlap considerably. Ethnic differences imply cultural differences and often linguistic differences as well. Furthermore, cultural differences frequently include religious differences. Even when, as in the plural societies of Lebanon and Northern Ireland, the segments are mainly described in religious terms, the differences between them encompass a great deal more and can also be legitimately described as ethnic differences. I shall therefore make the general assumption that segments are ethnic segments and, in particular, ethnic minorities. Finally, let me emphasize that I shall use the terms *consociational* democracy and *power-sharing* democracy synonymously and interchangeably.

RE-DISCOVERING AND RE-INVENTING CONSOCIATIONALISM

Three answers have been given to the question of how to provide peace and democracy in plural societies. The first is that this is an impossible task : successful democracy is assumed to require a minimum of homogeneity and consensus and hence cannot be established in plural societies. This answer has been given by social scientists from John Stuart Mill to Alvin Rabushka and Kenneth A. Shepsle. Mill states :

> Free institutions are next to impossible in a country made up of different nationalities... Among people without fellow-feeling, especially if they read and speak different languages, the united public opinion, necessary to the working of representative government, cannot exist.[1]

---

1. John Stuart Mill, *Considerations on Representative Government* (New York : Liberal Arts Press, 1958) at 230.

On the basis of similar arguments (although couched in modern game-theoretic terminology), Rabushka and Shepsle contend that "stable democracy [cannot] be maintained in the face of cultural diversity" and that to argue otherwise reveals wishful thinking.[2]

The main problem with the Mill and Rabushka-Shepsle argument is not that it is not logical but that there are numerous cases of plural societies where democracy has worked reasonably well. The argument requires two amendments. First, it must be stated in terms of probability democracy is less likely to be successful in plural than in homogeneous societies instead of in absolute and apodictic possible/impossible terms. Second, as I shall show in greater detail below, social scientists are not the only people who can understand the logic of this proposition. Politicians in plural societies can also grasp it and may want to try to take special measures to strengthen the probability of successful democracy. This means that the proposition can be turned into a self-denying prediction.

The second answer is that democracy in divided societies is possible provided that there is a majority that is firmly in control. A good example is Northern Ireland in the period from 1921 to 1972 when political power was firmly in the hands of the Protestant majority segment.[3] My objection to this second answer is not that it is empirically incorrect but that it seems highly questionable that we can speak of democracy in such cases. In Northern Ireland, Protestant majority rule spelled majority dictatorship rather than democracy in anything but the most superficial sense of the term.

The third answer is that peace and democracy are indeed possible in even the most deeply divided societies, provided that, instead of majority rule, consociational democracy is used. I discovered this answer in the late 1960s on the basis of my case study of the Netherlands and a subsequent extension of this study to Belgium, Switzerland, and Austria.[4] I have defined consociational democracy in terms of four basic principles: two primary principles (grand coalition and segmental autonomy) and two supplementary or secondary principles (proportionality and minority veto).

---

2. Alvin Rabushka and Kenneth A. Shepsle, "Political Entrepreneurship and Patterns of Democratic Instability in Plural Societies" (April 1971) 12:4 *Race* at 462.
3. See Ian Lustick, "Stability in Deeply Divided Societies: Consociationalism versus Control" (April 1979) 31:3 *World Politics* at 325-44.
4. Arend Lijphart, *The Politics of Accommodation: Pluralism and Democracy in the Netherlands* (Berkeley: University of California Press, 1968); Arend Lijphart, "Typologies of Democratic Systems" (1968) 1:1 *Comparative Political Studies* at 3-44.

A grand coalition is an executive in which the political leaders of all significant segments participate. It may take various institutional forms. The most straightforward form is that of a grand coalition cabinet in a parliamentary system. In presidential systems, it may be achieved by distributing the presidency and other high offices among the different segments. These arrangements may be strengthened by broadly constituted councils or committees with important coordinating and advisory functions.

Segmental autonomy means the delegation of as much decision-making as possible to the separate segments. It complements the grand coalition principle: on all issues of common interest, the decisions should be made jointly by the segments; on all other issues, decision-making should be left to each segment. A special form of segmental autonomy that is particularly suitable for divided societies with geographically concentrated segments is federalism. If the segments are geographically intermixed, segmental autonomy will have to take a mainly non-territorial form.

Proportionality is the basic standard of political representation, civil service appointments, and allocation of public funds. As a principle of political representation, it is especially important as a guarantee for the fair representation of minority segments. There are two extensions of the proportionality representation of small segments and parity of representation (when the minority of minorities are over-represented to such an extent that they reach a level of equality with the majority or largest group).

The minority veto is the ultimate weapon that minorities need to protect their vital interests. Even when a minority segment participates in a grand coalition executive, it may be overruled or out-voted by the majority. This may not present a problem when only minor issues are being decided, but when a minority's vital interests are at stake, the veto provides essential protection.

While I was discovering consociationalism in the Netherlands, two other scholars were independently discovering the same phenomenon in Austria and Switzerland: Jürg Steiner in the latter country and Gerhard Lehmbruch in a comparative study of the two countries.[5] But I should really use the word "re-discover," because another social scientist had preceded us by a few years: Sir Arthur Lewis in his pathbreaking short

---

5. Jürg Steiner, *Amicable Agreement versus Majority Rule: Conflict Resolution in Switzerland* (Chapel Hill: University of North Carolina Press, 1974); Gerhard Lehmbruch, *Proporzdemokratie: Politisches System und politische Kultur in der Schweiz und in Österreich* (Tübingen: Mohr, 1967).

book on West Africa.[6] Lewis defined the kind of democratic system he deemed desirable for the West African plural societies — which he did not give a distinct label — more narrowly than I have above, but it is clearly consociational: elections by proportional representation (leading to a multiparty system of ethnically based parties), broad and inclusive coalition cabinets, and autonomy for the different ethnic groups by means of a decentralized federal system. The term "consociation" goes back much farther; it was coined in the early seventeenth century by political theorist Johannes Althusius.[7] But Althusius was mainly an early federalist thinker and he cannot be regarded as a consociationalist. Lewis is clearly the intellectual originator of the theory.

What I have just stated requires one slight modification. Lewis formulated his concept of democracy on the basis of what he thought was needed, but not practised, in West Africa apparently in complete ignorance of the empirical examples of power-sharing elsewhere in the world. This means that he did not discover it; he invented it. Or, more precisely, he re-invented it. Politicians in different countries and at different times had already invented or re-invented it before him. The prize for the original invention should probably be given to the "peaceful settlement" of 1917 in the Netherlands, which was a comprehensive, thoroughly consociational arrangement, adopted at the same time that full democracy was being adopted.[8] Subsequently, it was re-invented in Lebanon in 1943 (National Pact), Austria in 1945 (grand coalition in what Lehmbruch has called "proportional democracy"), Malaysia in 1955 (government by the Alliance), Colombia in 1958 (the system of co-participation and pre-set alternation in the presidency), Cyprus in 1960 (the independence constitution), and Belgium in 1970 (drastic constitutional changes setting up a kind of "linguistic federalism").[9] What is striking about these repeated re-inventions of consociationalism is that, although they are substantively so similar, they appear to have occurred completely independently of each other. There is no evidence that the later instances of the establishment of power-sharing were based on the lessons of earlier cases. The fact that, without the benefit of social learning, plural societies have repeatedly opted for consociational democracy as a solution to the problem of deep divisions, adds considerably to the strength of consociationalism as a general model.

6. W. Arthur Lewis, *Politics in West Africa* (London: Allen and Unwin, 1965).
7. Johannes Althusius, *Politica Methodice Digesta* (1603).
8. See also Hans Daalder, "The Consociational Democracy Theme" (July 1974) 26:4 *World Politics* at 604-21.
9. See Arend Lijphart, *Democracy in Plural Societies: A Comparative Exploration* (New Haven: Yale University Press, 1977) passim.

VARIETIES OF POWER-SHARING

In my previous writings, I have emphasized that consociational democracy does not mean one specific set of rules and institutions.[10] Instead, it means a general type of democracy defined in terms of four broad principles, all of which can be applied in a variety of ways. For instance, as indicated earlier, the grand coalition can be a cabinet in a parliamentary system or a coalitional arrangement of a president and other top office-holders in a presidential system of government. The Swiss seven-member federal executive, which is based on a hybrid of parliamentary and presidential principles, is an additional example. Segmental autonomy may take the role of territorial federalism or of autonomy for segments that are not defined in geographical terms. Proportional results in elections may be achieved by the various systems of formal proportional representation (PR) or by several non-PR methods, such as Lebanon's method of requiring ethnically balanced slates in multi-member district plurality elections.[11] The minority veto can be either an absolute or a suspensive veto, and it may be applied either to all decisions or to only certain specified kinds of decisions, such as matters of culture and education. There is also the general difference, applicable to all four consociational principles, between laying down the basic rules of power-sharing in formal documents — such as constitutions, laws, or semi-public agreements — and relying on merely informal and unwritten agreements and understandings among the leaders of the segments.

I have come to believe that one of the most important differences between consociational arrangements — and also one of the most important choices that consociational engineers have to make — is the difference between pre-determination and self-determination of the segments of a plural society. Should these segments be identified in advance, and should power-sharing be implemented as a system in which these pre-determined segments share power? This appears to be the simplest way of instituting consociationalism, although, as I shall show below, it entails several problems and drawbacks. The alternative, which is necessarily somewhat more complicated, is to set up a system in which

---

10. See Arend Lijphart, "Consociation: The Model and Its Applications in Divided Societies," in Desmond Rea, ed., *Political Co-Operation in Divided Societies: A Series of Papers Relevant to the Conflict in Northern Ireland* (Dublin: Gill and Macmillan, 1982) at 166-186. See also Heinz Kloss, "Territorial prinzip, Bekenntnixprinzip, Verfügungsprinzip: Über die Möglichkeiten der Abgrenzung der Volklichen Zugehrigkeit" (1965) 22 *Europa Ethnica* at 52-73.
11. Arend Lijphart, "Proportionality by Non-PR Methods: Ethnic Representation in Belgium, Cyprus, Lebanon, New Zealand, West Germany, and Zimbabwe" in Bernard Grofman and Arend Lijphart, eds., *Electoral Laws and Their Political Consequences* (New York: Agathon Press, 1986) at 113-123.

the segments are allowed, and even encouraged, to emerge spontaneously — and hence to define themselves instead of being pre-defined.

The crucial importance of this set of alternatives has become especially clear to me as a result of my thinking about the best way of setting up a democratic power-sharing system in South Africa. The first problem, of course, is to induce the different groups in South Africa to start negotiations on a peaceful and democratic solution for their country, and the second problem will be to secure agreement on the principle of power-sharing. Assuming that these problems can be solved, I have tried to address the next question: what kind of power-sharing system should be adopted? Here the main problem is that, while there is broad agreement that South Africa is a plural society, the identification of the segments is both objectively difficult and politically controversial. The root of this problem is that the South African system of minority rule has long relied on an official and strict classification of its citizens in four racial groups (African, White, Coloured, and Asian) and the further classification of the Africans into about a dozen ethnic groups. The racial classification has served the allocation of basic rights: for instance, the current "tricameral" system allows Whites, Coloureds, and Asians to elect separate chambers of parliament, and excludes Africans from the national franchise. The ethnic classification has been the basis of the "grand apartheid" system of setting up, and encouraging the eventual independence, of a series of ethnic homelands (formerly called Bantustans).

As a result of this policy of artificially forcing people into racial and ethnic categories, it has become quite unclear what the true dividing lines in the society are. The South African government appears to continue to think mainly in terms of race when it speaks of group rights and a sharing of power among groups. My own feeling is that the ethnic groups, including the two White ethnic groups of Afrikaners and English-speakers, are the strongest candidates to be considered the segments of the South African plural society, but I admit right away that the situation is more complicated. For instance, the English-speaking Whites appear to be a residual group rather than a cohesive and self-conscious ethnic segment. Another example concerns the Coloureds: should they be considered a separate segment or, since most of them speak Afrikaans and have an Afrikaans cultural background, do they form a single ethnic segment together with the White Afrikaners? Others have argued that modernization, industrialization, and urbanization have had a "melting pot" effect, and that South Africa today is no longer a plural society and has become a "common society".[12]

---

12. Heribert Adam and Kogila Moodley, *South Africa Without Apartheid: Dismantling Racial Domination* (Berkeley: University of California Press, 1986) esp. at 196-214.

Furthermore, the White government's insistence on African ethnic differences in connection with its widely despised homelands policy has had the ironic effect of making ethnicity highly suspect among most Africans. This sentiment is expressed clearly in Archbishop Desmond Tutu's statement: "We Blacks (most of us) execrate ethnicity with all our being."[13] Similarly, the African National Congress, the most powerful Black party in South Africa (although officially banned), both rejects ethnicity, since it regards ethnicity as a White divide-and-rule policy, and denies even its existence and hence its political relevance.

How can we resolve these disagreements about the identity of the segments and about whether South Africa is a plural society or not? My answer is that these disagreements do not need to be resolved, since we can design a consociational system on the basis of self-determined segments. First of all, I recommend elections by a relatively pure form of PR which will allow representation for even very small parties. Its rationale is based on the definition of a plural society that I gave earlier. This definition implies that one of the tests of whether a society is genuinely plural is whether or not its political parties are organized along segmental lines. We can turn this logic around: if we know that a society is plural but cannot identify the segments with complete confidence, we can take our cue from the political parties that form under conditions of free association and competition. PR is the optimal electoral system for allowing the segments to manifest themselves in the form of political parties. The beauty of PR is not just that it yields proportional results and permits minority representation — two important advantages from a consociational perspective — but also that it permits the segments to define themselves. Hence the adoption of PR obviates the need for any prior sorting of divergent claims about the segmental composition of South Africa or any other plural society. The proof of segmental identity is electoral success. We can go one step further: PR elections can also provide an answer to the question of whether South Africa is a plural society or not. If it is a plural society, the successful parties will be mainly segmental (and presumably ethnic) parties; if it is not a plural society, the parties that will emerge will be non-segmental policy-oriented parties. PR treats all groups, segmental or non-segmental, in a completely equal and even-handed way.

All of the consociational principles can now be instituted on the basis of self-determination. A grand coalition can be prescribed by requiring that the cabinet be composed of all parties of a specified minimum size in parliament; since these will be segmental parties, the

---

13. Desmond Mpilo Tutu, *Hope and Suffering: Sermons and Speeches* (Grand Rapids, Michigan: Eerdmans, 1984) at 121.

cabinet will automatically be an inter-segmental grand coalition. The proportional allocation of public service jobs and public funds can also be based on the relative strengths that the several segments have demonstrated in the PR elections. And instead of granting a minority veto to all pre-determined segments, such a veto can be given to any group of legislators above a certain specified percentage.

Segmental autonomy can be organized along similar lines. Any cultural group that wishes to have internal autonomy can be given the right to establish a "cultural council," a publicly recognized body equivalent to a state in a federation. One of its main responsibilities will be the administration of schools for those who wish to receive an education according to the group's linguistic and cultural traditions. The voluntary self-segregation that such schools entail is acceptable as long as the option of multicultural and multiethnic education is also made available and provided that all schools are treated equally. It should be emphasized that this kind of non-territorial self-determined segmental autonomy can either be an alternative or an addition to geographically-based federalism. The two are eminently compatible. In the South African case, territorial federalism makes a great deal of sense because many of the ethnic segments have clear geographical strongholds and also because of the great diversity of the country in other respects. At the same time, however, there is so much group inter-mixture that territorial federalism by itself is insufficient to satisfy the demands of segmental autonomy.

In their book *South Africa Without Apartheid* Heribert Adam and Kogila Moodley make similar recommendations.[14] And such proposals have also been formally placed on the political agenda of South Africa by the Progressive Federal Party (PFP). In its constitutional plan adopted in 1978, the PFP proposes the following procedure to effect a grand coalition cabinet: The lower house of a bicameral legislature will be elected by PR, and the lower house will in turn elect the prime minister by majority vote. Then a power-sharing cabinet will be formed by requiring that the prime minister appoint cabinet members "proportional to the strength of the various political parties" in the lower house and that "in doing so the Prime Minister will have to negotiate with the leaders of the relevant parties". Segmental autonomy is proposed by the PFP in the following self-determined form: "A cultural group may establish a Cultural Council to assist in maintaining and promoting its cultural interests and apply to have that council registered with the Federal Constitutional Court". These cultural councils will be publicly recognized

---

14. *Supra*, note 12 at 215-263.

bodies almost on a par with the states in the federal system that the PFP recommends; in the federal senate, where the states will be represented by equal numbers of senators, each cultural council will be able to name one senator, too.[15]

The PFP proposal of cultural councils was inspired by the Belgian example of non-territorial federalism (or, more accurately, partly non-territorial federalism), but it differs significantly from the Belgian model in that the Belgian cultural councils are based on pre-determination: three, and only three, councils — Dutch, French and German — were established. Similarly, the Belgian constitution prescribes that the cabinet be composed of equal numbers of Dutch-speakers and French-speakers — again an example of pre-determination of segments. There are a number of other well-known examples of pre-determined segments, particularly the Greek and Turkish segments which are explicitly specified in the 1960 Cypriot constitution and Maronites, Sunnis, Shiites, and other religious sects recognized in the 1943 National Pact in Lebanon. However, the pre-1970 Belgian system of inter-religious and inter-ideological consociationalism was largely of the self-determined kind. The same generalization applies to the Dutch, Swiss and Austrian cases of consociational democracy.

A final, particularly interesting, but much less well-known example of self-determination is the 1925 Law of Cultural Autonomy in Estonia. Under its terms, each ethnic minority with more than 3,000 formally registered members had the right to establish autonomous institutions under the authority of a cultural council elected by the minority. This council could organize, administer, and supervise minority schools and other cultural institutions such as libraries and theatres, and it could issue decrees and raise taxes for these purposes. The councils also received state and local subsidies, and public funding was provided for the minority schools at the same level as for Estonian schools. The German and Jewish minorities quickly took advantage of the law and set up their own autonomous cultural authorities. As Georg von Rauch writes, "these cultural authorities soon proved their worth, and the Estonian government was able to claim, with every justification, that it had found an exemplary solution to the problem of its minorities".[16]

ADVANTAGES OF SELF-DETERMINATION

In the case of South Africa, because of special South African conditions and circumstances, self-determination of the segments is

---

15. Arend Lijphart, *Power-Sharing in South Africa* (Berkeley: Institute of International Studies, University of California, 1985) at 66-73.
16. Georg von Rauch, *The Baltic States: Estonia, Latvia, Lithuania — The Years of Independence 1917-1940* (Berkeley: University of California Press, 1974) at 141-142.

almost certainly the only way in which a consociation can be successfully established and operated. In most other cases, self-determination and pre-determination may both be reasonable options for consociational engineers. I would argue, however, that self-determination has a number of great advantages over pre-determination and hence that, unless there are compelling reasons to opt for pre-determination, the presumption should be in favor of self-determination. In this final section of my paper, let me list the advantages of self-determination:

1. The very first point in favor of self-determination is that it avoids the problem of invidious comparisons and discriminatory choices. Deciding which groups are to be the recognized segments in a power-sharing system necessarily entails the decision of which groups are not going to be recognized. In Lebanon, for instance, should the Moslem and Christian communes or the Maronites, Sunni, Shiite, Greek Orthodox, etc., sub-communes be made into the basic building blocks of the power-sharing system? In Belgium, since the small German-speaking minority was given its own cultural council, should not the Spanish, Turkish, and Moroccan minorities be given the same privilege? Even in cases that appear to be completely clear and uncontroversial, I would still argue that self-determination has no disadvantages compared with pre-determination in this respect.

2. The problem of potential discrimination is especially serious in countries where there are two or more large segments, which will obviously be recognized as participants in the power-sharing system, but also one or more very small minorities. These minorities run the risk of being overlooked, disregarded, or worse. Cyprus provides a good illustration. During the negotiations about the constitution and the electoral law, the question of how to define membership in the Greek majority community and in the Turkish minority community and the question of how to deal with the other, much smaller, minorities such as the Armenians and Maronites were discussed with "extraordinary intensity," as S. G. Xydis reports. Xydis speculates that the Turkish Cypriots may have been "anxious to prevent any other minority in Cyprus from acquiring the status similar to that of the Turkish community with all its political implications".[17]

3. Pre-determination entails not only potential discrimination against groups but, as a rule, also the assignment of individuals to specific groups. Individuals may well object to such labelling. If fact, the very principle of officially registering individuals according to ethnic or other group

---

17. Stephen G. Xydis, *Cyprus: Reluctant Republic* (The Hague: Mouton, 1973) at 490-492.

membership may be controversial, offensive, or even completely unacceptable to many citizens. Self-determination avoids the entire problem of placing people in groups and of establishing procedures for making decisions in individual cases. The New Zealand system of guaranteed Maori representation in parliament can serve as an example here. For many years, Maoris were placed on separate voter registers and voted for Maori candidates in four exclusively Maori districts. This entailed the problem of deciding whether particular individuals should be placed on Maori or the general voter registers and the additional problem that many Maoris preferred not to be singled out for this special treatment. In order to alleviate these problems, it was decided that the special Maori seats would be retained but that, for Maoris, registration on the Maori register would be optional. Clearly the entire problem could be solved by the introduction of PR; reserved Maori seats would no longer be necessary. This is what New Zealand's Royal Commission on the Electoral System proposed in 1986.[18]

4. Self-determination gives equal chances not only to all ethnic or other segments, large or small, in a plural society but also to groups and individuals who explicitly reject the idea that society should be organized on a segmental basis. In the Lebanese case, Theodor Hanf has suggested that the consociational arrangement could be strengthened considerably if secularly-oriented groups and individuals could be recognized on a par with the traditional religious communities:

> A formula which makes group membership optional instead of obligatory could perhaps reduce the fear of those who wish to preserve their group identity, and perhaps prevent pressure being exerted upon those who do not wish to define themselves as members of a specific community but as Lebanese.[19]

A system of self-determination would obviously make this possible. In the Netherlands, the self-determined system of segmental schools, primarily designed to accommodate the main religious groups, has also been taken advantage of by small secular groups interested in particular educational philosophies to establish, for instance, Montessori schools.

5. In systems of pre-determination, there is a strong temptation to fix the relative shares of representation and other privileges for the segments on a permanent or semi-permanent basis. Examples are the 1:1 (Dutch-French) ratio of representation in the Belgian cabinet, the 7:3 (Greek-Turkish) ratio in the Cypriot cabinet and legislature, and

---

18. Arend Lijphart, "The Demise of the Last Westminster System? Comments on the Report of New Zealand's Royal Commission on the Electoral System" (August 1987) 6:2 *Electoral Studies* at 97-103.

19. Theodor Hanf, "The 'Political Secularization' Issue in Lebanon" in *The Annual Review of the Social Science of Religion*, Vol. 5 (Amsterdam: Mouton, 1981) at 249.

the 6:5 (Christian-Moslem) ratio in the Lebanese parliament. Especially in Lebanon, this fixed ratio has become extremely controversial and it is one of the underlying causes of the breakdown of consociationalism in that country. Self-determination has the advantage of being completely flexible, since it is based on the numbers of people supporting the different parties and registering as members of cultural groups. It is naturally and continually self-adjusting.

6. Even when ethnic groups are geographically concentrated, the boundaries between different ethnic groups never perfectly divide these groups from each other. This means that territorial federalism can never be a perfect answer to the requirements of ethnic and cultural autonomy. And, if we opt for autonomy on a non-territorial — that is, individual — basis, the most satisfactory method is to let the individuals determine their group membership for themselves. This consideration is becoming more and more important as individual mobility in modern societies increases and dilutes the geographical concentration of ethnic groups.

7. Finally, let me make an argument which is partly at variance with the main thrust of my reasoning so far. In many cases, the main segments of a plural society may be absolutely clear and uncontroversial, and these segments may want to be recognized as formally and specifically as possible. In these circumstances, it may make sense to use a combination of pre-determination and self-determination: for instance, a two-tier system of pre-determination of the large segments and self-determination of any other group that may aspire to similar, though not necessarily identical, rights of representation and autonomy. While my main argument remains that self-determination is to be preferred to pre-determination, many of the advantages of self-determination can be attained by using self-determination as a complementary method to pre-determination.

Are there any disadvantages to self-determination? The only genuine drawback is that it precludes the application of the principle of minority overrepresentation. As indicated earlier, the principle of proportionality is already favorable to minorities, especially small minorities, but it may be extended even further by giving minorities more than proportional representation. The 7:3 ratio in Cyprus is an example of such overrepresentation since the actual population ration of the Greek and Turkish segments is closer to 8:2. The advantage that minorities derive from overrepresentation should not be exaggerated, however. The stronger protection for minorities in power-sharing systems is provided by guaranteed representation, guaranteed autonomy, and, if necessary, the use of the minority veto. Compared with these strong weapons, overrepresentation is no more than a marginal benefit.

PRECEPTS FOR LINGUISTIC PEACE: THE CASE OF SWITZERLAND*

Kenneth D. McRae

It is quite probable that Switzerland is the best governed country in the world. I shall not try to prove this statement, but I can state with some confidence that it is the best governed, by a considerable margin, of the twelve Western democracies that I have seen and studied at first hand. In my view, and by my criteria of excellence, Switzerland is about as far ahead of Canada in its quality of democracy as Canada is ahead of the average Latin American republic. This superiority should not really surprise us. If we follow conventional dates, the Swiss polity has been developing for some 699 years, that is, since the original Treaty of Alliance of 1291. On a similar time scale, our own Canadian polity now is roughly where Switzerland was at the time of the Reformation, which was a period of much pain and strife for the Swiss Confederation.

From the current Swiss Constitution, we learn relatively little about Swiss language arrangements. A rather terse Article 116 informs us that there are three *official* languages (French, German, Italian) and four national languages (the three official languages plus Romansh). Another article requires all three official language groups to be represented on the Swiss supreme court, the Federal Tribunal. To see how language arrangements really work, one must look at some relatively scanty ordinary legislation, at a few key judicial decisions, at unwritten customs, and — perhaps most of all — at the spirit of the Swiss political system in a wider sense.

My brief sketch today will present a few essentials of that system as it applies to the peaceful co-existence of the four constitutionally recognized Swiss language communities. One can treat these essentials

* The broader research project upon which these remarks are based has been supported by the Canada Council's Killam Program and by the Social Sciences and Humanities Research Council.

as stemming from two broad principles of Swiss public life: the absolute legal equality of the official languages, and the decentralized quality of the Swiss federal system. I believe most aspects of Swiss language policy and language planning can be linked in some fashion to one or the other of these two principles.

THE PRINCIPLE OF LANGUAGE EQUALITY

Let us begin with the dimension of language equality. From the standpoint of the federal authorities, the three official languages are legally and constitutionally equal in all respects. Legislation is considered and enacted in all three languages, and the three resulting texts are considered of equal authenticity. The recognition of Romansh in 1938 as a national but not an official language was symbolically important but did not give Romansh the status of an official language of the Confederation. It is, however, one of the three official languages of the canton of Graubünden.

One must note and emphasize that language equality does not have territorial consequences, and that *cantonal* governments are not bound in any way by this principle. The Swiss political system considers that each language and language community has a traditional and historic territory, and that one major goal of language policy is to maintain this system in equilibrium. For centuries of Swiss history, the linguistic integrity of mountain valleys was naturally protected by geography, but the rise of an industrial society and the coming of an age of railroads, superhighways, and mountain tunnels has led to more active policies of governmental intervention in the interests of linguistic stability and security.

In the face of four language communities grossly disparate in numbers, the pure legal theory of equality has to be tempered by a certain sociological realism. Certain programs and institutions provide more, proportionally speaking, to the smaller and culturally weaker language communities than to the larger ones. Thus the Italian-speaking and Romansh-speaking areas receive supplementary federal grants for elementary education. They also receive special cultural grants, relatively modest in size but symbolically important. The broadcasting budget is disproportionately favourable to the Italian service. Such programs occur in the context of a federal system that provides other examples of resource redistribution from wealthier to poorer cantons.

Another aspect of linguistic equality is careful attention to appropriate linguistic proportionality in all federal appointments. The most important example of this is undoubtedly in the federal executive body, the Federal Council, where the long-run tendency has been to overrepresent the non-German-speaking groups in the ratio of either two out of seven or three out of seven. Proportionality is also closely monitored in the federal public service as a whole and in individual departments, though some central departments, for reasons that will be seen later, have been less successful than others in keeping to the proportions indicated by the population at large.

The Swiss political culture in general stresses the appropriate, duly-weighted representation of significant interest groups of all types in the democratic political process, and the ideal policy outcome is a kind of multi-dimensional Aristotelian distributive justice. There is an inherent mistrust of solutions based on straight majority rule, to a degree that many Canadians — including Canadian academics — probably could not understand.

DECENTRALIZED FEDERALISM

I turn now to the second major principle of Swiss language policy, the basic notion of decentralized federalism and some of its linguistic consequences. We have already noted that the four languages of Switzerland have historically delimited territories, and that Swiss public policy envisages the securing of these territories against unwanted linguistic change. The point to be stressed is that the cantons, not the federal authorities, retain a general competence in language matters, and this includes both policy content and the means used to achieve it. In technical terms, the cantons have *sprachenhoheit*, or linguistic sovereignty, subject only to Supreme Court review for compatibility between cantonal language policy and general constitutional norms. One consequence of this decentralization is that language policies can, and do, differ considerably from one canton to another, concerning both policy content and severity of enforcement.

Litigation over language matters in Switzerland is relatively infrequent, but two cases have become landmarks and are also interesting for Canada currently because they happen to concern commercial signs and the language of education. In 1932 the Supreme Court upheld a decree of the Italian-speaking canton of Ticino which required precedence of Italian over other languages on external commercial signs. However, it ruled invalid a further restriction on the relative letter size of inscriptions in other languages. One might interpret this as upholding the precedence, but not the complete predominance, of Italian in the canton.[1]

---

1. K.D. McRae, *Conflict and Compromise in Multilingual Societies: Switzerland*, Vol. 1 (Waterloo: Wilfrid Laurier University Press, 1983) at 123-24.

In the field of education, a Supreme Court decision of 1965 upheld the right of the German-speaking canton of Zürich to limit the duration of study in French in a *private* French-medium school to a normal maximum of two years, and to require sufficient teaching of German to enable pupils to enter a German-language program after this period. While some commentators felt the canton's policy was unduly restrictive, its legal right to impose such a policy in the name of the territoriality principle was accepted without question.[2]

The principle of territoriality causes problems in relation to the federal capital, the city of Bern, which lies in the heart of Bern canton in German-speaking Switzerland. In such a location, full language equality for federal public servants can scarcely be realized. The Swiss solution to this problem is to keep the central federal bureaucracy rather small and to decentralize many administrative tasks to the cantonal level, a practice entirely in keeping with decentralized federalism. For children of non-Germanophone public servants living in Bern, special arrangements provide primary and secondary education in French, but not in Italian. This solution is a rough compromise between territoriality and language equality, and a partial derogation from both principles. It has been blamed by some for difficulties in attracting sufficient Francophone public servants to Bern to fulfill the requirements of linguistic proportionality in certain departments.

In wider perspective, the Swiss system of decentralized federalism is a question of the public mentality, an ingrained characteristic of the political culture, a reciprocal willingness to tend one's own garden. This was well illustrated in the development and resolution of the most intense language conflict in recent decades, the Jura question, for even Switzerland is not immune to language conflict. The central point is that, for some three decades, the question of Jurassian separatism remained essentially a conflict within a single canton. Other cantonal governments carefully avoided becoming involved. Public opinion and the media in both French and German Switzerland behaved with great circumspection. The federal role in this lengthy dispute was limited to establishment of a federal mediation commission at one critical period and to neutral brokerage between the parties during the final stages of creating the new canton of Jura. The last step was popular approval by referendum, a vote that was collectively orchestrated by virtually every interest group in the country.

Like any other multilingual polity, Switzerland encounters other language problems from time to time. The formation of a new canton in the North Jura left some parts of the South Jura still in contention.

2. *Id.* at 124.

The measures so far taken to defend the Romansh-speaking areas can be criticized, and have been criticized, as inadequate to the gravity of the problem. In education, the growing pressures of English upon the third official language, Italian, have yet to be sufficiently addressed. Nevertheless, the main point is that these and similar problems are handled by a sensitive and finely-tuned political system, which identifies most issues at an early stage and devises efficient compromises that minimize alienation in any major section of Swiss society.

Should this finely-tuned mechanism break down, there is a safety valve. The approximate Swiss equivalent of the notwithstanding clause is the system of direct democracy, based on initiative and referendum and available whenever the delicately balanced system of elite politics is believed to have lost touch with the popular will. Initiative and referendum procedures are resorted to fairly frequently in Swiss politics, but the proportion of votation results that runs counter to governmental policy is relatively low.

How shall I summarize what is already a mere summary of an argument? Perhaps I can do so by indicating how Switzerland avoids some of the problems and tensions that beset current Canadian language policy. I suggest that significant differences between the Swiss and Canadian situations occur on the following six points:

1. There is no overall, countrywide "language plan" superimposed from the top, and consequently no federal pressure upon cantonal governments to conform to a single pattern of language policy. As a result, language policies are quite variable from one canton to another.

2. Because there is no overall plan, there is no general expectation of symmetry in relations among the language groups. Federal financial help is channelled to the smaller groups that need it most, and not according to criteria of symmetry or reciprocity or proportionality. Moreover, there is adequate public understanding of the needs of the smaller groups and of the rationale for asymmetry in federal financial assistance.

3. There is little evidence in Switzerland of overlapping language jurisdictions, of federal-cantonal policy divergences, or of federal and cantonal bureaucracies pursuing competing or conflicting objectives. Instead, the cantons are simply paramount in making language policy within their territory, though federal assistance may be sought in some circumstances.

4. There is little or no disposition for a cantonal government to criticize another canton's language policy, or its treatment of a linguistic

minority, because to do so would violate the canons of Swiss federalism. To use a canton's own linguistic minority as a bargaining chip against another canton would be quite unthinkable.

5. There is little governmental promotion of individual bilingualism in Switzerland beyond the teaching of languages in schools and a requirement — more stringent than Canada's — of knowing at least two official languages for the federal certificate of completion of secondary schooling. Beyond this, the acquisition of language skills is left to the self-interest of the individual, with reasonably satisfactory though not spectacular results.

6. The Swiss political system manages to combine political loyalties to the Confederation and simultaneous loyalties to cantons and to linguistic-cultural communities, without generating serious cross-pressures or incompatibilities.

I would end with a note of caution. I am not suggesting Swiss language policies could be transplanted to Canada, nor that they are a precise answer to Canada's current needs. What I do suggest is that Canadian language planners and policy makers could learn a great deal through thoughtful study of other multilingual systems, and especially of one that accommodates tensions and conflicts more smoothly and more successfully than their own. If Canadians would reflect seriously upon the Swiss system, they might well arrive at a language policy for Canada substantially different from that pursued by successive federal regimes.

REDUCING THE TENSIONS RESULTING FROM LANGUAGE CONTACTS: PERSONAL OR TERRITORIAL SOLUTIONS?

J.A. Laponce

Do languages that come into contact, either within the mind of a given individual or within the boundaries of a particular territory, become linked by collaborative or by conflictual relationships?

Obviously, one cannot, in the abstract, provide a yes or no answer. Between the extremes of pure conflict and pure collaboration stand the many different intermediate stages characterized by their specific mixture of the collaborative and the conflictual, a mixture resulting from the interplay of a complex set of factors — economic factors such as the 'purchasing' power of a language — ethnic factors such as the intensity of loyalty to a group defined by a common language — social factors such as variations of prestige associated with different languages.

But, through the complexities of many specific cases, a pattern emerges that enables us to answer our original question, a question that we shall now rephrase by asking: do languages behave like animals; are they territorially bound; do they fight for exclusive control over physical space?

The answer is *no* in the case of *diglossic bilingualism, yes* in the case of *bilingualism without diglossia*. In the first case, languages tend to enter into collaborative relationships and, almost necessarily, they mix territorially; in the second case they tend to do the very opposite.

Before providing examples of territorial and personal solutions, we need to consider the distinction between the diglossic and the non-diglossic.

Bilingualism with and Bilingualism without diglossia

The term diglossia was coined to describe the bilingualism of people who have two languages (two to simplify, the problem being the same with three or more), but two languages that do not meet because of

173

their being used in different circumstances, associated as they are with different social roles.[1]

The strong correlation between social role and language use which characterizes diglossia appears most clearly when a language such as Latin, Old Slavonic, or Hebrew is used as a sacred tongue while another language — English, Russian or Yiddish for example — is used in the secular domain. The separation is not as marked, but obvious nevertheless, when the diglossic contact is between secular languages that distinguish private from public domains and are used, the one to affirm one's local ethnicity, the other to participate instrumentally if not emotionally in the communication system of a wider community.

Unlike the Francophone Swiss who uses only standard French, the Germanophone Swiss uses two forms of German, the standard literary language that links the user to the greater German community, and a local Swiss German that is learned and spoken at home as well as in public life at the local level (Swiss German is spoken in the cantonal legislatures while standard German is used in the federal Parliament).[2] In Luxembourg, nearly all citizens speak three languages : Luxemburgese in private, and either French or German in public settings — French dominating in church and government while German dominates in the field of business. Similarly, many Africans or Indians will know a tribal or local language, a regional language that may, but need not, be a pidgin, and a national language that may, but need not, be an international language as well. Each of these languages will typically have their very specific social domain.

Diglossic bilingualism tends to be relatively stable when the languages in contact collaborate rather than conflict with each other, collaborate at separating social roles that the individual wishes to keep separated or at least does not mind being separated. The more the diglossic situation is wanted by the individual concerned — as in German Switzerland, Luxembourg, Andorra or Paraguay — the more the contact between the languages concerned will be collaborative, stable, and in lesser need of intervention by the political system.

By contrast, instability characterizes the cases where diglossia is imposed by circumstances and is perceived as a burden by the individuals who have to know two languages — one to communicate with their

---

1. See C.A. Ferguson, "Diglossia" (1959) 15 *Word* 325-40. See also J.A. Fishman, "Bilingualism With and Without Diglossia, Diglossia With and Without Bilingualism" (1967) 23 *Journal of Social Issues* 2 at 29-38.
2. See K.D. McRae, *Conflict and Compromise in Multilingual Societies: Switzerland*, Vol. 1 (Waterloo : Wilfred Laurier University Press, 1983).

parents for example, and the other to communicate with their own children — as in Britany in the early twentieth century. In such cases diglossia fades rapidly and relatively peacefully into unilingualism.[3]

Bilingualism without diglossia is a more frequent source of individual frustrations, hence of social and political conflicts. Extending as they do to all social roles, ready to be used in all or at least in most important social contexts, the languages are engaged in a competition for dominance.

If everyone in a given community preferred the same language, then there would be no reason — internal to the group — to retain another language. The latter would be abandoned, if not by the individuals who acquired it, at least by their children or grandchildren. That is the way most languages 'imported' into English-speaking North America keep being assimilated and are quickly annihilated in the absence of new migrations.

But if the individuals in contact do not all have the same preferred language, then differences between languages are very likely to become associated with differences in social and political power, differences that are likely to lead to the formation of ethno-linguistic minorities.

Asymmetrical power sharing between two language groups results in the dominant group having the power to decide how the burden of bilingualism will be borne and what language will have the greater social spread. In some rare occasions the dominant group decides to assume the cost of bilingualism. This happens when an invader, being comparatively small in number compared to the populations they conquered, adopts the latter's language to avoid the military and social costs of imposing its own tongue. The Roman conquerors spoke Greek in their Eastern empire and the Arabs who invaded Persia adopted Persian.[4] In Bolivia, in the early days of Spanish colonization, the ruling group decided to learn Quechua because the natives were thought unworthy, if not incapable, of learning Castilian.[5]

More frequently, the dominant group shifts the cost of bilingualism onto the ethnic minority. Flemish Belgians were and are still more likely to speak French than Walloons to speak Netherlandish; French Canadians are more likely to speak English than English Canadians to speak French; and in Switzerland, in the federal bureaucracy, the

---

3. W. Dressler and R. Wodak-Leodolter, "Language Death" (1977) 12 *International Journal of the Sociology of Language.*
4. W.F. MacKey, "Geopolitics: Its Scope and Principle" in C.H. Williams, ed., *Language in Geographic Context* (Clevedon: Multilingual Matters, 1989) 20-46.
5. R. Breton, *Géographie des langues* (Paris: Presses Universitaire de France, 1976).

Francophones are more likely to use German than the Germanophones to use French.[6]

These asymmetrical situations favoring the dominant group will produce resentment within the minority and will tend to produce among the latter an 'embattled fortress' mentality. Wanting to restrict as much as possible language contacts that are to its disadvantage (since the dominant group will normally impose its own language in all important transactions) the minority will seek to reduce its contacts with the dominant group by means of territorial concentration.

Territorial or Personal Solutions?

When seeking to regulate the contacts among languages the state has the choice of two fundamentally different solutions. *Territorial* solutions of the kind used by Belgium and Switzerland and *personal* solutions of the kind used by Estonia between the two world wars, and used also, to a lesser extent, by Finland and the Canadian federal government.[7]

The classic example of a territorial solution is offered by Switzerland where language boundaries separate German, Italian, and French areas in such a way that unilingualism is the rule in the operations of local government services, schools, and public life more generally. Swiss citizens are free to cross the language boundaries but, if they do, they are expected to change language as would the typical immigrant to a foreign country. The political strategy guiding these stringent regulations consists in separating languages as much as possible at the regional level and restricting bi- or multilingualism to the central level of government; a strategy that seeks, in other words, to prevent contact in order to prevent conflict. Belgium adopted a similar system by making Flanders Flemish and Wallonia French but it has not been able to apply fully the Swiss model because its capital, Brussels, is a predominantly Francophone city cast in Flemish territory. As an exception to the rule of territorial unilingualism, the Belgian capital has been set aside as a bilingual area.

The political justification for the system of fixed language boundaries is given by the following decision of the Swiss federal tribunal when

---

6. J.A. Laponce, *Languages and Their Territories* (Toronto: University of Toronto Press, 1987).
7. See J.A. Laponce, *The Protection of Minorities* (Berkeley and Los Angeles: University of California Press, 1960) and J.A. Laponce, "La répartition géographique des groupes linguistiques et les solutions personnelles et territoriales aux problèmes de l'État bilingue" in A. Martin, ed., *L'État et la planification linguistique* (Québec: Office de la langue française, 1981) 83-106. See also K.D. McRae, "The Principle of Territoriality and the principle of Personality in Multilingual States" (1975) 158 *Linguistics* 33-54.

it rejected the claim of a businessman who had argued that a local regulation forbidding him to advertise his products in the language of his choice was in violation of the equality clause of the federal constitution:[8]

> The linguistic borders of our country, once established, must be considered to be unchangeable. Safeguarding the harmonious relationship among the various segments (ethnic groups) of our country requires that each be guaranteed the integrity of the territory over which its language is spoken and over which extends its culture; and that each be given the right to prevent any encroachment...

Similarly, in 1965, the same tribunal rejected the complaint of an association of Francophones in a German canton who claimed that the language of instruction in the schools be recognized as an individual right of the parents rather than as a group right given to the local authorities. The Tribunal argued:[9]

> The risk resulting from foreign migration... is controlled only by means of linguistic assimilation of the immigrants... and it is in that regard that the school has an important role to play; it is its duty to impart to the students the knowledge of the language of their new home.

In the Swiss, and to a lesser extent in the Belgian case, the languages are rooted territorially. They are thus guaranteed secure territorial niches of their own and the power to protect the boundaries so created is given not to individuals but to collectivities — the cantons in Switzerland, the regions in Belgium.[10]

In marked contrast to the Swiss system of territorial allocation of language rights, the Baltic countries, notably Estonia, used a system of personal federalism between the two World Wars.[11] In Estonia, for example, the system allowed any ethnic group comprising at least three thousand people to set up a nation-wide community with institutions of its own; institutions with the power to tax its members and to administer its own public and private schools. These nation-wide ethnic governments resembled local governments except in their not being territorially grounded and having extensive language rights, in particular that of selecting the language of instruction in the schools. That system — which had its forerunners in the Polish-Jewish *kahal* and in the millets

---

8. Translated from G. Héraud, *L'Europe des ethnies*, 2nd ed. (Paris: Presses d'Europe, 1974) at 247.

9. *Ibid.*

10. See K.D. McRae, *Conflict and Compromise in Multilingual Societies: Belgium* (Waterloo: Wilfred Laurier Press, 1986) and *supra*, notes 2 and 7.

11. See K. Aun, *On the Spirit of the Estonian Minority Laws* (Stockholm: Societies Litteraturn Estonia, 1940).

of the Ottoman empire[12] did not survive the war and has not been replicated, at least not in the regulation of multilingual situations.

Between the extremes of the Swiss and the Estonian models, Finland offers the case of partially and temporarily grounded languages. Wherever the Swedish minority accounts for at least eight percent of the population of a given commune (the basic unit of local government), the public services are offered in the two official languages — Swedish and Finnish. But a bilingual district will normally become unilingual Finnish if the Swedish population is shown by the census to have declined below the required minimum. The Swedish territorial niche is thus not secure, first in its being bilingual rather than unilingual, and, second, in having fluctuating boundaries affected by demography and population mobility (In the Aaland Islands however, a rule of territorial unilingualism protects the Swedish minority as a result of the international treaties that regulate the status of that territory).

The Canadian federal government has by and large patterned its language policies on those of Finland rather than those of either Switzerland or Belgium, partly out of fear that a unilingual French Québec might be closer to secession than if it remained bilingual. One cannot deny that possibility but, interestingly, the increase in language security of the Québécois population as a result of the implementation of Bill 101 is correlated with a lowering of separatist fervor. This appears to confirm that the Swiss strategy of reducing contact between competing languages by juxtaposing unilingual areas, rather than merging the languages within the same territory, has the desired effect of lowering tensions — at least when the language cleavage is not reinforced by other non-linguistic cleavages that would make the ethnic groups concerned incompatible on too many grounds.

In short, in diglossic situations, such as those of Luxembourg or Paraguay, a territorial solution is typically not available and, if available, likely would be dysfunctional since the characteristic of diglossia is that it separates not individuals but social roles; the language divisions run not between people but within each person. The languages need to be territorially transportable.

By contrast, in non-diglossic bilingualism the languages in contact, having as their function the expression of all the social roles of each individual, compete for dominance. Since in that competition the language of the dominant group has the advantage, the minority will seek protection through territorial concentration. The minority will

---

12. See Laponce, *supra*, note 7.

typically seek to obtain unilingualism on what it considers to be its territory and will want to have the control of its language boundaries. The territorial solutions of the Swiss type recognize and satisfy this need.

In looking for models in Finland rather than in Switzerland, did Canada make a mistake? I think so.

THE POLITICS OF "PARTNERSHIP" IN THE NORTHWEST TERRITORIES

Gurston Dacks

THE SOCIAL BASIS OF PARTNERSHIP

While the rate of progress has been fitful, history will have no difficulty identifying the direction in which the government of the Northwest Territories (the NWT) has been maturing since World War Two.[1] The extension of representative government and the evolution of the conventions of cabinet rule, as well as the universal precedent set by Ottawa and the provincial and Yukon governments, would seem to anticipate the establishment in the NWT of a set of governmental institutions based on the Westminster model.

However, the majoritarian principle which underlies this model has not served Canada's aboriginal peoples well.[2] This fact has led aboriginal peoples to pursue certain political powers through their comprehensive claims and to seek through the national process of first ministers' conferences constitutional guarantees that legislatures, in responding to majority wishes, will not impair or deny to the aboriginal minority the enjoyment of their rights. The aboriginal peoples of the NWT share in this pursuit of protection as members of the national aboriginal minority. However, they differ from other aboriginal peoples in Canada in that they form such a large proportion of the population of their own territory that the majoritarian principle itself may protect them. This will be particularly true for the Inuit should division of the Territories occur. Because the territory, to be called Nunavut, which they would

---

1. Ken Coates, *Canada's Colonies* (Toronto: James Lorimer, 1985); Gurston Dacks, *A Choice of Futures* (Toronto: Methuen, 1981) at 89-94; Royal Commission on the Economic Union and Development Prospects for Canada, *The North* (Vol. 72) by Michael Whittington (Toronto: University of Toronto Press, 1985).
2. See, for example, J. Rick Ponting and Roger Gibbins, *Out of Irrelevance* (Toronto: Butterworths, 1980) c. 1; Canada, House of Commons, *Report of the Special Committee on Indian Self-Government* (Ottawa: Supply and Services Canada, 1983).

occupy would have a population over eighty percent Inuit, they would have no difficulty achieving a government which is both Inuit in sensibility and majoritarian in structure. The demographics of the western portion of the NWT are much more complex than those in Nunavut. According to the 1981 census, the Dene, Metis and Inuvialuit groups, including non-status Indians, comprise 43 percent of the population of the western NWT.[3] As a result, the majoritarian principle will not guarantee them a future government sensitive to their rights, let alone their needs. Moreover, a federal structure will not work for any of the cultural communities of the western NWT because they live in too dispersed a fashion to permit the drawing of any geographical boundaries which would create plausible cultural homelands.

However, and this fact is crucial to an understanding of the present constitutional debate, the cultural composition of the electorate offers no guarantees to the non-aboriginal population either. Their majority status favours them and likely will continue to do so. However, it would be most imprudent for them to discount the possibility that a higher aboriginal than non-aboriginal birth rate might undercut their advantage at the ballot box, as might a judicial ruling in favour of a two year residency requirement for eligibility to vote. In addition, the non-aboriginal population recognizes that Ottawa views the aboriginal population of the North as having a legitimate voice concerning the shape of the future governmental institutions of the territories. Non-native northerners appreciate that it will be very much easier to receive full self-government if the form of government to which Ottawa's power is devolved enjoys the support of the native peoples it will govern. Indeed, this may be an absolute prerequisite if northerners are to enter Confederation with a status constitutionally equal, or at least nearly equal,[4] to other Canadians. Finally, many non-native northerners themselves recognize the right of their aboriginal fellow northerners to make constitutional claims, even if they may not agree with all of what is being sought.

Constitutional planning in the western NWT, therefore, has focused on two goals. The first is to develop a form of government which will embody the majoritarian principle sufficiently to satisfy both policy-makers in Ottawa and the non-aboriginal population of the western territory to be created. Both of these groups are understandably anxious

---

3. Michael Asch and Gurston Dacks, "The Relevance of Consociation to the Western Northwest Territories" in *Partners for the Future* (Yellowknife: Constitutional Forum, 1985) 60.

4. Gordon Robertson, *Northern Provinces: Mistaken Goal* (Ottawa: Institute for Research on Public Policy, 1984).

about any deviation from the constitutional formula which they have always viewed as natural, if not divinely ordained. The second goal is to entrench constitutionally the collective rights which the aboriginal peoples of the new western territory will possess, and the structures of government which will ensure that legislation and public administration will respect and promote those rights. The purpose of this paper is to sketch the model which was developed to blend the principles of majoritarianism and collective minority rights and to relate it to the direction of future constitutional development in the western NWT.

Responsibility for developing this model initially lay with the Western Constitutional Forum (WCF). This body and the analogous Nunavut Constitutional Forum for the eastern portion of the territories was created in 1982 after a plebiscite found a slight majority of those who voted to favour division of the territories.[5] The WCF was composed of a representative of each of the aboriginal organizations and two members of the Legislative Assembly, one of whom was specifically responsible for representing the non-aboriginal population. From 1982 to 1988, the WCF devoted much of its effort to the difficult tasks of negotiating a boundary between the two new territories[6] and defining the issues which will comprise the agenda for constitution-building.[7] The former task was pursued through the Constitutional Alliance, which was simply the two forums meeting together. In 1988, the forums were disbanded in favour of a unified Constitutional Alliance which it was hoped would prove more effective than the preceding arrangement had been. At their first meetings, the members of the reconstituted Alliance agreed to constitutional principles which would apply to either the present NWT, if division does not occur, or to the two separate territories which would result from division. The most fully developed model other than the parliamentary system of southern Canada and the Yukon which the Constitutional Alliance has available for consideration is the one developed for the western NWT by the WCF.

CONSOCIATIONAL GOVERNMENT

This constitutional model draws heavily on the concept of consociation. This concept in political science evolved from efforts to

---

5. Frances Abele and Mark Dickerson, "The Plebiscite on Division of the Northwest Territories: Regional Government and Federal Policy" (1985) 11:2 *Canadian Public Policy/Analyse de Politiques* 1.
6. The complexities of this question are discussed in Gurston Dacks, "The Case Against Dividing the Northwest Territories" (1986) 12:1 *Canadian Public Policy/Analyse de Politiques* 202.
7. See *Partners for the Future* (Yellowknife: Western Constitutional Forum, 1985).

explain how certain European countries, such as Belgium, Austria and Switzerland, have managed to contain the conflicts within their culturally deeply divided societies and maintain political stability.[8] The structural details of political systems which are organized on a consociational basis or which display consociational elements are so varied that it is impossible to speak of a general consociational model. It is more useful to think in terms of the logic of consociation and to consider the ways in which it has been adapted to meet the particular needs of specific societies. The essence of this logic of consociation is to develop governmental institutions which emphasize negotiation and the seeking of consensus rather than competition whose outcome is determined by the majoritarian principle. Four devices or principles which are relevant to the situation of the western NWT are commonly applied to produce the political coalescence which is the goal of consociational constitutions.[9] Under the first, *grand coalition*, "...the political leaders of all significant segments of the plural society co-operate in a grand coalition to govern the society." The second, *mutual veto*, protects minority cultural communities in situations in which their participation in the coalition executive fails to prevent it from making a decision which significantly harms the minority's fundamental cultural interests.

The third principle, *proportionality*, allocates governmental offices and funding regarding certain functions in a fashion which reflects each cultural community's proportion of the total population rather than the domination of the majority. In Lijphart's words, this device "...as a neutral and impartial standard of allocation, removes a large number of potentially divisive problems from the decision-making process and thus lightens the burdens of consociational government."[10] It should be noted further that it qualifies the grand coalition principle by requiring not merely the representation of all minorities in the ruling coalition, but more particularly the proportionality of their representation. The fourth fundamental device of consociational constitutions which distinguishes

---

8. B.M. Barry, "Review Article: Political Accommodation and Consociational Democracy" (1975) 5 *British Journal of Political Science* 477; Arend Lijphart, *Democracy in Plural Societies* (New Haven: Yale University Press, 1977); Kenneth McRae, *Consociational Democracy: Political Accommodation in Segmented Societies* (Toronto: McClelland and Stewart, 1974). Some political scientists have attempted to explain aspects of Canadian politics in terms of consociationalism. Examples are Ed Aunger, *In Search of Political Stability: A Comparative Study of New Brunswick and Northern Ireland* (Montreal: McGill-Queen's University Press, 1981), and Kenneth McRae, "Consociationalism and the Canadian Political System" in K. McRae, ed., *Consociational Democracy: Political Accommodation in Segmented Societies* (Montreal: McGill-Queen's University Press, 1981).
9. Lijphart, *supra*, note 8 at 25.
10. *Id.* at 39.

them from majoritarian systems is *segmental autonomy*, the principle that each of the cultural communities will have sovereign legislative authority over certain matters which are most crucial to their cultural interests. This autonomy ensures that regarding these matters, they will not have to compromise their interests to achieve a consensus or be put in the possibly awkward position of having to exercise a veto to protect themselves. Their unlimited ability to plan and implement policies in areas of autonomy will ensure that these policies most closely meet their needs as they alone define them.

These devices are variables, not either-or propositions. They can be applied to varying extents in different cases, producing governments which diverge from the majoritarian ideal type to varying degrees. This variability suggests a sense in which they are logically interrelated: if one is pursued in a very thoroughgoing fashion, the necessity for the others is reduced. For example, the more the executive and legislature are structured on the basis of proportionality and mutual veto, the less will the minority cultural communities feel the need for their segmental autonomy to extend over a broad range of issues. Conversely, if consociationalism is achieved primarily through segmental autonomy, then the limited jurisdiction of the overall territorial government makes its structure relatively unimportant. It should be noted that the most complete form of segmental autonomy, short of secession, lies in the establishment of a federal state in which each cultural community clusters within its own self-governing territory. Indeed, the logic of the Inuit pursuit of Nunavut is to obtain Inuit self-determination and cultural guarantees through majority government. However, as noted above, their geographic distribution prevents the cultural communities of the western NWT from taking advantage of this federal solution to guarantee protection of their rights.

THE PARTNERSHIP MODEL

For these people, the only option to majoritarian government lies in some form of consociationalism, which the WCF renamed "partnership" because the term "consociationalism" strikes the ear as both awkward and uninspiring. The partnership model[11] rests on nine basic principles. *First*, the society of the western NWT is conceived of as a partnership of cultural communities. Thus, it is more than a set of individuals whose only relationship to the state consists of the rights and responsibilities of the individual. Presumably, the cultural

---

11. Asch and Dacks, *supra*, note 3 at 35-63.

communities will be the non-aboriginal, the Inuvialuit and the Dene/ Metis, although the latter grouping could split into its two parts for constitutional purposes. It is essential to the partnership model that the rights of these cultural communities as participants in the new government of the western NWT be equal and symmetrical because the purpose of the new constitution is to protect all cultural communities equally. Put more bluntly, the constitution is more likely to be accepted by all cultural communities if its guiding principle is not the protection of only certain of the cultural communities — the aboriginal ones. As they relate to the public government, all should be equal. Of course, the aboriginal communities will also enjoy aboriginal rights, but these flow from the *Constitution* of Canada, not from any preferred status under the territorial constitution. *Second*, the partnership constitution will contain a Charter of Collective Rights which will define the fundamental interests of each of the cultural communities. The Charter will enable the communities, as a matter of right, to protect and enhance themselves in order to ensure their control over the direction and future integrity of the evolution of their cultures. *Third*, each cultural community will enjoy a measure of segmental autonomy in the form of a council which will exercise complete legislative jurisdiction over those matters defined in the Charter as fundamental to the community's cultural interest.

Fourth, there will be a legislative assembly which will have jurisdiction throughout the new territory over all matters not assigned to the cultural community councils. The territorial electorate will be divided into separate cultural community voting lists, so that the members of the assembly will be elected by their respective cultural communities. To reduce the problems of individual members serving and relating to constituents over the whole of the new territory, multi-member constituencies, probably three in number, will be created. The number of seats allotted to each constituency will be roughly proportional to its total population and the number of members elected by each cultural community will also reflect its proportion of the territorial population, except that the constitution will entrench some minimum number of members below which a cultural community's representation will not be allowed to drop. The details of the electoral system have not been finalized. However, a general application of these principles would produce a thirteen-member assembly comprising four Dene/ Metis, two Inuvialuit, and seven non-aboriginals. If a larger legislative body were deemed desirable, the 1981 population of the territory and the general rules suggested above would produce a twenty-five member body of nine Dene/ Metis members, three Inuvialuit, and thirteen non-aboriginals.

Fifth, matters which do not touch on constitutionally-defined cultural concerns will be decided by a simple majority vote in the

Legislative Assembly. *Sixth*, legislative enactments which the members representing any of the cultural communities deem to affect significantly matters of cultural right must be approved by a majority of each of the cultural caucuses in the assembly. This provides a mutual veto structure, which should reduce the anxieties which any of the cultural communities ought to feel about being represented by a minority of members in the Assembly; majority rule will not dominate cultural rights. *Seventh*, the executive will be composed of aboriginal and non-aboriginal members. It might be required that they be equal in number or, for flexibility in cabinet formation, some inequality might be permitted. Within limits, this would not jeopardize either of the groups because of the requirement that all executive decisions will have to have the approval of a majority of the members of each of the cultural components of the executive. The exact procedure for structuring the executive and its relationship of responsibility to the assembly and to the cultural caucuses which comprise it remain to be decided. Much will depend on whether political parties develop. However, it is clear that both forming and operating the executive will involve the politics of inter-cultural coalitions. *Eighth*, a priority of the new territorial government would be, while respecting the rights of ongoing employees, to work to make the cultural composition of both the bureaucracy and the judiciary more representative of the composition of the population. *Ninth*, amendments to any of these arrangements would require the approval of either a majority of each of the cultural caucuses in the assembly, or a popular referendum showing majority support for the change in each cultural community.

This description highlights the general principles of the partnership model. It also suggests that a great many crucial questions remain to be answered. For example, the matters of fundamental cultural concern which must be protected by means of segmental autonomy and mutual veto need to be defined. Indeed, it will have to be decided whether the definition ought to be the same for both purposes; it might be argued that the need for cost-efficiency would suggest a narrow list of powers for the cultural community councils, with the bulk of the task of cultural policy being decided through the interaction of the caucuses in the assembly. In other words, the communities would rely more on their veto and less on their autonomy to pursue their cultural goals. In addition, to minimize the possibility of obstructionism and deadlock, a mechanism must be created to resolve disputes as to whether a particular bill or executive action affects a matter defined in the Charter as a cultural concern, enough to require agreement of all of the cultural caucuses. Another issue to be resolved is how aboriginal rights won as a result of either claims settlements or new constitutional arrangements made at the national level will relate to the new territorial constitution. Also, it will be necessary to confront the thorny problem of integrating the national *Charter of Rights and Freedoms* and the territorial Charter of Collective Rights; what is required is some formula which adequately protects the individual rights provided by the former but also limits the opportunities which their pursuit in the courts offer for dismantling the collective rights guaranteed by the latter. Should the Alliance resolve these issues, it will still face the task of public education and consultation, probably in the form of a referendum, in order to demonstrate to Ottawa that the partnership model enjoys the support of the people whom it is intended to govern.

THE ROAD AHEAD

Resolving these issues and gaining this support, particularly given the unfamiliarity of the form of government being proposed and the uncertain commitment of the members of the Alliance to it, will prove challenging. It is not possible to prescribe appropriate responses to the challenges of the future for a most important reason: consociation is a concept, not a model, much less a blueprint. Moreover, to the extent that it succeeds in containing social divergences, its success reflects a triumph of pragmatism, not ideology. As noted above, consociation is rooted in the specifics of particular societies. Because those specifics vary greatly, the consociational devices which have evolved in response to them display great diversity from one consociational system to another. Thus it is not possible to apply rigidly to the unique circumstances of the western NWT lessons learned in other societies. However, these lessons can help northerners and others think about the road still to be travelled. In undertaking this thinking, it is useful to note that observers of consociation group the many factors influencing its success into three general categories: social structure, particularly the pattern of social segmentation; political culture; and elite behaviour.[12]

Social Structure

The balance of power among social segments is the fundamental factor conditioning relations among them. Patterns of social segmentation can compel elites to seek consociational rather than majoritarian political processes and will determine the likely success of their efforts. In this regard, Lijphart argues,

> A multiple balance of power among the segments of a plural society is more conducive to consociational democracy than a dual balance or a

---

12. See, for example, McRae, *supra*, note 8 at 5-13.

hegemony by one of the segments because if one segment has a clear majority, its leaders may attempt to dominate, rather than cooperate, with the rival minority.[13]

Viewed in this context, the western NWT would appear to offer little prospect of successful consociation in that the non-aboriginal group will form a majority of its population. This factor can be anticipated to lead it to press constantly to revise constitutional arrangements in a majoritarian direction. Indeed, all other considerations aside, consociation will be more viable if the territories do not divide. In a unified NWT, the non-aboriginal population would only account for about 43 percent of the total, hence would find it less attractive to pursue a path of domination rather than compromise. Still, even if division does occur, an extended residence requirement for voting and uncertain population dynamics might dissuade the non-aboriginal community from pushing its advantage of numbers. It might also be dissuaded by the thought that if the aboriginal groups are dissatisfied with the future territorial form of public government, they might pursue their own separate institutions of self-determination. The result could be a territory with little holding it together and much wasteful and perhaps bitter conflict among cultural governments which have no constitutional reason to cooperate.

Even more important is the fact that Lijphart's dictum may not fit the reality of the new territory in that it is neither fully a European nor a third world political system. The western portion of the NWT has important elements of uniqueness. First, the fact that aboriginal rights are both constitutionally entrenched and undefined provides an element of flexibility and opportunities for trade-offs in the process of constitution building. Second, the unusual and still evolving structure of the region's economy offers the possibility of both complementary economic relations among members of the cultural communities and a degree of mutual independence which, if managed with statesmanship, good will and some luck, could reduce tension among the groups. Third, the role of the government of Canada as a mediator and ultimate judge of the process contrasts with most cases of consociation, whose partners had to work out agreements without reference to an external power, with the result that these understandings depend entirely on the internal demographic logic which Lijphart argues. The western portion of the NWT is different, quite possibly different enough to escape this logic.

Theorists of consociation argue that the tendency toward a politics of coalescence grows as external threats to the society in question loom

---

13. Lijphart, *supra*, note 8 at 55.

larger. The western NWT does not face the danger of armed invasion, but it does resent the impositions of Ottawa, whose definition of the national interest, for example the Meech Lake Accord, can appear highly unresponsive to the North. Devolution of jurisdiction northward has removed many irritants, but the wish to gain full self-government and better treatment from Ottawa motivates northern politicians from all cultural communities to cooperate in pressing demands on Ottawa. For example, all of the members of the Ninth Legislative Assembly flew to Ottawa immediately upon learning the contents of Section 42 of the *Constitution Act, 1982* to lobby against its requirement that new provinces could only be created if at least two thirds of the existing provinces agree.

A third factor, relationships among the members of the cultural communities, poses complex and apparently contradictory conditions for the success of consociational experiments. On the one hand, it has been argued that:

> ...clear boundaries between the segments of a plural society have the advantage of limiting mutual contacts and consequently of limiting the chances of ever-present potential antagonisms to erupt into actual hostility.[14]

To the extent that this hostility can be avoided, the pursuit of consensus among the cultural elites is not complicated by the need to respond to conflict between their respective followers or by the tensions which crises of relations at the mass level produce.

On the other hand, consociation cannot bridge the cleavages in totally fragmented societies, ones in which the members of the various cultural communities have no interests in common and many in conflict. Cleavages which relate to interests which cross-cut the lines of segmental, that is cultural, cleavage reduce the intensity of conflict among cultural communities. They do this by encouraging members of different cultural communities to work together for common purposes and thus develop a degree of mutual understanding and sympathy. Also, to the extent that cross-cutting cleavages define communities of interest based on factors other than culture, people will feel reluctant to push to the fullest extent against members of other cultural communities strategies which they might otherwise attempt if their only consideration was antipathy which is structured along cultural community lines. After all, it would not be in their interest to abuse people who in one sense or another are their colleagues, and upon whom they may be dependent at some time in the future.

---

14. *Id.* at 88.

Social patterns in the western NWT offer some promise because they display the complexities of the "ideal" consociational social structure. To a very significant extent, the cultural communities do live apart, the Inuvialuit in their own communities around the Beaufort, and the Dene and Metis in the small communities of the Mackenzie Valley. Fort Simpson, Yellowknife and Inuvik stand as the largest exceptions to this pattern. While their populations are culturally mixed, they satisfy the condition of segmental self-segregation to some extent in that the cultural communities tend to cluster in different neighbourhoods. Also, substantial numbers of aboriginal people are marginal to the dominant social processes and to the labour markets in these urban settings, hence do not greatly challenge the non-aboriginal population. These social patterns result in regrettable inequalities, but also lead to a degree of self-segregation among the cultural communities which seems likely to reduce conflict at the mass level during the important early years of consociational politics.

With time, as more aboriginal northerners gain the education and the confidence to challenge non-aboriginals in the wage labour market, hence reduce segmental segregation, it seems plausible that they will come increasingly to share some interests and attitudes with non-aboriginals. This will increase the degree of cross-cutting among the cultural communities. For example, as more aboriginal people become involved in the private sector wage economy, they will increase the interest in non-traditional economic development that they have already begun to share with non-aboriginal people. Indeed, a major contrast between the decade of the 1980s and the preceding decade is a growing consensus that all northerners will benefit if the future economy of the North contains a healthy wage-oriented sector which employs aboriginal as well as non-aboriginal northerners. Clearly, aboriginal support for these types of activity will depend on their compatibility with aboriginal rights and the terms of claims settlements, and the degree of confidence aboriginal people feel in the cultural protections they enjoy under the new territorial constitution. In any case, some aboriginals will choose not to take part in this sector of the economy. Still, the Dene and Metis now clearly accept the principle of participation in the wage economy and non-renewable resource development. This acceptance increases the degree of cross-cutting cleavage among the cultural communities of the western NWT.

For their part, non-aboriginal business people recognize that the financial components of aboriginal claims settlements are good for business; they can inject cash into the local economy. The business community resists provisions which favour aboriginal businesses, such as preferential contracting procedures, but welcomes contracts financed out of settlement money. In this way, it anticipates some direct financial benefit as a result of the settlement of the Dene/Metis claim, as well as the general benefits of a better-defined context in which to do business, once the uncertainties associated with the unsettled claims are ended.

In sum, the existing degrees of communal self-segregation and cross-cutting cleavage and the directions in which these patterns are changing suggest a social structure reasonably conducive to consociational success. At present, substantial self-segregation at the mass level should minimize the friction which would distract elites from the task of sorting out co-operative arrangements, while an evolution in the direction of increasingly shared interest will produce over time cross-cutting cleavages (and less self-segregation) which characterize a more mature form of consociation.

Observers of consociation note that its successes tend to be confined to states with relatively small populations.[15] Among their explanations of this phenomenon is the suggestion that the small size of such states brings the members of the elites of the various cultural communities together more regularly than would be likely in larger countries. This probability combined with the small size of each elite makes it easier for members of the various elites to get to know one another and to develop the cooperative relationships which lead to the consensus-seeking behaviour which characterizes consociation. In addition, because small states feel particularly vulnerable to external threats, their elites feel particularly intense about the need to achieve compromises in order to present a united front to these threats. Undoubtedly, the western NWT will be a jurisdiction with an exceedingly small population, even in contrast to such "small" states as Belgium and Austria. Since the 1979 decision of the Dene Nation to end the Dene boycott in the Legislative Assembly, and the acceptance of Ottawa's determination that political development in the North must be decided by all northerners, not at the aboriginal claims negotiations,[16] contacts between members of the aboriginal and non-aboriginal elites have multiplied. With time these contacts have shown increasing understanding and cooperation, as will be discussed below.

Size is also seen to promote successful consociation because of its impact on a related factor, the "decisional load" which government must bear. Consociation is often criticized as slow to make decisions because respect for minority interests requires that every effort be made to accommodate them through a process of compromise which is necessarily

---

15. For example, *id.* at 65-71.
16. Canada, Department of Indian Affairs and Northern Development, *In All Fairness* (Ottawa: Supply and Services Canada, 1981) at 19.

lengthy. While this sensibility to minorities respects the basic purpose of consociation, it weakens the ability of government to meet another fundamental goal, "decisional efficiency." This is a problem for any government, but becomes an increasingly severe problem to the extent to which the society faces a set of problems which are numerous, fundamental or critical. In one sense, the decisional load facing the western NWT today is very great; the most basic questions of political philosophy and governmental forms remain to be answered. However, it is to be hoped that the settlement of aboriginal claims and the resolution of the constitutional development process under way will remove much of this uncertainty, and allow territorial politics to resume a "normal" decisional load. Indeed, one goal of the process of creating a partnership constitution should be to foster patterns of behaviour and to distribute governmental responsibilities so as to reduce the decisional load which must be borne by the Assembly as much as is consistent with its role of providing a focus for the public government of the territory. Even if this future comes to pass, the new territorial government will be faced with most of the decisions which the provincial governments face, including, to an even greater extent than the provinces because of the extreme dependence of the territorial economy on external forces, the need to adjust to the impact of decisions taken outside its boundaries. This suggests that the decisional load on the future territorial government will continue to be substantial. The conclusion to draw, however, is not necessarily that consociation will not work, but rather that it must be made to work in order to contain the conflict which these issues are likely to provoke and which a majoritarian system is likely to handle more efficiently but much less satisfactorily. In this sense, negotiations leading to a consociational system must consider how to manage the decisional load which the future legislative assembly will have to bear.

Political Culture

The basic political attitudes of a society and its cultural communities help determine the success with which the consociational model can be applied to it. Specifically, the members of the various cultural communities need to view themselves as having a particular culture which does indeed define a community with which they identify in a meaningful way. Moreover, they need to believe that, since their cultural community is one of several with divergent interests, they need to organize and to develop structures of leadership in order to be able to pursue the politics of cultural protection. In almost all cases, this cultural self-consciousness obviously exists in that the cleavages which necessitate consociational solutions rest on precisely this type of identification. It is, however, not clear that the western NWT satisfies this condition because of the lack of cultural self-consciousness on the part of its non-aboriginal population:

> Non-natives have conceived of themselves as the majority and as representing majority culture, in large part because they have seen themselves in the context of all of North America. They will now have to accept that, for territorial purposes, they constitute one of several cultural communities. The psychological transition from a position of pre-eminence to one of shared status is likely to be difficult. So too will be the transition from thinking of themselves and others as individuals to thinking in terms of cultural communities. The non-native population has never organized collective organizations which speak for their cultural group in the way that the aboriginal organizations speak for theirs.[17]

At the same time, it must be noted that while non-aboriginals in Canada have little history of organizing as a cultural community, they do seem capable of doing so when the situation dictates. If Anglophones in Québec can organize the Alliance Québec to protect their collective linguistic interest, non-aboriginals in the western NWT have at least the potential to perform in a similar fashion, provided that they are convinced of its necessity.

The intense debate surrounding the Berger Inquiry and the need to pursue their claims has led the aboriginal peoples of the western NWT to organize their own representative institutions and to develop traditions of working through them. These institutions have enabled these groups to identify and to authorize spokesmen and to gain practice in deferring to them or at least pressing their claims through them. Thus, in contrast to the non-aboriginal population, the aboriginals' more institutionalized political processes make them more culturally attuned to the requirements of consociation.

Observers of consociationalism have tended to argue that it flourishes in the context of a political culture of elite dominance:

> The success of the elites in stabilizing a fragmented community... presumes that they are able to retain the support of their followers. This implies either widespread popular support for the specific cooperative policies, or sufficient autonomy for the elites to let them act independently... Where the elites are not entrenched, there is the risk, first, that they will not be able to carry their followers with them and, second, that they will be replaced by militant leaders more congenial to mass sentiments.[18]

---

17. Asch and Dacks, *supra*, note 3 at 56.
18. Aunger, *supra*, note 8 at 162. One of the major criticisms of consociationalism is that the elitism on which it rests is undemocratic.

There is not a great deal of evidence in the western NWT pointing to the culture of deference which observers of consociationalism elsewhere have seen as contributing so significantly to the capacity of elites to reach essential accommodations. As has been noted, elite-mass relations in the non-aboriginal community are too undeveloped to have evolved habits of mass compliance. For their part, the Dene value highly the self-determination of the individual and view the local community, rather than the overall Dene Nation, as the appropriate focus of decision-making, or at least as the source of the Dene Nations' authority.[19] This suggests a resistance to consociational elite practices.

However, this may be precisely one of those points at which the analysis of consociationalism elsewhere sheds little light on the western NWT. There, it may be the case that the Dene leadership has developed a great sensitivity to the expectations of its people to be consulted on important issues, has decentralized decision-making, and only commits itself when it is certain that it enjoys the support of the bulk of the Dene people. As a result, it may not be in the position to command deference enjoyed by leaders of cultural communities in other consociational systems. However, its closer linkage to its members ensures that it will not commit itself to undertakings which the Dene will not support or cannot be persuaded to see as reasonable. A redefinition of the consociational requirement in this instance would replace the notion of mass deference to the elite with intimate mass-elite linkage. Indeed, such a redefinition goes even farther than some commentators on consociationalism, such as Eric Nordlinger, who argues that elite predominance:

> ...is usually tempered with a good measure of responsiveness to nonelite wishes and demands. In open regime, nonelites generally set distinct outer limits to their leaders' demands and controls.[20]

Viewed in this context, the form of support which the Dene give their leadership is quite consistent with consociation. Also, the development of structures linking the non-aboriginal population with its leadership appears less formidable than the conventional interpretation of consociation suggests.

---

19. Lorraine Malloch, *Dene Government Past and Future* (Yellowknife: Western Constitutional Forum, 1984) at 11-15; Dene Nation and Metis Association of the Northwest Territories, *Public Government for the People of the North* (Yellowknife: Dene Nation and Metis Association of the Northwest Territories, 1982).
20. Eric Nordlinger, *Conflict Regulation in Divided Societies* (Occasional Papers in International Affairs, No. 29) (Cambridge, Mass.: Harvard University Centre for International Affairs, 1977) at 73-4.

A positive elite-mass relationship particularly sustains consociational politics if it involves a third orientation : mass acceptance of the politics of grand coalitions. Leadership style in consociations is coalescent whereas the British parliamentary model features adversarial behaviour.[21] For a coalescent style to succeed, elites must have the security of knowing that those whom they represent are willing to tolerate their avoiding the superficially gratifying politics of confrontation in favour of more productive formal co-operative arrangements with the leaders of contending social groups. The tactics of temporizing and compromise which are necessary to make these arrangements endure must be culturally acceptable. Most fundamentally, the mass of people must be able to accept that elite members can work together, indeed institutionalize their relationships, without losing their commitment to their respective groups ; leaders can compromise on issues without compromising on their commitment to their respective groups. It is still early in the political evolution of the western NWT to judge the degree to which this orientation characterizes the political culture of the region. While the electoral system encourages the development of coalition parties, they may represent a poor vehicle for communicating the needs of a fragmented society in that they fail to express directly the basic lines of social cleavage. These, as has been argued above, need to be well defined if they are adequately to be considered in the process of consociational politics. Perhaps more important is the fact that the parliamentary tradition of responsible government inclines Canadians against coalition cabinets. In the context of the western NWT, however, it is worth noting that the tradition of responsible government is only beginning to take root. Moreover, territorial leaders already have turned to devices more consistent with consociation than with parliamentary politics in order to manage relations among the cultural communities of the region. As will be discussed below, the process of selecting the Executive Council, the original structure of the Constitutional Alliance, and recent proposals to select government leaders alternately between the East and the West all reflect consociational assumptions. To the extent that these arrangements have not provoked opposition among the population, it would appear that northerners are willing to tolerate such deviations from adversarial politics, and that they may develop a tendency to look to such solutions in the future to similar needs as they arise, thus developing a culture of tolerance of rule by "elite cartel."[22]

---

21. Martin O. Heisler, ed., *Politics in Europe: Structures and Processes in Some Postindustrial Democracies* (New York : McKay, 1974) at 52.
22. Christopher Cooper, *French-English Subcultural Segmentation: An Analysis of Consociational Politics in Quebec* (Masters Thesis, University of Alberta, 1986) at 60.

In summary, three clusters of cultural orientations, relating to group identity, elite dominance and tolerance of decision-making by elite cartel, foster successful consociational politics. The western NWT presents a mixed prospect when viewed in terms of these orientations. Constitution-building in the region cannot rest with confidence on them. To succeed, the process of constitution-building will also have to be a process of cultural nurturing, exposing northerners to consociational solutions to practical problems, training them to work through these solutions and fostering in them a confidence in consociational approaches.

Elite Behaviour

Social structure and political culture define the challenges and the prospects for consociationalism; it is elite attitudes and behaviour which bring consociationalism to life. Social structure and political culture can be viewed as determining the *capacity* of the elites to engage in consociational politics. Equally important to the actual development of this form of politics is the *predisposition* of the elites of the various cultural communities to evolve forms of behaviour which bridge the gaps among them.[23]

The first element of this predisposition is an awareness of the costs of intercultural cleavage. The extent to which the elites judge the alternatives to consociation to be unacceptable will determine the vigour with which they pursue it. It would be naive to ignore the probability that most non-aboriginal northerners at present view the alternative to partnership to be a gradual evolution in the direction of the parliamentary system, with aboriginal self-governments wielding little power, primarily of the sort associated with municipal governments. This probably appears tolerable to them. However, they and the aboriginal people of the western NWT still bear the bitter memories of the conflict and social division generated by the proposal in the 1970s to construct a natural gas pipeline the length of the Mackenzie Valley. Their reflection on this episode in their history and the growing reality of crosscutting economic interests among aboriginal and non-aboriginal people has committed them to avoiding the extreme positions which characterized that period. This concern could lead them to reconsider their assessment of the parliamentary system and to realize that, to the extent that majoritarian politics promotes opposition of interests and a struggle for domination, it promises a return to a political atmosphere which they would not wish to see encouraged by future constitutional structures.

---

23. This approach to conceptualizing the relationships among the factors influencing consociational politics is taken from Aunger, *supra*, note 8 at 162.

Observers of consocation generally agree that "the willingness of the elites to engage in consociational practices is likely to be strongest where partisanship is weak or, at least, very moderate."[24] The western NWT satisfies this condition. It is true that most elite members belong to one of the national political parties and that some have achieved positions of substantial prominence in these parties. However, elections at the territorial level have never been fought in terms of party labels and the debate about the appropriateness of party politics in the assembly suggests a significant resistance to parties given the variety of prior issues which the territory needs to resolve. In this sense, the present antipathy to party politics resembles the nonpartisan approach to politics in the Northwest Territories before the creation of Alberta and Saskatchewan.[25] In place of party politics, what has been termed "consensus politics" has dominated the legislative assembly. While its practice has involved sufficient conflict to cast doubt on the appropriateness of the consensus label,[26] there is no doubt that it is consciously non-partisan and contains several elements which can be viewed as pre-consociational in nature.

These elements touch on another aspect of elite behaviour which is judged to promote the prospects for successful consociational politics, namely, a demonstrated willingness on the part of the elite to think in consociational terms and to respond to practical problems with consociational institutions. The approach which has developed to forming the executive exemplifies this willingness:

> ...(regarding the selection of ministers), there seems as yet no vying for office in the sense of teams competing to achieve a monopoly of all offices for a team's members. There is, however, a vying for place designed to secure an equal distribution of political offices as between eastern and western Members. The satisfaction of this political imperative has produced something of a 'grand coalition' government in which the vying for control of all offices has, at least temporarily, been avoided.[27]

Similarly, the Western and Nunavut Constitutional Forums were structured explicitly to guarantee representation to each of the cultural communities in the regions for which they are responsible. Moreover, each cultural community had to agree with policies in order for them to be adopted by a Forum. A further extension of this consociational

---

24. *Id.* at 172.
25. L.H. Thomas, *The Struggle for Responsible Government in the North-West Territories: 1870-1897*, 2nd ed. (Toronto: University of Toronto Press, 1978).
26. Gurston Dacks, "Politics on the Last Frontier: Consociationalism in the Northwest Territories" (1986) 19:2 *Canadian Journal of Political Science* 350-53.
27. G. Eglington, "Matters of Confidence in the Legislative Assembly of the Northwest Territories" Appendix A to Northwest Territories, 10th Legislative Assembly, Special Committee on Rules, Procedures and Privileges, *Third Report* (October 1986) 103.

form of thinking is contained in recommendations to the Legislative Assembly which the Constitutional Alliance of the NWT attached to its 1987 agreement on the boundary for division of the territories:

> ...the Constitutional Alliance of the Northwest Territories recommends to the Legislative Assembly of the Northwest Territories that serious consideration be given to the principle that representation from each of the proposed new territories be guaranteed equally on the Executive Council, among officers of the Legislative Assembly and on certain boards with a territorial mandate.
>
> And further, that serious consideration be given to alternating the Government Leader between each of the proposed new territories, and to holding alternate sessions of the Legislative Assembly in each of the proposed new territories.[28]

If, as Hans Daalder argues,[29] consociational behaviour is learned behaviour, these forms of recognition of the cultural diversity of the territories, endorsed by representatives of all of the cultural communities, including the non-aboriginal, suggest a growing capacity on the part of territorial elites to turn to consociational structures to meet the practical challenges of managing inter-community relations in the future. However, to realize the promise of this capacity, they must first decide that it is in their interest to pursue partnership.

THE PROSPECTS FOR PARTNERSHIP

Can the western or the whole NWT build a constitutional future based on consociation? Most of the factors canvassed above are equivocal and none appears to doom the concept definitively. The aboriginal population will be reluctant to compromise on the very important principle of aboriginal sovereignty, but may view partnership as the best expression of this principle which political realities will allow. In contrast, the non-aboriginal community will approach partnership less enthusiastically for two fundamental reasons. The first is that it will constitute a majority of the new territory's population, hence will find it very much in its interest to pursue a majoritarian constitution. The second reason, which reinforces the first, will be the difficulty non-aboriginals will encounter in thinking of themselves as members of a "cultural collectivity," one of several communities of equal status making

---

28. WCF and NCF, "Memorandum of Understanding Between the Nunavut Constitutional Forum and the Western Constitutional Forum Concerning Recommendations to the Legislation Assembly" (Iqaluit: WCF and NCF, 1987).
29. Hans Daalder, "On Building Consociational Nations: The Cases of the Netherlands and Switzerland," in K.D. McRae, *supra*, note 8 at 121.

up a truly pluralistic society. Finding the will to organize on this unfamiliar basis, particularly when the material advantage in doing so is hard to discern, will prove difficult.

The response to these problems could take two forms. The first is to structure the institutions of partnership so that they are as appealing as possible to the non-aboriginal population which is likely to be least enthusiastic about the general principle of consociation, hence to bargain hardest against threatening or unfamiliar aspects of its application. The second response is to recognize that, because consociational behaviour is learned behaviour, it may be possible to structure the process of constitutional negotiation to encourage among the non-aboriginal population, or at least its elite, a tendency to turn to consociational responses for particular problems, perhaps not initially with enthusiasm, but with a recognition that they represent the best available solution. In this way, the pragmatism which characterizes consociation can be the vehicle which builds non-aboriginal support for it. The process of negotiation is as significant as the outcome.

The need to obtain non-aboriginal support for a partnership constitution will probably dictate choices regarding certain of the structural options which consociationalism affords. It can be anticipated that the non-aboriginal community will feel particular concern over the prospect for deadlock in the assembly which the mutual veto provisions of a consociational constitution offer. Indeed, the pre-Confederation history of the two Canadas offers some precedent for this anxiety. Responding to this anxiety will require defining as narrowly and specifically as possible those cultural matters regarding which the legislative mutual veto procedures apply. It would help to emphasize segmental autonomy as the first line of cultural self- protection. Allocating to the cultural community councils relatively broad powers over matters of cultural interest will reduce both the decisional load of the Assembly and the potential for deadlock in it. Both consequences will promote its effective functioning. As will be argued below, the need to build overarching feelings of community among all people in the western NWT suggests that shared interests ought to be emphasized in the process of negotiating a partnership constitution.

However, substantial segmental autonomy may prove a necessary result of these discussions in that elite-mass relations and cultural orientations supportive of consociation are not obviously strong in the western NWT; autonomy will reduce the strain between elite members and the people they represent, which arise when the elites must pursue prolonged negotiations, by reducing the need for these interactions. In time, as these dealings prove themselves and as people come to accept them and the sharing of intercultural interest they embody, consociational practice may evolve in a more centralized direction, with the role of the community councils diminishing and that of the Assembly growing. In the Assembly itself it will probably be desirable to state as a principle of interpretation that residual power lies with the Assembly as a whole, rather than, as the aboriginal communities might prefer, with the cultural community caucuses. It is a different question whether the grounds for cultural community vetos regarding constitutional matters ought to be so narrowly drawn because the protections at issue are absolutely fundamental to the cultural future of the aboriginal communities and because society can tolerate a rigid constitution more easily than it can manage a deadlocked process. However, regarding other constitutional choices, the general rule that segmental autonomy is more attractive to the non-aboriginal population than is mutual veto suggests a very important consideration for negotiators.

The fear of deadlock in the assembly may also be reduced if the constitution contains some explicit budgetary formula or process which guarantees the proportionality of funding among the cultural community councils. This would secure one of the basic elements of consociational arrangements and reduce the likelihood of the Assembly being burdened by a potentially very divisive subject of debate.

These provisions are likely to appeal to non-aboriginal northerners: the most reluctant cultural community. In addition, constitutional engineering ought also to consider the technical issue, that is, to identify structural features which will enhance the operation of a consociational constitution once the principle of consociation is accepted. Of these features, the first is to avoid imposing upon the legislative assembly the parliamentary logic of party discipline and largely adversarial inter-party relations which impedes the formation of grand coalitions. Specifically, the practice of responsible government might have to be modified to make it easier for members of the executive to negotiate amongst themselves without fear of losing a vote of confidence before this sometimes necessarily lengthy process can be completed. For example, it might be provided that the Executive Council can only be defeated on an explicit motion of want of confidence, or even that such motions shall only be entertained once during each session of the Assembly, that is, twice a year. Because the members of a coalition cabinet will have to be able, if necessary, to represent publicly their social groupings, the practice of cabinet solidarity is another parliamentary element which cannot figure in any consociational governmental process. Indeed, the MLA's from particular cultural community caucuses may wish to be assured the power to remove an executive member representing their cultural community if they feel that he or she has failed adequately to represent that community.

A second feature of a consociational constitution will be to structure the Assembly to represent directly the various cultural communities. While separate electoral lists for cultural communities may trouble many Canadians because of their superficial resemblance to features of apartheid, the analogy is totally misplaced.[30] Indeed, it is mischievous, given that the goal of consociation is to protect rather than subjugate cultural minorities. Making legislators unequivocally dependent upon the votes of their cultural communities is the best guarantee that the concerns of the communities will form the basis of political debate, rather than being deflected and refracted as occurs when geography is made the sole basis of representation.

Partnership offers a real option to the western Northwest Territories. However, it is unlikely to be able to sell itself politically on its own merits, for reasons which have already been identified. This suggests that its success depends on political campaigns by those interests which are already convinced that it represents the best available option for future social harmony and constitutional development in the region. If the aboriginal people see partnership as their last best hope, they would be well advised to demonstrate to the non-aboriginal community the unattractiveness of the alternatives to partnership. The most credible alternative as well as the best fallback position should the pursuit of partnership fail is aboriginal self-government. If the non-aboriginal population felt that Ottawa might approve a form of aboriginal self-government which, together with rights gained as a result of claims settlements, might significantly limit the ability of the Government of the Northwest Territories to act in a variety of matters, they might be motivated to negotiate in order to avoid the frustrations which they would anticipate would follow from this excess of segmental autonomy. It is worth noting in this regard that the memorandum of agreement concerning the boundary for division specifies that the relevant aspects of the partnership arrangements to be worked out for the western territory's constitution "are designed to constitute together with provisions in lands claims agreements, the definition of aboriginal self-government in the western jurisdiction."[31] This suggests an anxiety on the part of the non-aboriginal population which offers the aboriginal backers of partnership the promise of real leverage, if they pursue it persuasively.

---

30. Asch and Dacks, *supra*, note 3 at 40-41.
31. WCF and NCF, "Boundary and Constitutional Agreement for the Implementation of Division of the Northwest Territories" (Iqaluit: WCF and NCF, 1987) at 5.

The most powerful player in the game is, of course, the government of Canada, whose role distinguishes the western NWT from all other experiences of consociational evolution. In other states, the contending cultural communities have had to manage their relations independent of any higher authority. In the Canadian context, whatever accommodations are reached in the North must be approved in Ottawa. Indeed, Ottawa can take a more active role in fostering successful negotiations by manipulating the dependence of various northern interests regarding a number of questions it controls. The fact that this involvement could alter the balance of factors described in this paper poses for Ottawa the very difficult problem of how to intrude on the process in a fashion which will be accepted as legitimate. Ottawa's delicate problem is how to square the political circle of providing leadership without being accused of paternalism or bias. Because this is probably an impossible task, Ottawa's best strategy may just be to keep directing the various cultural communities back to the bargaining table. It could contribute by maximizing the interest which all feel in finding a consociational bargain and making it work. For example, Ottawa might compel the non-aboriginal population to negotiate with greater commitment by compelling it to understand that Ottawa views a single public government based on the parliamentary system to be an inappropriate model for the constitutional future. Ottawa might accomplish this by enhancing the credibility of an aboriginal self-government in the territory, perhaps by allocating funds and personnel to developing this model in conjunction with the aboriginal people. Ottawa could also announce a suspension of planning for devolution of jurisdiction northward until the form of government for the new western territory is confirmed or suggest criteria it will apply when approving a constitution. Further, it could commit itself to a review of the operation of the constitution after a specified period of time so as to reduce anxieties based on a sense that decisions, including possible mistakes, which may be reached will be exceedingly difficult to correct once the constitution is in place.

Constitutional development is, as much as anything, a process of learning. At present, a variety of factors combine to obscure the relevance of partnership for the people of the region. Chief among them is the sense that such a great gulf separates the interests of the various cultural communities that there is insufficient will to make a consociational legislative assembly and executive function. The political reality as the 1980s close is not promising for the partnership model. It appears that the Government of the NWT is eager to extend its authority in ways which alienate the aboriginal groups. Their likeliest response is to pursue aboriginal self-government. Still, northerners may develop consociational attitudes. They are likelier to do so if the Constitutional Alliance emphasizes the shared rather than the separate and contending interests of the different cultural communities. If the Alliance wants to seriously pursue the possibility of consociation, the first item on its agenda ought to see the representatives of the various cultural communities trading lists of the fullest amount of jurisdiction which they think the shared structures of a partnership government ought to control and ideas as to how to promote the effective functioning of these joint structures of government. This is not the obvious strategy for approaching a situation in which all parties are anxious about protecting very fundamental interests, in which conflict is unavoidable, in which bargaining will inevitably figure, and in which the model which results from this bargaining will have to be checked against the bottom line of each of the communities. However, all people in the western NWT, or the whole NWT failing division, need to appreciate most fully the political interests which they share if they are to negotiate and support innovative constitution-building. If negotiators seek to evolve constitutional models with a strategy of pushing their own respective interests, they will reinforce the perception that what is taking place is a zero-sum game. What they ought to do instead is to seek a measure of success in their interactions. This will build mutual trust and their own confidence in the process, enable them to build support for the evolving model within their respective communities, and encourage them to persevere at difficult stages in their discussions.

CONCLUSION

The social structure of the western NWT and of the NWT all told makes a parliamentary form of government ill-suited to the needs of the region. It makes a system based on consociational arrangements more appropriate. However, such a system will not realize itself. It will have to be fashioned out of the political sociology of the region, through a process which itself must embody a consociational sensibility. The outcome of such a process cannot be predicted because it will be a pragmatic response to an evolving set of circumstances. The most that can be said by way of anticipation is that the social structure, political culture, and elite behaviour afford appropriate materials for a consociational future. Whether a viable structure is fashioned from these materials will depend on the wisdom and will of the Constitutional Alliance — the government and aboriginal leaders of the Northwest Territories.

Partie VI / Part VI

Minorités linguistiques : expériences internationales et canadiennes

L'expérience des minorités linguistiques varie souvent et ne se prête donc pas à des comparaisons aisées. Les tensions qui existent entre les groupes linguistiques dominants et les minorités, et la menace d'assimilation qui en résulte, sont cependant une expérience que partagent toutes les collectivités linguistiques minoritaires dont il est question ici.

Rudolfo de la Garza et Armando Trujillo examinent le débat relatif aux langues officielles aux États-Unis et étudient le mouvement politique qui a tenté de faire de l'anglais la seule langue officielle du pays. Les auteurs montrent que le mouvement a été motivé par des malentendus portant sur l'affluence des immigrants latins et la probabilité de leur assimilation. Relevant la difficulté constitutionnelle et le caractère indésirable de la reconnaissance d'une langue officielle, ils proposent que le gouvernement continue à poursuivre ses affaires en anglais, à quelques exceptions près, en attendant l'assimilation visée des communautés immigrantes par la vaste communauté anglaise.

Toivo Miljan parle des tensions linguistiques et ethniques existant en République socialiste soviétique d'Estonie. Miljan décrit la tentative soviétique d'assimilation et la résistance des Estoniens. L'affluence considérable de russophones en Estonie, lesquels font fonctionner l'appareil politique et économique soviétique, a donné lieu a de larges groupes de russophones opposés à l'idée d'une nation-État estonienne. Avec une opposition si imposante et si bruyante, l'Estonie n'évoluera probablement que vers une forme de souveraineté-association avec l'Union soviétique, dans un avenir proche.

La minorité anglophone du Québec définit depuis longtemps le débat linguistique comme la lutte des libertés individuelles contre les droits de la collectivité francophone. Ronald Rudin estime qu'il s'agit là d'une simplification exagérée, qui ne prend pas en considération la façon dont les intérêts collectifs des deux groupes sont régis par les lois linguistiques au Québec. S'il est vrai que ces lois reflètent la position du français comme langue de la majorité, elles respectent aussi les droits collectifs des anglophones en garantissant le droit à l'instruction en anglais, ainsi que le droit de faire affaires en anglais dans les petits établissements commerciaux et culturels.

Les communautés francophones hors Québec sont loin d'avoir subi le même sort. Kenneth Munro suit l'histoire des revendications en matière de langue française et de droits à l'éducation française en Alberta, et décrit les stratégies rhétoriques utilisées. Dans leurs luttes pour la reconnaissance du français comme langue officielle, les Franco-Albertains s'en sont remis traditionnellement à la loi. À partir de 1988, ils font surtout appel à l'«esprit de la Confédération». Jusqu'en 1982, les Franco-Albertains invoquent ce même «esprit de Confédération» pour obtenir le droit à l'éducation en français. Ils commencent ensuite à s'appuyer sur la *Charte*. Munro se montre plus optimiste en matière des droits à l'instruction — garantis par la Constitution — que dans le domaine du bilinguisme officiel, lequel requiert la coopération de l'Alberta.

Linguistic Minorities :
International and Domestic Experiences

The experiences of linguistic minorities are often very dissimilar and hence do not lend themselves to easy comparison. Tensions between the dominant language group and that of the minority and the resulting threat of assimilation are, however, an experience common to all of the minority language communities discussed in this part.

Rudolfo de la Garza and Armando Trujillo consider the official language debate in the United States and study the political movement to make English the country's only official language. De la Garza and Trujillo show how the movement has been motivated by misunderstandings about the influx of Latinos and the likelihood of their assimilation. Noting the constitutional difficulty, and undesirability, of recognizing an official language, they propose that the government continue to conduct its business in English, subject to certain exceptions, with the ultimate objective being the assimilation of those communities into the larger English Community.

Toivo Miljan discusses the linguistic and ethnic tensions in the Soviet Republic of Estonia. Miljan describes the Soviet attempt to assimilate the Estonians, who have so far successfully resisted those pressures. The large influx of Russian speakers into Estonia, to staff the Soviet political and economic apparatus, has resulted in large pockets of Russian speakers resistant to the idea of the Estonian nation state. With such a large and vocal opposition, Estonia is likely to move in the near future only towards some form of sovereignty-association with the Soviet Union.

The Anglophone minority in Québec has long characterized the linguistic debate as a battle of individual liberties versus the collective rights of Francophone Québecers. Ronald Rudin considers this an oversimplification which fails to account for the way in which the collective interests of both groups have been accommodated in Québec language laws. While those laws have reflected the fact that French is the language of the majority, they have also given expression to the collective rights of Anglophones by guaranteeing a right to English language education as well as to conducting business in the English language in small commercial and cultural establishments.

French language communities outside of Québec have not fared as well. Kenneth Munro traces the history of claims to French language and educational rights in Alberta and the rhetorical strategies that have been employed to advance them. In fighting for the recognition of French as an official language in Alberta, Franco-Albertans have traditionally relied on the law. Since 1988, Munro explains, that strategy has been converted into one stressing the "spirit of confederation". In fighting for French language education, until 1982 Franco-Albertans relied on the same "spirit of confederation" argument to advance their claims. After 1982, however, they began relying on *Charter* rights. Munro is more optimistic about the prospects of success in education, where constitutional rights can be invoked, rather than in the field of official bilingualism, where the cooperation of the province of Alberta must be obtained.

LATINOS AND THE OFFICIAL ENGLISH DEBATE IN THE UNITED STATES: LANGUAGE IS NOT THE ISSUE

Rodolfo O. De La Garza and Armando Trujillo*

INTRODUCTION

A major item on the American political agenda is the debate regarding making English the nation's official language. Although language issues are not new to American politics, they are now more particularly salient. Amendments to make English the official language have been introduced into Congress annually since 1981. In 1988, for only the second time in its history, Congress scheduled hearings on an English language amendment to the Constitution, and four Official English bills have been introduced for consideration in 1989 by the House of Representatives. Also, fourteen of the sixteen states that have passed some form of Official English policy have done so since 1981, and similar legislation is pending in eleven other states.[1]

It is easy to conclude mistakenly that this is merely the most recent instance of nativists bringing anti-immigrant issues to the national political agenda, as has occurred previously in the nation's history.[2] Supporting this view are the close links between U.S. English, the principal organization supporting an official language policy, and groups that support restrictionist immigration policy such as the Federation for American Immigration Reform, the U.S. Border Patrol, the National Unity Fund and the American Ethnic Coalition.[3] Leaders of such organizations have warned that continued immigration from Latin

---

* Thanks to Luis Fraga for his comments on an earlier version of this paper.

1. M. C. Combs and L.M. Lynch, "English Plus" (1988) 6:4 *English Today* 36-42.
2. S. B. Heath, "Language and Politics in the U.S." in M. Sanille-Traike, ed., *Georgetown University Round Table on Languages and Linguistics* (Washington, D.C.: Georgetown University Press, 1977) and S. B. Heath, "Language Policies" (1983) 20:4 *Society* 56-63.
3. M. C. Combs and L.M. Lynch, *supra*, note 1 at 36-42.

America could cause "a serious cultural decline"[4] and threaten the political status of the "present majority".[5] Because now Latin American immigrants are the targets of the Nativists, Latinos are leading the counterattack.

While there is no question that nativist sentiments are fuelling much of the current debate, many supporters of Official English are not nativists. Indeed, it is noteworthy that in 1988 both major presidential candidates spoke out against Official English, and in Arizona, Colorado and Florida, the electorate approved Official English amendments despite bipartisan non-Latino opposition by the major political leadership in these states.[6]

Rather than being motivated by nativism, it is more plausible to argue that a majority of voters has been persuaded by Official English advocates that current language policy has been designed to enable recent immigrants, most of whom are Spanish speakers, to remain monolingual in their native languages. These voters fear this will result in the breakdown of national unity and must therefore be resisted. Official English advocates use such rhetoric to rally non-nativist Americans to their cause and mobilize them into an inchoate political block with substantial and growing influence. These arguments ignore how civil rights policies have shaped state and federal language policies since the 1960s and inaccurately describe the linguistic behavior of the nation's Latino population, including new immigrants.

In order to participate effectively in the current debate it is essential to understand the origin and intent of current language policies and the actual linguistic behavior of U.S. Latinos. The objective of this paper therefore is to clarify the context that has given rise to the controversy regarding Official English. It will begin with a brief review of the history of American language policy. It will then suggest that there are constitutional arguments for opposing the establishment of any official language that merit further attention by opponents of Official English. It will also argue that while these historical and constitutional considerations are the basis for opposing the establishment of an official language, they are insufficient as guides for the development of national language policy. Such policy must be historically and constitutionally informed, but it should also be compatible with (or limited by) the objectives of the nation's immigrant policy and relevant domestic policies, especially with regard to civil rights and affirmative action. The final

---

4. J. Crawford "English Issue Hides Immigration, Population Agendas" *Mesa Tribune* (21 October 1988).
5. J. Crawford "Official English Would Promote Ethnic Disunity," *Arizona Tribune* (23 October 1988) D3.
6. 1 :4 *Epic Events* (Newsletter of the English Plus Information Clearinghouse) (September/ October, 1988).

section of the paper offers a broad outline for a national language policy that takes into account all of these factors.

THE ORIGINS OF U.S. LANGUAGE POLICY

The framers of the Constitution were pragmatists as well as theorists. They recognized (and some were concerned about) the multilingual character of their constituencies and thus understood how divisive any attempt to establish an official language would be. They also understood the nation's future need for immigrants, and perhaps they concluded that establishing an official language would suggest that some groups would be less welcome than others.[7] Their actions indicate that they also recognized the benefits that would accrue from a common language. So, they adopted a multi-faceted strategy that established English as the national language without declaring it official and thereby provoking controversy. First, they kept language issues out of the Constitution. Second, because the Constitution did not grant the federal government any specific authority on language issues, each state would be free to establish its own language policy. Third, the federal government would conduct all of its business in English and thus make English the language of public discourse. Since its founding, then, the United States has never been neutral in its language policy. It has instead established English as its national language while simultaneously opposing any legal provisions that would make English the sole or official language.[8]

Federal court decisions and state and federal policies have further institutionalized the status English enjoys as the national language. Beginning with the *Nationality Act* of 1906,[9] and continuing through the *Immigration and Reform Act* of 1986, with noted exceptions, aliens have been required to know English to become naturalized. Also, in a series of decisions in the 1920s culminating with *Meyer* v. *Nebraska*,[10] the Supreme Court upheld the right of states to make English the official language of instruction.

---

7. S. B. Heath, *supra*, note 2 and D. F. Marshall, "The Question of an Official Language: Language Rights and the English Language Amendment" (1986) *International Journal of the Sociology of Language* 60.
8. Notes, "Official English: Federal Limits on Efforts to Curtail Bilingual Services in the States" (1987) 100 *Harvard Law Review* 1345-1362; J. A. Fishman, *The Rise and Fall of the Ethnic Revival: Perspectives on Language and Ethnicity* (New York: Mouton Publishers, 1985).
9. A. H. Leibowitz "Language and the Law: The Exercise of Power Through Official Designation of Language," in W. M. O'Barr and J.F. O'Barr, eds, *Language and Politics* (The Hague: Mouton, 1976).
10. *Meyer* v. *Nebraska*, 262 U.S. 390 (1923).

In *Meyer* v. *Nebraska*, however, the Supreme Court also declared it unconstitutional to restrict complementary or supplementary second language efforts by various ethnic groups.[11] This decision may be seen as maintaining a line of reasoning begun by Chief Justice John Marshall which argues that any legal provisions that make English the sole national and official language run counter to constitutional provisions regarding freedom of speech and freedom of religion.[12]

At the center of the U.S. constitutional system is the principle preserving individual rights and freedoms from governmental encroachment. Since the nation's founding, the law regarding how individuals exercise those rights and freedoms has gradually expanded toward an increasingly clarified position of official state neutrality. That is, the law has continuously evolved to constrain governmental agencies from defining the content of an individual's rights and freedoms or limiting how they will be exercised. The evolution of the law regarding freedom of religion illustrates this point. Repeated challenges to state policies that either support a particular religious variant or infringe on the views of those who are not religious have resulted in a greatly reduced state role in the promotion of religious activities. The recent attacks by Christian fundamentalists on those policies is proof of the extent to which former pro-Christian state policies have been curtailed. The reasoning behind this curtailment is illustrated in Supreme Court Justice Sandra Day O'Connor's concurring opinion in *Lynch* v. *Donnelly*[13] which argued that the Establishment Clause of the Constitution "prohibits government from making adherence to a religion relevant in any way to a person's standing in the political community." The same consequence would result if government endorsed or disapproved of religion. "Endorsement sends a message to non-adherents that they are outsiders, not full members of the political community, and an accompanying message to adherents that they are insiders, favored members of the political community. Disapproval sends the opposite message." (Ironically, this decision upheld the right of municipalities to display creches on the grounds that they were national rather than religious symbols.)

Another area where individual rights have been expanded is illustrated by *Roe* v. *Wade*,[14] the case that upholds the right of women to make their own reproductive decisions. In this decision Justice Douglas argued that the Ninth Amendment creates a:

---

11. Leibowitz, *supra*, note 9.
12. J. A. Fishman, *supra*, note 8.
13. *Lynch* v. Donnelly, 465 U.S. 668 at 687-88 (1984).
14. *Roe* v. *Wade*, 410 U.S. 113 at 210-211 (1973) (emphasis removed).

catalogue of rights... First is the autonomous control over the development and expression of one's intellect, interests, tastes and personality. These are rights protected by the First Amendment and, in my view, they are absolute, permitting of no exception... Second is freedom of choice in the basic decisions of one's life respecting marriage, divorce, procreation, contraception, and the education and upbringing of children.

Court actions in subsequent related cases have prevented even hostile administrations from circumventing the intent of this decision. Again, the intensity of the right-to-life movement is testimony to the extent to which these decisions have emphasized individual freedoms over governmental authority. The principle that protects these individual rights and freedoms and the arguments by Justices O'Connor and Douglas also clearly extend to the private use of language. Nothing can be more personal or private than an individual's language. Language is key to an individual's identity and sense of community.[15] The State has always acknowledged this and thus has prohibited efforts to regulate private language use.[16] Individuals have with rare exceptions always been free to speak the language of their choice in private spheres and to develop and maintain institutions that promote those languages. The exceptions such as occurred during World War I[17] were short-lived aberrations explainable by wartime fervor that were subsequently declared unconstitutional.

The language rights issue is intrinsically more complex than the other issues we have discussed, however, because it is an issue on which it is impossible for the state to remain neutral. The state must use language to communicate, and through its choice of the language it uses to communicate, it endorses one language over another. To be truly neutral on language would require the state to conduct all of its business in all of the languages used by the populace. This is obviously an impossible burden today, as it was when the nation was founded. To be more "neutral" than what the federal government now is would be impractical: to be less so would violate the constitutional requirement that the government remain substantively neutral regarding the content and exercise of individual freedoms. This is why the state has no official language, and why together these historical and constitutional arguments offer solid foundations for opposing the establishment of an official language.

---

15. J. A. Fishman, *Language and Nationalism* (Rowley, Mass.:Newbury House Publishers, 1972) at 46.
16. J. A. Fishman, *supra*, note 8.
17. S. T. Wagner "The Historical Background of Bilingualism and Biculturalism in the United States" in M. Ridge, ed., *The New Bilingualism* (Los Angeles:University of California Press, 1981).

The ultimate objective of participating in the current language debate transcends beating back Official English, however. It also includes responding to the concerns of non-nativists about what the nation's language policy should be. The following section examines those concerns and offers a proposal for dealing with them.

THE NEW SOCIAL CONTEXT

The concerns about the need for a new language policy are a function of the interaction of three issues. The first is the belief that the nation is experiencing unprecedented increases in immigration. The second is that most of the new immigrants are from cultural backgrounds so distinct from mainstream American society that they will not easily become a part of the nation. Third and most significant is the perception that recently initiated governmental practices encourage these immigrants to retain their native language and eliminate the need to learn English. This will lead to their developing and maintaining distinct communities rather than integrating into mainstream society as have earlier immigrants. The first of these is incorrect, the second is empirically unverifiable and is essentially a racist proposition, and the last is unsupported by available data.

While immigration has been high in recent years, it has been higher in decades past. On the one hand, close to half of the approximately 10 million persons who have become permanent legal residents in countries other than their country of origin reside in the United States. Nonetheless, only 6.2 percent of U.S. residents in 1980 were foreign born; this is less than half the percentage of foreign born in 1910.[18] Thus, while in absolute terms the number of recent immigrants is high, the overall size of the immigrant population relative to the nation's total population would not seem sufficient to generate current controversy. Its importance is only understood when seen in association with the assumption that these new immigrants will develop and maintain linguistically and culturally separate communities.

The second factor to take into account is that the new immigrants are predominantly non-Protestant Western Europeans and non-English speakers. Exacerbating this is that while earlier waves of immigrants were from multiple language groups, recent immigrants are predominantly Spanish speaking. The fact that large segments of society bitterly protested against earlier waves of Southern European and Irish Catholics and yet the nation successfully absorbed them should illustrate that those

---

18. A. Anderson, *Illegal Aliens and Employer Sanctions: Solving the Wrong Problem* (Stanford: Hoover Institute, 1986).

characteristics alone also cannot explain current concerns.[19] Like the previous issue, this factor becomes important only when it is assumed that these immigrants will remain apart from society.

The third factor is the perception that recent policy initiatives encourage immigrants to retain their native languages and reduce or eliminate their need to learn English. This argument revolves around the following points. Unlike prior immigrants, recent immigrants will develop and maintain their own communities, retain their native languages and remain apart from the rest of society. In prior decades, government policies did not encourage or facilitate such separatist practices, and therefore there was no need to make English the official language. The development of recent policies has weakened the integrative processes of society and the status of English as the national language. Therefore, it is necessary to make English the nation's official language.

Studies of the linguistic behavior of Latinos offer no evidence supporting these assertions. To the contrary, among Latinos "assimilation to the English group occurs more rapidly now than it did one hundred years ago".[20] Also, a 1984 survey by the National Opinion Research Center found that 81 percent of Latinos believe that speaking and understanding English is "a very important" obligation of citizenship, and 17 percent think it important. Another study found that 60 percent of 14- to 17-year-old Latinos seldom use Spanish.[21] Other research has found that after fifteen years, approximately 75 percent of Latino immigrants speak English on a regular daily basis, that 70 percent of children of Latino parents become essentially English speaking, and that the third generation has English as its mother tongue.[22]

The concerns regarding the need for official English thus are rooted in a misunderstanding regarding the origin and objectives of the policies under question. As illustrated by the *Voting Rights Act* (VRA) of 1965, these policies were designed initially to insure that Blacks would enjoy equal access to governmental services and the political process. With the VRA, the federal government initiated procedures that altered its well established policy of promoting only English as the national language. Because states had with regularity used English literacy tests to deny Blacks and Mexican Americans (and in earlier periods Irish, Finnish,

---

19. L. Dinnerstein and D.M. Reimers, *Ethnic Americans: A History of Immigration* (New York: Harper and Row, 1988).
20. Combs and Lynch, *supra*, note 1.
21. *Ibid.*
22. M. Jimenez, "Official Use of English", *A B A Journal* (December 1988) 34-35.

and Asian immigrants) the right to vote,[23] the VRA prohibited English literacy as a condition for enfranchisement. The renewal of the VRA in 1975 extended additional linguistic protection to language minorities by requiring:

> distribution of bilingual voting materials in any jurisdiction where more than five percent of the citizens of voting age are members of a single language minority and the percentage of such persons who have not completed the fifth primary grade is higher than the national rate. In such jurisdictions, federal law requires state and local governments to provide bilingual ballots in the voters' primary language.[24]

As the Civil Rights Movement spread to the Southwest, the federal government required public agencies to provide services in languages other than English to language minorities who had historically been the victims of state sponsored or sanctioned discrimination. To Mexican Americans, this meant initiating bilingual education programs.[25] Although there was disagreement as to whether these were intended to produce stable bilingualism with maintenance of the home culture as well as of the home language, or provide a smooth transition from the native language to English, there was no demand for monolingual Spanish education. The demand for bilingual education, thus, is best understood as a demand for an end to discriminatory education which would result in Mexican American children learning English. It was only secondarily a demand for Spanish language and Mexican cultural education. Whatever Mexican Americans hoped for from bilingual education, what they got in the 1968 *Bilingual Education Act* "was primarily an act for the Anglification of non-English speakers and not an act for Bilingualism".[26]

The demand by Mexican Americans and other language minorities for bilingual education combined with the Supreme Court decision in *Lau* v. *Nichols*[27] to produce a major departure in national language policy.[28] The Lau decision requires all school districts in the United States

---

23. Leibowitz, *supra*, note 9.
24. Notes, *supra*, note 8.
25. A. Pifer, *Bilingual Education and the Hispanic Challenge* (Arlington, Va.: Center for Applied Linguistics, 1980); R. Salome, *Public Policy and the Law: Legal Precedents and Prospects for Equity in Education*, Report submitted to the Race, Sex and National Origin Desegregations Assistance Center (New York University, Rutgers University, Columbia University, 1982).
26. J.A. Fishman, "Language Policy: Past, Present, and Future," in C.A. Ferguson and S.B. Heath, eds, *Language in the U.S.A.* (Cambridge: Cambridge University Press, 1981).
27. *Lau* v. *Nichols*, 414 U.S. 563 (1974).
28. S.B. Heath, "Language Policies", (1983) 20:4 *Society* 56-63; D.F. Marshall, *supra*, note 7.

with more than 20 limited-English students from a single language background to inform the Office of Civil Rights regarding the programs they are offering to these students.[29] In effect, after *Lau*, national law required that schools with a minimum number of non-English speaking elementary school students design methods that would enable those students to participate in the schools' educational programs. To be certain, bilingual education is under constant attack and the number of students who participate in such programs is only a small percentage of those eligible to do so.[30] Nonetheless, the institutionalization of bilingual programs must be recognized as the first example of the federal policy explicitly supporting the use of languages other than English. It is also essential to reiterate that bilingual programs were one aspect of federal civil rights policy that was designed to break down the segregation Mexican American and other language minorities had experienced and to provide them a mechanism for equal educational access.

It was for similar reasons that the 1975 VRA mandated the use of non-English ballots and related electoral materials. As Congress reviewed the extent to which Mexican Americans had been denied access to the political process, it became clear that a major factor contributing to that exclusion was that the electoral process was conducted completely in English.[31] For generations, Mexican Americans had been denied access to school and were effectively segregated from all aspects of mainstream American life[32] and therefore as a population had been denied the opportunity to learn English. The requirement that they vote in English thus was tantamount to a "grandfather clause" for many Mexican Americans. Moreover, because the English requirement was part of a package of devices that included, among others, the poll tax and at-large election schemes, the English requirement was a symbol that Mexican Americans were not wanted in the political process.[33]

With the 1975 VRA, Congress required that non-English election materials be made available to voters in electoral districts with histories

---

29. G.P. Guthrie, *A School Divided: An Ethnography of Bilingual Education in a Chinese Community* (Hillsdale N.J.: Erlbaum, 1985).

30. United States, General Accounting Office, *Bilingual Voting Assistance: Costs of and Use During the November 1984 General Election* (GAO/GGD 86-134BR) (Washington, D.C.: General Accounting Office, 1986).

31. C.F. Garcia and R. de la Garza, *The Chicano Political Experience: Three Perspectives* (North Scituate: Duxbury Press, 1977).

32. Thomas Carter, *Mexican Americans in School: A History of Educational Neglect* (New York: College Entrance Examination Board, 1970); D. Foley et al., *From Peones to Politicos: Ethnic Relations in a South Texas Town, 1900-1970* (Austin: Center for Mexican American Studies, University of Texas Press, 1978); D. Montejano, *Anglos and Mexicans in the Making of Texas, 1836-1986* (Austin: University of Texas Press, 1987).

33. Garcia and de la Garza, *supra*, note 31.

of discrimination or with low levels of minority electoral participation. Again, the objective was to eliminate the barriers that governmental authorities had established to deny U.S. citizens access to the political process. With this legislation, the federal government once again was acting in explicit support of languages other than English.

In the Northeast, the same concern for the right of all citizens to have equal access to the political process motivated Congress to include Puerto Ricans within the 1965 VRA. With that legislation, Puerto Ricans who were not literate in English were allowed to register and vote by showing evidence of having completed six years of schooling in Puerto Rico.[34] A federal court expanded these rights in 1973 when it required New York to allow all non-English speaking Puerto Rican residents of the state to vote and provide them with Spanish language materials if they were needed.[35] This decision recognizes that both Spanish and English are the official languages of Puerto Rico and that Puerto Ricans are not required to know English.[36] As citizens, Puerto Ricans must be allowed to exercise their political rights. Given the particular linguistic situation of Puerto Ricans, therefore, it follows that the State must provide them bilingual ballots to insure that, as U.S. citizens, Puerto Ricans are not denied equal access to the political process.

It is noteworthy that these policies did not generate widespread protest when they were enacted. Indeed, except for designated areas in the South and Southwest, most U.S. citizens including local level officials may have been unaware of them.[37] The intended beneficiaries do not even make much use of them.[38] In 1988, for example, only 6 percent of Mexican American voters in the Texas presidential primary used Spanish language ballots exclusively.[39] It is only since the increases in immigration that these policies have come under attack.

When bilingual ballots and bilingual education were introduced, it was clear that they were intended to help historically discriminated groups overcome the societally imposed barriers that had prevented them from fully participating in American society. Also, immigration was not

---

34. J.P. Fitzpatrick, "The Puerto Rican Community in New York City" in F. Cordasco and E. Bucchioni, eds, *The Puerto Ricans 1493-1973* (Dobbs Ferry, N.Y.: Oceana Publications, 1973).
35. *Torres* v. *Sachs*, 381 F. Supp. 309 (S.D. N.Y. 1974).
36. I.S. Santiago, "Language Policy and Education in Puerto Rico and the Continent" (1984) 1:1 *International Education Journal* 61-90.
37. R. de la Garza and G. Cardenas. "The Impact of the Voting Rights Act in Uvalde County, Texas" in *Bilingual Elections at Work in the Southwest: A Mexican American Legal Defense and Educational Report* (1982).
38. G.A.O., *supra*, note 30.
39. II:2 *Southwest Voter Research Notes* (May 1988). (A Monthly Publication of the Southwest Voter Research Institute).

a national issue at that time. Today, however, immigration is an issue, and Official English advocates mobilize support for their cause by implying that these programs were designed to serve the new immigrants, and that their consequence is to retard if not completely prevent the integration of new immigrants into American society. For example, Linda Chavez, until recently the president of Official English, states:

> In the last few decades, we have drifted toward a language policy that places the maintenance of an immigrant's native language and culture ahead of efforts to promote the acquisition of English... If government pursues a policy primarily directed at native language maintenance and continues to expand efforts to provide government services in an immigrant's native language, the natural process of assimilation and language acquisition, which historically has always taken place, may not be repeated in the future.[40]

What is new, then, about the context in which these issues are being debated today is that the nation is at a point in its history where two types of policies that developed autonomously are now intersecting. On the one hand are policies such as bilingual education and bilingual electoral assistance that originated in the civil rights movement to provide language and ethnic minorities equal access to American society. On the other hand are immigration policies that have resulted in large numbers of immigrants who are thought to be participating in the expanded social service programs of the nation that have developed since the 1940s, including those generated by the civil rights movement. The consequence of the intersection of these independently developed policies has been to produce the perception that immigrants are enjoying all the benefits American society has to offer while remaining apart from that society.[41] That many Americans share this view is indicated by the often repeated charges that legal and undocumented immigrants participate extensively in government social service programs. In 1981, for example, 62 percent of the nation agreed that illegal immigrants "take more from the U.S. economy through social services and unemployment benefits than they contribute to the U.S. economy through taxes and productivity".[42] This same concern explains why legal immigrants, including those who received amnesty under the *Immigration Reform and Control Act* of 1986, are prohibited from participating in social welfare programs for at least five years.

---

40. L. Chavez, "Official English Amendment II: Should English Become Florida's Official Language?" *The Miami Herald* (6 October, 1988).
41. P. Schuck and R.S. Smith, *Citizenship Without Consent: Illegal Aliens in the American Polity* (New Haven: Yale University Press, 1985).
42. W.A. Cornelius, *America in the Era of Limits: Nativist Reactions to the 'New' Immigration* (San Diego: Center for U.S. Mexican Studies, University of California, 1982).

At issue, then, is the perception that current governmental policies have created an imbalance in the relationship between society and immigrants. Large numbers of Americans seem concerned that the obligations of society to the immigrant have expanded while the obligations of the immigrant to society have declined. It is that sentiment that is producing the demand that the language policies that developed in the last two decades be rescinded and that English be declared the nation's official language.

All nations distinguish between the rights of undocumented immigrants, legal resident aliens, and citizens.[43] Many, including Japan and the United States, also distinguish between the rights of native born and naturalized citizens. The convergence of the policies mentioned previously has blurred these distinctions in the United States and this blur is fuelling the current controversy. In other words, the language debate is less about language than about immigration policy.

THE POLITICAL ISSUES TODAY

To a greater or lesser degree, immigration is a voluntaristic action. Immigrants are in the United States ultimately because they choose to be. Those who are here legally have all the rights and privileges that the Constitution guarantees to "persons" and that are not limited to citizens. It should be noted that this means that the only rights and privileges enjoyed exclusively by citizens involve voting and holding public office and access to limited categories of jobs.

While there is no doubt that immigrants should enjoy all Constitutional guarantees, it is unreasonable to suggest that immigrants should be favored over citizens. That, however, appears to be the unintended consequence of the convergence of high immigration and policies such as affirmative action and new language policies produced by the civil rights movement. Immigrants, in other words, are perceived to be the beneficiaries of programs that were not intended for them but were instead designed for American racial and linguistic minorities. It is unlikely that such policies would have been enacted if it had been envisioned that they would be used by immigrants. But it is because of allegations that new immigrants are using these programs to resist integrating into mainstream society, that organizations such as FAIR and U.S. English have successfully rallied many Americans to demand that they be rescinded.

---

43. Schuck and Smith, *supra*, note 41.

It is important to emphasize that non-nativists who are concerned about these issues are not aware of the history of the language policies which so trouble them. They are, instead, concerned that the State is implementing policies that treat current immigrants, especially Latinos, preferentially relative to past immigrants and current citizens. U.S. English leaders protest that "European and African immigrants cannot get ballots in their native languages even in counties covered by the *Voting Rights Act*".[44] Voters do not understand why that should be so, think this unfair, and are mobilizing to terminate such policies.

The nation's political leaders must shoulder part of the blame for the current controversy since they have done nothing to explain the intent of the original policies. That silence has allowed Official English supporters to exploit the issue for their own purposes. Latino leaders have also contributed to politicizing and confusing the issue in that they too have been silent with regard to the original objectives of these policies. Moreover, instead of distinguishing between those Latino citizens for whom the programs were intended and recent immigrants, they have ignored the distinction between the two. By doing so, they may have abandoned the ethical high ground for a position that appears to be politically and philosophically untenable.

When Latino leaders were demanding that the State implement those measures to dismantle historical racism and enable U.S. citizens of Mexican and Puerto Rican origin to have full and equal access to American society, they could be confident about their ultimate triumph. By implicitly arguing that these measures be extended to recent Latino immigrants, Latino leaders have in effect made the claim that Latinos as a population should be treated differently from all other national origin groups in the United States. The only possible basis for such a claim is that all Latinos regardless of nationality and immigration history should be considered as having participated in the historical exclusion shared by Mexican Americans and Puerto Ricans. Such an assertion is politically and philosophically indefensible. The principles that necessitate special attention to the conditions of Puerto Ricans and Mexican Americans cannot be used to justify similar treatment for recent Latin American immigrants per se, whatever their country of origin.

Politically, Latino leaders have taken a precarious position that pits them unnecessarily against the rest of the nation. As was evidenced in Arizona, Florida, and Colorado, Latinos lost the vote on Official English amendments even when they had the support of the political leadership in these states. Indeed, the momentum behind Official English is such

---

44. Chavez, *supra*, note 40.

that the League of United Latin American Citizens, the oldest national Latino organization in the nation, has indicated that it may support an official language amendment in the hopes that this will make it possible to win concessions on minority language rights.[45] What, then, is the solution?

A GUIDE FOR NEW POLICY

The best way to end the controversy is to revise current practices so that they conform to the principles that have governed national language policy historically. That approach would maintain the distinction between rights and privileges of citizens and resident aliens while simultaneously protecting the constitutional rights of all "persons" residing in the United States. Conceivably, that approach would take the following form:

1. English could continue as the national language without being declared the official language. No group challenges that English is the national language. However, because certain minority groups have experienced (and continue to experience) language-related discrimination, to attempt to declare English the official language would cause political controversy akin to the controversy that such an effort would have engendered in 1787. Even conservative Republicans such as Governor Bill Clements of Texas consider demands for an official language unnecessary and insulting.[46] The nation's founders were wise enough to avoid unnecessary problems; the nation would be well served to follow their example today.

2. The government would remain neutral regarding the use of language for any purpose other than the conduct of elections and related political life. This means that all "persons" may continue to exercise their constitutional rights in the language of their choice. They may develop institutions to enhance their native language; they may worship in those languages. If they do not know English, they must be provided language assistance for whatever dealings they have with public agencies.

This requirement would seem to place an onerous obligation on government. However, that obligation is an inherent consequence of national immigration policy. It would be cruel to admit immigrants without requiring them to know English then, in effect, penalize them for not knowing English after they are here. As is evidenced by the

---

45. Letter from Arnold Torres to Congressman Don Edwards, 28 November 1988.
46. *American Statesman*, (2 November 1987) [Austin, Texas — Rodolfo O. de la Garza].

Court Interpreters Act of 1987,[47] the State has recognized and is acting on this obligation. The government could accelerate the integration of non-English speaking immigrants by sponsoring an effective, free adult English language acquisition program such as those European states provide for immigrants.[48] Indeed, under the *Immigration Reform and Control Act* of 1986, English competence is a requirement for amnesty. Currently, however, the English classes that are available are grossly insufficient to meet the demand. In 1988, the waiting lists for English classes in Los Angeles and New York were 40,000 and 25,000, respectively.[49]

Government neutrality also provides Latinos the opportunity to develop and maintain Spanish to the extent they choose. This changes the historical practices that led Latinos, especially many Mexican Americans in the Southwest, to discard Spanish in an attempt to avoid stigmatization and discrimination. As recently as the 1960s, many parents refused to speak Spanish at home so that their children would learn only English and avoid experiences such as having their mouths washed out with soap for speaking Spanish on school playgrounds and being ridiculed for accented English. Nonetheless, the nation's socio-linguistic processes and the state of Spanish maintenance among Latinos who are not recent immigrants suggest it will be difficult to establish stable bilingualism, even with the influx of immigrants and the increase in institutions such as Spanish media they have stimulated.[50]

3. Governmental agencies would continue to promote English as the national language. This would require all official activities to be conducted in English. Individuals who do not know English would, as argued previously, be provided linguistic assistance to insure that they have equal access to these services.

There would be several major exceptions to this policy. While schools would continue to conduct their programs in English, they would continue to promote the learning of languages other than English. They would also be allowed to conduct special programs for non-English speakers. The form these programs would take would be determined by local and state authorities. However, the primary objective of those programs would be to facilitate rapid English acquisition. This approach recognizes that

---

47. A.H. Leibowitz, *Federal Recognition of the Rights of Minority Groups* (Rosslyn, Va.: National Clearinghouse of Bilingual Education, 1982).
48. *Reviews of National Policies for Education: Sweden* (Paris: Organization for Economic Co-operation and Development, 1981).
49. M. Jimenez "Official Use of English" *A B A Journal* (December 1988) 34-35.
50. J.A. Fishman, *The Rise and Fall of the Ethnic Revival: Perspectives on Language and Ethnicity* (New York: Mouton Publishers, 1985).

the great majority of bilingual education programs will be transitional rather than maintenance. Because it is so clearly in the national interest that American children develop foreign language competencies, federal policy to promote foreign language teaching would also be strengthened. The United States has never been good at promoting foreign language teaching, however,[51] and there is no reason to expect it will successfully do so now. It must be tried, nonetheless.

The support for foreign language teaching while not advocating Spanish maintenance programs may seem contradictory, but it is not. The consequence of the former is to teach all children foreign languages. Educationally and politically, that is unobjectionable. The consequences of the latter are to emphasize only one language in ways that may be educationally acceptable but are ethically untenable and politically explosive. It results in treating Latino immigrants as if they were members of historically victimized ethnic groups, and the consequence of this is to benefit Latino immigrants over others. As was stated previously, this distinction is at the heart of much of the intensity of the current controversy. Eliminating this distinction should cool passions substantially.

The second exception applies to populations such as natives of Puerto Rico which the government has recognized have an autonomous and distinct historical identity and a national language other than English. The government has granted those populations the right to conduct some official activities in their native language rather than English. Moreover, the federal government recognizes their right not to learn English and does not require them to do so in order to exercise any of their rights as citizens. Furthermore, as in the case of Puerto Ricans, they carry this right with them wherever they go in the United States. Other groups that should be included under this exception are Native Americans (Indians) and the several indigenous populations of the Pacific islands. The status of these groups is such that the federal government must insure that they are allowed to exercise all of their rights and privileges in their native languages.

4. The federal government should not tolerate actions by any public agencies that in any way undermine, attack or discriminate against the use of languages other than English by individuals in their daily private activities. Private activities include religious observances, work, recreation, and all other behaviors that are not associated with the official conduct of the nation's electoral life. In the past, state and

---

51. G. Unks "Practically Speaking: The Perils of a Single Language Policy" (March 1984) 57:7 *Clearing House* 318-322.

local-level agencies systematically attacked the private use of Spanish. This requirement thus signals an important change.

5. All electoral activities will be conducted in English. This requirement emphasizes the distinction between citizen and resident alien. Resident aliens enjoy and are guaranteed the fundamental individual rights and privileges of our constitutional system. Participation in electoral life, however, is a right that may be legitimately limited to the citizenry.

With the exceptions that have been noted, requiring English to be the language of official political discourse should disenfranchise no one. Unlike in years past, now the native-born learn English as a matter of course. Resident aliens enjoy all the protection of the Constitution with no obligation to learn English. They are allowed to reside permanently in the United States without becoming U.S. citizens. If they choose to become citizens, however, current law already requires that they learn English. Therefore, the requirement that they vote in English is in no way a burden.

Requiring Puerto Ricans and other similarly situated groups to vote in English is, however, unjust. As has already been shown, these individuals are U.S. citizens by birth, and their unique relationship to American society allows them to retain their native languages. To require them to vote in English would in effect disenfranchise them. They should therefore have access to bilingual electoral materials.

The case of Mexican Americans is somewhat different. Although Mexican Americans were colonized similarly to the way that Puerto Ricans were, their relationship to American society has evolved very differently. The primary reason that Mexican Americans did not learn English historically is that they were segregated from all aspects of mainstream society, including schools, and thus were unable to do so. Nonetheless, since they were colonized, Mexican Americans have continuously struggled to gain access to U.S. institutions.[52] Puerto Ricans, on the other hand, struggled to remain apart and retain their distinct cultural and political identity. Thus, the reason for providing Spanish language electoral materials to Mexican Americans is, as was explained previously, to enable them to overcome the obstacles that states had created to prevent them from exercising their political rights. Mexican Americans, therefore, should have the right to bilingual electoral materials until it is clear that they have been allowed to acquire English, and until that generation that never learned English has passed on. A review

---

52. Garcia and de la Garza, *supra*, note 31; C. Allsup, *The American GI Forum: Origin and Evolution* (Austin: University of Texas Press, 1982).

of Mexican American language behavior suggests that there will continue to be a need for such materials approximately until the year 2000, and surely no later than 2025.[53]

The availability of Spanish language materials for Mexican Americans (and Puerto Ricans) would make it possible for naturalized citizens to use them. This would contravene the requirement that naturalized citizens be allowed to register and vote only in English. It would be possible to develop a process for limiting these materials to native-born citizens, but it would be cumbersome. While there are philosophical reasons for having such a policy, the costs may outweigh the benefits. If there is a need for such a policy, the least objectionable one would be to limit the use of bilingual election materials to those jurisdictions that were initially included in the 1975 VRA. Given how few bilingual ballots are used, however, it is not clear that such rigid control is needed. Whatever is done about bilingual ballots in the short run, in the long run this policy would explicitly recognize English as the national language. It would have the nation's elections conducted in English, but it would not penalize those who have either been denied the opportunity to learn English or who have an historically established special linguistic relationship to the polity.

CONCLUSION

This paper has developed the outlines of a language policy that will serve the nation as well as Latinos while also respecting the fundamental constitutional principles of the United States and its historical receptivity to immigration. This policy recognizes the need to treat the cultural rights of immigrants and citizens equally, while also protecting the fundamental freedoms of all persons who reside in the United States. It also emphasizes the distinction between the rights of citizens and the rights of resident aliens, as well as the differences in the obligations that the state has to its native-born citizens and to immigrant populations. Substantively, the result of this proposal will probably be as distasteful to those who want English to be declared the official language as to those who would raise the status of other languages to be equal to that of English. If we displease both it may be because this proposal is on the right track.

---

53. J.A. Fishman, *supra*, note 8; L.F. Estrada, "Languages and Political Consciousness Among the Spanish Speaking in the United States: A Demographic Study" in D.J.R. Bruckner, ed., *Politics and Language: Spanish and English in the United States* (Chicago: University of Chicago, Center for Policy Studies, 1980).

ETHNIC AND LINGUISTIC REVIVAL IN ESTONIA

Toivo Miljan

Estonia, one of the three Baltic states along with Latvia and Lithuania, was annexed by the Soviet Union in 1940 as a consequence of the secret annexes to the Molotov-Ribbentrop Pact of 1939. By the pact, Hitler and Stalin divided north-eastern Europe with the Baltic states allocated to the Soviet Union. Although Estonia is the smallest of the three it is larger than Belgium, Switzerland, the Netherlands, and Denmark, and about the size of Austria. Latvia is half again as large and Lithuania twice the size of Estonia.

The objective of this paper is to identify the process of national re-awakening in Estonia and to explain its historical and contextual background. To this end the paper is divided into four sections: the first addresses the problems of migration and settlement of foreign labour; the second provides historical comparisons of independent Estonia and Soviet Estonia; the third explains the Soviet nationality policy; and the final section describes the Estonians' drive for national self-expression — their aspiration for sovereignty-association.

THE MIGRANT PROBLEM

One of the basic driving factors of Estonian self-expression in recent years has been the instinctive negative reaction to the "migrants". These are the large stream of non-Estonians that have invaded Estonia from the rest of the Soviet Union during the past 35 years. A glance at the Table below will show the statistical cause of the Estonians' unhappiness with the "migrants". Whereas foreigners accounted for less than 3 percent of the population in 1954, about the same as during independence, five years later they constituted a quarter, and in 1988, 30 years later, non-Estonians form 40 percent of the population. In the capital, Tallinn, Estonians are in the minority.

NATIONAL COMPOSITION OF THE ESTONIAN POPULATION[1]

Total	Population	Estonians	Non-Estonians	Share of Estonians %
1954	854,000*	831,000	23,000	97.3
1959	1,196,791	892,653	304,138	74.6
1970	1,356,079	925,157	430,922	68.2
1979	1,464,476	947,812	516,664	64.7
1988	1,570,600*	851,800	618,800	60.6

* Estimates

None of this migration was generated as a result of indigenous Estonian immigration policy; it is wholly the result of Soviet nationality policy aided and abetted by Moscow-directed industrial and economic policy in which the Estonians have had no say. What has grieved Estonians for the past two decades is the statistical evidence that they are inexorably becoming a minority in their own country — against their will.

What is even more dramatic than the enormous influx of foreigners threatening to overwhelm the native population is the transient factor in this migration. During the Soviet period it is estimated that 7.2 million non-Estonians have passed through Estonia as migrants, staying between two and seven years before passing on to other parts of the Soviet Union. Because these transient migrants are exclusively industrial labourers, their typical temporary abode has been one of the large industrial complexes located in the capital and north-eastern Estonia, in the cities of Narva, Kohtla-Järve and Rakvere. The result is that these cities all look like large worn-down railroad stations where transients who have no commitment to the community have dropped tons of garbage during their brief sojourn, and then moved on. The migration data exists because the Soviets are inveterate keepers of precise information about everybody's residence. Every resident must be registered with the local government. Until recently this data was secret but *glasnost* made its publication possible.[2]

Two major problems with a majority of the migrants are the generally low educational (and what the Estonians refer to as the "cultural") level of the imported industrial labour; and the increasing cultural "incompatibility" of the newer migrants. The latter problem is caused

---

1. K. Katus, *Demographic Development in Estonia through Centuries*, (1989) [unpublished] 16.
2. See K. Katus and A. Piip, *Dannye Migratsii Naslenya Estonii*, (Tallinin: 1989).

by the general shortage of labour in the Soviet Union. Hence, the migration hinterland, not only for Estonia and the other Baltic republics but also for Leningrad, has been moving farther east and south, thus bringing labour from areas and cultures historically different from the European cultures of the Balts and the European orientation of Leningrad. Moreover, the newer migrants come from rural backwaters of the Union, and bring with them unsophisticated and "crude" habits and behaviour. The last straw for the Estonians is the refusal of these migrants to learn Estonian, and their insistence on speaking the working man's underdeveloped Russian everywhere. It is this very visible segment of migrants who have created the most disgust and vocal rejection among the Estonians.

The current 600,000 migrants may be divided roughly into three equal segments. Of the first 200,000, who have lived in Estonia longest, 80,000 speak fair to good Estonian and most tend to support the Estonians quest for economic autonomy. Basically, Estonians would accept large numbers of this group if they were to show greater sensitivity to Estonian language needs and reject the notion of *homo sovieticus* along with the Estonians. Parenthetically, it seems to me that as the Estonian demands become better known and as the Russian-speaking Soviet intelligentsia itself dissects Soviet culture and Leninist-statist values, this segment of better-educated and well-settled migrants, originally from Russian and White Russian areas of the Soviet Union, will "Estonianize" themselves and thus solve a large part of the "migrant" problem.

The second, or middle segment, is the most problematical and is currently creating the most vocal reaction on both sides of the "national" issue. This group consists of more recent migrants at all socio-educational levels heavily influenced by war veterans and retired senior officer ranks. On retirement, officers of lieutenant-colonel or higher rank may choose to settle wherever they wish. Second World War veterans have the same right. Such privileges are not allowed for ordinary mortals in the Soviet Union. The result is that the Baltic republics have disproportionately large numbers of war veterans and retired officers (together with their extended families), for not only is life more pleasant and "civilized", but food and consumer goods are more plentiful than elsewhere, except for Moscow. About 20,000 retired senior ranks live in Estonia, guard the values of Soviet civilization and give tone to the middle segment of migrants who represent most typically the de-nationalized *homo sovieticii*, of whom we will discuss more later. A second group of leaders in this middle segment is equally anti-Estonian but much smaller in size. This consists of the directors (the term in the Soviet Union is used to describe anybody in middle management or higher levels in industry or the different public services, including the Party apparat) sent from

Moscow to run local plants for a few years. These men (the Soviet Union has few women "directors") approximate the "organization man" in the Western world in that their loyalty is to the system and not to the local nation or state where they may be stationed temporarily. They have been very vocal antagonists and have organized the labour in their plants in opposition to Estonian nationalist efforts.

The third segment is the one alluded to at the beginning of this section. They are part of the flotsam and jetsam that floats around the Soviet Union looking for a better or easier job, or even any job at all. There is a conflict between this segment and the first, or settled one, in that they have entirely different attitudes to life and habits incompatible with European civilized life. In the case of the transient migrants some of their unacceptable habits include the dirtying of hallways and elevators in brand-new buildings so that within five years they look forty years old. Moreover, this segment is totally de-nationalized and Sovietized to the absolutely lowest common denominator of statist and assimilationist values as propounded by the institutions of propaganda.

The migrant problem may be condensed into a few words: there are too many of them; the Estonians did not invite them to come; they are insensitive to the Estonian language and culture; very large numbers are uncouth; and they treat Estonia as part of a de-nationalized Soviet Union where the Russian language is the only universal and truly "official" language. The seriousness of the numbers becomes apparent when we look at decade-old statistics. The census of 1979 shows that in the urban municipality of Tallinn 55.35 percent of the population was non-Estonian, in Rakvere 71.2 percent, in Kohtla-Järve 95.7 percent, and in Narva 94.7 percent. It is likely that the 1989 census data, when published later this year, will show that Estonians have become even a smaller minority in their own capital city of Tallinin. In so far as north-eastern Estonia, which contains the other cities listed, is concerned it is already considered lost to Estonians — a de facto Soviet enclave in Estonia.

The north-east is also a serious bone of contention between Estonia and Moscow for reasons that go much deeper than the migrant problem, which is but a symptom of the underlying conflict. This part of the country was industrialized heavily during the past two decades, much against the wishes of Estonians, by the centralized ministries in Moscow. Two developments in particular have united Estonians in opposition to Moscow. The first concerns the wasteful burning of the vast and kerogen-rich oil-shale deposits to produce electricity for Leningrad and Latvia. Not only is the expensive shale, which during independence was turned into oil and chemicals, merely burned but the electric power generated is sold to Leningrad at 24 percent below production cost, and to Latvia at 15 percent below cost, but to Estonia at 78 percent above cost![3] Why? Because the Moscow electric power ministry made these deals, because it controls electricity production and distribution. But the Estonians are even more incensed at the air pollution that this uneconomic exploitation of one of their scarce resources creates, not only for northern Estonia but for the southern coast of Finland, 75 to 100 km across the Gulf of Finland.

A second ecological disaster about to be created by another Moscow ministry, this time the fertilizers ministry, united Estonians as never before and mobilized the beginnings of the current revival of national self-determination. This was the planning by Moscow to exploit new deposits of phosphates by open-pit mining in the same already ecologically raped north-east, where the landscape of one twentieth of Estonia already looks like a cross between a moonscape and hell, with smoking, spontaneously igniting slagheaps covering the landscape. Moscow kept insidiously pushing its plans against local Estonian research findings which showed that not only was the phosphate of such low quality that its exploitation was uneconomic, but that the mining would lead to chemical reactions which would rapidly pollute the water-table of northern Estonia with a radium by-product. Gorbachev's need for *glasnost* allowed Estonian academics and journalists to begin publicizing this and make a public issue out of it during 1987, with the result that Moscow was forced by the newly-engaged reformist politicians in Estonia to hold up the plans during 1988, without, however, promising to shelve them. The Moscovite foot-dragging and patronizing insistence that they knew best made all Estonians into greens and united them in the conviction that if they were to save their homeland from certain destruction and preserve their nation then they had to act decisively, radically and together in demanding independence of decision-making. An important part of this is the emotionally satisfying, revulsive reaction against everything and everybody Soviet, especially the Leninist invention of the New Soviet Man.

HISTORICAL COMPARISONS: INDEPENDENT ESTONIA AND SOVIET ESTONIA

Although Estonians have been settled in their present territory for several thousand years and have a written recorded history since the early 13th Century A.D., they have had only two decades of political

---

3. "Kuhu lähed elektrimajandus?" (1988) 6 *Horisont* 6.

independence in their entire historical period. These decades (1918-40) were preceded by six (from the 1860s on) of national awakening and cultural development generated by the romantic nationalism that swept Europe at that time. Estonians discovered forgotten folk-dances, recorded folklore, wrote scores for folk music and developed modern educational structures and institutions, along with newspapers and a high degree of respect for their language and education. By the end of the century (1897) Estonian literacy stood at 96.2 percent while the Russian figure was at 29.6 percent.[4]

The period of the independent Republic of Estonia, which was admitted to the League of Nations in November 1922, saw the flowering of the aspirations of Estonian nationhood with vibrant cultural, economic, and political development that demonstrated the viability of its aspirations as a sovereign nation-state fully able to carry out its responsibilities as a member of the family of nations. By the end of the 1930s Estonia, with one third of the population, ranked ahead of Finland in the standard of living. Today, when Finland has reached the third or forth position in the world ranking of per capita GNP measured in purchasing power, Estonia has fallen to somewhere in the 50s, with the Soviet Union as a whole somewhere in the 70s. During independence, the Estonian economy achieved a high degree of industrialization but depended primarily on the premium meat and milk products of its agro-industry for export penetration of the West European markets. Today, its economy is totally controlled from Moscow, as is the economy of every part of the Soviet Union. Today, Moscow determines directly what, and how much, Estonian farms must produce. Moscow even determines what, how much and where to distribute the production, with over half of it allocated to other parts of the Union. The result is an endemic shortage and periodic unavailability of every foodstuff except bread, milk, butter and cabbages. Potatoes are endemically in very short supply in the very country that in the 1930s produced them in abundance, and even made a premium potato vodka !

The non-food sectors of the economy are similarly misdirected by the 120 ministries and coordinating committees at ministerial level in Moscow. The result is that Estonia has been covered with heavy industrial plants for which not only the raw materials apart from electric power but also the labour must be imported from other parts of the Union. Estonia still exports a much larger share of her economic production than 50 years ago, in fact, but it all goes to the rest of the Soviet Union.

---

4. Harald Haarmann, *Sotziologi und Politik der Sprachen Europas* (Munich: 1975) table at 179.

Moreover, the "export" prices are established by the same Moscow ministries, with the result that a large part of the sales are below production cost. The shortages are made up by the national Moscow budget, leaving very little for distribution to the health-welfare-education-culture segment of the budget allocated to Estonia. It should also be noted that the "sovereign" Soviet republics do not have any independent taxing power, and that "their" budgets are made up in Moscow and simply given to the republican ministries to implement. Naturally, consumer goods are in as short a supply as are cultural goods and welfare, health and educational services.

Culturally, the period of independence provides an even starker contrast to the present Soviet period. For one, in 1925 Estonia instituted Cultural Autonomy for any ethnic-linguistic minority with at least 5,000 members. Moreover, it was up to individuals to freely designate their ethnic identity. Cultural Autonomy provided state support for ethnic-language schools, museums, publishing, etc., in short, it assisted financially to keep alive the ethnic cultures of Estonian citizens of other ethnic origins. In the event, only the German and the Jewish minorities took advantage of these provisions. The Swedish minority, 20,000 strong, settled along well-defined coastal areas, did not need Cultural Autonomy since it already controlled local municipal councils and schools. With the Latvians settled in Estonia, special mutually acceptable arrangements were made in the border areas. However, the Russians, then as now the largest minority in Estonia, did not take advantage of Cultural Autonomy. Today, in contrast, Moscow wants to produce a single Russian-speaking *homo sovieticus* everywhere in the Union. Estonians who do not willingly accept de-nationalization are regarded as traitors and "nationalists". This word has a special meaning in the Soviet Union — it means a fascist, bourgeois traitor to the Leninist workers' values of collectivism as propounded by the Party propaganda workers (in Estonia with a population of 1.5 million there are 15,000 "propaganda workers") and from time to time reinterpreted and fixed by the Party leadership.

Politically, in the 1930s Estonia had a highly fractionated party system with over a dozen political parties regularly vying for support, producing thereby a richly variegated political atmosphere, even during the period of authoritarian rule between 1934 and 1938 when the president was given extraordinary powers in order to prevent a feared fascist coup (which hindsight shows was never a real probability). For nearly five decades, since the Soviet takeover, only one party has been permitted to exist — a party, moreover, that is not really an Estonian party, but the local arm of the CPSU, with directives and senior personnel provided by Moscow. The result was that politics for forty years was as barren as in the rest of the Soviet Union — until Gorbachev's need to mobilize popular support for *perestroika* led to *glasnost* and the revival of politics in defence of the Estonian nation.

Today, in the middle of 1989, there is not only the mass-based Popular Movement, which rivals the Communist Party of Estonia (ECP) informally as the most important political organization, but in June 1989, the Estonian government legalized other parties, by allowing them to register and hold bank accounts. Thus, in short order the Labour party was formed and the illegal Estonian Independence Party was legitimized. So far, however, under the existing election act only the ECP can contest elections as a party individuals may, of course, run for election, as provided by the 1989 Peoples Congress election law. The Estonians are, nevertheless, in the process of developing new electoral regulations and new parliamentary legislation which, ideally, would mirror Western democratic ones, where the Communist party has no pre-determined role but would have to earn its majority like any other political party.

Whether Moscow will allow this is moot. More to the point is the question of whether the Estonian Communist Party leadership is ready to give up the party's privileged position. There are indications, however, that a sizeable group in the ECP leadership consists of true democrats who are willing to move ahead cautiously, even at the risk of, again, being castigated by Moscow as revisionists in a hurry. Such charges are becoming repetitious to the Estonians and are not likely to affect the progressives. The liberals, those who, like Gorbachev himself, are true Party loyalists interested in reviving the moribund, aged Party do not want to give up the constitutional right of the Party to provide leadership for Soviet (and Soviet Estonian) society-polity-economy. Although we know that this group is in the dominant majority in the CPSU, we do not know their strength in the ECP. It is likely that the dividing line between the progressives and the liberals in the ECP is very fluid, moving with the perception of events and Moscow's tolerance. At this point it should also be noted that there are virtually no conservatives or reactionaries left in the ECP Central Committee or other leading circles. Moreover, all, with the exception of a small non-Estonian contingent, are Estonian patriots. This helps explain why national revival has moved so rapidly and why legislation is being passed to implement cultural, language and economic provisions guaranteeing national survival.

Unfortunately, all this is insufficient to actually guarantee non-interference by Moscow. For so far Moscow insists that it alone has the right to make policy changes on behalf of the republics; and, that it alone may delegate any rights on its own terms, at will and during pleasure. Hence, all the self-assertions of the Estonians are "mere" political games in many senior Moscow players' eyes. So far, politics, as Canadians well know, often takes on a life of its own and changes even the most stubborn minds and the best argued constitutional briefs.

SOVIET NATIONALITY POLICY AND ESTONIA

The basis of Soviet nationality policy is *homo sovieticus* — the New Soviet Man. He is a reality today and was developed consciously and deliberately on Leninist principles by his successors. At the XXIVth Party Congress in 1971 his existence was proudly announced: "During the years of building socialism a new and historic set of relationships developed in our country — the Soviet nation."[5] This "Soviet nation" consists of the New Soviet Man who has no loyalty to any of the more than 100 historic ethnic nations found within the borders of the Soviet Union, including the Russian, although they are all supposed to speak that language.

The formation of the New Soviet Man was begun in 1923 when Lenin issued his programme of cultural revolution, which had as its objective the restructuring of intellectual values in the Soviet Union free of "wrong" capitalist class-values and worthy of communism. The initial objects of this reprocessing were the leadership cadres of the Union. Soon, however, the whole population had been inculcated with the collectivistic values and beliefs centred on the Party and its leader, to such an extent that a personality cult developed only two decades after the revolution to wipe out inequality and privilege. The method employed was the forcible deculturation of the individual by cutting him loose from all his existing social and personal values, making him part of the herd — the collective — and then making the collective play the role that the individual had hitherto played in society. A similar method is used to produce instantly obedient super-soldiers in the U.S. Marine Corps, for example. The inevitable result in the case of the Marines is the subsuming of the individual and his personality to the Corps: he identifies himself as a Marine, first and always, even after leaving the Corps. In the case of the individual in the Soviet Union the experience of the Marine boot camp of six months became not just one lifetime but three generations, with a fourth being "trained" at this very moment. Moreover, unlike the marine the Soviet citizen cannot resign or ever retire — he can never escape the incessant socialization process. The degree to which this Sovietization is successful among the Russian-

---

5. Cited in Matti Nutt, "Homo Sovieticus'e sündroom" [The syndrome of *homo sovieticus*], 1989 2 *Looming* 221.

speaking population in Estonia is demonstrated by several recent opinion polls.[6]

A seminal part of this collectivization of individuals involved the rapid destruction of ethnic differences which would enable retention of loyalties to non-uniformized social values not created and directed by the Party. Hence, Stalin used genocide early on, not only on the Ukrainians and White Russians as part of his farm collectivization programme, but killed his own ethnic Georgians and deported and dispersed the Tatars from their ancestral home in the Crimea. Indeed, the latter method — dispersion — was a more efficient means of killing cultures and destroying non-state sanctioned loyalties than outright genocide since it preserved working bodies. Cultural destruction also presupposed the neutralization of the ethno-cultural elites, and the easiest way to do this was to send them to the Gulag, where they would provide raw labour power for the state while slowly dying. Leaderless, and deprived of cultural and spiritual nourishment, the Soviet peoples became easy targets for re-socialization into the New Soviet Man with only the Soviet Union as his "nation". The Estonians, Latvians, and Lithuanians were subjected to the same genocidal and cultural programme when they were annexed to the Union, with follow-up, or more correctly mopping-up, deportations of remaining cultural elites in 1949 and 1951.

However, the process of developing *homo sovieticus* did not end with the death of Stalin but continues to the present. The main — and vast — difference is that instead of deportation and genocide his successors have used forced assimilation. In the case of the Baltic nations this has taken the form of forced importation of labour, the mixing of army conscripts in multi-ethnic units far from home, and the repression of their languages. In fact, today only Estonian, Latvian, Lithuanian, and Georgian are fully developed ethnic languages in that they are still used daily and consistently by all their national elites in preference to Russian, which most speak badly. But even in these republics higher education suffers. In Estonia, for example, of the approximately 300 degree programmes sanctioned by Moscow only 100 are available in Estonian, with another 25 only in Russian, in Estonia. The course syllabuses are all programmed in Moscow to enforce uniformity of leadership values and approaches throughout the Union.

To compare the two decades of independence with the four of the Soviet period is to invite invidious contrasts. During 1936-39, 240 newspapers and periodicals were regularly published in Estonian and

---

6. The public opinion research division of MAINOR has conducted several surveys on this question; parts have been published periodically in *Rahva Hääl* during 1988-89.

1,600 to 1,700 new book titles appeared annually; today fewer than 100 newspapers and journals are published in Estonian and in 1986, 1,400 book titles were released in Estonian, the most since independence. Nevertheless, the Estonian reader still suffers: in 1986 in Estonia for each Russian reader 14 copies of books were printed, whereas only 12 copies were made available per Estonian reader. The situation, however, is a far cry from the early Soviet years (1944-53) when at least 10,000 volumes were removed from libraries and destroyed along with 5,000 annual volumes of newspapers and periodicals. The whole of the educational literature of the independence period was strictly forbidden. In fact, only since the third quarter of 1988 has it become possible to publish materials on the history of the independence period and to deal honestly with ethnic and language questions in Estonia. But even these modest moves toward normalization have created a strong negative reaction in Moscow among the Party apparat in the hard-core Russian hinterland and among local *homo sovieticii* in Estonia.

The anti-national or anti-ethnic bias of the Party continues unabated today, despite Gorbachev's promises to convene a much-delayed Central Committee Plenum on the nationality question. In fact, the apparachik in charge of the preparatory commission for the Plenum is Doctor of History M. Guboglo, who has made his mark as an articulate and vehement opponent of "nationalism", which he, like the ideology of *homo sovieticus* generally, equates with fascism and the perverted attempts to destroy the socialist collectivistic unity of the Soviet Union and its progressive "egalitarian" society.[7] In January of 1989 two prominent Soviet specialists on nationality questions, both members of the Institute of Building the Soviet State and Developing Policy, attacked the new Estonian language law as discriminatory against non-Estonian speakers and, in particular, against Russian as the national language of the Soviet Union. They appealed to the collectivistic "economic" argument as the basis for Russian's dominant status: "Because the existing single national economic complex and the fact of migration are undeniable necessities for the normal functioning of our federal state ... the rights of all ... Soviet citizens to freely use their mother tongue, or *any other language that they speak*, must be guaranteed."[8]

THE DRIVE FOR SOVEREIGNTY-ASSOCIATION

All the political activities that Estonians have engaged in since this became possible with the initiation of *glasnost*, though so far without

---

7. See M. Guboglo, "Na dvuedinoi osnove" *Sovetski Lei* (26 February 1985).
8. Cited in *Ohtuleht* (13 April 1989) italics added; see also *Edasi* (15 January 1989) for a longer review of the attack.

the open possibility of free contestation among freely established parties, have had one single overwhelming objective — survival of the nation. All Estonians, regardless of political conviction, are single-mindedly united on this. Of course, there are a few Sovietized Estonians, but their numbers are few — an estimated two percent of the Party membership.[9] National survival requires, first of all, the cutting off of the Estonian economy from the "single seamless" Soviet economy; only then can Estonians reorganize the economic and financial structures of the country to serve Estonian, and not Moscow's, interests. Only then can they acquire the wherewithal to restructure the educational system and the cultural industries to serve Estonian national interests. Only then can the Estonian government put a stop to the uneconomic, massive, heavy industrialization and the consequent massive importation of low-grade labour. Only then can the wholesale environmental degradation caused by insensitive central ministries in Moscow be stopped. Incidentally, the Estonian press and periodicals have for the past year written one horror story after another about the ecological rape of the country. For example, in the chemical valley of north-eastern Estonia, children under 10 have been losing their hair and the incidence of sickness among them is several times the national average. For example, the sulphur content of the air in the industrial parts of the country consistently exceeds the high Soviet standards, often several times. For example, the beaches of the resort town of Pärnu have been closed for years because of industrial effluent. For example, the effluent from very large-scale pig farming factories has severely contaminated a large area of the water table in central Estonia. These and similar stories have been published monthly in *Loodus, Horisont*, and *Aja Pulss* from mid-1988 on.

It should also be pointed out that Estonia is not unique. The whole of the Soviet Union has been environmentally degraded to such an extent that many home-grown experts believe that much of the damage is irreversible. What is worse, although laws to control the ecological impact of industrial decisions exist, they are routinely disregarded in the "national" interest of producing to quota. Moreover, fines are laughably low and are paid out of the miscellaneous fund in each enterprise's budget.[10] There is no worse sin in the Soviet economic lexicon than not fulfilling the quota prescribed by the Planning Commission and the central ministries. Until a year ago, directors of chronically quota-short

9. Private communication, Tiit Made, Edgar Savisaar, in May 1989. This is the generally accepted figure within the Party leadership.
10. Private communication, Vladimir Alexeev, Institute of Limnology, USSR Academy of Sciences, Leningrad (11 June 1989). He also pointed out that there are 100 cities in the Soviet Union where the air quality is "dangerous to life". The Union as a whole spews out 100 million tons of pollutants per year into the air.

enterprises not only lost their jobs but were liable for jail term for sabotaging their national economy. The result is that quotas are filled at considerable cost, often ecological, and nearly always at the cost of quality. But even when filled there is usually some element of fiction in the final production figures. And, there is always a fairly sizeable bookkeeping entry for bribes, under the miscellaneous rubric.[11]

These are some of the reasons why it is imperative that the Estonians gain unconditional control over their economy. What Gorbachev has so far proposed, the so-called Masljukov Plan — named after the Deputy Prime minister who chaired the commission that developed the plan — is totally unacceptable to the Estonians since it proposes the transfer of no more than a maximum of 70 percent of the economy to the republics, keeping control over all "essential" industries, including electric power and technology in general. Moreover, the plan makes no mention of transferring taxing power, which is completely in Moscow's hands. This is why the Estonians have rejected the plan outright and developed their own proposal, titled *Isemajandav Eesti*. The mellifluous acronym, *IME*, also spells wonder in Estonian. The closest English translation would be "Economically Autonomous Estonia" or Sovereignty-Association in the Canadian context. On 18 May 1989 the Estonian Parliament passed a resolution to implement Sovereignty-Association on 1 January 1990.[12]

As pointed out earlier, all this, however, will not suffice, for so far the All-Union Constitution arrogates the right to disallow the legislation of what it names the "sovereign" republics. To bring this matter to a head the Estonian Parliament, on 16 November 1988, passed a resolution and some small changes in its own constitution to confirm the independence of the Estonian constitution from the All-Union one and to arrogate exclusive jurisdiction over Estonian territory, air-space, the territorial sea, and the economic zone. Estonia also declared itself the "owner" of all the land, buildings, economic enterprises, and institutions on Estonian territory. Moscow rejected all these and asked the Estonian Parliament to rescind the amendments, laws and resolutions. The Estonians refused and passed a resolution that the Estonian Parliament "took note" of the communication from the All-Union Supreme Soviet.[13] On 18 May 1989 the Estonian Parliament formally requested the new All-Union Supreme Soviet to accept the Estonian Economic Autonomy proposal. The Lithuanians submitted a similar proposal on the same day, with the result that the Supreme Soviet formed a Social and Economic Problems Commission with the Lithuanian

---

11. Private communications, several nameless directors.
12. *Rahva Hääl* (21 May 1989).
13. See *Rahva Hääl* (17 November 1988 and 8 December 1988).

economist Eduardas Vilkas as chairman, and representatives from each of the 15 republics as members, to evaluate the Estonian, Lithuanian and Masljukov proposals. This commission began its work during the week of 19-23 June 1989.

Surprising though it may be, especially in contrast to the immobility of the Brezhnev years, political developments have taken place with bewildering speed in the Soviet Union. In this case the Estonian and Lithuanian proposals for implementing "self-management" were approved in principle by the Supreme Soviet on 27 July 1989. The approval did not come easily or without cost. Although both the Vilkas commission and the Council of Ministers had approved the proposals, a two-day debate in the Supreme Soviet showed extensive opposition in principle as well as on the pragmatic grounds of not wanting to be left behind. Nevertheless, because the leadership of the Soviet Union sees these proposals as the only probable, rapid moves towards *perestroika* in the whole Union, it has put its support, however conditional it may be, behind them and managed to persuade the majority of the deputies to cast a vote in favour of the proposals. But even this required a watering-down of the proposals, at least for the time being. Only a three paragraph resolution authorizing the All-Union Council of Ministers to begin negotiations with the Republican Councils of Ministers of the three Baltic republics in order to work out the details of initiating "self-management" on 1 January 1990 was approved. This was possible only because a clause was added to reiterate that All-Union economic regulations would continue to apply to the extent that they would not prevent these republics from implementing "self-management". Both the main clause and the codicil show the stong opposition to any dismantling of the Soviet economy and the fear of dismemberment politically among the majority of the deputies of the Supreme Soviet.[14]

In the meantime, the Estonians also passed a Language Act on 18 January 1989, in which Estonian was restored as the official ("state") language of Estonia, a status that it had lost in 1940. The Act is short and consists of only 39 articles which make the Estonian language the language of priority in all conceivable official, economic, educational, and cultural activities. A special section re-establishes Estonian place names and Estonian spellings using Latin script as the only legal ones. Russian or other languages may be used in translation as authorized by Estonian state regulations. Russian may be used in Estonia in commerce and in service relationships only if the client chooses to speak it.

---

14. This information was faxed to the author from the Estonian Radio and Television information centre on 30 July 1989. *Pravda, Izvestia* and *Rahya Hääl*, as well as most Baltic newspapers carried reports on the matter between 26 and 30 July 1989.

The article that has created the greatest negative reaction among Russian-speakers in Estonia and in the central news media is Article 4, which requires all persons in management positions as well as all foremen and lead-hands in industry to be able to speak Estonian. In addition, all public servants, in its widest meaning, must have knowledge of Estonian and be able to use it in varying degrees. This includes the police, medical personnel, journalists, and emergency service personnel. Article 37 requires the implementation of the language requirements for the categories enumerated in Article 4 over a four year period.[15] At the same time the Language Protection Commission reporting to the Parliament was established. The first responsibility of this body is the delineation of precise language proficiency requirements for 6 levels of knowledge, the application of these levels to the various job and position categories, and the development of testing procedures and language teaching regulations. At mid-summer 1989 the commission of 26 members, heavily loaded with language experts, has produced drafts of all of these and is waiting for the government to issue them as decrees, as provided by the Language Act.

A cautionary note is necessary here. The repression of Estonian usage was carried out over time, not by legislative, but by administrative means. This was usually achieved by the newly-appointed Russian-speaking director suggesting that it would be more efficient if Russian were used as the language of record and of internal communication since all could understand it and would make costly and time-consuming translation unnecessary. In any case, since so much material had to be submitted to Moscow, it would be more efficient to use Russian as the base language. The result of this process was that even in the Estonian Communist Party Central Committee apparat only Russian was used, even among Estonians whose Russian was barely adequate. At his first meeting as the new First Secretary, Vaino Vljas spoke only Estonian and made it clear that translation services would be provided only to the Second Secretary who, in the case of the republics, is always a Russian, appointed by Moscow to keep an eye on the ethnics. Moreover, he made it clear that within three months he expected all workers in the apparat to be able to use adequate Estonian in their work. I have given these examples of administrative fiat, which show that it is possible to move both ways easily at the whim of the boss in the Soviet system.

To prevent the use of administrative fiat in the future to repress Estonian as a language, the Estonian Parliament must be in full control of the economy. Only then can it prevent Moscow appointees from

---

15. See *Rahva Hääl* (22 January 1989).

overwhelming the carefully constructed long-term programmes of the Estonians to re-establish a viable Estonian-speaking Estonia. The ideal of a completely independent state is currently politically premature; sovereignty-association, however, appears to be politically achievable.

If the above review has done nothing else, it has at the very least graphically demonstrated the validity of Jean Laponce's[16] and Ken McRae's[17] claims that a language cannot long survive without political and legal control over its territory. Granted, the methods used by the Soviets are crude, but the sentiments are those of assimilationists everywhere, and the arguments for "efficiency" echo those of Anglophones in Canada.

16. See Jean A. Laponce, "Reducing the Tensions Resulting from Language Contacts: Personal or Territorial Solutions" in this volume.
17. See Kenneth D. McRae, "Precepts for Linguistic Peace: The Case of Switzerland" in this volume.

COLLECTIVE RIGHTS, THE ENGLISH-SPEAKING MINORITY AND THE QUÉBEC GOVERNMENT 1867-1988

Ronald Rudin

Late 1988 witnessed the revival of what is widely known in Québec as 'The Language Debate.' On 15 December the Supreme Court ruled[1] that the prohibition of English-language signs as set out in Bill 101[2] was a violation of certain provisions of the Québec *Charter of Rights*.[3] The Court would undoubtedly have also ruled that this prohibition violated the *Charter of Rights and Freedoms* of the Canadian Constitution had it not been for the fact that the Québec government availed itself of the "notwithstanding clause" of the Canadian *Charter* upon amending Bill 101 in 1983.[4]

Following the Supreme Court decision, the Québec government quickly moved to re-establish the prohibition of external English signs with the passing of Bill 178, a law which would be beyond the reach of the courts since it contained notwithstanding clauses that removed it from the jurisdiction of both the Québec and Canadian charters.[5] But while Bill 178 was drafted in a manner that assured that it would not end up in the courts, nothing could prevent it from becoming a hot topic of debate within Québec. The bill was seen by many French-speakers, concerned with the survival of their language in the midst of the North American sea of English speakers, as a retreat from the principles of Bill 101, adopted in 1977, which had forbidden the use of English signs by most commercial establishments. Bill 178, they claimed, was unsatisfactory since it allowed the use of English signs within most establishments as long as French signs were "markedly predominant." By contrast, most English speakers saw Bill 178 as insulting

---

1. *Ford* v. *Québec (Attorney General)* (1988), 54 D.L.R. (4th) 577 (S.C.C.).
2. *Charter of the French Language*, R.S.Q. 1977, c. C-11.
3. *Charter of Human Rights and Freedoms*, R.S.Q. 1977, c. C-12.
4. *Act to Amend the Charter of the French Language*, S.Q. 1983, c. 56, s. 52.
5. *Act to Amend the Charter of the French Language*, S.Q. 1988, c. 54.

because of the so-called 'inside-outside' formula. Since only French signs were permitted outside with the possibility of English signs inside, it seemed that English was acceptable as long as it was not visible to the general public.[6]

Beyond a sense of outrage or betrayal towards the provincial Liberal government that had been elected in 1985 committed to the restoration of bilingual signs, the reaction of the English-speaking population was also frequently expressed in terms of the primacy of individual rights. To many, the government's actions gave preference to the collective rights of the French-speaking majority over the individual rights of a merchant to post an external sign in his own language. Reflecting a more general perception among English speakers, *The Gazette* minced no words in describing the bill as an "offence against fundamental human rights".[7] There was nothing particularly novel about this assessment of the language debate as a conflict between individual and collective rights. As we shall see, English speakers defended their interests in a similar manner in 1974 when limits were placed upon the freedom of Québecers to choose the language in which their children could be educated.

The point of this paper is not to determine who has been right and who has been wrong in the language debate that has continued intermittently for twenty years. Nor is the goal to resolve the philosophical issue of where the line should be drawn regarding the infringement of individual rights in the name of collective ones. Rather, the objective here is to place the debate in a different light by showing that it is a gross oversimplification to equate individual rights with the interests of the English-speaking minority, while seeing collective rights as solely the concern of the French-speaking majority. An examination of the relevant legislation indicates a more complex situation in which the collective rights of both the French and English-speaking populations have been recognized.

The first evidence of the recognition of the collective rights of the English-speaking minority of the province came in the *British North America Act* (hereafter BNA) of 1867.[8] Many commentators have pointed to section 133 of the Act which accorded equal status to French and English in the courts and the legislature of the newly created province

---

6. Outside of Québec there were also negative reactions to Bill 178 since it suggested that the Québec government would be inclined to use the "distinct society" provisions of the Meech Lake Accord to suppress individual rights. In this context, the Manitoba government promptly withdrew its support from the Accord, thus throwing the future of the agreement into doubt.

7. *The Gazette* (20 December 1988).

8. Now the *Constitution Act, 1987*, (U.K.), 30 & 31 Vict., c. 3.

of Québec. Less well known, but perhaps even more significant to the issue of collective rights, was section 80 which restricted the ability of the Québec government to alter the electoral boundaries established in 1867 for the selection of members to the Québec legislative assembly. A schedule was appended to the BNA Act which listed twelve ridings, three-quarters of which had had English-speaking majorities at the time of the previous census and all of which were located in either the Eastern Townships or the Ottawa valley. It was stipulated that no alteration could be made to the boundaries of these ridings unless the majority of the twelve deputies in question agreed to the change. This was a recognition that the English-speaking population had the collective right to defend its representation against unfair intrusions by the Québec legislature, which was widely perceived by all parties at the time as the agent for the collective interests of the French-speaking majority.[9]

Section 80 was eventually repealed by the Québec government in 1970, with little reaction from the English-speaking population which had long since lost its majority within each of the twelve so-called 'privileged' ridings.[10] Nevertheless, by giving constitutional sanction to this 'legislature within a legislature' the precedent was set for much of the language legislation of the 1970s and 1980s which was passed by a provincial legislature intent upon advancing the collective rights of the French-speaking majority at the same time that it also established certain collective rights for the English-speaking minority.

This general approach to linguistic matters was first made evident in 1974 with the passage of Bill 22.[11] By and large, there was little language legislation worthy of note from the passage of the BNA Act to the adoption of Bill 22. To be sure, there were minor acts passed throughout the twentieth century which proclaimed French to be the only official language of certain small municipalities.[12] There was also Bill 63, passed in 1969 which feebly proclaimed the primacy of French at the same time that it supported the freedom of Québecers to choose for themselves the language in which their children would be educated.[13] In this sense Bill 63 was a ringing endorsement of individual rights. Bill 22, however, indicated that a new era had arrived in its assertion that French was the official language of the province. This rather symbolic proclamation

9. Arthur Silver, *The French Canadian Idea of Confederation* (Toronto: University of Toronto Press, 1982) at 55-6.
10. Jean-Charles Bonenfant, "Les douze circonscriptions privilégiées du Québec" (1962) *Cahiers de géographie du Québec* 161-6.
11. *Official Language Act*, S.Q. 1974, c. 6.
12. Claude-Armand Sheppard, *Régimes linguistiques canadiens et étrangers* (Québec: Editeur Officiel, 1974).
13. *Act to Promote the French Language*, S.Q. 1969, c. 9.

was given teeth by requiring firms in the private sector to secure francization certificates indicating that French was the primary language of internal communications. As for the public sector, there was to be no need in the future to publish public notices in a language other than French, and only the French version of statutes and regulations was to have the weight of law.

Beyond these efforts to support the ability of French speakers to operate in their language throughout Québec, there were other provisions which touched upon the collective needs of both the majority and the minority. For instance, in the realm of education, Bill 22 departed from Bill 63 in insisting that French be the language of instruction for all Québecers except for those who formed part of the English-speaking minority. Membership in the English-speaking community was determined by means of language tests which were administered to children before the beginning of their education to determine whether they possessed "a sufficient knowledge of the language of instruction."[14] Only if a child indicated a satisfactory knowledge of English, presumably an indication that English was the language in the home, was he to be admitted to an English school; otherwise the student would attend a French school.

There was widespread negative reaction to the educational provisions of Bill 22. Nearly all Québecers agreed that there was something improper about subjecting six year olds to language tests. At the same time, however, there was considerable support within the French population for the advancement of its collective rights which had been systematically compromised over the years under the system of 'freedom of choice'. That system had long permitted parents whose mother tongue was neither English nor French to send their children to English schools, in the process adding new recruits to the English-speaking minority. The strengthening of the English-speaking population was viewed with some alarm in light of the rapid decline of the birth rate among French speakers. Dire predictions were produced in the late 1960s and early 1970s that if nothing were done to protect the French population it would almost cease to be a majority in the Montreal region by the turn of the century.[15]

As for the English-speaking minority, it felt threatened by the potential loss of the clientele that had been bolstering its numbers since the end of World War II. Quite appropriately, the minority pointed to the fact that the French-Catholic schools of the province had

---

14. *Supra*, note 11, s. 41.
15. For example, see J. Henripin, *L'immigration et le déséquilibre linguistique* (Ottawa: Main-d'oeuvre et immigration, 1974).

systematically excluded immigrant children from their classes for generations.[16] In light of this history of neglect, how could the French-speaking majority now turn around, when circumstances changed, to claim its right to this clientele? This reversal of a long-standing practice was condemned as hypocritical by English speakers who were also bothered by Bill 22 because they perceived that it advanced the collective rights of French speakers at the expense of individual rights.

Safe in the knowledge that the economic attractions of English would always draw a large clientele to its schools in any system that permitted freedom of choice, the English community could present itself as the philosophical defender of the principle of individual rights, all the time ignoring the fact that its own collective rights were also recognized by Bill 22 in the statutory pronouncement that those who truly formed part of the English-speaking population (as defined by the language tests) had a right to an education in English. This principle had never previously been declared in Québec, where only the rights of denominational education had been guaranteed since 1867. Nevertheless, the English-speaking population had no reason to perceive the recognition of its communal existence as a victory since it had been doing quite well under the old system of 'freedom of choice'.

Quite aside from the issue of education, Bill 22 also recognized the collective rights of English-speakers in its provisions pertaining to the language of communications for local institutions such as school boards and municipal governments. Article 13 of the statute made it clear that French was to be the official language of public administration except for local institutions in which the "majority of persons administered are English-speaking". To assure that this provision would be put into force the *Régie de la langue française*, established to watch over the implementation of Bill 22, was empowered to "ascertain the number of English-speaking persons in each municipality and school board". Just as Section 80 of the BNA Act had established special rules in the interest of the English population in those parts of the province where it formed the majority, so too did article 13 of Bill 22 move in such a direction. In this fashion, the collective rights of both the majority and the minority were to be protected.

Following the rise to power of the Parti Québécois in the 1976 provincial election, Bill 22 was replaced by Bill 101 which was generally perceived within the English-speaking population as even less desirable than its predecessor. There was some justice in this observation given

---

16. See Donat Taddeo et Raymon Taras, *Le débat linguistique au Québec* (Montréal: Presses de l'Université de Montréal, 1987).

that the right to use English in the courts and legislature of Québec, guaranteed by section 133 of the BNA Act, was rescinded.[17] This right was restored in 1979 following a ruling of the Supreme Court,[18] but the annoyance of the linguistic minority remained, fuelled by such provisions as those which prohibited the use of English on most commercial signs. There is no reason why English speakers should have embraced Bill 101, but it is nevertheless important to recognize that it continued what Bill 22 had begun in attempting to define a situation in which French was the normal language of activity in the province, except in those specific contexts in which English speakers were likely to predominate. For instance, Bill 101, while banning the use of English on most commercial signs, made special provision for those settings in which the clientele of the firm might logically speak English. Accordingly, the rules did not apply to firms with fewer than five employees which could post signs in French and another language. This provision was designed to enable small stores catering to the local population to function in English. Similarly, there were exemptions for signs and posters advertising "cultural activities". In this fashion, English language bookstores had the ability to post signs in English. The same spirit of making French the language of business except where English speakers might dominate was also evident in the strengthened provisions for the francization of business, which were to apply only to firms with more than fifty employees; the small family-run, and possibly English, firm was not to be subject to these provisions.

Bill 101 also continued the thrust of Bill 22 in terms of education. Much to the delight of all Québecers, the tests to determine eligibility to English schools were abolished. In their place, hard and fast rules were established whose goal once again was to establish membership in the English-speaking population. According to Bill 101 access to English schools was largely limited to the children of parents who had been educated in English in Québec.[19] Following a Supreme Court decision taking into account the *Canadian Charter of Rights and Freedoms*, admissibility to English schools was extended in 1984 to include the children of Québecers educated in English anywhere in Canada.[20]

---

17. *Supra*, note 2, ss. 8-9.
18. *A.G. Québec* v. *Blaikie*; *A.G. Québec* v. *Laurier*, [1979] 2 S.C.R. 1016 (S.C.C.).
19. *Supra*, note 2, s. 73. There were some exceptions to this rule. For instance, parents educated in English anywhere in the world were allowed to send their children to English schools if they had been living in quebec prior to the proclamation of Bill 101 or if they were only residing in the province temporarily. Moreover, the rules were to be waived for the brothers and sisters of children already in English schools, independent of their parents' linguistic background.
20. *A.G. Québec* v. *Quebec Association of Protestant School Boards*, [1984] 2 S.C.R. 66 (S.C.C.).

As we have seen, there were two thrusts to the language legislation of the 1970s. On the one hand, the effort was made to establish French as "the common language of Québecers", which would be used "as the means of communications between Québecers of all languages and origins".[21] At the same time, however, there was also an attempt to give legal status to the rights of the English minority in those situations in which English speakers were predominant. In the 1980s this recognition was extended by both the Parti Québécois and Liberal governments. In 1983 the Lévesque government amended Bill 101, adding to the preamble an explicit reference to the need to respect "the institutions of the English-speaking minority."[22] This commitment was given greater substance by the Bourassa government in 1986 when it passed legislation that recognized that "every English-speaking person is entitled to receive health services and social services in the English language."[23]

In a curious sort of manner, Bill 178 was consistent with the earlier legislation of the 1980s in that it reaffirmed, and even strengthened, the Bill 101 provisions regarding commercial signs by prohibiting the use of English on the outside of establishments regardless of the number of workers employed.[24] As in Bill 101, there was an exemption for firms catering to a specific ethnic or cultural group.[25] Otherwise, however, external signs were to be in French only so as to make French "the common language" in settings such as the streets of Montreal where Québecers, independent of linguistic background, were likely to congregate.

As for internal signs, Bill 178 potentially opened the door for bilingualism within all commercial establishments, and not merely within those with fewer than five employees as had been the situation under Bill 101. In practice, however, the government appeared reluctant during the first months of 1989 to allow this deviation from Bill 101. Bill 178 forbade the use of English within franchise operations or chain stores with between five and fifty employees.[26] Moreover, regulations were on the horizon in early 1989 to prevent the use of English in all establishments with more than five employees. In terms of internal signs, this would effectively reaffirm the principle that English should be permitted in those settings, such as small neighbourhood stores, where English

---

21. Quebec, *Report of the Royal Commission of Inquiry on the Position of the French Language and Language Rights in Quebec* (Québec: Éditeur Officiel, 1972) I, 147.
22. *Act to Amend the Charter of the French Language*, S.Q. 1983, c. 56, s. 1.
23. *Act to Again Amend the Act Respecting Health Services and Social Services*, S.Q. 1986, c. 106, s. 3.
24. *Supra*, note 5, s. 1.
25. *Id.* s. 61.
26. *Id.* s. 1.

speakers were likely to predominate. Otherwise, in mixed settings, French was to prevail.

Bill 178 was in line with the evolution of linguistic policy since the 1970s that sought to establish the dominance of French in most contexts, while creating exceptions for those situations in which English speakers were likely to be in the majority. This approach was first given force in 1866 when Alexander Galt insisted upon the recognition of the collective rights of English speakers via section 80 of the BNA Act. In the 1980s a similar effort to negotiate for the collective interests of the linguistic minority has been undertaken by Alliance Québec, established in 1982 and immediately recognized by the Québec government as the official bargaining agent for English speakers.

Quite understandably, English speakers have been staunch supporters of individual rights given the economic and cultural power of their language in North America.[27] Accordingly, they have conveyed the impression that the language debate in Québec has been one between English advocates of individual rights and the French-speaking supporters of collective rights. As this paper has shown, however, this debate cannot be reduced to such simplistic terms. Over the course of nearly 125 years both linguistic groups have been involved in efforts to define the role of the two collectivities. Neither group has been entirely pleased with the outcome of these negotiations, but this is to be expected when two groups, one a minority in Québec and the other a minority in the North American context, perceive their survival to be on the line.

---

27. On this issue, see Michel Plourde, *La politique linguistique du Québec, 1977-87* (Québec : IQRC, 1988).

FRENCH LANGUAGE AND EDUCATIONAL RIGHTS IN ALBERTA : AN HISTORICAL PERSPECTIVE

Kenneth J. Munro

The intimate link between language and nationality has been a recurring theme throughout French Canadian history. In 1913, the noted French Canadian intellectual, Henri Bourassa, explained the nature of this symbiotic relationship. He stated :

> The day a race ceases to express its thought and its sentiments in its language, in that language which has grown with it and which took form with its ethnic temperament, it is lost as a race. The preservation of its language is absolutely necessary to the preservation of the race, of its genius, its character and its temperament.[1]

More recently, Francophones outside Québec reiterated this belief in their document *Les héritiers de Lord Durham*. In this report, signed by the Director-General of the Association Canadienne-Française de l'Alberta, the Fédération des Francophones Hors Québec stated :

> We are born French-Canadian. The people that we are must be able to live and develop in French or they are destined to disappear.[2]

Indeed, since the Quiet Revolution of the 1960s, the French language has become the "focus of group loyalty as well as the principal identity trait ...."[3] of French Canadians throughout the country. Consequently, French language and educational rights in Alberta are the essential factors for Franco-Albertans in discussing their survival and development as part of the larger Francophone community of Canada.

In the area of official bilingualism, Franco-Albertans have traditionally stressed the law, but since 1988 have emphasized the "spirit

---

1. Henri Bourassa, "Language and Nationality" as cited by J. Levitt, *Henri Bourassa on Imperialism and Bi-Culturalism, 1900-1918* (Toronto : Copp Clark, 1970) at 134.
2. Fédération des Francophones hors Québec, *Les héritiers de Lord Durham*, Vol. I, Ottawa, avril 1977, 12.
3. Edward M. Corbett, *Quebec Confronts Canada* (Baltimore : Johns Hopkins Press, 1967) at 84.

of confederation" in support of their rights; in the area of French education, Franco-Albertans have traditionally relied on the "spirit of confederation", but since 1982 have embraced the law to obtain justice. In 1877, the Northwest Territories became bilingual; in 1905, the bilingual nature of the Territories in the judicial and legislative spheres was carried forward into the new Province of Alberta and remained unchanged until 1988. Under the *Languages Act, 1988*, Francophones lost the right to have bills and statutes, the Standing Orders, records and journals of the Assembly printed in French.[4] In education, the story differs. Although never guaranteed explicitly in law until recently, French as the language of instruction in the Northwest Territories was a right that flowed from the "spirit of confederation". Interference with that right occurred in 1892 when the Legislature of the Territories granted permission by statute for only "a primary course to be taught in the French language ...."[5] Such action constituted a crippling grievance for francophones in the Territories that was perpetuated in the *Alberta Act* of 1905 and only redressed through *The Constitution Act, 1982* whereby instruction in the French language was granted legal status in Alberta through section 23 of the *Canadian Charter of Rights and Freedoms*.[6]

In attempting to understand the question of French as an official language in Alberta in the Legislature, before the courts and in schools, the argument must focus on legislation and parliamentary debate. The former provides the essential legal framework for the right to use French in everyday life in Alberta, and the latter reveals the intention of the builders of that legal structure. Language was an issue at the outset of the west's entry into Confederation. Canada assumed full power and authority over Rupert's Land on 15 July 1870. Simultaneously, Manitoba was carved out of this newly purchased area and entered Confederation as a bilingual province. The remainder of the territory became known as the Northwest Territories. These Territories were administered under an *Act for the Temporary Government of Rupert's Land*[7] and after 1875, under the *Northwest Territories Act*.[8] Both laws were silent on language. The 1875 Act established a dual school system, one based on religion, however, rather than language. Schools were voluntary and French was the language of instruction for those established in French-Canadian communities.[9]

---

4. S.A. 1988, c. L-7.5.
5. *An Ordinance Respecting Schools*, Consolidated Ordinances of the Northwest Territories 1898, c. 68, s. 109.
6. Part 1 of *The Constitution Act, 1982* being Schedule B of the *Canada Act 1982* (U.K.), 1982, c.11.
7. S.C. 1869, c. 3.
8. S.C. 1875, c. 49.
9. Keith A. McLeod, "Politics, Schools and the French Language, 1881-1931" in Norman Ward and Duff Spafford, eds, *Politics in Saskatchewan* (Toronto: Longmans Canada Ltd., 1968) at 124.

The language issue arose when the Liberal government of Alexander Mackenzie proposed a series of minor amendments to the *Northwest Territories Act*[10] in 1877. At that time, Senator Marc Girard of Manitoba proposed an amendment in the Upper House to place French on an equal footing to English:

> Either the English or the French language may be used by any person in the debates or said Council, and in the proceedings before the Court, and both those languages shall be used in the records and journals of the said Council, and the ordinances of the said Council shall be printed in both languages.[11]

This amendment was silent with respect to the language of instruction in schools. Although the wording of the Girard amendment differed slightly from section 133 of the *British North America Act* and section 23 of the *Manitoba Act* which likewise dealt with language,[12] no one disagreed with the fact that after 1877 the French language enjoyed the same status in the Northwest Territories that it possessed in Québec and Manitoba. Nine years later, this clause became section 110 of the *Northwest Territories Act*.[13] By allowing Senator Girard's amendment to pass,[14] the Mackenzie government signified the acceptance of an assumed commitment to recognize the permanence of the French fact within Confederation.

During this same period in which French became an official language through statute in the Council and courts, and later the Legislature and

---

10. S.C. 1877, c. 7, s. 11.

11. *An Act to amend the Northwest Territories Act, 1875*, S.C. 1877, c. 7, s. II.

12. Section 133 of the *British North America Act* (now the *Constitution Act, 1867* (U.K.), 30 & 31 Vict., c. 3) reads as follows:
"Either the English or the French Language may be used by any Person in the Debates of the House of Parliament of Canada and of the Houses of the Legislature of Quebec: and both those Languages shall be used in the respective records and Journals of those Houses; and either of those Languages may be used by any Person in any Pleading or Process in or issuing from any Court of Canada established under this Act, and in or from or any of the Courts of Quebec.
The Acts of the Parliament of Canada and the Legislature of Quebec shall be printed and published in both those languages."
Section 23 of the *Manitoba Act*, S.C. 1870, c. 3, reads as follows:
"Either the English or the French language may be used by any person in the debates of the Houses of the Legislature, and both languages shall be used in the respective Records and Journals of these Houses: and either of these languages may be used by any person, or in any Pleading or Process, in or from all or any of the Courts of the Province. The Acts of the Legislature shall be printed and published in both those languages."
See Claude-Armand Sheppard, "The Law of Languages in Canada" Marcel Trudel and Geneviève Jain, eds, *Studies of the Royal Commission on Bilingualism and Biculturalism*, Vol. 10 (Ottawa: Queen's Printer, 1970) at 67 and 77.

13. R.S.C. 1886, c. 50.

14. *Toronto Globe* (28 April 1877) 8.

courts of the Territories, the French language continued to enjoy recognition as a language of instruction in schools. In 1881, when the Territories began giving financial assistance to schools, no distinction was made between those with French or English as the language of instruction.[15] Although the first Territorial School Ordinances of 1884 and 1885 were silent respecting language of instruction, the Northwest Council explicitly stated under the 1884 Ordinance, petitions requesting the erection of school districts "must be in both the French and English languages."[16] After the first Territorial Assembly was elected in 1888, the Assembly stressed the importance of English by passing an Ordinance obliging Trustees of all schools "to cause a primary course of English to be taught."[17] In reality, the situation was not much altered because most French schools already taught an English course.

In the 1890s, however, change did occur as the French language came increasingly under attack. While on a speaking tour of the west during the summer of 1889, D'Alton McCarthy, an influential and distinguished Conservative backbencher from Ontario, launched his crusade "to have it perfectly understood ... that the English tongue is the language of the people of this Dominion."[18] The fact the west had failed to attract French-speaking migration lent credence to McCarthy's cry.[19] While there were equal numbers of British and French of the non-native population in the Territories in 1881, by 1891, only 2.36 percent of the inhabitants of the Northwest Territories were French Canadian in origin. In 1901, the French origin population remained less than 4 percent of the Territories as a whole, and 6.2 percent of what would become the Province of Alberta.[20] These figures apparently demonstrated there was little need to continue a policy of bilingualism in the west. Furthermore, McCarthy believed that recognition of duality through a dual school system and bilingualism prevented Canada from becoming a great nation. He lamented the fact that the great dream of Confederation, the building of a strong unified nation in North America,

---

15. *Supra*, note 9 at 124.
16. *School Ordinance of 1884*, Ordinances of the Northwest Territories 1884, No. 5, s. 15(1) and in Canada, House of Commons, *Sessional Papers*, (1894) 57 Vic., Appendix D at 69.
17. Manoly R. Lupul, *The Roman Catholic Church and the Northwest School Question: a study in church-state relations in western Canada, 1875-1905*, (Toronto: University of Toronto Press, 1974) at 45.
18. Canada, House of Commons, *Debates* at 3081 (30 May 1890).
19. Peter B. Waite, *Canada 1874-1896: Arduous Destiny* (Toronto: McClelland and Stewart, 1971) at 216.
20. Edmund A. Aunger, "Linguistic Problems of Western Canada: Language and Law in the Province of Alberta" (A paper prepared for presentation at the First International Conference on Comparative Linguistic Law, Montreal, April 22-29, 1988) at 5 and Table 2. Also see *Census of Canada 1890-91*, Vol. I, at 220-221.

had not been realized. The cause of Canada's problems was to be found in French Canada's ability to maintain a separate culture with its particular pretentions and special privileges within Confederation. McCarthy wanted unity through English supremacy and his crusade in the west was to alert Canadians to the dangers inherent in dualism.[21] Since the Territories had the ability to abolish schooling in the French language themselves, McCarthy left that issue aside and introduced a motion into the House of Commons to abolish French as an official language of the Territories early in January 1890.[22] In searching for a solution to this explosive language issue before the approaching federal general election of 1891, politicians sought a compromise. Accepting the Liberal party principle of local option, the Conservative government agreed to allow the Territorial legislature to decide, after the next Territorial elections, whether French and English should remain official languages in the Legislature, and in the printing of journals and debates of the Assembly of the Northwest Territories. In all other aspects, the 1877 law would remain. This compromise which did not affect the use of French in the courts or the publication of ordinances in French was passed by Parliament in 1891.[23]

With the lifting of some of the legal restrictions to the abolition of French, the legislators in the Territories were ready to tackle the language issue in the Assembly and in the schools. In 1892, following the Territorial elections, the leader of the Executive Committee, Frederick Haultain, proposed a motion "That it is desirable that the proceedings of the Legislative Assembly shall be recorded and published hereafter in the English language only."[24] The motion passed.[25] Apparently, this restrictive legislation was never proclaimed as the federal legislation of 1891 demanded. According to the 1891 amendment to the *Northwest Territories Act*, abolition of French in the Assembly could have effect only if "embodied in a proclamation ... forthwith made and published by the Lieutenant Governor."[26] Research has failed to discover such a proclamation or even the preparation of such a document.

---

21. Donald Creighton, *Canada's First Century, 1867-1967* (Toronto: Macmillan, 1970) at 72-73.
22. Canada, House of Commons, *Debates* at 38 (22 January 1890).
23. *An Act to amend the Acts respecting the North-West Territories*, S.C. 1891, c. 22, s. 18.
24. Northwest Territories, *Journals* (1891-92) Vol. IV at 110.
25. Grant McEwan, *Frederick Haultain: Frontier Statesman of the Canadian Northwest* (Saskatoon: Western Producer Prairie Books, 1985) at 70.
26. *Supra*, note 23, s. 18.

Consequently, French was never legally abolished in the Legislature of Territories.[27]

Such legal niceties were not at issue with respect to the abolition of schooling in the French language. In the fall of 1892, following the attempt to abolish French in the Legislature, the Assembly of the Territories turned its attention to the question of schools. David Mowat, the member for South Regina, proposed a bill demanding that all schools be taught in the English language but allowing school trustees to permit a primary course to be taught in French.[28] In effect, French could be used as the language of instruction in the first two years of schooling. Protests followed through petitions to Ottawa calling for disallowance of the Ordinance.[29] Charles B. Rouleau, a magistrate in Calgary, argued that the Ordinance was contrary to the spirit of section 110 of the *Northwest Territories Act*.[30] Amédee Forget, an advisory member of the Council of Public Instruction, stressed that Canada had two official languages and thus French Canadians had the right to learn the language of their ancestors.[31] To escape political conflict with local authority, Ottawa decided not to disallow the Ordinance.[32]

One further change was made with respect to the language of instruction in schools before Alberta became a province. As the west began to fill with people who were neither British nor French in origin, the Territories bowed to pressure to permit the use of languages other than English or French in schools. In the 1901 School Ordinance,[33] clause 136 provided that the primary course could still be taught in French and that the school board of any district could employ one or more competent persons to give instruction in a language other than English, but this course was not to supersede or interfere with regular school instruction.[34] Regulations provided for one hour of instruction between three and four o'clock of selected school days. Such instruction was to be confined to reading, composition, and grammar, and the textbooks

---

27. Sheppard, *supra*, note 12 at 85; Fédération des francophones, *supra*, note 2 at 52; and *Report of the Royal Commission on Bilingualism and Biculturalism*, Book I, (Ottawa: Queen's Printer, 1967) at 51-52.
28. Northwest Territories, *Ordinances of the Northwest Territories*, No. 22, 1892.
29. Canada, House of Commons, *Sessional Papers*, No. 40 (1894) at 4-11, 39.
30. *Id.* at 41-42.
31. Rev. H. Leduc, *Hostility Unmasked: School Ordinance of 1892 of the North-West Territories and its Disastrous Results* (Montreal: C.O. Beauchemin, 1896) at 39.
32. For an apologist's view of the federal position, see P.B. Waite, *The Man from Halifax: Sir John Thompson Prime Minister* (Toronto: University of Toronto Press, 1985) at 399-401.
33. *An Ordinance respecting Schools*, Ordinances of the Northwest Territories 1901, c. 75, s. 1.
34. *Supra*, note 8 at 130.

used were to be those authorized by the Department of Education.[35] Although these provisions were directed at the newly arrived immigrants from central Europe, Keith McLeod has argued that this Ordinance constituted a gain for the French-speaking population because French Canadians could now teach their language beyond the primary course.[36] Nevertheless, this Ordinance rejected the concept of Canadian duality that French Canadians upheld.[37]

Franco-Albertan education and linguistic rights became entangled with the larger struggle of French Canadian rights throughout Canada during debate on the *Alberta Act*[38] in 1905. The intention of the Liberal Laurier government was "to continue on the conditions existing in the Northwest Territories ..." in the new Province of Alberta as had been provided in section 110 of the *Northwest Territories Act* as amended in 1891.[39] The Minister of Justice, Charles Fitzpatrick, clearly stated that "we are continuing the conditions existing at the present time; we are perpetuating the rights, whatever they may be, in the Northwest Territories with respect to language, leaving it to the legislature to determine hereafter to what extent these rights may be maintained."[40] He maintained that "as an official language in the Northwest Territories in the courts of law ... there has not been a single document in the French language entered in a court of justice there for the last 15 years, not a single word of French spoken in the courts."[41] Rejecting the desire of French-Canadian nationalists to make Alberta explicitly bilingual,[42] Laurier carried over the bilingual section of the Northwest Territories Act in to the new *Alberta Act*[43] in a catch-all clause and enabled the provincial Legislature to amend those bilingualism provisions or abolish them outright.

By examining schooling in the French language during the debate of the *Alberta Act*, French Canadians recognized that there was no law assuring Francophones the right to education in the French language. Many accepted the reality that it was not explicitly stated in law but was "in the spirit of it".[44] Some claimed that the term "separate schools"

---

35. *Ibid.*
36. *Ibid.*
37. Kenneth Munro, "Official Bilingualism in Alberta" (Spring 1987) 12:1 *Prairie Forum* 42-43.
38. S.C. 1905, c. 3.
39. Canada, House of Commons, *Debates* at 8240 (27 June 1905).
40. *Id.* at 8633-34 (30 June 1905).
41. *Id.* at 8577 (30 June 1905) (Laurier).
42. *Id.* at 8539 (30 June 1905) (Bourassa); at 8530-31 (30 June 1905) (Monk); at 8582, 8577 (30 June 1905) (Laurier).
43. *Supra*, note 38, s. 16.
44. Canada, House of Commons, *Debates* at 3487 (30 March 1905) (Bergeron).

embodied the right "to authorize the use of the French language whenever thought convenient".[45] The Minister of Justice, Charles Fitzpatrick, however, was emphatic that the question of religious education and the question of the French language are entirely different. There is no connection between them.[46]

Consequently, because the *Alberta Act* was to preserve the school situation at the time of Confederation, as reflected in the Ordinance of 1901, French was permissible as a primary course only. That was the situation with respect to schooling in French as Alberta entered Confederation.[47] The first two years of schooling could be taught completely in French, except for English. From grades 3 to 9, one hour of French was permissible. French was also allowed to explain any concepts and ideas which students could not understand after being taught them in English. Also one-half hour of catechism was permitted and that one-half hour could be given in French in addition to the regular hour of French.[48] Clearly, as Alberta entered Confederation, the status of French in schooling, in the Legislature and before the courts remained unacceptable for Franco-Albertans.

For over sixty years after 1905, Franco-Albertans remained hesitant and wary about asserting their rights. Hovering between 5 percent and 6 percent of the population of the province,[49] they had never the force of numbers within Alberta nor the benefit of a secure, accepted French Canadian community throughout the rest of the country to support them in their struggle. Whereas the constitutional provisions for official bilingualism in the Legislature and before the courts were clear,[50] English so dominated that it appeared as if it were the only official language. Despite the fact that laws were to be enacted, printed, and published in French and English in Alberta, since 1905 English was used exclusively until the *Language Act*[51] of 1988 (a bilingual Act) sanctioned the use of English only. Following 1905, the records of the Legislature with few exceptions were published in English only. In 1987, the Legislature amended the standing orders of the Legislature to confirm this practice in the form of a resolution.[52] Again, in debate since 1905, English has

---

45. *Ibid.*
46. Canada, House of Commons, *Debates* at 8328 (28 June 1905).
47. Canada, House of Commons, *Debates* at 5174 (1 May 1905) (Boyer).
48. *La Survivance* (17 août 1949).
49. Aunger, *supra*, note 20, Table 2.
50. The case of Father Mercure as decided by the Supreme Court 25 February 1988 implied that Alberta was officially bilingual. See *Le Franco* (4 mars 1988) 24; *R. v. Mercure*, [1988] 1 S.C.R. 243.
51. *Supra*, note 4.
52. Aunger, *supra*, note 20 at 13.

been the language of usage in the Legislature, although a few French-speaking members have used some French for symbolic purposes.[53] To ensure English remained the language of debate, the Legislature adopted a resolution 27 November 1987 declaring English to be the working language of the Assembly.[54] As with bilingualism in the Legislature, the province disregarded the law and English was the language of the courts in practice, with few exceptions.[55] Because legislative authority for criminal law, including procedure, falls under the exclusive jurisdiction of the federal Parliament, on 1 January 1990 Francophones in Alberta will have the right in law to a criminal trial in French.[56] In the interim, Alberta experienced its first French-language trial in Vermilion in 1986 in which the judge heard testimony in French and addressed the lawyers in French; the first trial before a French-speaking jury in the province occurred in Calgary in 1987.[57] Section 4 of the 1988 *Languages Act* provides for all trials under provincial jurisdiction to be in French or English.[58] Thus, Alberta has moved from dragging its feet on bilingualism in court procedures to embracing bilingualism in both civil and federally imposed criminal court procedures.

In 1988, what rights the French Canadian had enjoyed in law were qualified and in part, abrogated. Since official bilingualism contained within the *Alberta Act* did not become part of the constitution in 1982 but rather remained part of the statutes of the province which could be changed through ordinary legislative procedures,[59] Alberta Francophones had to turn from basing their arguments for official bilingualism on the law, to basing their arguments on the "spirit of Confederation".

The reverse situation occurred in the area of schooling in the French language. After 1905, because there was no statutory right to French schools beyond grade two, Franco-Albertans promoted and protected French through various community organizations and institutions. French was encouraged with the founding of the *Société du Parler Français* in 1912 and later through the annual examinations of the *Association canadienne-française de l'Alberta* (l'ACFA) which consisted of a test in five different subjects: grammar, composition, literature, history and dictation. Private schools were opened for boys and girls

---

53. *Id.* at 14-18.
54. *Id.* at 17.
55. Sheppard, *supra*, note 12 at 170.
56. *Official Languages Act*, S.C. 1988, c. 38, s. 96.
57. *Edmonton Journal* (15 September 1987) B6.
58. *Supra*, note 4, s. 4.
59. *Le Franco* (4 mars 1988) 3 & 24; *ibid.* (8 avril 1988) 16; *Alberta Report* (14 March 1988) 17 & 19.

— the Jesuit College for boys in 1912 and Assumption for girls in 1926.[60] At the same time, close ties were maintained with the English-speaking community to preserve the privileges that existed. Consequently, in 1916 when the Department of Education adopted new regulations placing further restrictions on the teaching of languages other than English in Alberta schools, French was excluded from the Department's interpretation of those regulations.[61] Little changed from then until 1958. At that time, the Franco-Albertans were able to present their views when the government of Alberta established a Royal Commission to examine ways of reforming the educational system of the province. In a brief to the Commission, l'*ACFA* urged that teaching be given at least one-half day in grades 5 to 9 inclusive. This idea was rejected,[62] but could not be sustained throughout the 1960s.

As the 1960s dawned, Franco-Albertans benefitted from the larger struggle for French Canadian rights across the whole country. The question of the future of French Canadian society became acute as Québec felt alienation from Ottawa and when social changes within Québec produced by the Quiet Revolution came at a time when Québec adapted her institutions to meet the needs of an urban and industrial society. Committed to a fuller recognition of the French fact in Canada, Lester Pearson, Prime Minister of Canada in 1963, appointed a Royal Commission on Bilingualism and Biculturalism to recommend appropriate steps to further the equal partnership of the two founding peoples within Confederation. Appearing before the Commission, the Association of Bilingual Educators in Alberta urged the teaching of subjects in French during one-half of the school day.[63] Going beyond any proposals from either l'*AEBA* or l'*ACFA*, the Royal Commission recommended bilingual schools and unilingual French schools be established in provinces.[64] In response to the Royal Commission on Bilingualism and Biculturalism, the constitutional negotiations of the period and the heightened desire of Canadians to accommodate and resolve the question of French Canada's place in Confederation, the Social Credit government of Alberta in February 1968 gave permission for the teaching in French fifty percent of the time from grades 3 to 12. Grades one and two could naturally be taught completely in French,

60. (1913) *Canadian Annual Review* 655; E. J. Hart, *Ambition and Reality: The French-speaking community of Edmonton 1795-1935* (Edmonton: Le Salon d'histoire de la francophonie albertaine, 1980) at 132-133.
61. Brenda Gainer, *The Franco-Albertans and the First World War* (History Honours Essay, University of Alberta, 1974) [unpublished] at 30-31.
62. *La Survivance* (14 mai 1958 et 1 décembre 1959).
63. *La Survivance* (15 décembre 1965).
64. *Le Franco* (13 décembre 1967).

except for the subject of English.[65] In response to this change of policy, Jean-Maurice Olivier wrote in *Le Franco* that Francophones had again been granted a privilege, "but official acceptance of that which is and must remain a RIGHT ..." is what was required.[66]

From 1968 onwards, a change occurred in the emphasis of Franco-Albertans. Until the 1970s, they had been advocating bilingual schools, largely because Alberta was a province that was overwhelmingly English. They believed that only through teaching in English some of the time could their young people have the same advantage as English-speaking students. Yet, experience demonstrated, especially after the 1968 law came into effect, that bilingual schools could not achieve Francophone goals. This change in attitude is apparent in the views expressed by Father Breton in 1950 compared to those stated by Yvon Poulin in 1972. In 1950, Father Breton argued for "schools where all the primary courses will be uniquely French; where, in the subsequent years, we would have, not only one in eight, but at least four hours of French each day."[67] By 1972, Yvon Poulin was claiming that "if one wished that the French fact in Alberta remain a reality and not a folk phenomenon, the unilingual French school financed and administered by the province, is the first condition necessary."[68]

This forceful stand became the norm amongst the intellectual leaders of the Franco-Albertan community by 1974. That year, Guy Lacombe demanded French schools for the province, schools "where the totality of teaching in French, where the atmosphere is totally French not only because of the French language which is the only vehicle of communication, but also because of the authentic French or French Canadian culture which emanates from the administrators and the teaching staff." He also meant "schools where a very competent teaching of the English language is given, in order to take into account the Canadian and Albertan reality in which we live."[69] Noting the differences between immersion schools and French schools, Lacombe explained that immersion schools gave anglophones what they wanted — bilingual children "at the conversational level"; French schools would give French parents what they wanted — children "bathed in the French culture."[70]

---

65. *An Act to amend the School Act*, S.A. 1968, c. 89, s. 24 and *Le Franco* (février 1968).
66. *Le Franco* (28 février 1968).
67. *La Survivance* (20 septembre 1950).
68. *Le Franco* (22 novembre 1972).
69. *Le Franco* (22 novembre 1972).
70. *Le Franco* (28 avril 1976).

These opinions came to dominate the Franco-Albertan community as Confederation reached another crisis in 1976. As Québec separatism grew in popularity and the *Parti Québécois* prepared to take power, concrete action by English-speaking Canada appeared necessary to demonstrate to the Québécois that they had a place in Canada. Within that context, in November 1976, the Alberta Minister of Education announced that henceforth, teaching could be carried out in French for 80 percent of the school day.[71] This meant that theoretically, French schools were possible in Alberta. But, contrary to Franco-Albertans who asked for French education *rights*, this permission was granted to Francophones only as a privilege.[72] Yet again, national events served to benefit Franco-Albertans by 1980. Prime Minister Pierre Trudeau was determined to bring the Canadian constitution home and, in doing so, to demonstrate the good faith of English-speaking Canadians for constitutional change regarding French rights, all of which was in return for the majority of Québécois having rejected the separatist option in the Québec referendum. Trudeau was emphatic that in the new constitution "the entrenchment of linguistic rights ... was one of the two basic principles non-negotiable."[73] Consequently, against Alberta's objections, instruction in French was guaranteed to French minorities outside Québec in the new constitution under article 23 of the *Charter of Rights and Freedoms*.[74] The Franco-Albertan community rejoiced : "This linguistic right in education; at last we have it ...."[75] For the first time in their history, Franco-Albertans had the right to French schools enshrined in law; the recognition of a right that had been enjoyed in practice but no law before 1982 had recognised because of the larger Canadian determination to ensure French rights across the country. Following this victory, Franco-Albertans turned to realize this right in practice within their province.

Following the passage of the *Constitution Act, 1982*, some Edmonton French-speaking parents requested the Minister of Education, and subsequently the Edmonton Public School Board and Edmonton Catholic School Board, to establish a French-language school "designed specifically for French-speakers."[76] In response to the refusal of this request by all three authorities, the parents established a French-language private school, L'Ecole Georges et Julia Bugnet in 1983. They also took their case to court claiming that section 23 of the *Constitution Act,*

---

71. *Le Franco* (10 novembre 1976).
72. *Le Franco* (21 september 1977 & le 1 février 1980).
73. *Le Franco* (13 juin 1980).
74. *Le Franco* (13 juin 1980; 27 février 1981; 7 octobre 1981).
75. *Le Franco* (11 novembre 1981).
76. Aunger, *supra*, note 20 at 28.

1982 guaranteed them the right to a French-language minority school and "the power to create a school board to administer the school."[77] In this case, *Jean-Claude Mahé* v. *The Queen in Right of the Province of Alberta*,[78] the Alberta Court of Appeal found that School Boards were permitted to provide French-language instruction but made no provision for a distinct and separate French-speaking school board to administer these schools.

A year earlier, Alberta had recognized the distinction between minority and immersion schools by having the Edmonton Catholic School Board open a French minority school, l'École Maurice Lavallée. Since then, another French minority school, l'École Sainte-Anne, has been established in Calgary and in September 1988, l'École Héritage opened at Jean Côté. These three primary schools remain the only French minority schools in the province. Yet, while the government of Alberta appears willing to guarantee the right of the French-speaking minority to instruction in French according to the Canadian Constitution, as seen in their revisions to the Alberta *School Act*,[79] it refuses to accept the proposition that these schools should be managed by the French minority through their own distinct school board.[80]

While the principles laid down in the *Constitution Act, 1982* have been accepted by the Alberta government, the battle continues for the creation of more French language schools and the right to distinct French minority school boards. In effect, progress is being made in the gradual establishment of French minority schools, but the provincial government refuses to accept the necessity of creating distinct French minority school boards to administer these schools. Victory in the former areas was made possible because the struggle was part of the larger Canadian struggle of securing French rights for Francophones throughout their country; victory in the latter area will be more difficult if history is any guide because Franco-Albertans must rely solely on their ability to convince their own provincial government of the justice of their cause. Since 1982, in the field of education, Franco-Albertans have emphasized the law to support their cause; but since the *Mercure*[81] case caused Alberta to adopt the *Languages Act* of 1988, Franco-Albertans have turned to the "spirit of Confederation" to obtain justice in the broader area of official bilingualism.

---

77. *Ibid.*
78. (1987), 80 A.R. 161 (Alta. C.A.), rev'd (1990), 68 D.L.R. (4th) 69 (S.C.C.).
79. S.A. 1988, c. S-3.1, s. 5.
80. Aunger, *supra*, note 20 at 29.
81. *Supra*, note 50.

Partie VII / Part VII

Allocution

Les conflits linguistiques canadiens apparaissent souvent sous le couvert d'un conflit de principes fondamentaux. Parfois, le différend est moins motivé par une question de principe qu'enflammé par l'intolérance et le manque de compréhension. À la lumière de deux événements historiques — l'un religieux, l'autre linguistique, Jules Deschênes met l'accent sur les tensions sous-jacentes de nos querelles linguistiques répétées.

Deschênes rappelle la controverse religieuse qui entoura l'affaire *Guibord* au dix-neuvième siècle. Joseph Guibord était un membre important de l'Institut canadien, que ses thèses politico-religieuses opposaient à l'Église catholique. Lorsque Guibord mourut, l'évêque de Montréal refusa l'inhumation en terre consacrée. La veuve de Guibord poursuivit l'évêque et porta la cause jusque devant le Comité judiciaire du Conseil privé, qui ordonna que Guibord fût enterré au cimetière de l'église. La décision souleva l'indignation véhémente de l'église et du public et l'opération n'aboutit que sous la protection d'une escorte militaire fédérale armée.

Deschênes examine ensuite la controverse à laquelle donna lieu l'usage du français dans l'espace aérien canadien. Invoquant des motifs de sécurité, contrôleurs de l'air et pilotes y opposèrent une farouche résistance. Deschênes décrit le débat dans ses grandes lignes ; il rappelle la création d'une commission d'enquête dont on limita sévèrement le mandat afin d'apaiser les pilotes et les contrôleurs, en grève illégale. Malgré la rhétorique des opposants, la Commission dut finalement conclure que l'usage du français ne posait aucun danger à la sécurité aérienne. Les craintes initiales se sont révélées sans fondement et, depuis dix ans, la circulation aérienne s'effectue dans les deux langues et de façon sécuritaire au Canada.

Conference Address

Language conflicts in Canada often have appeared in the guise of a conflict of fundamental principle. Sometimes, the conflict is less one based on principle than one inflamed by intolerance and misunderstanding. Drawing from two historical events, one regarding religious and the other linguistic controversy, Jules Deschênes highlights the underlying tensions of our recurring language disputes.

Deschênes recounts the nineteenth century religious controversy regarding the burial of Joseph Guibord. Mr. Guibord was a prominent member of a group which dissented from Catholic church doctrine. Upon his death, the Bishop of Montréal refused Mrs. Guibord's request that her husband be buried in the Catholic cemetary. Litigation was initiated and proceeded all the way to the Judicial Committee of the Privy Council who ultimately ordered that Guibord be buried in the church cemetary. The Privy Council's order was resisted vehemently both by church and by public. It was only with a federal military escort that Guibord's body was safely interred in consecrated ground.

The controversy over use of the French language in Canadian airspace is explored next. Bilingualism in the air was aggressively resisted by air traffic controllers and pilots, citing the potential danger to air traffic safety. Deschênes outlines this debate, including the appointment of a commission of inquiry whose mandate was severely circumscribed in order to appease illegally striking pilots and controllers. In spite of the rhetoric of safety invoked by opponents, the Commission ultimately found that French language use posed no danger to air safety. A decade of safe, bilingual air traffic movement in Canada has ensued, despite those fears.

BABEL AND GOLGOTHA

The Honourable Jules Deschênes

The *Canadian Charter of Rights and Freedoms* refers, in its s. 27, to "the preservation and enhancement of the multicultural heritage of Canadians."

Still more recently, our 1988 *Official Languages Act*[1] states, in its preamble, that "the Government of Canada recognizes the importance of preserving and enhancing the use of languages other than English and French while strengthening the status and use of the official languages."

La Sainte Bible recèle encore des mérites inattendus. Car c'est un peu grâce à la tour de Babel que nous nous trouvons réunis ce soir. En effet, à l'époque Yahvé confondit le langage des hommes et, nous dit la Bible, il les dispersa sur toute la face de la terre[2].

Aujourd'hui c'est encore trop souvent la division et la discorde que sème la confusion des langues : témoin le besoin qu'éprouve l'Organisation des Nations-Unies d'assurer la traduction simultanée de ses débats en anglais, arabe, chinois, espagnol, français et russe.

It took therefore a substantial dose of courage for the Centre for Constitutional Studies to convene this conference on *Language and the State*. Furthermore, the programme provides for the study of the topic under no less than eleven different angles : what relevant issue could be left unexplored? And was it not unrealistic to invite a guest speaker further to comment on language rights?

In this predicament, my first thought was that we could possibly draw some useful lessons from the very beginning of our times. The

---

1. S.C. 1988, c. 38.
2. Genesis, 11, 7 & 8.

267

Book of Genesis tells us that "Adam and Eve heard the voice of the Lord God walking in the Garden in the cool of the day"[3] and, as we all know, a fateful conversation ensued. Unfortunately, what language God and His creatures were using, the sacred writer neglected to record.

Later at the dawn of the Mediterranean civilization the Pelasgians kidnapped a number of Greek women. Convinced of the superiority of their usages, the Greek concubines insisted upon teaching their children the Greek language and traditions. A few years passed and the children of the Greek concubines made an alliance in order to dominate over the children of the legitimate Pelasgian wives.

The Pelasgians began worrying over what might happen when the children would reach adulthood and aspire to government: might not the Greek-speaking ones wish to perpetuate their domination?

The Pelasgians elected to resort to a radical solution: they killed by the sword all the male issue of their Greek concubines as well as the Greek concubines themselves. Thus the Pelasgians settled their bilingualism problem.[4]

Scores of centuries later some Canadians seem to harbour somewhat similar feelings when they rehash the ten-minute episode of the Plains of Abraham, 4000 kilometres away from here. "I am sorry, but the French have lost," an alderman of Esquimalt, B.C., is reported to have said two months ago after signing a petition presented to the Premier of British Columbia by the Alliance for the Preservation of English in Canada. Last month I have heard over the radio an Indian Chief who clamoured on Parliament Hill in Ottawa: "Our children will be denied higher education, because of federal spending in favour of Québec, the spoilt child of Confederation. Enough with Québec! They are the people that were defeated, they must learn to live with that lesson."

Well, the truth is: we shall not learn! This truth may be hard to swallow, especially for people who live closer to Anchorage to the West, or Queen Maud Gulf to the North, or Chicago to the East, or Los Angeles to the South, than to Montréal or Québec City. Yet that is the truth which found its way in 1976 into the judgment where I upheld the validity of Québec's Bill 22, the predecessor of Bill 101.[5] Let me quote from the original text:

---

3. *Id.*, 3, 8.
4. Herodotus, *The Median Wars*, Book VI, no. 138.
5. *The Protestant School Board of Greater Montréal* v. *The Minister of Education of the Province of Québec et al.*, [1976] 1 C.S. 430.

Nous vivons en effet un tournant majeur de l'histoire du Canada et du Québec. Il n'y a plus de vainqueurs ni de vaincus, plus de conquis ni de conquérants, mais deux peuples appelés par un accident de l'histoire à partager en permanence un meme coin de l'Amérique. Ils possèdent tous deux leurs traditions et leur culture qu'ils sont décidés à préserver. Tour à tour majoritaires et minoritaires, ils connaissent la volupté de l'autorité et la crainte de l'intolérance. La seule différence c'est que, chez le peuple francophone, cette crainte date d'une plus longue expérience tandis que cette volupté possède encore l'attrait du neuf, presque de l'inconnu.[6]

I would only add that to the two founding peoples must now be added the numerous new Canadians of so many ethnic origins who are gracing our country with the variety and the richness of their ancestral cultures and, in many cases, are witnessing with surprise and bewilderment the contest between English and French which since Lord Durham has never abated.

But why has it proven so difficult to quiet down this contestation? After all, many other countries are facing similar problems, and not all of them go to war on the issue.

Look at Ruanda, with one national and two official languages.

Take the opposite situation in Paraguay, with one official and two national languages.

Look at Singapore with one national and four official languages.

Look at Switzerland with its four national languages, of which three are official.

Turn now to India which aims at officializing Hindi, cannot do without English, and must acknowledge, in Annex VIII of its Constitution, no less than fifteen languages, several of which are spoken by a larger number of people than the population of Canada.

Then look at Yugoslavia with its six federated republics, its twelve nationalities, its three main languages and its two alphabets!

What laws can settle those problems? And should we not be ashamed, in this land of bounty, to let our respective majorities become hypnotized by recurring language disputes? And why are we so blind to our own foolishness?

---

6. *Id.* at 435.

A comparison may help. It is a trite saying that language and religion are the two fields where feelings will most easily run high. This has been my experience during the four years when I enjoyed the privilege of sitting in Geneva as the Canadian member of the U.N. Sub-Commission on the Prevention of Discrimination and Protection of Minorities. On every occasion when an issue would arise concerning the death penalty, or corporal punishment, or the apparent persecution of a religious minority in an Islamic country, or an event occurring in Jerusalem, at once a very emotional debate would start and it would take all the control that every member could muster to avoid a regrettable clash.

An example taken from the religious field may therefore help to illustrate the situation in the linguistic field. So as not to risk hurting anybody's feelings, I will take my example from last century, indeed from events which occurred in Montréal immediately following Confederation.

Msgr Ignace Bourget, Bishop of Montréal during thirty-six years, was the most powerful figure of the local Catholic Church during the 19th century. At a certain point in time, a group of prominent laymen established l'Institut canadien. This was a social and cultural society devoted to organizing lectures, setting up a circulating library, and generally promoting culture. L'Institut canadien and Msgr Bourget found themselves on a collision course in the field of religious doctrine. The Bishop put the members of the Institut in default to resign, under pain of severe moral sanctions. Several members bowed to the Bishop's instructions, but one Joseph Guibord resisted. Shortly afterwards, on 18 November 1869, Guibord died suddenly.

His widow asked that he be buried in the Catholic cemetery but, after consultation with the Bishop's office, the officials of the Parish of Notre-Dame turned the request down on the ground that, being a member of the Institut canadien, the late Guibord was liable to canonical sanctions, including deprivation of ecclesiastical burial. Pending settlement of the dispute, the body was buried in the Protestant cemetery.

But Guibord's widow was determined. Through the offices of Me Joseph Doutre, one of the tenors of the Institut canadien, she sued the Parish of Notre-Dame requesting a writ of mandamus to order the burial of her late husband's remains in the consecrated grounds of the Catholic cemetery. On 2 May 1870, after a highly publicized trial, Mr. Justice Mondelet found that the ecclesiastical authorities had failed to substantiate their grounds of defense and, at the end of thirty-eight printed pages without a single paragraph, he granted the mandamus and ordered the requested sacred burial.[7]

The Parish took the matter to the Court of Review. On 10 September 1870 the three-judge Court reversed the trial judge's decision and dismissed the widow's action.[8]

Guibord's widow was not to be so easily defeated; she brought the matter before the Court of Appeal. But a unanimous decision of a five-judge panel again dismissed her claim.[9] The judges, however, were not at one in their reasons for judgment. For Judges Drummond and Monk, the civil courts had no jurisdiction over matters involving spiritual rights. Judges Badgley and Duval rested rather their opinions on a defect in the procedure. Judge Caron concluded that the petition was wrong both as to procedure and as to substance.

By that time passions had been aroused and the case of the widow of Joseph Guibord had become a cause célèbre. Always through Me François Doutre, she appealed to the Court of last resort at the time: the Judicial Committee of the Privy Council, in London. But she did not see the results of their efforts: she died while the appeal was pending. She had, however, left all of her estate to the Institut canadien. The Privy Council granted leave to the Institut to pursue the appeal in the stead of the widow. Then, a little over three years after the judgment of the Court of Appeal, on 21 November 1874, the Privy Council, finding in the evidence no ground to support the plea of ecclesiastical sanctions against Guibord nor the alternate plea that Guibord qualified as a "public sinner," reversed the Court of Appeal and the Court of Review, restored the conclusions of the trial judge and, issuing the writ of mandamus, ordered that Guibord be buried in the consecrated grounds of the cemetery, with costs throughout against the Parish.[10]

Exactly five years had elapsed since the death of Guibord and one would have thought that the matter had come to an end; not so. Ten months after the final judgment, it still had not produced its effects. Doutre obtained the issue of a writ of execution addressed to the "curé" of the Parish of Notre-Dame. On 2 September 1875 a funeral procession, led by Doutre, left the Protestant cemetery for the Catholic cemetery. A large crowd had gathered. Doutre found that the gates of the cemetery were closed. He sent a call for the police, but to no avail: they were

---

7. *Brown v. Les curés et marguilliers de l'Oeuvre et Fabrique de Notre-Dame de Montréal* (1870), 21 R.J.R.Q. 169 at 178.
8. 2 R.L. 257.
9. 17 L.C.J. 89, 7 September 1871.
10. L.R. 6 P.C. 157.

attending the funeral of the chief of the fire department. Pistols could be seen flashing on both sides. Realizing that the situation risked to get out of hand, Doutre and his friends returned Guibord's coffin to the Protestant cemetery.

Polemics then erupted in the papers and among religious and civic authorities. English papers labelled French Canadians as rebels to the law and to the authority of the courts. Msgr Bourget, and then the whole episcopal college of Québec, published letters upholding the right of the Church to decide alone who is entitled to an ecclesiastical burial. Papers in Ontario and the Maritimes were asking whether the Pope could assert any legal authority in the British Empire. The Bishop of Toronto published two letters to defend the attitude of the Bishop of Montréal.

Finally, Doutre fixed the 16 of November 1875 as the definitive date for the Catholic burial of Guibord and he requested the protection of the municipal police. Mayor Hingston, who incidentally was an Irish Catholic, answered diplomatically that the cemetery lay outside the limits of the City of Montréal and that he therefore had no authority in the premises.

Doutre then applied to the Government of Canada. He was heard; and the military authorities of Montréal were instructed to take the necessary steps for the law to be enforced. One thousand soldiers, belonging to six different units, gathered on the Champ-de-Mars where they were reviewed by Colonel Fletcher, and then marched to their positions. The "curé" of the Parish protested against the planned violation of the Catholic cemetery:

> Si l'autorité ecclésiastique se résigne à une attitude passive, c'est pour éviter de plus grands maux; si la Fabrique consent à payer les frais du procès, c'est par respect pour la Reine; mais ni les autorités ni la Fabrique ne modifient leur attitude de principe.[11]

This time the gates were opened and Guibord's coffin was lowered into fresh concrete strengthened with steel rods. His journey to his final resting place had lasted six years, gone through the four tiers of the judicial establishment, and outlived his widow.[12]

Mais il est possible de faire une comparaison qui illustrera encore mieux la férocité des débats et l'exacerbation des passions dans l'affaire Guibord. Il ne fallut pas moins d'un millier de bayonnettes pour refroidir

---

11. Quoted by Rumilly, *Histoire de la Province de Québec*, Vol. II, at 78 & 79.
12. The Recital of the extra-judicial events in the matter of Guibord is drawn from Rumilly, *id.*, Vol. 1 & 2, passim.

les esprits et assurer l'inhumation de Guibord en conformité du jugement qui l'avait ordonnée. Or Montréal comptait alors environ 100 000 habitants.

Reportons-nous maintenant aux événements d'octobre 1970. Pour mater une insurrection appréhendée, le gouvernement fédéral dépêche au Québec, et essentiellement à Montréal, quelque 8000 hommes de troupe. Or Montréal compte alors environ un million d'habitants et l'ensemble de la région métropolitaine, le double.

En proportion de la population, on avait donc mis en état d'alerte une force armée plus imposante pour assurer l'enterrement de Guibord qu'on ne devait en requérir, un siècle plus tard, pour contrer un mouvement terroriste.

All that remains today of the sorrowful episode is a coffin-shaped gray stone, lying flat on the ground, fractured in two along its length and showing a rectangular hole which may, years ago, have held a plaque with an inscription. It is now totally anonymous, except for a registry number (N873) painted on it by order of the cemetery authorities. *Sic transit gloria mundi.* So vanishes the glory of the world.

That example shows vividly how deeply ingrained are religious passions and to what extents of stubbornness and violence they may carry otherwise law-abiding citizens. Linguistic passions are not essentially different. It is therefore no surprise that they have also brought us, peaceful Canadians, to regrettable excesses. A case in point occurred during the last decade: the sour debate on bilingualism in the Canadian airspace. This fully appears to be an appropriate case for study by this gathering. Part of the events are public knowledge; another part, though also publicily available, is not widely known; another part has never been revealed. I will attempt to make as fair and objective an exposé as is possible by someone who has been involved in the yet untold part of the events. The lessons to be drawn from this episode of our history should flow naturally from the naked recital of the facts.

From the beginning of aviation in this country English had been the only language of communication. However, on June 14, 1974 the Department of Transport announced that French could also be used for visual flights at the airports of Québec City and four other smaller centers in the Province of Québec.

On 13 December 1975 the Honourable Otto Lang, then Minister of Transport, gave a press conference outlining the efforts of his Department to promote progressively the use of French in air to ground communications.

On 1 April 1976 this use was officially extended for visual flights to the whole territory of the Province of Québec.

But not everybody was in agreement with this policy. At the very same time that it was being developed, the Canadian Air Traffic Control Association (CATCA) was negotiating with the Treasury Board. The parties concluded a collective agreement on 22 August 1974, but the Controllers' Union refused to sign the French version of the agreement. The Union further announced that it would fully support any member who would file a grievance against a decision of the employer that a position be designated as bilingual.

A member of the Union, Jean-Luc Patenaude, lodged a complaint against CATCA before the Public Service Staff Relations Board, alleging essentially that the Union was discriminating against its French-speaking members by refusing to officialize the French version of the collective agreement and by raising a systematic opposition to the Government policy that French become a working language in aerial communications in Québec.

On 12 March 1976 the Board dismissed the complaint of Patenaude by a majority vote of 5 to 2. Was it purely a coincidence? The five English-speaking members of the Board formed the majority; the minority was comprised of the two French-speaking members. What is still more surprising: after having dismissed the complaint, the majority saw fit to add a kind of footnote, a sort of consolation prize where they said:

> Nothing we have said in this decision is to be taken as in any way condoning the refusal of the Respondent to execute the French version of the Agreement.
>
> ...
>
> The course adopted by the Respondent flies directly in the face of the spirit of the declared policy of Parliament regarding the two official languages of Canada and is deplorable.
>
> ...
>
> In the absence of any explanations, the Respondent leaves itself open to the charge that it is cavalierly ignoring the interest of its French-speaking members and is inviting them to seek whatever remedies may be available to them for what they obviously regard as an intolerable situation.[13]

---

13. *Patenaude and Canadian Air Traffic Control Association*, before the Public Service Staff Relations Board, File no. 161-2-123, 12 March 1976, p. 11, unreported. Quoted in French in Jules Deschênes, *Ainsi parlèrent les Tribunaux I* (Montréal: Wilson & Lafleur, 1980) 200 at 203.

But Patenaude lost nevertheless and his Union did not forgive him. In July 1976 he was tried by CATCA on the charge of having urged the French-speaking controllers to leave CATCA and form their own union. Patenaude was found guilty and sentenced to a six-month suspension from his position of director of the Union for Québec.

Patenaude had a sense of humour. When he rejoined his post at the end of the year, he offered to the Board of CATCA a bottle of champagne to congratulate the controllers on the help they had given to the Parti Québécois in its recent electoral victory.[14]

In the meantime, events had started to move swiftly, and on several fronts at the same time. But an incident which had occurred towards the end of 1975 might help better to understand the atmosphere which was then prevailing. On an Air Canada flight, the pilot was English-speaking, the co-pilot was French-speaking. The co-pilot says "Bonjour" to a French-speaking controller in Québec and he is rebuked by his pilot. Later in the same flight the pilot says "Buenas tardes" to a Spanish-speaking controller in Cuba. The co-pilot cannot but notice the fact. From that moment the pilot ceased to speak to the co-pilot. Which one was to blame for the poisoned atmosphere in the cockpit?[15]

But let us revert to our story. On 20 April 1976 Air Canada publishes a regulation: "English only will be used on the flight deck, with the exception of passenger announcements".[16] Five weeks later, forty-one French-speaking pilots, joined by a member of Parliament, Mr. Serge Joyal, take Air Canada to court to obtain the cancellation of this regulation and an order of injunction allowing the pilots to use the French language in their work.

By that time the situation was reaching the crisis level. On 11 May 1976 a conciliation board had found that no solution to the language problem raised by the controllers could be worked out and that "an independent public commission of enquiry" was necessary.[17]

In June a strike vote was taken among the controllers. The strike was justified, they contended, by their concern for the security of the public which would be threatened by the use of French.

---

14. Sandford F. Borins, *The Language of the Skies*, 1983, Chenelière & Stanké, at 172.
15. This incident is quoted in the judgment rendered by the author in *Joyal* v. *Air Canada*, 1976, S.C. 1211; See Jules Deschênes, *Ainsi parlèrent les Tribunaux I*, *supra*, note 13 at 166.
16. Air Canada 500 Flight Regulations, Regulation no. 14 A (20 April 1976).
17. Report of the Board of Conciliation in the Canadian Air Control Association and Her Majesty in right of Canada, File no. 190-2-148, 11 May 1987, at 6, unreported. Quoted in French in Jules Deschênes, *Ainsi parlèrent les Tribunaux I*, *id.*, 219 at page 220.

In granting an injunction against the controllers on 19 June 1976, Mr. Justice Addy of the Federal Court, said tersely;

> ...it is very difficult, to say the least, for me to accept that the sole motive of all the members of the Association favouring this strike vote at the present time... is their altruistic concern for the safety of the public who might be landing in Québec some one year hence.[18]

> This is without the slightest doubt in my mind an artificial motive...

Two days later a similar order issued against the pilots who had launched an illegal strike.[19]

Another two days later, on 23 June, the Canadian Government resolved to set up a Commission of Inquiry into the safety of bilingual Air Traffic Services in the Province of Québec.[20] Two commissioners were appointed: the Honourable W. R. Sinclair, well known in these parts, and the Honourable Julien Chouinard, whose premature passing we all not long ago lamented.

But events then took a dramatic turn on June 28 with the signature of an agreement between the Minister of Transport and the two unions of pilots and controllers, the rescission by the Cabinet of the Order-in-Council setting up, five days earlier, the Commission of Inquiry and the passing of a fresh Order-in-Council providing for a Commission of Inquiry composed of three judges, namely the Honourable Sinclair, Chouinard, and D. V. Heald of the Federal Court.[21]

As Chief Justice of the Superior Court of Québec, I was then a member of the Canadian Judicial Council and of the Conference of Chief Justices of Canada. On 29 June I sent to the Chairman, the Right Honourable Bora Laskin, the following telegram:

> Je demande la convocation d'urgence du Conseil Canadien de la Magistrature ou de la Conférence des Juges en Chef du Canada pour considérer s'il est opportun que des juges agissent comme commissaires-enquêteurs sur le bilinguisme dans les communications aériennes au Canada vu les conditions et les limitations extraordinaires que le Gouvernement fédéral a imposées hier à leur liberté de pensée, d'action et d'expression / Copie expédiée aux membres du Conseil et aux trois commissaires-enquêteurs.

The reason for my request was clear: "In view of the extraordinary conditions and limitations which the Federal Government has imposed yesterday on their freedom of thought, action and expression."

---

18. *R.* v. *Livingston*, [1977] 1 F.C. 368 at 375.
19. *Air Canada et al.* v. *Maley et al.*, [1977] 1 C.F. 368.
20. P.C. 1976-1576, June 23, 1976.
21. P.C. 1976-1588, June 28, 1976.

Now, lest I be charged with having waited until after the death of the Chief Justice to tell, without fear of contradiction, only my side of the story, let me say that the Chief Justice drafted a memorandum of our conversations which he circulated to all members of the Canadian Judicial Council in July 1976. Whoever is interested can therefore easily check the accuracy of the picture which I am about to draw.[22]

An extraordinary situation had suddenly developed which, in my view, called for an urgent consideration by the Canadian Judicial Council.

Indeed we all know that there exists in Canada a long-standing tradition of separation of powers between the executive and the judiciary, which must be most jealously cherished. Now the future of this tradition was put in jeopardy when the Federal Cabinet unveiled the amended conditions under which it wanted three members of the Canadian judiciary to perform the duties of Inquiry Commissioners.

By way of comparison, I have examined the Orders-in-Council which have set up fifteen commissions of inquiry at the federal level between 1931 and 1969.

In *all* those instances, spanning over a third of a century, the government of the day spelt out the mandate of the commissioners in most open and generous terms; in *none* of those instances did the government try to restrict the freedom of the commissioners or to impose upon them rules of conduct or of evidence; and in *all* of them the government expressly allowed the commissioners to "adopt such procedures and methods as they may from time to time deem expedient for the proper conduct of the inquiry" and to "engage the services of such counsel, staff and technical advisers as they may require."

All of this was highly proper and quite consonant with judicial independence, so that, of those fifteen commissions, thirteen were chaired with distinction by members of the judiciary and no objection was ever raised to their rendering that kind of public service to the country.

It was in the same spirit and with an equal broadness in the terms of reference that the Honourable W. R. Sinclair and Julien Chouinard were appointed, on June 23, 1976, to inquire generally into the safety of bilingual air traffic in the Province of Québec.

But this unobjectionable situation did not last even five days, and it is with the action of 28 June that strong issue must be taken.

---

22. This memorandum, of which the author holds a copy, is part of the relevant file of the Canadian Judicial Council, whose offices are situated in Ottawa.

I will not deal with the right of veto conceded by the Government to the Air Traffic Controllers over the choice of the third commissioner, though such a condition precedent to the appointment of a judge as commissioner might well be frowned upon, since it could easily be considered as going to his impartiality.

But I do wish briefly to look into three aspects of the matter which should have been of grave concern to the Canadian Judicial Council.

1. Clause number two of the "Memorandum of Understanding" between the Minister and the two associations reads as follows:

> That a prerequisite to the expansion or introduction of any bilingual air traffic service be a unanimous report of the Commission declaring the proposed expansion or introduction to be consistent with the maintenance of current safety standards in Canadian air operations.[23]

This raises a question not of legality, but of policy. Here is a government which appoints a three-man inquiry commission. It pretends to grant them all possible leeway and not to encroach upon their freedom of thought and expression. But before they set down to their task, the Government warns them that, failing unanimity, their report will not be worth the paper on which it will be written: "a unanimous report" shall be "a prerequisite" to positive action by the Government.

The Commissioners may not be legally bound to unanimity, but they are morally coerced into it. It is only natural for anybody to wish one's work and recommendations to be followed by practical implementation. On the part of the Government, so to submit the course of nature to the prerequisite of unanimity, was a perversion of the judicial process and an intolerable attempt at bending the reasoning of one or the other of the Commissioners by inducing them to reach unanimity under pain of reducing their inquiry and their report to an exercise in futility.

This should have been a matter of immediate concern for Council when it was announced.

2. Paragraph g) of the Amended Order-in-Council provides:

> The Commissioners shall not in any of their reports indicate that safety has been demonstrated unless they can justify beyond a reasonable doubt why any contrary view expressed by CATCA or CALPA should not prevail.[24]

---

23. Quoted in The Commission of Inquiry into Bilingual Air Traffic Services in Québec, *Interim Report*, June 23, 1977 (Ottawa: Supply & Services, 1977) at 2.
24. P.C. 1976-1588, June 28, 1976.

This is a sample of an extraordinary provision imposed upon three members of the judiciary.

The Commissioners are put under a strict prohibition: "They shall not" demur from the views expressed by the controllers or the pilots unless they can justify beyond a reasonable doubt why such views should not prevail.

This was a provision insulting to the judiciary. It put the Commission on the defensive. Even before the inquiry began, it clearly implied that, in principle, the views of the controllers and the pilots must prevail. It even went so far as to import into the work of the Commission a rule of criminal law and to impose upon the judges the burden of justifying themselves beyond a reasonable doubt.

Never in our history, at least in modern times, had a government dared write into an Order-in-Council a provision so offensive to the judges whom it was appointing, a provision showing such a lack of confidence in their ability and their impartiality. Never before had members of the Canadian Judiciary been told in such blunt terms that they should bow to the opinions of two of the parties involved in their inquiry, barring a justification to the contrary beyond a reasonable doubt.

Again, Council should have been concerned about the role which thus devolved upon three members of the Canadian Judiciary.

As a matter of fact, three days after the Order-in-Council, the Minister himself saw fit to play down that particular provision in a letter to l'Association des Gens de l'Air:

> ...This in no way gives either organization a veto: they do not have to be convinced or say so; the Commission need only explain why they disregard the arguments...[25]

The Commission of Inquiry welcomed the opening and, on 6 July 1976, wrote to the Minister, after quoting his letter:

> This seems to us to mean that reasons must be given in our report, and such an interpretation of the clause is acceptable to us.[26]

Of course any commission of inquiry ought to give reasons in support of its recommendations; but that is a far cry from what the Order-in-Council enjoined this Commission from doing or instructed it to do.

---

25. *Supra*, note 23 at 2.
26. *Ibid.*

3. Finally, paragraph f) of the amended Order-in-Council reads as follows:

> The Commissioners shall append to their reports any statement on the aspects of the inquiry reported upon, received from CATCA or CALPA within a specified period of time designated by the Commission.[27]

Now the Government takes upon itself to meddle in advance with the report of the Commission and to order the Commission to append to its report any statement received from two of the parties involved. There is a world of difference between the possibility for the Government to publish whatever documents it sees fit out of those which have been collected by the Commission — a right which nobody questions — and the duty which it imposes upon the Commission to attach to its report certain specific documents coming from two particular parties.

This again was an overt intrusion into the independence of the Commission which should be free to draft its report as it sees fit and to attach to it such documents, and such documents only, as in its judgment, and in its own judgment only, it deems proper.

Those three particular aspects of the mandate of the Commission clearly show that the Commission was not set up according to the objective pattern that had been consistently followed in previous years, but that obvious political considerations drove the Government to write into the terms of reference conditions and limitations which, in my humble view, were incompatible with the truly unfettered application of the judicial mind to the subject at issue.

I am comforted in this view by the opinion of Professor Sandford F. Borins in his book of 1983 *The Language of the Skies*. At page 236 the author writes:

> The Commission of Inquiry also had its rules of evidence established for it beforehand, in terms of the unanimity requirement and other aspects of the Lang-CATCA-CALPA agreement designed to put the burden of proof on the government.

At the very least, the situation was so novel and the risk so great that the point was deserving of the preferred interest of the Canadian Judicial Council and ought to have been looked into with despatch. This was a unique opportunity for the judiciary to take a strong stand, through its Council, on the conditions of the use of its members as Inquiry Commissioners.

Unfortunately this did not happen. I had some four telephone conversations with Chief Justice Laskin during that weekend, when he

---

27. P.C. 1976-1588, June 28, 1976.

told me that he had consulted with the majority of the members of the Executive Committee of Council. In their opinion the matter did not fall within the statutory authority of Council, and it was not appropriate to convene a meeting of the Conference of Chief Justices for three reasons:

1. The Judges who accepted appointments to the Commission were acting within the law in so doing.

   This, I answered, was not contested, but irrelevant.

2. Each of the Judges ... had consulted with his Chief Justice and the matter was one essentially between them.

   On this second point, I answered that we were dealing with a matter of national interest where it was quite appropriate that the Chief Justices should exchange their views at the level of the Conference of Chief Justices of Canada which had been set up for that very purpose.

3. Any issue as to the propriety of the Terms of Reference of the Commission was a matter between the Commissioners and the Government.

   With this third point I strongly disagreed. The amended terms of reference were a matter of public record and since, in my opinion, they purported to affect the conduct of the Commissioners, the Judiciary in general and the Chief Justices in particular could not wash their hands of the matter.

Our further conversations led nowhere and the Chairman stood fast in his negative answer to my request. He added that there was no urgency and that I should be satisfied with dealing with the matter at our September meeting.

In final analysis, the Chief Justices of Canada not only decided not to speak up, but took the extreme attitude of even actually refusing to meet in order to look into the matter. This left me, should I confess, with a sad heart and a disillusioned mind.

In the meantime, however, life was going on: both pilots and controllers were cited for contempt of court for having allegedly violated the injunctions issued in June previous. Four different sets of procedure were started and — as could be expected — they ended in four different ways.

The first case was decided in Federal Court on 15 July 1976 in Vancouver; it involved three pilots. The three pilots testified that their refusal to fly was based on a question of security, not of bilingualism.

The Court dismissed the motion for contempt, on the basis of the benefit of the doubt.[28] But the president of the Court added:

> I feel obliged, however, to indicate some scepticism. I have a suspicion that the decision they individually reached was not motivated solely and pristinely by safety considerations...[29]

The second case was decided in Winnipeg on 6 August 1976. It involved sixteen air traffic controllers.[30] The Court found that they had committed a "deliberate disobedience of the injunction." The Court added, however, the following startling comment:

> With respect to the public it can be assumed that every passenger would prefer to survive through the use of English rather than be killed by a misunderstanding caused by the imprudent use of French.

The Court concluded:

> In view of the nature of the issue which gave rise to the strike I have decided that I should let by-gones be by-gones. I find you guilty of contempt of court but I impose no penalty.

Let me now break the chronological order, so as to deal immediately with the two other cases of contempt.

The third case was decided on 7 February 1977. It involved an undisclosed number of controllers posted at thirteen different locations from Gander to Vancouver. This time the Federal Court dismissed even the original application to cite the respondents for contempt.[31]

The fourth case involved CALPA and three pilots and was decided in Ottawa on 16 February 1977.[32] The Court found all respondents guilty of contempt, because their opinion as to the inadvisability of using two languages in air traffic control in Canada could not excuse them from disobeying an order of the Court. CALPA was sentenced to the maximum fine, $ 5,000, and the three individual respondents to fines of $ 500, $ 750, and $ 1,000.

Thus in the first contempt case, the respondent pilots were acquitted; in the second case the respondent controllers were found guilty but not punished; in the third case the respondent controllers were not even summoned to answer the charge; in the fourth case, the respondent pilots and their union were found guilty and fined.

---

28. *Air Canada et al.* v. *Maley et al.* (1976), 7 C.L.L.C. 206.
29. *Id.* at 215.
30. *R.* v. *Livingston et al.*, Federal Court of Canada, Bastin, J., 6 August 1976, unreported; reproduced in Jules Deschênes, *supra*, note 13, I, at 237.
31. *R.* v. *Livingston*, unreported, Federal Court of Canada, 7 February 1977; reproduced in Jules Deschênes, *supra*, note 13 at 238.
32. *Air Canada et al.* v. *Maley et al.* (1977), 8 C.L.L.C. 85.

But the story is not yet over. Let's get back to the fall of 1976. The Air Canada pilots had sued Air Canada in the Superior Court, seeking the annulment of an Air Canada regulation which imposed the sole use of English. L'Association des Gens de l'Air du Québec, having some one thousand three hundred members, had sued the Canadian Government before the Federal Court, seeking the annulment of an order of the Minister of Transport published on 1 September 1976 which, in practice, imposed English as the only language in air communications.

Two hundred and two aeronautics workers had also sued Air Canada before the Superior Court in order that they be allowed to work in French and that the hiring practices of Air Canada to the contrary be cancelled.

The three cases gave rise to five judgments which it is now proper to survey in their chronological order.

The first judgment was rendered by the Superior Court, in the pilots' case, on 7 September 1976, i.e., shortly after the second of the four contempt of court cases. The Court found in the *Official Languages Act*[33] more than a mere expression of pious wishes; the Act contained executory provisions which allowed the Court to annul the impugned regulation and to order Air Canada to respect the right of its French-speaking pilots to use their maternal tongue in their work.[34]

Four months later the Federal Court disposed of the suit launched by the Association des Gens de l'Air du Québec. This time the Court saw in the *Official Languages Act* merely introductory measures, attuned to mere possibilities and even permitting a temporary freeze of the language policy previously announced by the authorities; hence the dismissal of the action.[35]

Both judgments were appealed but, as of necessity, to different courts. The Federal Court of Appeal decided the case of the Association des Gens de l'Air du Québec on 27 June 1978.[36] It found, in essence, that the federal statute had created between the two official languages not an absolute, but only a relative, equality and that the Minister's order did not therefore offend the relevant provisions of the Act.

The next judgment was rendered by the Superior Court in the aeronautics workers' case on 25 May 1981. The Court granted the plaintiffs' prayer in part, declared the *Official Languages Act* executory

33. R.S.C. 1970, c. 0-2.
34. *Joyal* v. *Air Canada*, [1976] 2 S.C. 1211.
35. *Association des Gens de l'Air du Québec* v. *Lang et al.*, [1977] 2 C.F. 22.
36. [1978] 2 C.F. 371.

and ordered that the measures announced by Air Canada to remedy the situation be completed by the end of 1983. An appeal was lodged in 1981 but was never actively pursued, though Air Canada filed its brief six years later, on 27 March 1987.[37]

In the meantime the Commission of Inquiry had produced a preliminary report on 23 June 1977 and had filed a final report on 10 August 1979.

Unbelievable as it may appear, it was only five and a half years after the judgment of the Superior Court, granting the pilots' prayer against Air Canada, that the Québec Court of Appeal issued its own ruling on 16 February 1982.[38] Even then, it was a split decision. By a majority of two to one, the Court of Appeal reversed the Superior Court and dismissed the pilots' action against Air Canada.

What was the overall effect of this jurisprudence? The Superior Court of Québec opened the door to the pilots and to the aeronautics workers, but the Federal Court of Canada and the Court of Appeal of Québec closed it. The last two Courts told the pilots and their fellow employees that the *Official Languages Act* did not offer them any protection; and the Québec Court of Appeal told Air Canada French-speaking pilots that they had no recourse against an English-only policy, that they could not obtain flying instructions manuals in French, and that they could not object to a directive prohibiting the use of French as a working language.

Yet in its 1979 report, which was splendidly ignored by the Court of Appeal, the Commission of Inquiry had vindicated the view that the use of French in air operations presented no particular danger and that the contrary contentions put forward in 1976 by the controllers and the pilots actually concealed ulterior motives. The Commission wrote, in its unanimous report:

> In the final analysis, in the cold light of day, the safety of any method of transportation must be measured by the number of accidents it produces. There are 79 countries throughout the world where air traffic control services are provided in varying degrees in two or more languages.
>
> ...
>
> If one stops to think of the number of flights that must have been made in those countries, of the miles flown and passengers carried, of the take-offs and landings safely accomplished, one is left with an abiding conviction that there is nothing inherently dangerous in bilingual air traffic control...

---

37. *Joyal & Tremblay* v. *Air Canada et al.*, S.C. 500-05-011542-766, unreported; reproduced in Jules Deschênes, *supra*, note 13, II, at 93.
38. [1982] C.A. 39.

And further:

> To the Commission's knowledge there has never been an accident in Québec
> related to the use of the two official languages in Air Traffic Control.[39]

This 1976 head-on collision bearing on the use of one of this country's
official languages in the skies of Canada has crudely shown the persistence
of the conflict, the seeds of which had been sown in our soil over two
hundred years ago. Yet events have later shown how pointless it had
been. The impugned orders and regulations have been rescinded, bilingual
air traffic has taken hold, and the earth has not stopped revolving around
the sun. The whole territory of Québec is now open to bilingual air
communications for both visual and instrument flights. According to
reliable sources which I have consulted, last year some 20 percent of
aircraft movements at the Dorval airport in Montréal have taken place
in French; at the Québec City airport, the proportion stands at 50 percent
of 125,000 movements. Yet, contrary to the so-called experts' warnings,
not a single mishap attributable to language has occurred. Traffic has
rather increased. We are now entitled to expect that bilingual air
communications will become a reality in the national capital a year from
now and, in the foreseeable future, in Northern Ontario and the
Maritimes.

Il faudra bien qu'un jour la raison prenne le pas sur les sentiments,
si l'on veut que ce pays qui est le nôtre reste gouvernable. Nous sommes
tous des frères humains, quelle que soit notre religion, quelle que soit
notre langue. Nous sommes tous des compatriotes, quel que soit le coin
du pays que nous habitions. Combien de temps encore allons-nous
continuer de nous déchirer pour savoir si l'on peut annoncer un commerce
dans une autre langue que le français, ou pour décider si l'on peut
s'adresser à une législature dans une autre langue que l'anglais?

Combien de temps encore allons-nous nous battre pour choisir la
langue de nos écoles ou pour fixer les principes de leur gérance ainsi
que les bases de leur financement?

Combien de temps encore allons-nous dépenser dans ces querelles
intestines des énergies précieuses que réclament tant de causes autrement
exaltantes?

Oublions ces querelles malheureuses et inutiles qui nous divisent.
Cessons de considérer comme des ennemis ceux dont le seul défaut est
de parler une langue différente de la nôtre. Comme l'épiscopat du Québec
nous y conviait dans sa *Déclaration* du 13 février 1989,[40] visons à instaurer

---

39. The Commission of Inquiry into Bilingual Air Traffic Services in Québec, *Final Report*,
    10 August 1979 (Ottawa: Supply and Services, 1979) at 117.
40. Published in *La Presse* (14 February 1989).

dans notre société une «amitié civique» fondée sur la «générosité sans démission».

Il faut créer la paix linguistique, il faut provoquer la paix chez nous; grâce à la force de notre exemple, nous pourrons alors espérer voir poindre la paix dans le reste du monde.

Partie VIII / Part VIII

Langue et culture

Au cours des récentes années, les questions d'importance légale et morale se sont multipliées. La société a commencé à prendre en considération les animaux et la protection de l'environnement. David Marshall et Roseann Gonzalez avancent qu'un des secteurs souvent ignorés, et cela consciemment, est celui des droits linguistiques, le droit de parler la langue de son choix. Ils proposent deux arguments pour démontrer que les droits linguistiques méritent leur part d'attention. Premièrement, les droits linguistiques devraient être perçus comme appartenant aux droits de la personne; ils sont en effet le moyen premier par lequel nous définissons notre identité personnelle et celle de notre groupe. À ce titre, la langue sert aussi à la distribution du pouvoir au sein d'une société. L'érosion des droits linguistiques est donc souvent liée à l'effritement des autres droits fondamentaux et peut le provoquer. Deuxièmement, les droits linguistiques devraient être perçus comme des droits de l'environnement. Marshall et Gonzalez soutiennent que les langues requièrent une protection écologique à cause de leur valeur intrinsèque. Le multilinguisme ajoute immensément à la riche tapisserie de notre monde et il multiplie les facettes sous lesquelles nous le contemplons.

Manoly Lupul présente une vision moins romantique de la question. Évoquant son expérience de Canadien d'origine ukrainienne, Lupul n'imagine pas que les intérêts de la puissante majorité céderont aux revendications linguistiques des petites minorités. Selon lui, la lutte linguistique et culturelle tourne essentiellement autour du partage des pouvoirs et des chances. Il propose une vue plus pragmatique, une notion élastique des peuples «fondateurs» et une politique de bilinguisme appliquée dans un cadre multiculturel. Le bilinguisme serait alors un phénomène local, reflétant la composition multiculturelle du pays; de ce fait, les deux langues parlées dans chaque région ne seraient pas nécessairement l'anglais ou le français.

Si la vision de Lupul semble plus conforme à la réalité canadienne, celles de Marshall et de Gonzalez se rapprochent davantage des principes théoriques énoncés par la Cour suprême du Canada quand elle se prononce sur la langue d'affichage. Les droits linguistiques sont fondés, d'après elle, sur le rôle essentiel que joue la langue dans l'existence, le développement et la dignité de l'être humain. Reste à voir si les conséquences à long terme de cette perspective peuvent faire une place à la vision multiculturelle de Lupul.

Language and Culture

We have seen in recent years an expansion of matters attracting legal and moral significance. Society has begun to accommodate concerns for such things as animals and the environment. David Marshall and Roseann Gonzalez argue that one area often overlooked, and sometimes conciously ignored, is that of a claim to language rights, the right to speak the language of one's choice. They present two reasons why language rights deserve a similar degree of concern. Firstly, language rights should be seen as a part of human rights, for they are one of the primary means by which we identify our own personal and group identity. As a social identifier, language is also used as a means of distributing power within society. The erosion of language rights is often tied, and can lead, to the erosion of other basic rights. Secondly, language rights should be seen as environmental rights. Marshall and Gonzalez argue that languages deserve ecological protection because of their intrinsic value. Multilingualism adds immensely to the rich tapestry of, and multiplies the lenses by which we view, our world.

Manoly Lupul is less romantic about the prospects of protecting language rights. Drawing from his experience as a Canadian of Ukranian origin, Lupul does not see powerful majority interests conceding to the linguistic demands of small minorities. For him, the struggle over language and culture is essentially a struggle over the sharing of power and opportunity. He advances a more pragmatic view, an elastic concept of "founding" peoples, and a bilingual policy within a multicultural framework. Bilingualism would be a local phenomenon reflecting the multicultural composition of the country, thus, the two languages spoken in each region would not necessarily be English and French.

While Lupul's vision may appear to be more reflective of the Canadian reality, Marshall and Gonzalez's insights come closer to the kind of theorizing we find in the Supreme Court of Canada decision dealing with the language of commercial signs. Language rights are considered by the Court to be "grounded in the essential role that language plays in human existence, development and dignity". Whether the long term consequences of this view can accommodate Lupul's multicultural vision remains to be seen.

WHY WE SHOULD BE CONCERNED ABOUT LANGUAGE RIGHTS: LANGUAGE RIGHTS AS HUMAN RIGHTS FROM AN ECOLOGICAL PERSPECTIVE

David F. Marshall and Roseann D. Gonzalez

The ecological perspective

The history of human and ethical rights is one of outward expansion slowly throughout history; starting by granting rights to themselves, some human beings gradually and sometimes erratically moved the circle outward to include others, the family, the clan, the tribe, the ethnic group, and sometimes lately to all human beings and beyond.[1] This expansion of rights is mirrored in the United States with the expansion of voting rights, first to land-owning males, then to non-landed males, then to women, then as guaranteed rights to citizens of differing races in the *Voting Rights Act* of 1965. Nash[2] argues that now we are in the process of expanding this circle outward further to include ethical and legal rights to animals, plants and nature itself (the endangered species and environmental laws). In this expansion, however, some rights have been either overlooked or sometimes consciously ignored, others little explored and ill-defined; a prime example of such rights (for humans) is the right to use the language of choice, either the mother tongue or some other.

This expansion of ethical and legal rights to the environment has provided in these last years of the 20th century an alternative to either the left or the right in political thought, where it becomes a "third way" between capitalism and socialism;[3] one example among many of this

---

1. Nash, R.F., *The Rights of Nature: A History of Environmental Ethics*, (Madison: University of Wisconsin Press, 1989).
2. *Ibid.*
3. Paehlke, R.C., *Environmentalism and the Future of Progressive Politics* (New Haven: Yale University Press, 1989).

alternative is the growing membership and political activity of the Green Party in the Federal Republic of Germany. Within such a milieu, the preservation of a small fish or an endangered flower, which can hold up the building of a highway or the construction of a major dam project, seems somewhat slight in comparison to the preservation of a unique human perspective for viewing reality — a perspective provided by a separate language. William S.-Y. Wang notes that "knowing more languages makes available to you more ways of looking at things, more ways of relating to things, to others".[4] Haugen reminds us that "each language has its shortcuts and its circumlocutions".[5] Many of these unique perspectives we call languages can be viewed as products of persons having unique rights within the politicalization of the environment. The increasing spread and diffusion of major world languages, which most often creates the death of less widely-spoken ethnic languages, causes the latter to be viewed as another type of endangered species, their loss making human understanding that much the poorer. It is from such an ecological vantage point that we might profitably examine the question of why we should be concerned about language rights.

The argument for the quality of human life

The interrelationship between language and identity has been explored extensively.[6] Language functions as one of the primary means for creating personal and group identity.[7] Language also functions in society as the means for creating power relationships, and the control of this linguistic creative process offers the possibility for the manipulation and the potential amassing of power, either personal or collective.[8]

From this perspective, language rights become highly important for several reasons. First, they are part of human rights, and the erosion of one endangers the others.[9] Second, they are an extension of intellectual purpose, for how we treat people is also how we treat ideas.

---

4. Restak, R.M., *The Mind* (New York: Bantam, 1988) 231.
5. Haugen, E., *Blessings of Babel: Bilingualism and Language Planning* (Berlin: Mouton de Gruyter, 1987) 141.
6. For insights as well as bibliographies, see Edwards, J., *Language, Society and Identity* (New York: Basil Blackwell, 1986); Grace, W.G., *The Linguistic Construction of Reality* (London: Croom Helm, 1988); Aboud, F., *Children and Prejudice: The Development of Ethnic Awareness and Identity* (New York: Basil Blackwell, 1988); and the soon to appear Harre, R. and Muhlhausler, P., *The Linguistic Construction of Reality: Pronouns and Selves* (New York: Basil Blackwell, 1989).
7. Edwards, J., *Language, Society and Identity* (New York: Basil Blackwell, 1986); Grace, W.G., *The Linguistic Construction of Reality* (London: Croom Helm, 1988); Aboud, F., *Children and Prejudice: The Development of Ethnic Awareness and Identity* (New York: Basil Blackwell, 1988).
8. Fairclough, N., *Language and Power* (London: Longmans, 1989).
9. Skutnabb-Kangas, T. and Phillipson, R., *Wanted! Linguistic Human Rights* (Roskilde: Roskilde Universitetscenter Lingvistgruppen, 1989).

A human being finds identity in the group and fulfils personal authenticity through language.[10] Denying a person's language rights can have the effect of creating social situations in which that person questions personal identity and feels alienation in family, ethnic, and national identification. An example or two might point out how this process creates a form of human suffering through intense emotional distress.

Kee, a Navaho Native American, provides our first example:

> Kee was sent to boarding school as a child whereas was the practice — he was punished for speaking Navajo. Since he was only allowed to return home during Christmas and summer, he lost contact with his family. Kee withdrew both from the White and Navajo worlds as he grew older, because he could not comfortably communicate in either language. He became one of the many thousand Navajos who were non-lingual — a man without a language. By the time he was 16, Kee was an alcoholic, uneducated and despondent — without identity. Kee's story is more the rule rather than the exception.[11]

Native American children were often educated in government boarding schools, most far from their homes. They were not allowed to speak their native languages and were often punished when caught doing so.[12] Effectively, their language development in their mother tongues was arrested, and the quality of education in English was not sufficient for them to master completely the language utilized for forced assimilation.[13] The denial of language rights to Native Americans led to many situations such as Kee's, situations where persons were caught between cultures and denied authenticity in either culture, blocked off from either because of the language barrier.

Another case illustrates the frustration that arises when a person is so caught; these are excerpts of the story of a Sami in Sweden, Johannes Marainen:

> As a child I had the opportunity to live and grow in an intact Sami environment. All of us in my village depended solely on our herds of

---

10. Edwards, J., *Language, Society and Identity* (New York: Basil Blackwell, 1986).

11. Platero, D., "Bilingual education in the Navajo Nation" in Troike, R.C. and Modiano, N. eds, *Proceedings of the First Inter-American Conference on Bilingual Education* (Arlington, Va.: Center for Applied Linguistics, 1975) 58; and Skutnabb-Kangas, T. and Phillipson, R., *Wanted! Linguistic Human Rights* (Roskilde: Roskilde Universitetscenter Lingvistgruppen, 1989) 33-34.

12. Leibowitz, A.H., "English literacy: legal sanction for discrimination", (1969) 45 *Notre Dame Lawyer* 16.

13. Platero, D., "Bilingual education in the Navajo Nation" in Troike, R.C. and Modiano, N. eds, *Proceedings of the First Inter-American Conference on Bilingual Education* (Arlington, Va.: Center for Applied Linguistics, 1975) 57-58; Skutnabb-Kangas, T. and Phillipson, R., *Wanted! Linguistic Human Rights* (Roskilde: Roskilde Universitetscenter Lingvistgruppen, 1989) 24-25; see also Cahn, E.S. and Hearne, D.W., *Our Brother's Keeper: The Indian in White America* (New York: New Community Press, 1969).

reindeer, and our way of living was still fairly uninfluenced by the Swedish society. We had our own language and our own culture and lived our own lives.

When I started school I took my first step from my Sami environment... I went to first grade in a summer — or tent school. The school looked exactly like my own home. It was a tent, made of canvas, stretched over tall slender birch poles with an opening for the smoke in the middle. We sat on boughs around the open fire with a slate or a book on our outstretched legs...

Thus our schooling was fit to Sami life, but I am sorry to say, that it was only the organized part that was fit. Culturally and linguistically the school was a shock to me. 'Mother tongue' was the domineering subject during the first school years, but I did not understand until much later that 'tongue' means language. The word 'mother tongue' did not mean anything to me, I just accepted that it mean Swedish. *Eatnangiella*, my mother's language, it definitely was not.

Like all other beginners I did not understand a single word of the 'mother tongue' and it would take many years before I was able to speak it. During school time we were not allowed to use our own language, not even during recess. We were supposed to become 'mother tongued' as soon as possible.

None of my friends had continued their studies. My teacher in the sixth grade suggested that I should go to Middle School in Kurina...

Again I got nice schoolmates who were not prejudiced, but they did not share the common misinterpretation that: 'Sami have all the rights and no obligations' with many other Kiruna dwellers.

Aside from that, school was the only place in town where I felt secure and safe. I soon learned that outside of school it was best for me to demonstrate my Sami roots as little as possible. Despite that, I was called 'Sami devil' every day. I tried to pretend that I did not hear, but each time a thorn stuck into my heart, and eventually I carried inside me a whole forest of thorns. I tried to suppress my feelings and wrapped all the thorns into all kinds of excuses, so they wouldn't hurt anyone. The worst of it was that all this Sami hate was concealed, nobody wanted to show their contempt openly. There were lots of Kiruna dwellers, who were unaware that it existed and who would have been hurt if someone had mentioned that there was a Sami hate in Kirun...

The 'mother tongue' became our language when we were together in town. Our own language was used only in our boarding rooms and in the Lapp Inn, which was the only hotel in those days which accepted Sami, and the Lapp cafe.

Thus I felt like a stranger among the Swedes and, unfortunately, felt a little bit like a stranger with my people who remained in the Sami village... I was no longer sharing their lives as active reindeer herders. They, on their side, were ignorant of my experiences in my new school.

We Sami in town learned fast that the best, and certainly the easiest way to cope was to adapt, and as far as possible become Swedish. Unfortunately this drove many of us to self-denial. Once I saw some Sami youths purposely avoiding their parents in order not to demonstrate their Sami origin. It hurt me unbelievably and filled me with feelings of shame. To be absolutely honest, it could have been me, who felt forced to act the same way! It is painful to remember that it was quite often necessary for me to force myself not to deny myself, which to me felt extremely humiliating.

I continued my studies and accepted myself as more or less Swedish... In time I became a teacher of the 'mother tongue' in a high school in Gothenburg, and I felt quite content with my life. I had not been discriminated against. I had received the same good education as other Swedes. I had a job which I liked. Did I have anything to complain about?

I soon realized that as a Sami, I was considered an exotic being in Gothenburg. There were requests that I give lectures on Sami. I hesitated long before I dared to stand up and talk, because in reality I knew nothing about Samis, nothing about my people. All I knew about were my own experience.

At last, I agreed to give a lecture, and in order to remedy my ignorance, I went to the library and borrowed a book about Samis. As I was reading the book I realized for the first time that we Sami indeed had our own history! I had not been allowed to read my history in nomad school. I had learned about King Karl, the young hero, and other brave Swedish kings, who had made the Swedish name fly in honour over the earth. For my history, it might possibly even have been favourable if the tyrant Danish King Christian had kept Sweden.

Well, my father happened to be visiting when I held my lecture on Sami in Gothenburg. As we were returning home, I asked him what he had thought of my speech. He answered: 'Well, I did not understand much of what you said, but they applaud, so I assume that it was good.' The answer did not surprise me, and I decided to translate my speech into Sami language for him. It was then that I got my life's greatest shock! I realized that my 'mother tongue' had taken over my *eatnangiella*. I realized in horror that *I could no longer in my own language relate the most common and everyday matters!*

That was the first time since I grew up that I realized the negative sides of my becoming Swedish. I started to comprehend that the Swedish Educational System had robbed me of something valuable, yes, maybe the most valuable thing I had owned: my language.

I can no longer talk to Father! This made me shiver. I became desperate, despondent. And then I became angry.

I had imagined that I still knew Sami language, but due to the broken continuous contact with my Sami environment and culture, my language had not developed in a natural way. I realized that I stood on a level comparable to a 7-year old's linguistic capabilities. I could still talk about certain matters in Sami, but I was not able to keep a conversation or a discussion going.

As I was unable to develop my language in a natural daily contact with other Sami, the school should have given me a chance to study my language. But what had it done instead?

It had forced a new 'mother tongue' upon me. I had been robbed of my language, my own history and my own culture. The school had substituted something that was now well known to me. What was foreign to me was I, myself. I felt cheated!

I realized that the first thing to do was to study my own language. I asked for leave of absence in order to study Sami, but that was not granted. A 'mother tongue' teacher asking for time off in order to study his mother tongue! Unthinkable! So instead, I studied my language at night as I kept working and teaching...

The most difficult part of my journey to my roots remained. I had to find my way to my Sami identity. I felt obliged to go back and analyze my development. I had to understand... the transformation from Sami to Swede... which hade made me choose the easiest way, accepting myself as Swedish and living like other Swedes. I went through all the painful memories as I tried to understand and realize what had happened. I no longer tried to erase, forget, and hide, nor did I pretend not to hear anymore.

It was hard enough to accept myself, but it was harder still to explain myself to others. I felt shame and guilt because I had betrayed my people. My people and myself. It hurt to remember and it was painful to tell others. I did it because I felt it was necessary for me, and maybe I could help others who were looking for their identity...[14]

Almost anyone would recognize that this narrative describes a situation where governmental educational policy and the well-intentioned but wrong disregard for language rights lead to a person's intense emotional distress. The same story with different settings can be found around the world; for example, in the United States with its Native Americans,[15] in Turkey regarding the Kurds,[16] in Kenya where English

14. Marainen, J., "Returning to Sami identity" in Skutnabb-Kangas, T. and Cummins, J., *Minority Education: From Shame to Struggle* (Clevedon: Multilingual Matters, 1988) 179-185; Skutnabb-Kangas, T. and Phillipson, R., *Wanted! Linguistic Human Rights* (Roskilde: Roskilde Universitetscenter Lingvistgruppen, 1989) 34-37.

15. Platero, D., "Bilingual education in the Navajo Nation" in Troike, R.C. and Modiano, N. eds, *Proceedings of the First Inter-American Conference on Bilingual Education* (Arlington, Va.: Center for Applied Linguistics, 1975); Cahn, E.S. and Hearne, D.W., *Our Brother's Keeper: The Indian in White America* (New York: New Community Press, 1969).

16. Clason, E. and Baksi, M., *Kurdistan* (Stockholm: Arbetarkultur, 1979).

was the forced language, in the Federal Republic of Germany regarding Turkish children of "guest workers",[17] just to name a few.

Many nations do not recognize the language rights of minorities for various reasons. Language rights are not currently clear-cut even in United States law, being dependent upon other human rights for action or preservation.[18] This ignoring of language rights seems tragic when we realize, as Deutsch reminds us, that "Language is an automatic signalling system, second only to race in identifying targets for possible privilege or discrimination".[19]

An international seminar on Human Rights and Cultural Rights was held in Recife, Brazil, in 1987. Organized by AIMAV (the International Association for Cross-cultural Communication) and UNESCO, the seminar published the celebrated Declaration of Recife which recommended that steps be taken by the United Nations to adopt and implement a Universal Declaration of Linguistic Rights, requiring "a reformation of national, regional and international policies".[20]

Joshua A. Fishman states the environmental argument for preservation of endangered languages when he writes:

> [I]f we are sensitive to the loss suffered by our collective 'quality of life' on this planet when endangered animal species are further decimated, if we strain to do something on their behalf so that their natural habitats will be protected and their life chances improved (like holding off the repair and replacement of the West Side Highway in New York for over a dozen of years because certain species of fish would never recover if their current breeding grounds were destroyed), then the need to look steadfastly and act affirmatively in connection with endangered languages should be even more obvious.[21]

From Fishman's argument, we can find our first reason for being concerned about language rights; it is an argument for "quality of human

---

17. Skutnabb-Kangas, T. and Phillipson, R., *Wanted! Linguistic Human Rights* (Roskilde: Roskilde Universitetscenter Lingvistgruppen, 1989).
18. See Marshall, D.F., "Federal language rights in the United States" in *Minority Language Rights and Minority Education: European, Australian and North American Perspectives* (Ithaca, N.Y.: Cornell University Western Studies Program, 1988) for a discussion; also Leibowitz, A.H. ed., *Federal Recognition of the Rights of Minority Language Groups* (Rosslyn, Va.: National Clearinghouse for Bilingual Education, 1982).
19. Deutsch, K.A., "The political significance of linguistic conflicts" in Savard, J.-G. and Vigneault, R. eds, *Les États multilingues* (Québec: CIRB, Laval, 1975) 7.
20. Gomes de Matos, F., Personal communication (October 1987).
21. Fishman, J.A., "Language spread and language policy for endangered languages" in Lowenburg, P.H. ed., *Language Spread and Language Policy: Issues, Implications, and Cases Studies. Georgetown University Round Table on Languages and Linguistics 1987* (Washington: Georgetown University Press, 1987) 3-4.

life". Language rights are part of human rights, and the eroding of one of these rights leads to the loss of others. We dare not ignore the human suffering that arises when persons are alienated from their personal and ethnic identity by language policies that do not safeguard individual language rights; we cannot do so without also facing up to the concomitant loss in our own "quality of life" and the resultant loss each person faces by such loss, which leaves a less diversified and less colorful culture, less pluralistic and, therefore, more drab world.

The argument for the benefit of the body politic

Multilingualism aids in the creation of that rich mosaic that is each nation's culture. The phenomenon of multilingualism has been viewed differently in the western tradition than in the eastern.[22] While the western tradition many times has seen multilingualism as something to be avoided, the eastern has seen it as a resource that enriches the quality of life and offers a multiplicity necessary for cultural appreciation. As Pattanayak states:

> Many languages are like petals of a lotus. Many languages form a national mosaic. If some petals wither and fall off or some chips are displaced from the mosaic, then the lotus and the mosaic look ugly. With the death of languages a country will be poorer.[23]

Skutnabb-Kangas and Phillipson[24] argue that the western view of multilingualism which espouses the benefits of monolingualism is really a form of linguicism, "ideologies and structures which are used to legitimate, effectuate and reproduce an unequal division of power and resources (both material and non-material) between groups which are defined on the basis of language". Analogous to racism, linguicism creates a "hegemonic structure which permits the dominance of certain groups or classes and their languages over others". One of the myths supporting linguicism, they argue, is that "many languages divide a nation".[25]

---

22. Pattanayak, D.P., "Forward"in Annamalai, E., Jernudd, B. and Rubin, J. eds, *Language Planning: Proceedings of an Institute* (Mysore and Honolulu: Central Institute of Indian Languages and East-West Center, 1986), "Monolingual myopia and the petals of the Indian lotus: do many languages divide or unite a nation?" in Skutnabb-Kangas, T. and Cummins, J. eds, *Minority Education: From Shame to Struggle* (Clevedon: Multilingual Matters, 1988).
23. Pattanayak, D.P., "Monolingual myopia and the petals of the Indian lotus: do many languages divide or unite a nation?" in Skutnabb-Kangas, T. and CUMMINS, J. eds, *Minority Education: From Shame to Struggle* (Clevedon: Multilingual Matters, 1988) 379.
24. *Wanted! Linguistic Human Rights* (Roskilde: Roskilde Universitetscenter Lingvistgruppen, 1989).
25. Skutnabb-Kangas, T. and Phillipson, R., *Wanted! Linguistic Human Rights* (Roskilde: Roskilde Universitetscenter Lingvistgruppen, 1989) 5-6.

A slightly different view is provided by Fishman, where he writes about the view of ethnicities in western thought:

> To this very day ethnicity strikes many Westerners as being particularly related to "all those little people and languages out there", to the unwashed (and unwanted) of the world, to phenomena that are really not fully civilized and that are more trouble than they are worth.[26]

Fishman argues that there are two conflicting concepts within the western tradition, one which arises from the Classical Hebrew emphasis on the "perfectibility of ethnicity, i.e., an emphasis on its highest realization via sanctification", and the other view embodied in that theory of the state which sought total assimilation and acculturation as the authenticating test of national loyalty (examples being the Western Roman Empire and some western nations today).[27] This conflict in western thought is seen in the question of whether multilingualism is beneficial or detrimental to a nation's unity.[28]

Of course, there is no necessity that language spread will kill the languages with smaller numbers of speakers; there is always the chance that a situation of diglossia will arise where the H (higher) language will be used in certain domains and the L (lower) in others, but the chances of establishing such stable diglossia are not great, as Fishman notes: "[T]he diglossic solution to the problem of endangered languages is a very difficult one to arrive at under any circumstances, whether philosophically or empirically, all the more so under typically modern circumstances".[29] The "nationist"[30] concerns in forcing assimilation through language shift can come into conflict with the concerns of the various nationalities which find their individual languages authenticating,

---

26. Fishman et al. (1985) 8.
27. Fishman et al. (1985) 3-13; 473-487.
28. Marshall, D.F. and Gonzalez, R.D., *"Una lingua, una patria?* Is monolingualism beneficial or harmful for a nation's unity?"* in Brink, D. and Adams, K., *Perspectives on Official English* (Berlin: Mouton de Gruyter, 1990); Fishman, J.A. and Solano, F., "Cross polity perspectives on the importance of linguistic heterogeneity as a 'contributing factor' in civil strife" in *Proceedings of the Hyderabad Conference on Language and Development* (Hyderabad: Osmania University, 1988a); Fishman, J.A. and Solano, F., "Cross cultural perspectives on the importance of linguistic product" in *Proceedings of the Heslington Conference on Sociolinguistic and Social Change* (Heslington: University of York, 1986b).
29. Fishman, J.A., "Language spread and language policy for endangered languages" in Lowenburg, P.H. ed., *Language Spread and Language Policy: Issues, Implications, and Cases Studies. Georgetown University Round Table on Languages and Linguistics* (Washington: Georgetown University Press, 1987) 4.
30. See Fishman, J.A., *Language and Ethnicity in Minority Sociolinguistic Perspective* (Clevedon: Multilingual Matters, 1989) 97-175; 269-367, for the distinction between nationalism and nationism.

and those who feel relative deprivation from non-participation in the nation's governance who often mobilize either politically or, sometimes regrettably, militantly.[31]

This concern about the interface between language rights and the nation's governing provides our second reason for being concerned about language rights from an ecological perspective. Far from being solely a source of conflict, it is possible for the creation of a policy of multilingualism in a nation to be extremely beneficial for that nation's political climate and governing. First and most obviously, such a policy enhancing multilingualism provides a prophylactic against ethnic mobilization around a language question, preventing one avenue of mobilization and its concomitant splitting of groups into vested interests more easily politically manipulated. Such a policy of enhancing multilingualism also creates a political atmosphere for greater participation by all its citizens in that nation's benefits.[32]

Second, an enlightened policy propounding multilingualism can actually create major national contributions, not only in the areas of national defense, where multilingualism becomes an asset or in the areas of world trade, where multilingualism is a pronounced necessity for increased trade, but also in the arena of the nation's contribution to ideas and new concepts.

This concept has been known for several years to linguists and language planners under the rubric of "Whorfianism of the third kind".

Benjamin Lee Whorf stands at the head of a long tradition of linguists and philosophers who examined the relation of language to culture and thought. Whorfianism of the first kind — linguistic relativity — is commonly espoused by many, perhaps most linguists; Whorfianism of the second kind — linguistic determinism — does not have such backing and is supported by few linguists today.[33] However, there is a Whorfianism of the third kind, a belief which espouses that:

---

31. See Marshall, D.F. and Gonzalez, R.D., "*Una lingua, una patria?* Is monolingualism beneficial or harmful for a nation's unity?" in Brink, D. and Adams, K., *Perspectives on Official English* (Berlin: Mouton de Gruyter, 1990) for the interrelationship between language rights and ethnic mobilization; see also Beer, W.E., "Toward a theory of linguistic mobilization" in Beer, W.E. and Jacob, J.E. eds, *Language Policy and National Unity* (Totowa, N.J.: Towan and Allanheld, 1985).

32. For examples, see Beer, W.E., "Toward a theory of linguistic mobilization" in Beer, W.E. and Jacob, J.E. eds, *Language Policy and National Unity* (Totowa, N.J.: Towan and Allanheld, 1985) and Marshall, D.F. and Gonzalez, R.D., "*Una lingua, una patria?* Is monolingualism beneficial or harmful for a nation's unity?" in Brink, D. and Adams, K., *Perspectives on Official English* (Berlin: Mouton de Gruyter, 1990).

33. Fishman et al. (1985), 474.

the entire world needs a diversity of ethnolinguistic entities for its own salvation, for its greater creativity, for the more certain solution of human problems, for the constant rehumanization of humanity in the face of materialism, for fostering greater esthetic, intellectual, and emotional capacities for humans as a whole, indeed, for arriving at a higher stage of human functioning.[34]

In this concept of Whorfianism of the third kind, it is believed by those scholars of sociolinguistics and the sociology of language who have studied the contributions of multilingualism, that the:

great forces that inspire all humanity do not emerge out of universal civilization, but out of the individuality of separate ethnic collectivities — most particularly, out of their very own authentic languages. Only if each collectivity contributes its own thread to the tapestry of world history, and only if each is accepted and respected for making its own contribution, can nationalities finally also be ruled by sense or reciprocity, learning and benefiting from each other's contributions as well.[35]

In this way, we can see that "the world's little languages and peoples are a treasure trove of wisdom and refinement. Only if this human treasure is valued and shared can biases be set aside and a genuine (rather than a self-serving imperialistic) universal perspective be attained".[36]

From such a perspective, which can only be termed ecological, any advocacy of the weak and as yet unappreciated ethnic groups and their languages has the effect of dignifying us as well as them; of safeguarding our own nations as well as their identity as nationalities. For it is precisely in that attitude that refuses to value them that one finds those concepts which render the idea of a nation asunder, and we must always remember that a nation, in its final analysis, is only an idea to which we have various attachments.[37]

The abiding contributions of a nation are in the form of ideas and specifically insights to human understanding; any policy that enhances such contributions would be beneficial for that nation in the oversight of history. Thus a concern for language rights, when viewed from a perspective of Whorfianism of the third kind, is ultimately a concern for allowing the individual nation to have its citizens bring the ideas that truly make a nation great.

---

34. Fishman (1985), 478-479.
35. Fishman et al. (1985), 479.
36. Fishman et al. (1985), 482.
37. Kelman, H.C., "Language as an aid and barrier to involvement in the national system" in Rubin J. and Jernudd, B.H. eds, *Can Language Be Planned? Sociological Theory and Practice for Developing Nations* (Honolulu: University of Hawaii Press, 1971); Anderson, B., *Imagined Communities: Reflections on the Origin and Spread of Nationalism* (London: Verso, 1983).

A moment's reflection will reveal how this nationist's concern fits into the overall scheme of looking at human rights environmentally, and how the nationist's concern is only another side of the concern we earlier referred to as "quality of human life". Besides Canada, with its Official Languages Commission in Ottawa, there is another nation which has taken this Whorfianism of the third kind a step further in nationist planning — Australia. Facing the challenge of "Asianization", Australia has formulated a national policy in which every child will become bilingual, one of the languages to be English, the other the child's mother tongue or a community language.[38]

A concomitant reason for adopting such a national policy in a democracy is that multilingualism provides optional ways to view issues and national questions; having two languages provides a person a means whereby that person can examine questions and issues from different perspectives.[39] With such an advantage, the bilingual are capable of understanding the issue in greater depth. The opposite of each situation is termed by Skutnabb-Kangas and Phillipson "monoculism",

> being able to see things with one pair of glasses only and having a poorly developed capacity to see things in another person's or group's point of view. It mostly means not knowing more than one culture from the inside, and therefore lacking relativity.[40]

It seems plausible that combating monoculism would be in the interest of any democracy, for it could create a more informed citizenry. The ecological analogy is self-evident; such a perspective only incorporates better informed voting into an overall view of the nation's health as a body politic.

The argument for the benefit of our children's future

Overcoming monoculism also has a benefit in educational policy, providing a third reason for our need to be concerned about language rights. A growing body of research has begun to hint at the cognitive advantage that is enjoyed by children who are bilingually educated.[41] Genesee summarizes that research when he writes:

> Notwithstanding myriad research problems, evidence from primary evaluations of individual bilingual programs indicates that bilingual

---

38. Australia: Commonwealth Department of Education, *Towards a National Language Policy* (Canberra: Australian Government Printing Service, 1982).
39. Grosjean, F., *Life with Two Languages: An Introduction to Bilingualism* (Cambridge: Harvard University Press, 1982).
40. Skuttnabb-Kangas, T. and Phillipson, R., *Wanted! Linguistic Human Rights* (Roskilde: Roskilde Universitetscenter Lingvistgruppen, 1989) 56.
41. Genesee, F., *Learning Through Two Languages: Studies of Immersion and Bilingual Education* (Cambridge: Newbury House, 1987); Willig, A., "A meta-analysis of selected

education can work.[42] It has also been shown, using statistically appropriate procedures to control for variation in both programs and research design, that in general students in bilingual programs outperform students in non-bilingual programs on measures of language and academic development administered in English or in the native language.[43]

An educational policy that refuses to recognize the potential cognitive benefits of bilingual or multilingual education is one that is detrimental to the nation that espouses it. It is in the area of educational policy that a concern for language rights can help to fulfil the human potential of the next generation. To not explore the advantages of bilingual education is to perpetrate a wasting of future resources. Again, the ecological analogy is clear cut; being concerned about language rights in education is being concerned about conserving and further enhancing our most precious resource — children, our hostages to the future.

The benefits of the ecological perspective

A concern for language rights, when viewed from an ecological perspective — one that incorporates the development of all human rights — shows us that such a concern is necessary for preserving and enhancing our current "quality of life" and enjoyment of a pluralistic and more enticing culture. Such a concern for language rights is also crucial in preserving and enhancing the potential contributions of citizens to their democracies, and the potential contributions of a nation to the global village through the generation of new ideas and concepts for human understanding. Being concerned about language rights in education is tantamount to preserving and enhancing the potential of those hostages to the future who are our children.

---

studies on the effectiveness of bilingual education", *Review of Educational Research*, (1985) 55:269-317; Crawford (1989); Hakuta, S., "The causal relationship between the development of bilingualism, cognitive flexibility, and social-cognitive skills in Hispanic school children" (Washington: National Institute of Education (NIE-G-81-0123), 1984); Hakuta, S., *Mirror of Language: The Debate on Bilingualism* (Cambridge: Newbury House, 1986).

42. See Baker, K.A. and de Kanter, A.A., "Federal policy and effectiveness of bilingual education" in Baker, K.A. and de Kanter, A.A. eds, *Bilingual Education: A reappraisal of Federal Policy* (Lexington, Mass.: Lexington Books, 1983); Cummins, J., "The role of primary language development in promoting educational success for language minority students" in *Schooling and Language Minority Students: A Theoretical Approach* (Los Angeles: Evaluation, Dissemination, and Assessment Center, 1981); and Troike, R.C., "Research evidence for the effectiveness of bilingual education", *NABE Journal*, (1978) 3:13-28, for examples.

43. Willig, A., "A meta-analysis of selected studies on the effectiveness of bilingual education", *Review of Educational Research*, (1985) 55:259-317; Genesee, F., *Learning Through Two Languages: Studies of Immersion and Bilingual Education* (Cambridge: Newbury House, 1987) 195-96.

As the circle of ethical and legal rights expands outward, it is possible to see that a concern for language rights, as for all human rights, is one that preserves and enhances our humanity. Where language rights are not observed and protected, there, we all are a little less human. For we are not only *homo sapiens*, human beings who think, but also *homo loquins*, human beings who use language to find our personal identity in collectivities and in the interrelated global village of shrinking natural resources, one of which is human cultural diversity. A disregard for language rights is a disregard for the human race, a disregard for an important part of the ecology — the quality of human life, the contribution of nations, and the promise of the future. To allow such disregard, legally or not, is foolhardily to place ourselves and our future generations in peril.

COMMENTS

Manoly Lupul

I was asked to comment on Dr. Marshall's paper from the Ukrainian perspective. I do so as a Canadian of Ukrainian origin whose grandparents came to Alberta in 1900. However, I will not really dwell all that much on the paper itself for reasons which will soon become apparent. I found the paper very congenial; in fact, I liked its sentiments very much, and I was especially struck by its ecological analogy. I had never thought of cultural diversity and cultural pluralism in quite that way.

The argument that we live, as Dr. Marshall puts it, in a global village of shrinking natural resources, one of which is cultural diversity, is both clever and true. And it is also easy to agree that language is a key element of culture. Some would even say, and I have heard it said, that language, in fact, defines culture. It is easy to accept also that language is an integral part of culture. The French Canadians are very fond of saying that language and culture are, in fact, inseparable. And most people of Ukrainian background in Canada have also found that to be a very congenial position. Certainly, I was raised on that thesis, and I have used it often in my own work, for the people of Ukrainian background in Canada have a linguistic predicament overseas that is explained very well in the Estonian context by Professor Toivo Miljan.[1] It essentially goes under the label of "Russification" in the Soviet Union. Because of this, and with language loss in Canada even more marked, Ukrainian Canadians could be said to be an endangered species, and that was the core of my argument when formulating the proposal for the Canadian Institute of Ukrainian Studies at the University of Alberta in the mid 1970s. In a recent blueprint for action, *Building the Future: Ukrainian Canadians in the 21st Century*,[2] there is a section

---

1. See Toivo Miljan, "Ethnic and Linguistic Revival in Estonia" in this volume.
2. (Edmonton: Ukrainian Canadian Committee, 1986) 11.

entitled "An Endangered People", an appropriate analogy with which most Ukrainians have very little difficulty.

While pleased with Dr. Marshall's paper, I concluded nevertheless that it is largely an exercise. It is a nice exercise, but it is still essentially an exercise, at least in the Canadian context. I will illustrate the point with quotations from the paper, neither of which should be interpreted as a critique of its basic orientation. The quotations are from Joshua Fishman, on whom Dr. Marshall leans heavily.

> ...great creative forces that inspire all humanity do not emerge out of universal civilization, but out of the individuality of separate ethnic collectivities — most particularly, out of their very own authentic languages.

Now, one could really get carried away with that point, but I will try to restrain myself. However lovely the thought may be, does anyone who is serious really believe it? Just think how often our great liberal democracies — Britain, the United States, Canada — with their centuries-old animus toward individual ethnic collectivities, have violated it. "Great creative forces that inspire all humanity" — all humanity! — "do not emerge out of universal civilization, but out of the individuality of separate ethnic collectivities". Really! Where is the evidence for such grandiloquence? And then again: "the entire world needs the diversity of ethnolinguistic entities for its own salvation..." Really! Who says so? Fishman? David Marshall? But how important are they in the eyes of the mighty? How would Conrad Black react to such a statement? The Eatons? The Irvings? "The entire world needs the diversity of ethnolinguistic entities for its own salvation." I wonder what Margaret Thatcher would think of such a position, in view of her problem up north with the Scottish nationalists. And I wonder what President George Bush would think of it, bearing in mind America's difficulties in Miami with ethnolinguistic minorities.

Later on, Fishman is quoted again:

> ...the world's little languages and peoples are a treasure trove of wisdom and refinement. Only if this human treasure is valued and shared can biases be set aside and a genuine (rather than a self-serving imperialistic) universal perspective be attained.

As if western civilization has ever been embarrassed by imperialistic universal perspectives! "The world's little languages and peoples are a treasure trove of wisdom and refinement." Again, what a lovely view of the world. Yet the entire histories of the United States and the Soviet Union have been testaments of opposition to just such views where minority cultures are concerned. The entire histories of both superpowers have been precisely to do in (to overcome) such little languages and peoples; the sooner, the better, with the school in the forefront and the church (in the United States) right behind. A nice thought, of course, but where has it ever been taken seriously?

I also found the pitch for multilingualism a most noble one. But how *does* one fight that part of the Western tradition whose concept of the state — to quote from the paper again — "sought total assimilation and acculturation as the authenticating test of national loyalty (examples being the Western Roman Empire and some western nations today)". How can one advocate multilingualism with such sincerity, with such obvious emotional attachment, on a North American continent with its long heritage of hostility toward all second-language learning — on a North American continent, that is, whose people cannot stand to learn one language, never mind two or three! I am, therefore, almost tempted to conclude that David Marshall is a maverick. He is unquestionably not a typical American, because Americans have no use for multilingualism. And Canadians are just like them. How can any one in his right mind really advocate multilingualism in Canada? It is a dirty word — not in the four-letter sense, of course — but it is a dirty word in Canada nonetheless. It is certainly such in Ottawa, especially among the civil servants. I found this to be the case — very much so — in my seven-year stint as a member of the Canadian Consultative Council on Multiculturalism in the 1970s. You simply did not mention the word. You could say any other thing you pleased, but you could not use the term 'multilingualism'. It was *verboten*, banned and ostracized for fear that some well-placed person might take it seriously.

In the end, I concluded that David Marshall's paper raised very many more questions than it answered in the Canadian context. I, therefore, decided that there would be much less risk of offending him if I concentrated on a safer subject — the Ukrainian-Canadian position, which will really be my position, since I wish to avoid the charge of being a self-styled spokesman for the Ukrainian-Canadian community in which I hold no office. My interest in the subject comes largely from my upbringing in Alberta's Ukrainian block settlement — the largest in Canada.

I began to develop a position on language and culture once the French Canadians began to stir up the country in the early 1960s. Their efforts were extremely important, for no other ethnocultural community at the time would have dared to articulate its cultural and linguistic aspirations as strenuously. And, from the beginning, the concern was how best to follow in their footsteps for the good of the whole country, for the good of all ethnocultural communities, not just the French Canadians. From the outset, the view held by thinking people within the Ukrainian-Canadian community was that Canada's two official languages were extremely important because they established the principle of bilingualism. But the promotion of bilingualism could not stop there. One had to build on official bilingualism. And that was the view that I, too, came to hold.

I took the view that in a polyethnic society, regional federalism — as I termed it[3] — was very important where languages and cultures were concerned. The term was especially appropriate since education — whose role in the transmission of language and culture would be crucial — was a provincial and, therefore, a local responsibility. In his paper on the Swiss experience, Professor McRae used the term "decentralized federalism", which I took to be the same idea.[4] Of course, there was no suggestion that Ukrainian, or any other language, could in any way hope to achieve official status. That would be nonsense, even at the provincial level. Nor would it follow that Ukrainian, or any other language, would be a factor in the provision of social services, although I might say that there are some people even in this room who might contest that statement.

Thus, I saw bilingualism — as well as multiculturalism — as umbrellas which embraced the whole country with the application of each varying specifically from region to region according to how the people themselves perceived their needs. In Alberta, this would have meant bilingualism that was English and Ukrainian, with French as a third language. And right away there was trouble because French cannot be a third language ! And, in Québec, it would have meant that French — whose primacy had to be recognized if one understood anything at all about the predicament of the French in Québec — would have been combined with Ukrainian as the second language, with English now the third language. Trouble again ! How in the devil could anyone ever move either one of these two linguistic giants into a position of 'thirdness'? It is the languages of "the others" that were third languages (if that), not English or French. Everybody knew that — and I think that by now even God has gotten the message !

From my standpoint, however, I just could not see how one could displace the language of one's culture and still achieve a meaningful multiculturalism. It was, of course, true that not much of a language

---

3. M. R. Lupul, "Canada's Options in a Time of Political Crisis and Their Implications for Multiculturalism", in M. R. Lupul, ed., *Ukrainian Canadians, Multiculturalism, and Separatism: An Assessment* (Edmonton: University of Alberta Press, 1978) at 151-67.
4. See Kenneth D. McRae, "Precepts for Linguistic Peace: The Case of Switzerland" in this volume.

or culture often remained: bits and pieces, remnants, rag-tag things that the assimilators happened to leave behind. Nonetheless, in western Canada, there were all kinds of people with this kind of nascent linguistic and cultural potential. It was not, of course, supposed to be there anymore. It was to have been killed completely, and if it was still there, that was a problem certain individuals had created for themselves. It was almost in the nature of an impairment and somehow rendered the individuals imperfect products. However, I just could not see how I could go among the Ukrainians and tell them: we live in Canada and therefore you are going to have to learn French rather than Ukrainian; you are not to build on what is still there; you are not to make better what still remains; you will have to substitute French language and culture for Ukrainian language and culture.

It was not that I did not understand the strong process of assimilation and that much died as a result. It was easy to see the many losses. It was just that I always believed that a people's language did not have to be one of the losses. Whatever else went — the sheepskin coats, for example — it was important that, along with Easter eggs and *pyrohy* (dumplings), the language, too, should remain. And not just on Heritage Days. I believed this passionately because I also believed that, apart from the numerous benefits to the human being of knowing a second language (described so well by Dr. Marshall in his paper), language is very important to the concept of being a Canadian. A Canadian should be understood to be a bilingual human being — French and English, but not necessarily French and English. So if one were to meet a Canadian in Sydney, Australia, for example, one could assume that, if the particular individual came from western Canada or Ontario, he/she might be able to speak English and at least one other language, and if from Québec — French and at least one other language.

The above followed naturally from the more elastic (liberal or expansionary) view of the concept of founding people which to me was always important. In eastern Canada, the "French" and the "English" were unquestionably founding peoples a long time ago — they engaged in the discovery, exploration, and the settlement of much territory. But in western Canada, I have always maintained that my grandparents and countless others like them, were also settler founding peoples. Wherever they settled on those one hundred and sixty acres which they obtained for ten dollars, they were the first to till that particular land. And before they made the 'desert bloom', they went through plenty! There is, therefore, no reason for the descendants of such people to take a back seat to anyone. While I do not dislike the concept of founding people, I just want it to be more elastic. When I told as much to John Evans, a member of the Pepin-Robarts Task Force in the late 1970s, he was at first aghast and then intrigued; then he became interested; and finally he found the concept congenial. He said he had never seen it quite that way. And I said it would help if more people did.

To end, let me say that I have now been seriously involved for some nineteen years in Canada's linguistic and cultural vineyard. Besides the academy, I have experienced my share of the trenches — the streets and the church basements, as well as numerous nice hotels once the C.C.C.M. had discovered that the microphones in the church-basement halls did not always work very well! And since I expect the coming academic year to be my last, what might one say? What might there be in the way of a "bottom line"?

First, the struggle over language and culture in Canada is essentially a struggle for the sharing of power and opportunity. It is almost a snatching of power and opportunity from the hands of those descended from the Anglo-Celts, who have always had the upper hand. I saw the Quiet Revolution in the province of Québec essentially as one of the French finally telling the Anglo-Celts to move over, in all respects. If you want a useful analogy, they met on a bench on which the Anglo-Celts had a monopoly, with the French-Canadians, especially in Québec, primarily on the grass. The Québecois were determined to sit on the bench. Maybe they would only get a little piece of it, perhaps the corner, or even just the edge. But the Anglo-Celts were going to have to move over.

But there were also others who soon spoke up. They were not supposed to exist as 'ethnics' past the immigrant generation, but somehow they had managed to survive. In the dialogue between the Anglo-Celts and the French, the latter unfortunately also turned out to be of very little help to these other 'ethnics'. At worst, one could say that the French were as arrogant as the Anglo-Celts. It is almost as if they wondered, "How dare you equate your ethnic concerns and problems with ours?" At best, they were merely indifferent, perhaps out of ignorance. But one hesitates to judge them too harshly, because the Anglo-Celts, as we all know, are pretty tough customers. They do not yield ground too easily. They have had it pretty good. The French-Canadians have, therefore, had to pursue their own agenda. They defined it carefully, perhaps deliberately so, with little regard to the aspirations of other ethnocultural peoples. It is very easy to sympathize with their approach against a well-entrenched, stubborn majority.

Second, most unfortunately, however, the narrow view of bilingualism and biculturalism continues to be very prevalent among most people in the academy, especially in the Arts faculties, and especially among most Canadian historians, and only to a slightly lesser extent among the social scientists who deal with the Canadian problematic. Most scholars appear wedded to a frozen concept of the two founding peoples with the season always winter ! The eastern Canadian intellectuals, in particular, find it difficult to take in the whole nation.

Third, this narrowness is most unfortunate because it ignores the real North American world. I do not think we recognize that very few in North America care a hoot about bilingualism or biculturalism, and even fewer value multilingualism. And I do not know what North Americans will make of multiculturalism. It has taken on some very strange shapes along the way. The masses in North America have imbibed well North America's basic, fundamental hostility toward second-language learning. They have imbibed well the view that languages are divisive in the nation-state. They have also imbibed well North America's conventional wisdom that languages promote ghettoization and Balkanization, that languages create towers of Babel. The masses have mastered all this well. And whenever they need any reminding, there are always plenty of 'intellectuals' around to ridicule multiculturalism or any official support for ethnic aspirations beyond the immigrant generation. The politicians are aware of that conventional wisdom, and they govern accordingly. The antidote, at least to me, has always been a more liberalized view of *bilingualism within a multicultural framework*, just the reverse of what presently exists. But that would make all collectivities equal and might even encourage multilingualism. And that, of course, must never be in Canada.

Partie IX / Part IX

Les revendications constitutionnelles des autres groupes linguistiques

La majeure partie des discussions relatives aux droits linguistiques constitutionnels vise inévitablement les droits de la *Charte* qui garantissent la prestation, sur les fonds publics, de l'instruction dans les langues officielles. Cependant, un certain nombre de stipulations autres, énoncées seules ou combinées à d'autres, peuvent servir à promouvoir les droits des groupes linguistiques non officiels. Chacune des communications suivantes traite de ce sujet.

Les langues autres que le français et l'anglais ont été reconnues dans le passé comme « langues ancestrales », selon le bon vouloir des autorités locales — les conseils scolaires notamment. Dale Gibson examine les prescriptions de la *Charte* qui peuvent servir à invoquer le droit aux langues non officielles ; il parle en particulier du droit à l'assistance d'un interprète lors des procédures judiciaires, des dispositions reconnaissant les droits des peuples autochtones, et de la clause d'interprétation reconnaissant notre patrimoine multiculturel.

Wayne MacKay examine les fondements moraux et juridiques permettant de faire progresser les revendications multiculturelles. Comme Gibson, il lit la disposition relative au multiculturalisme corrélativement à d'autres droits et libertés garantis par la *Charte*. MacKay se montre toutefois sceptique quant à leur éventuel succès, surtout lorsque le multiculturalisme contrevient à un droit des langues officielles.

Ian McGilp et Chris Dassios sont plus optimistes. Ils examinent comment la *Charte* peut servir à empêcher que les gouvernements fassent opposition aux groupes linguistiques multiculturels, à attaquer la question des fonds octroyés à d'autres groupes linguistiques ou à rechercher des fonds similaires pour un groupe oublié.

Si les droits — ancestraux et issus de traités — des peuples autochtones sont préservés par la Constitution, il n'est pas clair que cette reconnaissance inclut les droits linguistiques des autochtones. Brian Slattery affirme qu'il est impossible de parler de droits linguistiques découlant de la coutume, car c'est seulement quand une langue est menacée qu'il convient de parler de droits. Vu les relations historiques qui ont été établies entre les peuples autochtones et les représentants de la couronne, Slattery propose que les droits linguistiques des autochtones ont peut-être acquis un statut constitutionnel.

Constitutional Claims for Other Linguistic Groups

Much of the discussion concerning constitutional language rights revolve inevitably around those *Charter* rights providing for official language instruction at public expense. A number of other provisions, however, read alone or in combination, may be available to advance the language rights of unofficial language groups. Each of the following papers discusses this opportunity.

Languages, other than official languages, have been given recognition in the past, often as "heritage languages" and usually at the discretion of local officials such as school boards. Dale Gibson examines a number of *Charter* provisions which can give recognition to unofficial language claims, in particular, he discusses those that guarantee the right to an interpreter in legal proceedings, those that recognise existing aboriginal rights, and the interpretive clause recognising our multicultural heritage.

Wayne MacKay discusses the moral and legal bases for advancing multicultural claims. Like Gibson, he reads the multiculturalism clause in conjunction with a number of other *Charter* rights and freedoms. MacKay is sceptical, however, about the likelihood of their success, particularly when multiculturalism conflicts with an official language right.

Ian McGilp and Chris Dassios are more optimistic about the possibility of success. They discuss how the *Charter* can be used to prevent government interference with linguistic groups, to attack the provision of funding to other linguistic groups or to seek similar funding for an omitted language group.

While "existing" aboriginal and treaty rights are preserved in the Constitution, it is unclear whether this recognition also includes aboriginal linguistic rights. Brian Slattery argues that one cannot talk about customary language rights, for it is only when a language is under threat that it is reasonable to talk about rights. Due to the pattern of historical relations between aboriginal peoples and representatives of the Crown, Slattery argues that aboriginal language rights may have gained constitutional status.

HERITAGE LANGUAGES AND THE CONSTITUTION

Dale Gibson*

INTRODUCTION

The mother tongue of 3¼ million Canadians — just under 13 percent of the total population — is neither English nor French.[1] That percentage varies regionally from less than 1 percent in Newfoundland to 42 percent in the Northwest Territories. For Alberta the figure is more than 350,000 — slightly over 15 percent of the population. One factor common to almost every region is that the proportion of those with "other" mother tongues is gradually but constantly diminishing.

The right of 3¼ million people to enjoy the use of their mother tongue if they choose, and to help perpetuate it if they wish, is no small matter. Article 27 of the International Covenant on Civil and Political Rights stipulates that members of linguistic minorities must not be denied "the right, in community with other members of their group, to enjoy their own culture...or to use their own language." Yet the right has been little respected in Canada over the years. Horror stories have been plentiful: punishment of Indian children for speaking their first language in school,[2] Manitoba's 1916 abolition of the right to have children taught in "foreign" languages,[3] and so on. But the greatest harm has come from simple neglect — including the neglect of occasional pious promises and proposals concerning third languages. As early as 1873, the Council of the Northwest Territories resolved that all future ordinances of the

---

* I gratefully acknowledge the research assistance of Lee Gibson and Dr. Sandra M. Anderson.

1. These and the following figures are taken from the *1987 Annual Report of the Commissioner For Official Languages* (Ottawa: Supply and Services Canada, 1988). They are based on the 1986 Census.
2. D. Sanders, "Article 27 and Aboriginal Peoples of Canada" in Canadian Human Rights Foundation, *Multiculturalism and the Charter: A Legal Perspective* (Toronto: Carswell, 1987) 155 at 160.
3. Royal Commission on Bilingualism and Biculturalism, *Report* (Book IV) (Ottawa: Queen's Printer, 1969) at 104.

Council should be published in English, French and Cree, but the resolution was never acted upon.[4] In 1969 the Royal Commission on Bilingualism and Biculturalism recommended that "the teaching of languages other than English and French, and cultural subjects related to them, be incorporated as options in the public elementary school programme, where there is sufficient demand for such classes,"[5] but twenty years later progress in that direction is fetal at best.

A survey of the legislation of several Canadian jurisdictions (Alberta, Manitoba, Ontario, Canada, Yukon and Northwest Territories) discloses some improvements in the recognition and status of heritage languages — much of it very recent — but precious little in the way of legal rights respecting those languages.

The Alberta situation is typical. On the educational front, the provincial government has announced, as one of its "policies," that:

> Alberta Education supports the provision of opportunities for students who wish to acquire or maintain languages other than English or French so that they may have access to a partial immersion (bilingual) program or second language courses in languages other than English or French.[6]

But the policy is entirely permissive; the *School Act* leaves the decision to provide such courses to the discretion of local school boards.[7] The role of the provincial government is limited to encouragement, co-operation, consultation, and the development of certain educational resources.[8] What this policy has produced in practice is a 1987-88 enrollment for all forms of heritage language courses in Alberta public schools of 9,251 pupils, only about 1.6 percent of the total student population[9] and roughly 10 percent of those with mother tongues other than English or French. The vaunted "partial immersion" programs in heritage languages turns out to be offered only in one language — Ukrainian — and provided to only 1/5 of 1 percent of the school population.[10] The only other legislative concession to heritage languages

---

4. C. A. Sheppard, *Law of Languages in Canada* (Ottawa: Information Canada, 1971) at 82.
5. *Report, supra,* note 3 at 141, Recommendation 3.
6. Government of Alberta, *Language Education Policy for Alberta* (Edmonton: Government of Alberta, November 1988) at 16.
7. *School Act,* S.A. 1988, c. 5-3, s. 6(1). Manitoba and Yukon have similar provisions: *Public Schools Act,* R.S.M. 1987, c. P-250, s. 79 (2); *School Ordinance,* Con. O. Y.T. 1976, 5-3, s. 115(1).
8. Policy statement found in *supra,* note 6 at 17.
9. *Id.* at 22.
10. *Ibid.* It should in fairness be added that an additional 1/5 of 1% of the students are enrolled in what is described as "locally developed bilingual or partial immersion programs." How these differ from the Department's Programs is not clear from the Policy Statement, but most appear to involve a combination of public and private resources.

in Alberta is a section of the *Election Act* which permits deputy returning officers to appoint interpreters to explain voting procedures to voters not conversant in English, but does not require them to do so.[11] Records of the proceedings of municipal councils, on the other hand, are required to be in English.[12]

In Ontario the legislative picture is slightly better. The provision relating to the assistance of interpreters at polling stations has recently been re-cast in terms of a "right" of the voter,[13] though it acknowledges the possible "inability to secure an interpreter", and denies the right to vote in that event. Heritage language instruction in Ontario public schools, which has until now been a matter within the discretion of the Minister of Education,[14] has been up-graded with the announcement by the Minister that such instruction will be mandatory for all school boards, as of September 1989, if requested by parents of 25 or more pupils.[15] It must not be forgotten, however, that a similar arrangement in Manitoba in the early part of the century was ended peremptorily under the influence of World War I jingoism.

It is in the federal bailiwick that the fragility and political sensitivity of heritage language protections is perhaps most noticeable. No legal guarantees could be found in any federal legislation, and governmental policies have vacillated over the years.

The annual reports of the Commissioner for Official Languages provide an interesting barometer of the political weather affecting the non-official languages in the federal domain. Reports for the years from 1970 to 1978 contain no references to third languages. In 1979 it was acknowledged for the first time that "Canada has an incalculable resource in its multiplicity of languages, and should recognize this fact."[16] In 1981 the message became much more emphatic:

> For too long Canadians were content to treat these languages almost as charity cases whose survival could best be left in the hands of family

---

11. *Election Act*, R.S.A. 1980, c. E-2, s. 72. Manitoba has similar provisions: *Elections Act*, R.S.M. 1987, c. E-30, s. 88(1); *Local Authorities Election Act*, R.S.M. 1987, c. L-80, s. 87(1).

12. *Municipal Government Act*, R.S.A. 1980, c. M-26, s. 58(a).

13. *Election Act*, S.O. 1984 c. C-54, s. 56; *Municipal Elections Act*, R.S.O. 1980, c. 308, s. 64 remains permissive, however.

14. *Education Act*, R.S.O. 1980, c. 129, s. 10(19).

15. "Heritage Languages Becoming Mandatory Ontario Schools Told" *Globe and Mail* (24 October 1988) 9.

16. *1979 Annual Report of the Commissioner for Official Languages* (Ottawa: Supply and Services Canada, 1980) at 28.

piety and cultural curiosity, and to ignore linguistic resources that are just as valuable and just as hard to replace as any of the other resources Canadians are born to. We are beginning to see that such an approach was not only patronizing but improvident.[17]

Neglect of aboriginal languages came in for special criticism and the Report ended by recommending that:

All of Canada's language resources are valuable. Governments should go beyond the encouragement of cultural diversity by increasing instruction in languages other than English and French, and by providing institutional support for their use in the communities concerns.[18]

The tone began to change in the 1983 Report, however. While the importance of "heritage languages" (so designated for the first time in the 1982 Report) continued to be stressed, it was admitted that "some members of the official language communities are less than warm toward institutionalizing heritage language support."[19] By 1987 there was a decided chill in the Report's discussion of heritage languages:

The proposition that Canada should evolve institutionally speaking, as a multicultural but bilingual nation is fraught with ambiguities... (T)he national respect and support which is due to the many languages other than English and French which are spoken in Canada cannot be the same as those given to our official languages. That could never work, and actively or passively to encourage new Canadians...to believe that their cultural behaviour need suffer no significant adaptation toward Canadian norms is to do them a disservice.[20]

Although paying homage to the fact that aboriginal and other heritage languages contribute a "special cultural richness in which most Canadians rejoice", the 1987 Report concluded that they are not entitled "at the national level at least" to "the same institutional treatment — and promotion — as the official languages." The strongest support that Report could offer was that:

it is in the national interest that individual Canadians be permitted and enabled to acquire, retain and use those languages to the extent that the fundamental bilingualism of our institutions makes this feasible and affordable.[21]

---

17. *1981 Annual Report of the Commissioner for Official Languages* (Ottawa: Supply and Services Canada, 1982) at 33-34.
18. *Ibid.*
19. *1983 Annual Report of the Commissioner for Official Languages* (Ottawa: Supply and Services Canada, 1984) at 38.
20. *Supra*, note 1 at 10-11.
21. *Ibid.*

The alleged "flagship" of the Government of Canada's current multicultural program is the 1988 *Multiculturalism Act*,[22] which asserts the government's policy to "preserve and enhance the use of languages other than English and French," and arms the Minister with permissive authority to take steps in that direction. It creates absolutely no linguistic or cultural *rights*, however. This flagship is no dreadnought; it is, rather, an insubstantial sailing skiff, highly responsive to changes in the political breeze, and utterly unsuited for stormy seas.

The one occasion which the Government of Canada has had a hand in the legislative protection of heritage language rights was actually closer to a situation of having its hand forced. When Parliament proposed amendments to the *Northwest Territories Act* and the *Yukon Act* entrenching protections for French and English, it encountered angry resistance from the Government of the Northwest Territories, on the ground, among others, that aboriginal languages, spoken by a high proportion of the people of the Territory, were at least equally deserving of protection. Negotiations ensued, resulting in an agreement that the proposed amendments would be withdrawn and that the Territorial Legislature would enact legislation recognizing both that English and French are official languages, and that several native tongues are "official aboriginal languages".[23] The *Northwest Territories Act* and, consequently, the *Yukon Act*, were then amended to reflect this agreement.[24] The Federal Government put up a substantial sum of money for support of aboriginal languages, and the Territorial Government established a Task Force to inquire into appropriate methods of enhancing their use.[25] Subsequent legislation of the Northwest Territories has provided for the use of aboriginal languages in such matters as elections[26] and jury service.[27] Education in heritage languages has been possible for some time, though only, as in Alberta, as a matter of school board discretion.[28] Significant though these developments are, it must be pointed out that the "official" status accorded to Inuktitut, Dogrib, North and South Slavey, Chipewyan, Cree and Loucheux as "official aboriginal languages" is considerably more limited and dependent upon further developments than that which is enjoyed by English and French.

22. S.C. 1988, c. 31.
23. *Official Languages Act*, R.S.C. 1985, c. 0-3.
24. R.S.C. 1985, c. 31 (4th Supp.), s. 98-99.
25. Government of Northwest Territories, *Report of Task Force on Aboriginal Languages*, 1986.
26. *Elections Act*, SI-051-87, s. 204-5; *Local Elections Act*, SI-090-87, s. 17(1).
27. *Jury (Amendment) Act*, S.N.W.T. 1986(1), c. 7 (unproclaimed).
28. *School Ordinance*, R. O. N.W.T. c. 86, s. 103.

The fact that both federal and provincial governments have been loathe to grant legal rights to third languages is by no means the whole story, of course. Increasing *de facto* recognition is now being accorded to heritage languages in most jurisdictions, and increasing expenditures are being made to support them in several jurisdictions. Illustrative of the numerous heartening events in recent months was the publication by the Montreal newspaper *Le Devoir* of a special edition in Inuktitut dealing with the April 1989 election of a regional Assembly for Nunavik.[29] The point of dwelling upon the paucity of *rights* in the foregoing discussion has been to stress the evanescence of current benefits. No assurance can be offered that the political motivation will persist to maintain present levels of support, much less to improve upon them.

Only a constitutional guarantee could provide such assurance. The object of this paper will be to explore the possibility that a degree of protection for heritage language rights might be entrenched in the *Canadian Charter of Rights and Freedoms* and related constitutional guarantees. It is not an obvious possibility, except in one relatively small respect, but there are several potentially significant, if less than obvious, sources of constitutional protection.

Only one guarantee of third-language rights in the *Charter* is undeniable: the right under section 14 of parties and witnesses in legal proceedings to have the assistance of an interpreter if they need one. Another important form of protection in the case of native languages might well also reside in the guarantee of aboriginal rights in section 35 of the *Constitution Act, 1982*. There is also a substantial possibility that the *Charter*'s guarantees of free expression (section 2) and equality (section 15), and a number of the other *Charter* provisions, can be invoked in aid of heritage language rights, if those guarantees are read in light of sections 22 and 26, which stipulate that the *Charter* may not be construed to derogate from existing rights, and in light of section 27, which requires that the *Charter* be interpreted consistently with the preservation and enhancement of Canada's multicultural heritage.

These various possibilities will be examined in turn.

RIGHT TO INTERPRETER

The only provision of the *Charter* that creates a clear-cut right with respect to languages other than English or French is section 14:

> A party or witness in any proceedings who does not understand or speak the language in which the proceedings are conducted or who is deaf has the right to the assistance of an interpreter.

---

29. "Inuktitut Edition Heralds Arctic Election," *Globe and Mail* (1 April 1989) 4.

Section 2(g) of the *Canadian Bill of Rights*[30] embodies a right that is substantially similar, but differs in that it : (a) does not mention deafness explicitly; (b) expressly includes administrative tribunals as well as courts ; (c) appears to apply to everyone "involved" in proceedings, not just to parties and witnesses; and (d) is restricted to matters under the jurisdiction of the Parliament of Canada.

Although this right is a comparatively minor one, in the sense that it applies only to a very limited area of human activity, the Supreme Court of Canada has made it clear that it considers the right to be important wherever it is relevant. Failure to grant the right to an interpreter can result, for example, in a deportation order being quashed,[31] or a criminal conviction being set aside.[32]

The entitlement to an interpreter is not an absolute one ; it depends upon the claimant's lack of understanding or ability to speak the language in which the proceedings are being considered. It appears, however, that the claimant's initial onus of establishing this entitlement can be met by a simple request and assertion of inability; the court is not required to conduct an inquiry into the good faith of the assertion.[33] It has been held that the right should be given a "large and generous interpretation."[34] Indeed, even if a request has not been made by the person affected there may be a responsibility on the court to make the assistance of an interpreter available if it appears that such assistance is needed.[35] Opposing parties are entitled to challenge the need for an interpreter in a *voir dire* but a request for such assistance should be denied only if cogent and compelling evidence is adduced that the request is not made in good faith.[36] Merely establishing that the claimant can speak and understand the language for simple communications is not sufficient to refute his or her right to an interpreter :

> A person may be able to communicate in a language for general purposes while not possessing sufficient comprehension or fluency to face a trial with its ominous consequences without the assistance of a qualified interpreter.[37]

While the right may be capable of waiver in some circumstances, the Ontario Court of Appeal has stated that there is a presumption against such waivers.[38]

---

30. R.S.C. 1985, App. III.
31. *Leiba* v. *Minister of Manpower and Immigration* (1972), 23 D.L.R. (3d) 476 (S.C.C.).
32. *R.* v. *Reale* (1976), 58 D.L.R. (3d) 560 (S.C.C.).
33. *R.* v. *Petrovic* (1984), 10 D.L.R. (4th) 697 (Ont. C.A.); *R.* v. *Tsang* (1985), 16 W.C.B. 341 (B.C.C.A.).
34. *Re Roy et al.* (1987), 45 D.L.R. (4th) 415 (Ont. C.A.).
35. *R.* v. *Tsang, supra,* note 33.
36. *Id.*; *R.* v. *Petrovic, supra,* note 33; *Re Roy et al., supra,* 34.
37. *R.* v. *Petrovic, supra,* note 33 at 704-5.
38. *Id.* at 706. See also : *Winnipeg School Division* v. *Craton,* [1985] 6 W.W.R. 166 (S.C.C.).

Section 14 of the *Charter* grants the right of interpretation to "a party or witness" only, and this has been held to mean that a *lawyer* who is unable to understand the language employed does not have the same right.[39] This ruling is possibly open to challenge on the ground that lawyers are the alter egos of their clients in litigation, and that denying a lawyer access to interpretation is effectively denying that right to his or her client. In any event, it should be remembered that the equivalent provision of the *Canadian Bill of Rights* (applicable to proceedings under federal control) extends the right beyond parties and witnesses to anyone "involved" in the proceedings, which the Federal Court of Canada has found to include lawyers.[40]

The fact that the language of the *Charter* guarantee is somewhat narrower than that of the *Bill* with respect to the type of proceedings covered may indicate that the former does not apply to administrative proceedings, as the latter clearly does. It should be borne in mind, however, that there is nothing in the wording of section 14 of the *Charter* that would exclude administrative hearings; the term "proceedings" is certainly capable of including them if given a "large and generous interpretation." The Ontario Court of Appeal has held that although section 14 does not apply directly to arbitration proceedings it is nevertheless incorporated indirectly as one of the requirements of "natural justice" which arbitrators must respect.[41]

The expression "language in which the proceedings are conducted," which is common to both the *Charter* and the *Bill* probably means more than just the language used by the court or tribunal itself: it appears to include languages used by witnesses and others in the course of the proceedings. It is clear that deprivation of an interpreter's help for even a portion of the proceedings violates the constitutional right.[42]

Nor is a mere summary translation sufficient. The Federal Court of Appeal has held that an accidental failure to translate a portion of the evidence adduced at a deportation hearing could not be rectified by a translated summary of the evidence in question :[43]

> (T)he failure to interpret verbatim the testimony of a witness called on her behalf deprived the applicant of her fundamental right to know what was being said in an essential part of the inquiry... The applicant was entitled to know exactly what was said...[44]

---

39. *Cormier* v. *Fournier* (1986), 29 D.L.R. (4th) 675 (N.B.S.C.).
40. *Re Canadian Javelin Ltd. et al.* (1980), 117 D.L.R. (3d) 82 (F.C.T.D.).
41. *Re Roy et al.*, *supra*, note 34 above. See also the discussion of section 7 under the heading "Other Possibilities," below.
42. *R.* v. *Reale*, *supra*, note 32; *Re Weber et al.* (1977), 69 D.L.R. (3d) 473 (F.C.A.).
43. *Re Weber et al.*, *id.*
44. *Id.* at 476.

It is also well established that the right is to have the assistance of an independent interpreter. Offering an accused person translation by a Crown counsel is not sufficient.[45]

Whether the right guarantees *simultaneous* translation is in doubt. In a case under the *Bill of Rights* where simultaneous translation (not just "an interpreter") was requested, the Federal Court of Canada held that refusal of the request was justified:

> Notwithstanding that interpreters translate and translators interpret and that interpretation and translation, interpreter and translator, are, in their relevant meanings, synonymous, simultaneous translation is but a method by which an interpreter may function. It is not the only method, nor is it the mandatory method unless...the *Official Languages Act* applies. A right not to be denied the assistance of an interpreter and a right to be provided with simultaneous translation cannot be equated.[46]

It is not altogether clear what the Court meant by "simultaneous translation." Perhaps it was referring only to the electronic arrangements that are commonly designated by that term. If the comment was intended to mean more than that, and to reject any form of simultaneity as an aspect of the right, the ramifications could be serious and questionable. The most important purpose served by the right to have an interpreter is undoubtedly to enable the individual to respond in an appropriate and timely fashion to evidence, questions or submissions that require response in order to ensure that the person's legitimate interests are protected, or position is fairly represented. If an understanding of what is being said in an unfamiliar language is not conveyed instantaneously, or nearly so, it may well be too late to make an effective response. This is especially so where an objection may be called for to a question or a line of questioning being advanced in the ill-understood language. A reasonable degree of simultaneity would therefore seem to be implicit in the right to be assisted by an interpreter.

This conclusion might be challenged by reference to a statement made by Chief Justice Laskin, for the Supreme Court of Canada, in *R. v. Reale.*[47] In that case the accused had the assistance of an interpreter, seated in a chair next to him, throughout his trial for murder, until the judge's charge to the jury. At that point the judge ordered that the interpreter cease translating because he thought it might distract the jury during his charge. No other provision for interpretation of the charge was made. The Supreme Court of Canada held by a majority that the

---

45. *R. v. Sadjade* (1984), 1 D.L.R. (4th) 384 (S.C.C.).
46. *Re Canadian Javelin Ltd., supra,* note 40 at 84, per Mahoney J.
47. *Supra,* note 32.

accused's right to an interpreter had been contravened. Two judges dissented, on the ground that the judge's order was a reasonable way of ensuring compliance with the right to "fair hearing," which is also guaranteed by the *Bill of Rights*.[48] Chief Justice Laskin acknowledged that the right to "concurrent interpretation" may sometimes have to yield to other considerations:

> Assuming that there may be cases where the trial judge may reasonably apprehend that the jury will be distracted from attention to his charge by a concurrent interpretation to the accused and that he may thereupon be justified in refusing to allow his charge to be interpreted while he is giving it, such apprehension does not relieve the trial judge from giving effect to (the right of interpretation) in some other way.[49]

The Chief Justice did not indicate what "other ways" of satisfying the accused's right might have been appropriate, but one method might have been to record the charge and call an adjournment immediately after the charge so the accused could hear a translation and raise possible objections before the jury began its deliberations. In that way the accused would not have been deprived of the right to respond in a timely way through counsel to anything in the charge he felt required response. An even better method of meeting the right to an interpreter without distracting the proceedings would be, of course, to make use of electronically transmitted simultaneous translation. But it is submitted that, whatever means are employed, the persons in need of translation must be accorded the capability to make effective response. Nothing in the Laskin dictum in *Reale* contradicts that submission.

Who is to pay for the cost of providing an interpreter? There are several lower court rulings to the effect that section 14 of the *Charter* does not guarantee "free" access to interpretation facilities as, for example, section 1(6) of the European Convention on Human Rights does.[50] Those who have need of translation services are generally expected to pay for them, at least in civil litigation. Presumably the expense could be included in any award of costs that was made. In criminal proceedings it is to be hoped that the service would be provided at state expense. It may also be that even in civil proceedings the "user pay" principle does not apply to impecunious litigants. This possibility was conceded in *Wyllie*

---

48. *Id.* at 564, per de Grandpre J., Judson J. concurring.
49. *Id.* at 561-2.
50. *Wyllie* v. *Wyllie* (1987), 37 D.L.R. (4th) 376 (B.C.S.C.); *Marshall* v. *Gorge Vale Golf Club et al.* (1987), 39 D.L.R. (4th) 472 (B.C.S.C.); *Re Roy et al.*, *supra*, note 34 above. In *Gill* v. *Canada*, [1988] 3 F.C. 361 (F.C.T.D.), it was held that the right to an interpreter had been complied with by permitting the individual to have his own interpreter present.

v. *Wyllie*, the first decision imposing the cost of an interpreter (for a deaf party in that case) on the user:

> The submission that the court order the Crown to pay the interpreter's fee was not based on impecuniosity....
>
> ...
>
> The question that remains unanswered is, is there an obligation upon the court or the Crown in civil proceedings to pay an interpreter's fee upon the court being satisfied that the litigant requiring an interpreter is unable to pay the necessary fee? The wording of s. 14 is bold and unequivocal and it might well be that upon the basis of impecuniosity that a court would so order.[51]

This is an important qualification. If impecuniosity were allowed to prevent the exercise of one's right to an interpreter under section 14 of the *Charter*, one could justifiably claim to be the victim of systemic discrimination contrary to section 15(1) of the Charter. It is also possible that a denial of free translation services in criminal and administrative proceedings would violate "principles of fundamental justice," contrary to section 7 of the *Charter*.

ABORIGINAL RIGHTS

Aboriginal rights are expressly recognized twice in the Constitution once negatively and once positively. Within the bounds of the *Charter*, there is a stipulation in section 25 that *Charter* guarantees of other rights are not to be "construed so as to abrogate or derogate from any aboriginal, treaty or other rights or freedoms that pertain to the aboriginal peoples of Canada...." Outside the *Charter*, in section 35(1) of the *Constitution Act, 1982*, is an even more significant affirmative guarantee:

> The existing aboriginal and treaty rights of the aboriginal peoples of Canada are hereby recognized and affirmed.

The phrase "aboriginal peoples of Canada" is defined, for both contexts, to include "the Indian, Inuit and Metis peoples of Canada."[52]

Regrettably, the Constitution offers little guidance as to the meaning and content of the term "aboriginal rights." Section 25 states that the rights to which it refers include those recognized in the Royal Proclamation of October 7, 1863, and those acquired by way of land claims's settlements. Section 35 carefully avoids even that degree of

---

51. *Wyllie, id.* at 376-7 (L.J.S.C.), Skipp J.
52. *Constitution Act, 1982*, s. 35(2), being Schedule B of the *Canada Act (U.K.)*, 1982, c. 11.

specificity, however, and modifies the rights affirmed by it with the word "existing." It was hoped that the meaning and extent of the rights and freedoms protected by these provisions could be determinated by negotiation, but attempts to do so have been unsuccessful so far.

For the purposes of this paper, the question is whether the rights embraced by sections 25 and 35 include linguistic rights. I am of the opinion that they do. The 1863 Royal Proclamation contains no reference to language.[53] Some land claim settlements have included protections for aboriginal languages,[54] but many have not. In any event, the positive guarantee in section 35 does not refer directly to land claim settlements, and post-1982 settlements could be excluded by the word "existing." It is submitted, however, that the notion of "aboriginal rights" includes cultural and linguistic rights.

Central to the purposes served by the recognition of aboriginal rights is the preservation of a way of life — or at least those aspects of it that are capable of survival in the modern age. Central to any way of life — both as a component and as a preservation tool — is language. The affirmation of aboriginal rights by section 35 of the *Constitution Act, 1982* must, therefore, include entrenchment of the right to use and preserve aboriginal languages.

The inextricability of native cultures and languages from the question of aboriginal rights has been acknowledged by the Government of Canada. The 1984 First Ministers' Conference on Aboriginal Rights had before it a proposal that Parliament and the provincial Legislatures proclaim their commitment to "preserving and enhancing the cultural heritage of the aboriginal peoples of Canada", and to:

> respecting the freedom of the aboriginal peoples of Canada to live within their heritage and to educate their children in their own languages, as well as in either or both of the official languages of Canada.[55]

While no agreement was reached on this (or any other substantive) proposal, and while it has not yet resurfaced in subsequent negotiations, Prime Minister Trudeau left no room for doubt in his opening statement to the 1984 conference as to his government's acceptance of the linkage between aboriginal rights and native languages:

> Aboriginal peoples are deeply concerned, and rightly so, about the maintenance of their cultures and languages, including arts, religion and

---

53. W. P. M. Kennedy, *Documents of the Canadian Constitution, 1759-1915* (Toronto: Oxford University Press, 1918) at 20-21.
54. E.g.: Government of Quebec, *James Bay and Northern Quebec Agreement* (Québec: Éditeur Officiel du Québec 1976) s. 16.0.10 and s. 16.17.0.59.
55. Quoted in D. Sanders, *supra*, note 2 at 159.

above all the education of their children. This is a concern that all Canadians can readily comprehend. In due course self-governing institutions will prove to be important bulwarks for culture and language. The design of the necessary social, cultural and economic programs and services can be tailored so as to protect and enhance aboriginal cultures and languages. I suggest that it is the responsibility of us all to see to it that it be done.[56]

Should the question of constitutional protection for native cultures and languages come to the courts before the politicians get around to fulfilling that responsibility, it is to be hoped that linguistic survival will be judicially recognized as one of the most fundamental of the "existing aboriginal ....rights of the aboriginal peoples of Canada".

NON-DEROGATION AND INTERPRETATION CLAUSES

The *Charter* contains several assurances that rights and freedoms embodied in it are not to be construed as derogating from other rights. Section 25, which extends such protection to aboriginal and related rights, has already been mentioned. Additional protection for heritage languages can be found in sections 22 and 26 :

22. Nothing in sections 16 to 20 abrogates or derogates from any legal or customary right or privilege acquired or enjoyed either before or after the coming into force of this Charter with respect to any language that is not English or French.

26. The guarantee in this Charter of certain rights and freedoms shall not be construed as denying the existence of any other rights or freedoms that exist in Canada.

For most, if not all, purposes relating to heritage languages, section 26 may be redundant, since section 22 seems broad enough to cover most conceivable forms of derogation on language rights.[57]

In addition to the "non-derogation" clauses, the *Charter* contains an important direction to interpret its provisions in a manner that respects multicultural interests :

27. This Charter shall be interpreted in a manner consistent with the preservation and enhancement of the multicultural heritage of Canadians.

The protection afforded by non-derogation and interpretation clauses is limited, of course. They do not create positive rights in themselves, but merely call for interpretations of *Charter* guarantees that

---

56. *Ibid.*

57. S. 22 does not refer to "freedoms," as s. 26 does, but that is not likely to be significant, for these purposes.

will be consistent with other entitlements or privileges. This indirect type of protection could nevertheless be quite significant in some circumstances.

Consider section 17, for example. It provides that: "Everyone has the right to use English or French" in the debates or proceedings of the Parliament of Canada and the Legislature of New Brunswick.[58] Grammatically, it would be possible to infer from those words that *only* English or French may be used, and that a speech in Ukrainian or Cree would not be proper. That is not a permissible interpretation, however. Speeches have been made in Canadian legislative chambers in languages other than English or French from time to time. The use of Inuktitut in Parliament by M.P. Jack Anawak was recently noted by the news media, for example,[59] and although described as a "new twist", it was not the first time that language had been heard in the House of Commons.[60] This practice could be considered, under section 22, a "customary right or privilege" that should not be abrogated by a narrow application of section 17. In any event, a narrow interpretation would clearly offend section 27's injunction to respect the "preservation and enhancement of the multicultural heritage of Canadians."

There is an important difference between sections 22 and 26 on the one hand, and section 27 on the other. The protection provided by the non-derogation clauses is purely negative: they merely prevent *Charter* rights from undercutting other rights and privileges. Section 27 has the additional potential to provide a degree of *positive* protection, by encouraging interpretations of Charter guarantees that will contribute affirmatively to the preservation and enhancement of multiculturalism. It cannot perform this function all by itself, of course, but it can play a useful role in tandem with certain other guarantees, the most important of which are freedom of expression (section 2) and the right to equality (section 15). These guarantees will be considered next.

FREEDOM OF EXPRESSION

Section 2(b) of the *Charter* guarantees, as a "fundamental" right "freedom of ...expression." It would be difficult to conceive of anything

---

58. This right was first embodied, so far as Parliament is concerned, in s. 133 of the *Constitution Act, 1867* (U.K.), 30 & 31 Vict., c. 3. That section continues to be the basis for the same right in the Legislature of Quebec. The Manitoba Legislature is governed by a provision to the same effect in s. 23 of the *Manitoba Act, 1870* (U.K.), 33 Vict., c. 3.
59. "M.P.'s Speech New Twist" *Winnipeg Free Press* (21 December 1988) 11.
60. "M.P.'s Applaud Inuit's Speech in Native Language" *Winnipeg Tribune* (17 October 1979) 6.

more closely allied to one's right to express one's thoughts fully and freely than the capability to speak or write in one's mother tongue. That capability can also be vital to the transmission of cultural values to one's children and others. As the Supreme Court of Canada stated in *Ford* v. *A.-G. Québec*:

> Language is so intimately related to the form and content of expression that there cannot be true freedom of expression by means of language if one is prohibited from using the language of one's choice. Language is not merely a means or medium of expression; it colours the content and meaning of expression. It is ...a means by which a people may express its cultural identity. It is also the means by which the individual expresses his or her personal identity and sense of individuality.[61]

The *Charter's* guarantee of free expression, read in the light of section 27's admonition to interpret the document in a manner consistent with "the preservation and enhancement of the multicultural heritage of Canadians," offers much promise for the protection of heritage languages.

Small victories are probable. The Alberta requirement that municipal council records be in English[62] could well be struck down, or at least "read down" to preclude the interpretative implication that English must also be used in the debates of municipal councils. Permissive provisions concerning the availability of translation facilities at polling places[63] stand a good chance of being given mandatory interpretations.

Situations like "l'Affaire Piquette," described by Dean Christian,[64] in which the use of languages other than English in the Alberta Legislature was denied, are open to section 2 scrutiny, whether the language in question is French or any other. If Alberta were to experience in the future an "Ironquill Affair," or a "Takihira Affair," involving the use of Cree or Japanese in the Legislature, exclusionary Speaker's rulings or House Rules could be challenged as a denial of free expression. While the courts have traditionally been deferential to Parliament and the Legislative Assemblies with respect to their internal proceedings, it must be kept in mind that section 32(1) of the *Charter* now expressively subjects even sovereign legislatures to *Charter* responsibilities:

> This Charter applies...to the legislature...of each province with respect to all matters within the authority of the legislature of each province.

All Charter rights are, of course, subject under section 1 to "such reasonable limits, prescribed by law, as can be demonstrably justified

---

61. (1988), 54 D.L.R. (4th) 577 at 604.
62. *Supra*, note 12.
63. *Supra*, notes 11 and 13.
64. See T. Christian, "L'affaire Piquette" in this volume.

in a free and democratic society," and it might be contended that the long-standing immunity of autonomous legislatures from judicial review respecting their internal affairs is such a "reasonable limit." I doubt, however, that a blanket argument to this effect would stand up in face of the unequivocal wording of section 32(1). More limited restrictions, however, calling for reasonable prior notice in order to arrange appropriate translation services, for example, or requiring question period queries to be accompanied by a translation, or to be followed by one before a response is required, might well be found to be justified under section 1.

A more contentious application of the right of free expression with respect to third languages would be to assert that it entitles the users of heritage languages to greater access to Canadian Broadcasting Corporation radio and television facilities. This possibility will be examined more fully below in relation to the right to equality.[65] In the context of section 2(b), however, it is worth noting that freedom of expression is stated to include: "freedom of the press and other media of communication." This is usually construed to refer to the freedom of journalists and the news media themselves, which it undoubtedly does. But it could also refer to the freedom of all Canadians to have adequate access to public news media in their mother tongue.

EQUALITY RIGHTS

Section 15 of the Charter reads:

(1) Every individual is equal before and under the law and has the right to the equal protection and equal benefit of the law without discrimination and, in particular, without discrimination based on race, national or ethnic origin, colour, religion, sex, age or mental or physical disability.

(2) Subsection (1) does not preclude any law, program or activity that has as its object the amelioration of conditions of disadvantaged individuals or groups including those that are disadvantaged because of race, national or ethnic origin, colour religion, sex, age or mental or physical disability.

Here are further possible constitutional protections — both positive and negative — for heritage languages.

The negative, or "shield," type of protection comes from subsection 15(2). That provision guarantees that a special "affirmative action" program created by governments to ameliorate disadvantages suffered by the users of particular minority languages (say a program to train

---

65. See below, text accompanying note 71 ff.

teachers of aboriginal languages) cannot be successfully attacked under subsection 15(1) as a violation of the equality of rights of those who do not have the benefit of similar programs. (This view assumes that "disadvantages" refers to *cultural* disadvantage as well as *economic* disadvantage, a point that has not yet been confirmed judicially. It would be astonishing, however, given the existence of section 27, if cultural disadvantage were excluded from section 15(2)). It must be remembered, however, that this is a negative protection only: it creates no positive right to be given the benefit of affirmative action.

The users of heritage languages may nevertheless have a positive constitutional "sword" available, thanks to subsection (1). If, for example, a school board provided instruction in Ukrainian for children whose parents requested it, but did not provide it in German in comparable circumstances, the equality of the German-speaking group might be contravened. This is not to say that the Ukrainian program could be struck down by the courts; section 15(2) precludes that. It might mean, however, that other heritage groups in similar situations would be entitled to have similar programs made available to them.[66]

The qualification that the groups being compared must be "similarly situated" is important.[67] Circumstances would have to be such within the particular school district that the demand for German language instruction was as significant, and could as feasibly be met, as that for Ukrainian language instruction.

Whether a heritage language could ever be considered "similarly situated" to a minority official language is an interesting question. In my view it could. Although the special guarantee of educational rights granted to French and English minority populations by section 23 of the *Charter* constitutes a major difference between heritage languages and minority official languages in this regard, it is not necessarily a conclusive difference. Consider the relative positions of French and German in Alberta, for example. According to the 1986 Census, 3.3 percent of the Alberta population are of French ethnic background,[68] and 2.4 describe French as their mother tongue.[69] German ethnic origins are claimed by 7.8 percent of the population,[70] and a German mother-

---

66. For a good discussion of the right to use heritage languages in schools, with some American comparisons, see: D. Schmeiser, "Multiculturalism in Canadian Education," in *supra*, note 2, 167 at 172 ff.
67. See: D. Gibson, *Law of the Charter: Equality Rights* (Toronto: Carswell, 1990) c. 3.
68. *Supra*, note 6 at 20.
69. *Supra*, note 1.
70. *Supra*, note 6.

tongue claim is probably also significantly larger than that for French. Section 23 of the *Charter* guarantees French-language instruction and facilities to the children of French-speaking parents "where numbers warrant". If the City of Edmonton provided such benefits to Francophones, it is not unlikely that a group of German-speaking parents could successfully invoke section 15(1) in support of a claim to have their children similarly treated. Assuming that the German-speaking and French-speaking populations of Edmonton were roughly equivalent to their province-wide proportions, the two groups would be dissimilar in respect of section 23, but highly similar in regard to: (a) the importance to the parents of perpetuating their heritage; (b) the demand for non-English instruction and; (c) the feasibility of meeting the demand.

It is true that section 15 does not mention "language" among the expressly prohibited grounds of discrimination or disadvantage. It is nevertheless highly likely that linguistic discrimination is proscribed. Even if the ambit of the equality guarantee were restricted, as some have proposed, to the listed grounds and those that are analogous to them,[71] discrimination based on language is so closely akin to discrimination based on "ethnic origin" as to be virtually certain of inclusion.

Let us return to the possibility of challenging the limited facilities available for heritage language broadcasting from the Canadian Broadcasting Corporation. Could section 15(1) be used successfully in an area of Canada where the Chinese-speaking population outnumbers the Francophone population to support a legal claim for Chinese-language service equivalent to that provided to Francophones? The answer, I think, is: "Yes, provided that the cost of doing so and other practical obstacles were not prohibitive". A legislatively prescribed limit on service in non-official languages might well be found to be reasonable and justifiable under section 1 of the *Charter* in the light of such practical considerations, however.

OTHER POSSIBILITIES

We have not exhausted the possible sources of constitutional protection for heritage languages.

The right to associate with others of similar linguistic backgrounds is assured by section 2(d); the guarantee of freedom of association. The right of citizens to vote without regard to language skills might well be embedded in the "democratic rights" guarantees in section 3, and the same provision, by stipulating that every citizen has the right "to

---

71. See D. Gibson, *supra*, note 67, c. 4.

be qualified for membership" in Parliament and the Legislatures could imply a right to participate in the debates of those bodies without linguistic restrictions. Section 6(2) permits every citizen and landed immigrant to take up residence in any province and to pursue a livelihood there, which probably prohibits language proficiency tests as conditions precedent to provincial residence. The guarantee in section 7 that no one may be deprived of his or her "liberty" or "security of the person" except in accordance with principles of fundamental justice probably has important implications for heritage languages — both with respect to the "liberty" of using such languages, and the right to have "just" translation facilities made available in any legal or administrative process affecting one's other liberties or other aspects of personal security. There is a right, under both sections 10(a) and (b) and section 11(a), to be "informed" of certain things (reasons for arrest, right to counsel, reasons for prosecution) and since one cannot be realistically "informed" of anything by being told it in a language one doesn't understand, these provisions probably require that reasonable steps be taken to transmit the information in a language that is meaningful to the individual affected.

REMEDIES

What type of relief could heritage language users expect to receive from the courts if they were successful in *Charter*-based litigation? The possibilities are numerous.[72] Section 24(1) of the *Charter* empowers the courts to award victims of *Charter* contraventions "such remedy as the court considers appropriate and just in the circumstances." Section 24(2) calls for the exclusion from legal proceedings of evidence obtained in a manner that infringed or denied *Charter* rights, if the administration of justice would be brought into disrepute by its admission. Section 52(1) of the *Constitution Act, 1982* ordains that laws inconsistent with any provision of the Constitution, including the *Charter*, are of no force or effect to the extent of the inconsistency.

Criminal convictions can be quashed, and civil verdicts or administrative verdicts set aside, for failure to provide the interpreter required by section 14. Evidence obtained as a result of an unjustified failure under section 10 to inform an arrested person in a language he or she understands of the reasons for the arrest and of his or her right to counsel can be excluded. Legislation that violates *Charter* guarantees with respect to heritage languages may be struck down under section 52(1). School boards, government agencies like the C.B.C., and administrative officers and boards may be ordered to desist from activities

---

72. See, generally, D. Gibson, *Law of the Charter: General Principles* (Toronto: Carswell, 1986) c.6.

that infringe the constitutional rights of heritage language users, or may be required to take positive steps to make suitable heritage language facilities and services available. The payment of monetary damages may be ordered where appropriate. The ability of courts to order autonomous legislative bodies or their officers (such as the Speakers of Parliament or the Legislatures) to do or refrain from doing anything is not yet entirely certain (though section 32(1) clearly extends *Charter* obligations to them). It is undeniable, however, that declaratory judgements may be made with respect to any situation whatsoever, including internal legislative matters, and the political weight of a declaration that constitutional rights have been violated by an organ of government can be as effective a means of righting the wrong as any formal legal remedy.

In short, success in establishing before the courts that a constitutional right respecting heritage languages has been infringed or denied can be expected to result in appropriate and efficacious relief. What is less certain is the extent to which the courts will be willing to go in recognizing substantive rights in this area.

CONCLUSION

This paper has been an attempt to identify possible constitutional tools for breaking free from the French/English linguistic dichotomy that has long dominated language policies in this country. It can be safely predicted that not all the tools discussed will prove effective. It would be highly regrettable if none of them failed to attract judicial favour, however.

Legal and constitutional norms are all too prone to dichotomous tendencies. Accused persons must be either guilty or innocent: witnesses often must answer questions "yes" or "no"; legislative schemes must be within either federal or provincial jurisdiction; to qualify for minority language education rights under the *Charter* a person must be either English or French. Real life is much more complex and much more interesting than that, though, and the courts would be gravely remiss if they permitted constitutional rights to be unduly dichotomized in regard to matters as subtle and sensitive as language and culture.

As a very minor poet once said, with much more wisdom than poetic grace:

> For the venomous, full-fanged falla-
> cious dichotomy is more to be feared
> than a frontal lobotomy.[73]

---

73. D. Gibson, "Beasts of Academe" *The National* (November, 1986).

MULTICULTURALISM, HERITAGE LANGUAGE RIGHTS AND ALL THAT: THE SITUATION OF ALLOPHONES IN CANADA

A. Wayne MacKay*

I. INTRODUCTION

Within the context of the recent debate in Canada about the proper role of bilingualism in Canadian society, the issue of the constitutional protection to be accorded unofficial or heritage language groups has arisen. A consideration of the claims of these groups to constitutional protection requires an examination of the relationship between the Constitution and Canadian society and culture. Both the *Constitution Act, 1867*[1] and the *Charter*[2] contain important statements about Canadian culture. The *Constitution*'s preamble to section 91, with its emphasis on "Peace, Order and Good Government", suggests a Canadian culture based on a British, liberal model. The *Charter* reinforces this impression with its recognition of traditional liberal individual rights and freedoms. In addition to these individual rights in the context of a Parliamentary democracy, I would submit that there are four pillars of culture that distinguish Canadian culture and warrant constitutional recognition.

The first pillar of culture is language. The language guarantees in section 133 of the *Constitution Act, 1867* and the recognition of two official language groups in the *Charter* have a direct impact on Canadian culture. Second, religion is obviously a significant component of culture. Section 93 of the *Constitution Act, 1867* guarantees certain rights and privileges to denominational schools, which is in sharp contrast to the rigid separation of church and state found in the United States Constitution. These rights have been reaffirmed in section 29 of the

---

* Professor MacKay of Dalhousie Law School in Halifax made the original presentation of this paper at the conference but he gratefully acknowledges that the final version of this text was prepared by him in conjunction with Paul Morrison, a 1990 graduate of Dalhousie Law School.
1. (U.K.), 30 & 31 Vict., c. 3 [hereinafter *Constitution Act, 1867*].
2. *Canadian Charter of Rights and Freedoms*, Part 1 of the *Constitution Act, 1982*, being schedule B of the *Canada Act 1982* (U.K.), 1982, c. 11 [hereinafter *Charter*].

Charter. Third, education has been singled out for special consideration in the Canadian constitutional framework. Section 93 grants exclusive jurisdiction over education to the provinces, indicating the importance attached to local influence and control over education. The *Charter*, however, has created a role for the courts in education with its guarantee of official minority language education in section 23. Finally, and this is particularly true with respect to unofficial language claims, one cannot speak about culture in the constitution without referring to the role played by autonomous groups in culture. Autonomy guarantees a degree of independence from governmental interference in areas considered vital to a group's cultural identity, in order to prevent assimilation and ensure the continuing vitality of the minority.[3] There is obviously a great deal of overlap between these four aspects of culture; components of language, religion, education and autonomy would all be involved in a consideration of minority language in schools, for example. It is significant that the rights based on these pillars are for the most part collective rights enjoyed by particular groups, as opposed to individuals. The task of juggling these different constitutional aspects of culture with the broad guarantees of equality and fundamental justice in sections 15 and 7 of the *Charter* will obviously be a difficult one.

Another important thread in the cultural fabric of Canada is the recognition of Canada's multicultural heritage in section 27 of the *Charter*. The recognition of multiculturalism is seemingly at odds with the privileges enjoyed by the two official language groups and the denominational school systems. The difficulty, of course, lies in balancing the claims supported by these various constitutional guarantees with the aspirations of groups which have not been granted special constitutional status. Is the inevitable conflict of these constitutional guarantees a symbol of a healthy tension which is properly found within a constitution, or a poorly reasoned ambiguity replete with contradictions?

In order to deal with these complex questions, an accommodation will have to be made between the competing constitutional visions of bilingualism, biculturalism, and multiculturalism. In the bicultural view of Canada, the relationship between the people and the exercise of government power is primarily concerned with the connection between the two "founding" cultures. This is particularly true with respect to language although, as noted above, this is not the only component of culture.[4]

---

3. See J.E. Magnet, "Collective Rights, Cultural Autonomy and the Canadian State" (1986) 32 *McGill L.J.* 171.

4. W. MacKay and C. Beckton, "Institutional and Constitutional Arrangements: An Overview", in Beckton and MacKay, eds, *Recurring Issues in Canadian Federalism* (Toronto: University of Toronto Press, 1986), Vol. 57 of the Royal Commission on

Multiculturalism, however, envisions a Canadian mosaic with the promotion and preservation of many different cultures. The contradiction between attempting to have a bilingual, yet multicultural society has not yet been resolved, or even clearly articulated. One of the most significant problems in Canadian federalism today is the apparent gap between the *de jure* vision of a bilingual Canada, given expression and form in the *Charter* and legislation such as the *Official Languages Act*,[5] and the *de facto* experience of most Canadians who live within either an Anglophone community or in communities with an Anglophone minority or a Francophone majority. For many heritage language groups, the primacy accorded to official languages is alien to their experience of Canadian society, particularly in the West. The position of official language minorities within this system, like Acadians, is even more problematic. The sense of alienation among heritage language groups leads to demands for many of the same privileges accorded official language groups, particularly in education and government services. The main basis for such claims will be the acknowledgement of Canada's multicultural heritage in section 27. However, the fact that the guarantees accorded to the bilingual nature of Canada have been given substantive protection, while the multicultural guarantees are present simply in the form of an interpretive clause, illustrates that, at the end of the day, the issue is one of political power.

II. MORAL BASIS FOR HERITAGE LANGUAGE CLAIMS

The crucial question with respect to multiculturalism is whether section 27 is merely a rhetorical commitment, or a basis of real political claims for a multicultural Canada. There are two major moral bases for the recognition of claims of unofficial linguistic minorities. The first is rooted in the traditional liberal approach to privacy, that people should be free to use the language they wish, free from state interference. With respect to many unofficial language claims, however, such an approach would in all likelihood lead to a "freedom to assimilate". The second moral basis of heritage language claims would require a more affirmative role for the state in the promotion of the unofficial language in the context of multiculturalism. Given the key role of education in the promotion and preservation of culture, it could be argued that if there is a duty on the state to provide education, in some cases there would be a right to education in unofficial or heritage languages. This would be a revolutionary development in the context of a bilingual government strategy.

Economic Union and Development Prospects for Canada (*Macdonald Commission*) at 3-16.

5. R.S.C. 1985, c. O-3, as rep. *The Official Languages Act*, S.C. 1988, c. 38.

The two moral bases must be examined in light of the constitutional dichotomy in Canada between individual and collective rights. Certain collective rights were recognized in section 93 and section 133 of the *Constitution Act, 1867*, as part of the Confederation compromise.[6] New collective rights were recognized in the *Charter* for official language minorities, such as Acadians, in section 23.[7] While official linguistic minorities may have their constitutional niche, non-recognized collectives must base their claims on section 27 alone or in combination with other constitutional provisions. Constitutional recognition is based on historic collective rights within Canada: mere status as a collective will not guarantee rights. Is the answer to abandon the collective approach, and take on a liberal, individualistic approach, or is the proper solution that of Professor Magnet, who advocates a more tolerant and pluralistic approach to collective rights based on group autonomy?[8] Insofar as Section 27 is not a source of substantive rights itself, but a statement of an interpretive principle only, it is likely that the explicit rights of official linguistic minorities will prevail over the multicultural vision.

III. LEGAL AVENUES

Despite the preeminent role of official linguistic groups in Canada's constitution, it is possible to build a legal foundation for the claims of heritage groups. The following will provide only an outline of a constitutional basis for heritage language claims.

A. Freedom of Expression

Section 2(b) of the *Charter* guarantees:

> freedom of thought, belief, opinion and expression, including freedom of the press and other media of communication;

It should be observed that the freedom guaranteed by section 2(b) is defined quite expansively, not merely being restricted to the traditional notions of freedom of "speech" or the "press". It could be argued that the language of the section could support a broad right to express oneself in any language. In the case of *A. G. Québec* v. *Chaussure Brown's Inc., Valerie Ford et al.*,[9] the Québec sign law case, the Supreme Court accepted

---

6. As characterized by the Supreme Court of Canada in *Reference Re Roman Catholic High School Funding* (1987), 40 D.L.R. (4th) 18 at 60 (S.C.C.).

7. *Société des Acadiens du Nouveau Brunswick Inc.* v. *Minority Language School Board No. 50*, [1986] 1 S.C.R. 549 at 578. (S.C.C.).

8. *Supra*, note 3.

9. (1988), 90 N.R. 84 (S.C.C.).

the invitation implicit in the text to make a broad statement concerning the fundamental right to speak a particular language:

> ...Language is so intimately related to the form and content of expression that there cannot be true freedom of expression by means of language if one is prohibited from using the language of one's choice. Language is not merely a means or medium of expression; it colours the content and meaning of expression. It is, as the preamble of the *Charter of the French Language* itself indicates, a means by which a people may express its cultural identity. It is also the means by which the individual expresses his or her personal identity and sense of individuality. That the concept of "expression" in s. 2(b) of the Canadian *Charter* and s. 3 of the Québec *Charter* goes beyond mere content is indicated by the specific protection accorded to "freedom of thought, belief [and] opinion" in s. 2 and to "freedom of opinion" in s. 3. That suggests that "freedom of expression" is intended to extend to more than the content of expression in its narrow sense.[10]

Given the recognition of the role language plays in the preservation of the cultural identity of both groups and individuals, and that it is a fundamental right to speak a particular language, it is possible that the guarantee of freedom of expression could provide a constitutional foundation for the use and promotion of unofficial as well as official languages.

Section 27 could play a significant role in the interpretation of section 2(b).[11] Assuming that culture does include components of language, religion and education, section 27 could be used to buttress the claims of unofficial linguistic minorities to certain language rights. An interpretation may be accepted that would not have been made in the absence of the mandate of multiculturalism in section 27 of the *Charter*. The caveat to this approach is that section 27 is an interpretive clause only. It is not a source of substantive rights by itself, such as the *Charter* guarantee of official minority language educational rights in section 23. Thus section 27 will likely be limited to the expansion and interpretation of other rights in the *Charter*. Given this approach, it could be argued that an expansive interpretation of substantive *Charter* rights would already take the multicultural heritage of Canada into consideration, thus reducing section 27 to a superfluous declaration of principle. The pattern so far has been that it is at least a useful hook upon which progressive interpretations of other *Charter* sections can be hung.[12]

---

10. *Id.* at 124.
11. See G.L. Gall, "Multiculturalism and the Fundamental Freedoms: Section 27 and Section 2" in Canadian Human Rights Foundation, *Multiculturalism and the Charter* (Toronto: Carswell, 1987).
12. One example is the use of section 27 as a support for s. 23 rights in *Lavoie* v. *A.G. Nova Scotia* (1989), 58 D.L.R. (4th) 293 (N.S.S.C.,A.D.) at 315.

In the recent case of *Reference Re Roman Catholic Separate High School Funding*,[13] the Supreme Court of Canada's decision would seem to suggest that arguments based on interpretive clauses would not prevail in the face of substantive constitutional guarantees. This is particularly true with respect to those guarantees concerning education and language that are considered crucial to the original Confederation compromise, regardless of the seeming unfairness of ignoring significant groups. This again is a clear statement of the political reality in Canada, that certain groups will continue to enjoy a privileged constitutional position. The recognition of multiculturalism will likely remain secondary to the principle of linguistic duality.

B. Multiculturalism and Equality Rights

The guarantee of equality in section 15 could have a significant effect on the preservation and promotion of Canada's unofficial linguistic minorities. At first glance, the combination of section 27 and section 15 may seem curious. The essence of section 27 is the preservation of the cultural distinctions within the Canadian mosaic, while equality theory has traditionally been concerned with the elimination of distinctions based upon race or culture. However, equality does not necessarily imply that homogeneity of society is a desirable result.[14] Section 15, with its broad wording, can embrace varying degrees of equality on both listed and unlisted grounds. The first and broadest formulation is "substantive equality", in which special measures above and beyond the treatment accorded the majority are warranted in order to protect the minority. The second, less expansive, view of equality is "formal equality", in which the minority would enjoy access to programs equal to those of the majority. Either approach could be used to ground a claim for unofficial language claims, assuming that language is an unlisted prohibited ground of discrimination in section 15.

A complex constitutional argument in favour of third language claims could be devised using a combination of section 15, section 27, and the official language guarantees in the *Charter*. For example, if there are sufficient numbers of Francophone children to qualify for minority language education under Section 23, and section 15 mandates equal benefit of the law, then should not an equal number of Ukrainians qualify for instruction in Ukrainian especially in light of the acknowledgement of Canada's multicultural heritage in section 27? Or will the unique political position of English and French as the two

---

13. *Supra*, note 6.
14. A. Wayne MacKay, "The Equality Provision of the *Charter* and Education : A Structural Analysis", (1986) 11 *Can. J. of Education* 293.

'founding'[15] cultures be sufficient justification for the special treatment accorded French and English minorities?

This 'building-block' approach to constitutional interpretation is probably the most fruitful avenue for unofficial linguistic minorities to pursue. The scope of the approach may have been limited by the decision of the Supreme Court in *Andrews* v. *Law Society of British Columbia*.[16] While the *Andrews* approach to equality is quite broad and purposive, the decision also makes it clear that the unlisted grounds must be analogous in nature to the listed grounds to warrant constitutional protection. Language is a strong candidate for inclusion as an unlisted ground, given its strong connections with personhood and individual identity. In *McDonnell* v. *Fédération des Franco-Colombiens*,[17] the British Columbia Court of Appeal held that official language is not an unlisted ground within section 15, given that official languages are separately considered in sections 16 to 23 of the *Charter*. However, the court held that discrimination based purely on language could be within the purview of section 15. In *Reference Re Use of French in Criminal Proceedings in Saskatchewan*,[18] the Saskatchewan Court of Appeal held that both official and unofficial languages could be considered as unlisted grounds in section 15. The trial decision of Purvis J. in Mahé[19] concluded that unofficial languages could be an unlisted ground under section 15. Given these decisions, there is clearly some scope for building on section 15. However, the reasoning employed in the *Roman Catholic Funding Reference*[20] could be used to scuttle this approach.

C. Section 7 and Language

Section 7 of the *Charter* guarantees the right not to be deprived of life, liberty or security of the person, except in accordance with the principles of fundamental justice. In the context of language, it could be argued that the right to security of the person could encompass the right to speak one's own language, particularly when the survival of the language is at stake. Again, section 27 could be drafted in support of such a claim. The difficulty with this approach is that the decision in the *B.C. Motor Vehicle Reference*[21] case made clear that the rights

---

15. I do not accept the concept of 'founding' cultures and people, which is an insult to Canada's aboriginal people who were here long before the Europeans. Nonetheless the concept of 'founding' groups does animate some aspects of constitutional interpretation.
16. (1989), 56 D.L.R. (4th) 1 at 13 (S.C.C.).
17. (1986), 31 D.L.R. (4th) 296 (B.C.C.A.).
18. (1987), 44 D.L.R. (4th) 16 (Sask. C.A.).
19. *Mahé* v. *R. in Right of Alta.* (1985) 22 D.L.R. (4th) 24 (Alta. Q.B.).
20. *Supra*, note 6.
21. *Reference Re s. 94(2) of the Motor Vehicle Act (B.C.)*, [1985] 2 S.C.R. 486.

to life, liberty and security of the person do not stand alone, and that these rights can be limited if such limitation is in accordance with the principles of fundamental justice. Justice Lamer in the *Reference* also made clear that section 7 extends to substantive fundamental justice, so it would simply be a matter of considering linguistic security as a matter of substantive fundamental justice.

With respect to the provision of education rights for unofficial linguistic minorities, it could be argued that the right to an education is included in section 7's guarantee of liberty. In her dissent in *R.* v. *Jones*,[22] Wilson J. adopted a definition of liberty broad enough to include the right to education:

> I believe the framers of the Constitution in guaranteeing "liberty" as a fundamental value in a free and democratic society had in mind the freedom of the individual to develop and realize his potential to the full, to make his own choices for good or ill, to be non-conformist, idiosyncratic and even eccentric — to be, in today's parlance "his own person" and accountable as such.[23]

If the constitutional right to an education is accepted,[24] only a short leap is required to the necessity that such education be in the heritage language as a security of the person interest. The recognition of a right to an appropriate education in section 7 could also be used to support the equality right argument to minority language education for unofficial linguistic minorities, discussed above.

D. Language and Freedom of Religion

The guarantees of freedom of conscience and religion in section 2(a) of the *Charter* could also serve as a basis for unofficial language claims. Douglas Schmeiser argues that, based on the guarantee of equality rights in section 15, the availability of publicly financed denominational schools should be extended to any religious group with sufficient numbers and interest to make a school viable.[25] Given the decision in *R.* v. *Jones*,[26] that parents should have some say in the education of their children, it is not unrealistic to suggest that parents should have input into the

---

22. [1986] 2 S.C.R. 289.
23. *Id.* at 318.
24. I have argued elsewhere that there is a constitutional right to education in Canada. W. MacKay, "Public Education in Nova Scotia: Legal Rights, Fleeting Privileges or Political Rhetoric" (1984) 8 *Dal. L.J.* 137 and W. MacKay and G. Krinke, "Education as a Basic Human Rights: A Response to Special Education and the Charter" (1987) 2 *Can. J. of Law and Soc.* 73.
25. D. Schmeiser, "Multiculturalism in Canadian Education" in Canadian Human Rights Foundation, *Multiculturalism and the Charter* (Toronto: Carswell, 1987) at 167, especially at 172.
26. *Supra*, note 22.

language of instruction. In most cases, religious education would be provided in English or French, but if there is a religion in which the language of instruction is not English or French, for example a Jewish education in Hebrew, it could be argued that it is a component of religious freedom to have a child's education provided in that language. As religion is clearly a component of culture, section 27 could also be enlisted in support of this argument. Once again, the 'building block' approach must be employed, which is of course vulnerable to the reasoning in the *Catholic School Funding* case.[27]

IV. CONCLUDING THOUGHTS

It appears that there will continue to be minorities in Canada who will be accorded special privileges based on their historic position in the Confederation compromise. These rights have been extended and reinforced in the *Charter*, and may be reinforced further by the provisions of the Meech Lake Accord.[28] The minorities which have not received explicit, substantive constitutional protection will be forced to make a legal case through analogy and the combination of constitutional provisions. While the moral vision of the rights of multicultural groups may be present, and the legal foundations are available (although somewhat shaky), the political power of multicultural groups to implement their claims is lacking.

The claims of Aboriginal Canadians which have been so shamefully ignored by Canadians are the topic of another article in this book,[29] so I have not explored their constitutional status. However, I would be remiss if I did not at least acknowledge that there is emerging a clear, articulate, and powerful Aboriginal vision of Canada, which does not fit within either the bicultural or multicultural vision of Canada.[30] Issues of language and culture in Canada have generally been resolved on the basis of political power rather than in accordance with moral or legal principles. While I see signs that things are improving, Canada has a long way to go in reconciling its conflicting constitutional visions about the cultural fabric of the country. Difficult days lie ahead.

---

27. *Supra*, Note 6.
28. By the date that this manuscript was finalized, the Meech Lake Accord had failed to pass constitutional muster. This leaves doubt about the status of Quebec in the Canadian Confederation and the future of bilingualism and biculturalism in Canada. One of the reasons the Meech Lake Accord died was the stand of Elijah Harper and the Aboriginal people of Canada that it is time to recognize "Canada's true distinct society". Where Canada is going has never been less clear than at present.
29. See Brian Slattery, "Aboriginal Language Rights" in this volume.
30. These issues are ably explored by my colleague, Mary Ellen Turpel, in "Aboriginal Peoples and the Canadian Charter: Interpretive Monopolies, Cultural Differences" (1989-90) 6 *C.H.R.Y.B.* 3.

POTENTIAL CONSTITUTIONAL CLAIMS BY LINGUISTIC GROUPS OTHER THAN FRENCH AND ENGLISH

Ian McGilp and Christopher Dassios*

The *Canadian Charter of Rights and Freedoms*[1] has generated new concerns about the rights of linguistic minorities in Canada, and new hopes that minority language rights will be respected and enhanced by government. This paper will explore possible constitutional claims against the state by linguistic minorities other than the French and English in Canada.

Prior to the enactment of the *Charter*, limited provisions relating to language already existed in the constitution : s. 133 of the *Constitution Act, 1867*, s. 23 of the *Manitoba Act, 1870*, and s. 110 of the *Northwest Territories Act*. Although worded in slightly different ways, the Supreme Court of Canada has held that the substance of each of these provisions is essentially the same.[2] They provide for :

1. The right to use either English or French in Parliamentary or legislative debates.

2. The right to use either English or French in Court proceedings and issuances.

3. The use of both English and French in statutes.

4. The use of both English and French in Parliamentary and legislative records and journals.

The above rights apply federally and in Québec and Manitoba. The Supreme Court of Canada recently determined in *André Mercure* v.

---

* We would like to thank Maureen Webb for her valuable contribution to the writing of this paper.

1. *Canadian Charter of Rights and Freedoms*, Part 1 of the *Constitution Act, 1982*, being schedule B of the *Canada Act, 1982* (U.K.), c. 11 [hereinafter, the "*Charter*"].

2. *Infra*, note 3.

A-G Sask.[3] that these constitutional provisions also apply in the province of Saskatchewan. Due to the way in which s. 110 of the *Northwest Territories Act* became part of Saskatchewan's constitution, however, it was held that it was open to Saskatchewan, unlike Manitoba and Québec, to amend its constitution and remove these restrictions. Alberta has already amended its constitution to pre-empt the application of s. 110 in that Province.[4]

Sections 17 to 19 of the *Charter* appear to be similar in nature and scope to the above provisions. Indeed, the Supreme Court of Canada has confirmed this connection, at least with respect to ss. 17 and 19(2).[5] Sections 17 to 19 differ only in that they apply to Parliament, New Brunswick and such provinces as choose to opt into the scheme set out in ss. 16-20 and 23 of the *Charter*.

The *Charter*'s expansion of language rights is focused in the areas of government services and minority language educational rights. These rights are contained in ss. 20 and 23 of the *Charter*. Like ss. 17 to 19, they apply only to French and English, the proclaimed "official languages" of Canada and New Brunswick (see s. 16).

In contrast to the rights of French and English linguistic groups, the rights of non-official language groups are not specifically protected by any provisions in the Canadian *Constitution*. Accordingly, such groups are restricted to attempting to found claims on provisions such as ss. 2(b), 7, 14, 15 and 27 of the *Charter*.

There are three kinds of constitutional claims that might be made by a non-official language group or a member thereof:

1. Claims preventing direct government prohibition of, or interference with, the exercise of linguistic rights. This could be characterized as a "negative right" to be free from government interference.

2. Claims attacking government funding or provision of services to linguistic groups other than the group bringing the claim.

3. Claims seeking government funding or services for its members.

Each of these three types of claims is discussed in turn.

---

3. [1988] 1 S.C.R. 234.
4. *Languages Act*, S.A. 1988, c. L-7, s. 7.
5. *Société des Acadiens du Nouveau-Brunswick Inc.* v. *Association of Parents for Fairness in Education* (1986), 27 D.L.R. (4th) 406 (S.C.C.).

I- PREVENTING DIRECT GOVERNMENT INTERFERENCE WITH THE EXERCISE OF LANGUAGE RIGHTS OF MINORITY GROUPS

Claims which challenge direct government interference with an individual's right to liberty or free speech are the most likely to succeed. Examples of direct interference are laws or government practices that prohibit the teaching of any language but English to school children, or laws or practices that prohibit the establishment of private schools. Such laws are unlikely to exist in Canada today outside Québec, although they were prevalent in Ontario and the Western provinces in the early part of the century.[6] Indeed, in Saskatchewan an "English only" law of instruction in schools existed as late as 1974.[7] "French only" laws still exist in Québec.[8] There is a possibility that administrative practice amounting to interference could exist anywhere in Canada.

a) Section 7

Section 7 of the *Charter* guarantees the right not to be deprived of "liberty ... except in accordance with the principles of fundamental justice". In the United States a long line of cases suggests that the "liberty" interest provides a fruitful avenue for bringing language rights claims.

The constitutionality of "English only" and anti-private school laws were litigated in the United States in the 1920s in two seminal cases, *Meyer* v. *Nebraska*,[9] and *Pierce* v. *Society of Sisters*.[10] *Meyer* involved a state law which made it a crime to teach foreign languages to children who had not passed the eighth grade. The Supreme Court struck down the law and held that the teacher's "right thus to teach and the right of the parents to engage him so to instruct their children" were components of the concept of liberty protected by the 14th Amendment. Justice McReynolds writing for the majority stated:

> While this Court has not attempted to define with exactness the liberty thus guaranteed, the term has received much consideration and some of the included things have been definitely stated. Without doubt it denotes not merely freedom from bodily restraint but also the right of the individual

---

6. J. Berry, R. Kalin and D. Taylor, *Multiculturalism and Ethnic Attitudes in Canada*, (1976) at 10, cited in M. Hudson, "Multiculturalism, Government Policy and Constitutional Enshrinement: A Comparative Study" in Canadian Human Rights Foundation, *Multiculturalism and the Charter: A Legal Perspective* (Carswell: Toronto, 1987) at 61-62.

7. *School Act*, R.S.S. 1965, c. 184, s. 209(1) as am. *Education Act*, R.S.S. 1978, c. E-0.1 (supp.), s. 180(2).

8. *Charter of the French Language*, R.S.Q., c. 11; see also the *Education Act*, R.S.Q. 1977 c. I-14, s. 16(7) and regulations thereunder (Bill 101).

9. 262 U.S. 390 (1923).

10. 268 U.S. 510 (1925).

to contract, to engage in any of the common occupations of life, to acquire useful knowledge, to marry, establish a home, and bring up children to worship God according to the dictates of his own conscience, and generally to enjoy those privileges long recognized at common law as essential to the orderly pursuit of happiness by free men.[11]

In *Pierce*, a state criminal law required parents or guardians to send their children to public schools, thus precluding the choice of a private school. The Court relied on the reasoning in *Meyer* to invalidate the law.

In Canada, the majority of the Supreme Court has so far been reluctant to define the concept of liberty under s. 7. In *R. v. Morgentaler*,[12] the majority relied on "security of the person" in s. 7, not "liberty". In *Jones* v. *The Queen*,[13] which involved a pastor's failure to seek the approval of provincial education authorities to educate his children privately, the majority stated, "even assuming that liberty as used in s. 7 does include the right of parents to educate their children", Mr. Jones was not deprived of it in a manner which violated the principles of fundamental justice.[14]

In contrast to the majority of the Supreme Court of Canada, Wilson J. has not shrunk from the task of interpreting the liberty interest in s. 7. In her dissenting judgement in *Jones* she quoted the above passage from *Meyer* with approval, and concluded that s. 7 includes the right to raise and educate one's children "in accordance with one's conscientious beliefs". She elaborated:

> The relations of affection between an individual and his family and his assumption of duties and responsibilities towards them are central to the individual's sense of self and of his place in the world. The right to educate his children is one facet of this larger concept. This has been widely recognized. Article 8(1) of the *European Convention for the Protection of Human Rights and Fundamental Freedoms*, 213 U.N.T.S. 222 (1950) states in part "Everyone has the right to respect for his private and family life" ... Particularly relevant to the appellant's claim is Article 2 of Protocol 1 of the *Convention*:
>
>> No person shall be denied the right to education. In the exercise of any functions which it assumes in relation to education and to teaching, the State shall respect the right of parents to ensure such education and teaching in conformity with their own religious and philosophical convictions.[15]

---

11. *Supra*, note 9 at 399.
12. (1988), 82 N.R. 1 (S.C.C.).
13. (1986), 69 N.R. 241 (S.C.C.).
14. *Id.* at 259.
15. *Id.* at 279.

In *Morgentaler*, Wilson J. said that a "critical component" of liberty is the "right to make fundamental personal decisions without interference from the State".[16]

It seems probable that when a majority of the Supreme Court of Canada comes to determine the scope of "liberty" under s. 7 they will do so having some reference to American jurisprudence and international law. Accordingly, one might ask what limits could be placed on parents' rights to choose the education of their child. For example, do parents have the right to decide that their children will not learn an official language? This is the type of question a court would be forced to answer under s. 1 of the *Charter* if it were to accept the prevailing American definition of liberty as including a right to choose the language of education of one's children.

In *Jones*, the majority of the Supreme Court of Canada observed that the state, like the individual parent, possesses a significant interest in the education of children:

> Whether one views it from an economic, social, cultural or civic point of view, the education of the young is critically important in our society.[17]

The majority went on to adopt the following passage from *Brown* v. *Board of Education of Topeka*:

> Today, education is perhaps the most important function of state and local governments. Compulsory school attendance laws, and the great expenditures for education both demonstrate our recognition of the importance of education to our democratic society. It is required in the performance of our most basic public responsibilities, even service in the armed forces. It is the very foundation of good citizenship. Today it is a principal instrument in awakening the child to cultural values, in preparing him for later professional training, and in helping him to adjust normally to his environment. In these days it is doubtful that any child may reasonably be expected to succeed in life if he is denied the opportunity to an education.[18]

Although the above passages refer to the state's interest in education generally, they may also apply to the state's interest in having its citizens receive education, to some degree, in an official language.

Where, then, would a court draw the balance between the competing interests of the individual and the state with respect to the linguistic education of a child? If for example, Parliament or a legislature allowed extra-curricular education in a non-official language but required the

---

16. *Supra*, note 12 at 119.
17. *Supra*, note 13 at 253.
18. 347 U.S. 483 at 493 (1954).

curricula of all schools to include a minimum amount of education in one of the official languages, would this be upheld as constitutionally valid?

In *Meyer* the purpose of the impugned statute was to "promote civic development by inhibiting training and education in foreign tongues and ideals of the immature, before they could learn English and acquire American ideals".[19] The United States Supreme Court rejected the suggestion that the State had the power to "foster a homogeneous population".[20] Interestingly, however, the Court observed that "the power of the state to compel attendance at some school and to make reasonable regulations for all schools, *including a requirement that they shall give instructions in English* is not questioned" (emphasis added).[21] Similarly, in *Pierce*, the Court stated:

> No question is raised concerning the power of the State ... to require ... that certain studies plainly essential to good citizenship must be taught.[22]

In view of the above, it appears that American courts would uphold a 'minimum official language instruction' law. The manner in which Canadian courts would draw the balance, however, is by no means clear. As s. 27 of the *Charter* suggests, Canadian society is distinctly different from American society. In Canada, partly but not only because of Québec, cultural and linguistic freedom has much greater currency than in the U.S. In Canada, arguably there is a stronger commitment to allowing minority groups such as Doukhobors and Hutterites to be "left alone".

Even American courts have shown that they are not insensitive to cultural and linguistic concerns. Professor Laurence Tribe has observed that, among later interpretations of *Meyer* and *Pierce*, "one subsequent explanation of their joint import has been that they demonstrated judicial solicitude for the Catholics in Oregon and the Germans in Nebraska against whom the invalidated statutes had evidently been directed because of the inability of those groups adequately to safeguard their interests through the political processes of their states".[23] This explanation was set out in *United States* v. *Carolene Products Co.*,[24] where the Court indicated that special constitutional protection is owed to "discrete and insular minorities". Tribe has noted:

---

19. *Supra*, note 9 at 401.
20. *Id.* at 402.
21. *Id.* at 402.
22. *Supra*, note 10 at 534.
23. L. Tribe, *American Constitutional Law*, 2nd ed. (Mineola, New York: The Foundation Press, 1988) at 1319-20.
24. 304 U.S. 144 at 152-153 (1938).

[The] notion is worth stressing as illustrative of a general technique that of assessing alleged invasions of personhood in their historical and social context. The character and extent of the personal affront, and indeed even the degree to which government is in fact usurping judgments crucial to personal definition and development, are powerfully shaped by the circumstance that the government has targeted an insular group for its requirement. A rule that might be sustained as a proper expression of community interest were it to affect the population as a whole might thus be invalidated as a violation of personality when it operates to single out, if not to submerge, a distinct group in the society.[25]

The "discrete and insular minority" concept has already been utilized by the Supreme Court of Canada in the context of s. 15 of the *Charter*.[26] This test may also find favour with the Court in instances where it must decide whether a law restricting language rights should be sustained under the *Charter*. One can imagine the Court being unsympathetic to language laws which have a detrimental effect on groups that fall within the definition of "discrete and insular minority".

In the end, whether minority language rights will be afforded protection by s. 7 of the *Charter* will depend largely on the definition of "liberty" that is eventually developed by the Supreme Court of Canada. Based on American jurisprudence and international law, there is some hope that the Court's definition will be broad enough to afford some protection to these rights.

b) Section 2(b)

Language laws impugned under s. 7 might also be attacked under s. 2(b). Precedent exists on which parents, teachers or students might found s. 2(b) claims. Recently, the Supreme Court of Canada has held that "expression" includes expression in the language of one's choice.[27] In the United States, *Meyer, Pierce* and other cases also treat language rights as free speech issues implicating the First Amendment. In both American and Canadian jurisprudence the right to free speech has been held to extend to both speaker and listener.[28] In American jurisprudence

---

25. *Supra*, note 23 at 1318.
26. *Andrews* v. *Law Society of British Columbia* (1989), 56 D.L.R. (4th) 1 (S.C.C.); *Turpin and Siddiqui* v. *R.* (1989), 96 N.R. 115 at 160 (S.C.C.).
27. See *Allen Singer* v. *A.-G. Quebec*, [1988] 2 S.C.R. 790; *Ford* v. *A.-G. Quebec*, [1988] 2 S.C.R. 712. These cases involve challenges to Quebec's Bill 101 which prohibited the public display of signs or advertisements in a language other than French.
28. See *Re Ontario Film and Video Appreciation Society and Ontario Board of Censors* (1983), 147 D.L.R. (3d) 58 (Ont. Div. Ct.), aff'd 5 D.L.R. (4th) 766n (C.A.); and *R.* v. *Videoflicks Ltd.* (1984), 14 D.L.R. (4th) 10 (Ont. C.A.), aff'd 35 D.L.R. (4th) 1 at 29; *Ford* v. *A.-G. Quebec*, *supra*, note 27 at 766; and *Irwin Toy*, *infra*, note 30.

a distinction is drawn between "content-based" abridgement of speech and "content-neutral" abridgement. The former attracts a stricter standard of scrutiny under which the law will not be upheld unless it is "necessary to serve a compelling state interest and is narrowly drawn to that end".[29]

Canadian courts have so far avoided different levels of scrutiny under s. 1. *R.* v. *Oakes* determined that the same s. 1 tests apply in all cases. The recent Supreme Court decision in *Irwin Toy* v. *Québec*,[30] however, may mark the beginning of a "different levels of scrutiny" approach. At the very least it adopts the American distinction between content-based and content-neutral regulation of speech, and determines that there is always a *prima facie* infringement of s. 2(b) where legislation is content based. If content-based regulation is a more serious infringement, and in our opinion it is, then it will take a more pressing and substantial governmental objective to justify it. A law that has an impact on the content of speech should be scrutinized more carefully than a law which does not.

The Supreme Court of Canada has made it clear that it considers restrictions on the freedom to speak the language of one's choice to be "content based". In *Ford*, the Court stated:

> Language is so intimately related to the form and content of expression that there cannot be true freedom of expression by means of language if one is prohibited from using the language of one's choice. Language is not merely a means or medium of expression; it colours the content and meaning of expression. It is, as the preamble of the *Charter of the French Language* [Bill 101] itself indicates, a means by which a people may express its cultural identity. It is also the means by which the individual expresses his or her personal identity and sense of individuality ... "freedom of expression" is intended to extend to more than the content of expression in the narrow sense.[31]

The Court went on to adopt a quote by J. Fishman, from *The Sociology of Language*:

> Language is not merely a *means* of interpersonal communication and influence. It is not merely a *carrier* of content whether latent or manifest. Language itself *is* content, a reference for loyalties and animosities, an indicator of social statuses and personal relationships, a marker of situations and topics as well as of the societal goals and the large scale value-laden arenas of interaction that typify every speech community.[32]

---

29. *Perry Education Association* v. *Perry Local Educators Association*, 460 U.S. 37 (1983).
30. *Attorney General of Quebec* v. *Irwin Toy Ltd.*, [1989] 1 S.C.R. 927, 58 D.L.R. (4th) 577 at 605-8.
31. *Supra*, note 27 at 748-749.
32. J.A. Fishman, *The Sociology of Language: An Interdisciplinary Social Approach to Language in Society* (Rowley Mass.: Newbury House, 1972) at 4.

In light of the Court's view of the content-based nature of language regulation, it is perhaps not surprising that the Court found in *Ford* and *Singer* that the "French only" sign law was not justified under s. 1. The Court accepted that there was an important governmental purpose to the law, to protect the vulnerable French language and "[assure] that the reality of Québec society is communicated through the 'visage linguistique'". Nonetheless, it found that the means employed by the law were not proportional to the end sought, and suggested that a law requiring the visual predominance of French rather than the exclusive use of French would be more "proportional".[33]

Given the Supreme Court's analysis in *Ford* and *Singer* it is unlikely that an "English only" sign law elsewhere in Canada would be sustained under s. 1. English is not a vulnerable language in Canada. Nor is it easy to imagine what other "pressing and substantial" government purpose could be advanced to support such a law.

It is interesting to compare the position of Canadian law relating to linguistic rights with European law. In Europe a principle of territoriality has been used to justify unilingual laws. Simply put, this principle allows majority language groups within a given territory to impose official unilingualism. Each group is thus provided with an "area of linguistic security" within which it is sheltered from "linguistic competition" from other groups.[34] This principle has been upheld as a justifiable limit on freedom of expression by the European Court of Human Rights,[35] and by Switzerland's Tribunal Federal.[36]

This is not, of course, the framework for language rights which Canada has chosen to adopt, as reflected by our Constitution. It seems from *Ford* and *Singer* that the Supreme Court of Canada is clearly not applying a principle of territoriality as conceived above, because it held that mandating exclusivity of French within Québec is not an acceptable governmental limit on freedom of speech. Nevertheless, the Supreme Court does seem to be applying a "territorial" concept of some kind, through the concept of a "visage linguistique" — a visual linguistic environment that reflects the existence of a French majority in the territory of Québec.

---

33. *Ford* v. *A.-G. Quebec, supra*, note 27 at 779.
34. J. Woehrling, "Minority Cultural and Linguistic Rights and Equality Rights in the Canadian Charter of Rights and Freedoms" (1986) 31 *McGill L.J.* 51.
35. *Case relating to Certain Aspects of the Laws on the Use of Language in Education in Belgium* (the Belgian Linguistics Case) (1968) 11 *Eur. Y.B. Hum. Rts.* 832.
36. See for example, *Association de L'École française und Mitbeteiligte* v. *Regierungsrat und Verwaltungsgericht des Kanton Zurich* (1965) 91 (1ère partie) Arrêts du Tribunal fédéral suisse at 480 ff.

It can be expected that the Supreme Court of Canada will continue to protect the rights of linguistic minorities as it continues to view language as part of the content of speech. Notwithstanding that the *Ford* and *Singer* case dealt only with English and French, they offer significant hope to non-official language groups who wish to challenge laws or government practices that restrict the use of their languages, especially in the field of education. In Québec, this protection will be balanced against the recognized right of that province to protect its "visage linguistique". As defined by the Supreme Court of Canada, however, visage linguistique represents only a weak form of the territoriality principle.

c) Section 15

The thrust of s. 15(1) challenges would be that a minority language group is being discriminated against by restrictions on its fundamental freedoms.

The recent Supreme Court of Canada decisions on equality rights, *Andrews* v. *Law Society of B.C.*, and *Turpin and Siddiqui* v. *R.*,[37] held that in order to succeed under s. 15(1) the claimant must show:

1. That the distinction created by the impugned legislation violates one of the equality rights protected by s. 15(1);

2. That the law has a discriminatory effect or purpose, based on the grounds set out in s. 15(1) or grounds analogous to them.

The Court also suggested one analytical tool to be used in determining whether a case falls within 'analogous' grounds cases. In order to fall within an analogous ground the claimant must show that he or she belongs to a group that is a 'discrete and insular minority'; that is, a minority disadvantaged in society generally, apart from the legislation at issue.[38]

In our opinion it would not be difficult to establish 'language' as an analogous ground. Language is often an important aspect of one of the enumerated grounds, ethnicity. Linguistic minorities suffer much the same disadvantages as ethnic minorities do. In his 1965 book *The Vertical Mosaic*,[39] John Porter posited that the following hierarchy exists in Canadian society in terms of political, economic, and social power:

(a) English and French (founding populations) and British and Western European immigrants at the highest levels;

---

37. *Supra*, note 26.
38. *Andrews, id.* at 32-33; *Turpin, id.* at 160.
39. J. Porter, *The Vertical Mosaic* (Toronto: University of Toronto Press, 1965).

(b) later immigrant populations, largely from Southern and Eastern Europe at the middle levels; and,

(c) aboriginal peoples at the lowest levels.

To Porter's groupings could be added the most recent immigrant populations of Asian, East Indian, and Latin American origin. Porter observed that, although change occurred in the middle levels, the ethnic composition of the upper and lower levels remained relatively stable. The inferior status ascribed to certain ethnic minorities subjects them to stereotyping and prejudice, and reduces their opportunities for upward mobility. Minority group reactions to inferior status include inferior self-image, psychological and social maladjustment, and the rejection of group language, customs, and values.[40]

The second component of the test enunciated by the Supreme Court of Canada in *Andrews* involves looking beyond the form of discrimination to its impact. McIntyre J. states:

> [I]n assessing whether a complainant's rights have been infringed under s. 15(1), it is not enough to focus only on the alleged ground of discrimination and decide whether or not it is an enumerated or analogous ground. The effect of the impugned distinction or classification on the complainant must be considered. Once it is accepted that not all distinctions and differentiations created by law are discriminatory, then a role must be assigned to s. 15(1) which goes beyond the mere recognition of a legal distinction. A complainant under s. 15(1) must show not only that he or she is not receiving equal treatment before and under the law or that the law has a differential impact on him or her in protection or benefit accorded by the law but, in addition, must show that the legislative impact of the law is discriminatory.[41]

McIntyre J. describes a 'discriminatory' effect as one which imposes "burdens, obligations, or disadvantages" on individuals or groups not imposed on others, "or which withholds or limits access to opportunities, benefits, and advantages available to other members of society".[42] The "English only" laws, anti-private school laws, and sign laws discussed earlier in this paper could all be described as having a 'discriminatory' effect on non-official language groups.

The s. 1 analysis of laws challenged under s. 15(1) would raise essentially the same issues and concerns as discussed above in the context

---

40. B. Ramcharan, *Racism: Non-White in Canada* (Toronto: Butterworths, 1982) at 100-103. See also R. Anand, "Ethnic Equality" in Bayefsky and Eberts, eds, *Equality Rights in the Canadian Charter of Rights and Freedoms* (Toronto: Carswell, 1985) 81 at 89.

41. *Andrews, supra*, note 26 per McIntyre J. at 23-24.

42. *Id.* at 18; *Turpin, supra*, note 26 at 158-159.

of s. 7 and s. 2(b). Whether a claim is based on s. 7, 2(b) or s. 15 of the *Charter*, where a non-official group challenges direct government interference with the exercise of minority language rights, a strong case can be made for Court intervention.

II- ATTACKING FUNDING OR PROVISION OF SERVICES TO SOME LINGUISTIC GROUPS BUT NOT OTHERS

A plaintiff who successfully attacks selective government support for particular linguistic groups may induce government to include the claimant's linguistic group in the support scheme. Such a claim should be contrasted with one where a claimant asserts a positive constitutional obligation on the part of government to support a non-official language group, whether or not the government supports other groups. The most difficult claims to establish will be the latter, which will be examined in the section below. In the context of non-official language rights, both kinds of claims may arise under ss. 7, 2(b) or 15 of the *Charter*.

The question of attacking funding for other groups is of no small importance, since governments in Canada presently fund numerous minority language programs. In Ontario, for example, the Heritage Language Program provides "third language" classes on request where the number of students warrants it. In 1988, 68 school boards offered classes in 62 heritage languages to 93,000 students. Grants totalled more than $11 million.[43] Similar heritage language programs exist in each of the Western provinces with the exception of British Columbia.[44]

In Ontario, certain government services and advertisements are available in non-official languages.[45] Some provinces have adopted federal legislation providing accused persons with the right to a trial in the language of their choice.[46] In addition, academic chairs in universities have been established for a number of language minorities, for instance, Gaelic, Ukrainian and Hungarian.[47]

---

43. Ministry of Education News Release dated October 22, 1988, at 1-2. Legislation to support "on demand" policy Bill Number 5(G) proclaimed in force July 13, 1989: *Education Amendment Act*, 1989, S.O. 1989, c. 33.
44. M. Hudson, *supra*, note 6 at 86-96.
45. Ontario Ministry of Citizenship and Culture, *Ontario and Multiculturalism Survey of Recent Developments* (Toronto, 1983) at 43-45, cited in M. Hudson, *supra*, note 6 at ff. 85, 91.
46. See Part XVII of the *Criminal Code of Canada*, R.S.C. 1985, c. C-46, "Language of the Accused": proclaimed in force in New Brunswick, Yukon Territory, Northwest Territories, Ontario, and Manitoba on June 20, 1985; proclaimed in force with respect to summary conviction matters in Nova Scotia, Prince Edward Island and Saskatchewan, and with respect to indictable offenses in Saskatchewan on September 1, 1987.
47. Canada, *Multiculturalism and the Government of Canada* (Ottawa: Supply and Services, 1984) at 11, cited in M. Hudson, *supra*, note 6 at ff. 22, 40. See also, Canada, *Report of the Standing Committee on Multiculturalism* (Ottawa: Supply and Services, 1987) at 34.

In his article "Multiculturalism, Government Policy and Constitutional Enshrinement — A Comparative Study", Michael Hudson has studied federal policy and funding for non-official language groups. According to Hudson, federal funds have been made available for provincial heritage language programs throughout the 1980s, although the sums have been small in comparison to the entire budget for multiculturalism, and "minuscule" compared to funding for French and English minority education.[48] Hudson has noted that broadcasting is another area where non-official languages have been accommodated by the federal government: in the 1980s broadcast permits were issued by the CRTC for multilingual television in several centres, full-time multilingual radio broadcasting across the country, and third language programming for most metropolitan areas.[49]

Given that funding and services exist, the question arises whether it must be distributed equally among groups in accordance with some kind of pro-rata formula. What would be the result under the *Charter* if Latvians, for example, challenged the University chair provided to Ukrainians, or *vice versa*?

Broadly speaking, the United States Supreme Court has developed two divergent streams of cases regarding the positive obligations of government with respect to speech, liberty, and equality claims. In the first type of case, the Court has been reluctant to review government expenditure decisions and has characterized government decisions to subsidize or not to subsidize particular activities as a legitimate exercise of the state's broad spending power. The viewpoint these cases express is sometimes termed the 'preferred choices doctrine', as it permits the government to use its fiscal policy to implement normative judgments.[50]

In the second stream of cases, the Court has refrained from applying this reasoning, and has imposed constitutional restraints on government use of public funds. A review of the cases reveals the difficulty of predicting when the preferred choices doctrine will be applied, and when it will not. The cases are difficult to reconcile, but are instructive as to the types of issues that may arise where government spending power is constitutionally challenged.

Pierce v. *Society of Sisters* upholds a state's right to choose what conduct it will support in these terms:

> It cannot be that because government may not prohibit the use of contraceptives, or prevent parents from sending their child to a private

---

48. M. Hudson, *supra*, note 6 at 68; see also *Standing Committee Report, id.*
49. M. Hudson, *supra*, note 6 at 69-70.
50. *Maher* v. *Roe*, 432 U.S. 464 at 470 (1977).

school, government therefore, has an affirmative obligation to ensure that all persons have the financial resources to obtain contraceptives or send their children to public schools.[51]

Similarly, in *Norwood* v. *Harrison*,[52] a case involving the lending of textbooks by government to racially discriminatory private schools, the Court explicitly rejected the argument that the equal protection clause gives private or parochial schools a right "to share with public schools in state largesse". The Court noted that "[i]t is one thing to say that a state may not prohibit the maintenance of private schools and quite another to say that such schools must, as a matter of equal protection, receive state aid".[53]

As indicated, in *Meyer* v. *Nebraska* the Court suggested that the power of the state to prescribe the curriculum for publicly supported schools, even one that includes English and excludes German, cannot be questioned.[54] In *San Antonio Independent School District* v. *Rodriguez*,[55] the Court held that the state is not obliged to ensure that public schools receive equal funding. The case involved a Texas scheme that funded the provision of school services at a minimum level, which was to be topped-up by property taxes from the local community. The scheme resulted in poor communities having inferior schools. In its reasons for judgment, the Court noted that judicial restraint is appropriate where "delicate and difficult" questions of local taxation, fiscal planning, and educational policy are involved.[56]

The preferred choices doctrine has also been applied outside the context of education. The United States Supreme Court has held that there is no positive right to receive government funding for abortions, even if the mother's life or health are in danger, and even if the state pays all health care costs incident to childbirth.[57] According to the Court, a state's decision to fund childbirth and not abortion is an exercise of its power to make policy choices.

The United States Supreme Court has also held that the state may spend its money where it chooses in several cases dealing with indigent persons involved in criminal proceedings or the welfare system. In *Ross* v. *Moffit*,[58] for example, the Court refused to impose the cost of counsel

---

51. *Supra*, note 10 at 518.
52. 413 U.S. 452 (1973).
53. *Id.* at 462.
54. *Supra*, note 9 at 402.
55. 411 U.S. 1 (1973).
56. *Id.* at 40-44.
57. *Harris* v. *McRae*, 448 U.S. 297 (1980); *Williams* v. *Zbaraz*, 448 U.S. 358 (1980); *Maher* v. *Roe, supra*, note 50.
58. 417 U.S. 600 (1974).

for discretionary review on states which determined that "other claims for public funds within or without the criminal justice system preclude the implementation of such a policy at the present time".[59] In *Dandridge* v. *Williams*,[60] the Court upheld a state policy choice to discourage poor people from having large families by conferring welfare benefits below assessed need.

On the other hand, in *FCC* v. *League of Women Voters*,[61] the Court held that government restricts freedom of expression when it extends funding to broadcasters subject to a condition that they not engage in editorializing. In this instance at least, government was not permitted to use its spending power to encourage some kinds of speech at the expense of others. Similarly, in *Speiser* v. *Randall*,[62] the Supreme Court struck down a property tax exemption that was available only to those who would sign a declaration that they did not advocate forcible overthrow of the government.

In *Sherbert* v. *Verner*,[63] the Court held that denial of unemployment benefits to individuals who refuse to work Saturdays on religious grounds violates their freedom of religion. In *Babbit* v. *Planned Parenthood Federation*[64] a prohibition against channelling state family planning funds to agencies offering abortion services or counselling was held to abridge First and Fourteenth Amendment guarantees. In all of these cases the Constitution limited government's ability to use its spending power to encourage some course of conduct preferred by government.

These cases have attracted considerable controversy in American legal circles, and may or may not be reconcilable. It is our submission, however, that one principal distinction explains the different results. Although American courts readily apply the preferred choices doctrine in cases that do not involve expression or advocacy, for example the school and abortion funding cases (*Rodriguez, Maher*), they do not apply the same reasoning in expression cases, such as *FCC, Speiser*, and *Babbit*, which do involve expression. Further, in our opinion the Unites States Supreme Court is correct in treating speech funding cases differently than other funding cases. Governmental preference in the world of ideas and beliefs fundamentally threatens the democratic process and the "search for truth", whereas governmental preference in the provision of other services, even education and abortion services, does not skew

---

59. *Id.* at 618.
60. 397 U.S. 471 (1970).
61. 468 U.S. 364 (1984).
62. 357 U.S. 513 (1958).
63. 374 U.S. 398 (1963).
64. 107 S.Ct. 391 (1986).

so directly the marketplace of ideas. The thesis we advance here is that government must be neutral as to ideology in exercising its spending power, even if it has free rein to make policy choices in most other funding contexts.

This analysis may be relevant to the protection of linguistic rights of cultures other than French and English in Canada. As indicated, the Supreme Court of Canada has held that freedom of expression includes the right to use the language of one's choice, and has stated that "language is not merely a means of interpersonal communication ... [or] a *carrier* of content ... Language is content."[65] Thus, governmental programs which fund one language group, but not another, in the schools or for public advocacy purposes, constitute a direct interference with the content of individual thought, belief and expression. As such, Canadian governments should not be permitted to "prefer" particular language groups in expending public funds because to do so is akin to a government "preference" for particular ideas or beliefs. Government must be neutral with respect to ideology, and, in our opinion, also with respect to culture and language.

This is not to say that government is not entitled to considerable latitude in setting school curriculum. It is to say, however, that when public authorities prescribe a language of instruction for schools, or provide third language instruction in the schools, they are making choices that may have to be justified under s. 1 of the *Charter*, because they are directly regulating speech in a way they do not when they prescribe the content of math or geography courses. Literature courses also raise s. 2(b) issues, as demonstrated by *Board of Education* v. *Pico*[66] where the United States Supreme Court held that school boards may not remove books from the school library because they are deemed to be "un-American".

The point is that government intrudes on individual thought and belief when it prescribes language curriculum in much the same way as it does when it prescribes the content of the school library. In our opinion, laws or practices which make English or French the language of instruction in schools, or which provide funds for third language instruction in one language but not another, amount to content-based regulation of expression, and for that reason should not be justified by application of a "preferred choices" doctrine which would give the government full license to prefer one language over another for whatever reasons.

---

65. See *Ford, supra*, note 27 at 748-750.
66. 457 U.S. 853 (1982).

Our thesis here, to some extent, contradicts *obiter dicta* in the United States to the effect that "the power of the state to prescribe a curriculum that includes English and excludes [other languages] in its free public schools is not to be questioned".[67] In Canada, however, language rights are perhaps more important than they are in the United States. Perhaps the necessity of accommodating both English and French in the *Constitution*, and to some extent in day-to-day life, has made Canada and its courts more sensitive to the relationship between language and freedom of thought, belief and expression. *Ford* and *Singer* articulate that sensitivity eloquently. We also suggest that s. 27 of the *Charter*, which protects multiculturalism, adds additional weight to the proposition that in Canada government must be even-handed in providing funds or services to non-official language groups. Accordingly, it is our opinion that under the Canadian *Constitution* government action preferring one language over another indeed can be "questioned".

At the same time, we recognize that in many cases language curriculum or funding provisions probably can be justified under s. 1 of the *Charter*, even though content based. For example, where "minimum official language instruction" laws are concerned, the fundamental right to use one's mother tongue must compete with the important public interest in fostering social values and democratic participation through the education system. If government must justify its actions under the ordinary tests of s. 1, however, rather than being able to rely on a preferred choices doctrine, it must demonstrate that the provisions at issue serve a pressing and substantial public objective. It must also demonstrate that there is no less intrusive way of achieving that objective.

Similarly, we recognize that many language curriculum or funding provisions which favour certain third language groups over others may be justified under s. 15(2). Again, however, under the ordinary tests of s. 15(2) the government must justify its actions by establishing that the favoured language group is a disadvantaged one on enumerated or analogous grounds.

III- SEEKING FUNDING OR SERVICES

Non-official language groups probably cannot successfully assert that s. 2(b) of the *Charter* imposes a positive obligation on government to provide funding, because of the view often expressed by American Courts that the First Amendment operates negatively to prevent government interference with expression, but not positively to impose an obligation on government to fund expression. Section 15, however, may be of more assistance, at least in the context of education.

---

67. *Maher* v. *Roe, supra*, note 50 at 477.

In the United States, education has been accorded special constitutional recognition because courts have viewed it as an essential prerequisite to the meaningful exercise of other fundamental rights. In *Plyler* v. *Doe*[68] the Supreme Court stated that education is not "merely a government 'benefit' indistinguishable from other forms of social welfare legislation".[69] It went on to consider, "the inestimable toll of th[e] deprivation [of basic] education on the social, economic, intellectual, and psychological well-being of the individual, and the obstacle it poses to individual achievement", and held it impossible "to reconcile the cost or the principle of a status-based denial of education with the framework of equality embodied in The Equal Protection Clause."[70] In the Court's opinion, no rationale advanced by the state could justify the "creation and perpetuation of a subclass of illiterates within our boundaries".[71]

Although *Plyler* involved a law which denied education absolutely to children of illegal aliens, the Court reached a similar result in *Lau* v. *Nichols*,[72] where non-English speaking Chinese-American students successfully alleged that classes taught only in English prevented them from obtaining a meaningful education. The Court held that the school board in question was discriminating against Chinese-American students in violation of the *Civil Rights Act*, which prohibits discrimination by any organization receiving federal funds. Absent analogous Canadian legislation, it may be possible to advance the same kind of claim under s. 15 of the *Charter*, so as to require school boards to develop bilingual or bicultural programs for students whose mother tongue is not one of the official languages. Such programs were developed by the school board in the *Lau* case following the court's ruling.[73]

This type of claim is potentially important in Canada where many new immigrants cannot speak either official language. A 1988 survey by the Vancouver School Board, for example, designated 46.9 percent of the school population as "ESL" (English as a Second Language) students. In Toronto, 25 percent of students are ESL, the next highest percentage in an Anglophone city in Canada. The Vancouver School Board has estimated that high levels of immigration into the city (mostly Asian) will continue for at least the next 20 years. Educators are learning that while immigrant children acquire "survival" English or French quickly, it can take five to eight years for them to achieve sufficient

---

68. 457 U.S. 202 (1982).
69. *Id.* at 221.
70. *Id.* at 222.
71. *Id.* at 230.
72. 414 U.S. 563 (1974).
73. See Woehrling, *supra*, note 34 at 63.

command of one of these languages to express themselves in abstract terms. Thus, without special assistance, immigrant children may emerge from schools cognitively illiterate.[74] Based on American precedent, s. 15 of the *Charter* may provide a remedy.

In the context of positive-funding obligations, s. 27 of the *Charter* must also be considered. Section 27 provides:

> This Charter shall be interpreted in a manner consistent with the preservation and enhancement of the multicultural heritage of Canadians.

If full meaning is given to the words "preservation" and "enhancement" it is possible that s. 27, combined with ss. 7, 2(b), or 15(1), mandates affirmative action by government with respect to cultural minorities. Some writers are pessimistic about the substance of s. 27, and admittedly it is easy to view s. 27 as protecting very little.[75] Others, however, are of the view that s. 27 may produce modest benefits for minorities. Professor Tarnopolsky, as he then was, believes that s. 27, being somewhat similar to a preamble or "aims" provision, is not legally binding in the narrow sense but has "great psychological value". He believes that s. 27 in conjunction with s. 15(1) will assist groups in invalidating government action which provides unequal funding for cultural activities. He does not believe, however, that s. 27 will assist in claims for positive obligations on the part of government.[76]

There is little case law on s. 27 to date. In *Ref. Re Education Act of Ontario and Minority Language Education Rights*, the Ontario Court of Appeal utilized s. 27 in its interpretation of the minority education provision in s. 23(3)(b) of the *Charter* to include cultural as well as language education.[77] In *R. v. W.H. Smith Ltd.*,[78] Jones J. of the Alberta Provincial Court stated:

> [Section 27] in my opinion directs that a measure of equal treatment be dispensed when interpreting any problem involving multicultural considerations. [79]

The Court did not indicate that "equality" entails affirmative obligations by government.

---

74. "A Lesson in Communication", *The* [*Toronto*] *Globe & Mail*, (11 March 1989) D1-2.
75. See for example, P.W. Hogg, *Canada Act 1982 : Annotated* (Toronto : Carswell, 1982) at 71-72.
76. W. Tarnopolsky, "The Equality Rights" in Tarnopolsky & Beaudoin, eds, *The Canadian Charter of Rights and Freedoms : Commentary* (Toronto : Carswell, 1982) 367 at 441-442.
77. (1984), 10 D.L.R. (4th) 491 at 528-529 (Ont. C.A.).
78. [1983] 5 W.W.R. 235.
79. *Id.* at 258.

Section 27 is patterned, in part, after Article 27 of the *International Covenant on Civil and Political Rights*[80] which states:

> In those States in which ethnic, religious, or linguistic minorities exist, persons belonging to such minorities shall not be denied the right, in community with the other members of their group to enjoy their own culture, to profess and practice their own religion, or to use their own language.

It has been widely held that Article 27 requires only that States allow minority private schools, not that they finance them.[81] For example, in the *Belgian Linguistics Case*, the European Court of Human Rights stated:

> [T]o interpret [the *Convention*] as conferring on everyone within the jurisdiction of a State a right to obtain education in the language of his choice would lead to absurd results ...[82]

By contrast, a United Nations study on the implementation of the Covenant[83] suggested that Article 27 requires that, where numbers warrant, all minorities be given the right to use their own language in dealing with government (at least for the most important administrative services). It may be, however, that this recommendation would carry little weight in international law. It would more likely be viewed as expressing an ideal towards which states should strive.

Perhaps the biggest obstacle to asserting an obligation to provide funding or services to non-official language groups under s. 27 is that the concept of multiculturalism in s. 27 is part of a constitutional scheme in which the principle of duality, not pluralism, predominates. In the Canadian *Constitution*, duality pervades guarantees relating to the legal system, the educational system, religious instruction, the operation of government and the provision of government services.[84] While multiculturalism suggests that all cultures and languages are to be treated equally, duality suggests that only two of them are.

The tension between multiculturalism and duality is reflected in the history of s. 27. That history began in the early 1960s when a Royal

---

80. 19 December 1966, 1077 U.N.T.S. 172 (in force in Canada 19 August, 1976).
81. Y. Dinstein, "Cultural Rights" (1979) 9 *Israel Y.B. Hum. Rts* 58 at 118-120; V. Van Dyke, "Equality and Discrimination in Education: A Comparative and International Analysis" (1973) 17 *Int'l Stud. Q.* 375.
82. *Supra*, note 35 at 866.
83. F. Capotorti, *Study on the Rights of Persons Belonging to Ethnic, Religious and Linguistic Minorities* (New York: United Nations, 1979) Doc.E/CN4/Sub.2/384/Rev.1.
84. See for example, *Constitution Act, 1867* (U.K.), 30 & 31 Vict., c. 3, ss. 133 and 93; and *Charter* ss. 29, 16-20, 23, 41(c), 41(d).

Commission was appointed to address growing tensions between English and French Canada. The mandate of the Commission, essentially to report on "Bilingualism and Biculturalism",[85] seemed to many to ignore the pluralistic reality of Canadian society. Spokespersons for the substantial non-English and non-French portion of the population reacted vigorously.

The Commission's final recommendation to the government was that it pursue a policy of "multiculturalism within a bilingual framework".[86] This recommendation was adopted by the Trudeau government in 1971. Under the new policy, ethnic groups were to be assisted in preserving their distinct identities, and discriminatory barriers to their integration into Canadian society were to be removed. As Michael Hudson has observed, however, a "plurilingual Canada was not to be encouraged at the expense of the linguistic rights of the French and English".[87]

When the first draft of the *Charter* was released in 1980 it did not include a reference to multiculturalism.[88] In the Special Joint Committee sessions that followed, over 100 witnesses were heard.[89] Nearly one in four of them made submissions regarding multiculturalism.[90] Of these, nearly all called for some recognition of multiculturalism in the *Charter*. No clear consensus emerged, however, about the meaning of the word. The words "culture" and "language" were often used interchangeably by witnesses, and "multiculturalism" was often used as a synonym for linguistic plurality.[91]

Many witnesses advocated express protections for non-official languages. Their position was perhaps understandable given Statistics Canada reports showing a rapid assimilation of linguistic minorities. For example, in Alberta, populations of German and Ukrainian origin have been historically significant since the turn of the century. Nevertheless, the numbers of people speaking these languages as a mother tongue has declined steadily since the 1940s (for German, from 7.9 percent in 1941 to 3.2 percent in 1986; for Ukrainian, from 9.4 percent in 1941

---

85. Canada, *Report of the Royal Commission on Bilingualism and Biculturalism* (Ottawa: Queen's Printer, 1969).
86. *Id.* Book IV, "Cultural Contributions of the Other Ethnic Groups".
87. See M. Hudson, *supra*, note 6 at 62-63.
88. Canada, House of Commons, "Proposed Resolution for Joint Address to Her Majesty the Queen Respecting the Constitution of Canada" (Oct. 6, 1980).
89. Canada, Special Joint Senate-House of Commons Committee on the Constitution of Canada, *Final Report* (Ottawa, 1981).
90. Canada, *Minutes of Proceedings and Evidence of the Special Joint Committee on the Constitution of Canada*, 9:105 (20/10/80).
91. See M. Hudson, *supra*, note 6 at 76,78.

to 2.0 percent in 1986).[92] Speaking on behalf of the Canadian Polish Congress, Mr. Federorowicz stated:

> [T]he question of language is key... . The question of third languages needs to be reviewed. The Government of Canada says that it accepts the multicultural nature of this country and yet it ignores the issue of language without which culture per se is meaningless ...[93]

Speaking on behalf of the Ukrainian Canadian Committee, Dr. Manoly Lupul proposed an amendment to the minority language education section of the *Charter* that would allow parents to demand third language schooling where numbers warranted:

> [I]f the Government of Canada can invade provincial rights in education on behalf of one minority in Québec and in other provinces, we would submit that it can do the same for other ethno-cultural minorities whose linguistic and cultural needs are equally pressing ... We would submit that if a Canadian Constitution is to guarantee minority language rights in provincial education systems, that guarantee should not be confined to one linguistic combination but embrace all that are viable ...[94]

The Council of National Ethno-Cultural Organizations, a broad coalition of ethnic groups, proposed a number of amendments, among them:

(1) The inclusion of "mother tongue" as a prohibited ground for discrimination under s. 15(1);

(2) The amendment of s. 15(2) to allow programmes to ameliorate and protect "any linguistic or cultural rights";

(3) The inclusion of a provision which would allow provinces to extend the "status or use of other languages other than English or French".[95]

Some groups explicitly rejected the principle of duality manifested in ss. 16-20 and 23 of the draft *Charter*. In its brief, the Canadian Polish Congress asserted:

> [A] document which singles out the so-called 'founding races' for special mention and special privilege will become increasingly objectionable and irrelevant .... [It is] an insult to Canada's smaller ethnic groups whose partnership in this country is of legally equivalent validity.[96]

---

92. *Infra*, note 99 at Table 1, and *Census Reports 1881*.
93. *Supra*, note 90, 9:105-106 (20/10/80).
94. *Id.* 14:56-57 (27/11/80).
95. *Id.* 22:78-102 (9/12/80); see also M. Hudson, *supra*, note 6 at 75-76.
96. Canadian Polish Congress, "Brief on Constitution Reform" (1980), presented to the Special Joint Committee of the Senate and House of Commons on the Constitution of Canada.

The federal government's response to the Committee hearings was s. 27 of the *Charter*. Certainly it seems to have been the government's intention at the time s. 27 was drafted that the concept of multiculturalism would not confer on non-official language groups the same rights or benefits as English and French groups. In introducing the text of s. 27 to the Special Joint Committee, Jean Chrétien, speaking for the federal government, did not deny that multiculturalism may encompass language. He did say, however, that "[m]ulticulturalism is not a question of the official languages of Canada which are French and English".[97] Similarly, Premier Allan Blakeney of Saskatchewan speaking before the Joint Committee stated:

> Saskatchewan is the only province in which those of British or French origin combined form less than half the population. That makes us particularly conscious of our multicultural heritage, and it gives us a strong commitment to policies and programs that will ensure the continued vitality of languages and cultures other than French and English, all the while agreeing that this is a country of two official languages.[98]

It is perhaps not obvious that duality would subordinate multiculturalism in a constitution that protects both concepts. The Polish Congress' view that a dominant principle of duality "will become increasingly objectionable and irrelevant" is understandable if one recognizes that while the first provinces to join Confederation were inhabited primarily by people of English and French origin, other provinces, particularly the Western ones, were not. At the turn of the century the western provinces had significant non-English and non-French populations. Moreover, statistics show continued increases in the immigration of people of non-English and non-French origin, and a steady decline of the French population in all parts of Canada.[99] For example, in 1870 when Manitoba joined Confederation, a slight majority of the population was French. Today only about 4.3 percent are Francophone, less than the percentage of German Manitobans.[100]

On the other hand, if one views Confederation as stemming from an original compact forged between two founding races, the idea that duality must be a dominant principle gains credence. On this view, Canadian history demonstrates that Confederation was a political compromise, carefully designed to ensure that the French language and

---

97. *Supra*, note 90, 50:17 (31/1/81).
98. *Id.* 30:15 (19/12/80).
99. Statistics Canada, *Mother Tongue: 1911-1986* (Ottawa: Supply and Services, 1989).
100. J.E. Magnet, "The Charter's Official Languages Provisions: the Implications of Entrenched Bilingualism" (1982) *Supreme Court L. Rev.* 163 (special edition); Statistics Canada, *id.*

culture would have the protection it needed to survive in a dominantly English continent. In *McDonald* v. *City of Montreal*[101] the Supreme Court of Canada left no doubt that this is the preferred view of the Canadian *Constitution*.

> What [the] historical record demonstrates is that the Fathers of Confederation were quite familiar with the old and thorny problem of language rights; they knew or must have known of the various experiments that had been attempted in this area; and they were provided with a whole panoply of legislative models from which to draw...[I]n a historic constitutional agreement [s. 133]...,which was carefully redrafted several times, the Fathers of Confederation chose the last-mentioned system... Section 133 has not introduced a comprehensive scheme or system of official bilingualism, even potentially, but a limited form of compulsory bilingualism.... . This incomplete scheme is a constitutional minimum which resulted from an historical compromise arrived at by the founding people who agreed upon the terms of the federal union...it is a scheme which can of course be modified by constitutional amendment. But it is not open to the courts, under the guise of interpretation, to improve upon, supplement or amend this historical compromise.[102]

Later in his judgment Beetz J. confirmed that the French and English languages have special status under the *Constitution*. Speaking about language rights that may flow indirectly from the right to a fair hearing, he warned:

> This is not to put the English and the French languages on the same footing as other languages. Not only are the English and French languages placed in a position of equality, they are also given a preferential position over all other languages.[103]

Section 16 of the *Charter*, of course, makes English and French the "official languages of Canada", and provides that "Nothing in this *Charter* limits the authority of Parliament or a legislature to advance the equality of status or use of English and French". In *Société des Acadiens*, Wilson J. commented on the relationship between s. 16 and 27 of the *Charter* in these terms:

> I do not believe that s. 27 was intended to deter the movement towards the equality of status of English and French until such a time as a similar status could be attained for all the other languages spoken in Canada. This would derogate from the special status conferred on English and French in s. 16.[104]

---

101. (1986), 27 D.L.R. (4th) 321 (S.C.C.).
102. *Id.* at 347-349; in a similar vein see Ford, *supra*, note 27 at 40; and *Quebec Association of Protestant School Boards* v. *A.-G. Quebec* (1984), 10 D.L.R. (4th) 321 at 331 (S.C.C.).
103. *McDonald, supra*, note 101 at 351.
104. *Supra*, note 5 at 457.

The foregoing suggests that Courts are unlikely to interpret s. 27 as imposing a positive obligation on government to fund or "enhance" non-official language groups. Even if such a claim were recognized, the obligation to support the non-official language would be subordinate to the obligation to support the equality of status of English and French. Section 15(1) of the *Charter*, therefore, provides more hope. Based on the American precedent *Lau* v. *Nichols*,[105] it may be argued that immigrants who speak neither official language are victims of discrimination by school boards who provide instruction in English only. In general, claims asserting a positive obligation to provide support will be hardest to win. The *Lau* case, however, is an interesting precedent.

---

105. *Supra*, note 72.

ABORIGINAL LANGUAGE RIGHTS

Brian Slattery

I would like to explore the question whether the indigenous languages of Canada occupy a special place in the *Constitution*. We know that the guarantee of freedom of expression in section 2(b) of the *Canadian Charter of Rights and Freedoms*[1] ensures our right to express ourselves in any language we choose, including, of course, any indigenous language.[2] I would like to look beyond that section and consider briefly the prospects for arguing that aboriginal languages are in some sense official languages of Canada.

If you turn to section 16(1) of the *Charter*, you find the flat statement that English and French are the official languages of Canada, with the definite implication that there are no others. However, this impression is dispelled by section 22, which provides that nothing in sections 16 to 20 "abrogates or derogates from any legal or customary right or privilege acquired or enjoyed either before or after the coming into force of this Charter with respect to any language that is not English or French." You also find in section 25 a provision that explicitly shields from the adverse impact of *Charter* guarantees "any aboriginal, treaty or other rights or freedoms that pertain to the aboriginal peoples of Canada", which would clearly cover language rights. But these two sections do little more than clear a constitutional space for aboriginal language rights; they do not provide a foundation for them. For that, I think, you have to look outside the *Charter*.

The obvious starting point is Part II of the *Constitution Act, 1982*,[3] which deals specifically with the rights of aboriginal peoples. Section

---

1. Part I of the *Constitution Act, 1982*, being Schedule B of the *Canada Act, 1982*, (U.K.) 1982, c. 11 (hereafter referred to as the *Charter*).
2. *Ford* v. *Quebec (Attorney-General)* (1988), 54 D.L.R. (4th) 577 (S.C.C.).
3. *Supra*, note 1.

35(1) states that the "existing aboriginal and treaty rights of the aboriginal peoples of Canada are hereby recognized and affirmed". And subsection (2) explains that the term "aboriginal peoples of Canada" includes the Indian, Inuit and Metis peoples of Canada. The question is to what extent this section provides a constitutional foothold for aboriginal languages.[4] But since the topic is a large and complex one, I'm going to leave to one side treaty rights and focus exclusively on aboriginal rights. Treaty provisions would, at best, provide a partial, uncertain, and fragmentary basis for indigenous language rights. The category of aboriginal rights is much more promising.

There are two families of theories about aboriginal rights: we will call them "historically-based theories" and "principled theories". Historically-based theories argue that existing aboriginal rights are rights that can be identified by reference to particular historical practices, customs, laws, or contexts that existed in Canada prior to 1982 and continued to exist in some form at the time the *Constitution Act, 1982* came into effect. Principled theories, by contrast, suggest that existing aboriginal rights are rights that can be identified by reference to first principles or basic human goods, such as, in the case of language, the value of linguistic security or the value of being able to transmit one's culture and world-view to one's children.[5]

I do not mean to imply, naturally, that these families of theories are internally homogeneous; to the contrary, like human families, they include members with very different characteristics. And I should also note there is no compelling reason to think that section 35(1) allows for only one or other of these two basic approaches. In fact I am inclined to think that a blended approach, which makes use of both, might be the best of all.

---

4. For general discussion of this section see: Slattery, "The Constitutional Guarantee of Aboriginal and Treaty Rights" (1982-83) 8 *Queen's L.J.* 232; Slattery, "The Hidden Constitution: Aboriginal Rights in Canada" (1984) 32 *Amer. J. Comp. L.* 361; Lysyk, "The Rights and Freedoms of the Aboriginal Peoples of Canada", in Tarnopolsky and Beaudoin, eds, *The Canadian Charter of Rights and Freedoms* (1982), pp. 467-88; Hogg, *Constitutional Law of Canada*, 2nd ed. (1985), c. 24; McNeil, "The Constitutional Rights of the Aboriginal Peoples of Canada" (1982) 4 *Supreme Court Law R.* 255; Sanders, "The Rights of the Aboriginal Peoples of Canada" (1983) 61 *Can. Bar Rev.* 314; Emery, "Réflexions sur le sens et la portée au Québec des articles 25, 35, et 37 de la Loi constitutionelle de 1982" (1984) 25 *Cahiers de Droit* 145; O'Reilly, "La Loi constitutionelle de 1982, droit des autochtones" (1984) 25 *Cahiers de Droit* 125; Pentney, "The Rights of the Aboriginal Peoples of Canada and the Constitution Act, 1982" (1988) 22 *U.B.C. Law Rev.* 21, 207. For recent jurisprudence on the section see esp.: *Sparrow* v. *R.*, (1990), 70 D.L.R. (4th) 385 (S.C.C.); *R.* v. *Agawa* (1988) 53 D.L.R. (4th) 101 (Ont. C.A.); *Denny* v. *R.*, (1990), 94 N.S.R. (2d) 253 (N.S.S.C.A.D.).

5. See, for example, the illuminating discussion in Leslie Green, "Are Language Rights Fundamental?" (1987) 25 *Osgoode Hall Law Journal* 639.

Here, I can only deal with historically-based theories, leaving others to deal with the rather quarrelsome family of principled theories. Let me cast a quick eye now over three historically-based theories and consider what promise they hold for aboriginal language rights. I will then conclude with some brief remarks on the proper bearing that principled theories have on their historically-based cousins.

The first historical approach argues that existing aboriginal rights are those rights that were affirmatively recognized in 1982 in Canadian law, which, on this view, is confined to European-derived systems of law. That is to say, in order to assert that something is an existing aboriginal right under section 35(1), you have to show that it was recognized in an existing enactment or, alternately, under English common law or Québec civil law. Only then, argues this approach, could you say that something is an existing aboriginal right.

Needless to say, this rather blinkered approach does not offer much solace for aboriginal language rights, or indeed for aboriginal rights generally. The kind of affirmative legal recognition it requires was, in 1982, patchy, niggardly, and often uncertain. Fortunately, there are good reasons for rejecting this approach, which I cannot pause to explain fully here.[6] Suffice it to say that it ignores the fact that section 35 speaks of the existing *aboriginal* rights of aboriginal peoples, and not simply their existing rights. The repetition of the word "aboriginal" is significant. It indicates that aboriginal rights are not just whatever rights happen to have been held by aboriginal peoples under the law in force in 1982. They are a particular kind of right, identified in a particular sort of way. More importantly, this approach fails to come to terms with the strong case that the words "recognized and affirmed" in section 35(1) have the effect of constituting new legal rights and not merely adopting old ones.

Let me move on now to a second historically-based approach, which has the merit of looking beyond European-derived law for the source of aboriginal rights. It argues that existing aboriginal rights are those rights that were recognized under the customary law and practice of aboriginal peoples and that still survived in some form in 1982. This approach holds more promise for aboriginal language rights for the obvious reason that most aboriginal nations across Canada continued to speak their maternal tongues in 1982. It also gives full meaning to the word "aboriginal" in the phrase "aboriginal rights". But there is a possible deficiency in this approach, which I can refer to only in passing.

---

6. See: Slattery, "The Constitutional Guarantee of Aboriginal and Treaty Rights" (1982-83) 8 *Queen's L.J.* 232; Slattery, "The Hidden Constitution: Aboriginal Rights in Canada" (1984) 32 *Amer. J. Comp. L.* 361

It seems both true and yet misleading to say that under the customary law of an aboriginal group its members had the *right* to speak their own language. For this is like saying that under customary law people had the right to breathe or eat or sing or dance. Such mundane matters did not ordinarily attract much attention at the level of law. They were simply assumed to be the natural ways in which members of the community carried on their lives. The right to speak one's own language, if it could be said to have existed in customary law, would have risen to a conscious level only when it was in some way challenged or threatened, most likely by forces from outside the group.

So aboriginal rights should perhaps be seen as stemming in part from inter-societal contact and conflict than simply from internal custom. Under this view, aboriginal language rights should be located in a body of legal principles governing the relations between indigenous groups and incoming settler groups. In other words, they are bound up with inter-societal norms.

This reflection brings us to the third historically-based approach. This maintains that aboriginal rights, or at least a range of such rights, are the product of customary practices that emerged to regulate the relations between the original nations of America and incoming European nations. This body of custom developed over a long period of time, extending from the first tentative contacts in the sixteenth century to the grand treaty settlements in the nineteenth. It was not exclusively English or French in origin, nor on the other hand was it purely aboriginal. Both aboriginal and settler groups contributed to its formation; so doing, they produced something genuinely new and distinctively Canadian.

This body of inter-societal custom secreted certain basic principles and rules, which in turn reflected certain rights. For example, as I have argued elsewhere, if you look at the period running up to 1763, you find that under the emerging practice of the time aboriginal peoples were considered the effective owners of the lands they possessed, unless or until they voluntarily transferred their title to the Crown by treaty, and that this viewpoint was reflected in the aboriginal Magna Carta, the *Royal Proclamation of 1763*.[7] This rule held true even if (as some have argued) under aboriginal legal systems land could not be owned or transferred, and under English and French legal systems title to land could not be gained simply by possession. This unique body of custom, whose roots lay in inter-societal dealings, passed into an autonomous body of Canadian common law, which is distinct from both English common law and the civil law of Québec, and which underpins the

---

7. See: Slattery, "Understanding Aboriginal Rights" (1987) 66 *Can. Bar Rev.* 727.

Constitution.[8] A view similar to this was first presented by Justice Strong of the Supreme Court of Canada in the last century,[9] but it languished in near oblivion for nearly a hundred years. My reading of the Supreme Court's decisions in the *Guerin*[10] and *Roberts*[11] cases suggests that a version of the argument has now been officially accepted.

Coming now to language rights, can it be said that under inter-societal practice as it developed from 1500 onwards aboriginal languages were accepted in effect as official languages or as languages with a special constitutional status? The current state of my research does not allow for more than a tentative answer. But I would draw attention to the frequent parleys, negotiations, and treaties which took place between first nations and settler communities, and in particular to the ceremonial structure that gave these exchanges shape and meaning. This structure was in large part aboriginal in inspiration, although it also drew on European precedents. It usually involved the formal exchange of greetings, presents, ceremonial belts, statements of grievance or intent, and reciprocal oral promises. The negotiations were conducted in at least two languages and sometimes a number of languages, and so involved interpreters in important roles. Insofar as these exchanges can be seen as the forge of the constitutional structure that eventually bound first nations to the Crown as allied and protected nations, they can plausibly be seen as recognizing that aboriginal languages occupied a special constitutional status, consistent with the unique constitutional position occupied by aboriginal groups. On this view, this special status is now confirmed and guaranteed in section 35(1) of the *Constitution Act, 1982*.

But I am not one of those people who think that we can read history, much less understand it, without a grasp of the human values at stake or a sense of underlying narrative. Much less, then, can we hope to sift through the voluminous records of aboriginal-European relations in search of an historically-based theory of aboriginal language rights without some notion of the basic goods served by language and the principles that should inform relations between different linguistic groups. But if this realization draws us down the path toward the philosopher's den, we should be on guard lest we be devoured at the end of our

---

8. I have developed the general argument for a common law basis to the Constitution in "The Independence of Canada" (1983) 5 *Sup. Ct. L. Rev.* 369.

9. See *St. Catharines Milling and Lumber Co.* v. *The Queen* (1887), 13 S.C.R. 577 at 607-616.

10. [1984] 2 S.C.R. 335, (1984), 13 D.L.R. (4th) 321; discussed in Slattery, *supra*, note 7.

11. [1989] 1 S.C.R. 322, (1989), 57 D.L.R. (4th) 197; discussed in Evans and Slattery, "Comment: Federal Jurisdiction — Pendent Parties — Aboriginal Title and Federal Common Law" (1989) 68 *Can. Bar Rev.* 817.

journey. For I fear that that philosophical reflection pure and simple, apart from an appreciation of historical context, can be misleading and unhelpful. Reflection on basic goods and principles by itself can give us no grasp of the historical realities which must shape all human action. In a word, if history needs philosophy to give it meaning, philosophy needs history to save it from irrelevance. With that thought, I leave you to the tender mercies of the philosophers.

Partie X / Part X
Langue, culture et éducation

Un groupe linguistique est plus qu'un ensemble de personnes identifiables parlant une langue donnée. C'est aussi une collectivité unie par certaines traditions, aspirations et le sens de sa dignité commune. C'est par l'éducation que ses valeurs culturelles se transmettent et se maintiennent de génération en génération.

L'enchâssement constitutionnel de 1982 qui garantit la prestation, sur les fonds publics, de l'instruction en français quand le nombre le justifie, est vu par beaucoup comme le moyen de revitaliser les communautés francophones. Angéline Martel décrit la lutte juridique menée par un groupe de parents albertains. Non seulement ont-ils porté leurs griefs devant les tribunaux, mais ils ont également exercé des pressions politiques — conférences de presse, sondages, lobbying. Les plaignants devaient finalement avoir gain de cause et d'autres communautés ont également réussi à faire valoir leurs droits depuis 1986. Mais Martel craint que les relations sociales ne se réduisent au mode judiciaire et que les minorités ne soient forcées de recourir uniquement aux tribunaux, à l'exclusion de tout autre instrument politique.

Frank MacMahon souligne l'importance de l'éducation pour le développement du milieu culturel de l'enfant. Mais il ne suffit pas d'enseigner le curriculum en français pour transmettre les valeurs fondamentales des communautés francophones et garantir leur survie. MacMahon revendique d'autres institutions sociales, plus symboliques, qui réaffirmeront la légitimité des communautés francophones. Le programme scolaire devrait aussi célébrer les expressions littéraires et artistiques de la culture française.

On présume que la prolifération des programmes d'immersion en langue française permettra l'avènement d'un pays réellement bilingue et qu'elle permettra de sauvegarder le français. Eric Waddell examine la philosophie qui sous-tend l'immersion française et ses résultats pratiques. S'il est vrai que ces programmes forment des élèves capables de parler français, ils ne contribuent pas à augmenter l'effectif des écoles françaises ou à soutenir la culture française. En fait, l'acquisition d'une langue seconde détruit la relation existant entre langue et culture, entre langue et communauté. Ce pourrait être une piètre victoire pour les collectivités francophones isolées dans une marée d'anglophones pratiquant le français langue seconde.

Language, Culture and Education

A language group is more than an assemblage of identifiable language speakers. It is also a community with certain traditions, aspirations, and a sense of common dignity. It is through education that these cultural values are transmitted with the ultimate aim of having them maintained through the generations.

The constitutional entrenchment in 1982 of the right to publicly funded French-language instruction where numbers warrant, has been viewed by many as a means of revitalizing French-language communities. Angeline Martel outlines one such legal challenge by a group of parents in Alberta. The parents' tactics included not only a court challenge, but also political pressure by means of press conferences, polling data, and lobbying. Ultimately, the parents succeeded in court, as have a number of other French-speaking communities since 1986. But Martel sees a danger in the judicialization of our social relations, for minority communities may come to rely solely on courts to the exclusion of other political means.

Frank McMahon underlines the importance that education has for the development of a child's cultural milieu. While a curriculum in the French language imparts fundamental values, and may safeguard survival, of French-speaking communities, language instruction alone is not sufficient. He calls for the appropriation of other, more symbolic, institutions of society so as to reclaim legitimate French-speaking communities. Simultaneously, curriculum should celebrate literary and artistic expressions of French culture.

Presumably, the proliferation of French-language immersion programs across Canada will help foster a truly bilingual country and help sustain the French language. Eric Waddell examines the underlying philosophy and practical results of French immersion instruction. While these programs do create French speakers, they do nothing to add to the declining numbers enrolled in French-language schools. Nor do they sustain French culture. That is, the acquiring of a second language ruptures the relationship between language and culture, between language and community. Ultimately, it may be a hollow victory for embattled Francophone communities in a sea of French-as-a-second-language Anglophones.

PROCESSUS INITIÉ PAR LA PROMULGATION DE L'ARTICLE 23 DE LA CHARTE CANADIENNE DES DROITS ET LIBERTÉS : LES REVENDICATIONS SCOLAIRES DE LA MINORITÉ DE LANGUE OFFICIELLE FRANÇAISE

Angéline Martel

INTRODUCTION

Depuis l'avènement de la *Charte canadienne des droits et libertés* (1982)[1], les contestations judiciaires occupent de plus en plus de place ; la vie professionnelle des juristes et des constitutionnalistes est non seulement inspirée par une nouvelle loi, mais encore, la vie quotidienne du grand public et de ses individus s'en voit modifiée. Que ce soit passivement par l'influence des médias qui font état de contestations judiciaires ou encore activement par l'action professionnelle ou personnelle, les membres de la société canadienne vivent une «judicalisation» des rapports sociaux. Nous nous permettons ce néologisme parce qu'il exprime bien le rôle accru que sont portés à jouer les tribunaux et les lois dans la régie des rapports entre individus, groupes et gouvernements depuis la promulgation d'une constitution canadienne. Par judicalisation[2], nous entendons donc un processus par lequel le domaine juridique et judiciaire vient fonder, motiver et guider les actions entreprises par les individus et les groupes concernés.

Nous documentons ici un aspect particulier du processus de judicalisation des rapports sociaux canadiens tel que nous l'observons depuis 1982 : ceux entre les minorités[3] de langue officielle française, leur

---

1. Partie 1 de la *Loi constitutionnelle de 1982*, constituant l'annexe B de la *Loi de 1982 sur le Canada* (R.-U.), 1982, c. 11.
2. Le phénomène de «judicalisation» est quelque peu analogue à la «médicalisation» des rapports avec notre corps qu'analysait Illich en 1975 dans *Némésis médicale : L'expropriation de la santé* (Paris : Éditions du Seuil, 1975).
3. Dans ce texte, nous désignons la minorité de langue officielle française du Canada comme étant formée de onze minorités provinciales ou territoriales ayant leurs caractéristiques particulières. Nous adoptons donc le terme «les minorités de langue officielle française».

majorité provinciale respective et le gouvernement fédéral. Nous limitons nos propos aux événements entourant l'article 23 de la *Charte des droits et libertés*. L'article 23 est à l'origine d'une nouvelle forme de revendications, celles appuyées par des contestations judiciaires; son implantation illustre notre thèse sur le processus de judicalisation des revendications des minorités eu égard à la problématique de l'éducation. Nous décrivons un cas particulier : celui de l'Association Georges-et-Julia-Bugnet dans l'affaire *Mahé et al.* c. *La Reine* en Alberta. Puisque les revendications de cette association furent les premières à être déposées auprès de la Cour suprême du Canada, elles constituent un précédent historique important pour la minorité de langue officielle française de l'Alberta et pour celle du Canada.

Notre exposé se fera en trois temps. Tout d'abord, nous situons les circonstances entourant la judicalisation des revendications scolaires : nous décrivons donc le contexte légal et démolinguistique influençant l'éducation des minorités de langue française au Canada. Deuxièmement, nous relatons les actions initiées par l'Association Georges-et-Julia-Bugnet pour illustrer l'ampleur des revendications nouvelles basées sur un processus judiciaire. Troisièmement, nous formulons quelques constatations en regard des résultats préliminaires du processus ; nous tirons également quelques conclusions portant sur la judicalisation des revendications des minorités de langue française.

Quant à la méthodologie de cette présentation, nous sommes consciente des dangers qui nous guettent puisque nous avons été intimement liée au sujet de nos propos en initiant et en participant à une contestation judiciaire[4]. Conséquemment, afin de conserver l'objectivité nécessaire, nous adoptons une approche à trois niveaux. Tout d'abord, notre analyse est fondée entièrement sur des documents publics dont des articles de journaux, des lettres et des documents d'archive[5]. Ensuite, nous vérifions les conclusions de nos analyses auprès des écrits d'autres chercheurs-es sur le sujet ; cette procédure nous permet de considérer divers points de vue et d'ainsi rendre plus explicites pour nous-même les hypothèses sous-jacentes à notre expérience. Enfin, l'*épochè* phénoménologique qui veut que la connaissance que l'on a des choses se transforme en « étonnement devant le monde » (Merleau-Ponty, 1945, p. viii) nous est importante ; elle nous permet de prendre un retrait et de réviser descriptions, analyses et conclusions avec un oeil nouveau.

---

4. La cause *Mahé et al.* c. *R.*, (1985) 64 Alta. R. 35 (B.R.) a été portée par trois individus : Jean-Claude Mahé, Angéline Martel et Paul Dubé, et une association : l'Association Georges-et-Julia-Bugnet.
5. Cette documentation est disponible au Musée provincial d'Edmonton, Alberta.

En somme, nous apportons une double perspective au sujet de notre étude : celle de l'intérieur et celle de l'extérieur — à la fois « insider » et « outsider ».

LES CIRCONSTANCES ENTOURANT LA JUDICALISATION DES REVENDICATIONS SCOLAIRES

Dans cette section, nous retraçons les circonstances entourant la judicalisation des revendications des minorités de langue française telle qu'elle fut instituée par la promulgation de l'article 23 de la *Charte*. Nous exposons tout d'abord le contexte légal de l'article 23 : son origine historique, les droits conférés, les bénéficiaires des droits et la source d'appui financier à la contestation judiciaire. Ensuite, nous décrivons le contexte démolinguistique des minorités de langue officielle française du Canada et de l'Alberta au moment de la promulgation de la *Charte* en 1982. Enfin, nous présentons l'intériorisation de ces circonstances propices à la judicalisation des revendications par les membres de l'Association Georges-et-Julia-Bugnet.

1. Le contexte légal

Depuis la promulgation de l'article 23 en 1982, les minorités de langue officielle française et anglaise du Canada se sont effectivement toutes deux prévalues des circonstances légales favorables aux revendications judiciaires. Quoique nos propos ne portent que sur les minorités de langue française, notons toutefois que la minorité d'expression anglaise du Québec s'est également prévalue du système judiciaire pour appuyer ses revendications scolaires. Le jugement de la Cour suprême du Canada en 1984 dans l'affaire *Québec Association of Protestant School Boards* c. *P.G. Québec*[6] a d'ailleurs réaffirmé les objectifs de l'article 23 tels qu'ils furent énoncés par ses rédacteurs.

- *L'origine historique et la confirmation des objectifs de l'article 23*

L'article 23 de la *Charte des droits et libertés* est l'aboutissement d'un processus historique qui en marqua la formulation, l'esprit et l'intention. Par une brève description de l'origine de cet article, nous indiquons les objectifs visés et démontrons les intentions qui en ont guidé l'élaboration. En général, cette période historique qui précède l'enchâssement dans la constitution des droits à l'instruction pour les minorités de langue officielle est une période de négociations entre les gouvernements fédéral et provinciaux.

---

6. Pour une liste complète des jugements relatifs à l'article 23, voir la liste en appendice.

Pour la première fois, les besoins éducationnels des minorités de langue officielle font partie des débats publics dans le rapport sur l'éducation de la Commission royale d'enquête sur le bilinguisme et le biculturalisme en 1968. Dans ce rapport, la commission, bien connue sous le nom de la Commission Laurendeau-Dunton, accorde à l'école de la minorité un double objectif : (1) celui de permettre l'acquisition de la langue comme moyen de communication efficace et (2) celui d'assurer la continuité du groupe en fournissant un milieu de promotion sociale et culturelle aux minorités de langue officielle (1968, p. 8). Ces deux objectifs sont au coeur de l'histoire de l'article 23 de la *Charte* et serviront de leitmotiv aux discussions subséquentes.

Lors de la Conférence constitutionnelle de 1971 et suite aux recommandations de la Commission Laurendeau-Dunton, les premiers ministres provinciaux consentent à enchâsser le droit des minorités de langue officielle de recevoir un enseignement « principalement » dans leur langue. Cet enseignement serait financé par les fonds publics dans des régions bilingues[7]. Ce consentement constitue l'embryon de l'article 23 de la *Charte*. Plus tard, à la 18e Conférence des premiers ministres provinciaux à St. Andrews (1977), ce désir fut réaffirmé. La position officielle des premiers ministres était alors :

> Conscients de l'importance d'assurer le maintien et, au besoin, l'essor des droits linguistiques minoritaires au Canada ; et
>
> Conscients que l'éducation est la base même de la langue et de la culture ;
>
> Les premiers ministres conviennent qu'ils feront tout leur possible pour offrir l'enseignement en français et en anglais, sous réserve que le nombre le justifie. (*Déclaration sur la langue*)

Ces paroles démontrent l'*intention* des gouvernements provinciaux et fédéral de fournir aux minorités de langue officielle des droits éducationnels *équivalents* à ceux dont jouit la majorité[8].

La Conférence des premiers ministres provinciaux de 1978 reconnaît à nouveau que l'éducation constitue la base sur laquelle reposent langue et culture ; ils affirment encore que *chaque enfant* des minorités de langue officielle a droit à l'enseignement dans des écoles primaires et secondaires partout où le nombre le justifie.

---

7. Une région bilingue est une région dont une majorité de résidents-es en auraient choisi le statut et dont le nombre est suffisant pour justifier les établissements nécessaires.
8. Cette interprétation est confirmée en 1988 par le juge Wimmer de la Saskatchewan dans le jugement sur l'affaire *Commission des écoles fransaskoises et al.* c. *P.G. Saskatchewan*, [1988] 3 W.W.R. 354 (B.R.).

La même année, le gouvernement fédéral propose le projet de loi C-60 et publie le document *Le temps d'agir*. La protection des minorités linguistiques française et anglaise et le droit à l'éducation là où le nombre le justifie sont toujours au coeur des débats. Prime également le contexte de l'unité nationale ; il est clairement énoncé que cette unité n'est possible que dans le respect de la diversité et de l'égalité linguistique des minorités de langue officielle (Kerr, 1983).

Ces événements explicitent un processus menant à la reconnaissance des droits éducatifs des minorités de langue officielle. En 1982, cette reconnaissance par l'article 23 avait donc antérieurement fait l'objet de diverses interventions de la part des gouvernements fédéral et provinciaux ; l'article 23 repose alors sur trois objectifs principaux : (1) l'unité nationale par (2) un système éducatif semblable pour les minorités francophone et anglophone afin de permettre (3) leur épanouissement linguistique et culturel. Au Comité mixte spécial sur la Constitution, le ministre de la Justice d'alors dit :

> ... c'est que nous voulons, une fois pour toutes protéger les droits à l'éducation des Francophones hors Québec.[9]

> C'est cela qui est l'initiative et ce que nous recherchons, c'est de donner aux Francophones hors Québec à peu près l'équivalent de ce que les Anglophones ont ou avaient au Québec autrefois.

En 1982, les jeux sont faits : les gouvernements provinciaux et fédéral procèdent à la reconnaissance officielle des droits éducatifs des minorités de langue officielle dans la nouvelle constitution. D'une part, les tribunaux peuvent entrer en scène et arbitrer la reconnaissance ou la non-reconnaissance de ces droits. D'autre part, les minorités reçoivent une arme de taille, une épée de Damoclès, qui peut servir devant les tribunaux ou encore qui peut être étalée comme preuve de la validité de leurs revendications. De plus, les objectifs que visent l'article 23 sont explicites pour les minorités et pour les gouvernements.

---

9. Alors que le ministre de la Justice proclame l'intention de protéger les minorités de langue française du Canada, les ressemblances entre l'article 23 de la *Charte* et la section VIII aux articles 72 et 73 de la *Loi 101* du Québec prouvent également que le sort de la minorité de langue anglaise du Québec et son accès au libre choix de la langue d'enseignement sont également au coeur des objectifs : J.P. Proulx, « Les normes périjuridiques dans l'idéologie québécoise et canadienne en matière de langue d'enseignement », (1988) 19 *R.G.D.* 209. Le Québec est d'ailleurs la seule province qui, en 1982, établit des critères d'éligibilité à l'instruction dans la langue de la minorité ; certaines provinces dont Terre-Neuve, la Colombie-Britannique n'ont alors aucune législation sur la langue d'instruction : A. Monnin, « L'égalité juridique des langues et l'enseignement : les écoles françaises hors Québec », (1983) 24(1) *C. de D.* 157. Notons que l'article 23 (1) a) ne s'applique pas encore au Québec qui y est soustrait par les dispositions de l'article 59 de la *Charte*.

Les jugements émis depuis l'avènement de la *Charte* sont d'ailleurs venus renforcer et préciser les objectifs initiaux de l'article 23[10]. En effet, tout en reprenant l'objectif principal d'épanouissement des minorités de langue officielle, deux précisions sont apportées. La première est que l'article 23 doit créer un régime uniforme pour permettre l'épanouissement des minorités officielles d'un bout à l'autre du pays. Cet objectif affecte la juridiction provinciale exclusive en matière d'éducation et donc est assez difficile à mettre en oeuvre. D'autre part, les mesures découlant de l'article 23 doivent remédier à une situation historique ayant causé l'assimilation des minorités. En 1984, la Cour suprême du Canada édicte,

> ... le constituant a manifestement jugé déficients certains des régimes en vigueur au moment où il légiférait, et peut-être même chacun de ces régimes, et il a voulu remédier à ce qu'il considérait comme leurs défauts par des mesures réparatrices uniformes, celles de l'article 23 de la Charte, auxquelles il conférait en même temps le caractère d'une garantie constitutionnelle. (*Quebec Association of Protestant School Boards* c. *P.-G. du Québec*, 1984, p. 79-80)

L'article 23 vient donc, non seulement conférer des droits aux minorités en visant leur épanouissement mais il rappelle également que ces minorités, surtout la minorité francophone, ont subi le poids d'une situation historique à laquelle il faut remédier.

Depuis l'avènement de la *Charte des droits et libertés*, le Gouvernement du Canada a, en quelque sorte, consolidé les dispositions de l'article 23 dans la *Loi sur les langues officielles* entrée en vigueur le 15 septembre 1988 en prenant l'engagement, aux termes de l'article 41, de promouvoir la langue des minorités de langue officielle et l'épanouissement de leurs communautés[11]. De plus, l'article 42 vient entériner cette orientation en donnant au secrétaire d'État du Canada le droit de prendre les mesures estimées nécessaires pour «favoriser la progression vers l'égalité de statut et d'usage du français et de l'anglais dans la société canadienne». Parmi ces mesures, nous retrouvons l'encouragement aux gouvernements provinciaux visant à permettre aux minorités de recevoir l'instruction dans leur propre langue :

> 42. d) ... encourager et aider les gouvernements provinciaux à favoriser le développement des minorités francophones et anglophones, et

---

10. Pour une étude détaillée des interprétations subséquemment données par les tribunaux, voir notre étude *Les droits scolaires des minorités de langue officielle au Canada : De l'instruction à la gestion*, 1990 [non publiée].
11. L'article 41 de la *Loi sur les langues officielles*, S.C. 1988, c. 38, débute ainsi : «Le gouvernement fédéral s'engage à favoriser l'épanouissement des minorités francophones et anglophones du Canada et à appuyer leur développement, ainsi qu'à promouvoir la pleine reconnaissance et l'usage du français et de l'anglais dans la société canadienne. »

notamment à leur offrir des services provinciaux et municipaux en français et en anglais et à leur permettre de recevoir leur instruction dans leur propre langue.

Ces dispositions qui entourent la promotion et la survie des minorités de langue officielle viennent donc régir à nouveau par la loi les rapports qu'entretiennent trois groupes : les minorités, les gouvernements provinciaux et le gouvernement fédéral.

Ce bref historique a servi a démontrer le climat politico-juridique qui a entouré la promulgation de l'article 23 de la *Charte*. Il a rappelé que les objectifs élaborés en 1982 quant à l'instruction des minorités de langue officielle ont été confirmés par les jugements entre 1982 et 1989 et par la nouvelle *Loi sur les langues officielles*. Le processus de judicalisation des revendications, virtuellement enclenché par la promulgation de l'article 23, est actualisé dans les demandes des minorités après 1982.

- *Les droits conférés*

L'article 23 s'intitule « Droits à l'instruction dans la langue de la minorité ». Le titre anglais, pour sa part, reflète un objectif éducatif plus général et vient compléter et élargir, comme il est acquis en jurisprudence, le sens du terme dans l'autre langue officielle : « Minority Language Educational Rights ». Le mot « education » est plus global qu'instruction ; il signifie un ensemble de services à la minorité : (1) ceux de l'instruction, (2) ceux des écoles homogènes et (3) ceux de la gestion de cette instruction et de ces écoles.

Le droit à l'instruction dans la langue de la minorité est défini aux paragraphes 23 (1) et 23 (2) en général, et à l'alinéa 23 (3) a) en particulier où il nomme : « Le droit reconnu aux citoyens canadiens par les paragraphes (1) et (2) de faire instruire leurs enfants, aux niveaux primaire et secondaire, dans la langue de la minorité ... ». Pour expliquer la signification de ce droit, nous retrouvons plus loin dans le texte les mots suivants : « instruction », « faire instruire » et « enseignement ». En anglais, les mots « instruction » et « educational » sont employés. Cette instruction doit être « financée sur les fonds publics » (paragraphe 23 (3)). L'instruction visée par l'article 23 est donc d'ordre public et les écoles privées sont exclues lorsqu'elles ne sont pas pleinement subventionnées.

D'autre part, les termes « établissements d'enseignement de la minorité linguistique » apparaissent à l'alinéa (3) b) de l'article 23. Le sens du mot « établissement » a fait couler beaucoup d'encre parce qu'il dénomme un double champ d'application et donc un double droit. En effet, son interprétation recoupe généralement deux aspects de l'éducation : le premier concerne les établissements physiques (« physical facilities ») communément appelés les « écoles homogènes ». Le second se rapporte au droit de gestion scolaire. L'étendue de ces droits sera déterminée par les tribunaux.

C'est ainsi qu'en 1982, les minorités de langue officielle peuvent prendre conscience que des droits leur ont été conférés et qu'elles pourront potentiellement en soumettre la requête aux tribunaux. L'octroi de droits est la pierre angulaire d'un processus de judicalisation des revendications scolaires.

- Les bénéficiaires des droits conférés par l'article 23

L'influence d'un processus judiciaire entre principalement dans la vie des catégories de personnes auxquelles des droits sont conférés. Puisqu'il vise un objectif particulier que nous avons précédemment décrit, à savoir l'épanouissement des communautés des minorités de langue officielle, l'article 23 identifie clairement au paragraphe (1), alinéas a) et b) et au paragraphe (2) les catégories de personnes auxquelles il accorde les droits à l'instruction, à des écoles et à la gestion.

Pour être éligible aux droits conférés par l'article 23, il faut tout d'abord répondre *obligatoirement* à trois critères généraux : (1) citoyenneté canadienne, (2) résidence dans une province canadienne où la langue est celle de la minorité (anglais au Québec, français à l'extérieur du Québec), et (3) parent d'enfant(s) du primaire ou du secondaire. L'éligibilité est alors conférée si le parent répond ensuite à *l'un* des trois critères linguistiques identifiés : (1) la première langue apprise et encore comprise, (2) la langue d'instruction primaire, ou (3) la langue d'instruction d'un autre enfant de la famille est celle de la minorité. Le Tableau 1 résume ces critères.

TABLEAU 1

Bénéficiaires des droits conférés par l'article 23 de la *Charte*

Critère	Référence
Critères généraux (obligatoires)	
1. Citoyens-nés du Canada,	article 23 (1)
2. Résidant dans une province canadienne où la langue est celle de la minorité,	article 23
3. Parent	article 23(1)

Critères linguistiques (répondre à un seul critère suffit)

    1. Première langue apprise et encore comprise
       par le parent,   article 23 (1)a)

ou 2. Langue d'instruction primaire du parent,   article 23 (1)b)

ou 3. Langue d'instruction d'un frère ou d'une
       soeur   article 23 (2)

- *Le Programme de contestation judiciaire*

La loi entérine des droits pour des catégories précises d'individus ou de groupes et les tribunaux précisent la portée de ces droits. Cependant, pour poser un troisième jalon à la judicalisation des revendications des minorités, les moyens financiers de se prévaloir des droits conférés doivent être fournis aux bénéficiaires. Le choix de se prévaloir du système judiciaire pour revendiquer le respect de ses droits dépend tout d'abord de la disponibilité d'un financement adéquat. En effet, les individus ou même les groupes subventionnés disposent rarement de fonds leur permettant d'entamer le processus fort coûteux des revendications judiciaires. C'est ainsi qu'entre en jeu un programme du gouvernement fédéral destiné à promouvoir le respect et la reconnaissance des droits conférés par la loi : le Programme de contestation judicaire.

Historiquement, suite à la cause de Monsieur Georges Forest au Manitoba, le gouvernement fédéral donne naissance à un Programme de contestation judiciaire en février 1978. C'était la réponse à une inquiétude du gouvernement fédéral face à l'érosion possible de certains droits garantis aux minorités par la constitution du Canada (Conseil, 1989). Le programme, mis à jour lors de l'entrée en vigueur de la *Charte* et administré par le Conseil canadien de développement social depuis 1985, démontre l'intérêt que suscitent les contestations judiciaires pour l'obtention de services éducatifs chez les minorités de langue officielle. En effet, les minorités se sont prévalues de cette source de financement pour porter devant les tribunaux leurs requêtes reposant sur l'article 23. Entre 1982 et 1989, ce programme a subventionné onze interventions ayant reçu des jugements dont six jugements de cours de première instance, deux renvois constitutionnels, trois de cours d'appel provinciales et un jugement de la Cour suprême du Canada (Tableau 2).

TABLEAU 2

Résumé chronologique des jugements sur l'article 23 de la Charte, par province

	1982	1983	1984	1985	1986	1987	1988	1989
C.B.						Whittington : Cour supérieure de la C.B.		
ALTA				Mahé : Cour du banc de la reine		Mahé : Cour d'appel		
SASK.							Commission des écoles fransaskoises : Cour du banc de la reine	
MAN.								
ONT.			Renvoi : Cour d'appel		Marchand : Cour suprême de l'Ontario (4 jugements)			
QUÉ.	QAPSB : Cour supérieure		QAPSB : Cour suprême du Canada					
N.-B.		SANB : Cour du banc de la reine						
Î.-P.-É.							Renvoi : Cour d'appel	
N.-É.						Lavoie : Cour suprême de la N.-É. (4 jugements)		Lavoie : Cour d'appel de la N.-É.
T.-N.								

La disponibilité de fonds a joué un rôle majeur dans la judicalisation des revendications scolaires des minorités. En effet, l'enchâssement de droits dans la constitution aurait pu offrir une coquille vide sans l'accès à des fonds publics pour faire reconnaître la portée des droits et en dicter l'implantation. Le Programme de contestation judiciaire a permis aux principaux intéressés, les bénéficiaires, d'entrer en scène et de se prévaloir des droits enchâssés.

Le processus de judicalisation que nous décrivons prend donc ses origines dans la promulgation de droits par l'article 23 de la *Charte* à des individus appartenant aux minorités de langue officielle. Nous avons décrit l'origine, les objectifs et la nature des droits conférés par cet article ; nous avons ensuite énuméré les critères d'éligibilité qui en définissent les bénéficiaires. Enfin, nous avons signalé la disponibilité de fonds auprès du Programme de contestation judiciaire ; ces fonds permettent la revendication des droits auprès des tribunaux. Ce sont là autant de circonstances qui favorisent l'avènement du processus judiciaire dans les revendications des minorités. Au contexte légal que nous venons d'exposer, nous ajoutons maintenant la situation démolinguistique des minorités de langue officielle française.

2. Le contexte démolinguistique des revendications scolaires

Historiquement, l'entrée du processus judiciaire dans les revendications des minorités de langue officielle française venait fournir un nouveau champ d'actions à des minorités en perte de vitesse. En 1982, la situation démolinguistique n'était pas très encourageante pour ces minorités qui revendiquaient depuis longtemps et de façons variées des moyens d'assurer leur survie.

- La situation des minorités de langue officielle française en 1981 au Canada

Selon Statistique Canada, entre 1971 et 1981, la population minoritaire de langue maternelle française avait peu augmenté en comparaison à la population totale du Canada qui, elle, avait augmenté de 12,9 pour cent (de 21 568 310 à 24 343 180 personnes). Pour leur part, les minorités francophones avaient augmenté de 1,7 pour cent (de 926 400 à 942 085 personnes) en dix ans (Statistique Canada).

Au chapitre de l'instruction dans la langue de la minorité, les données de Statistique Canada (1989) démontrent une situation encore plus inquiétante que celle de la population minoritaire totale. Le Tableau 3 en fait état pour les écoles élémentaires et secondaires financées par les fonds publics du pays. En 1971, quatre provinces et territoires (la Colombie-Britannique, l'Alberta, les Territoires du Nord-Ouest et le Yukon) ne dispensaient pas ou peu d'instruction à leur minorité de langue française. Entre 1971 et 1982, les programmes d'immersion, alors en grande croissance, dispensaient l'enseignement à la minorité francophone et à la majorité dans trois provinces ; en effet, la Colombie-Britannique, l'Alberta et la Saskatchewan ne distinguaient pas entre ces deux clientèles pendant presque une décennie. En 1981, l'Alberta demeure la seule province à ne pas faire cette distinction.

En général, alors que les effectifs scolaires des provinces anglophones canadiennes, à l'exception de l'Alberta et des deux territoires, sont en chute de 9,7 pour cent, les effectifs dans les classes et écoles dispensant l'enseignement dans la langue de la minorité française diminuent à un rythme doublement rapide (19,6 pour cent en moyenne). C'est d'ailleurs grâce à la décroissance moins rapide en Ontario, (18,4 pour cent) et au Nouveau-Brunswick (19,9 pour cent), provinces qui comptent les plus

grands effectifs, que cette moyenne se situe sous la marque de 20 pour
cent. En effet, cette décroissance est supérieure à 30 pour cent dans
trois provinces : le Manitoba, l'Île-du-Prince-Édouard et Terre-Neuve/
Labrador. Nous constatons donc qu'en 1982, la situation éducative des
minorités de langue française est loin d'être florissante.

TABLEAU 3

**Comparaison des effectifs scolaires provinciaux et territoriaux*, et effec-
tifs dans les programmes de la langue des minorités françaises, 1970-71
et 1981-82**

Effectifs	Provinciaux 1971	Dans la langue de minorité 1971	Provinciaux 1982	Entre 1971/ 1982	Minorité 1982	Change- ment entre 1971/1982
C.B.	526 991	**	503 371	-4,5 %	785	
ALTA	425 987	**	442 176	+3,8 %	**	
SASK.	247 332	765	202 094	-18,3 %	1 403	
MAN.	246 946	10 405	200 619	-18,8 %	6 411	-38,4 %
ONT.	2 022 401	115 869	1 802 487	-10,9 %	94 557	-18,4 %
N.-B.	175 912	60 679	149 417	-15,1 %	48 614	-19,9 %
N.-É.	214 897	7 388	181 758	-15,4 %	5 308	-28,2 %
Î.-P.-É.	30 622	796	26 184	-14,5 %	529	-33,6 %
T.-N./ LAB.	160 915	185	145 185	-9,8 %	127	-31,4 %
T.-N.-O.	10 006	0	12 581	+25,7 %	0	
YUKON	4 634	0	5 121	+10,6 %	0	
TOTAL	4 066 643	196 087	3 670 993	-9,7 %	157 734	-19,6 %

Source : Statistique Canada. 1989. *Langue de la minorité et langue seconde dans
l'enseignement, niveaux élémentaire et secondaire.* Tableau 8.

* : Les données sont fournies pour les écoles et les programmes subventionnés
   entièrement par les fonds publics au sein d'écoles dites « publiques ».
** : Données non disponibles ; les ministères de l'Éducation ne compilaient pas
   ces données.

- *La situation de la minorité de langue française en Alberta en 1981*

Puisque notre propos touchera plus particulièrement la minorité de langue française en Alberta, nous donnons ici un bref aperçu démolinguistique de sa situation en 1981, date du recensement et aube de la promulgation de l'article 23 de la *Charte*.

En 1981, une forte vague d'immigration de francophones, venues surtout du Québec et du Nouveau-Brunswick, avait renforcé les rangs de la minorité officielle à 62 145 personnes alors en hausse de 17 705 personnes (40 pour cent) depuis 1976.

Depuis 1968, l'instruction en français était autorisée pour toute la journée scolaire sauf exception d'une heure obligatoire d'anglais en première et en deuxième années. De la troisième à la neuvième années, l'enseignement en français était autorisé pour 50 pour cent de la journée scolaire. En 1981, ces modalités prévalaient pour les écoles dites «bilingues»[12] et pour les écoles d'immersion qui accueillaient quelque 12 802 élèves. Le gouvernement albertain, ne faisant pas la distinction entre langue maternelle (de la minorité) et langue seconde (immersion), il était impossible d'estimer le nombre de ces élèves appartenant à la minorité française.

Autre fait permettant de bien cerner l'importance accordée par le gouvernement albertain aux services éducatifs de la minorité francophone, toutes les langues autres que l'anglais avaient été placées sur un pied d'égalité; l'instruction en avait été permise jusqu'à la douzième année en 1971. En 1978, le Language Services Branch avait été établi au ministère de l'Éducation afin d'appuyer les programmes de langues secondes: français, anglais, allemand, ukrainien. C'est donc dire que la minorité française ne recevait pas de traitement distinct de celui accordé à toutes les minorités ethniques.

Par ailleurs, comme le démontrent les journaux d'alors regroupés dans le *Dossier de presse I*, les organismes francophones oeuvraient à obtenir des écoles bilingues ou d'immersion et à faciliter le transport des élèves de la minorité à ces mêmes écoles[13]. Les organismes francophones, comme le gouvernement albertain, n'avaient pas encore pris adéquatement conscience des événements nationaux qui avaient mené à la promulgation des droits éducatifs de l'article 23 sur l'instruction, les écoles homogènes et la gestion.

---

12. Ce sont des écoles qui conservaient de fortes proportions d'étudiants-es francophones qui étudiaient dans la même école avec des groupes anglophones. Les programmes d'études étaient ceux de l'immersion.

13. Voir à ce sujet le rapport annuel de 1981 de l'Association canadienne française de l'Alberta dans *Le Franco* (novembre 1981).

3. Les francophones de l'Alberta et les droits conférés par l'article 23

La situation démolinguistique des minorités de langue française en 1981 au Canada et en Alberta est vécue quotidiennement par les membres de la communauté minoritaire, surtout par les parents. C'est ce vécu quotidien qui peut inciter les principaux intéressés à se prévaloir des dispositions légales de la *Charte*.

En 1982, un groupe de parents d'Edmonton s'est réuni pour faire le point sur la conjoncture de cette époque : (1) l'entrée en vigueur de l'article 23 et de la *Charte*, (2) l'inexistence de services éducatifs adéquats pour dispenser l'instruction aux jeunes franco-albertains-es, (3) l'apathie ou l'étapisme endémique des organismes minoritaires et (4) la faible importance accordée par le gouvernement albertain aux services éducatifs distincts pour la minorité francophone. Ce groupe de parents a subséquemment pris avantage de la proclamation des droits éducatifs conférés par l'article 23 ; il en a assumé la revendication auprès des tribunaux et des autorités compétentes.

Les parents réunis se sont d'abord donné une structure officielle viable ; l'Association Georges-et-Julia-Bugnet est née. Il s'agit d'une société incorporée depuis 1983, régie par la « Societies Act » de l'Alberta sous l'égide du ministère des « Consumer and Corporate Affairs ». Elle est composée de neuf membres formant son conseil d'administration. Les membres sont choisis par le conseil selon des critères de représentativité (géographique et sociale) et de dévouement à la cause de l'avancement de l'éducation française. La structure simple et restreinte de l'Association Bugnet lui a permis de réagir rapidement aux événements, d'être en contact direct avec les parents et de travailler de façon efficace et convaincue. L'Association Bugnet s'est également donné un nom symbolique, celui d'un couple de pionniers ayant immigré en Alberta en 1904. Monsieur Bugnet est bien connu comme romancier, poète, commissaire d'école et horticulteur.

En 1983, lors de sa fondation officielle et encore aujourd'hui, les buts de l'Association sont définis dans sa constitution : (1) promouvoir l'épanouissement des valeurs éducatives, politiques et culturelles des parents francophones en Alberta, (2) voir à la formation d'un système d'écoles françaises et (3) réclamer la gestion des écoles françaises. Ces buts sont directement inspirés des droits conférés par l'article 23 de la *Charte*.

Pourtant, ces buts n'ont pas la même signification pour les parents que pour les juristes. En effet, ce que revendiquent les parents, c'est en réalité une éducation *totale de qualité en français* pour leurs enfants. C'est d'ailleurs le thème principal de la publicité de l'Association Bugnet.

L'avenir de jeunes enfants motive les parents à l'action. Les besoins ressentis sont donc plus immédiats et plus urgents que pour les gouvernements ou encore pour les associations officielles francophones. L'assimilation linguistique et culturelle des enfants est observée et vécue quotidiennement. La création d'une ambiance de communication et de compréhension avec les enfants est alors détruite par l'érosion de la langue et de la culture familiale d'origine. Enfin, la restitution d'une justice sociale en permettant aux enfants de la minorité de langue française d'accéder, à part égale avec ceux de la majorité, à ce que nous pourrions appeler «une qualité de vie», est une préoccupation des parents. Ce sont là les motifs qui incitèrent une association composée de parents, l'Association Bugnet, à initier une série d'interventions communautaires appuyées par le processus judiciaire. Nous décrivons ces interventions dans la section suivante.

LES REVENDICATIONS NOUVELLES : EXEMPLE D'UN PROCESSUS EN ALBERTA

Les revendications de l'Association Bugnet s'appuyent directement sur l'article 23 en demandant :

- l'établissement d'écoles homogènes gérées par la minorité ;

- la reconnaissance par le gouvernement albertain des droits conférés par l'article 23 ;

- l'interprétation publique de ces droits afin que tous et toutes en comprennent la portée et l'ampleur.

Ces revendications visent cinq champs particuliers : (1) une contestation judiciaire, (2) des requêtes auprès des diverses instances, (3) une campagne d'information, (4) des recherches et (5) une mise en oeuvre directe par l'ouverture d'une première école française, l'école Georges-et-Julia-Bugnet.

1. Les étapes de la contestation judiciaire dans la cause Mahé et al. c. La Reine de l'Alberta

- La Cour du banc de la reine

En octobre 1983, une requête est déposée auprès de la Cour de première instance, la Cour du banc de la reine de l'Alberta. Pour l'essentiel, elle réclame du gouvernement albertain la reconnaissance du droit à l'instruction dans des établissements (écoles) de la minorité, de la gestion de ces établissements et de l'accès aux fonds publics pour un système d'éducation en français. C'est lors de l'interrogatoire préalable de mars 1984 que le gouvernement albertain prit amplement connaissance de ces questions. Un an plus tard, lors du troisième anniversaire de la promulgation de la *Charte* (du 13 au 17 avril 1985), l'Association Bugnet présente ses arguments au juge Purvis. Les manchettes des journaux[14] font état de cet événement en ces mots :

Language rights to face new test (*The Globe and Mail*, 4 avril 1985);

French schools case tests charter's equal-right section (*Edmonton Journal*, 6 avril 1985);

Des francophones de l'Alberta réclament la reconnaissance de leurs droits scolaires (*Le Devoir*, 11 avril 1985);

Insidious lessons (assimilation) criticized (*Edmonton Journal*, 18 avril 1985);

Le gouvernement albertain soutient pouvoir déléguer ses responsabilités constitutionnelles aux commissions scolaires (*Le Franco*, 17 avril 1985);

Le procès Bugnet aura été le procès de l'assimilation (*Le Franco*, 24 avril 1985);

Ignore Ontario language ruling, court urged (*The Globe and Mail*, 20 avril 1985).

Le gouvernement albertain croit que les revendications légales de l'Association Bugnet sont un coup d'épée dans l'eau (*Le Franco*, 17 avril 1985) et qu'elles n'apporteront rien à la minorité de langue française.

Pourtant, le jugement rendu le 25 juillet 1985 reconnaît le droit de la minorité à l'instruction dans des écoles homogènes et à un degré exclusif de contrôle de ses écoles. Selon les médias, c'est la victoire. Les manchettes le disent en ces mots :

Francophones win Alberta case (*Winnipeg Free Press*, 25 juillet 1985);

Judge rules in favor of French-speaking parents: School Act violates rights (*Edmonton Sun*, 25 juillet 1985);

French schools: a matter of rights (The *Edmonton Journal*, 26 juillet 1985);

Speedy action wanted on French education (The *Edmonton Journal*, 26 juillet 1985);

La loi viole la *Charte* des droits: Les francophones de l'Alberta ont droit au contrôle de leurs écoles (*Le Devoir*, 26 juillet 1985);

14. Nous employons ici les manchettes de journaux pour démontrer l'interprétation publique et médiatique accordée aux événements mentionnés. Nous invitons le lecteur ou la lectrice à prendre connaissance des articles compilés dans les Dossiers de presse.

Alliance hails Alberta French-rights ruling (*The Gazette*, 26 juillet 1985);

French schools required in Alberta (*The Globe and Mail*, 26 juillet 1985);

À l'ouest: le gain des francophones (*La Presse*, 27 juillet 1985);

La loi scolaire albertaine viole la *Charte* des droits: Les francophones de l'Alberta ont droit au contrôle de leurs écoles (*Le Franco*, 31 juillet 1985);

Décision Bugnet: Les droits sont rétablis (*Le Franco*, 31 juillet 1985).

Cependant, suite à des négociations avec le gouvernement albertain, l'intention de ce dernier semble claire: il n'entend pas légiférer pour reconnaître les droits acquis par la cour. En effet, dans un communiqué de presse du 27 juillet, le ministre de l'Éducation confirme que le gouvernement albertain n'entend pas légiférer quant à la gestion scolaire (*Le Devoir*, 1 août 1985).

- La Cour d'appel

Suite à ces événements, le 20 août 1985, l'Association Bugnet porte le jugement en appel tout en laissant la porte ouverte aux négociations:

French group pursues pledge on education (*Edmonton Journal*, 2 août 1985);

Le groupe Bugnet porte la décision Purvis en appel (*Le Franco*, 28 août 1985);

French group back to court on education (*Edmonton Journal*, 27 août 1985).

Les audiences de la Cour d'appel ont lieu un an plus tard, les 23 au 26 septembre 1986, avec l'appui de sept organismes provinciaux ou nationaux dont: le Commissariat aux langues officielles, le Gouvernement du Canada, Alliance Québec, l'Association canadienne-française de l'Alberta (ACFA), la Commission nationale des parents francophones (CNPF), la Fédération des francophones hors-Québec (FFHQ) et la Société des parents francophones d'Edmonton.

Le jugement rendu le 25 août 1987 s'avère une nouvelle victoire:

Une autre manche victorieuse, l'étape ultime: la Cour suprême (*Le Franco*, 4 septembre 1987);

Les Franco-Albertains auraient le droit de gérer leurs écoles (*Le Devoir*, 18 septembre 1987).

Mais, les trois juges de la Cour d'appel, par la plume du juge Kerans, interprètent la limite «du nombre suffisant» comme étant le nombre d'enfants alors inscrits à l'école Maurice Lavallée d'Edmonton, alors école mixte francophone et d'immersion. Par cette logique, ils estiment donc le nombre d'enfants insuffisant pour exiger l'établissement d'un système d'éducation comparable à celui de la majorité. La contestation judiciaire devait donc continuer.

- La Cour suprême du Canada

Une nouvelle étape est en voie de réalisation. Le 7 décembre 1987, la Cour suprême du Canada accepte d'entendre l'appel de la décision de la Cour d'appel de l'Alberta. Les audiences ont lieu le 14 juin 1989.

Les jeux sont faits : d'une part, l'Association Bugnet, d'autre part le gouvernement de l'Alberta. Entre les deux, les 13 parties intervenantes :

- les organismes fédéraux : le Commissariat aux langues officielles et le gouvernement du Canada ;

- les gouvernements provinciaux : le Nouveau-Brunswick, le Québec, la Saskatchewan, le Manitoba ;

- les associations minoritaires : Alliance Québec, l'Association canadienne française de l'Ontario, l'Association canadienne française de l'Alberta ;

- les associations professionnelles : l'Association française des conseils scolaires de l'Ontario, l'Association des enseignantes et des enseignants franco-ontariens, le Québec Association of Protestant School Boards, l'Alberta School Trustees' Association, l'Edmonton Catholic School Board.

Le résultat ? Le jugement de cette cour n'est pas encore rendu mais nous savons qu'antérieurement, dans le cas de la minorité de langue anglaise du Québec, la Cour suprême a tranché en faveur de cette minorité. Les chances sont donc bonnes qu'elle récidive dans le cas de la minorité de langue officielle française (infirmé par (1990) 68 D.L.R. (4th) 69 (S.C.C.)).

Pour l'essentiel, le processus de contestation judiciaire de l'Association Bugnet oblige la reconnaissance par les tribunaux et la mise en application par le gouvernement albertain des droits conférés par l'article 23 de la *Charte*. Jusqu'en 1989, ce processus a été favorable à la minorité de langue française de l'Alberta. Toutefois, les avantages de la contestation judiciaire pour la minorité francophone ne sont pas limités à ce domaine ; une contestation judiciaire justifie et rend crédibles les revendications menées sur d'autres plans.

2. Les requêtes

Une contestation judiciaire n'est donc jamais limitée au processus judiciaire. Elle fait également partie d'une panoplie d'actions et de réflexions qui touchent la communauté minoritaire tout entière. Nous documentons maintenant ce volet de la judicalisation des revendications puisque forts-es des droits conférés, une mise en oeuvre peut en être réclamée. Les membres de l'Association Bugnet se sont tournés vers les instances susceptibles d'entendre et d'accorder leurs requêtes que nous regroupons en trois catégories : (1) les demandes de services éducatifs, (2) les demandes de financement et (3) celles de soutien à la cause de l'éducation française en Alberta.

- Demandes d'une école française

En 1981, la *demande d'une école française* est présentée aux associations francophones qui oeuvraient traditionnellement en éducation (*Le Franco*, 1 décembre 1982). La demande portait sur l'élaboration de stratégies pour établir des écoles françaises en Alberta, prioritairement dans la capitale provinciale d'Edmonton qui regroupait alors 17 000 francophones. Le journal hebdomadaire de l'Alberta publie :

> L'ACFA s'impliquera-t-elle ? (*Le Franco*, 15 décembre 1982).

À cette époque, les membres de l'Association Bugnet n'entrevoyaient nullement la nécessité de mener eux-elles-mêmes les revendications : tout au plus croyaient-ils-elles nécessaire de faire connaître les besoins des parents aux organismes porteurs des dossiers sur l'éducation. Cependant, devant l'inertie des associations francophones, l'Association Bugnet doit agir :

> À Edmonton, l'école française : les parents agissent (*Le Franco*, 1 décembre 1982).

En effet, ces associations francophones n'avaient pas encore pris conscience de l'importance des droits conférés par l'article 23 de la *Charte*. En décembre 1982, *Le Franco* relate donc les refus essuyés par les parents. Les associations minoritaires prônent l'étapisme et craignent de revendiquer ouvertement des écoles françaises. La demande d'écoles françaises est donc portée directement par les parents de l'Association Bugnet auprès du ministre de l'Éducation d'alors. Ce dernier n'est pas, lui non plus, très sensibilisé à l'importance des droits conférés par la *Charte canadienne des droits et libertés*.

Tel que l'en avisa le ministre, l'Association Bugnet porte ses demandes auprès des conseils scolaires d'Edmonton[15] et effectue conjointement une campagne d'information auprès des francophones. Les demandes aux conseils scolaires catholiques et publiques d'Edmonton portaient sur trois points :

---

15. Il s'agit des conseils de l'Edmonton Roman Catholic School District no 7 et l'Edmonton Public School Board.

1) l'établissement d'une école pour francophones : School trustees question francophone school plan (*Edmonton Journal*, 8 décembre 1982) ; Francophone parents ask for own school (*Edmonton Examiner*, 13 décembre 1982) ;

2) un mécanisme de gestion de cette école par la minorité : Francophone group seeks parental control of school (*Edmonton Journal*, 7 décembre) et ;

3) le libre choix de cours de religion ou de morale afin de regrouper tous les francophones sous un même toit et une même langue.

Les refus des conseils scolaires se manifestent rapidement malgré les 128 inscriptions d'élèves de la première et la septième années recueillis par l'Association Bugnet :

Rejection of French-school plan advised (*Edmonton Journal*, 11 décembre) ;

Francophone school faces an F (*Edmonton Sun*, 14 décembre) ;

Board turns down francophone school (*Edmonton Journal*, 15 décembre) ;

French school nixed (*Edmonton Examiner*, 27 décembre) ;

RC trustees oppose new French School (*Edmonton Journal*, 18 janvier 1983) ;

L'école Bugnet essuie un autre refus (*Le Franco*, 19 janvier 1983).

L'Association canadienne française de l'Alberta (ACFA) suit l'exemple des conseils scolaires anglophones et déclare que les requêtes des parents sont irréalisables (*Le Franco*, 19 janvier 1983). Cette première épisode des requêtes d'école française et de gestion de cette école a duré un an et deux mois ; elle s'est soldée par un échec. L'Association Bugnet se verra donc dans l'obligation d'ouvrir sa propre école et de porter sa cause devant les tribunaux.

- Demandes de financement

Qu'elle soit communautaire ou judiciaire, toute action sociale, surtout toute action aussi globale que celle de l'Association Bugnet, ne peut se réaliser sans ressources financières. C'est ce que réalise l'Association. Six mois après le début de son action (novembre 1981) et, suite aux recommandations de l'ACFA[16] en juin 1982, le comité demande des fonds pour soutenir ses revendications. Les premiers fonds sont fournis par le Secrétariat d'État ; c'est le coup d'envoi de toutes les actions de l'Association Bugnet.

---

16. La correspondance de l'époque indique que l'ACFA ne souhaitait pas s'impliquer dans le dossier.

Par ailleurs, des revendications auprès des tribunaux sont fort coûteuses. En 1982, quelques jours après les refus des conseils scolaires d'Edmonton, un entrefilet du *Globe and Mail*[17] alerte les membres de l'Association Bugnet à la disponibilité de fonds du gouvernement fédéral, par l'entremise du ministère du Secrétariat d'État pour porter devant les tribunaux les lois contrevenant à la *Charte des droits et libertés*. L'Association Bugnet expose donc l'état de la minorité française de l'Alberta au Ministre d'alors, Monsieur Serge Joyal. En juin 1983, ce dernier accorde des fonds pour porter devant les tribunaux la conformité de la loi scolaire en regard des droits conférés par l'article 23 de la *Charte*.

Le geste du secrétaire d'État du Canada fut tout d'abord interprété par les journaux anglophones comme une ingérence de la part du gouvernement fédéral dans un domaine de juridiction provinciale. Les articles portèrent les titres suivants:

Ottawa funds francophone's challenge of Alta. law (*Edmonton Journal*, 15 juin 1983);

Feds to fight for French rights (*Edmonton Sun*, 15 juin);

Language case gets Ottawa aid (*Edmonton Journal*, 16 juin).

Toujours au chapitre des demandes d'aide financière, mentionnons celles reliées à l'ouverture de l'école privée fondée en septembre 1983. L'Association Bugnet demande alors au gouvernement provincial les subventions généralement accordées aux écoles de cette catégorie. Le gouvernement provincial est mal placé pour refuser les fonds généralement accordés à toutes les écoles privées; l'Association Bugnet reçoit donc les subventions de base de cette catégorie d'école mais seulement à la fin de l'année scolaire. Les parents doivent subventionner eux-mêmes l'école pendant l'année. Une subvention financée par les ententes fédérales-provinciales fait également l'objet d'une demande. Ces fonds octroyés par le gouvernement fédéral pour l'enseignement de la minorité sont également acheminés à la fin de l'année scolaire à l'Association Bugnet par le ministère de l'Éducation.

D'autres demandes de subventions portant sur des recherches de modèles de gestion scolaire en milieu minoritaire et sur l'organisation de conférences sont faites au secrétariat d'État et sont partiellement accordées.

---

17. «Ottawa to finance language cases», The [*Toronto*] *Globe and Mail* (22 décembre 1982). Il s'agit des fonds disponibles par le Programme de contestation judiciaire dont nous avons parlé antérieurement.

Les demandes de fonds de l'Association Bugnet ont généralement été fructueuses. Nous en notons pourtant les restrictions. Tout d'abord, le gouvernement fédéral s'avère la seule source de financement favorable aux demandes pour l'instruction de la minorité francophone. Ensuite, tout octroi de fonds est le résultat de nombreuses requêtes. Par contre, l'efficacité d'action de l'Association Bugnet lui valut une grande crédibilité auprès des organismes subventionnaires ; en effet, l'Association Bugnet, avec de minces ressources a réussi à éveiller la francophonie albertaine entière[18].

- Demandes d'appui à la cause de l'éducation française en Alberta

Un troisième domaine de requêtes, les *demandes d'appui à la cause de l'éducation française en Alberta*, touche toutes les associations et organismes susceptibles d'aider directement ou indirectement la minorité francophone de l'Alberta. C'est ainsi que la correspondance de l'Association[19] fait état de démarches entreprises auprès du Consulat de France à Edmonton et à Montréal, auprès du Bureau des Affaires intergouvernementales du Québec à Edmonton et à Québec, auprès du Commissariat aux langues officielles, de la Fédération des comités de parents du Manitoba, du gouvernement fédéral, de la Fédération des francophones hors Québec (FFHQ), du Secrétariat d'État, de l'Association canadienne d'éducation en langue française (ACELF).

Toutes les demandes d'appui effectuées par l'Association Bugnet ont comme arrière-plan les droits conférés par l'article 23 de la *Charte*. Elles ont en général comme but de créer un groupe d'intervenants-es qui puisse apporter un avis favorable aux revendications.

3. La campagne d'information

Devant le manque d'information sur l'éducation française en milieu minoritaire et face aux nombreux mythes circulant sur le sujet en Alberta, l'Association Bugnet lance une campagne d'information et de sensibilisation visant quatre secteurs :

1) la *communauté francophone* qui avait besoin de comprendre la différence entre les programmes d'enseignement en langue maternelle à la minorité et ceux de langue seconde par l'immersion ;

---

18. Pour une analyse complète des sources de financement et de la structure de subvention, voir P. Dubé, « Les conditions d'émergence du cas Bugnet et ses implications pour l'avenir des minorités francophones », dans R. Théberge et J. Lafontant, éd., *Demain, la francophonie en milieu minoritaire* (Saint-Boniface : Centre de recherche du C.U.S.B., 1987).

19. Cette correspondance est disponible aux archives du Musée provincial d'Edmonton.

2) le *gouvernement provincial albertain*, en particulier le ministère de l'Éducation, et plus généralement le public anglophone qui avaient besoin d'être alertés aux besoins et aux droits de la minorité de langue officielle française ;

3) les *organismes fédéraux* qui possèdent les ressources pour favoriser les actions d'une minorité jusqu'alors moins revendicatrice ;

4) le *gouvernement du Québec* qui potentiellement dispose de ressources essentielles pour les minorités francophones du Canada.

Nous décrivons ici les moyens d'information utilisés par l'Association Bugnet plutôt que d'énumérer les actions entreprises.

Tout d'abord, les archives démontrent que, quel que soit l'individu ou l'organisme sollicité, les actions de l'Association Bugnet sont longuement préparées et menées : recherches préalables, appel téléphonique de contact, rencontres, suivi par lettre ou par téléphone. Ce processus a pour but de bien fournir à l'interlocuteur ou l'interlocutrice toutes les dimensions de la question de l'éducation française en Alberta. Bien sûr, les droits conférés par l'article 23 de la *Charte* sont au premier rang des informations fournies.

Pour informer le ministre de l'Éducation et pour lui indiquer que les parents étaient convaincus de leurs besoins, son bureau a été inondé de lettres de parents réclamant le droit à l'école française plutôt qu'à une école d'immersion. Parallèlement, entre septembre et décembre 1982, ces lettres sont publiées dans les lettres à l'éditeur du *Franco*, le seul journal hebdomadaire de langue française de l'Alberta :

> Monsieur le ministre « Je réclame mon droit » (*Le Franco*, 20 octobre 1982) ;

> Demande d'école française et non d'immersion (*Le Franco*, 17 novembre 1982).

Ainsi la communauté et le ministère de l'Éducation étaient sensibilisés à la question. À une autre occasion, en avril 1983, une pétition en règle de 528 signatures demandant au ministre de l'Éducation d'établir une école française à Edmonton lui est présentée.

La campagne d'information s'est également poursuivie par une abondante documentation écrite distribuée d'un bout à l'autre du Canada. Ces dossiers de plus de deux cents pages contiennent les documents suivants :

- proposition d'école française présentée aux conseils scolaires ;

- correspondance entre le ministre de l'Éducation et l'Association Bugnet ;

- lettres d'appui au projet de l'Association Bugnet ;

- proposition d'école et de financement au ministère de l'Éducation ;

- demandes de subventions ;

- historique du projet ;

- articles pertinents portant sur le besoin d'écoles françaises en milieu minoritaire et sur les modalités de l'éducation minoritaire.

Parmi les actions d'information, mentionnons également celles qui offrent une grande visibilité à la question de l'éducation française en Alberta : la participation à des conférences et colloques. Tout d'abord, les membres de l'Association croient que leur participation à de nombreux colloques est une occasion idéale de porter en public la question de l'éducation française et les revendications pour des écoles françaises et sa gestion.

L'Association Bugnet organise également plusieurs conférences. À titre d'exemple, en 1985, elle organise à Edmonton un colloque visant à informer les conseils scolaires anglophones, les membres du gouvernement, les universitaires et la communauté francophone des droits et des besoins de la minorité. Cent cinquante personnes des milieux juridique et éducatif participent à cette journée organisée de concert avec les facultés de droit et d'éducation de l'université de l'Alberta. C'est la rencontre de décideurs-es albertains-es et de spécialistes venus d'un bout à l'autre du pays. D'ailleurs, le président de cette université donne l'allocution d'ouverture. Les actes de ce colloque sont publiés (Martel, 1985).

Un deuxième colloque a lieu à Montréal en 1988. Intitulé « Mise au point sur l'article 23 de la Charte, » il regroupe des avocats-es et des représentants-es d'associations nationales et d'organismes gouvernementaux. Il a lieu grâce à la coopération du Commissariat aux langues officielles, du Conseil canadien de développement social et de la Télé-université du Québec.

4. La recherche

Estimant qu'une bonne connaissance des faits doit informer toute action, la recherche s'avère un outil et une activité fondamentale de l'Association Bugnet. Dès les débuts, les procès-verbaux des réunions du conseil d'administration de l'Association démontrent que les membres se documentent sur les aspects psycho-linguistiques et socio-linguistiques de l'éducation minoritaire. Ces réunions font office de lieu de lecture et de discussions avant de passer aux prises de décisions et à l'élaboration des requêtes.

Avant de lancer l'idée d'inscription à une école française, l'Association Bugnet a aussi effectué un sondage démontrant que, contrairement à l'opinion courante, les Franco-albertains-es d'Edmonton inscriraient leurs enfants dans une école française si elle était disponible (50 pour cent). De plus, ce sondage effectué en deux volets a permis de constater qu'en expliquant le concept de l'école française, 90 pour cent des parents seraient en faveur de cette école[20]. Cette constatation signifie qu'une forte partie de l'opposition à l'école française provient d'un manque d'information. Les résultats du sondage convainquent donc l'Association Bugnet de la viabilité de ses revendications et l'incitent à poursuivre sa campagne d'information.

Un deuxième sondage, effectué par l'Association Bugnet et publié par l'Association d'éducation en langue française (ACELF) en 1988, documente la situation albertaine sept ans après le premier sondage. Il permet alors de constater les progrès accomplis, notamment au chapitre de l'opinion publique quant à la gestion scolaire. En effet, la minorité francophone d'Edmonton appuie maintenant le principe de la gestion scolaire par la minorité francophone (69 pour cent).

5. La mise en oeuvre

Suite aux refus du ministre de l'Éducation, des conseils scolaires anglophones et des associations francophones de favoriser l'établissement d'une école française en 1982, les membres de l'Association Bugnet réalisent que la seule façon d'obtenir cette école est de la fonder. En 1983, l'Association Bugnet agit et met en oeuvre des mécanismes concrets en fondant un prototype d'école française en Alberta. En juin 1983, l'ouverture de la première école française est annoncée. « L'école française ouvre ses portes en septembre 1983 » dit la manchette du *Franco* du 15 juin 1983. En un premier temps, elle serait privée, puisque l'Association n'avait pas trouvé d'autre moyen d'instituer une école française. D'ailleurs, en conjonction avec la démarche judiciaire, cette action permettait de mettre déjà en vigueur un système de gestion par la minorité puisque cette école privée serait gérée par les parents de l'école. Il serait de plus, facile d'obtenir, par les tribunaux, la reconnaissance aux fonds publics expressément nommée dans l'article 23 de la *Charte*.

Tout enfant francophone est admis à l'école Bugnet et le cas des parents ne pouvant payer les frais de scolarité mensuels (50 $) est traité

---

20. Les résultats de ce sondage sont disponibles de trois sources. Tout d'abord, ils sont diffusés dans un communiqué de presse du 17 janvier 1983. Ensuite, « Une école française, 249 inscriptions sont prévues » *Le Franco* (19 janvier 1983). Enfin, ces données furent déposées auprès de la cour et du ministère de l'Éducation lors de l'enquête préalable tenue en mars 1984.

individuellement. La difficulté de survie financière de l'École Bugnet était une attestation manifeste de la nécessité de fonds publics pour financer l'éducation de la minorité. Les paris étaient élevés : en trois mois, les enfants de l'école étaient heureux[21], les parents épuisés, le ministère de l'Éducation sidéré et la francophonie divisée. L'école ne put réouvrir en septembre 1984, mais la commision des écoles catholiques d'Edmonton avait compris : cette année-là, elle transforme une école d'immersion en école française.

Un deuxième volet de mise en oeuvre porte sur la structure de gestion. En 1983, l'Association Bugnet met sur pied une association-soeur qui gère l'École Bugnet. Cette nouvelle association, l'Association albertaine des parents francophones, était destinée à devenir le premier conseil scolaire francophone de l'Alberta.

Les conclusions que nous tirons de cette mise en oeuvre sont les suivantes. Les revendications prennent une valeur accrue quand une action concrète en prouve non seulement la faisabilité comme projet, mais également la nécessité. Sans ces mises en oeuvre, les pressions pour agir auraient été moindres ; les conseils scolaires, le gouvernement, l'ACFA et le public, tant anglophone que francophone, n'auraient pas estimé l'urgence des besoins des enfants de la minorité française. D'ailleurs, cette double mise en oeuvre est intimement liée à la contestation judiciaire. Nous revenons donc ici à notre propos de judicalisation des rapports de la minorité. En effet, la double mise en oeuvre d'une école et d'un embryon de conseil scolaire est possible grâce à la sécurité accordée par les droits conférés par l'article 23 de la Charte.

CONSTATATIONS SUITE AU PROCESSUS DE JUDICALISATION DES REVENDICATIONS SCOLAIRES

Si nous avons détaillé une partie des démarches entreprises par l'Association Bugnet, c'est bien pour illustrer combien difficile et tentaculaire est la judicalisation des revendications de la minorité française. Elle se fait au prix d'inconcevables énergies réparties entre cinq champs d'action que nous venons de décrire. La proclamation des droits a incité à un engagement profond qui a mobilisé, chez les parents de l'Association Bugnet, beaucoup d'énergie, de temps, de réflexion, de recherche, d'investissement émotif entre autres.

Paradoxalement, la proclamation des droits éducatifs de l'article 23 devait faciliter l'obtention des services affirmant l'épanouissement de la minorité française en Alberta et partout au Canada. Face au processus

---

21. « Une rose pour l'école Georges-et-Julia-Bugnet », *Le Franco* (2 mai 1984).

que nous venons de décrire, la question des résultats devient donc essentielle. Nous avons démontré que le processus de judicalisation des revendications est enclenché lorsque les circonstances légales sont propices et que les minorités de langue française sont en perte de vitesse au Canada et en Alberta. Nous avons décrit l'ampleur d'un processus de judicalisation dans le cas de l'Alberta. Nous nous demandons maintenant si le processus fournit des résultats en proportion des énergies mobilisées. Quels sont donc les changements occasionnés par le processus de judicalisation des revendications ?

1. La minorité officielle de langue française en Alberta

Voyons tout d'abord si la minorité de langue officielle française de l'Alberta a bénéficié du processus de judicalisation des revendications décrit plus haut.

Généralement, les relations inter-groupes au sein de la communauté francophone ont été modifiées par l'avènement de l'article 23 et par les revendications qui en découlent. Nous ne pouvons faire ici état des résultats obtenus par les revendications des associations francophones traditionnelles[22] de l'Alberta avant 1982 ; ce serait pourtant nécessaire afin de démarquer clairement comment le nouveau processus de judicalisation s'en distingue. Nous pouvons cependant faire une première constatation : les revendications judiciaires sont passées du statut d'une action difficilement acceptée par les associations francophones traditionnelles à celui d'une action souhaitable, voire même souhaitée par les membres de la francophonie.

Tout d'abord, avec l'avènement de l'article 23, un groupe nouveau, plus informé, plus revendicateur et plus impatient est venu s'ajouter, non sans friction, à la vieille garde francophone. En conférant des droits aux parents, l'article 23 a clairement incité ces derniers à dépasser les craintes, l'étapisme et les stratégies de négociations des associations traditionnelles. C'est ainsi qu'en 1983, la communauté franco-albertaine s'est trouvée divisée. Des manchettes contradictoires en témoignent :

Aller en cour, pourquoi pas ? (*Le Franco*, 26 octobre 1983) ;

Aller en cour, et puis après ? (*Le Franco*, 9 novembre 1983) ;

La contestation juridique : c'est normal (*Le Franco*, 16 novembre 1983).

---

22. Nous référons le lecteur ou la lectrice à l'article de Paul Dubé, *supra*, note 18, ou encore aux écrits de J-W. Lapierre et A. Prujiner, « Le pouvoir des mots : Les conflits ethno-linguistiques : un cadre d'analyse sociopolitique », (1985) 79 *C. internationaux de sociologie* 295 et S. Constantinidis, « De l'autonomie relative de l'ethnicité en tant que construit social », (1986) 18 *Can. Ethnic Studies* 102.

Au coeur du débat : l'acceptation du processus de judicalisation des renvendications. Cette acceptation ne fait pas, à l'origine, l'unanimité des membres de la minorité de langue française. Pourtant, en 1989, ce processus est devenu normal et activement recherché par les divers groupes. D'ailleurs une deuxième poursuite judiciaire a été intentée par un groupe de parents de Saint-Paul dans le centre-est de l'Alberta.

Sur le plan communautaire, les revendications de l'Association Bugnet ont été largement contestées. Elles étaient claires, directes et menaçantes pour le statu quo. Cependant, si l'Association Bugnet avait pris une position moins ferme, les progrès qu'accomplit la francophonie albertaine entre 1982 et 1989 seraient moindres sinon faibles. D'ailleurs, si l'Association était perçue comme radicale en 1982, aujourd'hui, ses revendications sont vues comme étant tout à fait légitimes et acceptables. Deux des trois objectifs de l'Association sont aujourd'hui monnaie courante dans les demandes des Franco-albertains(es) : les écoles francophones et la gestion scolaire.

Depuis 1982, nous faisons un bilan et nous retenons les événements suivants qui auraient été impossibles sans la judicalisation des revendications scolaires :

- quatre écoles françaises ont vu le jour ;

- d'autres écoles françaises sont en voie de réalisation ;

- un conseil scolaire francophone gère une de ces écoles ;

- le gouvernement albertain a reconnu, quoique insuffisamment, les droits des francophones dans sa Loi sur l'éducation ;

- une politique ministérielle prévoit la probabilité d'un nombre suffisant d'enfants pour une école française dans cinq régions de la province ;

- deux cours ont reconnu les droits à l'instruction et aux établissements ;

- le député Léo Piquette s'est exprimé en français devant l'Assemblée législative ;

- les parents ont organisé un « sit-in » dans les locaux du conseil scolaire catholique d'Edmonton pour l'obtention d'une école secondaire francophone ;

- des manifestations organisées par Francophonie jeunesse ont eu lieu à l'Assemblée législative ;

- la Faculté Saint-Jean offre un programme de formation d'enseignant-e dans les écoles de la minorité.

Les revendications et les exemples de l'Association Bugnet ont contribué largement sinon inconsciemment à ces événements. La judicalisation des revendications a donné à la minorité une fierté, une force et une vision renouvelées dans ses revendications.

Pour la minorité française de l'Alberta, la judicalisation des revendications portant sur l'article 23 a modifié ses rapports avec le gouvernement provincial et son public majoritaire. La judicalisation a obligé les organismes et les gouvernements à prendre partie. La plupart des organismes ont estimé légitimes les revendications de la minorité; ils ont ainsi contribué à légitimer les revendications et leur objectif principal, soit l'épanouissement de la minorité de langue officielle française.

Enfin, en documentant statistiquement les progrès des effectifs dans les programmes d'enseignement à la minorité de l'Alberta, nous notons qu'entre 1981 et 1986, le gouvernement albertain a reconnu la distinction entre ces programmes et ceux de l'immersion. Pour la première fois en 1983, le ministère de l'Éducation comptait 1 076 élèves dans les classes pour la minorité (Statistique Canada, 1989, p. 29). Avec l'année scolaire 1986-87, une augmentation de 48,2 pour cent s'était déjà fait sentir en deux ans; les effectifs avaient grimpé à 1 595 élèves (Tableau 4).

2. Les minorités de langue officielle française du Canada

Nous avons énuméré des événements qui, à notre avis, ont pris leur source dans la judicalisation des revendications de la minorité française de l'Alberta. Nous pouvons également dégager, sur le plan national, les résultats de cette judicalisation puisqu'elle n'est pas unique à l'Alberta. Nous avons d'ailleurs déjà indiqué que des revendications semblables à celles de l'Association Bugnet sont nées dans presque toutes les provinces canadiennes. Nous ne pouvons ici décrire les progrès qualitatifs réussis par les minorités de langue française des autres provinces et territoires canadiens. Nous pouvons cependant donner un aperçu statistique de l'évolution de la situation des effectifs dans les programmes d'enseignement à la minorité.

Le Tableau 4 fait donc également état des effectifs provinciaux/ territoriaux et de ceux de la minorité française en 1986 et effectue une comparaison avec les données du Tableau 3. Nous remarquons tout d'abord que les effectifs provinciaux se sont stabilisés; la baisse moyenne entre 1981 et 1986 est de 1,3 pour cent alors qu'elle était, rappelons-le, de 9,7 pour cent entre 1971 et 1981. Par ailleurs, la tendance à la baisse plus prononcée entre les effectifs de la minorité que ceux de la majorité se continue entre 1981 et 1986; à l'exception de la Colombie-Britannique qui enregistre une hausse spectaculaire de 129,7 pour cent des effectifs dans l'enseignement à la minorité, la baisse moyenne pour l'ensemble du pays est de 4,2 pour cent. Les baisses les plus marquées sont survenues en Nouvelle-Écosse (27,7 pour cent) et à Terre-Neuve/ Labrador (41,7 pour cent). L'Ontario a, pour sa part connu la moindre baisse de 3,0 pour cent.

TABLEAU 4

Comparaison des effectifs provinciaux et territoriaux*, et effectifs d'enseignement de la langue de la minorité, 1981-82 et 1986-87

Effectifs	Provinciaux 1986	% entre 1981**/ 1986	Minorité 1986	% entre 1981**/ 1986
C.B.	486 299	-3,4 %	1 803	+129,7 %
ALTA	451 419	+2,1 %	1 595	
SASK.	202 788	+0,3 %	1 164	-17,0 %
MAN.	199 037	-0,8 %	5 364	-16,3 %
ONT.	1 791 919	-0,6 %	91 728	- 3,0 %
N.-B.	139 465	-6,7 %	44 962	- 7,5 %
N.-É.	170 868	-6,0 %	3 840	-27,7 %
Î.-P.-É.	24 884	-5,0 %	497	- 6,1 %
T.-N./ LAB.	139 378	-4,0 %	74	-41,7 %
T.-N.-O.	13 296	+5,7 %	0	
YUKON	4 805	-6,2 %	36	
TOTAL	3 624 158	-1,3 %	151 063	- 4,2 %

Source : Statistique Canada. 1989. *Langue de la minorité et langue seconde dans l'enseignement, niveaux élémentaire et secondaire*, p. 28-29.

* : Les données sont fournies pour les écoles et les programmes subventionnés entièrement par les fonds publics au sein d'écoles dites « publiques ».
** : Pour un rappel des données de 1981-1982, voir le Tableau 3.

Voyons maintenant les progrès accomplis entre 1986-87 et 1988-89. L'augmentation spectaculaire des effectifs de la minorité française en Alberta entre 1983 et 1986 continue entre 1986-87 et 1988-89; elle est de 45,0 pour cent en deux ans (Tableau 5). Par ailleurs, le Tableau 5 présente une augmentation des effectifs dans les programmes de la langue de la minorité dans huit provinces et territoire: la Colombie-Britannique (6,3 pour cent), l'Alberta (45,0 pour cent), le Manitoba (5,8 pour cent), l'Ontario (3,2 pour cent), le Nouveau-Brunswick (0,1 pour cent), l'Île-du-Prince-Édouard (2,0 pour cent), Terre-Neuve/Labrador (243,2 pour cent) et le Yukon (52,8 pour cent). Cette hausse est surtout attribuable à l'établissement d'écoles françaises.

Quant aux effectifs provinciaux ou territoriaux, la tendance à la baisse depuis 1971 s'est résorbée: les effectifs des écoles publiques sont maintenant en hausse de 2,4 pour cent entre 1986 et 1989. D'ailleurs, si nous excluons les deux territoires dont la tendance à la hausse est notoire depuis 1971, nous remarquons que deux provinces avaient des effectifs scolaires à la hausse entre 1981 et 1986, l'Alberta et la Saskatchewan. Entre 1986 et 1988, quatre provinces sont maintenant à la hausse: la Colombie-Britannique (2,8 pour cent), l'Alberta (2,1 pour cent), la Saskatchewan (0,7 pour cent) et l'Ontario (4,3 pour cent). Quant aux autres provinces accusant une baisse, elle est maintenant faible entre 0,01 pour cent et 2,3 pour cent.

En comparant les effectifs provinciaux et territoriaux et ceux de la minorité française, nous constatons que seules deux provinces accusent des baisses plus marquées pour la minorité: le Manitoba (1,7 pour cent) et la Nouvelle-Écosse (1,0 pour cent). Ces chiffres permettent donc de constater que des progrès tangibles se font sentir d'un bout à l'autre du Canada quant aux effectifs scolaires de la minorité. Ce n'est pas là une preuve indubitable d'une grande amélioration des conditions d'épanouissement des minorités officielles de langue française. Par contre, c'est sûrement un indicateur que la situation est en voie de changement et qu'elle devrait être surveillée régulièrement pour attester des résultats de la judicalisation des revendications scolaires des minorités de langue française.

TABLEAU 5

Comparaison des effectifs provinciaux et territoriaux*, et effectifs d'enseignement de la langue de la minorité, 1986-87 et 1988-89

Effectifs	Provinciaux 1989 a	% entre 1986**/ 1989	Minorité 1989 b	% entre 1986**/ 1989
C.B.	499 994	+2,8 %	1 916	+6,3 %
ALTA	460 832	+2,1 %	2 312	+45,0 %
SASK.	202 492	+0,01 %	1 154	-0,1 %
MAN.	198 792	-0,01 %	5 676	+5,8 %
ONT.	1 868 211	-4,3 %	94 661	+3,2 %
N.-B.	136 639	-2,0 %	45 396	+0,1 %
N.-É.	167 600	-1,9 %	3 800	-1,0 %
Î.-P.-É.	24 743	-0,1 %	507	+2,0 %
T.-N./ LAB.	132 995	-4,6 %	254	+243,2 %
T.-N.-O.	13 449	+1,2 %	49	
YUKON	4 992	+3,9 %	55	+52,8 %
TOTAL	3 710 739	+2,4 %	155 780	+3,1 %

Source :
a : Statistique Canada.
b : Ministère de l'Éducation des provinces et territoires

* : Les données sont fournies pour les écoles et les programmes subventionnés entièrement par les fonds publics au sein d'écoles dites « publiques ».
** : Pour un rappel des données de 1986-1987 voir le Tableau 4.

CONCLUSION

Après sept années de contestations judiciaires, nous sommes en mesure de dégager des avantages et des inconvénients de la judicalisation des revendications des minorités de langue officielle française. Tout d'abord, la proclamation de la *Charte* et de l'article 23 en particulier a redonné force et vigueur aux minorités qui, croyant à la possibilité d'épanouissement, misent sur l'action, tant judiciaire que communautaire.

Ces communautés ont pris en main les revendications, comme le leur permettait la *Charte* : processus judiciaire, requêtes, recherches, campagne d'information, mise en oeuvre. Les résultats, tels que nous les avons esquissés, sont positifs et donc favorables à l'épanouissement des minorités de langue française.

Quelques dangers, tels que nous les estimons, guettent cependant les minorités de langue officielle. Le premier fait que la minorité elle-même risque, à long terme, de trop compter sur l'expertise légale et donc de délaisser les initiatives politiques et communautaires parallèles. Une manchette du *Franco* de mars 1989 nous porte à croire que ce danger est réel : « La contestation judiciaire : seul moyen de faire avancer l'éducation de la minorité francophone ». Nous sommes d'avis, suite à l'expérience de l'Association Bugnet, que le jour où les minorités croiront que la contestation judiciaire est le seul moyen d'obtenir les services nécessaires à sa survie, elles connaîtront une nouvelle situation historique à réformer. Elles seront alors à la merci des tribunaux et des experts-conseils ; elles ne décideront plus de leur sort[23] comme le favorise l'article 23. La contestation judiciaire est un moyen privilégié de faire avancer le dossier de l'éducation minoritaire mais les minorités doivent se garder d'en faire une panacée. La judicalisation de leurs revendications risque alors de devenir une aliénation entre le vécu minoritaire et l'action posée par les experts-es juristes.

D'autre part, le danger demeure également que les gouvernements provinciaux ou territoriaux s'en remettent au strict minimum et aux décisions des cours pour l'offre de services aux minorités de langue officielle. Ainsi, il faudrait d'innombrables causes dans chaque province et territoire pour obtenir la reconnaissance des droits conférés par l'article 23. Dans ce contexte, la judicalisation des revendications favorise la loi du moindre effort pour les autorités scolaires.

Toutefois, il nous semble que la judicalisation des revendications, avec ses avantages et ses résultats, doit devenir une seconde nature pour les minorités officielles de langue française. Le processus est légitime en fonction de ses objectifs et de ses résultats.

---

23. C'est d'ailleurs l'inconvénient du phénomène de la « médicalisation » de nos rapports avec notre corps, comme l'indique Ivan Illich, *supra*, note 2.

LISTE DES ARRÊTS ET DÉCISIONS RELATIFS
À L'ARTICLE 23

Commission des écoles fransaskoises et al. c. *P.G. Saskatchewan,* (1988) 48 D.L.R. (4th) 315 (B.R.).

Laurent Lavoie et al. c. *P.G. Nouvelle-Écosse et Cape Breton District School Board,* (1989) 91 N.S.R. (2d) 184 (C.A.).

Laurent Lavoie et al. c. *P.G. Nouvelle-Écosse et Cape Breton District School Board,* (1988) 90 N.S.R. (2d) 16 (C.S. 1re inst.).

Laurent Lavoie et al. c. *P.G. Nouvelle-Écosse et Cape Breton District School Board,* (1988) 50 D.L.R. (4th) 405 (C.S. 1re inst.).

Laurent Lavoie et al. c. *P.G. Nouvelle-Écosse et Cape Breton District School Board,* (84 N.S.R. (2d) 387), 10 février 1988.

Mahé et al. c. *R.,* (1987) 42 D.L.R. (4th) 514 (C.A.).

Mahé et al. c. *R.,* (1985) 39 Alta L.R. 215 (B.R.).

Marchand c. *Simcoe County Board of Education,* (1986) 55 O.R. 2d. 638 H.C.

Quebec Association of Protestant School Boards c. *P.G. Québec,* 1982, Cour supérieure.

Quebec Association of Protestant School Boards c. *P.G. Québec,* [1984] 2 R.C.S. 66.

Ref. re Education Act of Ontario and Minority Language Education Rights, (1984) 10 D.L.R. (4th) 491 (C.A).

Ref. re Minority Language Educational Rights, (1988) 49 D.L.R. (4th) 499.

Société des Acadiens du Nouveau-Brunswick c. *Minority Language School Board no. 50,* (1983) 126 A.P.R. 361 (N.B.B.R.).

Whittington c. *Board of School Trustees of School District no. 63 (Saanich),* (1987) 44 D.L.R. (4th) 128 (C.S.).

BIBLIOGRAPHIE

BASTARACHE, Michel. 1986. *Les droits linguistiques dans le domaine scolaire.* Ottawa : Fédération des Francophones hors-Québec.

BEAUDOIN, Gérald. 1987. « La question de l'établissement d'un conseil scolaire homogène francophone en Ontario. Un commentaire succinct. » *Revue générale de droit,* 18, 481-494.

Comité mixte spécial sur la Constitution. 1980. Procès-verbaux et témoignages.

Commissaire aux langues officielles. 1988. *Rapport annuel.* Ottawa : Ministère des Approvisionnements et services.

Commission royale d'enquête sur le bilinguisme et le biculturalisme. 1968. *Rapport de la Commission royale d'enquête sur le bilinguisme et le biculturalisme. Livre II, Éducation.* Ottawa : Imprimeur de la Reine.

Conférence annuelle des premiers ministres provinciaux. 1977. Déclaration sur la langue.

Conférence des premiers ministres provinciaux. 1978. Communiqué de la conférence.

Conseil canadien de développement social. 1989. « Le programme de contestation judiciaire : Historique ». Monographie.

CONSTANTINIDIS, S. 1986. « De l'autonomie relative de l'ethnicité en tant que construit social.» *Canadian Ethnic Studies*, 18(2), 102-113).

Dossier de presse I. 1982-1984. *L'éducation française en Alberta.*

Dossier de presse II. 1984-1985. *L'éducation française en Alberta.*

Dossier de presse III. 1981-1986. *L'Association Georges-et-Julia-Bugnet.*

DUBÉ, Paul. 1988. « Vivre un cas de cour : un processus d'éveil et de maturation ». Communication à la Fédération albertaine des parents francophones, Edmonton.

DUBÉ, Paul. 1987. « Les conditions d'émergence du cas Bugnet et ses implications pour l'avenir des minorités francophones » dans R. THÉBERGE et J. LAFONTANT, éd., *Demain, la francophonie en milieu minoritaire*, Saint-Boniface, Centre de recherche du C.U.S.B.

FOUCHER, Pierre. 1988. « Six ans après : L'article 23 de la *Charte* et les tribunaux. » Monographie.

FOUCHER, Pierre. 1985. *Les droits scolaires constitutionnels des minorités de langue officielle du Canada.* Ottawa : Ministère des Approvisionnements et Services Canada.

Gouvernement du Canada. 1978. *Le temps d'agir : Sommaire des propositions du gouvernement fédéral visant le renouvellement de la Fédération canadienne.*

ILLICH, I. 1975. *Némésis médicale : L'expropriation de la santé.* Paris : Éditions du Seuil.

KERR, Robert. 1983. « The Future of Language Rights under Canada's Constitutional Options » dans BECK, S. et I. BERNIER, (éd.), *Canada and the New Constitution : The Unfinished Agenda.* Volume 1. Montréal : L'institut de recherche politique.

LAPIERRE, Jean-William et Alain PRUJINER. 1985. « Le pouvoir des mots : Les conflits ethno-linguistiques : un cadre d'analyse sociopolitique.» *Cahiers internationaux de Sociologie*, 79, 295-311.

MARTEL, Angéline. 1990. *Les droits scolaires des minorités officielles au Canada : de l'instruction à la gestion.* (à paraître)

MARTEL, Angéline. 1988. « Analyse du discours médiatique sur l'article 23 de la *Charte des droits et libertés.* » Communication au Centre pour le journalisme d'enquête, Toronto, le 26 mars 1988.

MARTEL, Angéline. 1988. « Profil de la francophonie d'Edmonton. » *Nouveau regard sur l'égalité linguistique.* ACELF, 16 (2), 21-35.

MARTEL, Angéline (Ed.). 1985. *Constitutional Rights for Minorities and a Changing Educational Structure in Alberta: Proceedings of the Minority Language Education Rights and the Constitution Conference*, Edmonton, March 22, 1985. Edmonton: Université de l'Alberta.

MARTEL, Angéline. 1984. «Minority-Majority Relations in Second Language Education and the New Canadian Charter of Rights and Freedoms.» *Educational Research Quarterly*, 8 (4), 113-122.

MERLEAU-PONTY, M. 1945. *La phénoménologie de la perception*. Paris: Éditions Gallimard.

Ministère de la Justice du Canada. 1986. *Codification des Lois constitutionnelles de 1867 à 1982*. Ottawa: Ministère des Approvisionnements et Services Canada.

MONNIN, Alfred. 1983. «L'égalité juridique des langues et l'enseignement: les écoles françaises hors-Québec.» *Les Cahiers de Droit*, 24 (1), 157-167.

PROULX, J.P. 1988. «Les normes périjuridiques dans l'idéologie québécoise et canadienne en matière de langue d'enseignement.» *Revue générale de droit*, 19, 209-223.

Statistique Canada. 1989. Langue de la minorité et langue seconde dans l'enseignement, niveaux élémentaire et secondaire.

VERS L'ENSEIGNEMENT DE LA CULTURE

Frank McMahon

Il est important de préciser comment il faut entendre ce concept de la culture quand on aborde la question de l'enseignement de la culture, cette mer semée d'ambiguïtés pour employer l'expression de Robert Choquette (1980). Le terme a deux notions générales qu'il n'est pas difficile de séparer : culture au sens de cultivé, l'ancien sens de culture qui vient des Romains, au sens de « *cultura animi* » et qui est définie par Larousse comme « *l'application que l'on met aux choses de l'esprit... soins donnés à l'esprit, aux facultés intellectuelles de l'homme, pour les développer, les perfectionner...* » et que Fernand Dumont appellera : culture-horizon (Dumont, 1979). Depuis l'oeuvre d'Edmond Tyler au XIXe siècle, *Primitive culture*, on en est venu à appeler la réalité propre à un groupe social sa culture (Beneton, 1975 ; Geertz, 1973), ce que Dumont appellera culture-milieu. Cette notion des sciences sociales de culture est devenue monnaie courante au Canada plus particulièrement depuis les travaux de la Commission royale d'enquête sur le bilinguisme et le biculturalisme. Celle-ci la définit donc comme « *une manière globale d'être, de penser, de sentir ; c'est un ensemble de moeurs et d'habitudes, c'est aussi une expérience commune ; c'est enfin un dynamisme propre à un groupe qu'unit une même langue* » (Commission, 1967, p. xxi).

Partiellement à cause de cette ambiguïté, les scientifiques utilisent le terme d'ethnicité pour se référer au concept de culture-milieu, lorsqu'il s'agit de groupes distincts en fonction de leur origine. C'est une fausse solution devant le problème de l'enseignement ou de la transmission de la culture dans les écoles francophones car ces derniers n'ont pas encore accepté de se voir comme un groupe ethnique. Ils y voient une diminution inacceptable de leur statut de peuple fondateur ou de « communauté de langue officielle ». Une deuxième raison pratique pour maintenir le mot de culture, c'est de tout simplement reconnaître qu'avec les développements du multiculturalisme (Breton, 1986), le mot ne disparaîtra pas.

Une troisième raison pour le maintenir dans le domaine de l'éducation, c'est de souligner que le rôle de l'école dans la transmission de la culture-milieu d'une communauté donnée devra se faire à l'intérieur d'un projet de développement de l'enfant (culture-horizon). Devant les excès du nationalisme et du cléricalisme dans l'histoire des écoles françaises (Comeau, 1979), il n'est pas inutile d'insister sur ces dangers. En plus, les minoritaires dans leur lutte se doivent de pouvoir articuler leur action culturelle quand on les attaque de racisme, de ghettoisme ou d'élitisme. Il est critique de souligner que le développement de l'enfant, son perfectionnement, doit demeurer au coeur de toute action qui veut par l'école maintenir la façon de penser, de sentir, d'agir d'un groupe particulier. C'est ce que permet plus facilement le terme culture par opposition au terme ethnicité.

Cependant, dans nos sociétés libérales, on oublie plus souvent que le développement de l'enfant, sa culture-horizon, se situe toujours à l'intérieur d'un projet de culture-milieu. Déjà Dewey (1916) notait que l'éducation peut se définir fondamentalement comme l'équivalent de la reproduction biologique sur le plan social. L'éducation est inscrite dans l'instinct le plus fondamental de toute société, celui de sa survie. À partir des années soixante la nouvelle sociologie a souligné que l'école publique, telle que fondée un peu partout dans l'Occident au XIXe siècle était un instrument privilégié par lequel les groupes dominants dans la société maintenaient leur pouvoir. C'est une opération délicate mais nécessaire de faire découvrir par mes étudiants idéalistes que le système des écoles, fondé par Ryerson et toujours louangé par nos rapports officiels, l'a été avec l'idée de rendre les pauvres et les ouvriers heureux de leur sort (Curtis, 1988 ; Mifflen & Mifflen, 1982).

Aussi, devant les échecs scolaires systématiques des enfants de certains groupes sociaux, les scientifiques proposent des transformations dans le système pédagogique plutôt que des mesures pour compenser «*les lacunes chez les élèves*» (La Maîtresse d'école, 1979 ; Cummins, 1985 ; Méthé, 1983). Pour employer l'expression de Cummins, il s'agit d'assurer à l'élève un sentiment de puissance en valorisant sa propre perception du monde, comme étant tout aussi créatrice, c'est-à-dire de le conscientiser au sens de Paolo Freire. Je crois que Cummins ne fait pas erreur en rattachant à ce même courant, les recherches centrées autour du bilinguisme additif et soustractif qui intéressent vivement les groupes culturels dont la langue n'est pas celle de la majorité, soucieux d'un système scolaire équitable pour leurs enfants (*ibid.* ; Landry & Allard, sous presse).

Si j'ai bien compris la problématique, toutefois, il s'agit fondamentalement d'une stratégie pédagogique de culture-horizon, assurer que l'enfant maîtrisera les compétences nécessaires pour fonctionner dans la société, sans remettre en question la culture-milieu dominante, sauf dans la mesure où celle-ci le réduit à ce qu'Ogbu appelle une minorité de caste (1978). C'est également la stratégie dominante dans l'éducation multiculturelle où l'insistance est d'assurer que tous les enfants puissent s'intégrer à la société canadienne sans souffrir de discrimination ni cachée, ni ouverte dans leur progrès scolaire et social.

Une autre problématique surgit, toutefois, quand on aborde l'école francophone où le projet de l'école n'est pas tout simplement la culture-horizon de l'enfant en fonction de ce que Fitouri appelle la modernité : accès à la science, à la compétence linguistique, aux sciences mathématiques (1983). Car l'école francophone doit servir au maintien de la culture-milieu ; elle doit assumer une tâche particulière de reproduction de la communauté culturelle au sens de culture-milieu (Cour d'appel, 1984). C'est ce qui a motivé la Cour d'appel de l'Ontario à interpréter l'article 23 comme devant assurer à la communauté une forme de gestion de l'école, soit son rôle d'animation et de reproduction de la culture-milieu.

Avant de l'aborder, toutefois, soulignons l'importance capitale des écoles francophones pour assurer cette fonction de culture-horizon pour les enfants dont le français est la langue maternelle. Une communication récente de Claudette Tardif à l'American Educational Research Association (1989) documente, à partir tant de l'Alberta que du Manitoba et de l'Ontario, le faible rendement scolaire des francophones dans des écoles mixtes ou d'immersion, et les possibilités de changement par la création d'écoles francophones. En revenant maintenant au domaine de l'enseignement de la culture-milieu dans une école francophone, je me permets une assez longue citation qui souligne un paramètre de cet enseignement, paramètre relativement bien connu dans plusieurs milieux, mais malheureusement ignoré chez plusieurs.

Yolande Grisé rapporte le tableau final de théâtre « *La Parole et la Loi* », montée par une troupe de Vanier, Ontario. Il s'agit d'une brève cérémonie, au cours de laquelle les comédiens viennent en procession enterrer symboliquement tous les clichés traditionnels qui illustrent ordinairement l'identité collective franco-ontarienne. Ces clichés : boîte de soupe aux pois, vieille ceinture fléchée, grenouille, petits pains, etc. ne correspondraient plus à la réalité vécue par la jeunesse d'aujourd'hui. Grisé écrit :

> Par ce geste libérateur, la troupe veut signifier le rejet contemporain des vieilles images stériles d'un passé figé, dépossédé de lui-même et attirer l'attention sur les réalités que doit affronter le Franco-ontarien d'aujourd'hui confronté à de nouvelles valeurs, à de nouveaux problèmes, à une nouvelle existence : à la VIE. (1982, p. 82)

On est ici devant un rejet de la notion folklorique de la culture, définie par le petit Robert, comme éléments «*pittoresques, mais sans importance*». Armé de ces quelques outils conceptuels: culture-milieu; culture-horizon; culture folklorisée; culture scolaire comme reproduction de la culture dominante, j'ai pu faire une étude ethnographique d'une école francophone à Cornwall en Ontario dont le rapport de recherche a été soumis à l'Université de Montréal (McMahon, 1986). Utilisant les outils dont je disposais à l'époque, j'ai surtout analysé les résultats en fonction de la nouvelle sociologie, dont plus particulièrement, l'égalité des chances. Une autre interprétation de ces données m'apparaît désormais plus complète devant d'autres données qui m'ont amené à dépasser le premier cadre.

Ce que j'avais surtout noté dans mon premier rapport, c'était d'un côté un leadership francophone très puissant au plan politique, ayant réussi dans un milieu particulièrement difficile à: a) implanter une très bonne école, au point qu'elle m'apparaissait entourée d'une auréole dans le milieu; b) réorganiser tout le système scolaire au niveau élémentaire; et; c) lancer un mouvement, qui se continue, de refranciser les autres institutions dont surtout les institutions religieuses. D'un autre côté, depuis la fermeture des usines de textiles, l'économie de la ville de Cornwall demeure particulièrement fragile et très dépendante des autorités politiques. Or, le leadership francophone ne participait pas aux prises de décisions politico-économiques de la ville. Il fallait donc expliquer ce peu d'intérêt pour le pouvoir politique et économique. Une culture-milieu, pour être authentique, pour dépasser le folklore, doit représenter un moyen par lequel une collectivité se situe face à son environnement, obtient accès aux biens tangibles dont la société dispose.

Ce qui m'est apparu clair à l'époque, c'est que ce leadership parfaitement moderne, capable de réussir à atteindre des objectifs politiques cherchait un pouvoir réel, dépassait la culture des vieilleries dénoncée par les jeunes de Vanier, en cherchant à s'approprier ce que Breton a appelé le capital symbolique de la société (1984). Il n'y a pas que le capital économique et politique d'une société, mais il y a aussi son capital symbolique: sa façon de se définir, de se dire. C'est ce qui expliquerait ces curieux phénomènes de la Société pour la préservation de l'anglais et le *Bilingual today French tomorrow* (Andrew, 1977). Ce qui est en jeu est le prestige qu'on accorde à certains particuliers et que les autres groupes acceptent mal.

L'idéologie des francophones, selon laquelle la *Loi sur les langues officielles* n'a de sens que dans la logique de la Commission sur le bilinguisme et le biculturalisme, soit qu'il existe au Canada deux sociétés nationales distinctes et qu'aucun autre groupe culturel ne peut aspirer à s'établir comme société nationale, est menacée selon certains, par l'engouement dans les milieux politiques pour le multiculturalisme (Bastarache, 1988). S'il faut en croire M. Trudeau que le Canada n'a pas de culture officielle, mais a deux langues officielles, il est certain qu'il n'entend pas culture telle qu'on l'entend dans les sciences sociales. Pour ne citer que Lévi-Strauss, «*le langage est à la fois le fait culturel par excellence (distinguant l'homme de l'animal) et celui par l'intermédiaire duquel toutes les formes de la vie sociale s'établissent et se perpétuent*» (1958, p. 392). La déclaration de M. Trudeau n'a de sens que comme solution politique aux conflits de pouvoir suscités par cette redéfinition du pays comme étant officiellement bilingue.

L'insistance par ces bilingues de Cornwall d'obtenir des factures municipales en français, d'obtenir des services hospitaliers en français, ces gestes cent fois répétés et «tannants» d'attendre au téléphone quelqu'un qui pourrait répondre en français, représenterait donc un désir d'être reconnu comme une société française légitime. L'enseignant «en boule» devant le fait que le Collège Saint-Laurent n'avait pas de réceptionniste bilingue, pouvait fonctionner en anglais. Il affirmait explicitement s'objecter surtout au fait que la réceptionniste n'était pas consciente que son unilinguisme était un problème pour le Collège et non pour le client. Compréhensif devant ses limites à elle, il refusait absolument que ce soit son problème.

Tout en interprétant ces phénomènes comme une recherche légitime du capital symbolique de la société, j'ai beaucoup questionné les stratégies d'enculturation de la jeunesse développées par les enseignants. Elles m'apparaissaient survaloriser l'importance de la langue car les enseignants et les milieux professionnels travaillaient certes en français, mais en plus ils travaillaient le français. Aussi, la dimension de vitalité, de nouvelles valeurs auxquelles les jeunes de Vanier aspiraient ne pouvait pas être rejointe par le projet culturel de l'école dans la mesure où celui-ci n'englobait pas un sens particulier au travail d'usine et plus généralement à la productivité matérielle.

Dans deux études ici en Alberta, dont une faite en collaboration avec Madame France Levasseur-Ouimet (McMahon et Levasseur-Ouimet, 1987) et une autre avec Lawrence Fedigan (McMahon et Fedigan, 1988), l'établissement des écoles francophones est apparu comme étant absolument critique dans la perception de la situation par les militants francophones, et surtout, contrairement à l'hypothèse dégagée de Cornwall, chez les non-enseignants. Alors qu'il y a de plus en plus de données empiriques pour justifier l'école francophone ou homogène à partir des besoins académiques des enfants francophones, ce sont les chefs de file non enseignants qui soulignaient l'importance d'une maîtrise de la langue et surtout d'une fierté que seule l'école française pouvait assurer.

Aussi, en revenant à Cornwall, l'option des militants pour une action au niveau du symbolisme ou du capital symbolique, malgré les moyens dont ils disposaient pour récupérer le capital politique et économique, m'est apparue, finalement, comme un instinct naturel d'encadrer la culture dans les institutions dont dépendent les réalités plus matérielles d'une société et non comme une déviation professionnelle. L'établissement des écoles françaises devient donc autant une récupération du capital symbolique qu'un outil de culture-horizon pour une clientèle particulière. L'étude de Curtis (1988) déjà notée permet de découvrir dans l'établissement de l'école publique au milieu du XIXe siècle, la construction d'un espace qui appartiendrait à l'état pour consolider l'état canadien capitaliste et la domination de cet état par l'élite bourgeoise traditionnelle. C'est également la thèse de Breton en privilégiant parmi les incarnations du capital symbolique les institutions publiques et plus particulièrement l'école (1984, 125-129).

Ces considérations d'ordre très général doivent évidemment s'incarner dans un programme, dans un curriculum, dans une « culture-milieu » chez les enseignants. Aussi, il faudra y venir. Toutefois, il apparaît d'importance primordiale que l'école française s'oriente inévitablement vers une autonomie de plus en plus grande, dans ce sens de création d'un espace de « l'état ». L'élément de contrôle qui dans notre société est perçu comme étant neutre, comme provenant du peuple souverain, mais au service de l'élève, permettra à l'école française de se déclarer multiculturelle dans le sens de la Constitution canadienne, soit au service de tous les enfants qui veulent s'intégrer à la société canadienne d'expression française quelque soit leur origine ethnique. L'exercice d'une certaine « souveraineté », par contre, assurera aux Franco-albertains l'accès au capital symbolique qu'ils recherchent. S'il faut envisager tout changement comme l'occasion de conflits, l'école française en proposant cette politique de multiculturalisme pourra faciliter sa recherche d'autonomie.

Avant de conclure, il faut souligner deux aspects de la programmation qui apparaissent importants à partir des études déjà faites. D'un côté, s'il est important en sociologie de l'éducation de souligner que la langue est pouvoir, il faut qu'elle ne le soit que de façon implicite. Une idéologie est puissante dans la mesure où elle n'est pas trop visible. Concrètement, il faudrait insister sur l'importance d'enculturer les enfants dans la tradition littéraire, artistique et créatrice d'expression française. Si la langue est pouvoir, elle est aussi poésie.

D'un autre côté, il faut souligner une pédagogie de célébration. Il faut savoir à quel point c'est épuisant d'insister dans un milieu comme l'Alberta pour obtenir des services bilingues. L'insistance de nos répondants tant en Ontario qu'en Alberta sur la fête comme lieu privilégié pour distinguer la culture française de la culture anglaise en Alberta, ne provient pas d'une légèreté dans les moeurs, d'une tendance folklorisante de la culture, mais d'un besoin d'exprimer de façon positive son sentiment d'être différent là où le milieu dans son ensemble cherche à nier sa légitimité. L'affirmation de cette légitimité demeure une lutte constante pour s'assurer plus de prestige ou de pouvoir symbolique. La vie de cette communauté doit permettre à ses membres de rebâtir leurs forces pour continuer cette lutte.

Pour résumer, je dirais que lorsqu'il s'agit d'enseigner la culture en milieu minoritaire francophone, le premier problème est celui de l'ambiguïté du concept culture. J'ai noté qu'un programme culturel doit se soucier de transmettre l'héritage artistique, scientifique et littéraire d'une tradition afin d'assurer le développement du potentiel de l'enfant : une culture-horizon. L'optique des sciences sociales permet d'éviter une folklorisation de la culture, car selon cette optique, une culture-milieu donne aussi accès aux biens de l'environnement et de la société globale. Selon cette perspective, les études accordent une priorité sur la recherche du capital symbolique : une reconnaissance des francophones comme peuple fondateur ou comme communauté nationale. Il faut encore inventer le programme qui répondrait à cette priorité. Cependant, j'ai noté deux dimensions de ce programme qui s'imposent devant la dimension antagoniste de cette idéologie face à la société globale. La première dimension serait une recherche d'autonomie face aux autorités anglophones. J'ai appelé la deuxième dimension une pédagogie de la célébration.

En terminant, je noterais que la recherche et la science n'en sont qu'à leurs débuts dans ce domaine. Beaucoup de progrès s'est fait, cependant, depuis une quinzaine d'années et on peut espérer que si le même rythme de progrès se maintient, on pourra répondre à la question avec beaucoup plus de précision au tournant du siècle.

RÉFÉRENCES

ANDREW, J.V., *Bilingual Today, French Tomorrow*. Richmond Hill, Ont. : BME Publishing, 1977.

BASTARACHE, M., *Dualité et multiculturalisme : deux notions en conflit ?* Revue de l'*ACELF*, 1978, *16* (2), 36-40.

BENETON, P., *Histoire de mots: culture et civilisation*. Paris: Presses de la Fondation nationale des sciences politiques, 1975.

BRETON, R., *The Production and Allocation of Symbolic Resources: an Analysis of the Linguistic and Ethnocultural Fields in Canada*, *Canadian Review of Sociology and Anthropology*, 1984, *21* (2), 123-144.

BRETON, R., *Le multiculturalisme et le développement national au Canada*, dans A. Cairns & C. Williams, *Les dimensions politiques du sexe, de l'ethnie et de la langue au Canada*. Les Études / Commission royale sur l'union économique et les perspectives de développement du Canada. Ottawa: Ministre des Approvisionnements et Services Canada, 1986.

CHOQUETTE, R., *L'Ontario français, historique*. Montréal: Etudes vivantes, 1980.

COMEAU, G.L., *La question des écoles du Manitoba un nouvel éclairage*, *Revue d'histoire de l'Amérique française*. 1979, *(33)* 1, 3-23.

Commission royale d'enquête sur le bilinguisme et le biculturalisme. *Les langues officielles* (Vol. 1). Ottawa: Imprimeur de la reine, 1967.

Cour d'appel de l'Ontario, *Reference Re Education Act of Ontario and Minority Language Education Rights*, (1984) 10 D.L.R. (4th) 491, 527.

CUMMINS, J., *Empowering Minority Students: A Framework for Intervention*, *Harvard Educational Review* 1986, *56* (1), 18-36.

CURTIS, B., *Building the Educational State: Canada West, 1836-1871*. London, Ont.: Falmer Press, 1988.

DEWEY, J., *Democracy and Education. An Introduction to the Philosophy of Education*. New York: Macmillan Co., 1916.

DUMONT, F., *L'idée de développement culturel: esquisse pour une psychanalyse*, *Sociologie et Sociétés*, 1979, *11* (1), 7-32.

FITOURI, C., *Biculturalisme, bilinguisme et éducation*. Genève: Delachaux et Niestlé, 1983.

FREIRE, P., *Pédagogie des opprimés*. Paris: Maspero, 1974.

GEERTZ, C., *The Interpretation of Cultures*. New York: Basic Books Inc., 1973.

GRISE, Y., *Ontarois, une prise de parole*, *Revue du Nouvel Ontario* (4) (1982) p. 81-90.

La Maîtresse d'école: Le projet de pédagogie progressiste. Montréal: Faculté des Sciences de l'éducation, Université de Montréal, 1979.

LANDRY, R. et R. ALLARD, *Can Schools Promote Additive Bilingualism in Minority Group Children?* dans L. Malave & G. Duquette (éd.), *Language, Culture and Cognition* (sous presse).

LEVI-STRAUSS, Claude, *Anthropologie structurale*, Paris: Plon, 1958.

McMAHON, F., *Signification de la culture dans l'école française hors Québec: le cas de la Citadelle*, Ph.D. Thesis, Université de Montréal, 1986.

McMAHON, F. et F. Ouimet, *S'approprier ses réalités culturelles*, Rapport de recherche, Faculté Saint-Jean, University of Alberta, 1987.

McMAHON, F. et L. FEDIGAN, *École et culture: le projet culturel des Franco-Albertains* dans *Ecriture et Politique*. Actes du Colloque, CEFCO, 1987.

MÉTHÉ, L., *Les stratégies face aux inégalités scolaires* dans R. Cloutier, J. Moisset & R. Ouellet, *Analyse sociale de l'éducation*. Montréal: Boréal Express, 1983.

MIFFLEN, F.J. et S.C. MIFFLEN, *The Sociology of Education Canada and Beyond*. Calgary: Detselig Enterprises, 1982.

OGBU, J., *Minority Education and Caste*. New York: Academic Press, 1978.

TARDIF, C., *French Language Minority Education: Political and Pedagogical Issues*, Paper presented to the American Educational Research Association, San Francisco, California, 1989.

SOME THOUGHTS ON THE IMPLICATIONS OF FRENCH IMMERSION FOR ENGLISH CANADA

Eric Waddell

Tout le monde veut être bilingue, mais
personne ne veut être francophone

I intend to address the phenomenon of French immersion. My inquiry into this highly relevant and understudied topic has grown from my current interest in the relations between Québec and Francophone minorities across the continent. Discussing the societal implications of immersion within English Canada, leads necessarily to a reflection on Francophone minorities as much as on Francophiles, hence, the title of my paper. Finally, it provides a welcome occasion to express ideas, thoughts and opinions as distinct from a simple presentation of data. Specifically, my concern is to cast a cold look on a radical innovation in language instruction and education in general in English Canada — an innovation that dates back a quarter of a century now — and to cut through some of the self-satisfied back slapping that is constantly voiced about it.

We know how successful immersion is in terms of growth and diffusion: an estimated 256,370 students in 1,592 schools across the country or around 6.9 % of the total Anglophone public school population according to the 1989 *Annual Report* of the Commissioner of Official Languages.[1] According to Canadian Parents for French predictions, the figures should continue to rise to about 10 % of the school population and then level off.[2] Already in certain parts of the country they significantly exceed that figure: 20 % in New Brunswick and in excess of 22 % in the Ottawa area (with 55 % at pre-school level).[3] This is

---

1. Tables D.1, "Second-Language Enrolment in Public Schools" and D.2, "Minority Language Education Programs", pp. 256-61 in Commissioner of Official Languages *Annual Report 1989* (Ottawa: Minister of Supply and Services, 1990).
2. Kathleen Moore, personal communication, April 1989.
3. K. Moore, *Diffusion du phénomène d'immersion au Canada: 1965-1987* mémoire de maîtrise en géographie, Université Laval, 1990 at 66-67.

essentially the fruit of an explosive development in the late 1970s and early 1980s when, according to the September 1982 issue of *Winnipeg Magazine*, "[l]ike jogging, it was an idea whose time had come." The diffusion process has been essentially what geographers describe as hierarchical, that is from Montréal to other large metropolitan centres and provincial capitals in the country, then filtering down to small urban centres and ultimately into rural areas.

The immersion experience has spawned a mass of laudatory statements with claims like "French immersion is a Canadian success story of the first order"[4] and there is no doubt that the significant increase in the level of bilingualism in this country between 1971 and 1986, as expressed in census counts, is largely attributable to the phenomenon.[5] It constitutes a clear and positive response to the objective established in the late 1960s of creating a bilingual Canada. Yet this fascination with French as a second language in English Canada has a darker side best expressed in a remark made by a Fransaskois couple to a journalist from the Québec newspaper *Le Soleil*: "Tout le monde veut être bilingue, mais personne ne veut être francophone."[6] It is a harsh — indeed tragic — reality that is again clearly expressed in school enrollment figures. In every province of English Canada, with the exception of New Brunswick, the number of Anglophones registered in French immersion significantly exceeds the number of Francophones registered in minority language programmes. The order of difference in some instances is as much as 10 or 15 times!

---

4. Maxwell Yalden, former Commissioner of Official Languages, in his foreword to *The Immersion Phenomenon*, a special issue of *Language and Society*, 12, 1984.
5. 16.2% of the population declared themselves to be bilingual in 1986 compared with 13.4% in 1971. See J. Henripin, "The 1986 Census: Some Enduring Trends Abate", *Language and Society*, 24:8, 1988.
6. M. Giguère, "La Saskatchewan ne sera jamais bilingue", *Le Soleil* (18 March 1989) B-11.

COMPARATIVE ENROLLMENT IN FRENCH-LANGUAGE
EDUCATION PROGRAMMES, 1989-90

	Immersion programmes (Anglophones)	Minority language programmes (Francophones)
Nfld.	4,000	250
P.E.I.	3,300	520
N.S.	5,000	3,200
N.B.	17,400	45,000
Ont.	124,000	94,200
Man.	19,000	5,500
Sask.	10,400	1,150
Alberta	27,000	2,150
B.C.	26,500	1,910
Yukon	370	40
N.W.T.	400	30
Total	*256,370	153,950

* Includes 19,000 in Québec.

Source: Commissioner of Official Languages, *Annual Report 1989* (Ottawa: Minister of Supply and Services, 1990) Tables D.1 & 2, pp. 256-61.

Further, the number of students registered in minority language programmes has declined significantly since the end of the 1960s (although there is evidence now that the decline is levelling off), a reflection of the continuing erosion of the Francophone mother tongue population beyond Québec.[7] In other words, French immersion is apparently having

---

7. 196,087 Francophones were enrolled in minority language education programmes in 1970-71. By 1988-89 this figure had fallen to 153,437, while the estimated figure for 1989-90 is 153,950 (Commissioner of Official Languages, *supra*, note 1, Table D.2 at 260-61).

no effect on the assimilation of Francophones and the two curves seem to be functioning completely independently of each other. The implications of this development are serious for the language, the culture it transmits ... and for Canada.

In a geolinguistic sense what we are presently witnessing in English Canada is a progressive shift from French-speaking communities to communities containing French speakers. The former are generally rural, characterised by declining and aging populations, and are economically and institutionally marginal. The latter are urban, "modern", dynamic and politically and economically powerful. In a sociolinguistic sense we have been witness to a marked increase in the status of French, but in terms of numbers this is accompanied by a shift from French as a first language to one of French as a second language.

Putting these changes — or rather spheres of change — together we find that they affect the two groups differently. Where French is on the increase, i.e., among Anglophones, it involves individuals acquiring a second language. Where it is on the decrease, i.e., among Francophones, it involves collectivities struggling to maintain their first language which has already become in many cases a second language, Taken together, the two processes result in a greater diffusion of French across the country, and through English Canada's population as a whole, but at the same time its dilution, as its spheres of operation are eroded. Further, both categories of French speakers are increasingly assuming the profile of reactive as distinct from active speakers of the language, that is they will respond in French when addressed in the language but they will rarely initiate conversations or other actions in it. This is clearly true of immersion students; all studies point to that fact. For their part, the French mother tongue populations are becoming more and more reactive as their social space explodes and becomes increasingly permeable to outside (majority) influences. In sociolinguistic terms, the two language groups are evolving in different directions with respect to the French language, but the end product is the same: each is tending to use French as a second (and secondary) language. Finally, from a geolinguistic perspective, the language is quite clearly being deterritorialised.

Another fundamental development that is intimately associated with, and a product of, these changes is the rupture that has been effected between language and culture. By virtue of immersion the French language is in the process of becoming a commodity that belongs somehow to Canada as a whole, to everybody...or to no one in particular. It is quite clear that the immersion experience is designed uniquely to transmit language skills and provide bilingual competence to its students. Studies such as Arthur Leblanc's *Bilingual Education : A Challenge for Canadian Universities in the '90s* are quite clear on the subject. Leblanc considers it up to the country's English language universities to cater to the needs of such students rather than steering them to French language universities. Why? because these students are, perhaps, not interested in (or equipped for?) "a different cultural experience".[8]

This separation is a radical one and can only have profound consequences in the long term. It goes against everything that is expressed in the social science literature about the necessary, intimate relation between language and culture and, indeed, even contradicts the Supreme Court judgment with respect to *La Chaussure Brown's*: that "language is not merely a means or medium of expression; it colours the content and meaning of expression."[9] Language is something that is rooted in place and in collective experience. It assures the transmission of knowledge, of values and of visions of the world around us from one generation to the next. The French of immersion students is imbued with what kind of cultural content and vision? Indeed, do they even possess the language sufficiently to be able to communicate effectively in it? According to Leblanc "at least 90 % of graduates of high school immersion programs are not capable of coping in classes which are conducted entirely in French".[10] Is it any wonder that they are reticent to frequent French language universities? A colleague of mine has described the group in the following manner:

> It seems that a new "race" of half-breeds has been born in this country: the Francophiles — and no one is really conscious of the fact. ... They are no longer entirely Anglo, but they are not culturally Franco either, which means that they can only exploit their new identity in a manner which resembles playing a sonata composed by someone else. Their roots are roots learned in school, which results in their being some kind of bilingual and bicultural illiterates uncertain as to where the sun goes down and the moon rises.[11]

Given such a situation of what I would consider to be extreme fragility in both "Francophone" communities (Francophile and Francophone minority) remedial action needs to be taken. Otherwise long term maintenance will be impossible. Immersion, like jogging, will wind down as some kind of passing fad, while the Francophones that

---

8. (Winnipeg: Continuing Education Division, The University of Manitoba, 1986) at 52.
9. *Attorney General of Québec* v. *La Chaussure Brown's Inc.* (1988), 54 D.L.R. (4th) 577 at 604.
10. A. Leblanc, *supra*, note 8.
11. J. Morisset, *Post-Conférence — Cefco 1987 — Edmonton* (Extrait du Cahier — é mouvance/ II — automne-hiver '87) at p. 9 (My translation).

are beyond the bilingual belt around Québec will pursue their slow death. (As one Fransaskois said recently to the same journalist from *Le Soleil*: "Le français, c'est pareil comme on sait qu'on va mourir, mais ça presse pas.")[12]

For the Francophone mother tongue populations, this action involves abandoning the marginalised rural ghettos and "occupying the city" — acquiring modern institutions and skills, making the language (the knowledge and the skills it transmits) crucial to current social and economic advancement. It means creating exclusive spheres of action, or as the sociologist Raymond Breton said a couple of decades ago, moving as closely as possible to institutional completeness in the new environment.[13] It also involves, as Louis Balthazar indicates elsewhere in this volume,[14] integrating networks that emanate from Québec. Québec is, after all, a modern state and in such a perspective, it has every reason to wish to "possess" Montréal and to impose a predominantly French personality upon the city. Obviously, certain minority communities have clearly understood this, notably the Acadians with their historic concern to make Moncton into an (indeed the only) Acadian town and their more recent decision to open an office in Québec City for political, economic and cultural representation. Franco-Ontarians have also understood it in taking full advantage of the recently established Government of Ontario's official representation in Québec City and in assuring a dynamic presence in Toronto.[15] But in the game of power with the Anglophone majority (and as we have heard on many occasions thus far, language and culture are ultimately questions of power) they have a slim chance. I am not sure that the Francophone minorities in the other provinces have any chance at all.

In so far as the Francophiles — the products of immersion — are concerned, for cultural content and "sense" to be given to their language learning process they need quite obviously to interact and develop shared interests with the francophone minorities if not, indeed, with French-

---

12. M. Giguère, "Le français, langue du confessionnal", *Le Soleil*, (18 March 1989) A-4. Such reflections are often to be heard in the isolated Francophone minority communities of this country, and the tragic resignation voiced by Monique Giguère's retired Saskatchewan farmer reminds me of another that I heard in La Grand'terre, a small fishing village on the west coast of Newfoundland, in the early 70s: "Quand vous retournez à Montréal vous direz que vous avez rencontré les derniers français de Terre-Neuve..."

13. R. Breton, "Institutional Completeness of Ethnic Communities and the Personal Relations of Immigrants", *American Journal of Sociology*, 70 : 193-205, 1964.

14. See his "History and Language Policy" in this volume.

15. This latter point is perhaps best illustrated by the fashionable and highly successful weekly newspaper, *L'Express de Toronto*, which does not rely on Federal government subsidies and is now even distributed in Québec.

speaking Quebecers. However, the question is, given the strict separation of language and culture that characterizes their educational process, can they? Further, are they interested or, to pose the question more brutally, is it in their interests? According to the Commissioner of Official Languages' *Annual Report 1988*[16] there are some isolated attempts in this sense but, if Arthur Leblanc's study is any indication, the answer is quite definitely no. The reasons are as much linguistic as cultural. He says some quite astounding things about Anglophones mixing with Francophone students,

> ...in universities which have been founded to provide French education to young Francophones from minority areas. Though they are of French Canadian background, most of these students have *not yet mastered standardised French*. ...They are easily discouraged *when put down by Anglophone students who have never been exposed to vernacular French*. It has also been suggested that immersion students in all-French classes have the effect of reinforcing feelings of inferiority which Francophone students already experience *because they do not share the majority language and culture* (my italics).[17]

In other words, the author seems to be asserting that the two groups not only possess different cultures but they speak different "qualities" of French. To draw the different threads of this study together we must conclude that immersion graduates possess poor but "better" French and express little interest in the culture that lies beyond the language. Further, it adds up to a limited interest in using the language, an observation that is borne out by a study cited in the 1987 Annual Report of the Commissioner of Official Languages. This study of French immersion graduates of the Ottawa and Carleton Boards of Education (that is, of a part of the country where French is a real, living language in the sense of being present in the immediate environment) reveals that,

> ...the frequency with which these first-year university students actually use French is quite low, both in their studies or in leisure or other pursuits. ... [They] reported an average of two television hours per month in French, one French book read in three months, one French movie every two months and approximately 4.4 hours per month spent in other uses of French.[18]

If what I have said thus far is true, why are English Canadians so attracted to French immersion? In spite of the claim of Arthur Leblanc and numerous others that "eminent researchers have studied almost every facet of the immersion phenomenon",[19] the reader will perhaps be

---

16. (Ottawa: Minister of Supply and Services, 1989) at 245-46.
17. A. Leblanc, *supra*, note 8 at 80.
18. Commissioner of Official Languages, *Annual Report 1987* (Ottawa: Minister of Supply and Services, 1988) at 203.
19. A. Leblanc, *supra*, note 8 at 6.

surprised to learn that little consideration has been given to the motives underlying the selection of French immersion by parents for their children. Scholarly inquiry has dealt almost exclusively with immersion as it affects the individual (the learning process as a whole, French language acquisition, etc.); virtually nothing has been done on the broader, societal dimensions.[20]

Generally speaking, explanations are provided in terms of educational privilege (immersion schools are better), pragmatism (improved career opportunities) and patriotism (being better Canadians).

I can well appreciate the social class consideration, that it is English Canada's public sector alternative to the private school, hence the concern of privileged and education-oriented parents to send their children to them. However, French is only an incidental attribute in such a perspective. The schools could just as easily teach in German or Japanese — or one could create écoles internationales, placing an emphasis on the acquisition of three languages, as certain school boards have started doing in Québec.

Pragmatism? I do not really accord much importance to this explanation and certainly do not envisage the Canadian work world making active use of a quarter of a million Anglophone speakers of French in the coming decades! There are relatively few opportunities in the Federal Public Service, the demand for services in French is much more limited than one is led to believe, while as a general rule the private sector makes no use of French within English Canada. French is something to have on one's curriculum vitae at application, but hardly something to use once employed.

As for patriotism, it is a nice idea, but if it doesn't lead to increased interaction between Francophones and Anglophones or to some kind of cultural sharing, it doesn't translate into anything very concrete within the country. In other words, I have difficulty translating the sentiment into practice.

I have another theory, largely inspired by Raymond Breton's seminal paper entitled "The production and allocation of symbolic resources: an analysis of the linguistic and ethnocultural fields in Canada"[21] which proposes that the post-war reformulation of Canadian identity — from a British Commonwealth to a continental connection — has resulted

---

20. There are, of course, some exceptions but they are of an exploratory nature. See, particularly, R. Bienvenue, "Ethnolinguistic Attitudes and French Immersion Enrollments", *Canadian Ethnic Studies*, 16(2): 15-29, 1984, and M. Genty, "Le trillium et le lys ou quelques observations sur les classes d'immersion en français, à Toronto et en Ontario", *études canadiennes*, 22: 81-102, 1987.
21. *Canadian Review of Sociology and Anthropology*, 21(2): 123-44, 1984.

in the elaboration of a totally new symbolic order. In this context, French has become a major marker of national difference within an essentially North American context. A new national anthem, a new flag, new names for government departments and crown corporations, new coins, new stamps...and a new language. Hence the rocketing status of French and the development on the part of English Canadians of an ideological committment to the language.

However, its strength is largely that of a symbol and its importance ceases there. Those bilingual signs as we enter or leave Edmonton airport or cross the 49th parallel; the "code" that Canadians can introduce into their conversations or pull out of their briefcases. As an international message — a national boundary marker — directed principally at our omnipresent neighbours, it does not need and indeed cannot be used. It functions simply as a public manifestation of difference as Lester Pearson so aptly recognised in his remark that "When an American asks you the difference between Canada and the United States...answer him in French!"[22]

It is in this sense that the French language has been appropriated by English Canada, and its adoption by large numbers of Anglophones may well constitute a hollow and ultimately deceiving victory for Francophone minorities since it does little to advance their cause as a collectivity and provides no avenue for controlling the duration of English Canadian interest in the language.

The strategy of actively promoting a language for symbolic purposes to deal with a powerful neighbour is not unique to Canada. Two examples from the British Isles — Ireland and Wales — readily come to mind. Exactly the same paradoxes are evident: of a continuing decline of mother tongue speakers in the language core areas, but an increasing interest in and knowledge of the national language (Gaelic or Welsh) on the part of white-collar professionals, intellectuals and civil servants in the cities. Hence, constitutional or state commitments to the language, a great deal of rhetoric, accelerating bilingualism (where the school becomes the principal agency for the acquisition of skills and the promotion of language), etc. at the same time as there is a constantly declining functional usage of the language. There are only a few thousand surviving mother tongue speakers of Gaelic in Ireland and no longer any unilinguals, and yet almost 40 % of the country's population claims to speak the language! Bilingual junior and senior schools in Wales are not best developed in the anglicised parts of the country and they typically recruit three-quarters of their students from non-Welsh-speaking homes.

---

22. The remark was originally made in a Canadian Press interview and is cited in M. Morin "La langue au chat", *Le Devoir* (5 April 1986).

Quite obviously the reasons are much the same as for English Canada: national pride and national difference, the other nation being in this instance England.

What are the implications of all this? Where does it lead? I hesitate to say, but obviously we are witness to, in English Canada as in Ireland and Wales, a process of atomisation of language territories and, hence, an eroding of their functional significance. It is a process which can be tolerated so long as the language core areas remain. Their very existence justifies the considerable investments in the national minority language. But if those "core areas" (or language heartlands) disappear from the map, as the Gaeltacht, the Welsh heartland and the majority of the Francophone minority communities located beyond the Soo-Moncton bilingual belt are in the process of doing — and this for economic and political as well as linguistic and demographic reasons — what will happen? What will be the point in carrying on?

To pose such a question is, of course, to assume the role of the devil's advocate and bring English Canada's attention to three major issues. Firstly, social scientists — and indeed the intellectual elite in general — needs to look critically at the immersion phenomenon, asking themselves why, at a certain point in the history of this country, a specific social class is attracted to it. Such criticism involves, of course, self criticism and this is unlikely to be an easy task since social scientists as a group are judges in their own cause, actively supporting and largely committed to placing their own children in such programmes. Secondly, serious doubts should be raised about the proposition that French immersion and Francophone minority students are natural allies. If they have nothing to say to each other when they meet, have different attitudes to the French language and have different goals with respect to insertion in the larger society, what do they have in common? Thirdly, the permanence of French immersion should not be taken for granted. As someone raised at my dinner table during the conference: "Shouldn't we in the West be learning Japanese instead?" And I know Keith Spicer[23] already has the answer to that question, that, of course, we should be learning both!

French immersion is in a very real sense the fruit of a dream of the intelligentsia of English Canada, an ideal that evokes the rebirth of a nation. The irony, indeed the tragedy, as it unfolds is that this ideal is not necessarily shared by the Francophone minority communities, confronted as they are by the harsh realities of the cohabitation of languages and cultures on this continent.

---

23. The first Commissioner of Official Languages, now Chairman of the Canadian Radio-Television and Telecommunications Commission and Chairman of the Citizen's Forum on Canada's Future.

Partie XI / Part XI

L'Accord du lac Meech

L'échec de l'Accord du lac Meech entraîne des conséquences évidentes pour l'avenir des politiques linguistiques canadiennes. Sa ratification possible était perçue par certains comme l'enchâssement d'une politique étroite de dualité linguistique effectuée aux dépens de valeurs nationales importantes. Son échec éventuel était ressenti par d'autres comme une humiliation supplémentaire et le rejet final des aspirations minimes du Québec. Mais les conséquences dépassent le cadre linguistique. Le débat a permis à beaucoup de se prononcer sur l'avenir respectif du Canada et du Québec. Les contributions suivantes prennent position à cet égard et reflètent la gamme d'opinions les plus répandues. Toutes ont été énoncées avant l'échec de juin 1990.

Deborah Coyne avance que l'opposition à l'Accord Meech s'appuie sur deux thèmes de base : l'affaiblissement inacceptable du gouvernement fédéral d'une part et de la Charte d'autre part. Mais elle ne se borne pas à critiquer les dispositions de l'Accord. En constatant que l'assurance des Québécois grandit, elle cherche à discréditer le point de vue selon lequel ils sont mécontents du fédéralisme. Coyne estime que la fin du lac Meech nous permettra de commencer à élaborer de meilleures façons d'assurer l'évolution du Québec tout en faisant progresser d'autres réformes constitutionnelles importantes.

Selon Claude Morin, la valeur de l'Accord aux yeux du public québécois est avant tout symbolique, le caractère distinct du Québec étant finalement reconnu dans la Constitution. Il trouve ironique que l'opposition du reste du Canada envers l'Accord ait été motivée par le recours à la clause «nonobstant» du Bill 178, vu qu'il s'agit de la clause qui a permis à toutes les provinces de parvenir à un pacte constitutionnel excluant le Québec en 1981. Morin estime que, si Meech échoue, les Québécois porteront leur attention sur des problèmes plus importants ; les questions linguistiques représentent en effet une plus grande priorité que le symbolisme du lac Meech.

Bryan Schwartz défend la vision nationale du Canada que menaçait l'Accord. Selon lui, la clause de la société distincte assurerait aux communautés minoritaires hors Québec et à la minorité anglophone québécoise le statut de citoyens de seconde classe. Il se déclare en faveur d'une communauté plus large, dévouée au bien-être social national. C'est afin d'éviter une désintégration nationale qu'il milite contre l'Accord.

Selon le point de vue de McRobert, l'Accord ne menace guère la vision nationale canadienne. Il la refléterait plutôt et constituerait une articulation réaliste du *statu quo*. Plus important encore, il signifierait l'adhésion du Québec à la *Loi constitutionnelle de 1982*. McRoberts affirme que toutes les questions soulevées dans l'Accord relèvent des paramètres raisonnables du fédéralisme renouvelé et qu'elles sont, en fin de compte un bien petit prix à payer et un geste important à poser envers le Québec.

The Meech Lake Accord

The demise of the Meech Lake Accord has obvious implications for the future of Canadian language policy. Its threatened passage was seen by some as the entrenchment of a narrow policy of linguistic duality over other important national values. Its failure was seen by others as a further humiliation, and a final rejection, of Québec's minimal aspirations. But its demise has more than linguistic implications. It was also a time when many took sides on Canada and Québec's respective futures. The following contributions assume positions on that terrain and reflect a range of widely-held opinions. All were written before the Accord's failure in June 1990.

Deborah Coyne argues that widespread opposition to the Accord revolved around two basic themes: the unacceptable weakening of the federal government and the unacceptable undermining of the *Charter*. But she is not content to rest her case on a critique of the Accord's provisions. By establishing that there is a growing confidence amongst Québecers, she seeks to discredit the view that they are discontent with federalism. Coyne believes that with Meech Lake out of the way we can begin to discuss better ways of securing Québec's evolution while advancing other important constitutional reforms.

Claude Morin characterizes the appeal of the Accord to the Québec public as primarily symbolic; finally, constitutional recognition would be given to Québec's distinct character. He finds it ironic that objection to the Accord was building because of Québec's use of the notwithstanding clause in Bill 178, for it was that same clause which sealed the constitutional deal amongst all provinces, to the exclusion of Québec, in 1981. Morin believes that, if Meech failed, Québecers would move onto more important matters, language issues being of greater priority than the symbolism of Meech Lake.

Bryan Schwartz champions the national vision of Canada that was threatened by the Accord. The distinct society clause, in his view, entrenched minority communities outside of Québec and the Anglophone minority within it as second class citizens. He argues in favour of the greater community dedicated to the national social welfare. In order to avoid national disintegration, he argues against the Accord.

In Kenneth McRobert's view, the Accord does little to upset Canada's national vision. Rather, it is reflective of it, a realistic articulation of the status quo. More importantly, it is a means whereby Québec's signature would formally adhere to the *Constitution Act, 1982*. McRoberts argues that all of the matters raised in the Accord were within the reasonable parameters of renewed federalism and, in sum, were a small price to pay for the important gesture the Accord made towards Québec.

BEYOND THE MEECH LAKE ACCORD

Deborah Coyne

INTRODUCTION

Now that the Meech Lake Accord is clearly well on its way to being buried, it is time to discuss both the immediate and longer term implications of the popular rejection of the Accord, and the alternative ways to accommodate Québec's special concerns for constitutional guarantees of linguistic and cultural security. In particular, it is critical to build credible arguments to counter the apocalyptic, false assertions of the Accord's proponents that this is a once in a lifetime chance to "bring Québec into the Constitution", and that to reject the Accord will be interpreted in Québec as the rest of Canada saying no to Québec, which will then boost separatist claims that Québec cannot evolve securely within the Canadian federal system.

To begin with, it is dangerously misleading and wholly irresponsible for the Accord's proponents, including none other than the Prime Minister of Canada, to refer continually to the isolation of Québec as if Québec were not now part of Canada. The Supreme Court of Canada has held, in a case instigated by the Parti Québécois government in 1982, that Québec continues to be bound by the *Constitution*, as it has been since 1867, despite the refusal of the Québec government to consent willingly to the constitutional reforms of 1982.[1] Thus, among many other things, all federal laws continue to apply in Québec.

Journalist William Johnson has succinctly noted that, in 1982, "Québec spoke with two voices. Its strong federal voice joined with nine provinces to patriate the Constitution, by which Québec has been bound ever since... Québec was not isolated in 1981 and is not isolated today. The provincial *government* of Québec is."[2] Moreover, as La Presse columnist Marcel Adam concedes, the Québec government itself is responsible for this so-called isolation. "Le Québec n'a pas été isolé par

---

1. *Re A.G. (Québec) and A.G. (Canada)* (1982), 140 D.L.R. (3d) 385 (S.C.C.).
2. *The Montreal Gazette* (18 February 1989).

ses partenaires, c'est plutôt le gouvernement péquiste qui s'est isolé à cause de son option souverainiste."[3]

Second, it is equally misleading and irresponsible for the Accord's proponents to allege that the opposition to the Accord is "anti-Québec". As the well-known Québec commentator, Lysiane Gagnon, emphasizes : "Cet accord ne tourne pas qu'autour de la question québécoise; il chambarde toute la dynamique canadienne." Gagnon goes on to deplore the fact that "le compromis boiteux que constitue l'Accord du Lac Meech soit devenu une telle vache sacrée... Bien sûr, c'est le seul compromis constitutionnel qui existe, le seul qui soit en vue... Mais rien ne dit qu'un compromis bâtard produit par les tractations de dernière minute et inspiré par le besoin d'en finir davantage que par une vision politique digne de ce nom, soit mieux que rien."[4]

In this paper, I will argue that the widespread opposition to the Meech Lake Accord is oriented around two basic themes: first, the unacceptable weakening of the federal government and, second, the unacceptable undermining of the *Charter*. In analyzing the opposition, I will suggest why a majority of Québecers should share these deep concerns with the Accord and, with appropriate leadership, can be persuaded that the Accord is not desirable in its present form.

I will also suggest that Québecers have developed a new sense of self-assurance and confidence in themselves and in their future within the federal system. This tolerant, outward-looking perspective greatly enhances the prospects of successfully pursuing new directions for constitutional reform that take us beyond the flawed Meech Lake Accord. Thus, the rejection of the Accord in its present form will *not* boost the separatist forces in Québec and, instead, will lead to a more acceptable and effective constitutional accommodation of the Québec demands that were put forward as the basis for negotiating the Accord.

For example, better ways can be found to ensure Québec's secure evolution as the principal source of the French language and culture in Canada, rather than through the opaque "distinct society" clause in the Accord. To this end, we must carefully analyze and debate exactly what elements of the French-Canadian identity are threatened and then exactly what sort of special protection Québec requires. Among other things, this will involve building on the already existing special protections for Québec in our *Constitution Acts* of 1867 and 1982.

In addition, the renewed constitutional negotiations with Québec can be successfully integrated with discussions of other critical reforms,

---

3. *La Presse* (14 mars 1989).
4. *La Presse* (11 mars 1989).

notably, the abrogation of the notwithstanding clause in the *Charter*, the strengthening of minority language and education rights, Senate reform, a new amending formula with a referendum mechanism, and progress on aboriginal rights. Again, with appropriate leadership, all this could have the support of a majority of Québecers who recognize that the best guarantee of the survival of the French language and culture in North America is a strong Canadian federation firmly committed to bilingualism, rather than a tiny separate Québec alone in a sea of over 250 million Anglophones. The majority of Québecers recognize that survival depends on having a strong federal government working together with a strong Québec government to protect and promote the interests of both the Francophone majority and Anglophone minority in Québec and the Francophone minorities outside Québec.

These interests, however, are not simply of a linguistic or cultural nature. Of course, federal government assistance is and will continue to be critical in areas directly concerned with language and culture. These include ensuring that the arts and cultural community in Québec has sufficient financial assistance (particularly at this time when the Québec government has refused to fulfil its 1985 election promise to significantly increase spending on cultural affairs), and assisting in the promotion of excellence in education (for example, through financial support for universities as well as the much-needed expansion of library facilities), and in radio and television broadcasting (see, for example, Lysiane Gagnon, "Où s'en va Radio-Québec?", *La Presse*, le 16 mars 1989).

But an equally important element of protecting and promoting the French language and culture is maintaining a vibrant, dynamic social and economic life both in Québec and elsewhere in Canada. This is essential to nourish and sustain a vibrant, dynamic French language and culture to which new generations of Canadians in particular will want to contribute.

In all these areas, Québecers need to participate in a strong federal government that views Québec as much more than "une carte électorale qui produit de l'électricité", as author Yves Beauchemin puts it in a pungent criticism of Robert Bourassa.[5] Québecers need to participate in a strong federal government that will forcefully resist the disintegrative continentalist forces now exacerbated under the bilateral trade deal, and that will prevent internecine economic conflicts among provinces as they compete in unseemly fashion for a piece of the American pie.

Finally, Québecers need to participate in a strong federal government with other Canadians who share the same history, the same values and the same commitment to respecting and promoting basic human rights,

5. *La Presse* (11 mars 1989).

to building a fairer more compassionate society and to pursuing a steadily improving quality of life. Only if we can continue to act together coherently as Canadians will we be able to resist the fatal attraction of the American colossus and the very real danger that the desperate pursuit of a 'level playing field' with the United States will result in unacceptable constraints on both the federal and provincial governments. This will lead to a patchwork quilt of ineffective lowest common denominator public policies in critical areas ranging from acid rain and environmental protection to social security changes designed to eliminate child poverty and homelessness.

The renewed constitutional negotiations proposed above will obviously take time since the process must be opened up to permit the meaningful involvement of all concerned Canadians. But building a country has never been easy or painless. Moreover, unless the current Prime Minister and Québec Premier demonstrate some flexibility and admit that there are possibilities beyond Meech Lake, concrete progress will be stalled until after they pass from the political scene. In the meantime, however, it is critical to sustain the ongoing debate at the provincial and territorial levels and within the opposition at the national level in order to strengthen the broad popular consensus for the proposed reforms. In this way, we can ensure legitimate durable constitutional change and the ongoing evolution of Canada as a progressive dynamic nation.

I. OPPOSITION TO THE ACCORD: THE UNACCEPTABLE WEAKENING OF THE FEDERAL GOVERNMENT

It is important to emphasize that the opposition to the Accord is not directed against the original demands made by the Québec government as its condition for signing the *Constitution Act, 1982*.[6] Indeed most Canadians would agree with the Accord's proponents that the demands are perhaps the most reasonable ever put forward by a Québec government. Rather, the opposition is primarily directed against the generalization to all the other provinces of all concessions made to Québec and the failure of the federal government to discharge its unique responsibility to represent the interests of the people of Canada.

In effect, in negotiating the Accord, the Prime Minister did not speak for Canada and showed little, if any, national leadership. Of course, it is much easier to make a deal by giving everything to all the provinces and demanding nothing in return. But that is not leadership. Moreover, it reveals a complete absence of any sense of the distinct national identity of Canada, and abandons the pursuit of our vision of a bilingual, multicultural nation.

6. Being schedule B of the *Canada Act, 1982* (U.K.), 1982, c. 11.

A brief examination of how the Accord addressed the demands of Québec with respect to immigration, appointments to the Supreme Court of Canada, the federal spending power, and the constitutional amendment formula, illustrates clearly the unacceptable abdication of federal powers in favour of all the provinces, and the failure to deal specifically with Québec's special concerns. Québec's fifth demand — the recognition of Québec's distinctiveness in the preamble to the Constitution — will be discussed separately in the context of the *Charter*.

In addition, brief mention will be made of two other elements of the Accord that will equally result in an irreversible shift of political dynamism from Ottawa to all the provinces and that were not even part of Québec's proposals: entrenched First Ministers' Conferences and appointments to the Senate.

1. Immigration

Under the Accord, rather than address Québec's objective of ensuring sufficient reinforcement of the Francophone community through immigration, significant powers over immigration were given to all provinces. As Québec journalist Michel Vastel observed in a satirical open letter to the Minister of Immigration: "transférer à ces provinces-là les mêmes pouvoirs qu'au Québec, ce n'est pas seulement nier le caractère 'distinct' de la société québécoise, c'est aussi insulter le premier ministre du Québec... En fait, ce sont les petites provinces du Canada anglais qui ont le plus gagné, grâce au Québec, et chaque capitale provinciale devrait ériger une statue à Robert Bourassa."[7]

Thus, just at the moment when we require a coherent national immigration policy to help meet the demographic challenge of our aging population, the spectre is raised of eleven (federal and provincial) different and competing immigration policies and a severe weakening of the federal role in providing new Canadians with a sense of attachment to Canada as opposed to the particular province to which they initially immigrate.

2. Appointments to the Supreme Court of Canada

Similarly, rather than address Québec's special concerns for a constitutional guarantee of three civil law judges on the Supreme Court of Canada, the power to appoint judges to Canada's highest court was effectively ceded to all provinces. This means that, henceforth, the final adjudicators of, among other things, federal-provincial constitutional disputes and *Charter* challenges will owe their positions to provincial governments.

---

7. *Le Devoir* (11 mai 1987).

It is inevitable that the provincial appointments will be ideologically inspired — something that will subtly influence the approach of the Supreme Court of Canada to the resolution of disputes. For example, one cannot imagine a future Parti Québécois premier putting forward the names of judges who were particularly sympathetic to the federal government.

In effect, the Meech Lake provisions have simply transferred the patronage powers to appoint judges from the federal to the provincial levels. A valuable opportunity to negotiate a more open and acceptable appointment mechanism involving, for example, a non-partisan nominating council at the federal level, was lost. Equally important from Québec's perspective, although Québec gained control over the three Québec appointments, it lost all influence that it currently exerts over the other six appointments — the majority of the Court — by virtue of its representation in the federal cabinet.

3. The Federal Spending Power

A third area where the Accord fails to address Québec's special concerns and, instead, significantly weakens federal powers in favour of all the provinces, is in respect of the spending power. There is no doubt that federal government spending in areas of provincial jurisdiction, notably with respect to social welfare matters, has been a source of concern between the Québec and federal governments for many years. But in most situations to date, mutually satisfactory special administrative arrangements have been concluded which allow Québec to receive federal payments related to certain national shared-cost programs like the Canada Assistance Plan by way of compensating 'tax room' or adjustment payments, rather than conditional grants. Despite this, however, Québec governments have continued to demand explicit constitutional protection against unilateral federal action.

The other provinces have not expressed the same degree of concern. This is because, in general, they acknowledge the value of the spending power in facilitating national social and economic programs in critical areas in which the division of powers between the federal and provincial governments is not clear. These areas include health care, social welfare, post-secondary education, and environmental protection.

We often forget how important national programs are in sustaining and strengthening our sense of national community, securing equality of opportunity for all Canadians and ensuring our mobility. This occurs through the establishment of minimum national standards and the assurance that we can go anywhere in Canada and get the same or similar level of a public service, like medicare. To find evidence of the broad support for such programs, one has only to remember the national debate over the *Canada Health Act*[8] in 1983-84 and the strong resistance across Canada to the erosion of the universal medicare program through extra-billing and user fees. The same sort of debate is now occurring over child care, environmental protection — especially in the wake of the Brundtland Report[9] — a national education and training strategy, a national science and technology strategy, a comprehensive disability insurance scheme, and the creation of a national securities commission. And much of the widespread concern with the bilateral trade deal relates to the unacceptable constraints placed on the federal government that may prevent such important national initiatives in future.

But just when it is more critical than ever to ensure the capacity of the federal government to undertake new programs with firm national standards, the Meech Lake Accord would cripple it. The excessive ambiguity of the spending power provisions and the ease with which provinces can opt out of any proposed national program with compensation will mean that we will end up with a patchwork of programs across the country, with the federal government relegated to playing a sterile game of cash register politics. In addition, we will have transferred inappropriate powers to an ill-equipped judiciary to determine such key political issues as whether a province has complied with "the national objectives".

When this is then combined with the Meech Lake provisions permitting all provinces to opt out with financial compensation of all future constitutional amendments that may transfer power to the federal government, such as those in the past dealing with unemployment insurance and pensions, we will wind up with little sense of national purpose in an increasingly balkanized Canada. It will now be far too easy for a province to opt out of future adjustments to the division of powers that may be required to meet the critical challenges that lie ahead, notably, in the areas of environmental protection, telecommunications, financial services, and the integration of our employment and social assistance policies.

But, proponents of the Accord say, only heavy — handed centralists who do not really believe in the federal principle could possibly object to restrictions on federal spending in areas of exclusive provincial jurisdiction.

Yet this is simply wrong. On the contrary, we value our federal system of government and our diversity. But we believe in a dynamic

---

8. Now R.S.C. 1985, c. C-6.
9. World Commission on Environment and Development, *Our Common Future* (Oxford, New York: Oxford University Press, 1987).

federal system with both strong federal and strong provincial governments. It is the creative tension between the two levels of government that allows us to strengthen our distinct Canadian identity, accommodate our diversity and create a caring, compassionate society.

We believe that only the federal government is capable of recognizing and acting in the national interest and rising above the limited provincial perspective. Only the federal government can ensure the mobility of all Canadians and equal opportunity for all Canadians. But to focus on the unique and important role of the federal government does not imply rigid uniformity across provinces. It does involve, however, effective minimum national standards and effective coordination of provincial policies and programs.

We must, of course, acknowledge that the federal government is not always in the forefront of progressive policy initiatives. As in the case of medicare, the provinces are often ahead. Indeed, we have a less than satisfactory federal government at the moment, witness the ineffective minimalist response to major issues like environmental protection, child care, and the Acquired Immune Deficiency Syndrome (AIDS). But we must ensure that, whatever the current political situation, our constitutional arrangements will still permit the federal government to take the necessary steps to enable all Canadians to benefit from progressive policies, when the national interest so justifies.

The critical point to note in connection with the Meech Lake Accord is that even Québec does not benefit from the substantial decentralization and the fatal weakening of the federal government. Most Québecers, like the rest of Canadians, appreciate the value of both strong federal and strong provincial governments. One need only ask the residents of Saint-Basile-le-Grand who called for strong federal action in the wake of the PCB disaster in September 1988; or ask child care and social policy activists in Québec who know that the provincial government cannot always be relied on to adequately protect and promote their rights and interests. Finally, ask the writers and other members of the cultural community in Québec who have benefited from the federal government's decisions in March 1989 to compensate writers who lost royalty payments following the bankruptcy of the Québec publishing company Éditions Leméac, and to intervene vigorously in the so-called "dubbing dispute" with France to ensure that a much greater proportion of dubbed French language television programs aired in Québec are dubbed in Québec.

Lysiane Gagnon emphasizes this point, that Québecers would not benefit from the decentralization implicit in the Meech Lake Accord. According to Gagnon: "Il est préférable que les pouvoirs qui échappent au Québec restent concentrés au fédéral plutôt que éparpillés entre les neuf autres provinces, parce que le fédéral est le seul gouvernement, hors du Québec, où les Québécois sont présents. Le gouvernement d'Ottawa est le seul sur lequel Québec peut exercer une influence réelle, à travers ses députés et une fonction publique partiellement francophone, et à cause de sa force électorale."[10]

In other words, we must not forget that Québec representatives in Ottawa have a significant interest in and influence on the formulation and implementation of national policies, including those that depend on the exercise of the federal spending power. Thus while we must address the Québec government's concern to restrict federal powers, we must be careful to maintain an adequate balance of federal and provincial powers and we must avoid irreversibly weakening the federal government. For example, we could consider restrictions on the federal spending power but only in the broader context of revising the current outdated division of powers and clarifying, among other things, exactly what is meant by the Accord's reference to "areas of exclusive provincial jurisdiction". Any constitutional amendment must also ensure, in clear and unambiguous terms, the federal ability to establish effective national programs with minimum standards.

4. Constitutional Amendment Procedures

A fourth area where the Accord fails to address Québec's special concerns is in respect of the constitutional amendment procedures and Québec's demand for a constitutional veto. Rather than introduce an amendment formula that would give Québec a veto over all constitutional change, the Accord gives extensive veto powers to all provinces in respect of federal institutions and the addition of new provinces. It also loosens the current general amending formula to permit all provinces to opt out with fiscal compensation of any amendments to the division of powers, not simply those involving "education and other cultural matters" as permitted by the *Constitution Act, 1982*.

The extensive veto powers of all provinces will effectively freeze our future constitutional evolution. Among other things, it precludes meaningful Senate reform and the creation of new provinces. It also increases provincial bargaining leverage across the whole range of federal-provincial issues, thus enabling provinces to use the threat of a veto to extract concessions in unrelated areas.

Furthermore, the Accord proposals are not in Québec's interests. As Gérard Pelletier succinctly noted in 1965 with respect to the Fulton-

---

10. *La Presse* (10 décembre 1988).

Favreau formula, and repeated in 1987, "le Québec est désormais enfermé dans le cadre juridique de 1867 qu'il ne pourra jamais plus modifier puisqu'il suffit pour l'empêcher que l'Île-du-Prince-Édouard (125,000 inhabitants) décide de se trainer les pieds."[11]

Similarly, Québec does not gain from the ability to opt out with fiscal compensation of changes to the division of powers. This only gives Québec the "negative" power to reject certain amendments, but no "positive" power to influence the contents of the amendments. According to many Québec critics of the Accord, such as former PQ minister Jacques-Yvan Morin, securing and enhancing Québec's bargaining leverage is all the more important since Québec has yet to engage in a serious renegotiation of the division of powers. Thus in Morin's view, Bourassa should not agree to the Meech Lake Accord and particularly the new amending formula unless prior agreement is also reached on adjustments to legislative powers.[12]

Many current Québec politicians, however, are reluctant to admit the inadequacy of the Meech Lake amendment proposals and how, in fact, the Accord simply makes worse an already flawed amendment procedure in the *Constitution Act, 1982*. In large measure, this is because they would also have to criticize equally Bourassa's predecessor, René Lévesque, who in April 1981 abandoned Québec's longstanding claim for a constitutional veto and agreed, for tactical reasons, to the so-called Vancouver formula that has now been effectively incorporated in the Meech Lake Accord. It was also René Lévesque who was the first premier to abandon Québec's longstanding position of insisting on a meaningful transfer of legislative power from the federal to the provincial government before agreeing to entrench any amending formula in the *Constitution*.

In light of this close link between the Meech Lake Accord and Lévesque's demands in 1981, it is not surprising to find that the Accord is supported, albeit somewhat ambiguously, by several influential participants in the 1981 decision to abandon the veto and a prior renegotiation of the division of powers, notably, Claude Morin. In an extraordinarily one-sided self-justificatory account of the 1980-81 negotiations in *Lendemains Piégés*,[13] Morin claims that the Meech Lake provisions are a step forward and indeed were facilitated by the exercise of Québec's "passive veto" in refusing to accept the constitutional

---

11. *La Presse* (16 septembre 1987).
12. *Le Devoir* (19 et 20 janvier 1988).
13. Claude Morin, *Lendemains Piégés*, (Les Éditions du Boréal, 1988). (See also Gilles Lesage, "Claude Morin opine que le lac Meech découd du "veto" exercé par Québec", *Le Devoir* (1 octobre 1988).

settlement of 1981. At the same time, however, Morin candidly admits that the Parti Québecois strategy throughout the negotiations was not to participate constructively in order "de faire une fois de plus la preuve qu'il n'y a rien à espérer de ceux qui ne veulent rien offrir... Il ne veut pas que le public finisse par souhaiter l'arrivée sur la scène politique d'un remplaçant désireux de défendre ses intérêts à Ottawa."[14]

Fortunately, there are other less self-interested commentators who generally do not share Claude Morin's rosy assessment of the Meech Lake amendment provisions and are not reluctant to criticize the Lévesque strategy any more than the Bourassa one. But many of them go on to conclude that perhaps a constitutional veto for Québec in all matters is now an impossible goal in light of the reluctance of the other provinces to concede such a special role to Québec. Lysiane Gagnon, for example, argues persuasively that: "L'atomisation du droit de véto est anti-démocratique (elle va contre le principe «un homme, un vote») et impraticable. Elle risque de bloquer toute réforme constitutionnelle." She then points out that a constitutional veto for Québec is an essential component of Québec's historical claim for a special status, but that in her view, "La nature du Canada fait qu'il est impossible au Québec d'obtenir un statut particulier complet à moins qu'au moment des négociations, le rapport de force ne lui soit extraordinairement favorable."[15]

In my view, however, Gagnon and others should not be so pessimistic. The failure of the Meech Lake Accord and the still urgent need to resolve Québec's constitutional concerns will enhance both Québec's and the federal government's bargaining leverage in future constitutional discussions.

With effective national leadership, we can build on the widespread popular concern with the unaccountable anti-democratic process leading to the Meech Lake Accord whereby eleven men attempted unilaterally to fundamentally change the nature of the Canadian federation. We can then persuade the provinces of the need for a major revamping of the current amending procedures to include a constitutional veto for Québec. Among other things, this will mean implementing a referendum mechanism to ensure respect for the fundamental principle of the sovereignty of the *people*, something that was apparently forgotten at Meech Lake, and to allow the people of Canada to have the final word on changes to our *Constitution*.

---

14. *Id.* at 18-19.
15. *La Presse* (10 décembre 1988).

This referendum mechanism can be adapted to the federal principle and must accommodate the special needs of Québec through a requirement of regional majorities that will give Canadians in Québec the veto over constitutional change that their importance clearly justifies. In this connection, the 1971 Victoria Charter amendment formula and the federal government referendum proposals in 1978 and 1980 can provide some guidance. Most importantly, such a constitutional veto for Québec will enhance Québec's bargaining leverage and permit it to influence positively the substance of any constitutional change — something that will ensure that Québec will play, as it should, an integral part in our future evolution as a progressive dynamic nation.

5. First Ministers' Conferences and Appointments to the Senate

There are two other elements in the Accord that also involve generalized concessions to all the provinces on the part of the federal government, and were not even among Québec's original demands. These are the entrenchment of annual First Ministers' Conferences on both the *Constitution* and the economy, and the ceding to the provinces of the power to appoint senators.

The proposal to entrench at least two annual First Ministers' Conferences will have a subtle but potentially very damaging impact on the ability of the federal government to articulate and implement policies in the national interest. This is because inevitably the focus of attention with respect to matters of national policy will shift away from the federal Parliament, where it belongs, to an unaccountable third level of government — the First Ministers' Conference.

Parliament and the provincial legislatures will be relegated to mere ratification chambers, and Canada's position whether on international or domestic issues will be reduced to the lowest common denominator of rival provincial interests. In effect, we will no longer elect the federal government to articulate and pursue the national interest. Instead, eleven governments (federal and provincial) will speak for Canada, and crucial matters of national policy will be determined in regular First Ministers' Conferences, rather than by the federal cabinet.

As already noted, Québecers, like all other Canadians, will not benefit from this irreversible degree of decentralization. Moreover, one wonders why the entrenchment of First Ministers' Conferences is included as part of the constitutional accommodation of Québec, since it was not among the original demands. It appears that this was yet another short-sighted concession made by the federal government primarily to gain the support of recalcitrant Western provinces and Newfoundland with the promise of mandatory annual discussions of Senate reform and fisheries jurisdiction *ad infinitum.* But a more restrictive or bizarre provision would be difficult to find given the absurd requirement that the constitutional conference agenda cannot include any other topic unless "as agreed upon" by all other provinces !

The other concession made to all the provinces was the effective transfer of the power to appoint senators. Inevitably, this will totally transform the Senate into a body that simply reflects the untidy sum of rival provincial government interests, unable to bring any sort of constructive perspective to bear on the critical national issues facing the country. And it must not be forgotten that the Senate has the power to paralyze federal action through its veto in all matters except constitutional change.

Over the years, there have been a number of constructive Senate reform proposals that would involve either an elected Senate, or at least increased provincial involvement in the selection of senators. However, the ultimate aim has always been to maintain the national character of the institution while making it more effective at bringing the regional/ provincial perspectives to bear on national issues and legislative proposals in a way that may not be possible in the primary legislative forum — the House of Commons.

The proponents of the Accord claim that the Meech Lake provisions are only a temporary expedient pending meaningful reform of the Senate. But with the extension of a veto over Senate reform to all provinces, the prospect for any reform is virtually nil. Once again, this freezing of our constitutional evolution benefits neither Québecers nor other Canadians. Effective Senate reform must be negotiated as an integral part of the constitutional accommodation of Québec and not postponed to an indefinite string of First Ministers' Conferences.

II. OPPOSITION TO THE ACCORD: THE UNACCEPTABLE UNDERMINING OF THE CHARTER OF RIGHTS AND FREEDOMS

To understand the widespread concern with the Accord's "distinct society" clause, it is necessary to understand the impact of the *Charter of Rights and Freedoms*[16] and the broader constitutional environment that had emerged by 1987 when the Meech Lake Accord appeared on the scene.

---

16. Part I of the *Constitution Act, 1982*, being schedule B of the *Canada Act 1982* (U.K.), 1982, c. 11 (hereinafter *Charter*).

Despite the fact that the *Charter* is now over half a decade old, we have yet to realize how profoundly it has altered the relationship between the individual and the state and the political and socio-economic fabric of the country. The *Charter* is now the key component of our *Constitution* that articulates the fundamental values that are common to all of us and that define us as Canadians, our concept of the Canadian federation and our commitment to a fairer, more compassionate society.

The *Charter* is a uniquely Canadian document — one that must be interpreted in light of Canadian political traditions. It is also a late twentieth century document — one that is not preoccupied, for example, with how to limit government as was the case 200 years ago when the American Bill of Rights was adopted. Rather, the *Charter* reflects a belief that there need not be any contradiction between state regulation and individual liberty and that freedom, where appropriate, is enhanced by our public institutions and state action.

The *Charter* also blends an emphasis on individual freedom with respect for community values. For example, it requires us to take into account cultural, religious, linguistic and aboriginal communities in interpreting the rights guaranteed to individuals.

These unique aspects of the *Charter* are most obvious in the broad guarantees of equality, minority language and education rights, mobility rights and our commitment to multiculturalism, all of which are subject "only to such reasonable limits prescribed by law as can be demonstrably justified in a free and democratic society".[17] In addition, the *Constitution* now entrenches the principle of equalization and the affirmative commitment of all governments to promote equal opportunities for the well-being of all Canadians.[18]

It cannot be doubted that the *Charter* is having a transforming effect on the general conduct of politics and our language of political discourse. We are increasingly conscious of individual and group rights, and our collective identity now incorporates more fully our commitment to bilingualism and our multicultural heritage. A new dynamic element has been injected into our federal system: the courts have become major political actors, something that was illustrated most vividly by the recent Supreme Court of Canada decisions striking down the federal abortion law[19] and certain provisions of the Québec language legislation.[20]

---

17. *Id.*, s. 1.
18. *Constitution Act, 1982, supra*, note 6, s. 36.
19. *R.* v. *Morgentaler* (No. 2), [1988] 1 S.C.R. 30.
20. *Ford* v. *Québec (Attorney-General)*, [1988] 2 S.C.R. 712.

The impact of the *Charter*'s focus on rights and fundamental values in shaping the public policy agenda is not simply the result of legal challenges to legislative and administrative action. It shapes the agenda through the increased sensitivity of policy-makers who are determined to "Charter-proof" any proposed legislation or other government action in order to preempt such legal action. It also shapes the agenda through the activities of groups and individuals who use the *Charter* as a symbolic document in their lobbying efforts with governments.

The *Charter* influence is perhaps most obvious with respect to our approaches to dealing with the inequality and inequities in society, notably, our employment and social assistance policies. For example, we are increasingly conscious of the needs of disadvantaged groups such as women, visible minorities, native Canadians, the disabled, and are taking steps through employment equity/affirmative action and pay equity initiatives to improve their well-being. We also more frequently speak of a person's right to a decent minimum standard of living and a decent quality of life as something that is as worthy of protection as traditional property and constitutional rights.

More broadly, the *Charter* is having a subtle nationalizing effect as it gives expression to a national citizenship that transcends regional identities. It does this through its appeal to our non-territorial identities, for example, ethnicity or gender, something that is gradually diminishing the traditional regional or provincial/territorial focus of Canadian politics.

At the same time, the ability to challenge successfully a wide range of government action is enhancing the role of the citizen in the democratic political process in a way that was not possible before 1982. This, in turn, has given rise to new popular coalitions with national constituencies that draw their inspiration from the *Charter* and the *Constitution* and that cannot be ignored in the process of constitutional change.

In discussing the profound impact of the *Charter* in the context of the debate over the distinct society clause in the Meech Lake Accord, particular reference must be made to the minority language and education rights. These illustrate not only the unique character of the *Charter*, but also the perennial debate over how best to protect and promote both minority rights and the French language and culture in Canada that is surfacing yet again with the question of how to accommodate Québec's special concerns in the *Constitution*.

The decision in 1982 to vest minority language and education rights in individuals represented an important historical compromise, and was a critical element of "renewed federalism". Canadian history is littered with examples of the dangers of having to rely on benevolent government action to protect minority rights. For example, when Ontario moved to eliminate French language instruction in schools in the early part of the century, the federal Liberal Party leader, Wilfrid Laurier, could only plead unsuccessfully for a "regime of tolerance". So the answer in 1982 was to provide members of the minority language groups with legally enforceable rights that could be asserted against both levels of government.

The *Charter* guarantees of minority language and education rights are unique, however, because they reflect a blend of individual and group rights. More specifically, the individual rights are contingent on membership in the relevant community or collectivity. This is because language rights do not exist in a vacuum — to provide meaningful protection we must ensure the preservation and promotion of linguistic communities. So, the language guarantees, while accorded to individuals, reflect a positive, rather than negative, idea of freedom and place a positive obligation on the courts and our legislatures to promote the opportunity to use and develop one's language.

Already, we have seen several important court challenges, such as those instigated by members of Francophone minorities outside Québec, that are successfully forcing provincial governments to expand the availability of French language services and French language education. This new proactive role for the courts is perhaps usefully compared to the American experience with desegregation in the wake of the landmark U.S. Supreme Court decision in *Brown* v. *Board of Education*.[21]

The important point to note is that the success of the Francophone minorities outside Québec in galvanizing governments to promote their interests and the bilingual character of Canada, sends positive signals to French-Canadians in Québec and helps to build up their confidence in both themselves and Canada. As Lysiane Gagnon notes, the entrenchment of language rights was "une façon de permettre aux francophones de se senter chez eux à travers le Canada et d'enchâsser à jamais le caractère bilingue du pays."[22] This is the most durable way to address the reconciliation of Québec's position within Canada over the long term.

But this is where the Meech Lake Accord comes in. According to the Commissioner of Official Languages, D'Iberville Fortier, in his 1987 Annual Report, the Accord disrupts the linguistic equilibrium that has gradually emerged over the years and will potentially halt future progress

---

21. 347 U.S. 497 (1954).
22. *La Presse* (11 mars 1989).

toward strengthening the bilingual character of Canada as a whole.[23] This is because the Accord specifies that only the Québec government has the obligation to preserve and promote Québec's distinct society and identity, while all other governments, including the federal government, need only "preserve" the Anglophone minority in Québec and Francophone minorities outside Québec. It therefore denies the all-important federal role in promoting the distinct identity of Québec and weakens the commitment of all governments to advance bilingualism across Canada. Already this danger has been demonstrated by the action taken by the Alberta and Saskatchewan governments in 1988 to reduce rights enjoyed by their Francophone minorities, while all the time professing to be acting in the "spirit of Meech Lake".[24]

More generally, the Meech Lake Accord undermines the idea that all Canadians have common rights and freedoms regardless of where we live because it directs that the entire *Constitution*, including the *Charter*, be interpreted in light of geographic and socio-cultural considerations. In other words, the nature of our basic rights will henceforth vary depending on which province we live in, which linguistic group we belong to and so forth. This is clearly not a desirable course for a democracy that has always prided itself on our ability to sustain a diverse yet tolerant society and to promote bilingualism and multiculturalism throughout Canada.

The explanation for these deeply flawed Meech Lake proposals is not difficult to find. The Prime Minister and the premiers clearly did not appreciate the depth of the impact of the *Charter* on Canadians. They falsely assumed that they could deal with the question of the Québec government's place in the federal system and adjust legislative, executive and judicial powers on an intergovernmental level with little regard to the impact of such changes on our rights and freedoms and to the concerns of the new popular constituencies that have emerged since 1982. Thus they addressed only the so-called "Québec agenda" for constitutional change and the five conditions set out by Robert Bourassa.

But the critical point to note is that the Québec agenda is fundamentally an agenda focussed on the French-speaking majority in Québec and enhancing the legislative supremacy of the Québec government. It reflects the perennial Québec aim to obtain a "special status" within the federal system and to increase its constitutional powers to promote the interests of the French collectivity whether with respect to language and culture, social policy, the admission of immigrants, or international relations.

---

23. Commissioner of Official Languages, *Annual Report 1987* (Ottawa : Supply and Services Canada, 1988) at 7.

24. See Joseph Magnet, "Comments" in this volume.

The debate over whether Québec has obtained such "special status" under the opaque distinct society clause continues to be intense, especially within Québec. Most Québec nationalists argue that, at best, it will have a minimal symbolic impact and, at worst, enormous powers have been transferred to an ill-equipped judiciary to decide matters of central societal importance. Claude Morin, for example, speaks of other "lendemains piégés"[25] and warns Québecers not to be deluded into thinking that they have achieved any substantive enhancement of Québec's constitutional powers. Ironically perhaps, these nationalist critics draw support from the comments of federalist proponents of the Accord who insist, notwithstanding the weight of academic opinion to the contrary, that the distinct society clause is only an innocuous interpretive clause and is not intended to have any substantive impact on the exercise of legislative powers.

In contrast, Robert Bourassa and others certainly believe that Québec has gained something significant in terms of substantive powers. For example, since Bourassa invoked the notwithstanding clause in the *Charter* to override basic rights of freedom of expression in order to require unilingual outdoor French signs, it has been widely suggested that, had the distinct society clause been in effect, Québec would have had the constitutional power to sustain the controversial Bill 101 provisions and effectively to suppress the rights of the Anglophone minority, without resorting to the notwithstanding clause.

It is difficult to conceive of two more irreconcilable interpretations of such a critical constitutional provision and even more difficult to understand how our leaders could possibly even propose to entrench the provision before clarifying its scope. As political scientist Denis Monière emphasizes: "Ce jeu de dupes n'est pas sain pour le débat démocratique, et la confusion des esprits n'est certainement pas la meilleure façon de promouvoir les intérêts du Québec." [26]

Fortunately, the renewed language debate and the controversy over the notwithstanding clause in the *Charter* have now crystallized the widespread concern over the distinct society clause and, in particular, its inadequate protection for minority rights. And with it the last nail has been hammered into the coffin of the Meech Lake Accord.

It is now clear that the majority of Canadians do not support giving Québec undefined special powers to override the *Charter* and to promote its "distinct society" as the price of obtaining Québec's willing signature

---

25. Morin, *supra*, note 13 at 327-29.
26. *Le Devoir* (17 mars 1989).

on the *Constitution Act, 1982*. To do so will allow Québec to increasingly isolate itself from the rest of Canada. It will facilitate the emergence of provincial institutional structures to preserve and promote Québec's "distinct identity" in a wide range of areas. This in turn will inevitably facilitate the eventual separation of Québec, something that has already been publicly acknowledged by the leader of the Parti Québécois, Jacques Parizeau. Even Robert Bourassa, during his recent tour of Europe in January 1989, is already referring to building on the distinct society status to assure some "international autonomy" for Québec in the *Constitution*, and has insisted on some form, however diluted, of separate Québec representation under the Québec flag at the forthcoming Jeux de la francophonie in Morocco in July 1989.

But it is not good enough simply to say no to the distinct society clause approach in the Meech Lake Accord. A large number of Québecers continue to believe that Québec must have special constitutional guarantees to give the Québec government the necessary manoeuvering room to protect and promote the French language and culture in Québec.

The critical challenge for future constitutional discussions is to devise other ways to accommodate Québec's special concerns that will allow us to maintain a strong federal government and the primacy and integrity of the *Charter*. In seeking these alternatives, however, we must remember that the majority of moderate Québecers also share our concerns about federal powers and the integrity of the *Charter*. This quiet majority of Québecers belongs to neither the provincialist nor nationalist extremes and still believes that it is as important to have a strong federal government to defend the French language and culture within the framework of a bilingual Canada, as it is to have a strong provincial government.

Finally, as the renewed language debate in Québec is demonstrating, the majority of moderate Québecers believe that their interests can be assured without undermining our *Charter of Rights and Freedoms*. Indeed, in presenting Québec's original demands, Gil Rémillard emphasized that the *Charter* was "un document dont nous pouvons être fiers comme Québécois et Canadiens",[27] and that it was important that Québecers have the same rights and freedoms as all other Canadians. For this reason, the Bourassa government has stopped the Parti Québécois' systematic use of the notwithstanding clause in all legislation.

---

27. Texte du discours prononcé par M. Gil Rémillard, in *Une collaboration renouvelée: le Québec et ses partenaires dans la Confédération* (Institut des relations intergouvernementales, Université Queen's, 1987) Annexe A, 50.

The remainder of this paper will discuss the political situation in Québec and Québecers' new sense of self-assurance and confidence in themselves and the future of the French language and culture within the Canadian federal system. This discussion will show that the prospects are very good for successfully pursuing new directions for constitutional reform beyond the flawed Meech Lake Accord.

III. BEYOND MEECH LAKE: A CONFIDENT QUÉBEC FACES THE FUTURE

The current language debate in Québec has provided Canadians with an interesting opportunity to assess both the degree of nationalist support in Québec and the sense of cultural security on the part of the majority of Francophone Québecers.

To begin with, it is widely acknowledged by informed observers of all political stripes, both within and outside Québec, that Bourassa's inept technocratic approach to language issues is largely responsible for the reemergence of language tensions. Even a Francophone cabinet minister in Bourassa's government, Michel Gratton, has said that if the government had acted soon after its election in 1985 to permit bilingual signs, little controversy would have been generated, but that having delayed unnecessarily the government now lacks credibility on the language issue in the eyes of both Anglophones and Francophones.[28]

Despite the noisy outcry of a vocal minority of nationalists following the decision of the Supreme Court of Canada striking down the provisions of Bill 101 requiring unilingual French commercial signs, most Québecers feel secure enough that the "visage français" of Québec can be preserved without having to override the right of freedom of expression of the Anglophone minority. The evidence of this is increasing daily.

For example, Louis Dussault, a former conseiller linguistique et commissaire-enquêteur à la Commission de protection de la langue française, is co-president of an organization called l'Entente Cordiale with Hugh MacLennan. He and many other influential Québecers, including nationalists such as writer Jacques Renaud, have called on the Québec government to withdraw the legislation requiring unilingual French commercial signs and not to use the notwithstanding clause in either the Canadian or Québec *Charters* to sustain it.

To support this position, Dussault makes the following salient points: To begin with, "le visage français de Montréal et du Québec

---

28. *La Presse* (18 mars 1989).

est une realité vivante, mouvante et stimulante aux yeux de tout observateur le moindrement objectif". The French language can be promoted without infringing the freedom of expression of the Anglophone minority. English is an official language and has historic rights in Québec recognized in section 133 of the *Constitution Act, 1867*, the *Constitution Act, 1982*, and indeed the preamble to Bill 101.[29] No other country in the world penalizes the use of another language for commercial signs as does Bill 101. Finally, "l'unilinguisme français au Québec finira par correspondre à l'unilinguisme anglais partout ailleurs au Canada avec d'éventuelles conséquences néfastes: disparition de l'ethnie canadienne-française, démantèlement du Canada, faillite de l'accord de libre-échange etc."[30]

In the lead editorial in l'*Actualité*,[31] Jean Paré also sharply criticizes Bourassa's Bill 178 that imposes unilingual French signs outdoors and permits only limited bilingual signs indoors.

> Le visage unilingue français d'un realité qui ne l'est pas, c'est une masque. Un mensonge.... Une illusion. Toute illusion est dangereuse. L'unilinguisme est le sable des autruches politiques. L'affichage unilingue escamote les problèmes, incite à croire que tout est réglé, qu'il n'y a rien d'autre à faire sur le front de l'éducation, des médias, du travail...

Paré emphasizes that:

> Chaque fois qu'on entend des voix d'origine vietnamienne, haitienne, sud-américaine, parler le français ici....on comprend que l'avenir passe bien ailleurs que dans l'affichage. L'avenir, il se joue dans la vitalité des institutions culturelles et économiques. Dans le système scolaire, qui a bien besoin et depuis longtemps, d'une nouvelle réforme. Dans la sélection, l'accueil et l'intégration systématique des immigrants. Au travail où la loi 101 a exempté trop d'entreprises d'avoir le français comme langue de travail. Dans le développement économique et technologique: le départ de jeunes diplômés qui doivent chercher du travail à Toronto affaiblit le Québec bien davantage qu'un malheureux panneau bilingue. Dans le financement des universités et de la culture. Dans la puissance des médias.

Paré concludes that Bourassa should have opted for the bilingual solution with a clear predominance of French, as proposed by the Supreme Court of Canada. "[Cette solution] aurait apporté davantage au français et au Québec. Le paysage linguistique aurait rendu évident, de la façon plus éloquente, que le français est la langue principale du Québec."

---

29. *Charter of the French Language*, R.S.Q., c. C-11.
30. *Le Devoir* (30 novembre 1988).
31. Février 1989.

A former editor of *Le Devoir*, Gérard Filion, has also weighed in against Bill 178 and the infringement of minority rights. In an interview with *La Presse*,[32] he emphasized that "la loi 101, dans ses dispositions essentielles sur la langue d'enseignement et la langue de travail, n'enlève rien aux anglophones. Par contre, la loi 178 qui oblige à l'unilinguisme français dans l'affichage mais permet le bilinguisme à l'intérieur, non seulement est-elle pour lui 'stupide' et 'ridicule', elle est aussi 'injuste' parce qu'elle enlève quelque chose à une minorité."[33]

Finally, Paul Pipier, the president of le Comité scientifique à l'institut international de droit linguistique international, makes the important point that there is no proof that the imposition of unilingual signs will even aid the survival of the French language. "Il semble que la politique d'immigration, la 'langue de travail' et 'langue de l'État' constitue des domaines beaucoup plus cruciaux pour le développement du français... Les gens se battent ici sur l'affichage, mais ils sont discrets sur le libre-échange avec le colosse américain. Même le Parti indépendantiste l'appelle de ses voeux : et, pourtant, la sauvegarde du français dans ce nouveau marché sans barrières répresente un coût supplémentaire, que les américains ne devraient pas plus être prêts à payer que la réduction des pluies acides."[34]

Even among nationalists committed to ultimate political sovereignty for Québec, there are many who believe that the collective survival of the French language and culture can be assured while respecting basic rights and freedoms. Even before the Bill 101 dispute emerged, Isabelle Courville, the former president of the Comité national des jeunes du PQ, wrote that :

> Au Québec, même si la vigilance reste vitale, nos fondations linguistiques et culturelles sont consolidées et ne constituent pas une source d'insoutenable insécurité, sentiment qui a longtemps alimenté l'action des nationalistes fortement motivés par leur 'instinct de préservation'. Les énergies déployées à la protection de la langue et de la culture, par le biais de l'attente d'un statut constitutionnel indépendant, ont été recanalisées vers d'autres projets, plus individuels que collectifs... La force motrice du 'nouveau nationalisme' sera moins la réalisation de l'indépendance que l'élaboration de 'projets québécois' visant la maîtrise des éléments essentiels à notre développement, la souveraineté réelle... C'est la poursuite de l'excellence dans tous les domaines, c'est conquérir de nouveaux marchés pour nos produits. C'est aussi l'actualisation de nos valeurs sociales comme pouvoir accéder facilement aux niveaux supérieurs

---

32. Quoted in Marcel Adam, "Gérard Filion n'aime pas la loi 178", *La Presse* (2 mars 1989).
33. *Ibid*.
34. *Le Devoir* (18 janvier 1989).

d'éducation et de formation, bénéficier d'un système de santé adapté et accessible, pouvoir intégrer le marché du travail en tout temps, évoluer au sein d'une société juste et équitable.[35]

As for the ultimate goal of independence, Courville concludes by saying: "Le cadre constitutionnel aujourd'hui nous limite, mais il n'est pas sans possibilités. L'indépendance? Bien sûr ... lorsque le Québec est prêt. D'ici là, il ne faut pas cesser de progresser."[36]

This tolerant perspective, this belief in an open just society in which collective goals are compatible with respect for basic rights and freedoms, this new focus on social and economic development as providing the durable basis for the survival of the French language and culture, appear to be characteristic of most Québecers, including many nationalists, the current leadership of the Parti Québécois notwithstanding. For example, former PQ leader Pierre Marc Johnson recently stated that it is regrettable that Québec again finds itself in the grip of a "psychodrame linguistique" when so many other urgent questions are being neglected. According to Johnson: "L'énergie qu'on passe là-dessus, on ne peut la dépenser ailleurs sur les questions environnementales et sociales, par example. Il y a des gens ici qui ne savent pas où dormir."[37]

Of course, no one denies the broad support for Bill 101. Bill 101, for example, has undoubtedly been an important contributing factor to what Lysiane Gagnon describes in one of her forceful critiques of Bill 178 as the transformation of Montreal from a city where English was dominant to one where French now predominates.[38] Gagnon further notes that: "Ce que j'observe dans ma vie quotidienne reflète très bien les dernières données de Statistiques Canada, qui montrent qu'en 1986 la majorité (60 p.cent) des Québécois de langue maternelle anglaise connaissent le français. Les gens les plus bilingues au Québec, sont maintenant les anglophones. (Seulement 40 p. cent des francophones connaissent l'anglais.)"[39]

More generally, Bill 101 has also been an important contributing factor to the emergence of Québec as "l'un des territoires les plus dynamiques en Amérique" in which Francophone Québecers lead fulfilling lives in all spheres whether business, social, or arts and cultural.

---

35. *La Presse* (28 novembre 1988).
36. *Ibid.*
37. *La Presse* (12 janvier 1989).
38. See also a 1988 study prepared for the Conseil de la langue française ("La situation démolinguistique du Québec") which concluded that the Quebec population will continue to become increasingly French-speaking into the twenty-first century. Quoted in William Johnson, "Hysteria Beats Real Figures," *The Gazette* (14 February 1989).
39. *La Presse* (10 janvier 1989).

To quote Gagnon again, this is "le Québec de 1989 où, selon tous les faits verifiés et toutes les statistiques connues, le français ne s'est jamais aussi bien porté (sous l'angle quantitatif en tous cas), le Québec de la Caisse de dépôt, de Lavalin, et de Provigo, le Québec de Vigneault et de Marjo, le Québec des HEC, des 'best sellers' et des 'success stories'."[40]

Thus, to its credit, Bill 101 has reinforced the French language and culture in Québec and given the Québec government the ability and the manoeuvering room to promote the 'visage français'. But, in addition, it has given a majority of Québecers greater confidence in their future and a sense that their legitimate interests can be secured within the Canadian federal system. Indeed many observers argue that the 'success' of Bill 101 has in fact muted the claims of indépendantistes that Québec cannot survive with dignity and respect within Canada.

However, this result would not have been possible without concurrent developments at the national level, notably, the active commitment of the federal government to promote bilingualism throughout Canada, the steadily increasing number of young Canadians in French immersion, and the substantial progress made to assure the survival and indeed the expansion of Francophone communities in New Brunswick and Ontario, together with the proactive use by all Francophone minorities outside Québec of their new *Charter* rights. All this has combined to make the federal face of Canada more acceptable to Québecers and to strengthen the sense of common destiny among all Canadians.

Admittedly, much remains to be done by all governments. For example, the minority language and education rights need to be strengthened in light of recent judicial interpretations, something that Québec also supports, and the time is long overdue for Ontario to declare itself officially bilingual. But clear progress toward bilingualism has been made and a collective commitment has taken root across Canada to avoid any territorial approach to language issues whereby Canada develops into two essentially unilingual enclaves with all the disintegrative, destructive potential that Belgium now faces.

In all this, the Québec government must of course continue its legitimate and vigorous role in promoting the French language and culture in all spheres, but in ways that respect minority rights and that reflect Québecers' desire to expand their horizons and work within the Canadian federal structure. This is particularly important as Québec, like the rest of Canadian society, becomes ever more multicultural.

---

40. *La Presse* (4 février 1989).

In this connection, Jean Taranu, the president of la Fédération des groupes ethniques du Québec, eloquently puts the case against the use of the notwithstanding clause to suppress minority rights in an article entitled "Nous voulons choisir le Québec sans craindre pour nos libertés". According to Taranu:

> Le défi d'un Québec français est plutôt d'accepter un pluralisme socio-culturel à partager entre les différents groupes qui le composent. L'immigrant n'est pas un handicapé social obligé de se réhabiliter, de se déchirer ou de se déraciner pour vivre ensemble avec les autres et faire partie de la cohésion sociale....Il est nullement question pour nous de remettre en cause la nature même de notre société francophone, ni de vouloir la remplacer par un cosmopolitisme insipide. Le projet national québécois d'une société francophone ici en Amérique du Nord, dans le respect d'autrui et de sa culture, nous attire... Les anglophones de souche ou d'autres origines...ont parfaitement compris le message qu'au Québec, la langue et la vie se passent en français. Fallait-il pour cela leur enlever les droits et libertés protégés par deux Chartes à la merci d'une règle dérogatoire? Depuis la loi 101, 65 pourcent des Anglais parlent le français, et 95 pourcent de leurs enfants fréquentent l'école française.[41]

More generally, our political leaders in Québec and elsewhere in Canada must recognize that Québecers clearly share an internationalist, outward-looking perspective with all Canadians and a common concern for the international and domestic challenges that we face. These include the challenge of eliminating the threat of nuclear Armageddon; the challenge of our aging population and the emerging inter-generational tensions; the challenge of pursuing sustainable development that respects our vulnerable environment; and the challenge of eliminating poverty, ensuring meaningful work for all, and reducing the now widening gap in wealth and opportunities between more affluent and poorer Canadians.

As popular rock star of 'Beau Dommage' fame, Michel Rivard, stated in reply to former PQ cabinet minister, Lise Payette, after she accused him of abandoning the nationalist project: "my universe is the whole planet." The themes of Rivard's songs are universal ones ranging from racism ("C'est un mur") and urban violence ("Libérer le trésor") to creating a better future for our children ("Je voudrais voir la mer", beautiful poetry in which Rivard writes of the importance of "le rire de cent millions d'enfants qui n'ont pas peur de l'eau, qui ont envie de vivre sans tenir un drapeau.") Rivard and franco-manitobain Daniel Lavoie participated with Bruce Springsteen and Sting in the September 1988 Amnesty International "Human Rights Now" concert in Montreal

---

41. *Le Devoir* (16 mars 1989).

that attracted some 60,000 persons. For Rivard, "it's important to show the rest of Canada there's something to Québec they could learn to live with — even to love... We can learn to live in harmony."[42]

More recently, Rivard participated in a highly successful concert with another popular rock star, Paul Piché. Like those of Rivard, the themes of many of Piché's most well-known songs focus on the universal ones: environmental degradation ("J'appelle"), peace and friendship ("La haine", "Le temps d'aimer"). Both Rivard and Piché commented on the importance of taking pride in the French language and defending it, and they enjoined the spectators "de parler 'plus et mieux' le français, afin d'assurer la survie de la langue."[43]

What is important to note, however, is the absence of the strident nationalist discourse of the 1970s and the implicit assumption that Québecers can assure the survival of the French language and culture in ways that do not entail the destructive disruptive consequences of political independence. Indeed, during the concert Rivard deliberately seized the opportunity to respond again to his nemesis, Lise Payette. In February, Radio-Canada had aired Payette's apocalyptic documentary entitled "Disparaître: le sort inévitable de la nation française d'Amérique". In almost fascist-racist terms, Payette predicted the disappearance of the French language and culture shortly after the turn of the century, prompted by a disastrously low birth rate and the unacceptable cultural dilution that increased immigration will entail. Fortunately, the documentary elicited a wave of protest and criticism from all sectors of society and from persons of all political stripes. And Michel Rivard was able to exploit this brilliantly by appearing on stage with a candlelabra and recalling ironically that "Madame Payette l'avait investi d'une mission périlleuse: reprendre le flambeau de notre destinée avant de 'disparaître'".[44]

Like Rivard and Piché, another popular singer, Robert Charlebois, is concerned about the future of Québec and the French language. But he too emphasizes that:

> Ce ne sont pas des lois qui défendront le mieux la langue française, ou
> plus particulièrement québécoise. C'est le prestige des Québécois qui

---

42. *Globe & Mail* (3 December 1988).
43. *La Presse* (11 mars 1989).
44. *La Presse* (13 mars 1989). Rivard also referred to Payette as "une immense dame de coeur" an allusion to her popular soap opera series, les Dames de Coeur. Coincidentally it has just been announced that the series will be discontinued at the end of March 1989. Thus, perhaps next time Rivard can also mention that the only thing in danger of imminent extinction is les Dames de Coeur, something that will be of no enduring loss to the French language and culture notwithstanding humourist Nathalie Petrowski's amusing post-mortem "Y a-t-il une vie après les Dames de Coeur?" *Le Devoir* (25 mars 1989).

l'utilisent. Les jeunes cherchent ce que disent Michael Jackson ou Madonna, comme je cherchais à comprendre le langage d'Elvis ou de Chuck Berry. C'est depuis que Julio Iglesias a une renommée mondiale qu'on sait comment se prononce le J espagnol. Et ce qui m'avait fait le plus grand plaisir, il y a quelques années, c'est quand un ami de l'Ouest m'avait confié qu'il avait le goût d'apprendre le français à cause de 'Lindberg'.[45]

Beyond the world of music, in other spheres Québecers display a similar confidence and outward looking sense of cultural security. In Québec theatre, according to observers like Matthew Fraser, collective themes have been replaced by a greater interest in the individual. And a fascination with form and technical experiments characterizing many of the brilliant productions of Robert Lepage and René-Claude Dubois has replaced the emphasis on setting and text evident in such plays as Michel Tremblay's "Les belles soeurs".[46]

Quebec cinema has also literally taken off with successful films such as Yves Simoneau's "Pouvoir intime", Jean-Claude Lauzon's "Un zoo la nuit", and Denis Arcand's "Le déclin de l'empire américain". Québec films now have a well-earned reputation that extends far beyond Canadian borders, among other things, to most internationally renowned film festivals. Other examples of Québécois cultural excellence include Guy Caron's Cirque de soleil, and Alain Simard's Festival international de jazz de Montréal.

Finally, one must not forget the emergence of a dynamic Francophone business class as a critical factor in increasing Québecers' confidence in themselves and in their upward mobility prospects within the Francophone private sector. New models to which younger Québecers aspire include Bernard Lamarre of the engineering firm Lavalin and Pierre Péladeau of Québecor.

Political scientist Kenneth McRoberts notes that it is now the private sector that offers mobility, rather than the state sector as in the 1960s and 1970s.[47] In addition, Francophone business has steadily expanded into formerly Anglophone domains such as heavy industry and engineering; much higher proportions of Francophones are found at managerial levels; and the historical income differences between Anglophones and Francophones have largely disappeared. All this reinforces the business community as an influential opponent of Québec sovereignty, and a proponent of Québec's ability to prosper within a dynamic Canadian federation.

---

45. *La Presse* (30 mars 1989).
46. *Globe & Mail* (2 September 1988).
47. Kenneth McRoberts, *Quebec: Social Change and Political Crisis*, 3rd ed. (Toronto: McClelland & Stewart, 1988) at 429.

The challenge now for all our political leaders is to strengthen this sense that the future of the French language and culture is more secure within Canada's constitutional framework than it would be if Québec were alone in a sea of over 250 million Anglophones. We must strengthen this widespread sense of collective security in the Canadian federation and the belief, succinctly articulated by a young CEGEP student from Baie Comeau, that: "Quebec is better off as part of Canada — our culture is better respected in Canada. The Americans, they would eat us up in no time."[48] Finally we must move beyond the politicians' misplaced language fixation and focus, instead, on the critical challenges that unite us all as Canadians as we face the twenty-first century.

CONCLUSION

The foregoing discussion of the open, tolerant attitude of Francophone Québecers and their obvious sensitivity to and respect for individual and minority rights indicates that the current leadership in both Québec and Ottawa is sadly out of sync with the electorate. More specifically, in opting to mandate unilingual outdoor French signs and to invoke the notwithstanding clause in the *Charter* to override the right of freedom of expression, Robert Bourassa has gone beyond what most Québecers believe is required to protect the French language and culture in Québec.

In this connection, it is important to understand what the Supreme Court of Canada said when it declared that the relevant provisions in Bill 101 dealing with unilingual signs were a denial of freedom of expression. Once the Court determined that the requirement for unilingual signs infringed the basic right of freedom of expression, it turned to an examination under of section 1 of the *Charter*, and its Québec equivalent, to see whether the provisions could nevertheless be justified as reasonable limits. Among other things this required the Court to hear evidence from a range of socio-economic, demographic and other sources on the issue of whether the preservation of the "visage français" of Québec necessitated the limitation of the right of free expression.

The Court accepted the legitimacy of the legislative purpose of the provisions — the enhancement of the French language in Québec — and that the provisions were a response to a 'pressing and substantial' concern — the survival of the French language. But it concluded that,

---

48. Quoted in Stephen Hume, "A Westerner's View of Quebec" *The Montreal Gazette* (31 December 1988).

while the government could certainly require French to be used predominantly on all signs (the official position of the Québec Liberal Party), the prohibition of other languages could not be justified as a means of promoting the French language.[49]

The politicians obviously disagreed with this conclusion and immediately circumvented the Court decision with the use of the Québec and Canadian notwithstanding clauses and introduced the so-called inside-outside solution: unilingual French signs outside, predominantly French signs inside.

An intense debate over who was 'right' — the Court or the politicians — will clearly continue for the foreseeable future. The important point to note is that, in applying the *Charter*, the Supreme Court of Canada is required to analyse the special needs and concerns of Québec through the application of section 1 of the *Charter*. And as I have argued, the Court's conclusion as to the acceptable limits of the legislation was reasonable and, indeed, reflects the views of most Québecers. In other words, Québec's ability to preserve and promote the French language and culture is not adversely affected by the Canadian *Charter* and does not require the overriding of the *Charter*.

What this demonstrates is that the distinct society clause approach in the Meech Lake Accord is unnecessary and misguided, and to this the majority of Québecers would likely agree. Thus, as we move beyond the Meech Lake Accord, we must find another way to recognize that Québec is the principal source of the French language and culture in Canada, a way that does not undermine the *Charter* and does not result in Québecers having lesser protection of their basic rights and freedoms than other Canadians. At the same time, we must negotiate the abrogation of the notwithstanding clause in the *Charter*.

The alternative to the distinct society clause is to return to the original demand of Québec set out by Gil Rémillard in 1986 and to recognize the distinctiveness of Québec in the preamble of the *Constitution Act, 1867*. According to Rémillard, the revised preamble should also reflect the constitutional aspirations of all Canadians. In addition to the specific reference to Québec, it should express the socio-political composition of Canada and the general objectives of all Canadians living together in a federal regime.

The reference to Québec in the preamble of the Canadian *Constitution* would not have the substantive effect of the Meech Lake

---

49. *Ford* v. *Quebec (Attorney-General)*, *supra*, note 20.

Accord's distinct society clause, nor would it affect the *Charter*. This is because it is only one component of the constitutional accommodation of Québec in which Québec's special concerns in particular areas are dealt with separately in specific provisions. These include immigration, the appointment of Supreme Court judges, and the constitutional amendment procedures. Further concerns will arise in connection with Senate reform which will require, for example, the introduction of double majority vote procedures in respect of legislation affecting language and culture.

It is also important to realize, as Ramsay Cook succinctly notes, that the idea that the distinctiveness of Québec should be recognized constitutionally is far from new. He writes:

> Indeed the very act of creating the province in 1867 was, implicitly, a recognition of distinctiveness. But the British North America Act also included several explicit recognitions of that fact. For example, Section 94 recognized the civil law of Québec as distinct... In addition, the special character of Québec was recognized in Section 133 which not only made French, for the first time, an official language of Canada, but also made Québec, alone among original provinces, bilingual. In this, and in some other ways, Québec has never been a province exactly like the others for its historic characteristics have made some constitutional variations desirable.[50]

To these observations, one should add a reference to certain special provisions in the *Constitution Act, 1982*. Section 59 provides that the right to education of one's children in the "first language learned and still understood" by a parent who did not receive their primary school instruction in Canada in English, does not apply in Québec until authorized by the legislative assembly or government of Québec. Section 40 provides that a province that opts out of an amendment transferring provincial legislative powers relating to education or other cultural matters to Parliament will receive reasonable compensation. This was intended to address Québec's special concerns in these particular legislative areas.

In conclusion, we can do much better than the Meech Lake Accord. When it comes to changing our Constitution and influencing our evolution for years to come, Canadians must not settle for second best. Moreover, as Claude Ryan, the former Québec Liberal Party leader and current minister responsible for language and education issues, has admitted, the failure of the Meech Lake Accord would not be a catastrophe. "Le

---

50. "Alice in Meechland" in M. Behiels, ed., *The Meech Lake Primer* (University of Ottawa Press, 1989) 149-150.

climat du dialogue ayant permis la conclusion de l'entente continuera de prévaloir quoi qu'il advienne, et un retour à l'affrontement est peu probable."[51]

The Meech Lake Accord is unacceptable to Québecers and all Canadians as the basis for the constitutional accommodation of Québec. Not only does it fail to address Québec's special concerns for cultural and linguistic security, but it irreversibly weakens the federal government and undermines the *Charter of Rights and Freedoms*.

Québecers want to have the same rights and freedoms as all other Canadians. They want to play a meaningful role in a strong, dynamic national government and to ensure that Canada functions coherently as one nation. Finally, Québecers recognize that both the federal and provincial governments have responsibility for the protection and promotion of the French language and culture. But this does not simply involve linguistic rules and regulations. It involves the pursuit of excellence in all spheres, whether arts and culture, education, business and so forth, as well as vigorous social and economic development.

It is time for our leaders to move beyond the Meech Lake Accord and to renew constitutional negotiations. It is time for them to focus on the common challenges that we all face as Canadians, wherever we may live, and our shared commitment to pursue our vision of a bilingual, multicultural nation and a diverse, yet tolerant, society.

---

51. *La Presse* (23 septembre 1988).

COMMENTAIRE

Claude Morin

Pour quelles raisons sommes-nous réunis aujourd'hui ? Pourquoi ce débat sur l'Accord du lac Meech ?

Parce qu'en 1981, neuf provinces se sont entendues avec le gouvernement fédéral sans consulter la délégation du Québec (dont je faisais partie). Le Québec a rejeté cette constitution qui avait été préparée à son insu, sachant que, même soumis juridiquement, il forcerait ainsi éventuellement le gouvernement en place à réparer l'injustice commise en 1981.

En effet, l'accord constitutionnel conclu entre les neuf provinces et le gouvernement fédéral allait tout à fait à l'encontre des promesses référendaires que Monsieur Trudeau, les représentants fédéraux et les premiers ministres des provinces avaient faites au Québécois : « Si vous votez non au référendum, nous allons renouveler le fédéralisme. » Or, au Québec, l'expression « fédéralisme renouvelé » revêt un sens très précis ; elle signifie l'amélioration du système fédéral dans la voie de la reconnaissance de l'entité québécoise, de la société distincte québécoise. Voilà donc la première raison du refus québécois.

En second lieu, la constitution contenait une *Charte des droits*[1] dont l'un des objectifs était, de l'aveu même des négociateurs fédéraux de l'époque, d'empêcher le Québec de légiférer en matière de langue — et de protection de la langue française. Introduire dans la *Charte* des dispositions fondées sur les droits des individus et les opposer aux décisions des collectivités qui peuvent éprouver le besoin de se défendre, c'était une façon de torpiller la loi 101.

Troisièmement, en remettant ces décisions politiques à des juges non élus, la *Charte des droits* modifiait fondamentalement le fonctionnement de notre régime. Voilà donc les trois raisons expliquant le refus du Québec.

---

1. *Charte canadienne des droits et libertés*, Partie I de la *Loi constitutionnelle de 1982*, constituant l'annexe B de la *Loi de 1982 sur le Canada*, (R.-U.), 1982, c. 11.

Mais si nous sommes réunis aujourd'hui, ce n'est pas seulement à cause de ce premier refus québécois. En effet, le parti libéral du Québec, fédéraliste pourtant, a lui aussi rejeté l'accord de 1981-82. Comme pour le parti québécois, la décision de Monsieur Bourassa n'est pas partisane, mais bien québécoise — fait important à relever pour chasser l'impression selon laquelle le seul groupe au Canada qui s'est opposé au rapatriement de 1981, c'est le parti québécois à Québec.

Une fois élu, le gouvernement libéral a posé cinq conditions à son adhésion politique à la constitution de 1981-82. (Le parti québécois avait déjà présenté une quinzaine de conditions, si ma mémoire est exacte). Elles ont été en substance acceptées par monsieur Mulroney et les autres premiers ministres en 1987.

C'est ce qui m'amène à mon second point sur l'Accord du lac Meech.

Le premier élément frappant, c'est que Monsieur Mulroney ait étendu à toutes les provinces les demandes qui ne devaient initialement s'appliquer qu'au Québec. Le second, c'est que la notion de société distincte ne soit pas définie, qu'elle devienne une règle d'interprétation, précédée d'ailleurs par une autre règle d'interprétation qui la contredit en matière de dualité canadienne. Or, que signifie dans cette perspective la société distincte ? Quelle en est la portée ? L'effet concret ?

Au cours des deux dernières années, le public semble avoir franchi trois étapes dans sa façon de percevoir l'Accord du lac Meech :

1) Au Québec et dans le reste du Canada, l'accord a d'abord suscité un sentiment de satisfaction et d'étonnement. Étonnement, car, avec le souvenir de leur performance passée, le grand public a eu peine à croire que les onze chefs des gouvernements Canadiens, fédéral et provinciaux s'étaient finalement et réellement entendus sur un nouvel ensemble de propositions constitutionnelles visant la réintégration politique du Québec dans le grand courant politique canadien. Satisfaction, parce que cet accord semblait mettre un terme à la situation regrettable que le processus de rapatriement avait provoquée en 1981, lequel avait isolé le Québec et pouvait avec le temps engendrer une crise politique d'envergure.

2) Puis, au fil des mois, les doutes et les questions ont commencé à s'accumuler quant au vrai sens de l'accord et à son impact sur la dynamique du système fédéral canadien, et le processus de ratification s'est alors arrêté. Dans deux provinces, le Nouveau-Brunswick et le Manitoba, les premiers ministres nouvellement élus, qui n'avaient pas participé à l'accord, exprimèrent leurs réticences au sujet de la nature supposément imparfaite et incomplète de l'accord ; ils refusèrent de le ratifier sous sa forme

actuelle. Ici et là au pays, certains hommes politiques, observateurs et spécialistes bien connus, ainsi que divers groupes, firent également connaître leur opposition à l'approche de l'accord ou à certains de ces aspects. Selon eux, il fallait le réouvrir et l'« améliorer », ou même, pour certains, le mettre au rebut.

Tandis que ces critiques négatives faisaient leur chemin, l'opinion publique québécoise restait en grande partie favorable à l'accord, qui, par un processus classique de simplification, devint progressivement un *symbole*, le symbole de la reconnaissance officielle et concrète, pour la première fois depuis la Confédération, du caractère spécial du Québec en tant que société distincte — ou même de nation distincte.

3) Nous sommes actuellement dans une troisième phase et il semble de plus en plus probable que *l'accord ne sera jamais signé sous sa forme présente.* Ou, devrais-je dire, un certain accord sera bien signé mais ce ne sera pas celui dont il a été question jusqu'ici — l'authentique Accord du lac Meech. J'ai le sentiment profond que la pression deviendra si forte, d'ici à juin 1990, que le document politique sera réouvert, modifié et finalement ratifié. Pourquoi cela ?

a) Les doutes exprimés envers l'accord ont fini par ébranler les gens qui, même au Canada anglophone, avaient d'abord réagi favorablement ; ils ont maintenant le sentiment que le document est plus lourd de conséquences qu'ils ne l'avaient pensé en premier lieu. Ils craignent qu'il constitue un type de piège constitutionnel. Et le climat d'optimisme a fini par se dissiper.

Je me demande dans quelle mesure, pendant cette fameuse nuit où l'Accord du lac Meech a été accepté, les premiers ministres du Canada n'ont pas saisi différemment cette notion de société distincte. Si elle a d'abord été bien accueillie au Canada anglais, serait-ce parce qu'elle n'y signifiait rien ? Au Québec, au contraire, elle a été retenue parce qu'on l'estimait riche de sens : deux opinions à partir d'une même expression, et des conclusions contradictoires. Voilà pourquoi il est essentiel, selon moi, que la notion soit clarifiée.

b) Bien que la situation ne soit en rien liée à l'accord, le fait que le gouvernement du Québec ait eu partiellement recours à la clause « nonobstant » en décembre dernier, a fourni des munitions à ceux qui craignaient non seulement que l'accord affaiblisse le fédéral, mais encore que la clause de « société distincte » ne divise éventuellement le Canada ; en effet, si le Québec pouvait se « distinguer » de cette façon en piétinant les libertés fondamentales des citoyens anglophones, imaginez ce qu'il pourrait bien faire s'il était reconnu constitutionnel-lement et officiellement en tant que « société distincte » !

Ce qui me frappe ici, c'est qu'on veuille bien accepter le Québec comme société distincte, à condition toutefois qu'il ne se comporte pas comme telle... Notons que la clause «nonobstant» résulte d'une concession de Monsieur Trudeau envers les provinces telles que l'Alberta, la Colombie-Britannique, la Saskatchewan et, bien sûr, le Québec: si certains milieux rejettent aujourd'hui l'accord de 1987, c'est donc à la suite d'une décision prise à Québec en vertu d'un accord constitutionnel de 1982, étranger à celui de 1987.

Cette situation absurde exprime une perspective qui n'a jamais franchi les frontières du Québec: parce qu'il perçoit le Québec comme la plus importante des quinze minorités ethniques du pays, le Canada anglais s'attend à ce qu'il agisse en minorité et non pas à titre de peuple. Mais la loi 101 est bien la loi d'un peuple et la Caisse de dépôts est née, elle aussi, des décisions d'un peuple. Le fait indéniable et inéluctable, c'est que les Québécois sont et se considèrent, non pas en tant que «société distincte» (mot facile vide de sens), mais comme un peuple, une nation à part entière. Il est donc parfaitement illusoire d'imaginer qu'il puisse surgir un jour, au Québec, un parti fédéraliste prêt à traiter les Québécois en minorité ethnique.

c) Le NPD se prononcera éventuellement contre le lac Meech, retirant ainsi aux Conservateurs fédéraux l'appui qu'il leur avait jusqu'alors accordé. Dès le départ de Monsieur Turner, les Libéraux exigeront eux aussi des «améliorations».

d) L'élection, à Terre-Neuve, d'un gouvernement libéral opposé à l'accord à moins qu'il ne soit «réouvert et amélioré», a sans aucun doute donné une impulsion à ses adversaires dans divers milieux. Cet élément du tableau est important sur le plan psychologique et politique.

e) Le fait que Messieurs Mulroney et Bourassa refusent fermement de réouvrir l'accord les isolera lentement. Leur rigidité semblera injustifiée. Au cours des prochains mois, attendons-nous à ce que Monsieur Peterson, l'«honnête courtier» de l'Ontario, suggère que, après tout, il serait approprié de réexaminer le lac Meech pour tenir compte des aspirations légitimes des autres provinces. Et ainsi de suite. Éventuellement, fidèle à sa réputation de négociateur hors pair, Monsieur Mulroney annoncera qu'il est lui aussi prêt à se montrer «raisonnable», vu les circonstances. Monsieur Bourassa pourrait alors se retrouver isolé, dans une situation analogue à celle de Monsieur Lévesque en 1981-82... Bref, comme nous l'avons dit, un certain accord pourrait finalement être ratifié avec certains amendements, ajouts et corrections, avant la date limite de juin 1990.

f) En ce qui concerne le Québec, un accord « amélioré » ne serait certainement pas aussi avantageux que l'entente actuelle. Sous tous les rapports, son importance sera fortement réduite et de nombreux Québécois réaliseront évidemment, une fois encore, que les Canadiens ont fini par transformer et oublier un des engagements solennels qu'ils avaient pris envers eux. Tout comme en mai 1980...

4) Qu'y-a-t-il en fait de si dérangeant dans l'Accord du lac Meech ? Dans ce cas-ci, il semble exister un grave problème de perception.

a) Par exemple, contrairement à l'opinion actuelle, l'accord *ne reconnaît pas officiellement* le Québec comme une société distincte, en droit d'agir plus ou moins à titre d'état associé du Canada ! Il ne fait qu'introduire une règle d'interprétation constitutionnelle, elle-même liée à une autre règle la contredisant en partie : celle de la dualité canadienne. Ce qui signifie, en pratique, que la notion de « société distincte » pourrait s'avérer vide et sans conséquences tangibles. En poussant très loin l'imagination, on pourrait peut-être craindre qu'elle ne conduise à une définition juridique du Québec au sein (ou, peut-être à l'extérieur !) du système fédéral canadien. À mon avis, cette crainte est sans fondement.

Néanmoins, pour des raisons psychologiques et politiques légitimes, il est impératif que la notion de société distincte soit mieux définie. Si tel n'est pas le cas, la ratification éventuelle (bien qu'improbable) de l'accord tel qu'il est énoncé risque d'être fondée sur un terrible malentendu et pourrait entraîner de graves désillusions dans l'avenir. L'accord pourrait évidemment être accepté de part et d'autre : — par le reste du Canada parce qu'« il ne signifie rien » et ne changera rien de fondamental et d'important dans le fonctionnement du système fédéral actuel ; — par le Québec parce qu'« il signifie quelque chose » et représente le début d'une ère nouvelle.

Mais il est certain que l'accord ne peut à la fois être vide et significatif !

b) Dans de nombreux milieux, on estime que l'accord pourrait priver Ottawa de son rôle de leader dans les affaires canadiennes. En effet, les membres du Sénat et de la Cour suprême du Canada seraient nommés en consultation avec les provinces. Or n'est-il pas normal, dans un état fédéral évolué, que les parties constituantes partagent ce type de responsabilité ? Cette nouvelle procédure ne me semble pas menacer l'essence fédérale du Canada ni rendre les provinces omnipotentes. Ottawa demeurerait toujours le dernier ressort.

c) J'ai également apprécié, dans l'Accord du lac Meech, la modification apportée à la formule d'amendement constitutionnel, c'est-à-dire l'élargissement de la compensation financière. Qu'advient-il du pouvoir du fédéral en la matière ? Non seulement reste-t-il intact mais, pour la première fois, les provinces admettent qu'il peut s'appliquer aux juridictions provinciales *exclusives*.

Jamais auparavant le gouvernement fédéral n'était parvenu à extraire une telle reconnaissance des provinces en général et du Québec en particulier. Bien sûr, si jamais une des provinces résistait à une intrusion fédérale de ce genre, il lui serait toujours possible de se retirer (« opt out ») à condition toutefois de pouvoir offrir des services comparables à ceux du fédéral. En d'autres termes, dans les secteurs qui sont de son ressort, l'autonomie de la province n'est pas accrue, bien au contraire : pour recevoir les subventions fédérales, elle doit respecter les priorités du fédéral et éventuellement ses normes. Ainsi, Ottawa sera en mesure d'exercer une influence décisive sur les programmes sociaux et éducatifs, les provinces perdant tout argument constitutionnel contre ce type d'intervention fédérale dans leurs juridictions. Dans le cas présent, où trouver ce grand danger pour l'« Unité canadienne » ?

d) Je pourrais continuer à énumérer et à commenter les « dangers » que l'Accord du lac Meech est censé poser au système fédéral canadien actuel, mais je ne pense sincèrement pas qu'ils existent. Le caractère fédéral de l'État canadien s'en trouverait simplement augmenté.

e) Néanmoins, bien plus que les clauses concernant la « société distincte » et le pouvoir de dépenser, j'admets qu'un aspect de l'accord soit de nature à préoccuper les provinces de l'Ouest l'Alberta surtout : le Sénat. Quant à moi, ce groupe devrait être dissous ; je comprends toutefois que l'Ouest souhaite un Sénat triple-E (Efficace, Égal et Élu). Vu que l'Accord du lac Meech accorderait à chaque province, petite ou grande, un droit de veto pour toute réforme touchant cette institution fédérale, il est clair que le Sénat Triple-E ne verra pas le jour au Canada : jamais l'Ontario ni le Québec, quel que soit le parti au pouvoir, ne consentiront à une réduction aussi considérable de leur poids politique au Canada. Quelles que soient les déclarations des politiciens québécois actuels sur le sujet et la prise de position diplomatique qu'ils adoptent pour obtenir la ratification de l'accord, ils renverront le problème du Sénat à un second tour de négociations.

5) Dernière question : si jamais l'accord n'est pas ratifié, le Québec optera-t-il pour la souveraineté ? Je ne le pense pas et n'en vois pas la raison. Vu la valeur symbolique dont l'accord a été revêtu, on peut toutefois s'attendre à un certain désappointement, et ce sentiment minerait certainement le peu de confiance que le Québec peut avoir conservé envers l'ouverture possible des esprits au Canada de langue anglaise.

Mais selon ma propre évaluation, un seul sujet peut aujourd'hui provoquer le renouveau véritable des aspirations à la souveraineté : la langue, c'est-à-dire le statut du français au Québec. Cette question toujours présente dans le paysage politique québécois est le plus délicat de tous les problèmes possibles, beaucoup plus stratégique et de portée beaucoup plus vaste que le reste du Canada ne semble le réaliser. C'est pourquoi, comme nous l'avons dit, un gouvernement aussi prudent et aussi sensible aux sondages d'opinion que celui de Monsieur Bourassa a dû éventuellement trahir les promesses électorales faites aux Québécois anglophones et invoquer partiellement la clause « nonobstant ».

Une prise de position politique aussi surprenante de la part d'un parti fédéraliste ne peut s'expliquer autrement : s'il a agi ainsi, au risque de remettre en cause l'Accord du lac Meech, c'est parce que les Québécois sont infiniment plus préoccupés par la survie de la langue qu'ils ne le sont au sujet de l'accord même s'ils n'y sont pas indifférents.

Oui, les Québécois veulent que leur société, leur nation soit reconnue. Si cette reconnaissance est possible à l'intérieur du Canada, tant mieux. Quoi qu'il advienne, il faudra éventuellement expliquer aux Québécois en quoi consiste l'Accord Meech, les convaincre que la nouvelle version est meilleure que la première alors que tout aura été fait pour minimiser la notion de société distincte, la plus importante de toute même si c'est la moins claire. Et l'on finira par toucher au problème de la langue, lequel ralliera un nombre grandissant de Québécois au cours des prochaines années.

COMMENTS

Ken McRoberts

I want to develop some comments on the duality clause and the distinct society clause in light of some basic notions of sociology of language and language rights. But I would like also to respond to some of the comments made about Meech Lake Accord as a whole, including the process leading up to it and its possible effects on the Canadian political system. I will proceed fairly quickly through these issues.

It seems to me that the Meech Lake Accord would have introduced a healthy realism into our constitutional treatment of language in Canada. The concrete effects of the Accord may have been quite minimal but the symbolic effects could have been quite positive. I want to develop this train of thought in light of two general propositions from the sociology of language which were stated recently by Jean Laponce in his book *Languages and Their Territories.*[1]

The first proposition is that personal bilingualism, strictly defined, is very rare. To quote Jean Laponce, "perfect bilingualism is an ideal that is sometimes approached but almost never attained".[2] Most Canadians have a first language, French or English in most cases; some of them have a capacity in the other. According to the 1986 census as much as 16% of Canadians claim to know both languages.[3] It is doubtful, however, that most of them are truly bilingual in the sense of being able to speak with the same facility, the same ease, in both languages. The rarity of personal bilingualism seems to me a basic datum which is true of all multilingual societies, not simply Canada. It will not be altered by the best of efforts, including immersion schools and the many other initiatives of the last ten or fifteen years. With this in

---

1. J. A. Laponce, *Languages and Their Territories*, 2nd ed. (Toronto : University of Toronto Press, 1987).
2. *Id.* at 33.
3. Statistics Canada, *Language Retention and Transfer* (Ottawa: Supply and Services Canada, 1989) Table 3.

mind, it seems to me that the duality clause is really quite appropriately framed. It's a convoluted and awkward clause (I've yet to succeed in committing it to memory): "the recognition that the existence of French-speaking Canadians, centered in Québec but also present elsewhere in Canada, and English-speaking Canadians, concentrated outside Québec but also present in Québec, constitutes a fundamental characteristic of Canada".[4] At least it recognizes the reality of language in Canada: in the last analysis, most Canadians *are* English-speaking Canadians or French-speaking Canadians, with the obvious exception of people whose first language is neither. I would have preferred the earlier formation, "French-speaking Canada and English-speaking Canada", because it would have put the case more forcefully by recognizing the extent to which language is a shared collective experience. Language is not something that an individual can possess in isolation. Rather, it is acquired and maintained within a broad social network.

The second proposition that I would like to develop is that contact between two languages is never equal. In the last analysis, there always are going to be strong pressures for the predominance of one over the other. This may reflect the greater economic power or social prestige of one language as, for instance, the language that happens to be the language of work, or the language of economic and social mobility. It may also reflect the greater range of experiences of one language; if one language happens to predominate within the media and within cultural institutions.

The inequality of two languages in such contact can be seen in two ways. First, it can be seen in terms of patterns of assimilation. Usually, assimilation is strongly in one direction. This is certainly the case in Canada. By and large, assimilation has been overwhelmingly from French to English rather than the opposite. This has been the pattern of assimilation in all provinces, except in Québec. There, the absolute numbers switching from French to English is greater than the converse, but it draws from a much larger base. A second indication of the inequality of two languages in contact, lies in the choices that are made between the two languages by immigrants whose first language is neither. As we know, in the case of Canada, choice has been overwhelmingly for English in all provinces, including Québec.

As a result of these twin pressures, Francophone minorities have become so marginal in some provinces that their very survival is seriously in doubt — at least the survival of populations who speak French as a first language. I think this is sometimes overlooked in general discussions about language policy, especially discussions that are framed in terms

---

4. The Proposed *Constitution Act, 1987*, section 2(1)(a).

of a vision of Canada as being a bilingual country throughout. In all provinces but Québec, the proportion of the population whose mother tongue is French has continued to decline over the last 20 years despite the varying efforts of provincial governments and the federal government to support French. If we define the Francophone population in terms of the language used at home, according to the 1986 census, in all provinces but Québec, New Brunswick, and Ontario, Francophones represent three percent or less of the population.[5] On this basis, then, government actions to preserve dualism throughout Canada need to be concerned with actively reinforcing the position of the threatened language which is, indeed, French.

With respect to the persistence of French outside Québec, linguistic reforms in favour of the Francophone minorities have tended to miss the mark to the extent that they focused upon the formal equality of the status of languages within governmental institutions, as with the continuing debate about the desirability of generalizing s. 133 of the *Constitution Act, 1867*[6] to provinces such as Alberta and Saskatchewan. Even the Royal Commission on Bilingualism and Biculturalism did not go that far in its recommendations for a bilingual Canada. One can question the extent to which the fate of Francophone minorities in Saskatchewan or in Alberta would be seriously affected by the translation of provincial statutes into the other language. In the case of Saskatchewan, Francophones (understood as people who speak only French at home) now represent less than 10,000 people.[7] It is not clear to me that their fate would be seriously improved by the establishment of a truly bilingual legislature. Their fate is much more dependent upon government services that might alter their day to day lives, so that they would be less exposed to the strong assimilationist pressures that clearly now exist.

The *Constitution Act, 1982*[8] did make some progress in this direction in that the federal government and the New Brunswick government are now committed to provide a series of services in both languages. For all other governments, however, it is just a question of minority language education. And that, of course, is qualified by the phrase "where numbers warrant" in s. 23. The question then becomes whether the "duality clause" of the Meech Lake Accord could in any serious sense improve the situation. It is important to bear in mind that this is an interpretive clause that has no specific obligations contained within it. The fate of s. 27, dealing with multiculturalism, and other interpretive clauses suggests

---

5. Statistics Canada, *supra*, note 3, Table 1.
6. (U.K.), 30 & 31 Vict., c. 3.
7. *Supra*, note 3, table 1.
8. Being schedule B of the *Canada Act 1982* (U.K.), 1982, c. 11.

that the possible effect of such a clause is not too encouraging. There is, to be sure, the statement that it is the "role" of the Parliament of Canada and the provincial legislatures to "preserve" this fundamental characteristic of Canada. This has been criticized because the word "preserve" is used rather than "promote". I would think that, in face of the strong assimilationist pressures that exist, simply preserving the Francophone presence in many provinces would be a very ambitious objective that would certainly require a wide series of new programs. And, even then, one may ask whether even this is a realistic objective. The fact remains that the clause is an interpretative clause. It is unlikely that it could lead to the imposition of new obligations upon governments; conceivably it could strengthen the effect of s. 23. With the duality clause's clear distinction between "French-speaking Canadians" and "English-speaking Canadians", there might be a greater generosity on the part of courts when it comes to interpreting whether numbers are sufficient to warrant provision of minority language education *within separate institutions*, which I think is absolutely critical to the possibility of survival of Francophone minorities.

Turning to Québec, here too, historically it is French which has been in the weaker position due to the economic power of the Anglophone minority, the integration of the economy in the rest of North America, and the overwhelmingly Anglophone influences coming from beyond Québec. In the past, this favoured position of English was reflected in the choices that immigrants made when they came to Québec and their general tendency to assimilate into the English-speaking population. To the extent that there have been governmental efforts to bring the position of French closer to one of equality with English, they have come from the Québec government; the federal government being constrained by its commitment to formal equality in the status of the two languages. In these terms, at least, the Meech Lake Accord would have recognized the legitimacy of such actions on the part of the Québec government with the declaration of "the role of the legislature and the Government of Québec to preserve and promote the distinct identity of Québec", which is that of "a distinct society".[9] In linguistic terms, this could only mean the existence of a Francophone majority. On this basis, it would at least be legitimate for the Québec government to act to strengthen the position of the French language.

It is difficult to see what the concrete effects of that provision would be. Apparently, it would not have a significant effect on the division of powers, given s. 2(4) of the Accord which specifies that the application

---

9. The Proposed *Constitution Act, 1987*, section 2(3).

of the provision cannot derogate from "the powers, rights or privileges" of the federal and provincial governments. Conceivably, the distinct society clause could have an impact on the *Charter*, enabling the Québec government to stave off provisions of the *Charter* which it cannot affect through the notwithstanding clause. In particular, with regard to s. 23, the Québec government might be better positioned to make the claim that it is reasonable to limit access to English language schools, given the government's role of preserving Québec's distinct identity. To be sure, that kind of argument was made in the instance of the *Protestant School Boards* case,[10] and was unsuccessful. It would seem to me, then, that a fairly careful reading would suggest that there are real limits to any capacity of the distinct society clause to increase the ability of the Québec government to reinforce the position of French within Québec. Nonetheless, the clause at least would serve to legitimize the past and continuing actions of the Québec government to act in this fashion.

In English Canada, there is a widespread tendency to see an equation between the position of the Anglophone minority in Québec and that of the Francophone minorities in the other provinces. On this basis, such initiatives as Bill 178[11] seem to be clearly unacceptable. Yet, in terms of the sociology of language, the minorities clearly are in very different situations. Projections by Québec's leading demographer, Jacques Henripin, indicate that the Anglophone minority will continue to be a significant presence within Québec society, constituting at least ten percent of the population.[12] One would expect this in light of the broad institutional support that Québec Anglophones have enjoyed in the past, and appear likely to continue to enjoy, with few constitutional protections. Beyond this, there is the external support that the English language receives through the media, personal networks, etc. This points to the fundamental difference with respect to the Anglophone minority: it is part of a North American community in which the English language is clearly pre-eminent. On this basis, parallels between a Francophone minority in the other provinces and an Anglophone minority of Québec are seriously misleading.

In fact, it would seem to me that, in a larger context, the Québec Francophones are a minority rather than a majority. From a sociological or political perspective, there is a real arbitrariness in designating a group as a minority or a majority simply on the basis of provincial boundaries. It may well be much more appropriate to do so in terms of the place

10. *Quebec Association of Protestant School Boards* v. *A.G. of Quebec*, [1984] S.C.R. 66.
11. *An Act to Amend the Charter of the French Language*, S.Q. 1988, c. 54.
12. "Les anglophones pourraient ne représenter que 10,4% de la population du Québec en 2001" *Le Devoir* (28 Novembre 1984).

of a language group within the larger society and economy of the country or of the continent. The distinct society clause highlights the notion that the majority language in Québec may require protection and promotion by the Québec government: to reduce the impact of English on spoken and written French as with the efforts of *l'Office de la langue française*, and to ensure that opportunities are available to live all facets of life, including work, in French. Given the overwhelming predominance of English within North America, it would seem that the dynamism, the very survival, of French in Québec clearly requires government intervention. It would only be within the structures of a distinct society that one could imagine French surviving anywhere in North America. A recent authoritative demographic projection indicates that Québec Anglophones will continue to be significantly represented in Québec, constituting 10 percent of the population in 2021.[13]

So, the Meech Lake Accord at least would have established a more satisfactory symbolic definition of the status of languages within Canada. On that basis, it would have been a step forward, although a very small step forward. Apparently, it would have very little concrete effect in terms of added obligations on provincial governments to provide services to Francophone populations. As best as I can tell, it would not have a serious impact upon the prerogatives and powers of the Québec government. It is clear that there would not be any transfer of jurisdiction from the federal government to the Québec government through the distinct society clause.

Having made these points, let me turn to the real issue before this panel: the desirability or undesirability of the Meech Lake Accord in general. I am not persuaded that the Accord, if it had been adopted, would have seriously undermined the Federal government. I do believe that it would have responded to a serious problem: the continuing absence of Québec's signature to the *Constitution*. In 1982, it was seen as absolutely essential that the Canadian *Constitution* become truly Canadian, that it be repatriated. If it was important that this should occur, surely it is important that the second largest province should be signatory to the document. In practice, Québec is bound by the *Constitution*; the Supreme Court settled that question.[14] Nevertheless, in terms of a basic notion of the Canadian political community, it surely is desirable that this large province should be a formal signatory to our constitution. The Meech Lake Accord at least offered the possibility of this coming about.

---

13. Marc Termote and Danielle Gauvreau, *La situation démolinguistique du Québec*, le Conseil de la langue française (Québec: Éditeur Officiel, 1988), 255.

14. See *Re A.G. (Quebec) and A.G. (Canada)* (1982), 140 D.L.R. (3d) 305 (S.C.C.).

Having discussed the distinct society clause, the duality clause, and their possible implications, it would be worthwhile to review briefly the other elements of the Meech Lake Accord. I do not see them as seriously undermining the federal government. Rather, I think they can be seen as strengthening Canada as a federal system.

This is my interpretation, for instance, of the provisions having to do with the Supreme Court. A strong argument can be made that it would be desirable to have provincial participation in the selection of justices on the Supreme Court, given the role of the Supreme Court in arbitrating disputes between provincial governments and the federal government. In fact, this was one of the elements of the Victoria Charter in 1971 which would have allowed for provincial participation in the selection of justices. This power exists in other federal systems: in West Germany the landers are involved in the selection of members of the federal Supreme Court. I would have thought that this would have served to strengthen the legitimacy of the Supreme Court of Canada as a court within a federal system. With respect to the Senate, participation of provincial governments in the nomination of senators could also serve to strengthen the legitimacy of this institution within Canada, understood as a federal system.

In the case of the spending power, there would be a specification of the conditions under which provinces would be able to opt out of cost-shared programs within exclusive provincial jurisdictions. At the same time, there would be explicit constitutional sanction for the federal spending power. That could be seen as a strengthening of the federal government.

In the case of immigration, there are provisions requiring the formalization of what already has emerged within what is, in any event, a concurrent jurisdiction. In particular, the body of agreements that were developed between the federal government and the Québec government during the Trudeau years, culminating in the Cullen-Couture agreement, would now be entrenched. The same possibility would exist for other provinces. But there is no reason to believe that they would pursue agreements to the same extent that would Québec. The fact remains that this part of the Meech Lake Accord would have served to formalize what has already emerged on the basis of intergovernmental agreements between one government and the federal government. It is hard to see an argument here of a serious weakening of the federal government.

The Meech Lake Accord also provided for changes to the amending formula. Certain items that appeared under s. 42 of the *Constitution Act, 1982* would now require unanimity: matters involving the Senate, the Supreme Court and the House of Commons, as well as the creation of new provinces. Conceivably, this could complicate the chances of securing the kind of Senate reform that some provinces have wanted. But it should be borne in mind that even under the existing formula, which requires the approval of seven provincial legislatures representing at least 50 % of the population and Parliament, there may well be difficulty securing that kind of a change. The Québec government will contrive to oppose any constitutional change until it becomes a signatory to the *Constitution*. One must ask whether the federal government (or Ontario, for that matter) would be prepared to support a change as substantial as Senate reform, over the opposition of the Québec government.

As I understand the Meech Lake Accord, these are the basic elements: the distinct society clause, the duality clause, changes in procedures for nominations to the Senate and to the Supreme Court, specification of the spending power, formalization of existing agreements with respect to immigration, and an expansion of the items which come under the unanimity requirement for amendment. I do not see these as radical changes. Virtually all of them have been under discussion for a long period of time. Variation of some of these measures were in the Victoria Charter, and the federal government's proposal, *A Time for Action*.[15] The parameters of the Meech Lake Accord are well within the established discussion of renewal of the federal system and they offer the possibility of resolving a very serious problem: the fact that Canada has a repatriated constitution, but a constitution which does not have the formal adhesion of the second largest province. So, on that basis, I would continue to see the Meech Lake Accord as desirable, bearing in mind that, in all likelihood, it is dead. And I believe my time has also expired.

---

15. Canada, *A Time for Action: Toward the Renewal of the Canadian Federation* (Ottawa: Supply & Services, 1978).

COMMENTS

Bryan Schwartz

I'm not in the same position as my fellow speakers. I don't have a prepared text which I will not read from. I have, however, written on Meech Lake on a number of occasions, including the book *Fathoming Meech Lake*, which is published by the Legal Research Institute of the University of Manitoba, and "Refashioning Meech Lake", which you can find in the Manitoba Law Journal.[1] The article is an attempt to try and show what Meech Lake might have looked like if it had accommodated a vision of a coherent national community at the same time as trying to accommodate Québec's demands. I have taken seriously Professor Coyne's idea that it is not enough to say "no", but that you must try to propose constructive alternatives, although I am under no illusions about the facility with which we will achieve a new consensus.

On the opening day of this conference, I spoke about community from the point of view of a liberal individualist and one of the things I hoped to make clear is that I believe in the value of community as an instrument of individual self-realization. One of the things it is about time the proponents of Meech Lake realized is that there is not only one sense of nationalism in Canada which is held with conviction and passion and rationality: Québec nationalism. There is also a phenomenon called Canadian nationalism. It is the principal reason why the people of Manitoba, in a principled and honest fashion, overwhelmingly opposed the Meech Lake accord. As a democrat I do not believe that my vision of Canada should prevail if the overwhelming majority of Canadians are opposed to it. I would accept that. In fact, if an overwhelming majority of Québecers wanted to separate, as a democrat, I would accept that as well. But I hope it will be appreciated that there is this other vision that is entitled to tolerance and respect, and it may just have some attractive features to it.

---

1. (1989) 18 *Man. L.J.* 19.

During this conference, I have heard a number of speakers enthuse over a proposal that might be called "Let Canada be Switzerland". But I do not want to be confined to a mega-canton. I think the borders of Manitoba are quite small and the population fairly limited in numbers. My opportunities to do something exciting and important are amplified if I have the opportunity to participate not only in a local political community, Manitoba, but also to participate fully in the life of the Canadian political community. The Canadian political community would not be ethnically homogenous, would not be unilingually Anglophone, but would define itself in a number of other ways. One of them is through a system of national social welfare programs which express the sense of Canadian identity by embodying the caring for all Canadians by all Canadians. I regret that the Meech Lake Accord threatens to terminate the ability of the federal government to revise these programs, such as the *Canada Health Act*, and to initiate new ones. I do not believe you affirm the existence of the federal spending power by mentioning it and then gutting it. I believe that an important element of Canadian nationalism is respect for human rights and the establishing of a national system of human rights, which of course takes into account local facts and different circumstances, but nonetheless affirms the liberty and the individual equality of Canadians throughout the country.

My understanding of Canadian nationalism is that we respect minority language communities everywhere in Canada. One of my objections to Meech Lake is that it relegates the protection of minority language communities to second-class constitutional status, both outside of, and within, Québec. You don't have to be a constitutional lawyer to know that if you say "preserve and promote" the distinct identity of Québec and you say "preserve the existence" of these other communities, that the latter represent a second-class value. Yet it is the minority communities that are desperately in need of help.

That would be my sense of a Canadian nation. It would incorporate regional differences, it would respect the value of provinces as being closer to the people, more accessible, and vehicles for different linguistic expression. There would be an over-arching political community in which we could all participate, in which we could all care. Speaking of that community I would like to mention, which has gone almost without mention, that Canada is not simply the English fact and the French fact. It happens that you are sitting in one of them, but there are other communities, like western provinces and northern territories, who also want to participate fully in the life of the Canadian nation. Meech Lake is a cynical and undemocratic attack on the ability of northern Canadians to achieve the most elementary indicia of democratic rights in this country: to aspire towards provincehood. Do not reply by saying that they are not ready for provincehood today or tomorrow. The question is whether they will be ready in five, ten or twenty years. If you do not care what will be happening in five, ten or twenty years, do not change the constitution, because what you decide now you decide forever. Nothing in Meech Lake, once accomplished, could ever be undone.

We will not get Senate reform in the Meech Lake, but I will guarantee Senate deform under Meech Lake. Imagine yourself as travelling to another zone, the world of western Canada, in which provincial control has now been acquired over the senate. You will find a Senate which is more powerful than ever, but western Canada happens to be under-represented in the Senate, even on a straight representation by population basis. Premier Getty can get his six senators and send them to Ottawa and they can have a real good time dealing with twenty-four senators from Ontario and twenty-four senators from Québec, all with the certainty that the situation will remain the same, forever. I am in favour of the Senate reform which will provide a moderate counterbalance to the population dominance of central Canada, but which would not be an instrument of obstruction and which would continue to respect the principle of one person, one vote. A moderate counter-balance, but not an obstruction.

I have mentioned some of the problems with the current formulation of distinct society, this distinction between "preserve" and "preserve and promote". The other lack of recognition is that bilingualism might be a good. While dualism is recognized in the Canadian *Constitution*, and not bilingualism, I would like to see some recognition that governments have a role in building bridges, in giving people the opportunity to acquire a knowledge of the other official language. I have a problem with the Meech Lake Accord because I cannot understand what it means to say that it is merely interpretive if you have a completely undefined concept of distinct society. The last time I looked up the word "distinct" in the dictionary, one of the definitions was "separate". And these would not be just a couple of jargon words thrown into Supreme Court judgments. The primary interpreters of constitutions are not courts. Courts decide a very limited number of issues and most of the things that are very interesting have been and will be decided first and last by governments and by legislatures, not by courts. What counts far more than how the Supreme Court of Canada understands distinct identity and distinct society is the way it will be understood by the Government of Québec and the Government of Canada. And the Government of Québec will understand it increasingly as a mandate to pursue national affirmation with a consequent dissociation from the larger Canadian community. Whether that means repressing English in Québec, discouraging bilingualism among French-speaking Québecers, sending separate teams to the Francophone summit, increasing international recognition as a separate entity, opting out of national social welfare programs, acquiring control over unemployment insurance and retraining, you name it, distinct society will be taken as a political mandate to pursue it.

It is quite possible to recognize in the *Constitution* that each part of Canada, all the provinces, have distinctive characteristics and that among the distinctive characteristics of Québec are those of a French-speaking majority and an English-speaking minority, all operating under a civil system of law. I think it is possible to go a long way towards identifying certain features of Québec, its linguistic and cultural heritage that are distinctive, but the undefined mandate to promote the distinct identity of Québec is to use language that is quasi-separatist. To not limit it, and then to leave to future generations the fight over what is going to be left of the Canadian community, is unacceptable. Meech Lake says that nothing in the distinct society clause derogates from the powers of Parliament. But there are vast areas of concurrent jurisdiction that have already been recognized, and more may be claimed ; and Meech Lake will encourage aggressive claims by Québec governments to increase authority in these areas.

It may be that one concept in the Meech Lake Accord, also found in the Victoria Charter, was not such a bad idea. It is not so bad to have provincial participation in Supreme Court appointments. I do not know if Mr. Bourassa is a good negotiator. To say he is a good negotiator is like saying you are a brilliant gambler if you claim the prize in one of those "you-may-have-already-won-one-million-dollars-sweepstakes" that arrive unsolicited in the mail. It is not as though Mr. Bourassa went out and fought for this stuff. He got more than he asked for, and he got more than he asked for in Supreme Court appointments. He got primary control over one-third of the Supreme Court appointments, not the equal system of appointment found in the Victoria Charter. Not a situation which gave the federal government an equal voice with the provincial government, but a role which gave the provincial government overwhelming predominance. It is not very hard to find two or three hundred people of integrity in Québec who are trained lawyers, who would be very fine jurists and just happen to believe very strongly in Québec nationalism, in the superiority of collective rights over individual rights, and the importance of provincial community over national community. But I do not think that is the way one builds a balanced Supreme Court of Canada. I could live with the Victoria Charter. I cannot live with what is in Meech Lake.

I have spoken about the Senate, and I have spoken about the spending power. Maybe some of us in western Canada have an idea about this immigration stuff. It is not just affirming what was, it is also providing quotas, shares to different provinces, on immigration. Had these quotas existed in 1870, there would still be approximately 11,000 of us in Manitoba. The Accord has the potential of constraining overall levels of immigration into Canada, particularly at the expense of less populous provinces, and simultaneously guaranteeing the population inferiority of western Canada, all the while preventing the Senate from being reformed to be a political counterbalance. The Accord is a double whammy, which I do not think western Canadians should support, and the rest of Canada should not push because part of building a strong Canada is making every part of Canada, including the north, including the west, as well as Québec, feel comfortable within it.

I would like to conclude very briefly by reflecting on a few of the things I have heard at this conference over the last few days. I heard a lot about consociationalism, with four consecutive speakers endorsing it. I notice that it was without irony that a number of examples were given, and that they included Cypress, Lebanon, Austria, and the speakers said that it was strange that none of these people seemed to follow the earlier example. Well, given those particular examples, it does not seem the tiniest bit strange. [At this point, several members of the audience interjected, "What about Switzerland?"]. What about Switzerland? I heard yesterday that Switzerland is as far ahead of us democratically as we are compared to Latin America. I have a few questions about Switzerland: about the way it views immigrants; about the way a consociational society with rigid group boundaries treats its guest workers; about the track record of Switzerland with respect to sexual equality; about the policies of Switzerland with respect to open government, to banking secrecy and money-laundering, and to the regulation of multinational corporations. In some respects, some of the South American countries don't look so bad by comparison.[2]

---

2. In this printed version of my remarks, I would add to my impromptu comments on Switzerland that the drastic differences with Canadian conditions should not be overlooked. Contrary to the simplistic ideology of the "duality" approach to Canada, this country does not consist of two groups, but countless ones, including aboriginal people and "multicultural" ones. These complex conditions strengthen the claims that the supremacy, equality and freedom of the individual is the surest and most practicable basis for maintaining justice and unity. It should be obvious as well that with its vast expanse, large and disparate population, and the north-south attraction of the United States, Canada is in special need of a strong national government in order to maintain the cohesion of the country as a whole, and obtain the benefits that can result — including economic union, personal mobility, minimum standards of individual and minority rights, and a measure of social justice. By the way, notwithstanding the alleged glories of Swiss decentralization, there now appears to be a real possibility that Switzerland will, within the coming decade, join the European Economic Community.

I heard a lot about the English-speaking minority in Québec, the Westmount Rhodesians, the over-privileged class over which we should never shed a tear. Over the past decade, the Anglophone population in Québec declined massively. Where some time ago they were once 15 percent of the Québec population they are now 10 percent.[3] There is almost no immigration either from abroad or from the rest of Canada. I am not sure Canada can avoid the eventual extinction of the English-speaking community in Québec.

I have heard a lot about the "is-ought" fallacy, at least the endorsement of it, whatever is ought to be. Whatever is should be entrenched in the *Constitution*. Well good, let's entrench poverty, a lot of that in Canada. Premier McKenna, in the election campaign, said that "patronage is a way of life" in New Brunswick, well, let's entrench that in the *Constitution* too. But I thought what constitution-building was about not saying what is, it was about saying what ought to be: what our values are, what our principles are. Can Canada be Canada, or *le Peuple canadien*? *Le Peuple québécois*, is not something that just is, it is a question that we are going to decide, about what sort of Canada we are going to build. The choice is up to us about what Canada will be, what we make of Canada. All the natural forces of disintegration, for division along linguistic lines and ethnic lines, have only our political will to hold Canada together. They will lead us to a disintegrated Canada, but I think the notion of national community which I outlined earlier, and one I would not impose against the overwhelming wishes or even majority wishes of other Canadians, over the majority wishes of Québecers, is held with intense personal conviction in many parts of Canada and will not surrender easily, even to the polite *coup d'État* that took place at Meech Lake.

---

3. See Joseph Magnet, "Comments".

NOTES BIOGRAPHIQUES / BIOGRAPHICAL NOTES

Louis Balthazar

Professor in the Department of Political Science at Laval University (Québec) since 1969. He has published and lectured extensively on the topics of nationalism, United States foreign policy, and United States-Canada relations. Among his latest publications are Contemporary Québec and the United States (with Alfred O. Hero jr) (1988) and Bilan du nationalisme au Québec (1986).

Timothy Christian

Dean at the Faculty of Law, University of Alberta. Dean Christian has published in the area of Charter rights and has acted as legal advisor in a number of Charter cases.

Ramsay Cook, O.C., F.R.S.C.

Professor of History at York University in Toronto and general editor of the Dictionary of Canadian Biographies/Dictionnaire Biographique du Canada. His publications include Canada and the French Canadian Question (1966), Provincial Rights, Minority Rights and the Compact Theory 1867-1921 (1970), The Regenerators (1984) and Canada, Québec and the Uses of Nationalism (1986).

Deborah Coyne

Co-founder of the Canadian Coalition on the Constitution, a coalition of a wide range of groups and individuals opposed to the Meech Lake Accord. She is a lawyer and has taught constitutional law and public policy at the Faculty of Law, University of Toronto. She is currently the constitutional advisor to the Premier of Newfoundland and Labrador.

Gurston Dacks

Professor of Political Science and Adjunct Research Professor of the Boreal Institute, at the University of Alberta. His research interests

491

focus on the politics of the Canadian North, in particular, constitutional development processes and the political aspects of northern aboriginal claims.

Chris M. Dassios

Associate at Gowling, Strathy and Henderson, Toronto. His chief areas of practice are labour law and Charter litigation. He is a part-time faculty member at Osgoode Hall Law School, York University, Toronto.

Pierre Foucher

Professeur de droit, école de droit, Université de Moncton. Me Foucher a completé en 1985 une vaste étude des droits linguistiques en matière scolaire. Me. Foucher agit comme consultant pour diverses groupes francophones hors Québec.

Rodolfo O. de la Garza

C.B. Smith Fellow in Latin American Studies, Director of the Center for Mexican American Studies and Professor of Government at the University of Texas at Austin. He currently directs the Latino National Political Survey, the first national study of Latino political values and behaviour. Among his many publications are The Chicano Political Experience (1977), Ignored Voices: Latinos and Public Opinion Polls (1987), and The Mexican American Experience (1985).

Dale Gibson

Belzberg Chair of Constitutional Studies, University of Alberta and Professor of Law, University of Manitoba. He has published widely in the areas of torts, constitutional law, and legal history. His publications include The Law of the Charter: General Principles (1986) and The Law of the Charter: Equality Rights (1989).

Rosanne D. Gonzalez

She teaches at the University of Arizona and also serves as Director of the graduate program in ESL, Director of the Writing Skills Improvement Program, and Director of the Court Interpreter Program. Her research covers language discrimination in the courts, language rights, second-language acquisition, and methods for testing interpreting skills.

Jean A. Laponce

Professor of Political Science at the University of British Columbia. His works include The Protection of Minorities (1961) and Languages and Their Territories (1987). He is president of the Academy of Humanities and Social Sciences at the Royal Society of Canada.

Arend Lijphart

Professor of Political Science at the University of California, San Diego. His field of specialization is comparative politics, and his current research entails the comparative study of democratic regimes and of electoral systems. His most recent books include Democracies: Patterns of Majoritarian and Consensus Government in Twenty-One Countries (1984), Power-Sharing in South Africa (1985) and Electoral Laws and Their Political Consequences (with Bernard Grofman) (1986).

Manoly R. Lupul

Professor of Canadian Educational History, Department of Educational Foundations, and founding Director, Canadian Institute of Ukrainian Studies (1976-86), University of Alberta. His research interests are multiculturalism and the politics of language, culture, and education. He is the author of Roman Catholic Church and the North-West School Question... 1875-1905 (1974) and editor of A Heritage in Transition: Essays in the History of Ukrainians in Canada (1982).

Wayne MacKay

Professor of Law at Dalhousie University. He has published widely in the areas of constitutional law and education law and has been legal counsel in several Charter language cases.

Michael MacMillan

Associate Professor of Political Studies at Mount St. Vincent University in Halifax. He has published several articles on language rights and language conflict in the Québec and Canadian settings. He is currently preparing a book on the theory and practice of language rights in Canada.

Michael McDonald

He holds the Maurice Young Chair in Applied Ethics, Department of Philosophy, University of British Columbia. He was previously Professor in the Department of Philosophy, University of Waterloo. He has published widely in ethics, political philosophy, and the philosophy of law. He is English language editor of Dialogue and past president of the Canadian Section of the International Association for Philosophy of Law and Social Philosophy.

Ian F. McGilp

Partner at Gowling, Strathy and Henderson, Toronto. He is a part-time faculty member at Osgoode Hall Law School, York University and was Assistant Professor, Department of Philosophy, University of Alberta from 1969 to 1978.

M. Frank McMahon

Il est originaire de l'Alberta et travaille au sein de la communauté franco-albertaine depuis plus d'une vingtaine d'années. Ancien recteur et premier doyen de la Faculté Saint-Jean de l'Université de l'Alberta, il a beaucoup oeuvré avec d'autres parents francophones pour obtenir des écoles adéquates en Alberta. Il a déjà publié dans la revue Échanges et dans La revue canadienne d'enseignement supérieur.

Kenneth D. McRae

Professor of Political Science at Carleton University, Ottawa and was earlier a research supervisor for the Royal Commission on Bilingualism and Biculturalism. He has studied language policy and language conflict in several countries, and is author of Conflict and Compromise in Multilingual Societies, Vol. 1, Switzerland (1984) and Vol. 2, Belgium (1986). Two further volumes of this project, on Finland and Canada, are in progress.

Kenneth McRoberts

Associate Professor of Political Science at York University. He has published widely in the area of language policy and is the author of Québec: Social Change and Political Crisis, 3rd ed. (1988).

Joseph Magnet

Professor of Law at the University of Ottawa (Common Law Section). He has been a legal advisor in constitutional matters to federal and provincial governments and territories, as well as to both English and French language minority communities. He is the author of Constitutional Law of Canada, 2nd ed. (1989).

David F. Marshall

He has been a Lilly Visiting Scholar at Duke University and a National Endowment for the Humanities Visiting Scholar at Stanford University and the University of Wisconsin at Madison, as well as Visiting Professor at the University of Arizona and Fulbright Professor at Nanjing University, China. He is currently teaching at the University of North Dakota, writing on language rights, official languages, language and politics, and language planning.

Angéline Martel

Professeure de linguistique à la Télé-université du Québec à Montréal. Ses recherches visent principalement les droits éducationnels des minorités linguistiques. Elle est auteure d'une étude pancanadienne sur le sujet: Les droits scolaires des minorités de langue officielle au

Canada: De l'instruction à la gestion/ Official Language Minorities Education Rights in Canada: From Instruction to Management (1990).

Toivo Miljan

Professor of Political Science at Wilfrid Laurier University. Previously, he had been research officer for the Royal Commission of Bilingualism and Biculturalism. He has written extensively on the Soviet Union and Baltic States, including Bilingualism in Finland (1966) and The Political Economy of North South Relations (1987).

Claude Morin

Professeur à l'École nationale d'administration publique de l'Université du Québec. Ancien conseiller économique auprès du gouvernement du Québec de 1961 à 1963, il a été sous-ministre des Affaires intergouvernementales du Québec de 1963 à 1971 et ministre des Affaires intergouvernementales de 1976 à 1982. Il est l'auteur de *L'art de l'impossible: la diplomatie québécoise depuis 1960 (1987)* et de *Lendemains piégés: du référendum à la nuit des longs couteaux (1988)*.

Kenneth Munro

Associate Professor in the Department of History at the University of Alberta. His current research interests include the political History of late nineteenth century Québec and Franco-Albertan History. He is author of "L'Ouest dans la pensée politique de Chapleau" University of Ottawa Quarterly (1977) and "Official Bilingualism in Alberta" Prairie Forum (1987).

Denise Réaume

Associate Professor in the Faculty of Law at the University of Toronto. She has written several articles in the area of language rights, including "Education and Linguistic Security in the Charter", (with Dr. L. Green) (1990) McGill Law Journal and "Language Rights, Remedies, and the Rule of Law", (1988) Canadian Journal of Law and Jurisprudence. She has also written in the area of legal theory.

Ronald Rudin

Professor of History at Concordia University. He has published widely on the social and economic History of Québec in the nineteenth and twentieth centuries. Among his publications are the books Banking en français: The French Banks of Québec, 1835-1925 (1985), The Forgotten Québecers: A History of English-Speaking Québec, 1759-1980 (1985), and In Whose Interest?: Québec's Caisses Populaires, 1900-1945 (1990).

Bryan Schwartz

Professor of Law at University of Manitoba. He has been involved in, and written extensively about, the Canadian constitutional process in the modern era. His publications include First Principles, Second Thoughts: Aboriginal Peoples, Constitutional Reform and Canadian Statecraft (1986) and Fathoming Meech Lake (1987).

Brian Slattery

Professor of Law at Osgoode Hall Law School, York University. He has written widely in the fields of constitutional law, constitutional History, aboriginal rights, and criminal law and procedure.

Armando Trujillo

He has taught in the public schools and has partially completed his Ph.D. in anthropology at the University of Texas at Austin. His area of experience is educational anthropology and bilingual and migrant education and has authored numerous articles on education.

Eric Waddell

Professor of Geography at Laval University. His research interests are in the area of language and ethnicity, principally within the context of French-English relations in Canada and the French North-America in general. His publications include State, Language and Society: The Vicissitudes of French in Québec and Canada (1987) and The English of Québec: From Majority to Minority Status (1982).

INDEX*

- A -

Aboriginal

Rights, 15, 29, 369-374, 439, 451
   Also see *Northwest Territories;
   Natives; Charter of Rights*, section
   26
Relations with Ottawa, 268, 324, 325,
   373
   Also see *Northwest Territories*,
   relationship with Ottawa
Relationship with Settlers, 373
Self-Government, See *Northwest
   Territories*, self-government;
   Natives, self-government
Sovereignty, 152
   Also see *Northwest Territories*,
   self-government
Title, 15, 31, 152, 323, 372
   Also see *Natives*, land claims
Treaty Rights, See *Aboriginal*, rights

Acadians, 88, 90, 124-128, 136, 137,
   139, 146, 147, 336, 366, 428

Acadiens, 89, 93, 97, 99

Act Theory of Confederation, 77

   Also see *History*

Acton, Lord, 75

Affichage, Voir *Québec*, langue d'affichage

Affirmative Action, 30, 361, 451

   Also see *United States*, affirmative
   action; *Charter of Rights*, section
   15(2); *Injustice*, past

Africa

South, See *South Africa*
West, 157

African National Congress, See
   South Africa

Africans

Generally, 174
South, See *South Africa*
Tribal Languages, 174

Afrikaners, See *South Africa*

Afrique du Sud, 151

Air Canada, See *Language*, air traffic

Air Traffic and Language, See *Language*, air traffic

Alberta

Alberta Act, 111, 112, 120, 198, 252,
   254, 256-258, 344
Assimilation, 258, 260, 261, 263, 313,
   379, 479
   Also see *Assimilation*
(l')Association Albertaine des Parents
   Francophones, 402, 404
Association Canadienne Française de
   l'Alberta, See *Alberta*, Franco-
   Albertans
Bilingualism, 252, 254-263, 306, 314
   Also see *Bilingualism*
Calgary, 256, 259, 263
Courts, language in, See *Courts*,
   language in; *Alberta*, Languages
   Act, French language trials

---

* Indexation par / Index compiled by Glenn Solomon, Calgary.

Achevé d'imprimer
en mai 1991 sur les presses
des Ateliers Graphiques Marc Veilleux Inc.
Cap-Saint-Ignace, Qué.